CATHEDRALS OF ENGLAND AND WALES

1. Frontispiece *(overleaf) Lincoln from north-west: upper west front and base of central tower, c. 1225–55, by Master Alexander; top stage of tower, 1306–11, by Richard of Stow*

Cathedrals
of
England and Wales

John Harvey

B. T. Batsford Ltd, London

By the same author
HENRY YEVELE
GOTHIC ENGLAND
THE PLANTAGENETS
DUBLIN
TUDOR ARCHITECTURE
THE GOTHIC WORLD
ENGLISH MEDIAEVAL ARCHITECTS
A PORTRAIT OF ENGLISH CATHEDRALS
THE CATHEDRALS OF SPAIN
CATHERINE SWYNFORD'S CHANTRY
THE MASTER BUILDERS
THE MEDIAEVAL ARCHITECT
CONSERVATION OF BUILDINGS
EARLY GARDENING CATALOGUES

Bibliographies
ENGLISH CATHEDRALS—A READER'S GUIDE
CONSERVATION OF OLD BUILDINGS
EARLY HORTICULTURAL CATALOGUES—A CHECKLIST

Revised Muirhead's Blue Guides
NORTHERN SPAIN   SOUTHERN SPAIN

Edited with translation
WILLIAM WORCESTRE: ITINERARIES (1478–1480)

First published as *The English Cathedrals,* 1950
Second edition, revised and re-illustrated, 1956
Paperback edition, 1961; reprinted, 1963

THIS EDITION, COMPLETELY REVISED AND ENLARGED FIRST PUBLISHED 1974
© JOHN HARVEY 1974
ISBN 0 7134 0616 X
FILMSET BY SERVIS FILMSETTING LTD, MANCHESTER
PRINTED IN GREAT BRITAIN BY
BUTLER AND TANNER LTD, FROME, SOMERSET
FOR THE PUBLISHERS B. T. BATSFORD LTD
4 FITZHARDINGE STREET, LONDON W1H 0AH

Preface

The original version of this book has attained its majority, surmounting the hazards of successive revisions and of transformation to paperback form. In the course of revision the text had been somewhat expanded, but remained too short to be adequate as a treatment of the national flowering of a great art form. In this new edition the attempt is made to provide a thorough framework of reference and to take into account fresh discoveries both general and particular. In this context all other finds have been put in the shade by the complete excavation of the Saxon cathedral at Winchester. For the first time it is possible to make a specific assessment of what an English cathedral of the greatest type meant in pre-Conquest times. What has been found may, indeed, be regarded as relatively un- or even anti-architectural, but at last we do know the facts, just as contemporary lunar exploration has revealed to the world the real configuration of the other side of the Moon.

The excavation of one of the most important Saxon cathedrals has provided a noteworthy expansion in time. In space, the four ancient Welsh cathedrals have been added to 27 in England. Though of small scale, these buildings in Wales do not in fact differ in general character from English work, and must largely if not entirely have been designed by Normans and by Englishmen. It cannot be said that they share a national style even to the extent that is true of Scottish or of Irish cathedrals. Some further expansion is due to giving a more adequate consideration to the greater churches which are not cathedrals. Limitations of the possible scope of illustrations, rather than of space in the text, prevent this enlargement being taken to its logical conclusion. There is in fact little to be said for the inclusion of two of the three suffragan cathedrals to York (Ripon and Southwell) to the exclusion of the third, Beverley, simply because this has not been made the centre of a modern diocese. The difficulty lies in the fact that a policy of inclusion of all the churches architecturally relevant would double the effective total.

Comparatively little that is of significant importance has been discovered in the surviving cathedral fabrics during recent years. To this there is one major exception, York. There a massive programme of archaeological excavation linked to structural repairs in progress has revealed the earlier history of the post-Conquest cathedral, even though it has so far failed to discover positive traces of its Saxon predecessor. What does, however, appear certain is that the Saxon cathedral was on a quite different alignment. As at Winchester, an ancient sanctuary was totally destroyed to give place to another entirely new. As we shall see, conditions in England were very different from those which, on the continent of Europe, allowed surviving parts of early churches to be incorporated into, or dictate the plan of, later cathedrals and abbeys. The answer given by the last twenty years of research is that, so far as the cathedrals are concerned, the Norman Conquest made a clean sweep and art started afresh. This major cleavage was accentuated soon afterwards by the advent of the Gothic style.

Above ground, then, it is hardly likely that future discoveries will in any notable way upset the picture that has been formed of the development of the cathedral. It is also true that little may now be looked for in the way of startling documentary finds. Individual documents come to light from time to time, or their significance is recognized, but it is improbable that long lost series of fabric rolls will be found. The extensive work done by the National Register of Archives in the last 25 years, and more especially the survey of Cathedral Libraries by the Pilgrim Trust, tend strongly to confirm that most of the mediaeval sources are known. Generally speaking they have, in fact, been known for a very long time. Though much remains to be done in the adequate publication of the fabric records that do survive, they have for the most part yielded up their secrets in the matter of dating.

In the chapters now added to the present edition an attempt is made to bring up to date the correlation between the fabrics and the documentation, particularly in regard to the individual architects responsible. A high proportion of the significant names in this field is now known, and named persons rather than local schools appear as the agents of stylistic development. In passing, attention should be drawn to the fact that the surname of the great fourteenth-century architect to the Crown is now spelt as 'Yeveley'. This avoids phonetic misapprehensions and indicates the origin of his family at the little village of Yeaveley in Derbyshire; and also corrects an error of judgment of my own in adopting the spelling of the *Dictionary of National Biography* rather than that used by John Gough Nichols in his pioneer life of the architect, issued in 1864.

Apart from the archaeological investigations at Winchester and York, with attendant interim publications, there has not in recent years been much monographic study of individual cathedrals. The main exceptions are provided by the outstanding book on Chester cathedral *(The Monks of*

Chester) by Archdeacon R. V. H. Burne, and the detailed study of Lichfield Cathedral for the Victoria County History of Staffordshire undertaken by Mr D. A. Johnson. I am greatly indebted to both authors for personal communications, as also to Mr C. G. Bulman·in regard to Carlisle. Much other help has been received from persons too numerous to mention, but among whom I must name for the special value of their discussions: Professor George Zarnecki and Dr Peter Kidson at Bristol and Gloucester; also at Gloucester and concerning Worcester, Mr B. J. Ashwell; the Rev. Canon P. B. G. Binnall and Mrs Joan Varley at Lincoln; Mr and Mrs W. J. Carpenter Turner at Winchester; and Dr Eric Gee and Mr John Miller at York. Continued help has also been received from several of those mentioned in connection with the second edition of this book.

In regard to the discoveries at Winchester I owe much to the late Roger Quirk and to Mr Martin Biddle; and on the subject of the excavations at York to Dr Brian Hope-Taylor, Mr Herman Ramm, and Mr Derek Phillips. My wife has discussed many problems with me and has once more read the whole of the proofs. I would again express my thanks to my publishers, especially to Sam Carr; to Douglas Sellick for research on the illustrations, to Miss Miriam Wessel for design, and Michael Stephenson of the editorial department.

John H. Harvey
January 1974

Preface to the first edition

Books about the English cathedrals are legion, and range from the richly illustrated folios and quartos of the nineteenth century down to guide pamphlets. It would seem that little more could remain to be done, save for the dotting of the 'i's' and crossing of 't's' in matters of history and dating. Yet it is a singular fact that very few indeed of the existing works have dealt with our cathedrals as a unity; almost all have been content to accept them as units, and to give their several histories and descriptions with only a certain amount of cross reference from one to another. They have, too, been approached from many angles, the historical and the strictly architectural predominating, with some consideration of their liturgical use. It has not been common to regard them primarily as a series of related works of art: art consecrated to the service of God, truly, but still best to be apprehended as the creation of inspired human genius.

It is, after all, in this way that we appreciate the Masses of Byrd and Palestrina, the Passion Music of Bach, or the symphonies of Haydn. And to the Middle Ages, that ill-defined period which for England means the five centuries from Edward the Confessor to Henry VIII, the cathedral was the ruling art-form, as the symphony was in the Age of Taste. But there is this difference, that the symphony remains purely an art-form, while the cathedral is at the same time the outward and visible sign of an inward life; a shell made with hands, but still as natural a growth from the spiritual, invisible existence within as the chrysalid is from the butterfly in metamorphosis. However much room for admiration there may be in our post-mediaeval buildings, regarded purely as architecture, it remains true that they never, or hardly ever, can by the wildest stretch of imagination be said to stem from the soul and spirit of the people. I do not here use the word 'people' in its modern jargon sense, implying the masses as opposed to the classes, but as meaning the totality of the English community, bred in England and sharing the new, fresh English tradition which in the Middle Ages had only just emerged as a reality, and had not had time to grow stale.

It was during those Middle Ages that the modern nations took their rise, and from her island position, the close kinship of her folk, and the strength of her kings, England was the first of them all. We may therefore expect, and do find, that in English mediaeval art there is a greater unity, less diversity, of style than in any other country; yet, paradoxically, no country is so rich in variety of artistic invention. Steeped in one tradition, not torn between several, as were the French, the Germans, the Italians, the Iberians, and the Scandinavians, the English were able, within their all-rounding unity, to devote their time and energy to particular developments of tower and front and porch and vault and tracery; roof, pinnacle, niche and statue; painting, glazing and decoration of every kind.

Of this diversity of invention and unity of purpose the English cathedrals are the highest examples: the most complete and fully developed summation. The cathedral of the Middle Ages reigned supreme as the chief of all art forms, the co-ordinating centre of all spiritual culture. Greater than other churches in quality as well as in size, the cathedral was not a church alone: it was the greatest of art galleries, the noblest of lecture halls, sublimest of opera houses. The best of sculpture, of painting, of music and of verse were not too good for its service. Its enrichment provoked the finest flights of the decorative artists. It was in the cathedral, above all buildings, that architecture was truly the mistress art. And from this it follows that in the study of European and of English art and culture, chief place is taken by the cathedral.

Every serious student will wish to visit the cathedrals for himself; but much can be seen in photographs that is not normally visible on the spot. Much too can be learnt from the study of photographs correlated with written history, both before and after visiting the buildings. And in studying the whole body of English cathedrals as a unity, it is clearly desirable that the photographs themselves should form one whole and represent the viewpoint of a single artist. In the present series of views and details by Mr. Herbert Felton this end has been attained for the first time.

To the many persons who have indirectly contributed to this book I can give only a general acknowledgment; but I wish to thank especially the vergers and architectural and building staffs of various cathedrals for much kindness and help. To Mrs. M. E. Clegg and to Dr. D. F. Findlay I owe a special debt for the generosity with which they placed unpublished material from the Exeter fabric rolls at my disposal. My wife has throughout given her constructive criticism and advice, and has read the proofs. To my publishers I am grateful not only for valuable assistance, but in particular for their generous permission to reproduce the plans from their book on *The Cathedrals of England*.

J. H. H.

Note to the second edition

Changed conditions have now made it possible for Mr. Felton's collection of photographs of the cathedrals to be reproduced on a large scale in the manner which he originally envisaged. The plates to this new edition of the text have therefore been limited to those essential to a proper understanding of the development of the English cathedral as an architectural form.

Both text and notes have been carefully revised and the results of recent research incorporated. In this connection I have to thank many friends, critics and correspondents who have made suggestions and brought new facts to my notice, and especially Mr. Alec Clifton-Taylor. For assistance with the revision of my accounts of individual cathedrals I am indebted to Colonel Eric Ward in connection with Bristol; Mr. V. J. Torr, Dr. William Urry and Mr. Colin Walker at Canterbury; Canon W. K. Lowther Clarke and Mr. W. D. Peckham at Chichester; Mr. G. G. Pace and Canon J. E. W. Wallis at Lichfield; and Miss Kathleen Major at Lincoln. Even heavier is my debt to Mr. A. B. Whittingham, who has given me the benefit of his detailed knowledge of Norwich Cathedral; and to Mr. L. S. Colchester, whose largely unpublished researches at Wells have been so fruitful.

The historical notes on each cathedral have been considerably extended, and a Glossary and a note on sources added to this edition. Since the book was first published I have been able to re-examine the fabrics of all the cathedrals except Hereford.

J. H. H.

Contents

List of Illustrations

The illustrations to the original edition of this book were chosen from the very large collection taken by the late Herbert Felton, mostly in 1948–50. These provide the great majority of the present plates, since comparison with many other photographs, old and new, has demonstrated Felton's particular genius for bringing out architectural content and quality. In a few cases more recent views have been substituted to show structural improvement (e.g. the restored pulpitum at Chichester). In general the proliferation of intrusive fittings, notably acoustic apparatus, in recent years emphasizes the unique value of Felton's achievement as an irreplaceable record.

Acknowledgments

The Author and Publisher would like to thank the following for their permission to reproduce photographs:

A. F. Kersting, FRPS (Pls 3, 26, 40, 50, 52, 63, 89, 93, 108, 115, 128, 150, 164, 169, 171, 186, 188, 192); National Monuments Record (England) (Pls 2, 4, 9, 10, 12, 17, 18, 23, 24, 25, 33, 38, 47, 48, 51, 53, 56, 61, 62, 71, 83, 87, 92, 95, 98, 101, 104, 113, 118, 120, 131, 132, 133, 135, 144, 145, 147, 149, 155, 157, 161, 166, 170, 172, 173, 174, 178, 179, 180, 181, 182, 187, 189, 193, 194, 195, 197, 199, 200); Royal Commission on Ancient and Historic Monuments in Wales (Pls 78, 81, 100). The remainder are from the Publisher's collection.

The plans reproduced on pages 90 and 93 were based, by kind permission, on originals by Mr Martin Biddle and by Dr Brian Hope-Taylor respectively.

ENGLISH
AND WELSH
CATHEDRALS

Cathedrals discussed in
this book............ ■ CANTERBURY

Other cathedrals....⚬ GUILDFORD

Other churches mentioned •Tewkesbury

Boundaries of dioceses before 1541 -----

Lindisfarne

Alnwick

Brinkburn

Lanercost

NEWCASTLE

Hexham

Blanchland

CARLISLE

DURHAM

Darlington

Guisborough

St.Bees

Rievaulx

Cartmel

RIPON

Malton

Bridlington

Fountains

YORK

Bolton

Beverley

Kirkstall

BRADFORD

Selby

BLACKBURN

Howden

WAKEFIELD

MANCHESTER

SHEFFIELD

Blyth

Stow

LIVERPOOL

Worksop

Bardney

ST.ASAPH

CHESTER

LINCOLN

BANGOR

SOUTHWELL

DERBY

Binham

Elmham

St.Benet
Hulme

LICHFIELD

Croyland

NORWICH

Shrewsbury

LEICESTER

Thorney

Wymondham

PETERBOROUGH

Ramsey

Thetford

Dunwich

BIRMINGHAM

COVENTRY

ELY

ST.EDMUNDSBURY

Leominster

WORCESTER

Cambridge

Malvern

Pershore

HEREFORD

Evesham

Dunstable

Colchester

Llanthony

Tewkesbury

Abbey Dore

Winchcombe

ST.DAVIDS

BRECON

GLOUCESTER

Oseney

OXFORD

ST.ALBANS

CHELMSFORD

Cirencester

Abingdon

Waltham

Dorchester

LLANDAFF

NEWPORT

Malmesbury

Windsor

Eton

LONDON

Neath

Westbury

Ramsbury

SOUTHWARK

Margam

LLANDAFF

Reading

ROCHESTER

Redcliffe

BRISTOL

CANTERBURY

BATH

WINCHESTER

GUILDFORD

WELLS

Old Sarum

ROCHESTER

Glastonbury

St.Cross

Battle

SALISBURY

WINCHESTER

CHICHESTER

Sherborne

Romsey

Boxgrove

Arundel

CHICHESTER

Shoreham

Milton

PORTSMOUTH

EXETER

Wimborne

Christchurch

Selsey

Otter

Tavistock

TRURO

St.Germans

Scale of Miles

0   20   40   60   80   100

Introduction

What is a cathedral? The word is quite often used of any large church, as of Thaxted in Essex, and Altarnun in Cornwall, 'the cathedral of the moors'. But we are here restricted to the proper meaning, a church which contains the *cathedra* or throne of a bishop. In fact there was not during the Middle Ages any important difference, apart from the presence of the throne, between a cathedral and a large church belonging to one of certain other types. Architecturally, the churches of the greater monasteries, like Tewkesbury Abbey, or such collegiate churches as Beverley Minster, were of the same type as the cathedrals. That is to say, they were suited to processional and choral services, and the constant round of the *opus Dei*, 'God's service'; they were not directed to the needs of a lay congregation. So structural or artistic consideration of the mediaeval cathedrals implies comparison with these other churches built with a fundamentally similar purpose.

On the other hand, the present cathedrals of England are not all of this type: modern growth of population has caused the division of ancient sees, and many of the new cathedrals are normal parish churches, in which the bishop's throne and the choir services are functional intrusions. This book, considering the cathedrals as structures and as works of art, deals only with churches which are now cathedrals; thus excluding Westminster Abbey, a cathedral only from 1540 to 1550; but including St. Albans, an abbey church converted to cathedral use in 1878. Conversely, it deals with cathedrals built for choir services; the parochial churches recently erected into cathedrals are thus eliminated. The total number of churches left for inclusion is twenty-seven, and falls conveniently into three groups of nine.[1]

First come those ancient cathedrals which were always, as now, served by bodies of secular clergy, a chapter of canons presided over by a dean:

---

[1] The modern cathedrals of Truro, Liverpool, Guildford and Coventry have been omitted because historical judgment on a work less than a century old is impossible. Bath has been included because, though no longer a cathedral, it was built as such and still shares in the name of the see.

these are Chichester, Exeter, Hereford, Lichfield, Lincoln, London, Salisbury, Wells and York.[1] In the second place come the monastic cathedrals, those which before their 'new foundation' by Henry VIII had been served by regular clergy. In these the bishop of the diocese acted simultaneously as abbot of a great religious house, whose internal administration was headed by the prior. At the dissolution of the monasteries, all the monastic cathedrals then existing in England (except Coventry, which shared a diocese with Lichfield, as Bath did with Wells) were transformed into establishments of secular canons, on the same pattern as the first series: Bath, Canterbury, Carlisle, Durham, Ely, Norwich, Rochester, Winchester, Worcester. All of these had been houses of Benedictine monks, except Carlisle, which belonged to the Augustinian regular canons.

The third group consists of two sections: the five new cathedrals of Henry VIII which (with Westminster) were abbey churches made cathedral at the Dissolution: Bristol, Chester, Gloucester, Oxford, Peterborough. Bristol and Oxford had been Augustinian houses, the rest were Benedictine. The last four of our cathedrals were great churches surviving from the Middle Ages: Ripon and Southwell, always secular foundations; St. Albans, a Benedictine abbey; and Southwark, another priory of Augustinian canons. A curious point is that of the twenty-seven mitred abbeys whose abbots sat in the House of Lords with seventeen bishops (Bath and Wells having but one bishop between them) only four became cathedrals: Gloucester, Peterborough, St. Albans and, for ten years only, Westminster; and of only seven others is any part of the church still in use.[2]

Architecturally, the twenty-seven churches comprised in our three groups are the English cathedrals. They form a relatively compact body, having little in common with the parish-church cathedrals such as Birmingham, Chelmsford or Wakefield. But they are, as has already been mentioned, very closely related indeed to the non-cathedral greater churches which have by good fortune survived independently from the same period, some in a fragmentary state, and others almost complete. These churches could well form the subject of a separate volume, and deserve far more attention than they generally receive. Beverley, Tewkesbury and Westminster Abbey are world-famous, but there is a long list of former collegiate and monastic churches seldom visited in comparison with the cathedrals.[3]

[1] All four ancient Welsh cathedrals belong with this group.

[2] Croyland, Malmesbury, Selby, Shrewsbury, Tewkesbury, Thorney, Waltham. The others were Abingdon, Bardney, Battle, Bury, Canterbury St. Augustine's, Cirencester, Colchester, Evesham, Hulme St. Benet's, Glastonbury, Ramsey, Reading, Tavistock, Winchcombe, Winchester Hyde Abbey, York St. Mary's.

[3] In addition to the three famous churches named above, and the remains of six other mitred abbeys mentioned in the previous note, there are the following complete or fragmentary churches in use: Abbey Dore, Arundel, Binham, Blanchland, Blyth, Bolton, Boxgrove, Bridlington, Brinkburn,

Altogether, more than one hundred churches belonged to the cathedral tradition in English architecture: one quarter are now cathedrals, one quarter are totally destroyed, and the other half are wholly or partially in use, or represented by extensive ruins such as those of Fountains, Kirkstall and Rievaulx abbeys. This number is small compared with the vast total of cathedrals which existed upon the continent. In England there are only two archiepiscopal provinces; the area of present France (four times the size of England) was comprised within fifteen mediaeval provinces. The English provinces were made up of fourteen and three sees respectively, while in France the larger number would be nearer the average. In consequence, the English average of quality is relatively very high; for though we are accustomed to think of the vast cathedrals of the Ile-de-France and Champagne as typical of France, many of the ancient French cathedrals are architecturally insignificant, and have little to do with the main development of the cathedral as an art-form.

The great provinces of France were almost separate countries, and their arts and architecture were correspondingly diverse: in sharp contradistinction to this, English political unity, achieved very early in her history, brought with it a fundamental unity of art history, which nevertheless did not lead to a monotonous uniformity. On the contrary, though the English cathedrals form a homogeneous series, and the French do not, there is within this unity a greater diversity of individual treatment than in, for example, the great churches of the northern French Gothic. French logic and mental clarity were carried to such an extreme that the ideal of one perfect solution, and one only, of any problem was always kept in mind. The commonsense Englishman, working by rule-of-thumb, was not deterred by theory from doing just what he liked. The result is that England has no perfect type cathedral to set beside Chartres or Rheims; she has no portentous and structurally unsound extravagance such as Beauvais; no exquisite aspiration like Bourges.

The English temperament is uneasy upon the heights; at its best it still remains human, not bound to the earth, but firmly rooted in it; even in its flights of idealism it shuns the purely mystical abstraction and seeks some practical expression of its fervour. Like the ideal Chinese mirrored in Confucius, the Englishman rarely speaks of spiritual beings. Hence there is a warmth, a welcoming and homely quality in the English cathedrals which cannot be found elsewhere. French cathedrals dominate by their remoteness; German cathedrals crush by sheer superhuman size and strength; Spanish

---

Bristol St. Mary Redcliffe, Cartmel, Chester St. John's, Christchurch, Darlington, Dorchester, Dunstable, Hexham, Holme Cultram, Howden, Lanercost, Leominster, Malton, Great Malvern, Milton, Norwich Blackfriars, Ottery, Pershore, Romsey, St. Bees, St. Cross, St. German's, Sherborne, New Shoreham, Smithfield St. Bartholomew's (London), Wimborne, Worksop, Wymondham.

cathedrals are the dark and throbbing heart of a sombre mysticism; Italian cathedrals the theatrical properties of children at play. But the cathedrals of England took as their theme the exhortation to the weary and heavy-laden: the man of George Herbert's vision was an Englishman; deprived of rest in the outer world of everyday affairs, he would be driven to seek it in the church, and above all in the cathedral.

In modern times the English have ceased to find their home in the cathedrals; but the form taken by the buildings was due to this temperamental need of the English character. We must study them, first as works of man dedicated to the constant service of God; and secondly as works of Englishmen made to be transcendental homes. Thus they typify in the highest degree the English sense of balance which has been our greatest asset and the source of our worldly successes and of what is best in our character too: a feeling akin both to the moderation in all things inculcated by the Greek, and the doctrine of the golden mean taught by the Chinese sage.

Yet English art too has its excesses; and, in order to live, it is evident that all art must in some way depart from a mere state of equilibrium if it is to avoid the insipid balance of mediocrity. In a purely material sense, the individual excesses of the great nations of Europe can be traced in the extreme characteristics of their cathedrals: France excels in height, Germany in volume, Spain in area, Italy in colour. The English tendency is to length, in its churches as in its anglers' captures, or in those legendary 'Tales of the long Bow' so well epitomized by the authors of *1066 and All That* in their version of Robin Hood's last shaft, which 'hit the Sheriff of Nottingham again'.

Remembering that length without breadth is the property of the line, it can be seen that English length is essentially the outcome of the linear quality of our art. All the great achievements of our architecture, the finest features of our cathedrals, can be traced back to this preoccupation with outline and with the patterns formed by lines. And the principal, the main lines had to be straight lines. Thus we reached the typically and exclusively English development of the Perpendicular style, where straight lines subdivide windows, and equally form a pattern of blind tracery upon the surfaces of walls. Even in arches, where the form resisted to the utmost any attempt to reduce it to straight lines, we adopted first the acute and later the obtuse four-centred arch, whose curving arcs are minimized. This characteristic is seen in pronounced form in the acute vault of the nave of Winchester Cathedral, and in the obtuse vault, a century later, over the Divinity School at Oxford.

Before examining the chief features of the English cathedral, it may be well to consider briefly the outstanding qualities of the cathedrals of other European countries. To compare only buildings that are comparable, we must set aside the classical survivals and early revivals of Italy, and the Byzan-

2. *Ely from south: 1083–1130 and later*

3. *Peterborough from south-west: 1117–1230; central tower, c. 1335*

4. *York from south-east: central tower, 1408–23, by William Colchester, completed 1474*

tine domed types which spread from the eastern Empire through Venice to southern and western France. The remaining cathedrals are a family, a north-west European group of buildings sharing a common origin in the Lombardic and Romanesque churches of the early Middle Ages, and grounded in a common tradition of development. Most of these churches, even where they have retained part of the Romanesque fabric of the tenth to twelfth centuries, were profoundly modified after the adoption of the Gothic style.

Gothic architecture, whatever its ultimate sources, was first brought to something approaching an integrally fresh style upon French soil, though a major part of its invention is closely linked to England and to Normandy and the dominions of the English kings in France. While admitting the claims of France, or rather of the restricted domain of the French king close to Paris, to be the fountain-head of the great Gothic movement which in the thirteenth century was to spread the new art all over western Europe, we must not forget that it was in England, and to be specific, in the nave of Wells and the choir of Lincoln, both designed before 1200, that Gothic was first seen in a pure form, freed from survivals of Romanesque massing and detail. Among surviving works, the definite break with the Romanesque tradition is seen to have taken place between the design of the classic works of Sens, Laon and Paris cathedrals and the church of St. Remi at Rheims, and that of the choir of Wells. The vital date is close to 1175, or half a century from the first appearance of the germs of Gothic architecture.

The epoch of the great cathedrals of northern France opened with Notre-Dame at Paris, begun in 1163; it lasted for about one hundred years. These cathedrals share a common plan and a common approach to the problems of design. They are broad in proportion to their length, being frequently provided with double aisles which materially simplified the buttress system. The sanctuary terminates in a semi-circular or polygonal arcade surrounded by ambulatory and by radiating chapels. The transepts are of slight projection or altogether absent, and the crossing is seldom emphasized by a central tower. But externally emphasis is placed on the entrances by the provision of deep porches, usually in threes, flanked by nichework and sculptures of great importance and surmounted by towers in pairs, sometimes above the transeptal as well as the western fronts.

In proportion to their plan, these French cathedrals were extremely tall. By contrast, the height of the earlier Gothic cathedrals of England was moderate, but their breadth was also less, for single aisles were normal. Transepts were always of strong projection, the central tower was generally the point of greatest emphasis, and the eastern termination was almost invariably square. This was so even when it replaced a Romanesque ambulatory. Transeptal towers were not employed, and western towers seldom competed in importance with the central feature of tower or spired steeple. Only the west front was emphasized, and to a much slighter extent than in

5. *Winchester: west front, c. 1360–1400, completed by William Wynford*

France: the triple porch was most uncommon. Very often the main entrance was not through the western doors, as in France, but through a lateral porch on which the finest craftsmanship was expended.

Notwithstanding their great height, the French cathedrals rarely stand out from the landscape as well as the English, for two reasons: first, the greater sharpness and clarity of outline of the English churches; secondly, the much more solid grouping of the town round a French cathedral, contrasting with the relative isolation of the English close or, by accident of history, the levelled space on which the claustral buildings of a monastic cathedral once

7. *Gloucester: presbytery remodelled 1337–67*

8. *Wells: nave by Adam Lock, c. 1192–1230*

9. *Lincoln: Angel choir and porch, 1256–80, by Simon of Thirsk*

10. *Gloucester from south-west: south aisle 1318–29; porch 1421–37; tower 1450–60*

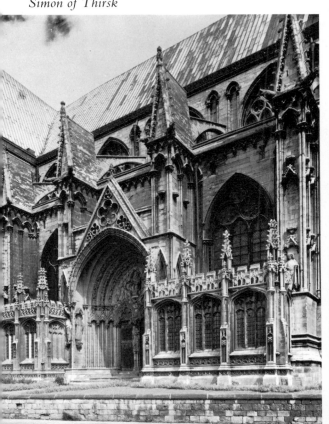

11. Lichfield from north-west: west front by Thomas Wallace, c. 1275–1320

stood. As we have seen, half of the ancient English cathedrals were monastic foundations, and stood at the centre of enormous institutions. The remaining, secular cathedrals tended more and more to borrow from the monastic type, building equally distinguished chapter-houses and cloisters, and even adding groups of houses, with hall and chapel attached on quasi-monastic lines, for their minor canons and vicars choral.

In the Low Countries the cathedrals adhere fairly closely to the French model, but tend to lose somewhat in coherence of composition while they gain in profusion of craftsmanship, and particularly in the development of the tower as an end in itself. In this they resembled English and German design, and their central position enabled them to bring together many of the

beauties of the surrounding schools. In Germany itself Rōmanesque forms lingered, and there was no adherence to one type of plan. Apses at both east and west ends; tri-apsidal terminations of sanctuary and transepts; and three parallel polygonal apses are found alongside the polygonal 'chevet' of French origin. Sheer mass is conspicuous in the greater German cathedrals, and as in England much thought was given to the effect of towers and spires, and to the decorative effect of ribbed vaults. Particularly national is the German hall-church of three aisles of equal height but different span, already employed in the thirteenth century, and towards the end of the Middle Ages becoming normal throughout Germany.

Austria, Hungary and Poland received direct impetus from France, and also further influences from Germany. Scandinavia too received Gothic art direct from France, and also from England, notably in Norway. Franco-Scandinavian influences reached the head of the Baltic, competing with the effects of German expansion and colonization. The number of mediaeval cathedrals in these parts of Europe is small, and it is impossible to speak of national types. In Italy the influence of classic Rome was always too strong to permit the full development of Gothic style, and most cathedrals of the period are strangely mongrel in effect. Apart from the general substitution of colour decoration for mouldings, and the almost total absence of the flying buttress, there are no major characteristics which define an Italian plan or school of design.

In Spain the case was different. During the Middle Ages the Mohammedan Moors were in full retreat from the Peninsula, and cathedrals were set up in the reconquered territories. For the most part these followed French models closely, and were designed by French architects, but later there was an influx of masters from England, the Netherlands and Germany. The churches are

13. Canterbury from south-west: nave by Henry Yeveley, 1379–1400; south-west tower by Thomas Mapilton, 1423–34; central tower, 1490–97, by John Wastell

wide-spreading and frequently, unlike those of France, have a central lantern supported on squinch arches above the crossing. Owing to the brilliance of the light, the window openings are usually small and the interiors dark. One of the most widespread features is the series of lateral chapels making a complete circuit of the outer walls, between the buttresses. This occurs both in cathedrals of the normal Franco-Spanish type, and in the aisleless churches of Catalonia and southern France, of which the outstanding examples are Gerona, with its single span of 73 feet, and Albi in France. Both this aisleless design, and the central lanterns, show a preoccupation with space, and with the appearance of spaciousness, otherwise rare in Gothic art except in its later years.

It has been common to describe the English cathedrals with undiscriminating eulogy, or else to depreciate them by means of carefully chosen contrasts with France. Neither of these methods results in a fair assessment of their value, either as witnesses to the English spirit, or as works of art pure and simple. In the last resort, judgment must be a matter of personal taste and opinion, but at least the evidence on both sides should be presented fairly, and given a patient hearing. And first it must be said that condemnation of the English cathedrals is usually abstract and theoretical. As abstractions, the great French cathedrals undoubtedly come nearer to perfection than any English example; yet this remote perfection tends of itself to remove them from the human scale of values to which works of art must be related.

With the outstanding exception of Bourges, the greatest of the French cathedrals are cold and aloof, fired only by a detached mental fervour akin to the passion of the higher mathematician and the astronomer for their lofty subjects. No concession is made to human frailty, the quality of mercy is absent from their terrible judgments upon the puny beings who pass through their doors. At Chartres the glorious windows, many of them given by the gilds of local craftsmen, infuse a different atmosphere; but the statues of the porches appal the spirit by their chilly disdain of mundane affairs. The French cathedrals fall under the great condemnation of French thought, despite their grandeur and logic: having all things, they yet lack charity.

The strict adherence of French art to prepared schemes of iconography; the refusal of the architects to countenance decorative elements such as stellar vaulting; the overburden of heavy flying buttresses to which they were constrained by insistence upon height: all bear witness to this hidden spiritual weakness in France. In the attempt to scale the heavens, the French cathedrals have lost contact with the earth; in seeking to express something above humanity they fall, by their almost Pharisaical excess, below the best aspirations of which mankind is capable. As temples of the great God preached by their stones, their glass and their colourwork, they suffer only from the one defect: they desired to be the first and greatest of all.

Having said so much, not in depreciation of the masterpieces of France, but in extenuation of other claims, it is time to look on the other side of the medal. The French cathedrals have all qualities but the one; they are the highest fruit of reason, their structures almost personify for us logic, unity of purpose, a complete and rounded aesthetic. In none of these can their English counterparts hope to compete. For, quite apart from the distinctions of national temperament, there is a great historical difference between the English and the French cathedrals. Whereas most of the great French churches were so fortunate as to be completed in one age and according to one design, this is in England an exception of the utmost rarity. There is not a single English cathedral, except the Renaissance St. Paul's, which was built from start to finish under the supervision of its original architect. Nor is there any mediaeval cathedral save the latest, Bath, which was in essentials finished according to the intentions of its designer, and still retains those essentials unchanged.

Most of our cathedrals resemble that other homely product of England,

15. Salisbury from north-west: west front 1258–66 by Master Richard

16. *Exeter from south-east, c. 1275–1308*

the patchwork quilt. Those which most nearly approach the ideal, in order of date are: Durham, essentially Norman, but with added Galilee, eastern chapels, and central tower; Lincoln, an Early English structure retaining a Norman front and with the addition of a Decorated retrochoir; Salisbury, more mature Early English, but with the major addition of a late Decorated steeple; Exeter, mostly Decorated, but keeping its Norman transeptal towers and adding a Perpendicular west frontal; Bristol, Decorated but with Perpendicular tower and modern nave. Finally there is Bath, a work entirely designed by Robert and William Vertue, but not completed until modern times, and suffering from extensive alterations and restorations. All the rest are veritable museums of the periods of English architecture.

We cannot therefore judge our cathedrals as complete, integral works of art: their individual parts have to be assessed on their intrinsic merits, and upon the contribution they make, partly intentional, partly fortuitous, to each building viewed as a whole. To some extent we must even form imaginative dream-pictures of a cathedral completed in accordance with the scheme of certain parts. At Canterbury we may mentally supply a nave in keeping with the French design of the eastern arm, or equally suppose a vast accession of funds to have destroyed this in favour of a total reconstruction upon the lines of the present nave, and to the designs of Henry Yeveley. The unfinished crossing-arches at Ripon suggest the completion of the late Perpendicular church under the supervision of Christopher Scune. And in almost every case, satisfied with our vain imaginings, we should awaken glad

17. *Bristol from south-east, c. 1311–40; central tower, c. 1466–71*

18. *Bath from south-west, 1501–39, by Robert and William Vertue*

*19. Ripon: nave by Christopher
Scune, 1502–22*

that the buildings are as they are. There is a beauty pleasing to the English
temperament even in the variety and the disjointedness. We have no desire
to be ruthlessly logical, to decide upon the appropriate scheme and eliminate
the rest. We much prefer (and surely our cathedrals are the supreme example
of an English habit) to muddle through.

It is unfortunately true that in the nineteenth century there arose a school
of architects in England who brought much dire destruction to the cathedrals
in the name of uniformity and of restoration to the supposed original concepts of the Gothic designer. It is to be feared that this campaign of holy
destruction was partly due to latent Puritanism; partly also it stemmed from
the mistaken desire (very natural in Victorian England) to render the English
monuments perfect, and so to surpass the rest of the world. But it did spring
too from a real love of our architectural heritage. In condemning the excesses
of Sir George Gilbert Scott we should remember that we owe to him, and
to his capacity for enduring exertion, discomfort and dirt in a good cause,
the rescue of the Chapter-house of Westminster Abbey. Much painful work
by Street is condoned by the loving care he expended on the new nave of
Bristol, to make it a worthy prelude to the truncated remains of the original
church.

Readers of this book, and still more, visitors to the buildings themselves,
must accept the cathedrals for what they are. Here our main attempt must

be to trace out the general course of development of their history and design, to show how it was that they became the monuments that we know. Unable to consider them as unities, we may still study their separate parts, and see how the great English architects made constant progress in their individual adaptations of the common tradition to the practical and aesthetic needs of their times. Never content with a method of vaulting, a column, a tower, a pattern of tracery, they used all their ingenuity to improve, to make each new specimen better than the last. And probably the most unusual feature of English Gothic is their continuous success. From Saxon times to the reign of Henry VIII there is no single work at any English cathedral which could be described as decadent. Sometimes inspiration flagged a little; the steps taken were uneven. But nowhere is there marked retrogression, not a work but bears plainly upon it the mark of a creative imagination.

This was true again of our single cathedral of the Renaissance, Wren's St. Paul's in London. Bitterly as we may regret the loss of Old St. Paul's, historically and stylistically the most interesting of all our cathedrals, its successor is unmistakably a great building. Even the heartiest loathing for the trappings of the classical revival cannot blind us to the fact that St. Paul's is a masterpiece in the foremost rank of the world's buildings. And Wren, its designer, never showed to better effect the vigour of his mind and his superb control of materials; while force of circumstances and the feelings of his clients saw that it was no foreign changeling, but an English cathedral church, that was to stand at the top of Ludgate Hill. Mentally shorn of its surface decorations, St. Paul's is indeed the star witness to the force and value of the English tradition.

20. *St. Paul's from south-east, 1675–1710*

I   The Building of Cathedrals

Before we can understand fully the English cathedral as a finished work of art, some general idea of cathedrals and of how they were built is essential. In the architectural sense we are here concerned only with buildings of a certain absolute size: many cathedrals are or have been of quite small proportions and can hardly be distinguished from other churches. It was the coming of the really large church, usually though not necessarily a cathedral, that introduced a new factor. It is not that mere quantity by itself is valuable, but that large scale involves a higher degree of complexity in organization. This complexity brings out the skill of the designer and his aptitude for composition in a way that small works seldom or never can. The opportunities for incorporating works of art of other kinds: sculpture, wall paintings, stained glass, can only be compared to the musical composer's power of associating in a single work the different qualities of the instruments of the orchestra.

The architect of a major cathedral is not simply a creative original artist, nor a supreme master craftsman; he is also the director of a team, captain of a ship, impresario and producer. Necessarily he receives assistance from many others, and his ideas are carried out by a body of craftsmen and labourers, but his are the ruling concepts which inspire and pervade the whole. In actual practice this has rarely happened, for the available funds have very seldom permitted the completion of a large cathedral within the lifetime of the original architect. It is at this point that sheer size in general causes the analogy with great works of music to break down. Whereas unfinished symphonies or concerti are rare, builds of only parts of cathedrals are a commonplace. We know that many of the great designs on the continent never were finished: Beauvais and Narbonne remain truncated fragments; Cologne was not complete until 1880. In England the only one of the cathedrals thus to remain unfinished over a long period was Bristol, without a nave for some four centuries. On the other hand, all our mediaeval cathedrals except Salisbury and Bath were built and rebuilt in sections.

The tradition of the great church inevitably owes something to the pagan temples of classical Greece and Rome, but in a strictly architectural sense it is dominated mainly by the Roman basilica. Nave, choir and transept may be regarded as basilicas joined together or interpenetrating, though the form was transmuted in the course of time, and underwent much variation. It is striking that even the greatest mediaeval churches were usually, regarded as units of structure, smaller in scale than the largest of the Roman basilicas. Thus, in spite of the requirement of large scale, the men of the Middle Ages demonstrated a higher refinement and a greater degree of sensibility than the Romans had possessed. It is also manifest that they surpassed in these respects most of their successors down to the present day. This paradoxical combination of refinement with the capacity to demand and to construct very large buildings of relatively great complexity, poses a fundamental problem.

What was the motive that caused really large churches to be built? Obviously one basic motive of a practical kind might exist, the need to accommodate large congregations. So far as places of worship were concerned, this was a new requirement in religion brought in by official Christianity. Pagan temples had not catered for the admission of layfolk: the roofed interior, even of a large temple, was a sacred cell to which the public of worshippers was not admitted. When the great sanctuaries of pre-Christian times were concerned with large bodies of worshippers, they were provided for in open-air courtyards. Such a courtyard or *atrium*, usually a colonnaded cloister, was built in front of the main doors of early Christian churches. At Old St. Peter's in Rome (AD 323–26 and later) there was an atrium of this kind with internal dimensions of about 180 by 150 feet, as a prelude to a five-aisled basilican church with an overall size of some 400 feet by 200, a *bema* or transept at the head in front of the high altar, and an apse behind the altar. For a very long period this was the model for almost all greater churches in the West, but many of them were in fact on a substantially smaller scale.

The intention of the large church was that it should be able to include, standing, the whole Christian population of a city. Before the growth of the parochial system there would normally be only the one major church, and that the bishop's, i.e. his cathedral. Beyond this there might be special sanctuaries at places of pilgrimage, where the crowds of pilgrims from a distance formed the congregations at special services. In Rome itself there were three churches of cathedral size built in the fourth century: the cathedral of St. John Lateran, and the two pilgrimage churches of St. Peter's and St. Paul's outside the Walls. Since Rome was the capital of the Empire, it was not likely that there would be any need for churches on such a scale elsewhere. In fact, early cathedrals built in late Roman cities generally do remain roughly proportionate to the population. As Christianity gained ground and became the only religion officially recognized, a bishop was appointed for each major city and a cathedral was built for him. Hence the concept of the cathedral as a really large church does go back to the very beginning of public Christian worship.

The downfall of the Western Roman Empire, however, changed both the normal requirements and the ability to fulfil them. The arts and crafts were in decline, and the large-scale organization demanded for the construction of great basilicas was no longer available. On the other hand, the same decay made it impossible to feed very large populations in big cities, and a new world of relatively small but self-supporting towns came into being. The church adapted itself to the new conditions, which meant that in many cases a bishop might have his church in a town or village of quite modest size. In the countryside still smaller churches served ordinary rural communities, and in course of time the system of parishes developed. For a long time it was not necessary, and perhaps not even desirable, for a multitude of people to come together inside a single building. For this reason the cathedrals of the Dark Ages were small by the standard set by Rome, and continued in Constantinople.

Up to now we have considered only the material reason for large churches. Undoubtedly there was as well a less obvious motive: the greater glorification of God by means of all the show and ingenuity of which the human artist was capable. The opportunities provided by a large cathedral for works of art of every kind were almost endless. The greater church became as it were a model or microcosm of the created universe, wherein men according to their talents did their best to imitate the handiwork of the Creator. The structural skills of building craftsmen united with the artistic gifts of carvers and painters, under the directional impetus provided by the creative imagination of the architect. As the figure of the Creator was depicted, compasses in hand, setting out the limits of land and sea and of the firmament above them, so also in humbler guise did the master mason declare himself by his pair of compasses and by his square. Not merely human imagination, but human capacity to realise the imagined concept in material form, was expressed in the greater church, of which the most familiar example to us is the cathedral.

As we shall see later on, in discussing English cathedrals before the Norman Conquest, this country had to wait a long time for the idea of the greater church. Even the importation, at intervals during the Anglo-Saxon period, of craftsmen from Rome or from the continent did not produce any major sanctuaries that can be set beside contemporary works in Italy. So any consideration of the building of cathedrals in England begins with the onset of the Norman period. This was rather before the Conquest, in the reign of

Edward the Confessor, who had spent most of his early life in Normandy and by 1050 had decided to rebuild Westminster Abbey in the up-to-date style of the Normans. The abbey church at Westminster, consecrated in 1065 just before the Confessor's death, was architecturally the first of the English cathedrals. Enough is known of its plan and character to show what a pace-setter it was.

Westminster derived its plan and general scheme from the latest abbey churches of Normandy: Bernay and Jumièges. It had an east end of three parallel apses, a central tower and two western towers and a nave of double bays with alternating compound piers and cylindrical columns. What is particularly striking at Westminster, however, is the great length of this nave comprising six double bays, that is twelve bays in all. This length seems to have had no continental precedents, though it was to have many followers in England. It would seem that a quality of longitude derived from the linear characteristics of earlier English art (see p. 22) was adopted, and perhaps too that King Edward was determined to outdo the greatest churches of Normandy itself. In any case it has to be remembered that fresh influences were at the same time transforming the social and artistic life of Normandy.

The Normans, who had been Viking pirates in the ninth century and had legalized their conquest of Normandy early in the tenth, were a relatively small caste of mounted soldiers. Like the Turks in the East, they were military adventurers who achieved rule over much larger subject populations. Neither Normandy nor England was Norman in virtue of any dense settlement, but by dominance based on victory in the field. The remarkable fighting qualities of the Normans, as well as their love of adventure, readily found them employment as mercenaries. Serving the Byzantine Greeks and the Lombards in that capacity, they found it possible within a single generation to take over the southern half of Italy and the island of Sicily. The Norman leaders throughout the fifty years of this Italian campaign, 1030–1080, were a band of brothers, the sons of Tancred of Hauteville, a Norman nobleman of Coutances. This close connection of the great Mediterranean expedition with the city of Coutances had particular significance.

It is at Coutances that the direct results of the Norman contact with the civilization of southern Europe are specified. The chronicler tells us that the bishop there, Geoffrey de Montbray (1049–1093), soon after his accession to the see went to visit his relatives in southern Italy, including their famous leader Robert Guiscard, sixth son of Tancred. Bishop Geoffrey came home loaded with gold, silver and precious stuffs; but also with spacious ideas derived from the Byzantine and Saracenic cultures which he had tasted on his journey. At a date before the Conquest of England in 1066 he had bought from Duke William a large estate in the suburbs of Coutances and there built a palace and planted a park. This was possibly the first introduction of the oriental 'paradise' into north-western Europe, and thus the very foundation of all subsequent developments of man-made landscape in France and England. But Bishop Geoffrey did a great deal more than this in connection with the cathedral for which he was responsible. He was one of the first to organize the life of the cathedral clergy on the basis of shares or prebends in the common stock. This, in contradistinction to the communal life of canons regular enjoined by the Lateran synod of 1059, was to become the normal system not only in France but in England. In addition to the clerics, 'a precentor and succentor, a schoolmaster, keepers of the church, clerks and prebendaries,' the bishop appointed at Coutances 'goldsmiths, blacksmiths, carpenters and a master mason.'

It is this model system set up in Normandy that has to be kept in mind when studying mediaeval methods of building and of maintenance. As a system it took its rise in the generation of 1060–90 and provided the human framework within which cathedrals were built and repaired for the next five centuries. The keepers of the church, with administrative responsibility for the fabric, were clergymen; but design and craftsmanship were provided by the laymen of different skills. The most significant point in the chronicler's description of the arrangements at Coutances is the opposition between the plural goldsmiths, blacksmiths and carpenters on one hand, and on the other the unique post of master mason. In spite of an occasional exception, where building works might be carried out under two or more directors in collaboration, it became usual for ultimate technical responsibility to rest with a single architect. This fact, inherently probable in any case, is sometimes obscured by the sharing out of praise by historians to the members of a group, and produces confusion between the clerical 'keepers' of the works, the architect himself, and the foreman of masons or (later) building contractor. Luckily full details were preserved in the case of one great cathedral, built in the relevant period (c. 1074–1122): Santiago de Compostela. Although in the remote north-western corner of Spain, Compostela was designed in Norman-French style and its technical masters bore the French names Bernard and Robert. The full account tells us that 'the masters of masonry who first built the church . . . were called Master Bernard the old the wonderful master, and Robert, with about fifty other masons who worked there diligently under the management of the most religious lords, Wicart, and the reverend canon Segered, and abbot Gundesund.' The last three were the clerical building committee; Bernard was certainly the designer; Robert the leading mason, foreman, warden or deputy of Bernard – perhaps even what we would now call a site-architect.

In the Latin text, two different words are used with the sense of 'master'. The phrase translated above as 'masters of masonry' is *didascali lapicidae*, literally 'teachers of stonecutting'; while Bernard is given the title of

21. St. Albans: tower and south transept, 1077–1115, by Master Robert

'Magister' and also described as *mirabilis magister,* the wonderful master because quite evidently recognized as the creative designer of the church. In just the same way the chronicle of St. Albans Abbey celebrated the original architect of our oldest surviving cathedral, Master Robert, as excelling all the masons of his time (1077–1115). All this helps when we try to interpret the rather vague references to the Confessor's building staff at Westminster, where three different men are named. One of them, Teinfrith, was the king's 'churchwright', and this can only mean that he was a carpenter skilled in setting up churches of timber, or the timber scaffolds and roofs for stone churches such as the Abbey. Leofsi Duddason, also called Leofsi of London, was specifically in charge of the masons who built the new church at Westminster; and this almost certainly means that, like Robert at Compostela, he was the warden or deputy of the architect. The third person named was Godwin Gretsyd, the master mason. He was a person of consequence, able to leave property of value to Westminster Abbey and also to Hyde Abbey at Winchester. There can be very little doubt that it was Godwin who was the designer.

What is puzzling is that the names of the three Westminster craftsmen all seem to be English rather than Norman, when it might have been expected that the king would have imported masters from overseas just as he had brought Robert of Jumièges to be his bishop of London in 1044 and later (1051) archbishop of Canterbury. Wherever they received their training, the church that Godwin, Leofsi and Teinfrith built at Westminster was quite certainly not Saxon, but Norman and up-to-date in the manner of the church at Jumièges as yet unfinished (1040–67). It has to be recognized that the adoption of a foreign style can be achieved in either of two ways: by the importation of foreign artists, or by the imitation of foreign models by native designers. In the latter case, residence abroad as part of a technical education is undoubtedly common. At any rate the invasion of England by Norman architecture some fifteen years or more before the Conquest is one main reason for the totally Norman character of all our cathedrals. Conservative details of the sort assigned to the 'Saxo-Norman overlap', frequent in smaller churches, are not found in works of grand scale. The greater church in the architectonic sense, whether monastic or cathedral, was an entirely new phenomenon in England.

The organization required to build a new architecture must have been present between 1050 and 1065 at the construction of Westminster Abbey. Since the earliest references to a royal palace at Westminster occur while the Confessor's abbey was in course of building, it is extremely likely that a single works organization was set up to build houses for the king and court as well as for the monks. Such methods of building were quite unparalleled in England at the time, and this helps to explain why there was a gap of twenty years or more before the next large churches were begun. These were Lanfranc's cathedral at Canterbury and the Minster at York, now destroyed; the abbey at Battle, and then St. Albans, not started until 1077. At St. Albans, however, a flying start was given to the works by the fact that the last Saxon abbots had been collecting Roman tiles from the ruins of Verulamium with a view to rebuilding. In most cases one of the first problems was to find a source of building materials such as a quarry within easy reach. Where no suitable stone was present in the district it had to be imported, and it is significant of the early dependence of England upon Normandy that very large amounts of stone were shipped from Caen for well over a hundred years after the Conquest. Though Caen stone is one of the best of the oolitic limestones, its use in Norman and early Gothic times demonstrates widespread ignorance in England as to the native supplies. It was only under the masters of the new age of Norman Romanesque architecture that English quarries of stone were sought and found.

It was not necessary to go abroad for timber, since England had already a strong tradition of carpentry, and extensive oak woods. But the large size of the timbers needed for greater churches of the new type undoubtedly meant that serious exploration of the forests had to be undertaken to find trees adequate for the permanent roofs and for the temporary scaffolds and centerings. That such exploration might not readily be productive is shown by the famous record of the works of Abingdon Abbey under Abbot Faritius (1100–35), when six wains, each drawn by 12 oxen, had to make a journey of six or seven weeks to Shrewsbury and back to get beams and rafters from Wales. More specific detail was recorded by Abbot Suger of St. Denis as to his search for long beams about 1140. His new western narthex required twelve tie-beams of such a length that the abbey's own carpenters and those of Paris agreed that they could not be found. Suger, after a sleepless night, describes how he set off in the early morning with his carpenters to the abbey's forest at Chevreuse. The foresters and keepers of all the woods in the district were questioned under oath, and grinned at the abbot's naivety in supposing that trees of that kind might be had. There was no help for it but for Suger to conduct his own search: in spite of tangled undergrowth and thickets of thorns he found one tree of sufficient size in the first hour, and all twelve by the end of the day. The timber then had to be felled, transported some 25 miles to the other side of Paris, and finally hauled up and placed in position.

Generally it was the master carpenter who went to the woods to find timber, and information as to resources must have improved as time went on. For any unusual work, however, special search had to be made, as for the eight great posts of the timber lantern built at Ely in 1328–40, and for the 13 great collar-beams for the new roof of Westminster Hall designed in 1394.

Transport was always a major financial problem and, whenever possible, stone and timber were carried by water rather than by road. Once the materials were on the boat the cost was low, even for such long journeys as that from Caen to Canterbury, of the order of 200 miles. There was of course the danger of storms at sea, and this was even recorded when it gave rise to a miracle on behalf of Abbot Scotland's building at St. Augustine's, Canterbury (c. 1070–91). Out of a fleet of 15 ships laden with Caen stone only one, destined for the abbey works, survived a storm which sank the rest, whose cargoes had been quarried for the palace of William the Conqueror at Westminster.

From Suger's story of the beams for his new work at St. Denis it might be supposed that the building had reached wall-top level before anybody began to worry about how it could be roofed. This may or may not have been true in that particular case, but it cannot have been the general rule. The methods of roofing and of vaulting mediaeval buildings were usually an integral part of their design from an early stage. The forms of piers and shafting differed greatly according to whether they were intended to support an open timber ceiling or a stone vault. Even in the eleventh century the architects were sophisticated enough to consider the problems posed by wide spans and the thrusts exerted at the tops of high walls. It is in this aspect of design that the cathedrals and other great buildings set questions that had not been posed before. The small house or chapel with a narrow span, smaller than the length of the timbers usually available, could be dealt with as a matter of routine. For such work the traditional skills of the village mason or carpenter sufficed. Once outside the scope of these everyday buildings, the craftsman depended upon the special knowledge of the man of higher training whom we should now call the architect. One of the most remarkable facets of the history of mediaeval architecture is the fact that, when the demand for larger and more complex buildings arose, and architects of extensive knowledge were required, they appeared on the scene.

The architectural ability to plan cathedrals must certainly have been rare or non-existent in England before the eleventh century. What is more, it was also absent from the rest of north-western Europe. Not until after the year AD 1000, looked upon beforehand with superstitious expectation of the end of the world, were churches of great size built. Under influences from Italy and from Byzantium there had been a few tentative efforts to build large churches in Germany under the Ottonian emperors after 962, and it is probable that masters were brought from East and South. The forerunners of the cathedral as we understand the term architecturally were great monastic churches, St. Martin at Tours (c. 1000–50), St. Remi at Rheims (1005–45), deliberately intended to be the largest church in Gaul (i.e. the whole of geographical France), and Hersfeld (1037–71) in the Hessian region of northern central Germany. The church of St. Michael at Hildesheim (1001–33) was built for Bishop Bernward immediately on his return from Rome, and indicates at least one source of inspiration. Major German cathedrals were built at Mainz (1010–36), Strassburg (c. 1015–50), and at Speyer from about 1030 onwards. All of these were afterwards much altered or rebuilt, but they were designed on a grand scale from the start.

There are faint historical indications of some continuity of architectural skill preserved by Roman guilds (collegia), and still operating under the Lombards through the Dark Ages, but fresh impulses were needed to account for the suddenly expanding architecture of the eleventh century. Travellers' tales, not merely of Roman buildings, but also of what had been seen in Cordova and Constantinople, Cairo and even Bagdad, must have been filtering through. Islamic influences came from Spain into south-western France, and through Sicily and Amalfi into Italy. Sophisticated knowledge of design and of stonecutting reached Constantinople from Armenia and Syria and was handed on to the West. Yet it is a striking fact that the first great cathedrals of the North-West were built in spite of seriously defective methods. The quality of work left a great deal to be desired, and structural collapse was far from uncommon. It was only at a late date in this epoch, shortly before 1100, that really high quality emerged in the new church of Cluny abbey (Cluny III, 1085–1121). Instead of small stones with wide and irregular mortar joints, very large stones and narrow joints were used. This presupposes not only greatly improved capacity on the part of the masons, but the use of forms of hoisting tackle hitherto unknown north of the Alps and west of the Balkans.

The revival of machinery at this time is a vital factor often overlooked. The outstanding point to notice is that a considerable degree of improvement had taken place a generation at least *before* the West acquired Latin versions of classical treatises. The book learning, which after the First Crusade of 1097–99 was to come from the ninth-century Arabic translations of Greek authors, came too late to account for the empirical improvement that had already taken place. This is not to exclude further improvements closely linked to the rise of Gothic architectural style, but the advance of engineering methods was beginning by the time of the Norman Conquest of England. Though there were in fact crusades before the 'First', and returning pilgrims from Palestine founded circular churches in imitation of the Holy Sepulchre from 1045 (Neuvy St. Sepulcre) if not earlier, some more specific source of knowledge has to be sought. It is probable that this source was the taking of Barbastro from the Moors in 1064. An expedition, one of the most important of the proto-crusades, was led by Duke William VIII of Aquitaine and included a strong contingent of Normans and northern Frenchmen. The outcome was not to be measured simply by the very short Christian occupation

of Barbastro which followed. Of far greater importance was the capture of
thousands of prisoners, including singers and other artists. It is recorded that
the victors refused to ransom their captives, but sent them into France, to
Constantinople and to Rome. Among so many Moors from one of the chief
cities of Aragon, there were certainly the members of the corps of military
engineers who had been responsible for its defence. The fact that they were
defeated should not lead us to imagine that their technical skill was not well
ahead of that of their conquerors. One of the most significant features of the
story is that the son and heir of William VIII, born in 1071, was to become
famous as the first of the troubadours, composing poems and songs in
Provençal but derived directly from Arabic models. He can have acquired
this knowledge only from some of the Moorish prisoners kept at his father's
court.

This massive acquisition of skilled slaves of various crafts reinforced the
body of less direct knowledge that was being brought back by Normans
returning from their conquests in the south of Italy and in Sicily. Bishop
Geoffrey de Montbray was no doubt only one of many who visited Italy
and brought back rich objects of art and information of various kinds. Thus
the emergent barbarism of the Normans themselves was no bar to their
gaining control over servants of high skill, and sources of technical knowledge. A great deal of the information obtained was vitally necessary to the
ascendancy of the Norman war-machine. Methods of siege warfare, the use
of different kinds of catapults, and means of transport of heavy objects over
great distances, were all involved. Much of this was equally relevant to
civilian life. By a paradox it is to the brilliant logistics learned by the Normans in their campaigns that we owe the rise of the great cathedrals and of a
building industry which provided the model for modern industrialism.

Just as architecture has a special significance among the arts because it
unites the aesthetic and the practical, so the cathedral as an art form stands
for two things at once. On the one hand it is the concrete realization of man's
highest religious aspirations; but on the other it strained to the limit his
powers of material organization and technique. At times the human limits
were even overreached, and collapse was the result. Before criticizing the
architects who ran such risks we have to remember that trial and error
provided the only available means for the expansion of their knowledge.
This was true not only during the Romanesque and Gothic periods, but also
down to the opening of the nineteenth century. The slow development of
mathematics to a point where adequate structures could be calculated by
purely theoretical means went on for more than seven centuries after the
building of the immense abbeys and cathedrals of Burgundy, Normandy
and England. Improvements were entirely empirical: it was found that
precisely cut masonry and lime mortar of the best quality permitted thinner

walls and more slender piers. The main supports of the church of St. Bénigne at Dijon, begun in 1001, had an area four times that of the piers of Santiago de Compostela designed less than 75 years later. In turn the Gothic reduction of shafts in the course of the twelfth century was proportionately greater still (see p. 80).

It is now a commonplace that mediaeval architecture in northern Europe came to depend upon balance: the counterplay between the thrust of arches and vaults and the return pressure of buttresses. In the invention of timber roofs for increasingly wide spans a different kind of balance was sought and found by the use of forms of cantilever or bracket such as the hammer-beam truss. Yet we must beware of exalting this principle into an automatic mechanism developing along lines akin to those of evolution by natural selection. The tendency to suppose that structural forms survive purely because of their efficiency has been carried much too far. A good deal of modern study of the arts and crafts has made a fetish of typology, in which a purely ideal series of successive developments is postulated. This series, in default of precise historical record, is then used to provide a chronology. Thus a process, of undoubted value in field archaeology when applied to prehistoric periods entirely devoid of documentation, is reduced to absurdity when its inductive rules are set against the actual facts of the great ages of artistic progress. Rapid change in any art appears to yield a precise typological diagnosis. But it fails to correspond with recorded events. The reason is that, at any time, works of art are produced in response both to the individual demands of patrons, and according to the individual abilities of artists. In any one generation there co-exist both advanced and conservative clients and architects: over many years in the Transition from Romanesque to Gothic style, the semicircular and the pointed arch were used simultaneously. One building, for a traditionalist patron or by a master of the elder generation, might have round arches alone; another, by a young man responding to a leader of fashion, would be all pointed. Perhaps even more frequent than either extreme was the hybrid in which both forms were used. The same phenomenon occurs again and again and can be seen at work at the present day.

Hence the story of the English cathedral as an architectural form must be considered in the first place as history, and only in a secondary degree as an example of archaeological development of a type or group of related types. At each cathedral every separate build, the outcome of creative imagination by one master, may represent a step forward, a step back, or occasionally a merely stagnant or static disinclination to depart from the pre-existing framework of the original design and details. In certain cases, of course, it is permissible and indeed essential to argue that a given work *could not* have been designed in ignorance of some other, and that its date must necessarily be later. In a number of instances this proves to be true only in respect of the drawings made for some building never, or not then, executed. Thus the pierced spires of Burgos cathedral, designed in the fifteenth century by a German master from Cologne, reflected his knowledge of the great parchment drawings there which were realized in stone only after rediscovery of the parchments in the last century. The tower of St. Mary Aldermary in the city of London, begun in 1510, was a modification of the design prepared about 1450 for the tower desired by Henry VI for King's College, Cambridge, but never built.

The echoes and re-echoes of buildings and designs now lost tend to confuse the scene, but in spite of these bewildering cross-currents a fairly clear thread of development can be discerned. Notwithstanding false starts and side-slips, it can be seen as an example of genuine progress. As opposed to the fossilization of Byzantine art over many centuries, and the failure of French Gothic inspiration after Beauvais, the course taken by the English cathedrals is remarkable for its continued invention, the novelty of its ideas, and the human scale and character of their realization. Unlike most of the excuses for nationalism, the English cathedral gives abundant reasons for a proper pride.

II Cathedral Builders – Architects and Craftsmen

It has already been emphasized that our cathedrals owe their quality to the human element of originality. The individual aspirations and decisions, of founders, patrons and architects, as well as of many subordinate artists, contributed to make a whole which has a life of its own. This substitute 'life', breathed in as it were into the inanimate materials of which they are formed, depends to some extent upon the continued use of the cathedrals for their original function. Although doctrine changed at the Reformation, the cathedrals and the great monastic and collegiate churches that have survived, represent still a living form. This form is that of the church which subsists for the purpose of regular and continued prayer and worship by a body of clergy attached to it. Fundamentally the cathedral exemplifies the unworldly, or other-worldly, 'uselessness' of religion. It is not directed to material or practical ends, even though it may very often serve them as well. The immense lay congregations brought into the Early Christian cathedrals were essentially there as witnesses to the ritual and worship of the new faith, rather than as participants.

The very fact that more or less continuous adaptation has been needed to enable the cathedrals to be so used, through changes of doctrine and usage, contributes enormously to their living quality. The cathedrals are, in a psychological as well as a structurally physical sense, dynamic rather than static. Their arches are literally flexed bows, but have a far wider symbolical value. This symbolical value was increased by the adoption of the pointed arch in the Gothic style, giving an upward vertical thrust pulsing through every part of the building. The culmination of this movement towards the sky was provided by tall spires. In the course of the first hundred years of Gothic architecture the tops of pinnacles and roofs of towers took on a steeper pitch. Instead of low pyramids there arose tall sharp cones, marking from afar the positions of the greater churches. By the thirteenth century and through the fourteenth the provision of spires was universal, and it must be accepted that the square-topped tower was never designed for religious buildings until a very short time before 1400 at the earliest. Even to the end of the Middle Ages and long afterwards, as Wren's steeples prove, the spire was the hall-mark of the church, and especially of the cathedral.

It is impossible to say whether the adoption of pointed arches and the development of tall spires were efforts of conscious symbolism. It is likely that they were at least partly conscious. The dome, certainly in use in the Middle East in pre-Christian times, and employed on a grand scale in Rome, was undoubtedly an artificial 'heaven' representing the firmament. Indeed, in the oriental languages the same words are used for the firmament of heaven and for a structural dome. There is no reason to doubt that such themes, regarded as elements in 'programme architecture', have always played a part in the imagination of creative artists. What is less certain is the extent to which the patrons of the Middle Ages, especially the higher clergy, actually demanded that ideas expressive of the religious thought of the time should be incorporated in churches. There were indeed works written in such a way as to be capable of interpretation as manuals of symbolism. Of these the most famous is the *De gemma animae* of Honorius of Autun, composed before 1130 and thus available before any Gothic architecture existed. But Honorius was perhaps using the parts of a church as texts for a sermon, and arguing from existing works rather than advocating particular forms. He tells us that churches are directed to the East, where the sun rises, 'because in them the Sun of justice is worshipped'; that the transparent windows which keep out the weather and let in light 'are the Doctors who resist the storm of heresies and pour in the light of the Church's teaching'; that 'the belfry placed on high is lofty preaching which speaks of heavenly matters.' From such remarks it would not be possible to design a church, or even very materially to affect its form.

A much greater influence was exerted on planning and general design by theories of number and proportion. These were of two main kinds. The first system was directly based on the observed Pythagorean intervals in music. It was held, with great probability, that such a natural law of harmony would be true throughout the creation and not merely in respect to concordant sounds. As further refinements of proportion the ratios of the side to diagonal of a square (1 : 1·4142) and of the side to diagonal of a regular pentagon (1 : 1·618) were used extensively. The latter, mean and extreme ratio or the 'Golden Cut', has continued to fascinate mathematicians and artists down to our own time on account of the perfection of its infinite repetition. Though this could be precisely achieved by means of an extremely simple geometrical process, it was also used in the approximate form of the Fibonacci series of whole numbers: 5, 8, 13, 21, 34, 55, 89, 144. In this every term is the sum of the two preceding and the proportion is thus easily memorized and also easy to set out with measuring rods or cords.

The second system, or group of systems, upon which numerical proportions were founded was not geometrical but mystical. It was based on the numerical significance of letters of the alphabet, Greek, Roman, Hebrew or Arabic. According to this system, or science of numerology, every word could be translated, letter by letter, into a number; and conversely, every number expressed a word or words. Though the roots of this theory went back to pre-Christian times, and it was especially prevalent in the teachings of the Sufis in the Islamic world, it had a particular appeal to Christians. For it gave inner meaning to the opening of St. John's Gospel: the Word that was God was the ineffable Holy Name, but from it proceeded everything else. The light of men could be put into numbers, and given material substance by employing those numbers in composition and design. The planning of cathedrals offered an even wider scope in this direction than harmonic music. Needless to say, the employment of several different proportional methods, whether by successive architects or at one time, left an obscure imprint on the building. Nevertheless, abundant evidence does exist in the form of precise dimensions which prove that at least the simpler systems of geometrical proportion must have been employed deliberately. Numerological symbolism and sacred cryptograms are less well attested, but very likely were used in some instances; a *prima facie* case can be made for them.

The study of mediaeval designs by mathematical analysis based on accurate survey has not yet proceeded very far. What has been clearly shown, and supported by documentary evidence regarding the rival views on proportion of the Italian, French and German masters concerned with Milan Cathedral, is that several different systems co-existed and were used by different schools of design. National, regional and local traditions all came into play. The individual contributions of great architects were, as always in art, conditioned by their upbringing. During pupilage or apprenticeship, and even more in the three years after 'graduation', the mediaeval artist of the higher ranks learned from his father, uncle or master a particular set of rules. These rules were seldom or never explicitly written down, but imparted by word of mouth. This was, at most times and places, a strict injunction of craft secrecy. In the course of wanderyears, however, or when called to execute work in foreign countries, a master might learn from his fellows in the same craft new and strange methods. Transmission of ideas was, to some extent, accidental.

Over and above the accidents of personal careers there was, all the same, a definite organization. This can be proved by explicit documents to have existed by the later thirteenth century; but it cannot have been a fresh departure at that time. The essence of the organization lay in the fact that building craftsmen tended to move from job to job rather than to live in one place. Hence they received a legally exempt form of jurisdiction and appeared before their own courts instead of local courts of justice. Historical records prove that in 1268 the mastery of the Masons of Paris, with rights of the lesser justice, was granted to Guillaume de Saint-Patu; that in 1275 the masons of Strassburg Cathedral constituted themselves a lodge of 'freed masonry according to the English fashion' under their master Erwin, who received confirmation from the Emperor Rudolf I in the next year; and that in 1305 Walter of Hereford, master mason at Caernarvon Castle, was there keeping his free court and taking the perquisites including the fines levied upon contractors and others in default. The case of Strassburg, though seven years later than the specific grant at Paris, implies that this form of organization was regarded as particularly English. Oddly enough, we know far more about the later history of the great architectural suzerainty exercised by Strassburg than we do of developments in England.

What England does uniquely preserve is the fourteenth-century text of the 'Constitutions of the art of Geometry', a legendary history of the mason's craft followed by explicit regulations for masters and journeymen. One of the most important provisions, attributed to King Athelstan (924–39), was that the masons should hold an assembly or congregation of all master masons and fellows once a year or once in three years 'from province to province and from country to country.' The word 'country' was certainly used as more or less equivalent to county, but whether 'province' meant any region, or specifically the ecclesiastical provinces of Canterbury and York, is quite uncertain. The practical outcome for architectural design is that the masters of a given county were likely to meet together every year; and those of a whole 'province' perhaps once in three years. That there were virtually national assemblies in the Germanic area in the later Middle Ages is a matter of record, together with the names of the masters representing each lodge. It can easily be seen how new ideas in design and forms of window tracery or mouldings could be disseminated over very wide areas within a short time.

We need not believe the fabled authority of King Athelstan, but the assemblies of masons in some form seem clearly to go back to the thirteenth century and quite possibly to an earlier date. Methods of bringing together building masters for consultation are implied by Henry III's instructions in 1245: his master mason and master carpenter were to advise upon works at York Castle after conference with other 'masters expert in the like skills.' In 1257 the king appointed his master mason and master carpenter to be chief keepers of the royal works south of the rivers Trent and Humber. This might well mean that there was already a southern province officially recognized, and perhaps its northern counterpart as well. Long before there

22. Canterbury: choir by William of Sens, 1175–78
east end by William Englishman, 1179–84

is any explicit evidence for the holding of assemblies for organizational or jurisdictional purposes, there had been specific conferences of masters to deal with the problems of a particular building. The most famous of these took place at Canterbury in 1174 when the monks of Christ Church cathedral, devastated by fire, 'called together both French and English architects.' Even granting the relative internationalism of the Middle Ages, it is interesting that this very close cross-Channel relationship should have persisted well over a century after the Conquest; and still more significant that the master chosen should have been one of the French delegation.

It was natural that, in the holding of occasional or regular assemblies of architects, the cathedrals should have played an important part. It was at the cathedrals and at the other great churches of the first rank that there was normally a permanent works organization. The 'lodge', though literally only the shed or shelter in which stones were cut, stood for the whole technical aspect of the works, the 'yard' in modern terms. Though subject to financial control by the clerical keepers of the works, canons or monk obedientiaries, and operating within the limits set by decisions of the chapter, the lodge under its master was autonomous for most architectural and all technical purposes. It was inherently likely that assemblies of masons would be called together at cathedrals or in cathedral cities far more often than elsewhere. The cathedral cities, from the late eleventh century, had tended to be the main administrative centres of the country; and this makes sense of the provision in the Constitutions that, if the masters needed support for their jurisdiction, the Sheriff of a county, the Mayor of a city, or the Alderman of a town might be 'fellow and associate' to the Master. In other words, the chief master mason of an assembly might have with him on the bench of his court the local chief magistrate. In England before the later fifteenth century there were very few places under cover where any really large assembly could be held. It is likely that many of these congregations actually took place in the nave of the cathedral, the principal meeting hall of the city. A smaller body might be accommodated in the chapter-house.

Although there is no evidence that the assemblies in any way dictated an imposed official style, they provided a regular means by which information on the latest fashion acceptable at Court and employed by distinguished contemporary prelates could be obtained. Resemblances between features of cathedrals within the same region: likeness between towers, or chapter-houses, or types of vaulting, can be explained by the more frequent meetings held at provincial or county centres and by simple emulation at one cathedral of components admired at another. The known journeys of mediaeval craftsmen and artists over long distances complete the picture. Architects might be sent by the Crown or by great patrons to do work at a building even hundreds of miles off; they might be impressed for official works or serve as military engineers in foreign wars; or they might obtain private commissions on the strength of their reputation.

The fact, abundantly attested in England and on the continent, that master masons of the Middle Ages were often men of considerable fame, raises the question of their origins. It has been common to refer to them, in somewhat patronizing manner, as 'craftsmen', but this really begs the question. It is of course true that they were not professional men in the sense that has grown up only since 1800. All of them had learned how to work with their hands at the materials of building before they added to this the knowledge of planning and design. Yet in some way they were able also to be, for the most part, literate men. Many of them could certainly read and write Latin after a fashion, presumably the fashion of the cathedral or other local grammar school. In England, and probably over a good part of Western Europe, they could speak some French in addition to their own vernacular. Practically all of them who were concerned with the design of cathedrals were exquisite draughtsmen. For it has to be remembered that, of whatever nature the drawings were, the actual stones that we see had to be cut to shape from the drawings made by the master. Of these the most important were the full-size drawings of the profiles of mouldings, drawn and then cut on thin boards (later on plates of lead, iron or zinc) as templates.

The famous album of Villard de Honnecourt, a Picard architect of the first half of the thirteenth century, and other surviving drawings on parchment and paper, prove that the masters could sketch freehand and draw to scale, as well as at full size. Their methods showed great economy of time, by indicating only one half of a front, one repeat of a pier or moulded opening, one severy of a vault pattern. This, at least, was their usage for working drawings. For the benefit of their clients show-drawings were made, roughly in perspective or bird's-eye view to explain the finished appearance to the layman (architecturally speaking). In this marked distinction between the draughtsmanship used in the tracing-house and lodge, and that produced for the nobility and clergy, we find an index of the gulf that separated (and for that matter still separates) the technically informed from the book-learned. It was rare in the Middle Ages, as at all other periods, for the building owner or the clergyman to understand drawings in orthographic projection.

Clearly the building masters were much more than mere craftsmen. They had a shared common ground with other artisans in their initial pupilage or apprenticeship, but at the end of their education they certainly formed a higher caste. The question is, to what extent they attained this privileged position because they were born into it? That is to say: were the upper grades of masters, capable of creative design, mostly drawn from a higher social class or from a more richly endowed stock, than the ordinary masons, carpenters and the rest? The answer is that many of them certainly were. In the general social context of the Middle Ages it already counted for a great deal that even ordinary masons had to be of free status and not of bond blood. In Germany there was a strict rule that the mason had to be of legitimate birth, a qualification otherwise insisted upon only for the priesthood. The rules laid down in the Constitutions are such as would apply to men of honour and call for 'gentlemanly' behaviour. It is impossible to pass this off as a mere affectation or snobbery. There are repeated documentary references to the honourable treatment to be accorded to craftsmen, and to the social distinction whereby masters of the crafts were entertained at the high table. In the fifteenth century two tables of official precedence group 'worshipful merchants and rich artificers' along with 'gentlemen well nurtured and of good manners' as sitting together at a table 'of good squires'; and placing 'an Artificer' immediately below a gentleman but above 'a yeoman of good name.' It has to be stressed that all the labouring classes ranked below the yeoman.

Not only the chief architects, the designers of cathedrals, but also many of their subordinates who might in turn rise to the rank of warden even if not of master, were men of standing. Their economic position, judged by pay and also by the evidence of deeds and wills as to their property, was far above that of the manual labourer or the smaller manorial tenant. Being freemen, they conveyed property by deeds under seal, and even those of their seals which made no pretence of being armorial were often works of art. Some of the greater masons used seals which were quite plainly heraldic, and in a few cases there is evidence that implies close blood relationship to families of the country gentry. To this limited extent at least there was justification for the boast in the legendary history (in the Constitutions) that the craft of masonry originated as a way of livelihood for the sons of great lords freely begotten.

One special skill possessed by a number of the masters was that of figure sculpture. Although it would be going too far to say that mediaeval architects were commonly sculptors as well, it is evident that in some cases the building master was also a carver of distinction. Those masters who, in private life, were also building contractors or had a shop, acted as monumental masons and provided tombs and effigies. Besides those in the round they produced incised slabs and in at least a few cases worked in brass or latten plate too. The fundamental reason for this lies in their skill in draughtsmanship. In the artistic world of the time, the master mason was so often the best available draughtsman that it would be his hand that produced full-size cartoons for effigies. Economy of labour suggested that the same cartoon might be directly transferred to a brass on the flat, instead of working a three-dimensional figure out of a solid block. In a less specific way it is probable that cartoons or sketches prepared by master masons with their own hands, or through their assistants, underlay a proportion of the designs for stained glass and for wall paintings. Both forms of decoration were considered, at any rate in the earlier part of the Gothic age, as integral contributions to the architectural unity of design.

Around the cathedrals, as at the greater monasteries, there grew up whole series of shops belonging to the various associated arts and crafts. The arrangements made at Coutances in the mid-eleventh century for gold-smiths, blacksmiths and carpenters were followed and expanded. All the minor arts likely to be concerned with the enrichment or furnishing of a cathedral were represented. This was particularly the case at the greatest churches, such as Old St. Paul's in London and York Minster. In some cases the cathedral close or yard offered the special attraction of being an exempt jurisdiction, where craftsmen could ply their trade and open shops without the expense of taking up the freedom of the city. In later ages this led to increasing pressure by the civic authorities, anxious to extend their control over all trading in the town; but though disputes occurred in the mediaeval period, the liberties and peculiars held their own.

The actual processes of building did not differ very greatly from the opening of the twelfth to the opening of the nineteenth century. In many ways there was even a closer link between the methods of say 1125 and 1925 than between those of 1925 and 1950. The almost complete disuse of tradi-tional construction has taken place mostly within the last quarter-century, so that the newly trained architect or builder of the present day is at a loss to understand the means by which the cathedrals were built. Only the tradi-tional craftsmen concerned with the day-to-day maintenance and repairs of the greater churches still maintain a continuity with the generations from whom they have learned their skills, without intermission, for the last eight or nine hundred years. Because of the gulf that has so rapidly widened between the old and the new, it seems advisable to give a brief account of the main stages of building a cathedral. (For finance, see pp. 81–2).

We are here concerned, not with the accumulation of the necessary finance, but solely with the operations under the architect's control, and reflected in surviving sets of accounts. First of all the design had to be prepared and approved, and in its final form at least sketched out as a diagram. The main dimensions were in most cases expressed in round numbers of feet or in rods. The length of the rod and of the foot differed in foreign countries, and also from place to place in England, but there is evidence of the use of the modern statute foot, and of the rod or perch of $16\frac{1}{2}$ feet, from the twelfth century. The earlier Norman buildings seem probably to have been set out with either Norman or Roman feet. The Roman foot measured about 295 mm and the Norman foot 297·77 mm; the comparison with the modern foot in a dimension of 100 feet is roughly 96′ 8″ for 100 Roman feet, and 97′ 8″ for 100 Norman feet. Dimensions in perches were complicated by the fact that they might contain 18 or 20 or 24 feet, even if the feet were of the normal standard.

However much geometrical complexity had gone into the production of the plan, the result was likely to be reducible to a simple grid of lines, easy to set out on the ground. The outer walls and the rows of piers were likely to be related to squares of 10, 25, 50 or 100 feet. The relationship might not be from centre to centre: the rows of columns, to reduce the span, would probably stand inside parallel lines 50 or 40 feet apart, while the external faces of the aisle walls would be aligned at 100 or 80 feet from each other. On a clear site, the first requisite was to settle the orientation by pegging out a line in the direction of the length of the building. The much disputed question of varying orientation has in recent years been settled in favour of the traditional facing towards sunrise on the patronal festival. Precise analysis, on the site, of every parish church in Oxfordshire, and of some of the cathedrals, by the Rev. Hugh Benson showed that the alignment must have been carried out by waiting for sunrise on the actual day at the time of the first building on a clear site. Taking into account the local horizon, refraction, and the changes in the calendar, it can be said, for example, that the orientation of Oxford Cathedral was to sunrise on Lady Day, 25 March, in the eighth century; that of Lichfield Cathedral is correct for St. Peter's Day, 1 August, in the twelfth century; while Rochester points exactly to sunrise on 30 November, the day of St. Andrew to whom it was originally dedicated, in the Norman period. Many dedications have been changed, and later additions made with fresh orientations.

From the first line, normally the central axis, everything else followed. At a point upon the line, probably corresponding to the east wall of the transept, another line had to be set out at right angles. Apart from other geometrical methods, the simple use of the triangle with sides in the proportions of 3, 4 and 5 was known to the Gothic masters. Greatly improved accuracy in the setting out of right angles is one of the sharpest marks of distinction between the earlier and later Romanesque periods, about 1100 or a few years later. The date of the improvement strongly suggests a fresh source of direct information from more competent architects in the Saracen lands visited by the First Crusade. Given the long axis and a north–south line representing one wall of the transept, all the other required alignments could be pegged out by simple measurement in the chosen units. Trenches of appropriate width were dug along the lines for foundations of walls, piers and colonnades. The depth to which the trenches were dug, and the nature of the subsoil, would determine the next step. In the Mediterranean and Oriental countries of ancient architecture, most important buildings took their rise from level shelves cut in the solid rock. This was unusual in England, and on fairly solid soils all that was done was to dig down some feet, throw in chalk or rubble stone, and pour on lime mortar to 'float' the top to a surface at the intended depth. On this the first course of dressed stones was laid. In the later Middle Ages there were certainly proportionate 'secrets' handed down among the masons, for determining the appropriate depth of foundations for a wall of a given height. Earlier work was probably rather rough and ready, and must have depended largely upon the individual judgement of the master as the trenches were being cut. On wet and boggy sites it was necessary to drive in rows of wooden piles and to form a boarded platform on top of them, on which the footings could be laid.

Since money tended to come in slowly, there was often a long interval between the first work on the site, which included the marking out and digging of trenches, and the stage when the first stones could be laid on the prepared foundation. The gap might be one of several years, and enabled supplies of stone and timber to be sought and found, brought to the site, and cut to shape. In general structural timber was not seasoned, so that no additional allowance for this had to be made. Part of the site would be set aside for workshops including the masons' lodge, and a shed for the master's tracing house, possibly with a plaster floor for drawing to full scale. Labourers for digging and other rough work, and craftsmen of various skills had to be taken on and placed on the payroll kept by a clerk. Highly skilled masons were set to hewing ashlar and moulded bases, ribs and shafts, while men at a cheaper rate rough-hewed rubble for infilling, retaining walls, or other less important purposes. Carpenters would in the first instance be concerned with taking dimensions from which they could design scaffolds and centerings for arches or vaults; with converting the logs and balks of timber to suitable scantlings; and with the actual making both of temporary and permanent timberwork. Sawyers, in pairs, were taken on to cut up the timber under the direction of the master carpenter.

A great deal had been done by the time that the work was ready for the ceremonial laying of foundation stones. These were not necessarily the first actual stones to be placed in position, but the ceremony was probably arranged for a date near the start of real walling above the level of the foundation platform. Where detailed records survive, as in the case of Salisbury Cathedral in 1220, it is made clear that the privilege of laying a foundation stone was offered to generous subscribers, local and other noblemen, as well as to the bishop and clergy. The bishop of Salisbury not only laid a stone for himself but two others by proxy, for the Pope and for the Archbishop of Canterbury. After this the local nobility, headed by the Earl and Countess of Salisbury, laid personal stones, and were followed in turn by the Dean, dignitaries of the cathedral, archdeacon and canons. Still more stones were laid at a later date by distinguished laymen who had been with the king to fight the Welsh at the time of the original ceremony.

At this point a short consideration of tools and plant is necessary. The master used a square and compasses in making his design. The working masons also used squares to mark out the edges and faces of stones, which they cut with hammer and cold chisels of various shapes in Gothic times. The Normans had hewn most sorts of stone with short-handled axes. The surface of ashlar stones was finished by driving across it a claw-tool with small teeth, or a narrow-bladed chisel at regular intervals. The softer stones were commonly surfaced at a late date with a length of fine-toothed saw-blade dragged across. A great deal can be deduced in regard to date from the use of these various kinds of tooling, and in some cases of margins of different widths 'drafted' around the face of the stone Carved work and enriched detail were done at the banker or bench, even in Norman times, not in position; but a small amount of finishing off of detail usually had to be done after the stones were in place. The instances of unfinished capitals commonly adduced as evidence of working *in situ* generally indicate a shortage of funds which meant that the intended carving had been abandoned altogether and the shaped block used as it was.

There were no bubble or spirit levels in the Middle Ages, the plumb-level being used. This was essentially a straight-edge with a rising 'bridge' above it, from which a short plummet hung in a slot. When the point of the 'bob' was exactly above a nick cut in the bottom of the slot, the straight-edge was level. Such levels have continued to be made up to late Victorian times and used even in recent years by conservative craftsmen. For the vertical faces the long plumb-bob has always been used. So far the work has been done below ground level, upon the foundations laid in the trenches, or up to four or five feet from the ground, in comfortable reach. Beyond this point scaffolding had to be put up, and might be of several kinds. In building walls it was possible to thread long poles horizontally through the wall and to tie platforms of wicker hurdles on both sides, balancing each other. Such scaffolds did not necessarily have to be supported by poles at the outer edges. Around piers and columns, and for higher walls or heavier weights, scaffolds of the more modern type were erected, with vertical poles a few feet from the wall and level putlogs lashed to the poles and supported in holes left in the wall at their inner ends. These small square holes, later blocked, are prominent in much mediaeval work.

For raising the stones and buckets of mortar various machines were used. The simplest kind had a windlass worked by two men at ground level, and a pulley suspended from scaffold or sheerlegs above the working stage. In building very high walls or towers it was common to place a large wheel, often a treadwheel, on top of the work, jacking it up from time to time as the job proceeded. Cranes with jibs were being used before the end of the Middle Ages, and there was a continuous development of pulleys and tackle which allowed heavier weights of material to be handled. After the end of the building work, the wheels were often used for raising the bells and for this reason have frequently survived. It seems to have been normal to limit the building of towers to about ten feet of height in a season, to allow for thorough settlement, so that a great tower standing 100 feet above the wall-top level would have taken at least ten years to build.

The mediaeval building season in England, on account of frost, was a strictly limited one. Even in the south, at Winchester, William of Wykeham laid down that building works should normally be done only between 1 March and 28 October. This meant that the unfinished work had to be protected with thatch at the end of each year; and also that men must either be laid off, or found indoor work such as cutting stones or making centerings for next year. Though much hardship was undoubtedly caused by seasonal laying off of men, it has to be remembered that many of them had a small farm of some kind on which they could work with their family and so get a bare subsistence at worst. The cathedrals and great abbey churches, when in funds, were able to keep many men in employment all the year round, and this was certainly a triumph of organization. The difficulty seems generally to have been to get enough skilled men when they were needed, and this led to the payment of fees to the Crown for licences to impress. Such a licence would specify a maximum number of men, perhaps masons only, who could be conscripted from any work except the king's or that of certain other privileged patrons, named in the licence. The pressed men, just as if directly taken into the royal service, had to be paid a fixed allowance by mileage for their journey from home to the works.

The greatly deformed shape of many Norman arches shows that the centering was often inadequate, and that it was taken down before the thick beds of mortar had set properly. Such defects are rare in Gothic work. For one thing, the thin joints set hard in a much shorter time; but the main reason was the excellence and precision of Gothic carpentry. Even temporary centerings must have been made exactly, and strong enough to carry the load without deflection. Hence there was no serious difficulty in turning the arches, including the main ribs of the vaults. What did present a problem was the infilling of the vaulting webs between the ribs, in the earlier period a wide expanse requiring full support. In relatively modern times this has been provided by building up a shaped centering to the exact curve of the vault and covering it with boarding, on which the vault stones are laid. This seems to have been done in the later Middle Ages for some greater vaults, such as those of the nave of Westminster Abbey, put up during the fifteenth century. An earlier, more rough and ready, expedient was to build a crude centering that filled up most of the space of the section of vault to be built, and then heap a pile of earth upon it, modelling the shape of the vault, and then laying the stones in mortar upon the heaped earth. Although only a comparatively shallow layer of earth was raised upon the rough timber centering, a misunderstanding of the facts produced the (modern) legend that earth was piled up in a great mound to the height of walls and vaults, instead of scaffolds and centres, to be dug away after the work had set firm!

Before the stone vaults were set it was usual in England to raise the great timber roofs. The vaulting could then be done in shelter, and the church used, at least in part. Although the outer roof covering of churches may sometimes be of thatch, clay tiles or slates, the use of lead has been almost universal on the cathedrals from an early date. The long life of cast sheet lead compares favourably with that of any other material, especially if well laid. The survival of at least some mediaeval lead roofing proves the ability of mediaeval plumbers, for in general even lead requires renewal at intervals of from one to two hundred years. Not only were the plumbers clever at their job; they were also courageous steeplejacks, undertaking periodical inspection of roofs and spires, fixing and re-fixing crosses and weathercocks, and fighting fires started by lightning. It need hardly be said that, in common with the master mason who sometimes accompanied them on these risky tours of high-level duty, they got a bonus of danger money for time so spent.

One of the more pleasing aspects of mediaeval life was its tendency to find excuses for holidays and for feasts of some sort. We still have in the building trade the last survival of this tendency in the ceremony of 'topping out' a house or building, when a flag or green branch is hoisted to show that it is time for the building owner to pay for a round of beer. The slow building of mediaeval cathedrals would have unduly limited the supply of beer had it been given only on completion; so that many excuses were found for repeating the ceremony. Closing a great arch, setting the keystone of a vault bay, and many other stages of the work are found to qualify in the account rolls. Apart from such occasional treats there was also a system of differentials which ensured that highly skilled masons and carpenters drew pay for certain holidays allowed to the trade. Furthermore, the beginnings of the English weekend can be traced back to the early fourteenth century if not earlier, when privileged men knocked off at noon on Saturdays. By such means then, and in such conditions, the English cathedrals were built.

III The English Cathedral

The English cathedrals as they now exist are a series of buildings made up of several groups. We have already seen that these groups correspond to two different original types, and to later additions made in the course of time.

Sixteen[1] of our twenty-seven churches have always been cathedrals, but they do not represent the earliest ecclesiastical division of England. The first Christian missionaries to the Anglo-Saxons found the country divided into a number of kingdoms, presently reduced to seven and thus known as the Heptarchy.[2] Each converted king granted rights to the missionaries, but naturally these grants were limited by his own frontiers. So it comes about that the boundaries of the older English sees represent a former political division of the country. Thus Canterbury and its early offshoot Rochester shared the kingdom of Kent, and Selsey occupied the whole of Sussex; Dunwich was the see for East Anglia (Norfolk and Suffolk).

These Saxon dioceses underwent much rearrangement, and it was not until after the Norman Conquest that the distribution of cathedrals became roughly what it was to remain for the rest of the Middle Ages. A number of the Saxon cathedrals had been sited in small country villages, such as Elmham in Norfolk and Ramsbury in Wiltshire. At the Council of London in 1075 it was decreed that all such cathedrals should be removed to large towns, and to this decision we owe the existence of cathedrals at Chichester, Lincoln,[3] Norwich, and Old Sarum, later removed to Salisbury. The diocese of Ely was carved out of Lincoln in 1109, and Carlisle, last of all the mediaeval sees, was created in 1133. Both at Ely and at Carlisle the earliest portions of the existing churches go back to dates before their erection to cathedral status.

---

[1] Ely did not become a cathedral until 1109, nor Carlisle until 1133.

[2] The number of kingdoms changed repeatedly, but the seven which gave rise to the name were: Kent, Sussex, Wessex, Essex, East Anglia, Mercia, Northumbria.

[3] This is uncertain; but the problem of the 'Saxon cathedral' at Stow is a vexed one.

23. *Hereford: nave, c. 1100–45, altered 1841–52*

24. *(below left) Hereford: south transept, c. 1100*
25. *(below) Chichester nave, 1123–48*

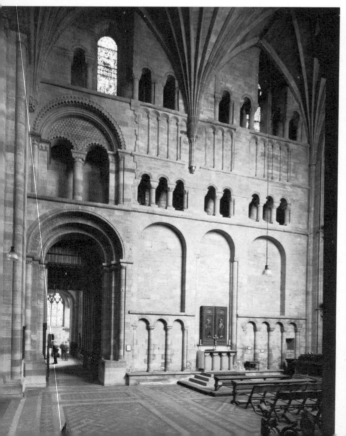

26. *Lincoln: west doorway, c. 1142–46; statues, c. 1360–75*

Before proceeding to detail the development of the English cathedral through the historical styles, it is necessary to consider the general types into which they fall, the methods by which they were built, and the fortuitous juxtaposition of parts built at different periods. To deal first with the ancient secular cathedrals, only at Hereford do extensive remains exist of the Romanesque building. At Lincoln there is a west front, much cloaked with later work, and at Exeter the strange towers which ended the transepts of the Norman church. At Chichester a large part of the church is in fact Norman, but has been extensively cloaked with work of later periods. Lichfield preserves foundations of its Norman eastern arm beneath the level of the paving. No type emerges from these scattered remains. Lincoln and Chichester both have paired western towers, Hereford had but one, Exeter

its transeptal pair. The eastern terminations are doubtful. Lichfield had an apse with ambulatory; Lincoln apparently a central apse, as had Chichester; Old Sarum had square-ended aisles flanking a central apse; Hereford three parallel apses. The two cathedrals which were originally great secular churches, Ripon and Southwell, differed again: Southwell had the unusual feature of a square-ended sanctuary between apsidal aisles, while Ripon, of later date, was square.

Turning to the monastic cathedrals, the Augustinian houses at Bristol and Carlisle, both relatively late, probably had square sanctuaries from the beginning. Of the Benedictine churches, only Rochester began with a square east end, though Ely is thought never to have completed the apsidal termination of which foundations have been traced. Oxford had a stepped termination, with square east end to sanctuary and aisles, which were kept back one bay. The rest were divided between the two common continental plans of the period, namely the triapsidal, with three parallel eastern apses; and the periapsidal, with central apse surrounded by a concentric aisle. The triapsidal plans were Durham, Peterborough and St. Albans, with Lanfranc's church at Canterbury. This was rebuilt by Conrad as a periapsidal church, and Chester, Gloucester, Norwich, Winchester and Worcester were peri-apsidal from the start.

The eastern terminations of several early cathedrals can be discovered from their crypts which still exist in spite of the rebuilding of the superstructures. Excellent examples of this are at Gloucester, Winchester and Worcester, while there are also early crypts at Rochester and York. At Canterbury there

27. *Chichester: west front, c. 1125–48; south-west tower, 1215–25; central tower, c. 1244–47*

28. *Gloucester crypt, 1089–1100*

29. *Canterbury: crypt under choir, c. 1073*

30. *Worcester crypt, 1084–92*

31. *Canterbury: eastern crypt, 1179–84, by William Englishman*

32. Rochester crypt, c. 1205–10

33. Hereford crypt, c. 1217–20

34. Canterbury: undercroft screens, c. 1372–77

is a whole series of subterranean chambers and chapels of various dates, including the very important lower Lady Chapel and the beautiful Chantry of the Black Prince. Originally designed on the analogy of Constantine's Church at Bethlehem, to house the chief shrine or object of veneration, crypts in England steadily fell out of use. When the whole tendency of the Gothic age was towards more space, light and air, it is hardly surprising that dark and damp undercrofts with low, gloomy vaults should have been disliked. The only Gothic crypts in the English cathedrals were beneath the choir of Old St. Paul's, those still extant at Hereford and Rochester, perhaps intended as bone-houses and that of the Lady Chapel at Winchester. At St. Paul's the crypt was necessary to accommodate the parish congregation of St. Faith.

All the cathedrals (except Exeter) had a central tower, and the usual arrangement was to have two western towers as well. At Winchester and Gloucester, perhaps also at Norwich, where there are now no western towers, they may formerly have existed. Nothing is known of the original west fronts of Bath, Bristol, Carlisle and Oxford; Ely has one western tower, like the secular Hereford and some non-cathedral churches such as Wimborne and Wymondham; Rochester, Southwark and Worcester had none. St. Albans was intended to have western towers, perhaps never completed.

The general picture of English Romanesque cathedrals, though like enough to that of the great continental churches of the same period, does show the beginning of several tendencies which were to grow, and thus to differentiate England from the rest of Europe. The universal emphasis on the central tower, in spite of its costliness, the obstruction caused by its great supports, and the risk of collapse, is the most noteworthy feature. But only second to it is the early appearance of the square east end, which in its earliest examples is quite certainly not due to Cistercian influence. This square eastern termination was in the Gothic period to become the chief mark of the English church, cathedral and other, in contradistinction to the apsidal chevet of the French model. Thirdly, and apparently linked to Saxon precedent, we have the instances of a single western tower; and another English peculiarity, that of placing a pair of western towers outside the aisles instead of in alignment. This plan was adopted at Wells, in the original front of Old St. Paul's, and was intended at St. Albans. Abroad it occurs at Rouen, and at Trondhjem in Norway, where it was imitated from St. Albans and Wells. Old St. Paul's seems to have been the earliest design of this type (c. 1110–30), while the continental series begins with Poitiers (c. 1161). Later examples occur at Bourges; in Spain at Santiago de Compostela, Sigüenza, Mondoñedo, León, Toledo, Astorga and several Renaissance fronts; and in the late fourteenth-century church at Kassa in Hungary.

35. Norwich from
north-east, 1096–1120;
tower, c. 1121–45;
spire, c. 1464–72 by
Robert Everard

We now leave the remains of the Romanesque cathedrals to dwell at greater length upon their Gothic successors: in most cases, the actual churches we now see. They vary in date from the mid-twelfth century Transitional St. Frideswide's at Oxford to the Tudor Bath Abbey, begun in 1501, and still unfinished at the end of the age. In all cases but three the extreme east end was square by the close of the Gothic period; the three exceptions are Canterbury, which has retained its unique circular Corona, and Wells and Lichfield, whose Lady Chapels have polygonal terminations. Norwich now has a somewhat similar modern chapel but this stands on the site of the thirteenth-century square-ended Lady Chapel destroyed after the dissolution of the monastery. And Wells, in spite of its polygonal termination, has a square high gable to the retrochoir, behind the Lady Chapel. This universality of the English square end contrasts everywhere with the continental usage, and goes far to justify the claims of England to a separate Gothic architecture independent of that of France.

The other almost ubiquitous characteristic, that of length, was due in part to the extended naves of the Romanesque churches, adopted by or rebuilt in the Gothic cathedrals. But it was still further emphasized by building eastern extensions equalling or even excelling the total length of the nave. This had already happened at Canterbury by the end of the twelfth century and was to take place everywhere else before the Reformation, except at Salisbury, where the new cathedral was built with the eastern arm slightly exceeding the nave in length; and Bath, where Bishop Oliver King's church was designed to take up only the length of the nave of the Norman cathedral. Usually the new building at the east end entirely destroyed the earlier termination, though Gloucester succeeded in retaining the outer wall of the ambulatory, Peterborough the inner arcade with the main apse, and Norwich both, merely hewing away the Norman eastern chapel to build a larger rectangular Lady Chapel in its place.

Setting aside the exceptional cathedrals whose high roofs terminate in an apse or polygon of some kind, and discounting Bath, which was the fresh composition of another age, the eastern extensions may be divided into two groups. Furthermore, these groups have a clearly marked geographical distribution. In the one type, the main roof is carried through at its full height to the end, and the east gable rises sheer from the ground to the apex. This type is confined to the area north and east of a line drawn from Bowness on the Solway Firth to the Thames at Westminster. South and west of this line the high gable is set back from the east end, which is formed by a Lady Chapel on a lower level, leaving space for a raised east window above the high altar. Within the south-western area are three exceptional cases, Worcester, Bristol and Oxford, where the high roof is carried on to the end; but in each case the eastern bay is aisleless, while in the north-eastern type the aisles continue throughout.[1] The distribution of the two types strikingly suggests the division of England between Wessex and the Danelaw in the late ninth century, but the complete destruction of all the greater Saxon churches renders a search for precedents hopeless.

The adoption of the square plan in England was so thorough that it can clearly have been no accident. It is a piece of deliberate policy. That it was not due to any inherent distaste for polygonal forms is proved by the English chapter-houses which differ from those of the continent in a precisely converse direction. Francis Bond showed convincingly that the reason for the ultimate adoption of the square chevet in England was due to a much stronger emphasis upon correct orientation here than in the rest of Europe. The

---

[1] At Bangor and St. Asaph the sanctuaries are aisleless; Llandaff and St. Davids conform to the normal south-western type.

Romanesque churches with parallel apses had correct orientation of their altars, but were awkward for processions. The periapsidal plan, both in its original Romanesque form, and as developed into the continental chevet, gave completely false orientations. The reason for this great attachment to correct orientation in England may well be due to the force of our pagan traditions. France, and the greater part of western Europe, had been strongly Romanized, and from the fourth century had been continuously Christian. England, on the contrary, was pagan from the fifth to the ninth century, wholly or in part. Great care had to be taken by the missionaries to England to adapt themselves as far as possible to traditional usage, and it seems likely that this would be especially the case with the central feature of solar worship.

But if this is the reason for our strict orientation, it must also account for the other prominent achievement of the square east end: the brilliant lighting of the high altar from an east window, instead of the gloom achieved in the French churches. It was not perhaps so much the desire that the congregation should be able to observe the movements of the celebrant that determined the English method, as the anxiety that both altar and celebrant might be bathed in the rays of the morning sun. This is further borne out by the English provision of eastern or choir transepts, so aligned as to throw still more light upon the altar, as well as to provide the additional subsidiary altars for which they were primarily built. Here again, though choir transepts do occur in France they were never popular; their development in England was so marked as to be yet another national peculiarity.

Outside the church itself was the chapter-house, a necessity both for monastic and collegiate establishments. In England they were often made the occasion for great artistic display, and the most famous of them are polygonal, with vaults either supported on a central pillar, or free-standing. There were not less than 25 of these polygonal chapter-houses in England and two in Scotland; but more than half have been destroyed. Ten of them are or were at cathedrals within our definition, as well as one at Manchester, of small size. The earliest known is that at Worcester, circular and of ten bays, 56 feet in diameter, and built early in the twelfth century. Next came one now destroyed at Alnwick, Northumberland; those at Margam and Abbey Dore were presumably inspired by Worcester. Then the form suddenly sprang into prominence with that at Lincoln, the largest ever built (59 feet span). So strange a leap in distribution would be hard to understand, if it were not that at that very time the master masons of Worcester and Lincoln cathedrals both bore the rather unusual name of Alexander. With other evidence of a connection between the two cathedrals this suggests that the two masters were one and the same. There is a noble apsidal chapter-house at Durham, and rectangular ones at the monastic Bristol, Canterbury, Chester, Gloucester and Oxford, as well as at secular Exeter.

36. *Worcester: chapter house, c. 1120; restored 1386–92 by John Clyve*

37. *Lincoln chapter house, c. 1220–35, by Master Alexander*

38. *Durham: chapter house, 1133–40*

39. *Bristol: vestibule to chapter house, c. 1154–64*

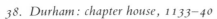

40. Bristol: chapter house, c. 1154–64

The cloisters, universal at monastic cathedrals, and commonly built for show by the secular chapters, are a study in themselves. The development of their design was constant, and shows particularly clearly the extent to which modifications of tradition in one part of the country were watched and adopted elsewhere. Cloisters, or some part of them, remain at Bristol, Canterbury, Chester, Chichester, Durham, Gloucester, Hereford, Lincoln, Norwich, Oxford, Salisbury, Wells and Worcester, as well as some fragments elsewhere, notably at St. Paul's in London. The secular cathedrals at Lichfield and York never possessed cloisters, while those at Chichester, Hereford and Wells did not form complete rectangles. At Salisbury alone the cloister equalled or surpassed anything produced by the monasteries.

Besides the disappearance of monastic and claustral buildings since the Reformation, there has been another serious loss in appearance suffered by many cathedrals: the destruction of spires. As we have seen, the typical English cathedral had three towers, one over the crossing, and two flanking

41. *Norwich cloisters: north walk, 1421–30, by James Woderofe*

42. *Gloucester cloisters: south walk, 1381–1412, by Robert Lesyngham*

43. *Worcester cloisters: west walk and lavatorium, 1435–38, by John Chapman*

44. *Oxford: nave and transept, 1158–80; tower, c. 1220–50; cloisters 1478–1503*

45. *Rochester: west front, c. 1150–60*

the west front. Of them all, only one now retains the three spires for which the towers were intended: Lichfield. Four central towers have kept their stone spires: Oxford, Salisbury, Chichester and Norwich; there are stone spirelets on the smaller western towers of Peterborough; Durham was preparing to build a stone spire in the early sixteenth century, but never finished it, though Wyatt again projected it in 1795. It is well known that the spire of Old St. Paul's was of timber and lead, and that it was never rebuilt after its destruction by lightning in 1561. According to Stow it was 520 feet high; and the central spire of Lincoln, blown down in 1584, is said to have been four feet higher still. Lincoln's western timber spires lasted until 1807. Ripon's central spire fell in 1660, and the two on the west towers were taken down four years later. Spires had been removed from Carlisle; from both towers at Exeter; from the western towers at Durham *c.* 1657; that on the single western tower at Ely lasted until 1801; the central tower of Hereford had a timber and lead spire until 1794. Rochester lost its spire in 1830, but regained it in 1904; Canterbury's Norman north-west tower was provided with a wooden spire in 1317, which lasted until 1704. The greater north-west tower of Peterborough also had a lead-covered spire; so had the central tower at Worcester and that at St. Albans.

It seems probable that the Norman central tower of Winchester was provided with a spire of timber and lead, and this may have been replaced in 1200 by the *turris* (a word found elsewhere in the sense of 'tall spire') recorded as begun and finished in a single season.

In addition to spires on the churches, there were others upon the many detached belfries which formerly existed, comparable to that which now stands spireless at Chichester. Such belfries stood by Old St. Paul's, Westminster Abbey, Canterbury, Norwich, Salisbury, and Worcester. The city parish and friary churches also were usually provided with spires, and the impression of the mediaeval civic skyline must have been very different from that to which we are accustomed; only in north Germany and the Baltic was the multitude of spires carefully preserved until modern times. Up to 1942, Lübeck still presented the picture which it made in 1482, when it was painted in the background of an altar-piece now or formerly at Reval, and which showed nine tall spires as well as innumerable smaller ones. The loss of atmosphere and purpose due to this great destruction of spires in England is incalculable; it amounts to the cancelling of a great part, possibly the most symbolic part, of the Gothic message. Even in spite of the Renaissance, Wren was consciously or subconsciously aware of this message when he so designed his London churches as to leave the city with more spires than it had before the Fire. More recent generations have been content that this message too should be lost in the monstrous upward surge of commercial premises.

From the story of loss and ruin, let us turn to the first building. In an age of cathedrals, how did cathedrals get built? Not only the cathedral churches themselves as we see them now, but in many cases enormous monastic buildings had to be financed and erected. The sheer size of the greater churches, in England as well as on the continent, was enough to daunt any constructor unendowed with faith as well as self-confidence. The late Professor Prior gave a number of valuable figures for the areas of the greater churches, in illustration of the immense scale upon which the Norman builders worked. The fountain-head of the later Romanesque was the abbey church of Cluny in Burgundy, with an area of 54,000 square feet; the early Gothic narthex brought the total to 66,000. The largest of the Norman cathedrals in England, Winchester, had been planned originally to cover as large a space, and the abbey church at Bury St. Edmunds was only just under 70,000 square feet. These areas are as large as those of the largest completed French cathedrals; Cologne was 90,000; but even this was surpassed by Old St. Paul's which with its Norman nave and Gothic choir and transepts reached 100,000 square feet. The vast size of Old St. Paul's can be appreciated by comparing it with the 70,000 square feet of Lincoln.

Another of Prior's illuminating comparisons is between the cross-sectional areas of the piers of Durham choir, laid out in 1093, and those of Canterbury choir of 1175. The Norman pier is seventeen times as big as the early Gothic one; a disproportion which evidences the enormous advance in constructive skill made in a couple of generations. This advance of skill is also shown by the large number of Romanesque towers which fell down, compared with the remarkable durability of Gothic work. Among the many collapses of Norman towers in England were two at Bury, central towers at Beverley, Ely, Winchester and Worcester, and the western tower of Hereford. There was naturally some trouble in Gothic times, and the first tower at Lincoln fell in 1237, while failure threatened at various periods at Peterborough, Salisbury, Wells and York. At Chichester the tower and spire actually fell, but after a life of five centuries, comparing very favourably with the fifteen years of the first Winchester tower, and the 200 of Ely. Furthermore the fall at Chichester was provoked by the pointless removal of the pulpitum ('Arundel' screen), which acted as a stiffener to the crossing piers.

Both the financing and the practical administration of building on such a scale were great problems. Generally speaking, English administration was more successful than English finance. There is no doubt that much of the patchwork character of our cathedrals is due to the inability of their founders to provide enough cash and credit to complete the work adequately upon the plan adopted. On the other hand it is permissible to wonder whether this was always the explanation. At Gloucester after 1328 the shrine of Edward II is said to have attracted for many years multitudes of pilgrims who made vast offerings to the abbey. Yet the building works actually carried out as a result were surprisingly meagre and slow. Fifty years were taken over the reconstruction, in a skilful but economical manner, of the presbytery and transepts; in another century only a new cloister, a new west front and two bays behind it; a reconstructed tower and a Lady Chapel of moderate size had been added. The offerings at Becket's shrine were astronomic, but never resulted in total rebuilding of Canterbury.

A suspicion is felt that the mediaeval clients and their building masters were less iconoclastic over ancient work than is often alleged. There were certainly prelates and others who wished to be in the front of fashion; but others loved the old churches they knew. It seems almost certain that the preservation of vast Norman churches at Durham, Ely, Norwich and Peterborough, and the early Gothic work at Canterbury, was due as much to affection as to lack of means. The careful adherence to earlier plans at Westminster Abbey and Beverley Minster, and the provision of a new porch scrupulously framing the precious Norman doorway of Malmesbury Abbey, point in the same direction.

Besides the offerings of pilgrims, funds were provided by wealthy laymen, anxious to take out a spiritual insurance policy; by bishops and abbots fond of their church, or of ostentatious temperament; by rents of endowed property; by casual gifts and bequests; and by carefully planned public appeals. These last were a most important method of attracting money, then as now, but contributions secured a definite return in masses and prayers, and other spiritual privileges for the donors. The chapters, secular and monastic alike, placed a responsible official in charge of these funds, and subjected his accounts to annual audit. There were two main methods of organizing the actual work of building: by direct labour, and by contract. In the direct labour system (which was the earlier), the administrator, possibly one of the monks or canons, had himself to arrange the purchase and transport of materials and the hiring of men. In practice he was able to delegate a good deal of this routine to the technical master of the works, normally an experienced master mason. This master was also the architect to whose plan and details the church would be built. Sometimes the chapter appointed one of their number or a clerical official, and the master mason jointly, to have full charge of the work, as happened in the late thirteenth century at Exeter cathedral.

In practice, the direct labour system was frequently modified by the introduction of task-work, when individual craftsmen were paid lump sums for performing set tasks, such as the cutting of so many feet of a moulded string-course, or erecting so many perches of plain walling. Gradually the tasks became larger and were introduced by written undertakings on the part of the craftsman to do the work to time, and of the client to pay the agreed sum at stated dates. By these stages the older methods gave place to the contract system more or less as we know it today. At the English cathedrals little major work was done by contract, though by the late fourteenth century prominent masons undertook large tasks: at Old St. Paul's in 1388 Henry Yeveley was paid the last instalment for his new front of the south transept. The whole task amounted to nearly £300, or in our values about £90,000–£100,000.

In the early Middle Ages it was customary for the master to reside at the job, and have full and constant control; later on, and certainly before the end of the thirteenth century, he had become a supervising visitor. This implied that he had control of more than one job at once, and the necessary corollary was a permanently resident undermaster or warden of the works on each job. For the work at Old St. Paul's above mentioned, Yeveley's friend and junior partner, and later his successor as King's Master Mason, was his warden: Stephen Lote. Both master and warden were bound by craft custom to take up an absolutely impartial position as between the interests of the client and those of their fellow-craftsmen, an interesting precursor of modern architects' etiquette, between client and builder. The warden had charge of the working masons who cut their stones beneath the shelter of a hut or open-sided pentice known as a 'lodge'. At the great cathedrals the lodges became permanent institutions, though the staff employed might fluctuate from one or two up to 100 or more, according to the available money and the time of year.

Besides the masons, a master carpenter had charge of a staff of carpenters to provide scaffolding, centerings, the wooden roofs, and later the choir fittings and doors. Glaziers might be directly employed, or the work might be sent out to glass-painters who had their own shops in the city. But in any case close touch had to be kept, that the glaziers might be provided at the right time with templates showing the exact size of the window openings they were to fill. The making of plans, details and cartoons went on in a separate room or shed known as the 'trasour' or tracing-house. Here there were drawing boards on trestles, and in some cases at least, a large slab of plaster-of-Paris,[1] on which full-size details could be set out with the help of a great pair of 3-foot dividers. Elsewhere, stone paving slabs have been found with the geometrical setting-out lines scratched upon them. At least one smith would be kept busy on the constant resharpening of the masons' tools, and the provision of necessary ironwork. Besides nails, hinges and stay-bars for the windows, this often included heavy wrought-iron bars of considerable length, for use as exposed tie-bars or as hidden reinforcement.

The master mason would have to visit quarries to find suitable sources of stone, and the carpenter would mark timber in the forests to be felled by his men. The clerical chief arranged transport for these and other materials and, as we have seen, had to give gratuities at suitable moments, to keep the works running smoothly. Rates of progress differed enormously: the whole eastern arm of Canterbury was rebuilt in the ten years 1175–84; the Lady Chapel at Salisbury took five years, and the rest of the church another forty altogether. On the other hand, the small cathedral of Exeter was about a century in its rebuilding, and the nave of Westminster Abbey was still not completed after 270 years of intermittent work. The great speed of the faster works, and their immense capacity of endurance, prove that neither jerry-building nor incompetence can have been common. The cathedrals of the Middle Ages are among the soundest, as well as the greatest works of man.

[1] Notably at Wells, where the plaster floor survives in the chamber or parvise over the North Porch, and is covered with the incised lines of a long period of use. At York there is a larger tracing floor in part of the room above the vestibule to the Chapter House.

IV Early Cathedrals

In spite of the very large number of fragments of English churches of the Saxon period, scattered all over the country, virtually no evidence for the architectural character of our early cathedrals survives above ground. Until ten years ago even the underground material recovered by accidental or intentional excavations was also extremely slight. A good deal of literary evidence has always been available, but its magniloquence was rightly suspect and now proves to have been misleading. The expectation, a good example of wishful thinking, that it would be found that pre-Conquest England was filled with noble minsters is unfulfilled and likely to remain so for ever. It is now all but certain that England before 1050 was absolutely devoid of the architectonic concept of the greater church.

Before proceeding to discuss what is now known of the Saxon cathedrals, it will be as well to go thoroughly into this question of scale. By what yardstick can we give some quantitative measure to the idea of a 'great church'? There are several sources of statistics from which varying answers may be drawn, but all these figures are of the same notional order. The sources of direct comparison are, firstly the early Christian basilicas of Rome and other classical churches of the fourth and fifth centuries; in second place the churches of Byzantium and the Eastern Empire; thirdly, Carolingian and Ottonian cathedrals of continental Europe; and finally the Norman and Gothic cathedrals of England which still survive. Beyond this corpus of directly comparable material it is permissible to consider the scale of pre-Christian temples and of the great mosques of Islam. Obviously it is impossible to institute precise comparisons on a basis of any one dimension such as overall length, since buildings of very different plan-forms are concerned. The volume of contained space would be a sound basis of comparison in theory, but in practice extremely hard to calculate, and subject to serious errors due to rebuilding and alteration. As a simple approximation which at least affords a standard not positively misleading, the figures given here are those of the rectangular plots of land which would be required to contain the external ground plan of the buildings considered. It should be noted that subsidiary buildings such as atria, cloisters and chapter-houses have not been included. The numbers are of thousands of square feet, imperial measure. For those who think metrically a rough idea of size can be obtained by dividing by ten (one square metre equals 10·7643 square feet). For our present purpose it is only the relative sizes that matter.

The great basilica of Old St. Peter's in Rome gives us an index figure of 126, and it will be seen that this is so close to the area covered by several of the largest mediaeval cathedrals as to leave no doubt that it was taken deliberately as a model for scale, even if for nothing else. St. Paul's outside the Walls, begun later in the fourth century, was about 4/5ths the size of St. Peter's, 100; but the basilica built for Constantine himself at Bethlehem was far smaller, only 15 – all these figures being exclusive of atria. In the later Eastern Empire scale increased slightly, as at Bosra cathedral in Syria, 21, the same as Justinian's S. Vitale in Ravenna. But with Hagia Sophia in Constantinople the factor rises sharply to 110. In western Europe no more really large churches were built for several centuries, until the Carolingian epoch around AD 800 was once more able to reach the smallest size of the classical churches: the much enlarged church at Nivelles in Belgium gives a figure of 14; that at Fulda in central Germany 18, the abbey church of St. Denis 20. Large enough to be impressive, these churches fell far short, as we shall soon see, of the size we consider appropriate to a cathedral.

A new outlook on scale appears about the year 1000 with a sudden leap to an index around 70: Hersfeld Abbey 67, St. Remi at Rheims 69, Speyer Cathedral 70, St. Martin at Tours 72. The new basilica at Nivelles, built in c. 1001–46 to replace the Carolingian church, reached 52. Norman work in Normandy was not outstanding, for Jumièges yields only 35, though further south St. Benoit sur Loire attained 43 and the pre-Gothic cathedral at Chartres about 64. This wave of enlarged design spread to Italy at Pisa Cathedral (72) and to Spain at Santiago de Compostela (70 or more). These were indeed greater churches, yet they were quite put in the shade by several designs of about 1080, of which the earliest was certainly the Norman Winchester Cathedral, set out in 1079 (122) and the second probably the abbey church of Bury St. Edmunds begun about 1081 (130). The new scheme for Cluny III may have been sketched out by this date, though more probably some five years later, and work did not begin until 1088. The plot to be covered by Cluny gives a factor of only 125, though the area was greatly increased by the early Gothic addition to the west end of the nave, not included in the original plan. As we have already seen (p. 80), the actual plan of Cluny was

46. *Winchester from east: tower, c. 1108–20; presbytery by Thomas Berty, c. 1520–32*

substantially smaller than that of Bury, even after enlargement, though Cluny exceeded Bury in volume owing to its greater height.

It is a matter of particular interest that the coming of Gothic architecture did not bring at first any attempt to exceed these remarkable figures. The substantial Cistercian abbey at Fontenay has a factor of only 27; Notre-Dame in Paris has 80; Bourges Cathedral 90, the metropolitan Rheims 96; the completed rebuilding of Chartres 114. Only in the second half of the thirteenth century was the enormous index of 135 attempted in the plan for Cologne, and this took more than six centuries to realise. Even Seville, generally regarded as the largest of Gothic cathedrals, and built in the fifteenth century, fails to beat Cologne when shorn of its subsidiary buildings (134). The Spanish metropolitan cathedral of Toledo was content with a factor of 92. Only after the Renaissance were all records beaten by the 354 of the new St. Peter's at Rome.

We now return to the English cathedrals of the Middle Ages, but need not consider each separately. Disregarding truncated and uncertain plans, the smallest to survive is Bath (32) and the largest Lincoln (129), with Winchester and York close runners-up (both 128). Apart from these three giants the ancient cathedrals fall into three sharply defined groups, large, medium, and small, with factors in the brackets 91–109, 61–76, and 21–47 respectively. In descending order of size the large churches are Salisbury, Ely, St. Albans, Peterborough, Durham, Canterbury and Norwich. The middle range includes Chester, Lichfield, Gloucester, Exeter, Chichester, Wells, Worcester and Hereford. The cathedrals which, by our standards, can be considered small are Rochester, Ripon, Bristol, Southwell, Southwark, Carlisle, Bath and Oxford. All four of the ancient Welsh cathedrals are in the smallest group and, apart from St. Davids (45), they are smaller than any English cathedral except the incomplete Oxford, ranging from an index of 27 at Bangor to 24 at both St. Asaph and Llandaff. It will be noticed that up to now no mention has been made of St. Paul's in London, old or new. The latter, in Renaissance style but making no attempt to emulate St. Peter's in Rome, has a factor of 143, rather narrowly excelling the biggest Gothic churches that survive. The real surprise is the vast figure reached (203) by Old St. Paul's after the completion of its new eastern arm in 1312. For some three hundred years the cathedral in London was a great deal larger than the basilicas of Rome itself.

We are now in a position to consider the minuscule scale of even the largest churches of Saxon England. Before the recent excavations at Winchester the largest known churches were the complexes at Glastonbury and St. Augustine's Abbey, Canterbury, which at their greatest extent within the century preceding the Conquest reached factors of 15 and 19 respectively. Neither of these complexes, however, had any kind of architectural unity, each consisting of two or more separate ancient churches linked by later communicating buildings. The single example of a Saxon cathedral with a deliberately composed plan, at North Elmham in Norfolk, has a figure of 7; but Elmham again is a very late building, probably built after 1000. Also of the earlier eleventh century was the Saxon abbey church at Peterborough, with a factor uncertain but not likely to exceed 15; roughly the same size as the contemporary church at Stow in Lindsey which may or may not represent the cathedral of Sidnacaster. Two other churches, of an earlier date, were the Jarrow basilica of St. Paul, completed in 685 (about 5) and the parish church at Brixworth which at its greatest extension rated as high as 11. This too was of the end of the seventh century, though enlarged somewhat later, and seems to represent more closely than any other building the continental techniques imported by bringing in masters from Rome and Gaul in the early period of Saxon Christianity. If Professor Ralph Davis is right in identifying Brixworth with Clofesho, as seems highly probable, this would have been a basilica of cathedral rank and the seat of several important church councils.

Another survival from the late seventh century is the existing crypt beneath Ripon Cathedral, said to have been built for St. Wilfrid about 670. Its central chamber and wandering passages are curiously reminiscent of the grottoes beneath the Church of the Nativity at Bethlehem, and the same arrangements are found at Wilfrid's other surviving crypt beneath Hexham Priory. It seems to be beyond coincidence that at the very same time the shipwrecked Gaulish bishop, Arculf, should have been at Iona relating his travels in the Holy Land and setting down plans of its sanctuaries. Arculf's narrative was sent to York as a gift to the Northumbrian King Aldfrith.

Before proceeding to a description of the Saxon cathedral at Winchester it may be as well to give a few examples of the scale of classical temples and mosques. Much the most famous of Greek temples, the Parthenon at Athens, of the fifth century BC, has a factor of 23, but it was far from being the largest of the classical temple buildings. The Olympieion at Athens, of the second century BC, had an index of 52, and still larger were the temple of Apollo at Miletus (75) and the Hellenistic temple of Artemis at Ephesus (about 82). In the Roman period few temples were very large: the Great Temple at Baalbek in Syria works out at 47, and was slightly exceeded by the double temple of Venus and Rome in Rome (50). The Basilica of Trajan, however, though a secular and not a religious work, bore comparison with the great cathedrals (112). In the Muslim world the covered areas of mosques tended to be relatively small in comparison to very large open courtyards. Of the earlier mosques, exclusive of courts, the Great Mosque at Damascus (AD 705–15) reached 68; the Dome of the Rock in Jerusalem only 32, though the Mosque El Aqsa is 48. The Mosque of Ibn Tulun in Cairo (876–79) was almost the same size (47), but all these were surpassed by the immense Mosque at Cordova which, after expansion at various dates ending in 990 (205 years from the foundation), attained the impressive figure of 169. The covered space of the mosque proper, without the patio, is thus far greater than that of any of the English cathedrals, but it is comparatively a very low building. Much higher, but with proportionately small areas, are the principal Turkish mosques, the Süleymaniye at Istanbul of 1550–57 (48) and the Selimiye at Edirne (Adrianople), built in 1569–75 (38). The classical temples and mosques are almost always greater works than the index figures suggest, because their rectangular plans filled the enclosing area instead of leaving a large proportion unbuilt.

The discoveries of the past ten years at Winchester are probably the most remarkable achieved in this country in the field of archaeological excavation. The work, directed by Mr. Martin Biddle, has redeemed this country from the serious slur of neglecting to modernize its approach to the mediaeval period. Great credit is due to those who made this achievement possible, notably to the late Roger Quirk, whose studies underlay the initial excavations; and also to members of two antecedent pressure groups. These, whose complementary efforts went on for several years unknown to each other, were led in the local field by Mrs. Barbara Carpenter Turner (subsequently Mayor of Winchester), and nationally by Professor Nikolaus Pevsner, who urged upon official quarters the need to exploit to the full post-war opportunities.

The opportunities afforded at Winchester, not only in connection with the Old Minster site, have indeed been taken, and the regular publication of clear interim reports has made it possible for scholars and the general public to make full use of the facts discovered. The detailed scientific reports have appeared in the *Archaeological Journal* (vol. CXIX for 1962) and in *The Antiquaries Journal* (vols. XLIV-L, LII); accounts of the discoveries on the Minster sites have also been given in the yearly issues of the *Winchester Cathedral Record* (Nos. 31–40 for 1962–71). These reports should be studied for the archaeological and historical implications of the discoveries. All that will be attempted here is to give some assessment of what has been revealed in the purely architectural sphere of interest, relying heavily on Mr. Biddle's final summary of 1970.

Notwithstanding the small size of the church revealed, the cumulative evidence is now overwhelming that what has been found is the royal church and Saxon cathedral of Winchester. In its final form (reached about 994) it incorporated several structures of different dates, in the way already familiar from the finds at Glastonbury Abbey and St. Augustine's, Canterbury. Disregarding minor alterations, five separate builds can be distinguished, belonging to three periods of construction. The first build is a small cruciform church with extreme dimensions of 100 feet from east to west, by 80 feet north to south, giving an index of 8. This can be linked with recorded history as the royal church built for King Kenwalh of Wessex, consecrated in 648 and doubtless begun soon after the king's baptism in 646. Though not a cathedral at the time it was built, this was an important church for its period. The nave was over 60 feet long, with an internal span of 24 feet. To the east there was a square 'chancel' with internal dimensions of about 20 feet each way, and there were smaller square chapels (*porticus*) laterally close to the east end of the nave, forming transepts on plan. The church was thus cruciform in appearance, though it had no true crossing.

The foundations of this whole building had been made at one time, of collected Roman material, and the archaeological evidence is explicit that

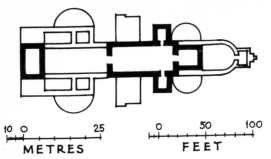
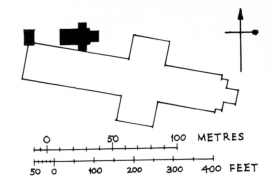
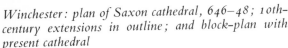

Winchester: plan of Saxon cathedral, 646–48; 10th-century extensions in outline; and block-plan with present cathedral

this was the first building on the site after the end of Roman occupation of central Winchester. Although the whole of the masonry superstructure had been robbed at demolition in 1093–94, chips of stone showed that the material used was oolitic limestone, probably from the Box Ground quarry near Bath. Considered simply as a church, without any specifically cathedral context, there are several important features. Relatively to a small Saxon church, such as Bradford on Avon (index 2), this was large, and the nave was about the same length as the much later one at Stow, though four feet narrower. The square sanctuary at the east end proves conclusively the early origin of the English tradition of avoiding apsidal terminations. From a liturgical viewpoint it seems that it was strictly a presbytery permitting a westward position of the celebrant on the east side of a high altar placed just within the eastern end of the structural nave.

There can be no doubt that this church became the see when Wine was consecrated bishop in 662 and Dorchester was abandoned as the West Saxon cathedral. Since it was already royal in origin there is no reason to regard it as in any particular way unworthy or unrepresentative by the standards then expected. It must be remembered that this was before the first building works of Benedict Biscop or St. Wilfrid, or the erection of the first parts of Brixworth church. The probable date of construction c. 647 was only 20 years after the beginning of the first stone church at York. Incidentally, both at York and at Winchester these early churches were dedicated to St. Peter. At Winchester there is no doubt that this church sufficed as the cathedral for a long period without any substantial alteration or extension, in fact until 971. At an unknown date within these three centuries one significant change did occur, the building of a free standing tower 65 feet west of the west front and on the same long axis. This tower, which constituted the second build, was oblong on plan, measuring externally about 38 feet from north to south by 26 feet, though the longer dimension depends upon the conjecture that the tower was axially placed. This is all but certain, since the north wall is in alignment with the nave of the church. The tower is known to have had a separate dedication to St. Martin by 970.

The third, fourth and fifth builds all belong to one final period of construction between 971 and 994. First came a link-building between the west end of the old church and the east side of the tower. This link was provided with large apses at the sides, having an internal diameter of about 28 feet; but it is doubtful if they were ever completed. A 'westwork' of a quite different kind was built in the next few years, 974–80, and cut across the apsidal foundations. The new transeptal westwork clasped the earlier tower to provide a wide west front some 75 feet across, and stretched eastward for some distance along the link-building. At an upper level it is likely that the westwork supported a royal gallery looking into the church from the west from a point almost immediately above the original tomb of St. Swithun, bishop for ten years until his death in 862, and buried in the open air between the old church and the tower. In total disregard of the saint's wish that his grave should be trodden on by passers-by and exposed to the rain, the structural link had certainly been designed to bring the tomb under cover and provide an outer casket to a shrine.

The last build at the Old Minster was mainly concerned with the east end, and was consecrated in 994. The body of the old church was doubled in length and given an apse; lateral apses were built on each side of the former sanctuary; and an unusual projection was built to the north (hypothetically also to the south) of the western part of the old nave, as if for a transept of three chapels on each side. The date and precise nature of this work remain obscure, though it undoubtedly formed part of the operations of the late tenth century. The result of the two main phases of this period was to give the cathedral by 980 an index of 19, and one of 25 by 994. Exactly as at Glastonbury and at Canterbury, these figures were achieved only by linking separate free-standing structures of earlier date, and at best reached only the notional scale of the very smallest of the mediaeval English and Welsh cathedrals. Even then, the impression of size is illusory, since the internal space was in reality excessively long and narrow, though like other Saxon churches it may have been relatively high.

With the possible exception of the first London cathedral on the site of St. Paul's, there is no likelihood that any other Saxon cathedral would notably exceed that of Winchester. We have to accept the strict limitations set by these remarkable finds, and restrain our astonishment at the disparity between the work and the unmeasured literary accounts of it which have come down. The fact is that the excellence of some of the minor artefacts of late Saxon times, and notably the very fine tradition of draughtsmanship, had raised expectation and made it possible to conceive that Saxon self-praise could be accepted in regard to architecture. Until the excavations of the season of 1969 at and around the west end of the Old Minster it was still possible to defend the possibility that there had been Saxon churches not unworthy of the main stream of architectural development. That view is now decisively rejected, and we are instead given a firm date of 1070, give or take a few years, for the beginning of the story of English cathedral architecture.

Before this conclusion had been reached at Winchester, another great series of excavations had begun under York Minster, where the chance came as a by-product of structural repairs to the fabric. It was naturally expected that the opening up of very large areas of the floor and foundations of the present Minster would reveal traces of the church begun for King Edwin of Northumbria after his baptism in 627. So far this expectation has been disappointed, and negative evidence strongly suggests that the Norman and later cathedral was built on a cleared site away from the position of the Saxon church. For the pre-Conquest period the outstanding discovery has been that beneath the south transept of the first Norman minster there was part of a late Saxon cemetery, with its graves following the alignment of the underlying Roman basilica in the military fortress. It can be accepted as all but certain that the earlier cathedral, therefore, was orientated diagonally across the true orientation of everything built after 1070.

The excavation at York has been of a very different kind from that possible at Winchester. At York the work had to be subservient to the structural needs of a vast programme of urgent repair, and the number of staff was strictly limited. Where York has benefited has been in the readiness with which the need for an archaeological investigation was accepted, and this was largely due to the climate of opinion which led to, and profited from, the earlier finds at Winchester. None the less, the fact that an emergency programme was able to start at short notice owed much to the local knowledge and influence of Dr. Eric Gee. Very soon after the state of structural emergency became known in 1966 a pilot excavation was begun under the direction of Dr. Brian Hope-Taylor, who subsequently became general director, while control of the excavations has been undertaken, successively, by Mr. Herman Ramm and Mr. Derek Phillips. The following brief account of the early Norman cathedral depends mainly on Dr. Hope-Taylor's recent publication *Under York Minster: archaeological discoveries 1966–71*.

From documentary sources it has always been known that the Norman cathedral was built as a result of the destruction of the city by fire in 1069, and while Thomas of Bayeux was archbishop (December 1070–November 1100). Thomas first repaired the Saxon Minster to serve for a time and afterwards built the new church from its foundation. It is now clear that his great church stood on a fresh site and was laid out on an axis due east and west. Though much smaller than the giant monks' churches at Winchester

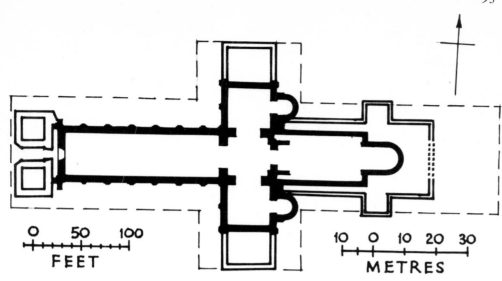

York: plan of Norman minster, c. 1080–1100; 12th-century extensions in heavy outline

and Bury, York was still a large secular cathedral, with overall external dimensions of about 370 feet by 160 feet across the transepts, and thus with an index figure of 59. The whole plan was certainly conceived at once, though the nave was built after the choir and transepts on a rather slighter foundation. As a design the church is most unusual, for it is essentially un-aisled, though the eastern arm may have had extremely narrow corridors, rather than true aisles, on each side. Each transept was internally a perfect square, as was the crossing between them. The nave, though without aisles, had the great span of 45 feet in the clear, and was divided into seven bays by flat buttresses of double projection. The east end had a semicircular apse, and apsidal chapels stilted on plan opened eastwards from each transept.

During the twelfth century the first Norman cathedral was expanded in all directions. Probably after the fire of 1137 both transepts were lengthened, and later a pair of western towers was erected outside the west front of the nave to form a wider front of about 95 feet. It is of particular interest that these extensions settled the limits of the later Gothic Minster, since the twelfth-century end walls of the enlarged transepts are under the present transeptal gables, while the western walls of the towers were aligned beneath the present front of the fourteenth century. Under Archbishop Roger de Pont l'Evêque (1154–81) an entirely new choir was built, of which part of the crypt survives. This, although stylistically late Romanesque rather than Transitional Gothic (as was Roger's church at Ripon), was a fundamental departure from the original concept. Its thinner walls and broad aisles, to-gether with small eastern transepts, belong to another age and reflect the atmosphere of the 'Twelfth-Century Renaissance' which reached England with Henry II. By about 1180 York Minster had increased in scale to a factor of over 107, though the precise form of the east end is still uncertain.

The origins of the very simple plan of the Norman church of *c*. 1075–1100 are not obvious, though there were precedents for wide aisleless naves in France, notably at Angers, where the cathedral had the immense span of some 52 feet, going back to a design of *c*. 1010. In England the nave of York was undoubtedly the inspiration for Archbishop Roger's early Gothic nave, without aisles, at Ripon, and perhaps influenced the later cathedral at Cashel in Ireland. Even more important is the fact that its great span accounts for the unusual width of the present central nave at York, where the Gothic arcades built after 1291 stand on the foundations of the Norman walls. Obviously there was no intention to vault the Norman nave, but the span must have given considerable difficulty to the carpenters called upon to roof it. With the exception of Angers Cathedral, where there must always have been a stone vault or a series of shallow domes, the Norman nave of York seems to have the widest clear span of any building erected down to the end of the eleventh century in northern Europe. The central aisles of the largest churches were not usually more than 35 or 36 feet wide.

These finds at York are of great interest for several reasons. They prove that almost immediately after the Conquest, and in a remote centre recently devastated by revolt and fire, it was possible to undertake the building of a really large cathedral. If any further proof were needed of the extraordinary skill of the Normans in organization and especially in logistics, it would be found here. Secondly, York Minster was a good deal bigger than the contemporary Canterbury Cathedral (1070–77) built for Lanfranc, with an index not more than 43 against York's 59. Here is an added demonstration of the utter seriousness of the York claim to primacy over Canterbury. This had possibly been reinforced by comparatively recent memories of its position as capital of a Viking kingdom from 875 to 954. Thirdly, Norman York Minster shows that a secular cathedral could then be a genuinely great church, even if not on the scale of the very greatest monastic foundations, such as Winchester. Finally, in its unusual plan, differing widely from all the other major churches built in this country at the time, York shows the possibility of individuality even in an age of relative uniformity. It is true that most Norman churches, large as well as small, tend to conform to one of several well known types. The warning against facile assumptions is a salutary one.

Mention has already been made (above, p. 59) of the use of the Norman foot in setting out. This seems to have been the case with Archbishop Thomas's church at York, for the plan can be deduced from a very simple squared grid ruled at intervals of 25 Norman feet and emphasizing the double squares of 50 feet. The crossing occupies one great or double square,

47. *York: Norman minster – masonry of c. 1090 showing external limewashed stucco with red joint-lines*

with the same allowance to north and south for each transept. The eastern
arm is fitted within three great squares but falls short because the eastern apse
(with its chord at $2\frac{1}{2}$ great squares from the east side of the crossing) sprang
from a narrowed central vessel. The nave took up $3\frac{1}{2}$ great squares, and the
buttresses which marked out its seven bays were placed at 25-feet centres.
This aid to design agrees with that demonstrated by Professor Kenneth
Conant for the slightly later design of Cluny III. The use of a Norman
measure seems clearly to indicate the origin of the architect employed by
Thomas of Bayeux for his new cathedral church.

   Finally, the remains of the Norman Minster at York provide a definitive
answer to the problem of appearance. The external wall surfaces were
covered with a fine white coating of plaster, on which imitation masonry
joints were picked out in red. This treatment, though very widely used
internally for several hundred years, had not previously been demonstrated

48. Oxford: chapter house – Norman arcading, c. 1160

as a finish able to stand weathering. The excellent state of preservation of several sections found, after exposure for two centuries and burial for nearly seven more, proves that by 1100 the Normans had mastered the use of lime stucco and of permanent pigments. It would now seem that the famous remark of Raoul Glaber that the globe during the eleventh century 'put on a white robe of churches' is to be understood literally: churches of the period were given a white overcoat, and the natural stone was not meant to be seen. That this was certainly true of the inside of buildings is repeatedly demonstrated by finds of wall paintings and of plain wall decoration. In the chapter-house at Oxford similar imitation joint-lines, painted about 1240, survived until general redecoration in 1968. What is more, a part of the internal arcading of the north wall of the earlier chapter-house was then discovered, bearing a rather cruder version of the same pattern. The fact that in all these schemes, external and internal, from the eleventh to the thirteenth century, the lines were neatly ruled, and on vaults as well as walls, shows that the decoration must have been carried out while the scaffolds were still in position. Even if its purpose was mainly aesthetic, the treatment was justified as a preventative of decay.

V Norman Cathedrals

Our earliest existing cathedrals are those built after the Norman Conquest of 1066. The first of the great churches built in the Norman form of Romanesque was the new abbey at Westminster founded by Edward the Confessor about 1049 and consecrated in 1065. Of the existing cathedrals, those with a mainly Norman structure are St. Albans, Rochester, Durham, Norwich and Peterborough, with extensive parts of Chichester, Southwell and Worcester. Ely and Gloucester are also very largely Norman, and Winchester retains its interesting early transepts and crypt. The nave of Old St. Paul's, now totally lost, was one of the most important of all. In spite of variations in detail, there is an extremely close family resemblance between all these churches.

In the first place, the Romanesque builders were still extremely ignorant of structural problems and the strength of materials. From this resulted the extreme solidity of the work, which gives to it its leading characteristic: massiveness. The proportion of wall and pier is enormous; of arch and window relatively slight. This exaggerated the tendencies of Roman and Early Christian basilicas, and produced an effect almost always lacking in grace. Commonly this failing was redeemed by excellent general proportions, and by the cumulative, soothing effect of tier upon tier of round-arched openings. There is another aspect of these buildings which had a practical as well as a spiritual effect. They were not merely churches, but in an age of insecurity, strongholds against savagery and barbarism. The thick walls could not quickly be undermined; the small openings were easily defended. Here was at least a spiritual line of descent from the catacombs.

Being a direct importation from Normandy, our Romanesque cathedrals have little about them that is exclusively English. They are not, to a significant extent, national works of art. They belong to European history, and especially to the history of Benedictine monasticism. For even the secular cathedrals of the late eleventh and twelfth centuries reflected in great measure the

49. *St. Albans: crossing, 1077–c. 1090, by Master Robert*

50. *Norwich ambulatory, 1096–1120*

traditions of the monks' churches. It was an age dominated by the Benedictine Order, and its Cluniac offshoot. Through five centuries of storm and stress, human values in western Europe had been preserved within the thick walls of the monasteries, and they were now being given out again to the public through the medium of the great churches. The age of monastic domination was passing away, but it was still able to build its enormous temples throughout the new country conquered for continental civilization.

It is significant that all the great churches which remain largely Norman in structure were monastic; while among our Gothic cathedrals it is the collegiate foundations that predominate. The concentration of influence and money in the hands of the Benedictines typified the earlier period; by the later twelfth century, when the new Gothic was sweeping the western world, it was the courtier-bishops who were in power. While the architecture of the thirteenth century was to express the relation of free men in a free world, bound together by the love of God, the Norman cathedrals show us the huddling together of wretches crazed by fear of the outside world, its murder and rapine. It is too easily forgotten that England had nearly fallen a prey to yet another assault of Scandinavian Northmen immediately before Hastings. That England was to be a part of civilization, not of splendid savagery, was due as much to the usurper Harold's success at Stamford

51. *Peterborough: north transept, c. 1130–55*

52. *Peterborough: nave, c. 1155–75; west end, c. 1193–1200*

53. *Southwell from south-east, c. 1108–50; presbytery 1234–50*

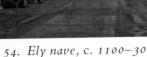
54. *Ely nave, c. 1100–30*

55. *Ely: Prior's door, c. 1140*

Bridge, as to his failure at Senlac. The Normans were already Northmen at several removes.

The dark world of outer barbarism was, nevertheless, still present in men's minds. Not until the fresh knowledge and the new Gothic spirit swept Europe in the succeeding century, were men to feel that they lived in a bright and open world. The sombre gloom of cave-dwelling and cave-worship hangs over the monks' choir of St. Albans, the long nave of Peterborough; flickers like a grey shadow glimpsed from the corner of an eye in the transepts of Winchester. Dark enough now, but with the opacity of early glass midnight must have reigned at noon. Most early windows, too, have been enlarged. Where, for climatic reasons, no floods of sunlight were allowed to enter even a Gothic church, we may recapture the intensity of this artificial night; as within Barcelona Cathedral. Better still, at the Church of the Holy Sepulchre, owing to the blocking of windows, the ambulatory is in total darkness, save for the sparks of wicks in oil, and the guttering candles of pilgrims and processions.

The outstanding achievement of northern art in the Middle Ages, and nowhere more than in England, was the progressive freeing of the churches from this atmosphere of the cell. The surest index of the movement of the times is the amount of new light admitted as one generation succeeded

56. *Gloucester nave, c. 1120–60; vault 1242–4*

58. *Durham choir, 1093–99; vaulting later*

59. *Durham nave, c. 1099–1128; vault 1128–33*

another. The ability thus to admit more light depended entirely upon advancing knowledge of construction and materials. The progress of knowledge was at first gradual, and resulted from experience of successes and failures in a large number of buildings all over northern Europe, but particularly in north France and in England. There can be no doubt that even in the Romanesque period there was a good deal of international intercourse among craftsmen, and the political link between Normandy and England inevitably caused much coming and going.

Of all the greater structural problems, that of providing a permanent stone covering was the greatest. And so difficult was the task considered in northern Europe that even where vaults of small span were built in crypts and aisles, the high clerestories of the churches were seldom vaulted. There is no example of a groined high vault in England, and even when the ribbed vault was introduced at the end of the eleventh century at Durham, it found few imitators. The only Romanesque high vaults in England, other than those of Durham and its neighbour Lindisfarne, which (so far as the evidence goes) may have existed, were at Hereford and Gloucester. A vault was also put up over the old nave at Lincoln in the 1140's, on the threshold of the Gothic

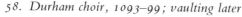

7. *Winchester: north transept, 1080–93*

60. *Gloucester: triforium of ambulatory, 1089–1100; screenwork 1337–67*

period. Nor was this lack of vaults the result of failure; it is plain from the plans of piers and shafts that vaults were never intended. In striking contrast, vaults formed an integral part of the scheme at Durham from its inception in 1093. Durham is therefore our only cathedral presenting a complete Romanesque scheme, perfect in all its parts.

As in many other Norman churches, the bay-design at Durham is of the double variety: only the alternate piers carry the vault, and are compound. The intermediate supports are great cylindrical columns. Even where there was no vault to carry, shafts were often carried up from base to summit of the wall inside the piers, and this gives a typical Norman scheme found at Ely, Old St. Paul's, Norwich, Peterborough and Winchester, as well as at St. Albans, where there are flat pilasters instead of shafts. A modified form of this type appears at Rochester, much altered by the work of later periods; before the even greater changes at Chichester its arcades were probably similar.

The other main type of Norman arcade is found at Carlisle, Hereford and Southwell, and consists of rather short cylindrical columns supporting a narrow strip of plain wall, on which stands a second range of triforium arches, and above these a range of clerestory openings. In this scheme there is no accentuation of the vertical bays, but a strong horizontal emphasis on the level line at the top of each stage. The same scheme was followed at Gloucester, but with a very big difference: the columns were made extremely tall in proportion to the height of the small triforium and moderate clerestory. This design, also followed at the neighbouring Tewkesbury, lessened the extreme horizontality of the walls and threw a cross-emphasis upon the height of the very tall side-aisles.

Durham apart, none of the Romanesque cathedrals can be considered remarkable as examples of design. Even such an idiosyncrasy as that of Gloucester and Tewkesbury, though it indicates an individual brain at work, does little to remove the church from its class. For this reason the anonymity of the Norman cathedrals is the less to be regretted. Even so, it is not to be supposed that in either the eleventh or the twelfth century such great buildings were put up without the intervention of an architectural supervisor. Amateurish as are some of the early methods when judged by the Gothic standards of 1150–1550, they still required a high degree of competence and organizing skill. Nor, in talking of anonymity, must we be misled into thinking that literally no names have been preserved. In several cases it is possible to connect the name of a master with the church he built.

61. Rochester nave, c. 1115–30   *62. Carlisle nave, c. 1092–1123*

Before the Conquest, Godwin Gretsyd had been the master mason of the Confessor's new abbey at Westminster, and was apparently a benefactor of Hyde Abbey at Winchester, as both he and his wife were to be prayed for there. Next comes the outstanding personality of Robert, the master of St. Albans Abbey from 1077 until 1100 or so. 'He excelled all the masons of his time', we are told by the chronicle of the Abbots, and considering the ingenuity as well as the beauty of his re-use of Roman materials, there is some truth in the statement. His employer, Abbot Paul, gave him for his skill and labour lands to the astonishing value of 60s. (say £900 or more) yearly; but the monastery murmured against so princely a gift; and Robert on his death-bed honourably restored the land to the abbey, renouncing the claims of his heirs. But he had another grant of land at Sopwell worth 8s. (£120 or so) a year, from Paul's successor, Abbot Richard. Robert, or Rodbert as he is also called, must in any case have been well off, for in the list of benefactors he is recorded not only to have worked faithfully about the building of the church, but to have contributed 10s. every year as long as he lived. At that date such a sum cannot have been worth less than £150 in our values, and was probably a great deal more.

Domesday Book tells us of Hugh the Mason of Winchester, apparently master at the building of Bishop Walchelin's great church of 1079–93, and tenant of two ploughlands of the bishop's manor at Chilcomb. About 1140 a certain Andrew was mason of St. Paul's in London; very likely he was the architect of the nave, which had been begun about 1110. Scanty as are these notices of the builders of our Norman cathedrals, they are enough to show that even then the masters in charge of the work were men of standing and highly esteemed. They could, and in some cases did, become wealthy, as we know their Gothic successors did. And these few are the first trickle of the flood of hundreds of the mediaeval masters known to us by name.

The interior of the Norman cathedral is best conveyed by Peterborough, for not only does it remain unvaulted, but it has retained most of its great apse. Everywhere else the insertion of Gothic windows or the total reconstruction of the eastern arm has made it impossible to visualize the eastward view. The effect is cumulative: bay follows bay as the vast naves drag their slow length along: ten bays at Peterborough, twelve at Ely, thirteen at St. Albans, fourteen at Norwich. In the 'horizontal' design, with three separate and superimposed storeys, the churches are much smaller, and one may wonder whether this design were not actually adopted to increase the perspective effect of length. In the monks' churches a solid screen wall divided the parochial nave from the convent choir, an effect which can still be seen in Romanesque naves at Norwich and St. Albans. This interruption of the vista has caused much controversy, not only in modern times. In the early twelfth century Abbot Suger swept away the interruption of a screen-wall

63. *Southwell nave, c. 1108–50*

64. (top left) Peterborough nave, c. 1155–75

65. (top right) Norwich nave, c. 1121–45; vault, c. 1464–72

66. St. Albans nave, c. 1090–1115, by Master Robert

from the ancient church at St. Denis. In our own time it has been done by the late Sir Ronald Storrs when governor of Jerusalem, at the Bethlehem Church of the Nativity. Since the Middle Ages a large number of screens have been abolished in 'aesthetic' improvements. Contrariwise, the pulpitum has recently been restored at Chichester. It is a knotty problem for which every-one must find his own solution.

The fragmentary state of most of our Norman cathedrals makes it difficult to discuss the intention of their designers. I have already referred to the standard type of external scheme, having in its perfect form three towers, one central and two western, and all surmounted by spires. In Norman times the spires were generally of rather low pitch, and at Southwell the modern spires on the two western towers are believed to be accurate reproductions of the original ones.[1] Southwell is in fact our only cathedral to preserve all three Romanesque towers, dating from the first half of the twelfth century. Owing to the small scale of the church, they hardly compare with what must have been intended at the greater cathedrals, but they do give a faithful picture in outline, as seen from western viewpoints.

Until 1834, long enough for Britton to have made measured drawings of it, an original Norman tower stood at the north-west corner of Canterbury Cathedral, the only survivor of the old nave. As in the case of the Southwell towers, it had clasping buttresses of slight projection, and stage after stage filled with different patterns of arcading. The smaller towers behind the eastern transepts at Canterbury are variations on the same theme. A more imposing arrangement of towers and recesses, unique of its time, was carried out at Lincoln, and still exists though much cloaked by work of various later periods. The free-standing transeptal towers at Exeter are more massive than the western examples, and have a well-graduated diminution of solid masses towards the top. Beside the light effect of the Gothic church, they appear rather blind and wall-sided.

Of central towers of Norman cathedrals we have three, at St. Albans, Winchester and Norwich, the last surmounted by a Gothic spire a little too small for it. All three towers are immensely successful; each is absolutely distinct from the others. St. Albans, the earliest of the three, is divided into three storeys of unequal height. In the lowest are arched recesses cleverly displaced towards the centre, thus increasing the apparent solid mass at the angles. Next comes a narrow band comprising four round arches on each face, and beneath each arch a pair of sub-arches. Above is another tall stage, with one arch on each side of the central pilaster on each face, each of these being sub-divided. The height of this tower above the abbey roofs is perfectly proportioned, and makes the distant view of St. Albans impressive and unforgettable. It is not for nothing that the Abbey boasted of Master Robert.

[1] They appear in Kip's view, c. 1724.

At Winchester, the first Norman tower fell in 1107, and the present one was built soon afterwards. Here there is no attempt to dominate the church by superior height, as in Robert's work at St. Albans. The Winchester tower has but one external storey, composed of three tall round-arched windows built in recessed orders, and somewhat set in from the angles of the tower. Again the proportions are admirable, and though less ambitious, the result is no less successful than at St. Albans. Lastly, at Norwich we have a far more complicated design arrived at in two stages. The lowest storey above the roofs belongs to the original church, built between 1096 and 1119. The angles are surrounded by a mass of attached shafts, giving great strength and emphasis to the verticals. Between these angle-turrets each face of this lowest stage is divided into nine tall openings, of which all but three are blind. Those which are pierced are the second from each end and that in the centre. Above this, and built between 1121 and 1145, is a massive cubical stage, continuing upwards the shafted corners. Between them comes first a series of nine blind arches interlaced with a second series, dividing the wall into eighteen panels altogether. Next is a much taller stage, repeating the motive of the nine panels, three of them pierced, but to a larger scale, and with ornament in the blind panels. Above this again comes a set of five panels, each containing two superimposed roundels, the upper set pierced. The total effect is impressive, but rather indistinct in detail.

All these towers were far surpassed, but not until the Transitional period, by the immense western tower at Ely. This is now surmounted by a Gothic lantern which formerly had a spire. Here the designer profited from travelled observation of the great towers we know, and doubtless others which have disappeared, such as those of the abbey at Bury St. Edmunds. The towered gateway at Bury is, in fact, clearly one of the main sources of the Ely design, giving the superimposed ranges of three windows, interspersed with narrower bands of minor arcading or roundels. The more pronounced corner turrets at Ely derive from Norwich. The whole vast front, with its western transepts as well as the lofty tower, was built in less than a quarter century, from 1174 to 1197. Though in process of translation into the idiom of the pointed arch, the western tower at Ely maintains the massive strength of Romanesque building.

This is also the case at Oxford, where the main structure of the cathedral is transitional in date, from 1158 onwards. Although retaining round arches, the columns are more slender, and the foliated capitals more dainty. Around the arches are narrower, more wiry mouldings. But the striking feature of Oxford is its unusual bay design, a forerunner of the Gothic attempts to merge the triforium into a vertical scheme. But while the later versions were to succeed by bringing the clerestory down to include the triforium, the Oxford architect had the somewhat unhappy notion of setting back his

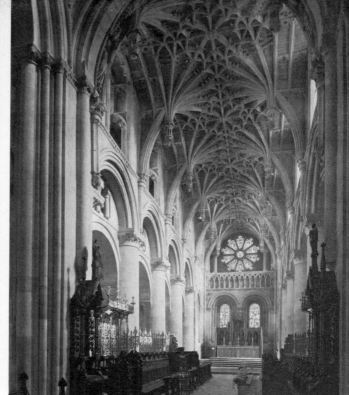

67. *Ely: west transept and tower, c. 1174–97; lantern 1392–, by Robert Wodehirst*

68. *Oxford choir, 1158–80; vault 1478–1503*

aisle-vault beneath tall arches which included the height of the triforium in the nave arcade. Unsuccessful as the experiment was, it was one of the necessary stages towards Gothic achievement.

The two great architectural features of the interior were the sanctuary and the bay design. We have seen that, with the partial exception of Peterborough, no original chevet of a Norman cathedral exists in a form in which we can appreciate it. The variations of bay design have been discussed. Similarly, we have examined the principal external features, namely the towers. But another feature of the outside which was of special importance, even where unemphasized by towers, was the front itself. In general the Norman churches do not seem to have laid great stress upon the western entrance of the church. There was, it is true, at least the one doorway, but this might not be an outstanding feature. Sandwiched between the two simple towers at Southwell, such a doorway is not impressive. On a rather large scale, Chichester must have been much the same; so was Chester before Perpendicular alterations. But there was another type of front, without towers, as at Norwich, Rochester and St. Davids, and formerly at Hereford. The place of towers was taken by pronounced turrets at the outer angles of the aisles, and there was also some decorative treatment of the ends of the arcade walls of the nave. There might be three recessed doorways, as at Norwich; or the side archways might be blind, as at Rochester.

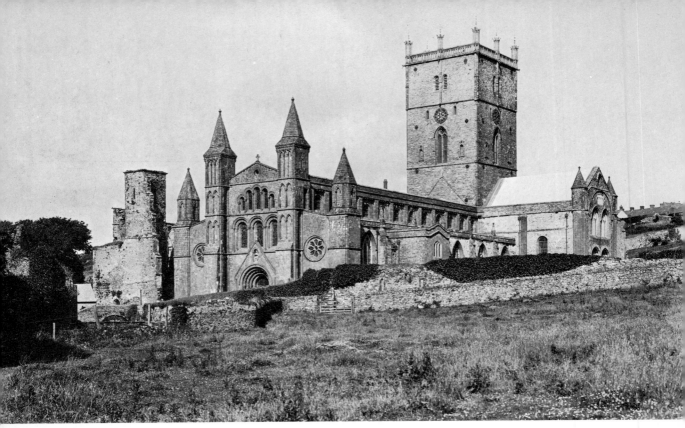

69. *St. Davids from south-west,*
1180–98; tower 1328–47 and
1509–22

70. *Rochester: west doorway,*
c. 1150–60

To make up for the lack of towers, these façades gave greater prominence
to the doorways themselves. We do not know what the original central
porch at Norwich was like, but that at Rochester is a splendid work of soon
after the middle of the twelfth century. The archway is in five recessed
orders, the innermost supporting a tympanum carved in high relief. All five
arch-rings are deeply carved, and a carved label-mould crowns all. The
tympanum, and the standing column figures supposed to be King Solomon
and the Queen of Sheba, may be later insertions of *c.* 1175. At Ely the Transitional front is an affair of many superimposed ranges of arcading, and the
entrance is cloaked by the early Gothic Galilee porch. But at Durham the
austere Norman front has before it a Galilee of another kind: Transitional,
and really a Lady Chapel. Intended for the east end of the cathedral, it was
destroyed by the supernatural misogyny of the long-dead St. Cuthbert, who
would have no women coming to worship near his bones. Consequently
it was rebuilt outside the west doors, where any number of females could
assemble without causing the Saint annoyance. Built for Bishop Puiset or
Pudsey about 1170, it is one of the latest round-arched buildings in the
cathedrals. But it bears witness at the same time to the coming of the Gothic

71. Ely: western Galilee porch, c. 1250

72. Durham: western Galilee, c. 1170–75, by Richard Wolveston

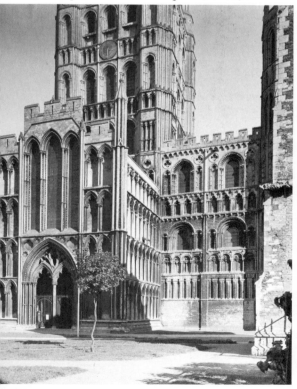

spirit in its attenuated columns and fine-cut zig-zags. It was probably designed by Puiset's great master mason, Richard of Wolveston, famous as an architect throughout the north country.

There remains only the front of Lincoln to describe. It is of its own kind, and, though it suggested the Gothic front of Peterborough, remains unique. It consists of three deep recesses containing doors now surmounted by Perpendicular windows; and at each side two smaller arches leading merely to deep niches. The central recess is much the highest. Behind the Gothic arcading which now crowns the work, rise the twin western towers, provided with corner turrets of strong projection. The Gothic extensions to north and south, with their system of arcading carried right across above the earlier recesses, seem to have been designed specially with a view to enshrining the ancient work. Clearly this is an instance where the old work was of such outstanding importance and interest that no one would allow its destruction. It is the only part surviving of the church of Remigius, built between 1075 and 1092. The master who designed this strange and impressive façade, whoever he was, was one of the first in England to strike a fully individual note. Not only this; his is the earliest solution, and one of the most satisfactory, of the problem of linking the outside of the church to what is within. Taken as a whole, English architecture was less successful in this respect than in most others, and there is some compensation in our possession of Lincoln. Dominant on its hill, Lincoln Minster shows us some of the most glorious lessons of Gothic: but to enter in we must pass through these strange portals, accepted as worthy even by the later builder, Chesterton's Architect of Spears.

Knowing what was to come, we cannot regard the Romanesque cathedrals as an end in themselves. In the curious mingling of styles which is above all typical of the English churches, it is the solemn and massive Norman which provides a foil for the light and airy Gothic. There is something satisfying about the static repose, even heaviness of the solid pillars, the dark aisles, the rough-dressed stones. Perhaps, being Saxon Englishmen and so not very far removed from Normans, we take a kind of pride in their crudity. We like the roughness, the emergent savagery of our Norman buildings. But even viewed from a more reflective standpoint, there is great virtue in the combinations and contrasts of style to which we are accustomed. It is fatally easy for one good custom to corrupt the world, and there is a certain smugness about the highly integrated perfection of some French cathedrals which grates upon us. It is this dehumanized perfection of the highest flights of France (Bourges always excepted) that puts it on a lower level. And we should above all be thankful to our forbears for the conservatism with which they held their hands. How easy it would have been to make a clean sweep of Lincoln, for example, and to build a newly designed front at little more cost.

73. Lincoln: west front, 1074–92; doorways 1142–46; with later additions

If the preservation of relics of earlier buildings were the result of pure chance in every case, it would indeed be extraordinary how so many vital clues have survived. It is rare for us to lack some evidence, often the most vital evidence, for the forms of the predecessors of our cathedrals. I except the Saxon churches, which admittedly have left little trace. But in most other instances there is enough to piece together the designs according to which successive masters worked. Every one of our cathedrals is a palimpsest. They have been worked on again and again, by master after master. Each has had in mind his own plan, and probably also that of his predecessor. Some were iconoclasts, others reverent in their handling of old stones, which they preserved and reset as far as possible. Much of the value of our cathedrals, at least to us, is their relative immunity from change.

The outcome of this reluctance to do more than is absolutely needful has given us the cathedrals as we see them. As we go on through the styles, we

74. Ripon from south: choir, c. 1288–97; central tower, c. 1460–

75. Ripon nave: original work of c. 1175–90, probably by Master Arthur

shall find a queer series of permutations and combinations. Norman combines with Early English at Chichester; with Decorated at St. Albans, Ely, Hereford, Southwell and Carlisle; Perpendicular is thrown upon earlier styles at Worcester, Gloucester, Winchester and Ripon; Early English stands almost alone at Salisbury and Southwark, and plays its part at Wells, along with Decorated and Perpendicular. And though in some of the buildings the Romanesque original is gone altogether, these are a minority. Not very often are we allowed to forget William the Conqueror; like the eternal record of his Domesday Book, the architecture of his followers is the base and corner stone of all that comes after.

VI   Early English Cathedrals

As we all know from the text-books, the great styles of English architecture each lasted for about a century; and in every case the appearance of a fully mature style was introduced by about a half-century of transition. Simply as a rough approximation, easily remembered, we may say that Norman lasted from 1050 to 1150; Early English to 1250; Decorated to 1350; Perpendicular to 1450; Tudor to 1550. The famous Transitional style was that towards Gothic, in the period 1150 to 1200. Even before 1150 there had been the first glimmers of a Gothic spirit in England. If we accept the view that the style first emerged as an entity at the abbey of St. Denis between 1132 and 1144, it is still true that all the three leading characteristics of the original Gothic, the pointed arch, the ribbed vault and the flying buttress (though this last in a concealed form) had been built at Durham between 1128 and 1133. So that all the Gothic essentials were present in England well before the middle of the century.

It was again at Durham that the slender and aspiring quality of Gothic art was seen in the western Galilee, even though the use of round arches was maintained. But before that time, pointed arches were becoming general in the great churches of the Cistercians such as Fountains and Kirkstall Abbeys. Finally, the massive composition and structure of the Romanesque church began to be discarded, and masons of experience took daring risks in building thinner supports of better quality. Our first Gothic cathedral, in this new sense, took shape at Worcester, where the western bays of the nave survive. Although their exact date is unknown, they seem to be of about 1175. Curiously mongrel in effect, these bays are yet our first Gothic composition. The clustering of narrow shafts, and the vertical emphasis which they give to triforium and clerestory, are a major landmark in style.

The bays are divided by shafts in series to carry the vault, a triplet flanked by an outside pair, making five attached rolls in all, running from base to capital, though interrupted by a moulding above the arcade. Even so, we

76. *Worcester nave: western bays, c. 1175*

77. *Wells nave: western bays, c. 1215–30, by Adam Lock*

have in embryo at Worcester the bay design of all the English cathedrals: a scheme which was even to provide the skeleton of Wren's St. Paul's. But there were still a number of subordinate round arches; and within a few years these were to disappear.

The first all-pointed cathedral was Wells, completely rebuilt between 1175 and 1260. So important is Wells in the history of English Gothic that we should particularize its dates. All that is certainly known of this first Gothic building is that it was begun by Reginald FitzJocelin, who was bishop 1174–91, and who had already endowed the fabric fund for the purpose at a date before 1186, and almost certainly by 1180 at latest. It seems reasonably certain that the choir was complete by 1190, and that the transept and east nave were finished by 1209; the west nave by 1230. All these works are built to a single design, though with slight changes of detail. Adam Lock, who died in 1229, may even have been the original architect. The west front was then built, and finished by about 1260, under Thomas Norreys.

Though small in scale, Wells is exquisitely proportioned. Its quality of workmanship is of the very highest, and perhaps nowhere are there so many foliage capitals of the first rank. The freshness of their carving and their

78. *St. Davids: nave looking east, 1180–98; screen 1324–47; roof, c. 1472–1509*

79. *St. Davids nave: note pointed arches in triforium*

immense variety are linked to a charming and genial humour, as where Farmer John is shown awakened by the sad news that 'the grey goose is gone, and the fox is off to his den-oh'. It was perhaps unfortunate that the architect contented himself with the storied scheme of arcade, triforium and clerestory in separated bands, but the height of the clerestory and the group of triple shafts clustering round the pillars do much to introduce the needed vertical element. The vaulting, with cross-arches and diagonal ribs, but no ridges, is of high pitch and suave curvature; it is one of the most excellent in design of all our early vaults. The natural development from Wells would be to consider Christ Church Cathedral in Dublin, begun soon after 1172 and completed by about 1215. It was designed and built by Somerset men, and even with exported Somerset stone; its resemblances are not only to Wells, but to the work at Glastonbury Abbey which began in 1185.

At St. Davids in the far west of Wales the nave was closely akin to the work at Worcester and at Wells. Building began about 1180 but the design retains much that is Romanesque. The main arcades are round-arched and so is the clerestory, but each bay of the triforium has two sharply pointed

arches recessed from the main face of the wall and thus incorporated into the
clerestory. Two of these round arches of the clerestory, comprising four of
the triforium arches, stand above each arch of the main arcade below. The
vertical line of each pier is carried up by triple wall-shafts. These and the
continuous roll-moulding surrounding the triforium arches mark the influence of the Somerset school, while the inset triforium points towards
unity of the bay. The Hereford retrochoir or vestibule to the Lady Chapel
also combines triple shafting with late Norman details and is an elegant build
of nearly the same date. The nave of Llandaff, though begun only about a
half-generation after St. Davids, is fully Gothic and extremely refined. The
problem of bay-design is solved by the almost flat roofs of the aisles, permitting the nave to be of only two stages. Each great arch of the pointed
arcade is surmounted by two lancets set in arcading to form a continuous
clerestory. In the latest western bays, triple shafts are carried up to the wall-
top, and triplet shafts are used on the piers throughout.

80. Hereford retrochoir, c. 1190   *81. Llandaff: chapter house, 1244–65*

82. Llandaff: nave, 1193–
1229, in two campaigns

83. Canterbury from south-east,
1175–84, by William of Sens
and William Englishman

84. *Canterbury: choir apse, 1179–84, by William Englishman*   85. *Canterbury: ambulatory by William Englishman*

Thus far we have been considering an internal transition from Romanesque, producing a (western) English Gothic. But now came the first great importation of Gothic style from France: the rebuilding of the whole eastern arm at Canterbury. A disastrous fire in 1174 led to a conference of building masters, who disagreed in their proposals. The monks appointed one of the foreigners present, Master William of Sens, and the outcome was a plan and design markedly unlike the English type which we have seen developing. In some senses the new French Canterbury was a retrograde step; the peri-apsidal plan and Corinthianesque columns of France were imported as they stood. And from comparison with Sens Cathedral, it is certain that Master William had indeed learnt his craft there. Sens was one of the earliest French Gothic cathedrals, mostly built in the twenty-five years from 1143 to 1168; it set a fashion which in France was adhered to throughout the early and classical period of the art. In England, fortunately, it was soon assimilated. This was partly due to the accident to William of Sens in 1178, which put control of the work into the hands of his English assistant, the second William. He rapidly developed his master's style and even in the strange Trinity Chapel

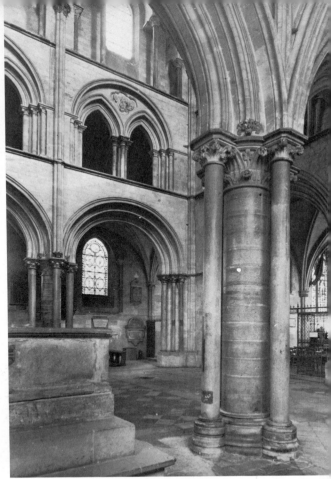

86. Chichester from north-east, 1187–99; tower, c.
1244–47; rebuilt 1861–66

87. Chichester: retrochoir, 1187–99, by Walter of
Coventry

and Becket's Crown imparted a certain national flavour, which a few years later was to be stronger still in the rebuilt retrochoir at Chichester.

But though indebted in certain details to Canterbury, Chichester was fundamentally English, with its square east end. And so was the other first-class work of the outgoing century: Lincoln. Francis Bond carefully analyzed the features which Lincoln derived from Canterbury, and showed that with one exception, the buttresses, these features from Canterbury were not French, but English. But analysis is at best only a series of finger-posts; it would hardly be possible for two great churches built in the same country almost at the same time to be less alike in feeling than are Canterbury and Lincoln. And it is in this feeling, an atmosphere not definable by analysis, that Lincoln is so richly and fundamentally English. Even more, it is supremely Gothic, in a way that no French cathedral had yet been: precisely because it discarded the last remains of the Romanesque tradition in columns, capitals and bases. Bourges, the first fully emancipated French cathedral, was the exact contemporary of Lincoln.

88. *Lincoln: south transept, 1215–30; 'Bishop's Eye'*
window, c. 1335–40

89. *Lincoln: nave, c. 1225–53, probably by Master*
Alexander

At Lincoln we have the supreme type of the Early English cathedral. Not as exclusively of the one period as Salisbury, it is by this very fact more typical of English development. Yet its whole design, apart from the preserved Norman front, forms a complete scheme, differing only in details. The bay design adopted to start with was carried through in essentials to the finish. And it is a bay design which, following on from the precedent of Worcester as much as from Canterbury, stands in the direct line of English development. Its one freakish eccentricity, the 'staggered' vault-ribs of the choir, was quietly dropped in the later continuations.

Many years ago J. H. Parker showed that there was no real reason to suppose that Geoffrey du Noyer, recorded as 'builder of the noble structure' (*nobilis fabricae constructor*), was a Frenchman imported by St. Hugh. The family of du Noyer were of Norman origin, but had been in Lincolnshire a hundred years before the building of Lincoln Cathedral, and long continued as a county family. But it is by no means certain that the description of du Noyer actually implies that he was the architect of the building. As so frequently happened in the accounts of architecture by mediaeval clerics, it may well be that Geoffrey was the administrative rather than the technical chief. And this tends to be borne out by Sir J. W. F. Hill's recent discovery that, during the last years of the twelfth century, one Master Richard the mason was holding land from the dean and chapter. Nowhere better than at Lincoln can we see the aspiring quality of Gothic art. We must, of course, reconstruct in the mind's eye the three spires of which the minster has been robbed: the central one the highest work of man ever erected in this country. If we do this, we shall see that everything is of one piece: the whole great church from east to west and north to south, the subsidiary chapels and the chapter-house, is beating against the sky with its spires, its spikes, its pinnacles. The lancet windows in the gables, the tall lights in the great tower, all are steadily and insistently surging up to heaven. And inside, the shafts, the vaults and the pale flames of the windows are doing the same. Sublime imagination of Master Geoffrey or of Master Richard, or of both together.

But Lincoln as first conceived by Master Richard (or by Geoffrey) was not fully English; its eastern end was a most unusual compromise between the French chevet and the English love of straight lines. It had long canted sides, off which chapels opened. This chevet was destroyed after 1256, and the existing Angel Choir substituted for it. Earlier in the thirteenth century there had been another English feature instituted at Lincoln: the polygonal chapter-house. The first chapter-house built in England with a central plan was the circular one at Worcester, going back to the first half of the twelfth century. Unlike the two belonging to Cistercian houses at Margam and Dore, it had ten instead of twelve bays, and this peculiarity was copied at Lincoln. The majority of the later polygonal chapter-houses had eight sides, except Evesham and Hereford, which certainly copied Worcester, and Bridlington, which may have borrowed its ten sides from Lincoln. Not only does Lincoln resemble Worcester in number of sides, but in dimensions also: the 56 feet of Worcester are just exceeded by the 59 feet of Lincoln; in both cases there is a stone ribbed vault resting on a central pillar; in both cases there is a surrounding wall arcade.

These close likenesses cannot be fortuitous; it is evident that the Lincoln work was directly inspired by Worcester, and was intended to surpass it in size, as in style. When we find that the master responsible at Lincoln bore the same name as one who had shortly before been at work at Worcester, the conclusion that he was the identical man is irresistible. The new work at the east end of Worcester Cathedral began in 1224, and the mason then employed is described as Master Alexander; at Lincoln, within the period 1235–57 appears Alexander the mason, master of the work. And there is no doubt that the works of the Lincoln nave, chapter-house and the lower stage of the central tower belong to the years between 1220 and 1255.

90. *Worcester: choir,*
1224–69, by Master
Alexander

Before the completion of Lincoln, another great eastern church, Peterborough, had been triumphantly finished. Its western porch, though inspired by the Norman arches of the Lincoln front, was pure Gothic. Nothing
more than the suggestion of deep niches came from Lincoln, and the
individuality of the design was carried so far as to make the central opening
the smallest instead of the largest of the three. This might have resulted in a
lack of balance, had not the crowning gables and pinnacled turrets been
carefully adjusted to a different rhythm. Among our early Gothic works, the
west front of Peterborough ranks very high indeed. Beneath the gables, it
seems to have been set out within a double square, and its parts are disposed
according to simple proportions. There is also a successful optical adjustment
in the stages of the shafting, as the spaces between the string-courses and rows
of annulets increase upwards.

Close to 1200 there was a period of great activity in the building of fronts.
In addition to the great porch at Peterborough, an ambitious front was

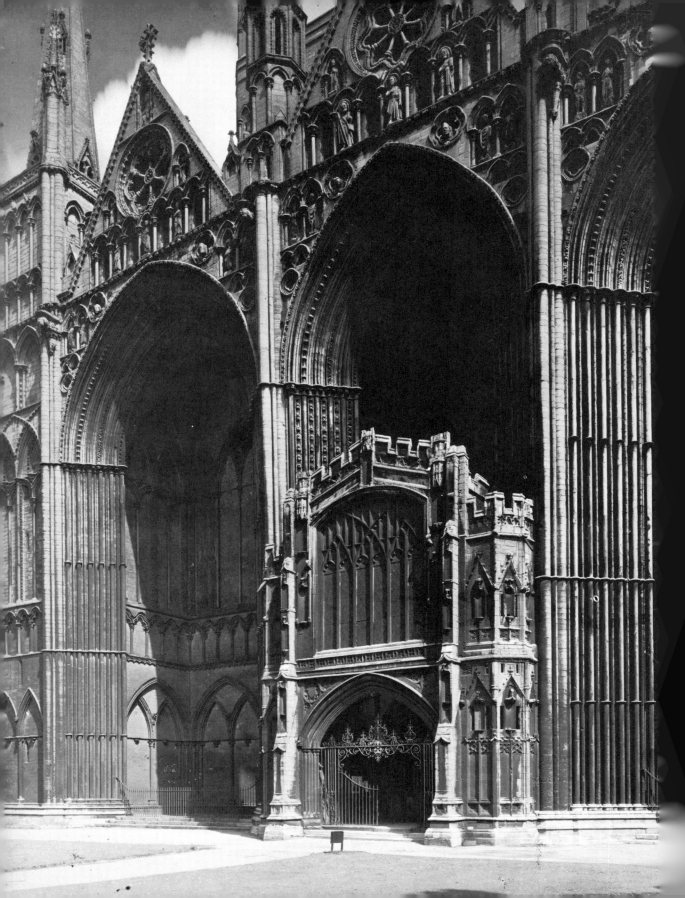

begun at St. Albans, and from about 1230 work started on the sculptured display at Wells. Both at St. Albans and at Wells the plan of flanking towers was adopted. Seen partly developed at Peterborough, this plan had been employed at Rouen Cathedral in Normandy, still under English rule, and seems to have been a modification of the western transept found at Ely and at Bury St. Edmunds and probably intended at Norwich. At St. Albans the flanking towers were never completed, probably owing to the defalcations of Master Hugh Goldcliff, the original master mason, whose work collapsed during winter frosts. But at Wells the front was developed by Thomas Norreys into another triumph of English originality.

As at Peterborough, the Wells front was designed to fill a double square, but its internal organization was utterly different. The three aisles and two towers were marked by six buttresses of deep projection, and the extremes

91. *Peterborough: west front, c. 1193–1230; porch, c. 1375*

92. *Wells: west front, c. 1230–60, by Thomas Norreys*

of the composition were taken up by the sides of similar buttresses facing north and south. Contrary to the precedent of the great three-porched fronts of France, and to that of the newly begun work at St. Albans, no stress was laid at Wells upon the entry to the church. The doorways are of very small scale, and hardly deserve to be called porches. Whether or not the local tradition that they symbolize the needle's eye is to be believed, they mark the contrast between puny human scale and the vast sculptured pageant of sacred history above. Except for the main range of windows and blind niches, practically the whole area of the front is devoted to the display of sculpture, by far the most elaborate single display ever devized. Exactly what the iconographic scheme was, cannot now be recovered, though William Worcestre, who saw it in 1478, states that it represented the Old and New Law; it is at least certain that the complete work was as much a triumph of painting as of carving. Every statue was painted and gilt, and at its completion it must have presented a dazzling sight, only comparable to the brilliance of the Parthenon in its first state. The front of Wells was the supreme triumph of the combined plastic arts in England. Henceforward the secondary arts were to

93. *Rochester: presbytery, c. 1200–27*   94. *Southwark: choir, c. 1213–35; reredos, c. 1520*

be pressed into the background, though with advantage to architecture considered on its own merits.

While the first wave of Gothic cathedrals reached the west fronts, a new wave was beginning to rebuild eastern arms. This rebuilding took the form of extension, the new work being carried up around the existing Norman apses or fronts. This had partly a practical significance; it allowed the existing sanctuary to be used for services continuously until the new was ready. But it also reflected a new emphasis laid on the sanctuary, eastern processional path and eastern chapels. Within the first quarter of the thirteenth century this transformation had been completed or at least begun at Lichfield, Rochester, Southwark, Winchester and Worcester. Of the masters responsible, only Alexander at Worcester is certainly known to us by name, and was probably identical, as we have seen, with the continuator of Lincoln. Peter des Roches, bishop of Winchester from 1204 to 1238, was the patron of the work at his own cathedral and of that at Southwark. The master, at least at Winchester, was probably that Richard the mason who was given 4 marks towards the work in 1208. Des Roches was closely connected with the king's court, and

95. Winchester: presbytery, c. 1315–60, by Thomas Witney; reredos, c. 1475–85

96. Southwark: retrochoir, c. 1213–35

97. *Salisbury: Lady Chapel, 1220–25, by Nicholas of Ely*

98. *Salisbury: nave, 1237–58, by Nicholas of Ely*

may later have employed the Master Stephen who was the principal mason in the royal service from 1213 to 1228 and perhaps for a longer period, and built the great hall at Winchester Castle. At Rochester another Richard Mason is mentioned, who was probably the designer.

But the great work of the time was the entirely new cathedral of Salisbury, begun when the city was removed two miles from the waterless mound of Old Sarum to the Avon valley. Salisbury is noteworthy as our only Gothic cathedral to have been built on an absolutely unencumbered site. Its planning and design could proceed without reference to existing buildings or the necessity of maintaining services. To this the building owes its exceptional symmetry and regularity of lay-out, and also its eccentricities verging on preciosity. Within five years from the start in 1220 the Lady Chapel had been completed, and this set the keynote for the whole cathedral. Supported on grouped marble shafts of almost incredible attenuation, the Lady Chapel is of greater ingenuity than beauty. There is no reason to doubt that the king's clerk Elias of Dereham had a large share in this rather pedantic scheme, while the master mason Nicholas of Ely deserves special credit for the constructional skill which overcame exceptional difficulties. Behind the eastern chapel the

church grew apace from 1225 onwards, and by 1258 was completed except
for the west front. The central tower and spire were not added until the next
century, but the 38 years of the principal construction compare very closely
with the 36 years of Wren's St. Paul's, our only other cathedral built in one
operation. In both cases the full completion of the original project occupied
about half a century. At Salisbury this included the building of very splendid
cloisters and chapter-house by Master Richard, in imitation of those begun
at Westminster Abbey. These were of Geometrical Decorated style, and
belong to a later phase.

Before the arrival of Geometrical work with the new bar-tracery invented
at Rheims between 1210 and 1240, there was an enormous burst of building
activity in England. In addition to the works already discussed, there are
extant buildings of the end of this period at Bristol, Carlisle, Durham, Ely,
Exeter, Gloucester, Hereford, Lichfield, Oxford, Ripon, Rochester, Southwell and York. These include lateral Lady Chapels at Bristol[1] and Oxford
and an eastern one at Hereford; north transepts at Lichfield and Rochester,
and both transepts at York; and chapter-houses at Exeter, Lichfield and
Oxford. Ripon built its version of the wide-spread west front, with triple
doors between towers, and two tiers of five lancet windows. But the most

[1] Where the Abbot asked for the loan of one 'L' from Wells *c.* 1220. Resemblances of detail are
to the west end of the Wells nave.

*99. Oxford: Lady Chapel, c. 1220–50, and north
choir aisle*

100. Llandaff: Lady Chapel, 1266–87

101. *Hereford: Lady Chapel, 1217–25*

102. *York: nave (1291) from south transept, c. 1230–41*

103. *Lichfield: chapter house, c. 1239–49, by Master Thomas*

important works were still concerned with the main eastern limbs of the cathedrals. Durham began its unusual eastern transept or Chapel of Nine Altars in 1242, under Master Richard of Farnham; Ely built its presbytery between 1239 and 1250; and Carlisle and Southwell were building their choirs. Carlisle and Southwell were both under the influence of York, and were probably designed by York masons. The presbytery at Ely, designed by one Sampson who had a long career as master mason to the cathedral through the mid-thirteenth century, became the type of the Eastern regional termination, as Salisbury did of the Western. This regional diversity of design is all the more interesting in view of close resemblances of detail between the work at Ely and at Salisbury, probably explained by the Salisbury mason's origin or training at Ely.

By 1250 the Early English cathedrals had taken shape and were awaiting the next progression of style. In less than a century the whole country had put off the heavy mass of Norman building and accepted an entirely new architecture. True, it was in places bound by the plan and disposition of

104. Ripon: west front, c. 1230–40

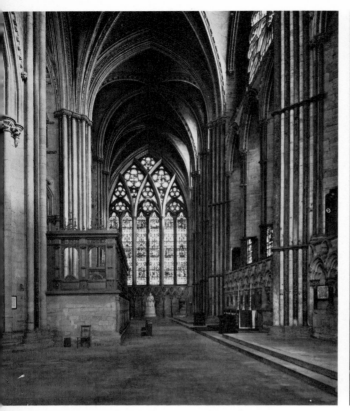

105. *Durham: Chapel of Nine Altars, 1242–80, by Richard Farnham*

106. *Ely: presbytery, 1239–50, by Master Sampson; and (left) choir, 1322–36*

earlier work preserved of necessity, as for instance at St. Albans and Durham, but there was nowhere any doubt of the radical nature of the change. Already the interiors of churches were infinitely lighter; in making comparisons it must always be remembered that our great Norman cathedrals, such as Peterborough and Norwich, have inserted later windows in place of those of Romanesque date. The gloom of a Norman cathedral must have approached that now only to be found in Mediterranean countries: the early Gothic church, even where it is completely lit through rich glass as at Chartres, glows with light. But the disposition of the new windows was still not fully satisfactory.

Owing to the structural division of the Romanesque church into the three stages of pier arcade, triforium or blindstory, and clerestory, the architects were at first committed to a major difficulty which stood in the way of unity in design. In the relatively low English churches, there was insufficient room for all three storeys to be fully developed. If the arcades were to be even of adequate height, as at Lincoln, without unduly reducing the lighted clerestory, the triforium became too small. At Lincoln this was well managed, but the arcades were not high enough to give full effect internally to the vertical quality of Gothic art. At Salisbury the designer was determined not to fail in this respect, and produced tall arcades and exquisitely proportioned triple lancets in the clerestory, with a well-arranged vault. But in doing so he cramped the triforium arcade into positive ugliness, and also left it sitting on top of the spandrels of the arcade in the same unfortunate way that had already occurred at Wells.

At Ely, the triforium is made the important stage, and is extremely beautiful, but the clerestory appears dwarfed, and the arcades do not occupy a sufficient proportion of the height. The design was in fact a poorer version of Master Alexander's for the Lincoln nave – the vault-springing, instead of being kept below the clerestory string-course, was made level with it as at Salisbury, while in the east gable an upper range of lancets rises from the same line. Vault and clerestory thus appear as the separate lid to a box, lacking cohesion with the work below. Even during the Transitional period attempts had been made at Oxford and at Glastonbury Abbey to eliminate the tri-

107. St. Davids: presbytery,
1221–

forium by absorbing it into the main arcade. This was not a happy experiment, but it was followed by another which was to yield fruit. Before the end of the period a two-storey design had been adopted at a number of Cistercian abbeys, at Christ Church Cathedral in Dublin and at St. David's and Southwell. In these cases the space of the triforium was absorbed into the design of the clerestory, to make only two stages of the interior elevation. The final and logical outcome, the bay of one stage only, was never fully attained in England, except at Bristol, by making the aisles the full height of the church. But it was hinted at in the stone grille applied to the choir at Gloucester, and in the recession of the clerestory behind the plane of the main nave piers at Canterbury. The best solution of all could not be applied to monastic churches requiring a processional path, but was accepted at the Chapels Royal, where St. Stephen's in Westminster Palace and King's College Chapel, Cambridge, dispensed with aisles. The final result also appeared in Spain and at Albi in southern France; it might well have been adopted for English cathedrals had a Catholic collegiate liturgy survived Henry VIII's anti-monastic reforms, and led to the building of a new series of great churches.

The best work of the Early English period has an incomparable freshness.

108. Southwell choir, 1234–50, looking east

109. Southwark from the south; lower stage of tower probably by Henry Yeveley, c. 1380–90

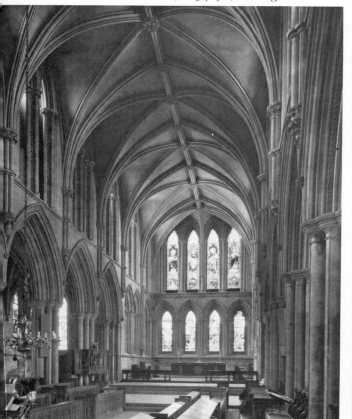

even where it forms part of a tentative and even ungainly design. It has the charm as well as the awkwardness of youth and immaturity: a coltish quality. Its finest flights were generally where the sculptor had free play, as in the leaf-capitals at Wells. It is certain that many of the early architects were themselves sculptors, and this was probably the rule. Only a sculptor could have devized the Wells west front as a gallery for figure-carvings; a gallery of display so exclusively that the actual doorways look almost like after-thoughts, even though this may symbolize the insignificance of human scale contrasted with the transcending importance of sacred history. As the child is father to the man, so is Early English the progenitor of the whole of English Gothic architecture, and even of our non-Gothic building as well. It contains the seeds of all our later developments, though often lying dormant and hardly perceptible.

To consider the chief parts of the English cathedral one by one, we can see the origins of future design in the bays, the vaults, the windows; doorways, fronts and steeples. As has just been mentioned, by the end of the period there were already bays which suppressed the triforium; even at the very start in the nave of Worcester, there had been unity of bay design. Master Alexander's vaults at Lincoln included not only ridge-ribs (which had already appeared in Master Richard's choir vault) but even a system of short cross-ridges meeting lateral intermediate ribs which gave rise to the whole elaborate system of later lierne and stellar vaulting. In the contemporary chapter-house, the circuit of ridge-ribs between the central pillar and the walls even more definitely foreshadowed the lierne or strut-rib. Long before the actual introduction of Geometrical bar-tracery from France, it had been largely anticipated in effect by the ornamental piercings of spandrel which formed plate-tracery of considerable elaboration.

The main types of doorways had been formed by 1250. In the Ely Galilee, for instance, there was the door opening partly veiled by a central shaft and a screen of tracery; at St. Albans were the English versions of the deep French porch; at Wells, Salisbury and Hereford were lateral porches highly typical of English tradition. Peterborough, St. Albans, Wells, Ripon and Lincoln were all producing versions of the wide spreading screen front, with or without lateral towers to flank the aisles. Salisbury continued the towerless tradition of Rochester and St. David's, but its front is a deliberately artificial screen thrown across nave and aisles. The narrow front with twin towers aligned on the aisles, a Norman design, was not favoured, but was to be adopted again at a later date. Central tower design suddenly leapt into prominence with the polygonal-buttress type at Lincoln, Oxford and Chichester. These towers were based on earlier precedents, such as the Norman central tower with round corner turrets at Gloucester, but had become entirely Gothic. The lower stages of the existing tower at Lincoln, designed about 1238 by Master Alexander, led to the more important of the two great divisions of tower design. The other, based on the tower of Old St. Paul's built between 1200 and 1221, is seen only at Bristol, Durham, Wells and York, and in hybrid form at Hereford, Gloucester and Southwark.

Among subsidiary buildings the chapter-house takes first place, and is represented by the rectangular example at Exeter and the magnificent decagon of Master Alexander at Lincoln, where the form was already almost perfect. Only at Peterborough and Canterbury are there considerable remains of Early English cloisters, in both cases restricted to the wall arcading. But here too enough is left to show that there was a completed Gothic form, not merely distinct from the Norman work that had gone before, but already susceptible of individual variations. This individuality is indeed one of the strongest characteristics of the time; there is no slavish copying, no adherence to sets of rules formulated by a man or a school. The customary code of proportions used by the designers was an elastic one and had not hardened into a strait-jacket. The vigour of Early English art is the vigour of English springtime, not confined to the regular blades of the young cornfields, but finding expression in an unending multitude of diverse forms.

Chichester: belfry,
c. 1410–40

VII   Decorated Cathedrals

The Early English period in our art had been a brilliant and sunny spring; Perpendicular, as Sedding wrote, was to be the harvest-time of our endeavour, Tudor the fading glory of the autumn leaves. The period of swiftly-maturing development which intervened between the early and the complete Gothic was the full blossom of our architecture. Notwithstanding the fire of criticism which has been levelled at Rickman's term Decorated as a name for this style, it has a certain appropriate ring. For though there is much 'Decorated' work that is restrained and even plain, the period does contain the peak of naturalistic carving and painting. Leaves, flowers and fruits, copied from nature, and then richly stylized into undulations, run riot over the more costly work of about 1300.

There are, it is true, two great divisions within the style, separated by the introduction (about 1290) of the ogee curve: the Geometric and the Curvilinear sub-periods. In the first of these, designers struck simple arcs and circles with their compasses; in the second, they joined their arcs into reverse curves and produced flowing, reticulated and flamboyant patterns. Foliage and natural forms are at first stiff, then towards the end of the Geometric period become intensely naturalistic, even photographic in their representation. In the Curvilinear style the crispness of natural leaves is lost, and the surfaces undulate more and more, producing strange nodules of rounded, globose form, connected by sweeping hollow surfaces which look as if they had been made with a vigorous thumb in moist clay. Before 1350 the quality of such work was becoming lush, decadent and even repulsive to the eye.

Superficially, the patterns of Geometric bar-tracery in the windows and upon wall surfaces are the outstanding mark of the new style; but they had far more than superficial importance. The introduction of bar-tracery meant another great lightening of the weight of stonework. Windows could be designed to consist mainly of glass, subdivided by very narrow mullions and bars, and supported largely by wrought-ironwork. This led directly to skeleton construction, where the weight and pressure from vaults and roof were concentrated upon a series of slender supports, and the intervening spaces of wall cut into window. This implied a further advance in structural knowledge, and was accompanied by a greatly extended use of metal reinforcement, which spread from the windows and arches into what was left of solid wall. Here was a revolution, tending towards the steel-frame building, the Crystal Palace, and all-glass solaria. At the same time it translated into stone and iron the methods of the framewright who set up mediaeval timber houses.[1]

[1] That there may have been a similar and roughly contemporary development in timber construction has recently been suggested by Dr. J. Quentin Hughes. He points out that the wooden vaults of the York transepts are independent of the roofs above, and depend for their strength and rigidity upon an unusual pattern of transverse and diagonal series of ribs: a system apparently not again exploited until the twentieth century (*Yorkshire Archaeological Journal*, pt. 152).

110. Lincoln: Angel choir, 1256–80, by Simon of Thirsk

111, 112. Salisbury chapter house, by Master Richard, c. 1275; (left) the doorway from the vestibule; (right) looking up into the vault

Much of this revolution, at least of its origins, was accomplished independently in England, but the decisive features were a fresh introduction from France in 1245, when the new church of Westminster Abbey was designed. The foreign flavour of Westminster, its great height, its chevet, its grandiose north front, did not find favour in England. But the new windows from Rheims, and the renewed feeling of verticality, were rapidly made integral parts of the English cathedral. At Lincoln, between 1256 and 1280, the lengthened presbytery or Angel Choir was built in place of the curious chevet of St. Hugh. It adopted just so much as was essential from the new scheme of Westminster, including the angels which give it its name; but in all respects it is a completely and even aggressively English building.

Similarly there is nothing French about the magnificent chapter-house and cloister indulged in by the canons of Salisbury between 1263 and 1284. Unburdened with monastic buildings, these secular canons were able to finish in 21 years a work which at Westminster, even on a rather smaller scale, took 120. What is equally remarkable, the non-functional Salisbury cloisters are actually the largest, as well as the earliest, of the cathedral

cloisters that remain. They may be considered as the starting-point of English cloister design, a highly specialized and interesting branch of our architecture. It became a point of honour to rebuild cloisters in the latest fashion, and much ingenuity was expended on them. Lincoln and Norwich followed Salisbury's lead before the end of the thirteenth century; in the fourteenth came Exeter, Old St. Paul's, Gloucester, Worcester, Durham and Canterbury. Peterborough, Wells, Oxford, Hereford, Chester, Ely and Bristol had all done likewise before the close of the Middle Ages.

The two great works of early Decorated are the Angel Choir at Lincoln and the nave of Lichfield. At Lincoln, where the designer was probably a Yorkshireman, Master Simon 'de Tresk' (Thirsk), the bold, broad northern scheme was adopted. The arches of the pier arcades are only just pointed; the windows of the clerestory are so wide as to be almost startling. The work is tentative, but remarkably successful as an essay in a style only freshly arrived in the country. At Lichfield the dates of the building cannot be precisely determined, and it is consequently impossible to relate the different parts to the succession of masters: Thomas (c. 1230–50); his son William (c. 1250–65); and Thomas Wallace or the Welshman (c. 1265–80). It seems probable that Thomas the elder was architect of the transepts and chapter-house, and Thomas Wallace the designer of the west front and scheme of three towers; he or William FitzThomas may have been responsible for the nave.

To whomsoever due, the Lichfield nave was another definite forward step in bay design. The arches are much sharper than at Lincoln, the triforium taller, while the clerestory has the beautiful and unusual feature of triangular windows formed of three equilateral arcs, and filled with three trefoil-cusped circles. From base to vault triple shafts rush upwards without a break, crossing a cinque-foiled circle which fills the spandrel between each pair of arches. As at Lincoln, there is arcading along the internal face of the aisle walls and above this three-light windows with traceried heads of three cusped circles. The reduction of the clerestory windows to tracery alone, without vertical lights, couples them to the triforium beneath, and again suggests the two-storied interior. There is another, more freakish but less successful, version of the same design in the north transept at Hereford, which is roughly contemporary. This has arches composed of arcs of such large radius as to be almost straight lines, and an unpleasantly harsh effect of saw-teeth is produced.

All of this activity was taking place at the secular cathedrals, and marks the change of emphasis of the thirteenth century, abandoning the great abbeys for the bishops' churches. This reflected an actual loss of power and influence by the monastic orders. In the diocese of Bath and Wells, where effective power had been transferred to the abbey at Bath in 1090, it finally went back to the secular church of Wells in 1218. The abbey of Coventry, joint-cathedral with

43. *Salisbury: cloisters, c. 1263–84, by Master Richard*

114. Lichfield: nave, c. 1265–93, probably by
William Fitz Thomas

115. Hereford: north transept, 1250–68

Lichfield of a great see, dropped more and more into the background. Baldwin, Archbishop of Canterbury in 1185–90, attempted to set up a secular college at Hackington, but the vested interests of the monks of Christ Church proved too strong for him. At Worcester, the bishops were so constantly at loggerheads with the monks that they withdrew to Westbury-on-Trym, near Bristol, and repeatedly tried to erect Westbury into a cathedral. The first of these efforts was made by Bishop Giffard towards the end of the thirteenth century, the age we are now considering. Another movement which was greatly lessening monastic influence was the spread of orders of friars, introduced to England early in Henry III's reign, and generously fostered by him.

Work went on apace. Lichfield continued its nave and reached the west front, while York began its new nave and Ripon an east front. Lady Chapels were built at Chichester, St. Albans and Wells, chapter-houses of great splendour at Wells, York and Southwell, the two last vaulted without a central pier. At York the great span of 58 feet would allow only of a timber roof, from which the vaulting is suspended. Essentially based upon the tie-beam and king-post truss, the roof is not a constructional novelty, but is a remarkable example of prefabrication on a very large scale. The Augustinian

canons at Carlisle remodelled the choir after a destructive fire in 1292, and
Rochester built its south transept. The chapter-house and Lady Chapel at
Wells are both of unusual interest. The plan of the former goes back to about
1255 and its octagonal shape and undercroft derive from Westminster. But
its treatment is entirely distinct, owing something to Lichfield and Lincoln,
yet still more to original inspiration. The central pier and wall responds are
no longer divided into stages by annulets and string-courses but rise from
base to capital unbroken, and the springing level of the vault is wisely kept
below that of the windows. The vault itself with its sheaves of ribs already
foreshadows the fan while the tracery, perhaps based on that in the London
chapel of St. Etheldreda, Ely Place, is poised on the brink of curvilinear
treatment. The Lady Chapel, also polygonal in plan, shows another marked
advance in style. Its elegant shafted piers with their singular pedestalled bases,
and the trefoiled tracery of its windows, closely resemble the works of
Thomas Witney at Exeter and suggest an identity for the Master Thomas in
charge at Wells in 1323.

116. York: nave, 1291–1322, by Master Simon

117. Carlisle: choir 1293–1322; east window, c. 1318–22, probably by Ivo de Raghton

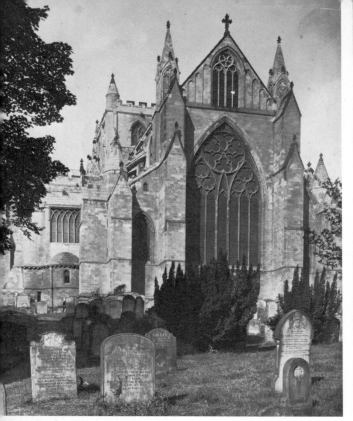

118. (top left) Ripon: east front, c. 1288–97

119. (top right) Ripon: choir, c. 1175 and 1288–97

120. Chichester: Lady Chapel, c. 1288–1304

121, 122. *York chapter house, c. 1265 and c. 1285–90; (left) exterior from east; (right) interior*

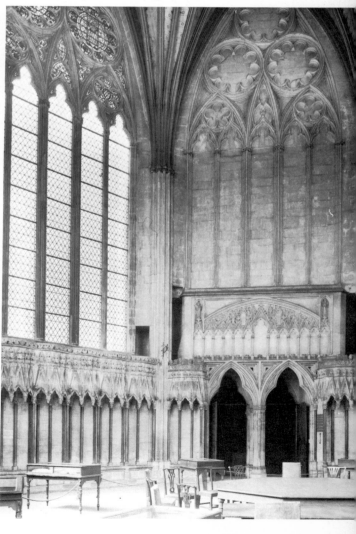

123. (top left) Wells: undercroft
of chapter house, c. 1255–65

124. (top right) Wells: staircase
to chapter house, c. 1286–90

125. (left) Wells: Retrochoir,
c. 1329–40, by William Joy

126. (right) Wells: interior of
chapter house, c. 1286–1306

Of the greater works, apart from the nave of York, by far the most important was the beginning of the total rebuilding of Exeter Cathedral, started in the eastern chapels at an uncertain date near 1275, and transformed into a scheme for a complete new church in 1288. Exeter and Bristol, which was not begun until ten or more years later, are our two complete Decorated cathedrals. Both, in their quite different ways, display the suavity and rounded qualities of the new style, now fully developed. The stiff, even hard crispness of Early English work has now altogether worn away, and everything speaks of the blown petal.

The approaching maturity of Gothic architecture in the later thirteenth century was shown not only in its decorative aspects, but in structure. A much larger proportion of the greater churches was intended from the start for high vaults. The building masters had proceeded beyond their tentative beginnings and had formulated a constructional system. Where before they had worked their way by guess and by God, they now piled stone on stone with well-founded confidence. Dissimilar in system as in detail as are Bristol and Exeter cathedrals, in both can be seen this assured and well-rounded technique, free from the disproportions, as well as devoid of the naive charm that had characterized the adolescent Early English. Exeter has a gracious generosity of form that typifies its Devon setting. Nothing is calculated to startle or astonish; everything is soothing, but with a well-assorted and various charm. The tracery patterns of the windows are as appetizing an assortment as a good box of chocolates. There is too perhaps a suspicion of the miniature perfection of bridal confectionery. This is one of the strange features of much Decorated work: that it seems less to have been built than to have been cast in a mould.

But the Exeter design unites beauties drawn from the examples of Lincoln and Wells, and carries a stage further the development of vaulting. Additional (*tierceron*) ribs are added to form a sheaf already approaching the fan in feeling. And though choir and nave were carried out according to the same scheme, the nave vault represses the flattened curve of the diagonal ribs, introducing a refinement at the expense of 'true' setting out. But this nave vault was not built until the middle of the fourteenth century, and such refinements in the interests of optical unity are really typical of Perpendicular Gothic. As in the Angel Choir at Lincoln, the Exeter arches are but slightly pointed, and so add to the broad and flowing qualities of repose which at Exeter are outstanding in the general impression. The new atmosphere of space and light is also noticeable, but there is not yet a fully satisfying resolution of the problem of bay design, and horizontal and vertical elements are too evenly balanced.

The chief connecting link between earlier and later, and eastern and western styles is lost: the new work of Old St. Paul's. This was in progress

127. Old St. Paul's: Lady Chapel, c. 1275–1312, probably by Michael of Canterbury; from the engraving by Hollar

through the whole of the second half of the thirteenth century and translated into almost aggressively English terms the French Geometrical style. Its great eastern rose set above seven narrow lights was a counterpart to the bay design at Lichfield, where spherical triangles took the place of the rose. For some reason the rose never achieved a lasting popularity in England as an architectural form, though Paul's window was paraphrased on a smaller scale, and appeared as a design on tiles and elsewhere. The vault was provided with single pairs of tierceron ribs in each direction. We know little of the

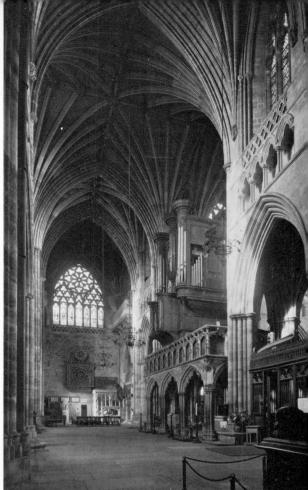

128, 129. Exeter: (left) presbytery, 1288–1308, by Master Roger; east window 1390–92 by Robert Lesyngham; (right) transept, 1308–17, by William Luve and Thomas Witney

130. Exeter: detail of pulpitum, 1317–25, by Thomas Witney

stages of the work or of its designers, though there is some reason for attributing the five eastern bays (the Lady Chapel) to Michael of Canterbury, and the work was completed in the years 1307–12 under John de Weldon, the cathedral's resident mason.

The building of Exeter was entirely finished in less than a century. Work began at the east end somewhere about 1275, with a Lady Chapel flanked by side chapels and backed by a retrochoir of one bay. Before these had been vaulted the presbytery, the 'new work' proper, had been founded in 1288. It was complete in about twenty years, the master for at least the last eleven being one Roger, who may well have been the designer of the whole scheme. He was succeeded in 1310 by William Luve, under whom the church reached the first bay west of the crossing. At this period stalls were made under Master John of Glaston and a bishop's throne of wood to the design of

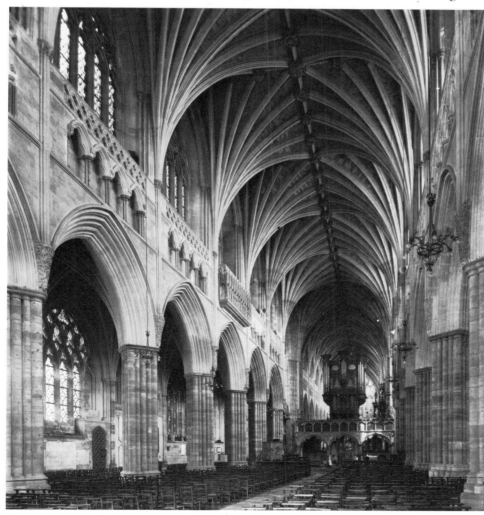

131. Exeter: nave, 1328–42, by Thomas Witney

Thomas 'of Winton'. He was presumably identical with Thomas of Witney, who came from Winchester to take charge from 1316 to 1342, and built the nave except for its vault, the high altar, sedilia and pulpitum, and eastern and northern cloisters.

It is an outstanding fact of the documentary history of Exeter that most of the principal craftsmen came from other counties. Master Thomas, presumably from Witney in Oxfordshire, had been in charge at Winchester; a master mason, William de Schoverville, from Salisbury, was called in in 1311. During the building of the western screen and the vaulting of the nave the masters were the two well-known Somerset men, William Joy and Richard Farleigh, and between 1376 and 1382 the cloisters were completed by Robert Lesyngham, a visiting architect from Gloucestershire, who also designed the new east window and the north-west porch. The intriguing possibility, suggested by the character of the Winchester presbytery, begun c. 1315, that the 'Master T. of W.' responsible was Thomas of Witney has now been proved by documentary evidence to be in fact the case. Furthermore, Witney was a manor belonging to Winchester Cathedral priory, and its noble church tower, with three windows and unbuttressed, is as if a Gothic translation of that at Winchester.

Within the century of its growth, at least five chief masters contributed to the development of Exeter, and yet they all adhered closely to the original concept of the first planner, who may have been Master Roger. The whole building is extremely regular and symmetrical, and embodies all the main characteristics of the age. Its eastern arm is built up on the lower surrounding chapels and eastern transepts, definitely a study in composition. The windows exhibit the ingenuity of the tracery designer; the vaults show the increasing preoccupation with pattern and with suavity of line as an aid to unity. The nave is provided with the English lateral porch, but also with a western feature which was new. This was the separate screen containing three porches, and standing in advance of the main gable. It is an alternative to the cavernous porches of the French cathedrals integrally planned as part of the front itself. The French scheme was to have been combined at St. Albans with the English lateral towers, but was never finished. At Lichfield and at Wells there were sculpture galleries on the fronts, but the doorways were not emphasized nor protected by porches. At Exeter it seems to have been William Joy, fresh from Wells, who devized this new departure, but like the rest of his work, it belongs strictly to the story of Perpendicular architecture, and must be discussed in the next chapter.

But the later Decorated period was one of lively experiment. Not only were the architects' compasses busy in the composition of tracery patterns; great structural features were beginning to take their final shape. Much of the underlying form of Perpendicular was present before its details started to appear in the fourth decade of the fourteenth century. Indeed, isolated details, not yet united in the Perpendicular manner, had been on view for nearly fifty years. The most noteworthy example of this tendency is the nave of York, begun in 1291 and finished, except for its timber vault, by 1345. Of unusual width, with relatively slender piers, this design at the same time greatly increases vertical emphasis by its pronounced vault shafts which run unbroken from base to springing, and even more by its incorporation of the triforium into the clerestory. The triforium gallery actually consists of downward prolongations of the window mullions. So definitely does this design foreshadow Perpendicular treatment that it was possible to adhere to it very closely in the eastern arm built after 1360. The designer of this great work was apparently Master Simon, who was already a wealthy man in 1301, and died in 1322.

The new east front of Carlisle and the west front of York went on under the same designer, Ivo de Raghton; and the breadth and space of the new idea were being simultaneously exploited by the king's masons in the south, where the immense church of the London Greyfriars was in progress by 1306. The lantern church was fast taking shape: piers were being reduced to the smallest practicable cross-section; windows were reaching their limits, as at Carlisle; and interiors were unified in treatment. The elimination of aisles was a logical step, but was not actually taken in any English cathedral. The architectural type, however, existed in the Chapel Royal of St. Stephen in the Palace of Westminster, begun in 1292, and followed by other chapels such as those of Eton College and King's College, Cambridge. Related to this aisleless scheme is the spacious eastern Lady Chapel at Lichfield, lit by very

132. *Lichfield: Lady Chapel, c. 1320–36, by William Eyton*

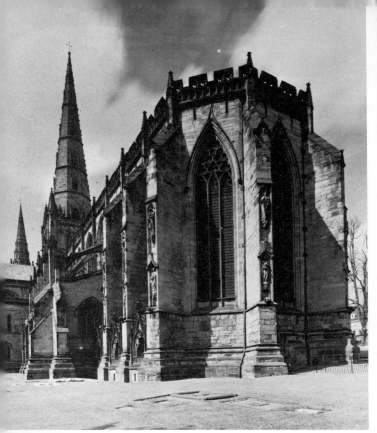

133, 134. Lichfield Lady Chapel: (left) exterior from east, (right) interior, c. 1320–36, by William Eyton

tall traceried windows. It was begun *c.* 1320, and finished by 1336; the mason was William of Eyton.

Following upon the example of Salisbury, large cloisters were undertaken at several cathedrals: those at Lincoln were begun in 1295, and those of Norwich two years later. Here too was an atmosphere of space and light, as well as much ingenuity of design expended on buildings wholly or largely for show. But the great example of English architecture for show is the design of towers. Most of the famous towers are later works of the Perpendicular period, but their types derive from earlier models. As we have seen, there were two great schools of tower design: the turreted form derived from Lincoln, and the buttressed scheme found at Old St. Paul's. The upper stage of the Lincoln tower was built by Richard of Stow between 1307 and 1311, and ranks among the finest in the whole country. Standing on the low arcading of the Early English storey, it achieves its effect in one tall stage composed of two pedimented windows each of two lights. At Lichfield, where two spires at least were up by 1323, the central tower was to carry a stone spire, and was kept low, but it developed this theme by dividing the space between the turrets into five parts, of which two contained windows of two lights. The Lichfield turrets were buttressed at a lower level, and this

two-stage buttressing was adapted to a non-turret tower at Hereford, built
about 1320. Hereford's tower is in two storeys, each of four panels, with twin
buttresses at the angles, giving a somewhat turreted effect. At Wells Master
Thomas (? Witney) built a tower of the turretless type, but quite unbuttressed, with three pairs of tall lancets on each face. The design was later
complicated by the insertion of tracery in the lancets, and the addition of
extra pinnacles. The original design undoubtedly derives from the great
tower of Old St. Paul's, possibly through that of Witney church, thus suggesting the identity of Master Thomas with Thomas Witney, also indicated by
resemblances between the Wells Lady Chapel and the Exeter pulpitum.
These four towers provided the elements from which the later towers were
to be derived by means of permutation and combination.

There was another experiment in a very different direction. This was the
great octagon at Ely, built to replace the Norman central tower which fell in
1322. Following on the wave of polygonal chapter-houses, the octagon
presents obvious analogies to them. But it must also reflect some knowledge
of the central plan abroad, and probably of the great buildings of Persia,

135. Norwich: cloister doorway,
c. 1310, by John Ramsey

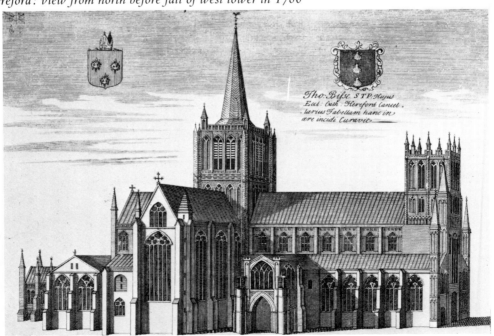

136. Hereford: *central tower, c. 1315, and north porch, c. 1520–30*

137. Hereford: *west front, c. 1140–45; and west tower, c. 1325*

138. Hereford: *view from north before fall of west tower in 1786*

through the medium of travellers' tales. It is at any rate an astonishing achievement, with no direct parentage, and no immediate progeny. Among the English cathedrals only Wren's St. Paul's adopted this singularity of the Ely plan. We are told by the chronicler that the plan was devized by Alan of Walsingham, the sacrist, but the accounts record payment made to 'a certain man coming from London to ordain the work', and show that the mason concerned was Master John. It is plausible to suggest that this was John of Ramsey, one of the important family of Norwich masons who were to lead the London fashion in architecture before the middle of the fourteenth century.

139. Wells: central tower, c. 1315–22, by Master Thomas (? Witney); altered 1439–50

140. Ely: octagon, 1322–46, by Master John (? Ramsey)

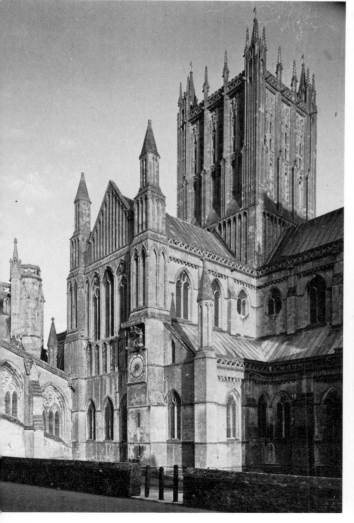

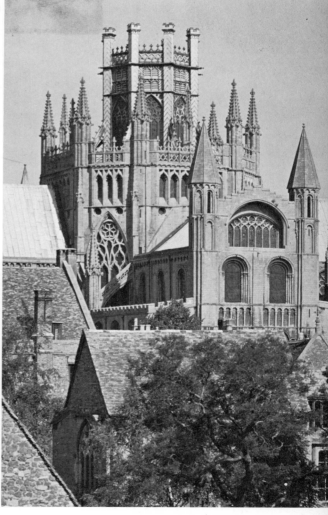

141. Ely: vault and lantern over octagon, 1328–40, by William Hurley

142. (left) Ely: detail of octagon

143. (top right), 144. (right) Ely: choir vault, c. 1335, and triforium, 1322–36, by Master John (? Ramsey)

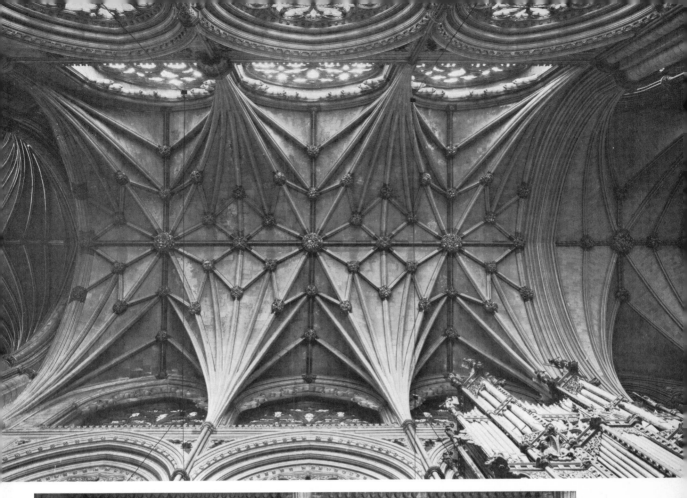

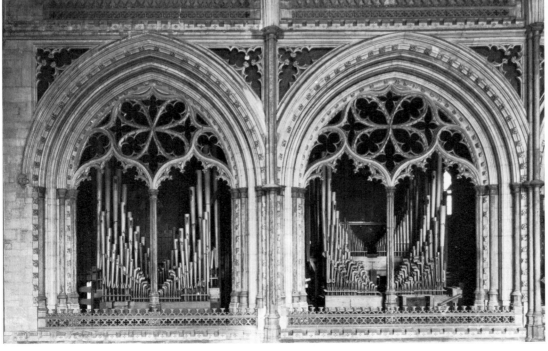

145. *Ely: Lady Chapel, 1321–49; east window, 1371–74, by Thomas Ufford*

146. *Ely: detail of Lady Chapel, c. 1330*

Original as the plan was, its scale proved to be beyond the mason's powers to vault. Nearly 70 feet in span, it also went far beyond the longest available timbers, and an entirely new method of construction had to be invented to cover it. This was the work of William of Hurley or Horley, who came from London for repeated visits and was paid the very high retaining fee of £8 a year, worth something like £2000 in the purchasing power of 1973. Although adapted to the octagonal plan, the wooden vault is analogous to a series of hammer-beam trusses whose hammerposts are the eight great uprights of the lantern. Though it had no direct results for the English cathedral, Hurley's adoption of the large-scale truss at Ely was to have far-reaching effects upon later English woodwork.

Ely: model of frame of lantern

Concurrently with the octagon, three bays of the choir destroyed by the falling tower were rebuilt, between 1323 and 1336. Just as the Exeter vaulting was important for its introduction of additional tiercerons, so is the vault of this choir at Ely for its lierne ribs. The vaulting plan of the undercroft of St. Stephen's at Westminster was adopted, but with extra ribs inserted to form a series of six-pointed stars. This vault may be considered the progenitor, not only of the later lierne and fan vaults of England, but also of the stellar vaults which became fashionable in Germany and were among the chief characteristics of the central European 'Sondergotik'. The third work which was proceeding at Ely alongside the new octagon and choir was the Lady Chapel, a large separate building running parallel to the north side of the choir. Here, beneath a single span of vaulting, and enriched with sculptured wall arcades, is the embodiment of the spatial idea of later Gothic.

A different interpretation was put upon this idea at Bristol, where the choir is unique among English cathedrals as an example of the hall-church. Certainly built between 1298 and 1340, its main period of construction did not begin until about 1311 and was over by 1332. The design is unusual in several ways. Not only are the three aisles of equal height, but the vault thrusts are brought down and equalized by a singular system of cross arches in the side aisles, supporting curious double vaults set sideways, This is structurally novel in England, and never was developed in that form. The piers too are a new version of the compound type developed into a series of mouldings rather than a collection of shafts. The arcades have no capitals, but sweep up as a single series of mouldings from base to apex and down again to base. For this characteristic there had been much earlier precedent in the West of England and South Wales, notably in the arcades of Llanthony Priory (*c.* 1180–1210) and the mid-thirteenth-century vestibule of the chapter-house at Chester. Here once more is a link with the methods of later German design, though the precedent continued to be followed in England to a limited extent. Finally, the central vault is formed with lierne ribs of another pattern, suggesting the netted complications of the retrochoir at

147, 148. Bristol: *(left) choir, c. 1311–40; (right) aisle, c. 1311–30*

149, 150. Bristol: *(left) transept, c. 1428–73; (right) vault of vestibule to Berkeley Chapel, c. 1310*

Wells. There is in fact a close resemblance between these works, and together they form the vanguard of the Somerset-Bristol school of design.

We shall discuss the fourteenth-century building at Wells in more detail as forerunning Perpendicular. All that remains to be done here is to mention the final expressions of Decorated style in the English cathedrals. Centred rather to the north of the Bristol area was a local school characterized by the very lavish use of the ball-flower ornament. It is found in profusion at Hereford on the central tower, and in the south nave aisle built at Gloucester between 1318 and 1329, as well as on the great tower of Salisbury begun about 1320. There are indeed remarkably close likenesses of detail between the towers of Hereford and Salisbury, and also in the disposition of the windows in each stage. The master at Salisbury for 25 years (? c. 1315–40) was Robert, joined in 1334 by Richard of Farleigh, already in charge of works at Bath and Reading, employing not only masonry flyers to spread the weight of the Salisbury steeple, but also hidden bands of wrought iron reinforcement.

Much of the building done during the period was of a tentative character: we have seen that several experiments had no progeny, at least in England. But this is not to say that they were fruitless. The full maturity of Gothic style in England was only reached after two centuries of constant endeavour;

151. Chester: vestibule to chapter house, c. 1230–50

and each and every experiment was of value. Certain steps were considered advantageous, repeated, and carried still further. Others were rejected and the mistake, if mistake it were, was not repeated. And the benefit of these experiences was cumulative. We do not know exactly how they were stored up for use by the building masters, but, arguing from the analogy of continental usage, we may suppose that each of the greater churches had a permanent masons' lodge and tracing-house, and that in the tracing-house was a collection of drawings. In no other way can we account for the nation-wide knowledge of past and current work possessed by the architects. Unprovided with printing or any means for the rapid and general dissemination of news as such, the building masters certainly had their own means of obtaining the information vital to their work. In some cases the facts of visits of inspection, or of the supervision of widely separated works by the same man, give a precious clue to the course of events.

This spread and exchange of knowledge was general throughout England by the early years of the fourteenth century. Local ideas were, at least in the greater buildings, giving place to national ones. The same mason or carpenter might also be at work on an abbey, a secular cathedral, a private house and the king's fortifications at one and the same time. No longer was art divided into almost hermetically sealed sections. There was an ebb and flow through all departments at once, a broader freedom and general interchange of ideas. This is certainly connected with the philosophic background of the new spaciousness and light of cathedrals and public buildings. The fourteenth century, like the nineteenth but with much better title, can be termed an age of enlightenment and progress.

It has been claimed by eager upholders of the dimmer age of faith in the Romanesque and early Gothic periods, lovers of the religious light which was but darkness made visible, that our late Gothic cathedrals lack spirituality. This claim, which might have some grain of truth if it were confined to the tentative harshness of the choir of Gloucester, or even the rather crude strength of York, has no general basis. There are no grander or more convincing monuments to belief in England than the naves of Canterbury and Winchester; and it is only by reason of immaturity that the slightly earlier Decorated work falls short of the same standard. Judged, as they should be, by the standard of their own times, Exeter and Lichfield and Bristol are outstanding monuments of piety as well as of aesthetics. And in such extraordinary buildings as the octagon at Ely or the steeple of Salisbury we are raised by the alchemy of their creators to a higher plane of sensibility.

52. Salisbury: crossing, c. 1237, with inserted
rches of c. 1415–23

VIII   Perpendicular Cathedrals

The period of English architecture known as Perpendicular is really twice as long as the rest, for it includes not only the true style of the fourteenth and early fifteenth centuries, but also its later offshoot which is sometimes called Tudor. Since this last Gothic style was in fashion roughly for the century 1450–1550, while the Tudor dynasty reigned from 1485 to 1603, the name is unsatisfactory. Here, in view of the small total of buildings concerned, we shall consider a period of two hundred years in the one chapter.

It is our misfortune that we have no one complete cathedral dating from the best period of early Perpendicular. What we have to exhibit this maturest and most complete of styles is divided between half-a-dozen cathedrals haphazard. Without counting the tentative work at Gloucester, there are the eastern arm and towers of York; the central tower, part of the nave, north porch and cloisters at Worcester; nave, transepts, south-west tower and cloisters of Canterbury; Winchester nave; and miscellanea at Norwich, Wells, Lincoln, Exeter and Chester. As is natural, considering the normal sequence of rebuilding from the east end, we are far richer in naves, porches, towers and cloisters than in sanctuaries or transepts. We have to go outside the cathedral group in search of comparable material, and even so find little of it, except at Bristol St. Mary Redcliffe, Christchurch Priory, Great Malvern and Sherborne, though these two last really belong to the later division of the period. It is only in St. Mary Redcliffe that we can savour to the full the spirit of unity which is the keynote of the style.

It is ironic that we should be unable to see a complete cathedral of that style which laid most stress on unity. The whole of Gothic development, and particularly in architecture in England, was working towards this end. The beautiful parts which to begin with were an end in themselves had to be framed into an integrated, universal whole. The same movement which was at work in politics to produce the centralized and strong government of

Edward I and the later Plantagenets, was also being applied to the plastic arts. The story of the progress of our architecture is the story of unification; its decline is written in a renewal of interest in the manifold parts of decorative pattern.

In considering the later Decorated cathedrals, we saw that the unifying tendency was already at work by 1290 or so; significantly also the date of the first ogee curves. For while the separated circles of Geometric art lacked unity, it was the ogee that made possible the lively subordination of branching traceries. A new style was carried to the threshold of the flamboyant by Ivo de Raghton from Carlisle, but was mainly followed in the north and east. The ogee and unity of bay design, with the first symptoms of Perpendicular detail, arrived together. The essence of Perpendicular architecture is that the mullions of windows shall rush up to the arch itself without deflection, and that they shall actually meet or cut at right angles the horizontals in their path. This tendency has also been described as rectilinearity.[1] As an accidental interpenetration of tracery on two planes this occurs in the wall-arcading of the Lady Chapel at Ely, designed between 1320 and 1330. As a deliberate feature of design, the very earliest instances in the world of the mullion being carried straight up to the arch are in the great window of the south transept at Gloucester, whose reconstruction lasted from 1331 to 1336; and in the windows of William Ramsey's Chapter House and surrounding cloister at Old St. Paul's, begun in 1332. Inasmuch as the side windows of the Gloucester transept show no sign of this characteristic feature, it may be doubted whether the design of the south window can date from the start of the work. If not, it was the metropolitan building, as might be expected, that first embodied the invention of the Perpendicular style.

But there had been examples of rectilinearity long before this. We have seen a trace of it in the triforium of the nave of York, begun in 1291, and it was even more clearly marked in the choir of Guisborough Priory and the south nave clerestory at Bridlington, both in progress from about 1290. Similar solutions were roughly contemporary in France; the York design is close to that adopted at Clermont Ferrand somewhere between 1262 and 1311; and almost the exact counterpart of the Bridlington triforium appears at Limoges in the choir begun in 1273 and completed in 1327. It may well be that England derived several of the basic ideas of Perpendicular from France, but it was only in England that they were ever brought together to form a complete style.

This style as seen in the cathedrals includes far more than the verticality of details which suggested its name. Its chief characteristic is the feeling of unity of space, no longer divided into bays longitudinally, into aisles trans-

[1] The stiffening of reticulated forms towards rectilinearity is well seen in the windows of the Carnary Chapel of Norwich Cathedral, designed c. 1320 by John Ramsey.

versely or into stages vertically. The progressive thinning of the supports reduced the obstructions which had divided the total space into compartments. Refinements of detail, such as the vault-shafts which ran from base to springing in one line, and the union of triforium and clerestory, all tended to group the individual parts together. And now the proportions of the whole building were being studied, to give a total cohesion which could not be attained by the additive method of building on bay after bay to an indefinite number. The proportions of the exterior also were considered, and the massing of aisles against nave and of towers against the sky and grouped with each other, was the result of careful planning and modelling.

The reduction of the piers laid an emphasis on space; that of the walls similarly stressed the access of light. Windows rapidly reached the limits of practicability, and at Gloucester the great east window was actually wider than the presbytery, being contained within a final bay whose sides were canted outwards to take it. Although the English cathedral remained low by French standards, its vertical lines were emphasized, and there was some actual increase in height over the Decorated norm. And in spite of the new emphasis on space, there was no abandonment of the linear qualities of English art, which were on the contrary increased. Vaults reached their limit in complicated patterns, and were then modified sufficiently to show their stellar or reticulated forms to the best advantage. Various devices were employed to increase the apparent height of the vault: thinning of the vault-ribs as at Canterbury, and the use of pendants at Oxford. The spandrels over arches, both internally and externally, became filled with vertical panelling.

Many of the antecedent features which led to the new style had been brought together at the Royal Chapel of St. Stephen in Westminster Palace, where work on the main upper chapel started in 1331. William Ramsey, a mason of standing in Norwich, had worked at St. Stephen's at an earlier date, and was certainly familiar with the most up-to-date knowledge of the King's Masons and of the Canterbury School then leading the fashion. In 1332 he was appointed master for the new chapter-house and cloister to be immediately begun at St. Paul's. The design of his work can be reconstructed from an engraving by Hollar, and from very considerable fragments recovered from the site in 1878. For the first time all the elements of Perpendicular were brought together, and the new style had arrived. It is important to realize that its origins had nothing whatever to do with the Black Death, so commonly invoked by those who would have us believe that the Perpendicular style is the product of penury and a shortage of skilled craftsmen.

Nothing could be further from the truth. The birth of Perpendicular was that of a genuine 'new art', the result of long experiment and of the ingenuity of the greatest architects of the age. It was the style's misfortune to have been invented so shortly before a major cataclysm that its brilliant promise was

153. Old St. Paul's: chapter house and cloisters, 1332–49, by William Ramsey; from the engraving by Hollar

partially enveloped in the great cloud of misery and fear. But there is no need to apologize for the best of the resulting works; they are able to stand comparison with anything produced in England, or indeed elsewhere. The first of the cathedral works to be considered is the reconstruction of the choir of Gloucester, where the Norman structure was largely retained, but cloaked over with a screenwork of the new masonry. After the south transept had been dealt with between 1331 and 1337 in an imperfect version of the new style, Gloucester immediately proceeded to the transformation of the eastern arm between 1337 and 1367. The north transept followed in 1368–74, and the whole of the cloisters between *c.* 1370 and 1412.

Coming at the very beginning of a period, the choir at Gloucester is a fantastic achievement. The gulf fixed between the mellow rounded effects of Exeter and this brilliant and clear-cut work of exactly contemporary date is immense. Far as Exeter had progressed along the road to Gothic fulfilment, its distance from Gloucester is not one hundred miles, but an age. Instead of accepting the existing division of the Norman church into three stages, the Gloucester architect cloaked the structure internally with a masonry grid, transforming the whole presbytery and choir into the semblance of an aisle-less chapel. The aisles still existed behind the grille, but were not included in the spatial scheme. In other words, the procedure at Gloucester was the converse of that at Bristol. In the earlier work the central area was extended to embrace the whole church within the outer walls; at Gloucester it was compressed, but in a translucent cage of stone and glass.

Gloucester is remarkable for the long continuance of its great building scheme. This was possible owing to the large sums contributed by pilgrims to the tomb of Edward II. We may perhaps be thankful that the renewal of the nave proceeded no further than the west front and two adjoining bays, with a lateral porch; the grand Norman columns are in impressive contrast to the lofty and brilliant work east of the screen. But the rest of the buildings are all admirably in keeping with the choir, though their completion took

154. Gloucester: choir, 1337–67; tower, 1450–60

155, 156. Gloucester: (left) presbytery, 1337–67; (right) Lady Chapel, c. 1457–83

over a century. The eastern Lady Chapel repeats the main motives of the choir on a smaller scale, while the central tower is a conversion of the Worcester design to the wholly buttressed type. The cloisters with their early fan-vaulting are a new invention.

The style of Gloucester is so closely akin to that of the chapter-house at Old St. Paul's that we must suppose William Ramsey to have provided designs, though the work was probably carried out under another resident master. From 1336 onwards, as King's Master Mason, Ramsey had the oversight of works at Gloucester Castle, and his wide fame is proved by the undertaking of 1337 by which he agreed to visit Lichfield Cathedral to give advice. There the Lady Chapel had just been completed by William Eyton, but had to be linked to the choir, which was on a different axis. Ramsey's presbytery compromises between the two alignments so skilfully that the breaks are not noticeable. He gave unity to the whole vista by rebuilding the choir windows to the same design as those of his presbytery, while retaining a simple tierceron vault design in keeping with that of the Lady Chapel. Vertical emphasis was provided by triple vaulting-shafts from base to springing without interruption, a theme borrowed from the earlier nave. At Hereford in 1359–70 a decagonal chapter-house was built, probably to the design of the

157. Exeter: west
front, c. 1335–42, by
Thomas Witney; and
porches, 1346 and later

master mason John of Evesham. A drawing of 1721 shows that it was fan-
vaulted to a design so closely similar to that of the Gloucester cloisters that
they too may well be assigned to the same architect, and the source of the
fan be traced back to the vast abbey of Evesham, now totally lost.

Another type of incipient Perpendicular, more allied to the style of Bristol,
was in progress at the retrochoir of Wells, where again an eastern Lady
Chapel of the early fourteenth century was linked to an existing choir. The
work dates from about 1329–45, and was carried out under William Joy,
who also appears at Bath and at Exeter within the period 1330–50. The east

window has two main mullions which cut the arch in Perpendicular fashion, and above the arcades and beneath the east window are vertical panellings forming nichework of great elaboration. Only the vault, a somewhat over-complicated attempt to improve upon that of Bristol, falls short of complete success. Joy was apparently responsible for the design of the engineering works to save the central tower though much of the actual work was not done until after his time.

Joy seems also to have supervized the beginning of the western screen and porches at Exeter about 1346 and the rich array of statuary may well have been inspired by the front of Wells. In type it was totally different, having only shallow buttresses and sheltering the doors behind porches with face-arches on the sculpture plane. But though on a much smaller scale, it does resemble Wells in ending on a horizontal line across the whole width of the church and aisles. The porches, though small, are of special interest, as they are the earliest examples of the typical Perpendicular 'welcoming' porch, seen at its best in the west fronts of Winchester and Canterbury Cathedrals, Westminster Abbey and the north entry of Westminster Hall. In a reduced form it also appears later at Gloucester, Norwich, Bath and formerly at Southwark. On the whole it seems probable that the design of the Exeter screen-front in its essentials must have been the work of Thomas Witney, though several hands were concerned in its detail, and the upper range of statues was not added until the beginning of the sixteenth century.

The west front of Winchester is a puzzling work, rather crude and un-formed, yet characteristically Perpendicular. The type features perhaps make an even too obtrusive appearance. It is certain that the standard west front with twin towers was disliked by our later Gothic designers. Even at York, where it had been adopted at the end of the thirteenth century, the front itself was finished off on a horizontal line, behind which the towers stand as if planted on top of a box. Salisbury had followed the much earlier example of Rochester in avoiding western towers altogether; so, later, did Exeter and Bath. At Gloucester and at Norwich, where Norman towers probably exist-ed, they were removed, and this certainly happened at Winchester. Every-where, except at Exeter, the attempt of the designers seems to have been to emphasize the central nave by building flanking turrets, and to minimize the aisles. This front has been termed parochial, but it is hardly likely that the architects of cathedrals and great minsters would be so strongly influenced by the least significant type of parish church. It seems far more probable that what was attempted was, as in the choir of Gloucester, an innovation based upon the turreted Chapel Royal, initiated at St. Stephen's and found also at Eton and King's College, Cambridge, and St. George's Chapel in Windsor Castle. If this view is correct, the 'welcoming' porch is a reminiscence of the western entrance of St. Stephen's Chapel.

How much of the Winchester front was built in the time of Bishop Edington is uncertain, but his will, of 1366, clearly states that he had already begun work on it. Its designer may have been the mason Thomas in receipt of an annual retaining fee in 1356. Considering the resemblances of the porches and west window to Gloucester choir, there seems no reason to dispute Willis's conclusion that the main scheme of the front belongs to Edington's time. But the heightening of the end walls of the aisles, the gable and perhaps the parapets, are later additions of Wykeham's time from the designs of William Wynford. The main work of the Winchester nave, not begun until 1394, will be discussed later.

At York the Lady Chapel was begun in 1361, and the master was William Hoton. The four easternmost bays were completed in twelve years, but for the last five the master was Robert Patrington, responsible for 'flamboyant' detail in the clerestory. The remaining five bays to the crossing were added between 1385 and 1405 to a different design by Hugh Hedon. In both cases the main lines of the original scheme laid down in the nave were adhered to, while the great east window closely followed the example of Gloucester, though with only nine lights instead of fourteen. The triumph of York, its immense lantern tower, was to come later. This was the only English tower (unless the octagon of Ely be included) which is broad enough to be com-

158. (left) York: west front, c. 1310–40; west window probably by Ivo de Raghton, c. 1338; towers 1432–74

159. York: choir, 1361–c. 1400

160, 161. Worcester: (left) nave, 1317–24 and c. 1360–95; (right) exterior from south–west; tower, c. 1365–74 by John Clyve

pletely satisfactory from within. But, unlike the rest of the Minster, it was not designed by a northern mason, but by William Colchester from Westminster Abbey, a pupil of Henry Yeveley.

Also connected with the Court School of masons was the architect of the fourteenth-century building at Worcester. Within little more than a genera-tion, some thirty years following 1365, the church was brought up to date with a new central tower, south nave arcade, nave vaults and lateral porch, and a new cloister. It is probable that all this work was designed by the Master John Clyve who was in charge from 1376 to 1392 and who had taken on several contracts at Windsor Castle from 1362 to 1365. The importance of his work is seen in the beautifully modulated cloisters, the north porch and the magnificent central tower. This tower has strong claims to be regarded as the finest individual tower design of the whole Gothic period in England. Its proportions are exquisite, and it blends in the happiest manner the turreted with the buttressed form. The contrast between the vertical panelling of the lower stage and the windowed scheme above is admirably managed, and its scale is perfectly in keeping with the bulk of the church below.

Also of the closing fourteenth century were the cloisters at Durham, begun in 1390 by John Lewyn and continued early in the next century by Thomas Mapilton. Lewyn had earlier vaulted the monastic kitchen in 1366–71 with an exquisite stellar polygon which recalls the Saracenic brick vaults of Persia. He was a great builder of castles in addition to his work for the bishop and monastery of Durham. Mapilton was later to become King's Master Mason, and to design the south-west tower of Canterbury Cathedral, built between 1423 and 1434. In considering work of first-class importance, such as almost the whole of our cathedral output is, it is no longer possible to speak of local schools. Communications in the later fourteenth century were excellent, and the greater architects were moving from end to end of the kingdom.

Among these great masons, the greatest were two of those in the royal service: Henry Yeveley and William Wynford. Born some twenty to thirty years before the great pestilence, they were able to seize the opportunity afforded by the ensuing shortage of artists. The essentials of the Perpendicular style had been laid down by William Ramsey before his death in 1349, and were being exploited in the years immediately following by successors such as John Sponlee, the chief mason at Windsor Castle. When Yeveley became King's Master Mason in 1360 he was able to diffuse throughout the country, by means of the official buildings under his control, a perfected version of the newly achieved national style. Lasting for forty years, his term of office included the period of highest achievement in the whole history of English art.

Slightly Yeveley's junior, William Wynford appears at Windsor Castle in 1360, and soon became joint master with the ageing Sponlee. Later he was to assume full control on Sponlee's retirement. Both Yeveley and Wynford were employed by the king, but Wynford's especial patron was William of Wykeham, for a time clerk of the works at Windsor, and then provost of Wells and bishop of Winchester. Through his patronage Wynford found opportunities second only to those of Yeveley. Appointed consultant master at Wells in 1365, he designed the western towers, of which the southern was actually built under his supervision. Here he showed his ability to design in harmony with earlier work, and to complete an existing composition in such a way as to raise it to a higher power. In this talent he followed the example set by Master Robert and Richard Farleigh at Salisbury and John Clyve at Worcester.

More important even than his work at Wells were Wynford's two colleges built for his patron at Oxford and Winchester. But we must here consider him as the architect of the nave of Winchester Cathedral, begun in 1394 and left in his charge at Wykeham's death ten years later. Although not finally

162. *Wells: Lady Chapel, c. 1310–19; and (on right) chapter house, c. 1286–1306; south–west tower, c. 1380–92, by William Wynford*

completed until many years after Wynford's death, he was the designer of the whole work, apart from the earlier sections of the west front. Like Gloucester, this was an attempt to alter without demolishing a Norman structure. But the two works were carried out by totally different methods. At Gloucester the inner faces of the Norman choir piers were pared off, and a skin of masonry applied as an internal cage. At Winchester the old work was at first cut down and worked to new mouldings all round, and later cut out and refaced with new stones. At Gloucester the Perpendicular building is mostly but skin-deep; from the other side, the original work appears unaltered. At Winchester almost everything was changed, and the very arches were replaced by others of different form.

Yeveley's methods were different again. Between 1375 and his death in 1400 he carried on the nave of Westminster Abbey, an adaptation of the early Decorated design of the choir. This was a new building on new foundations; the Norman nave was first utterly destroyed. The same process was adopted at his great cathedral design, the nave of Canterbury. Before the pulling down of the old nave, aisle walls were built, beginning in 1378.

After this there was a pause in the work, which was resumed in 1391. The design of the central arcade and clerestory, which differ in detail from the aisles, therefore belongs to that wonderful period around 1390. The moment was doubly fortunate: Richard II had just freed himself from the rule of the Appellants, surrounded himself with men of culture, and installed Geoffrey Chaucer as clerk of the royal works. And Yeveley, his chief mason, aged about seventy, had reached the final maturity of his powers, and could produce a design so mellow, so unassumingly perfect, that its perfection passes unnoticed.

For the nave of Canterbury Cathedral is the supreme triumph of English architecture, which is to say, of English art. Completed after Yeveley's death by his pupils and successors, Stephen Lote and Thomas Mapilton, the

163. *Winchester: nave, 1394–c. 1450, by William Wynford*

164. *Canterbury: nave, 1379–1400, by Henry Yeveley*

metropolitan cathedral became the exemplar of our own particular Gothic. And that it is so is because Yeveley's genius was big enough to break the rules of development which were becoming fixed in his time. We have seen the growth of the towerless but turreted west front, and the tendency to minimize the side aisles: Canterbury on the contrary has tall aisles and a twin-towered front which, though not built by Yeveley, was planned by him. And we can see how this movement against the tide happened.

Mr. Arthur Oswald has shown the very close resemblances between the naves of Canterbury and Westminster, and there can be no doubt that experience at Westminster was the decisive factor in Yeveley's design. Canterbury, still the church of a great Benedictine monastery, must have aisles; if they were low, according to the fashion, brilliant side-lighting would be impossible. It would not do to split the total height into two equal parts and on the north side the aisle windows had to stand above the cloister roof; so the aisles became very tall indeed, gaining much of the effect of Bristol without suppressing the clerestory altogether. The clerestory windows were still of importance, for, beside traditional value, they threw direct daylight upon the vault of the central nave. But, with so tall an arcade, something must be done to prevent the piers seeming to be disconnected and wavering; and the answer lay in the horizontal line of mouldings above the arches. This gives direction and at the same time brings together the whole arcade as one. So far as the limitations of the aisled scheme permit, the nave of Canterbury at last achieves the unity which the Gothic builders had been seeking for two hundred years.

Winchester, arrived at in a different way, and limited by the preservation of the Norman core, is hardly the equal of Canterbury, but it has the merit of providing an exactly contemporary solution that is altogether different. Instead of attempting the attenuated and brilliant glasshouse church, Winchester accepts the primitive sturdiness of its enormous piers, clothes them in the mouldings and details of the day, and sets above them a magnificently original vault. This vault with its upward leap is unlike that of any other cathedral, and seems only to be like the sweeping boughs of the beech trees on the neighbouring chalk downs.

After Winchester, the age of cathedral building was over. Within the limits of conservative English tradition, the last word had been said, and, just as the monasteries had lost ground to the bishops, so the bishops were being ousted as art patrons by lay courtiers founding new colleges of secular clergy. The wheel was sweeping round full circle. On the whole it seems fortunate that little remained to be done, and that there was little money available. For the work that was carried out in the fifteenth century was rarely on the level of what had been accomplished by Yeveley and Wynford. James Woderofe's west and north cloister vaults at Norwich are fine excep-

165. *Norwich: lavatorium in cloisters, 1444–47*

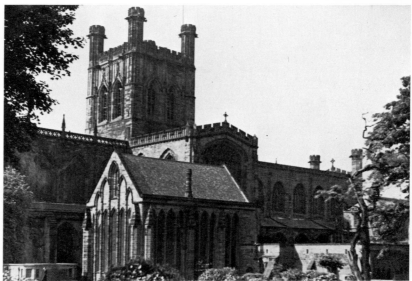

166. *Chester from the north: chapter house, c. 1249–65; tower, c. 1493–1537*

tions. There is a good deal of pleasant but uninspired work at Chester, and additions to other cathedrals such as the cloisters of Wells, Chichester and Hereford. The stone screen at Chichester, usually attributed to Bishop John Arundel (1459–78), belongs to the immediate School of Yeveley, and may well have been detailed by Walter Walton, whose work at Portchester Castle in 1396–99 appears to be of almost identical character. The one field of design in which outstanding things were still being done was the tower: York, Durham and finally Canterbury were supplied with central towers of absolutely the first rank, and interesting experiments were made at Bristol, Chester and Bath.

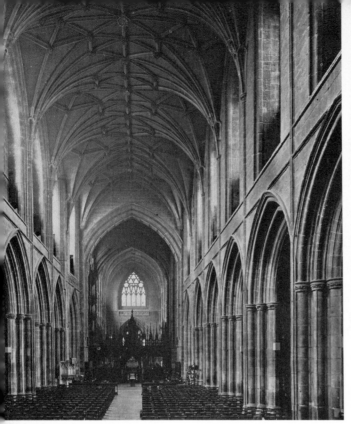

167. *Chester: nave, c. 1323–75 and c. 1485–92*

168. *Chichester: nave, 1114–48; pulpitum c. 1405–10*

169. *Chichester: cloisters, c. 1400, probably by William Wynford; and St. Richard's Porch, c. 1230*

170. *(right) Durham, tower 1465–75 by Thomas Barton; upper stage, c. 1483–90, by John Bell junior*

The four Welsh cathedrals all have late Gothic towers, but three of them are very simple. St. David's and St. Asaph both have central towers, completely unbuttressed. At St. David's the middle stage, built in the second quarter of the fourteenth century, has a central two-light window on each face between niches and beneath pairs of small lancets which relieve the plain walling. Above this an additional stage, with pinnacles and pierced parapet, was raised in 1509–22. At St. Asaph, where the central tower was mainly built in 1391–92 by Robert Fagan, a Chester mason, the only feature is a three-light traceried window on each side. Bangor has a western tower of the sixteenth century, buttressed diagonally at the free western angles and with very simple three-light windows in the top stage. It is at Llandaff that a Welsh cathedral achieved a really noteworthy tower, flanking the north side of the nave at the west front. This is a fine version of the Somerset tower, but incorporating the pinnacled 'coronet' (now a restoration) derived from the central tower at Gloucester. The Llandaff tower was begun after 1485 and was still unfinished in 1496.

171. St. Davids from the south-east: presbytery 1221–, altered 1328–47 and later

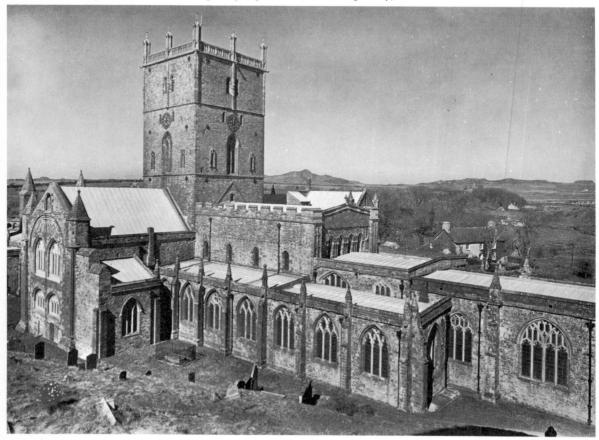

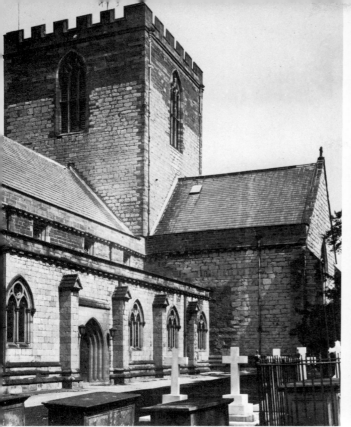

172, 173. *St. Asaph: (left) tower, 1391–92, by Robert Fagan; (right) nave aisle, c. 1320–52*

174. *St. Asaph looking east, 1284–1352*   175. *Llandaff: north-west tower, c. 1485–1500*

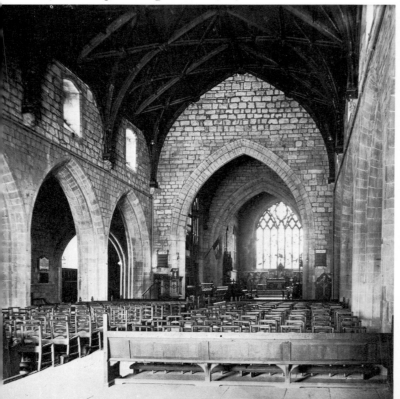

Towards the end of the century there was a revival, and Norwich vaulted first its nave (*c.* 1464–72) and then its presbytery (*c.* 1472–99). These vaults, of stellar lierne pattern, and approaching the fan-vault in feeling, are also among the finest in the country; they culminated in the exquisite pendant vault of the Oxford choir. At the extreme east end of Ely two bishops made delicately carved chantry chapels: that of John Alcock (*c.* 1488–1500), and that of Nicholas West, of 1523–36, already mixed with Renaissance details, designed

by Richard Lee and carved by Edmund More, who divided his time between Ely and Hampton Court Palace. At Peterborough a more ambitious work was carried out between 1496 and 1508: the New Work or eastern chapels surrounding the Norman apse, built and fan-vaulted by way of model for John Wastell's work at King's College Chapel, Cambridge. At Rochester the Lady Chapel of about 1500–12 was intended to have fan-vaults, but they were never built.

178. Oxford: vault of choir, c. 1478–1503, probably by William Orchard

179, 180. Ely: (below left) Bishop Alcock's chapel, c. 1488–1500, probably by Adam Lord; (below) Bishop West's chapel, 1523–36, by Richard Lee

181. Ely: vault of Alcock's chapel

182. Ely: vault of West's chapel

183. Peterborough: eastern chapels, c. 1496–1508, by John Wastell

These last works are Tudor rather than Perpendicular in the strict sense. All of them are enriched with surface decoration of a repetitive kind, much of it curvilinear or even flamboyant in character. Decorative crestings and scrolls of leaves and flowers in the mouldings run riot. The new national prosperity brought in by Edward IV and later reinforced by Henry VII was having its effect. Money could be and was lavished upon sheer display. The marvel is that so much of this virtuosity is upon a high plane regarded as art. Most of it was expended outside the cathedrals, upon colleges, parish churches and private mansions. But the cathedrals also benefited, and sometimes by the very finest works of the age. Such was the central or Bell Harry tower added to Canterbury between 1493 and 1505 by John Wastell, Cardinal Morton's master mason. Again striking the exact note required by the whole composition of the cathedral, Wastell's tower is almost as outstanding in its own age as Yeveley's nave.

The greatest products of the florid Tudor style are Henry VII's Chapel at Westminster Abbey, Wastell's completion of King's College Chapel, and among the cathedrals, Bath. Designed by the brothers Robert and William Vertue for Bishop Oliver King, the church takes up only the site of the nave of the vast Norman abbey. Nothing but the Tudor church is left. It was an attempt, still within the framework of a Benedictine abbey church, to produce a cathedral upon the lines of a Chapel Royal. As much earlier at Winchester and elsewhere, the fronts are turreted and the aisles depressed. At Bath the aisles are kept to the absolute minimum, while a series of vast clerestory windows achieves the desired glasshouse effect. Final achievement of the English masons, fan-vaults are employed throughout and in this instance we know of the deliberate effort made by the brothers Vertue to

184, 185. Bath: (left) west front, c. 1520–39, by William Vertue; (right) interior, 1501–39, by Robert Vertue and William Vertue

186. *Bangor from the south-west: nave aisles 1291– ; clerestory and west tower 1509–32*

improve upon what had been done before. 'Of the vaulte devised for the chancelle' they declared 'there shall be noone so goodely neither in England nor in France.' Bath has many beauties, and if it is not one of the most successful of the English cathedrals, the fault lies with its age, rather than in the undoubted genius of its architects. But even the common form of the age could have charm, as in Thomas Berty's remodelling of the Winchester presbytery.

That English architecture was tending to degenerate into lavish frivolities seems to have been widely realized at the time. Especially in the greater domestic architecture there was a strong counter-current of simplicity. This revulsion from florid ornament may in part have been due to lack of funds. At Bangor in North Wales the predominant works of the little cathedral were done between 1470 and 1530 in a simple Perpendicular. The western tower, a very late addition (*c.* 1510–32) is almost parochial in character, but well designed. The nave has a quiet and restful beauty, leading the eye towards the splendid fourteenth-century crossing arches. Among the English cathedrals there is, however, one major work of this period, the nave of Ripon, begun in 1502 and finished in twenty years. The master was Christopher Scune, who also appears in charge of the building of Louth spire in Lincolnshire, and as master mason at Durham Cathedral. Scune was a man

Durham: Kitchen vault, 1366–71, by John Lewyn

in the tradition of the great masters of construction; his work is sturdy and well proportioned, and quite devoid of contemporary mannerism. The aisles are tall, and their roofs of such low pitch that very little of the clerestory is obscured. Simple and unassuming, the nave would have formed a suitable prelude to the magnificent lancet arches of the new crossing, had that ever been completed. Built in what was then but a poverty-stricken suffragan cathedral, Scune's work cannot rank among the highest flights of Gothic architecture. But it remains one of the most intriguing of our artistic might-have-beens. While the perfected southern architecture was withering before the blasts of the Renaissance, this cruder building of the north was still strong, confident of its own powers. Given a kinder fate, Ripon might have been the germ from which sprang another and still more brilliant English architecture.

87. *Bangor: nave, 1509–32*

IX The Renaissance and Conclusion

A double blow was struck at the English cathedrals by the events of the sixteenth century. The Reformation dissolved the monasteries and jeopardized episcopacy and even the new English cathedral liturgy; and the Renaissance destroyed the country's living artistic tradition. It might be thought that the alteration in religious outlook would have had the more serious consequences, but this was not so. The Protestant countries of northern Europe, except Holland, all maintained a much greater degree of continuity with their mediaeval tradition than did we. And the reason lies in their modified acceptance of the classical Renaissance. There is no aesthetic compatibility between the English Gothic of 1525 and the English Mannerism of 1575.

The effects of the religious revolution upon the cathedrals were superficially good rather than bad. Although the monastic bodies were dissolved, no ancient cathedral was destroyed except Coventry; and five monastic churches (without counting Westminster Abbey) were made cathedral for the first time. All the cathedrals alike now had chapters of secular canons, and these chapters were provided with considerable endowments. But what had been destroyed was one of the chief incentives to building: the belief in the spiritual benefit of pious works which served no obviously practical purpose. One could no longer take out a spiritual insurance policy by endowing a chantry or by making a princely donation to the cathedral fabric fund.

Remarkably little structural work was carried out at any of the cathedrals during the hundred years following the dissolution of the monasteries. The only outstanding exception was Old St. Paul's where a new portico and a great deal of classic facing were added by Inigo Jones in 1631 to 1640. It is of some interest to note that, though in the classic style, this new west front adhered to the principles laid down by the Exeter and Winchester porch-screens, of a horizontal mass sweeping across the front and independent of it.

188, 189. St. Paul's: (left) choir; (right) south nave aisle, 1675–1710, by Sir Christopher Wren

Greatly as time-honoured Romanesque and Gothic St. Paul's was reverenced by Londoners, it is clear that it would have been completely classicized in the course of repairs, even had there been no Great Fire.

The state of the structure was already so alarming before the Fire, that a commission of survey, including Wren and Evelyn the diarist, was reporting on the fabric within its last few months of life. Wren had schemes for a central dome in the place of the great tower, and the influence of these pre-Fire plans can be traced in the design finally carried out for the present cathedral. It is profoundly interesting to examine the building to discover the extent to which Wren borrowed from the Gothic tradition in England. In spite of his attempts to force an original and completely un-traditional plan upon the Commissioners, the pressure of tradition was still strong enough to ensure that the new St. Paul's should be an English cathedral, though translated into new architectural terms. The plan, with well-marked transepts, and eastern and western arms both of considerable length, was the first and most fundamental concession to old usage. But no less significant is the section with its flying buttresses, and triforium and clerestory architecturally united. The west front has its towers placed outside the aisles, as had been intended at St. Albans and was achieved at Wells and in a half-hearted way at Old St. Paul's itself. East of this typically broad façade were chapels, as at Lincoln and Ely.

It was Ely that provided the inspiration for the central feature of the plan: the eight great piers and the four counter-forts which support the dome. Since Wren's uncle was bishop of Ely this is not surprising, but the fact again shows his indebtedness to the basic qualities of Gothic tradition. It is permissible to differ as to the aesthetic values of revived classic buildings in England, but probably few lovers of the English cathedral regard Wren's St. Paul's as altogether in keeping with its spirit. But it is at the same time possible to admire its brilliant composition and construction, and to feel affection for its massed grandeur towering over the spired city that its architect loved.

We would not pull down St. Paul's to rear a sham-Gothic structure on its site. And this is because we recognize its greatness in its own kind, and admit its survival value, even should we dislike and disapprove of its detail. Unfortunately, this attitude was not adopted by the church-restorers of the last century in their onslaught upon the cathedrals. Not only did they thoroughly 'do out' all remains of Renaissance and later alterations and furnishings, but they went so far as to impose a standard of orthodoxy upon Gothic itself. The destruction of a number of fine Perpendicular windows in the interests of sham Early English purity at St. Albans and elsewhere was the merest vandalism. And the effects of even well-meant surface reconstruction at Chester, Lichfield and Worcester are appalling.

On the other hand, things might be much worse. Had not extensive works been done, some cathedrals would have become heaped ruins, and even among the rash attacks of the restorers there is a good deal that is informed by a genuine love of Gothic and at least an attempt to grasp its principles. With the possible exception of St. Albans, the victim of Lord Grimthorpe's private massacre, no English cathedral was so severely wrecked as to lose its character. It is unwise to trust to detail for historical purposes without the most careful investigation, but generally speaking the cathedrals do preserve all the main features of their planning and design. In almost every case both the vices and the virtues of the 'great' restoration are due to Sir George Gilbert Scott. The exceptions are Bristol and York, where the architect concerned was G. E. Street; Wells, chastened by Anthony Salvin; Carlisle and Southwell, edified by Ewan Christian; and Southwark, where the new nave is by Sir Arthur Blomfield. Lincoln and Norwich were relatively fortunate in avoiding large-scale works during the nineteenth century.

The losses due to iconoclasm of every kind have been terrible, but so also are those caused merely by lapse of time and by the constant weathering of stone surfaces. Considering that four centuries of wear and tear have gone by since the end of the Gothic period, we must be thankful that so much is left. We should not be human if we did not regret the glories of mediaeval furnishings: the original statues, now so often 'restorations'; the paintings; the immense quantities of woodwork, treasures and plate; above all, the lost majority of the painted glass. Yet there is still an abundance of skilled craftsmanship left, and a good deal of high art. Dimly as these remains represent what there was in the reign of Henry VIII, the total quantity is still too vast to be set down in detail. The greater works of sculpture can, it is true, be numbered and described; but the lesser details, the roof-bosses, the corbel-heads, the little figures and grotesques which pepper the tombs and screens, run into many thousands and utterly defy calculation.

In 1948 the late C. J. P. Cave published a selection of nearly 400 roof-bosses out of a total of over 8,000 telephotographs taken by him. Not all of these were from cathedrals, it is true, but on the other hand there are in the cathedrals many other roof-bosses, and still more carvings of other types. Any one of the major cathedrals would provide work for an average lifetime, if every part were to be explored in detail and its stones made to yield up their secrets. Indeed, those who know the cathedrals best, the resident architects, surveyors, clerks of the works and foremen, can from intimate knowledge and affection speak most feelingly of the never-ending multitude of new facts constantly coming to their notice. There is no such thing as 'knowing' the whole of a cathedral. But this should not deter anyone from trying to see and to appreciate all that he may.

To give one more example of mere numbers: there are over 700 mediaeval carved misericords in the ancient cathedrals, often some 50 to 60 in one, or even over 100 at Lincoln. On the carved stone screen at Southwell there are over 50 carved heads of appreciable size on one side alone, as well as many more of minute dimensions. The same side of the same screen has over 200 large leaf-crockets, and some 100 foliated capitals or finials. Behind one stall set against this screen is a carved diaper of more than 150 repeats, all different. The quantity of glaziers' work involved can be hinted at by the size of the great west window of Winchester, which alone contains 44 great panels, besides smaller tracery lights. And each of the panels is 8 feet high by nearly 3 feet wide.

Of all the fittings which remain, probably the finest as well as the richest in detail are the series of carved stalls with their canopies and misericord seats. Beginning with some remains of early thirteenth-century work at Rochester, and fragments of shafting from canopies at Chichester, we only reach a complete set at Winchester. These were carved by William Lyngwode in 1308–10; he had been brought for the purpose from Blofield near Norwich, evidence of his fame. The design with its pierced gables leaps forward from the lancet arcade with level coping which had been used at Westminster Abbey by Jacob the joiner about 1253. The horizontal type of stall canopy

190, 191. *Southwell: (left) choir looking west, 1234–50; (right) pulpitum, c. 1320–35*

192. *Salisbury: old pulpitum, c. 1240*

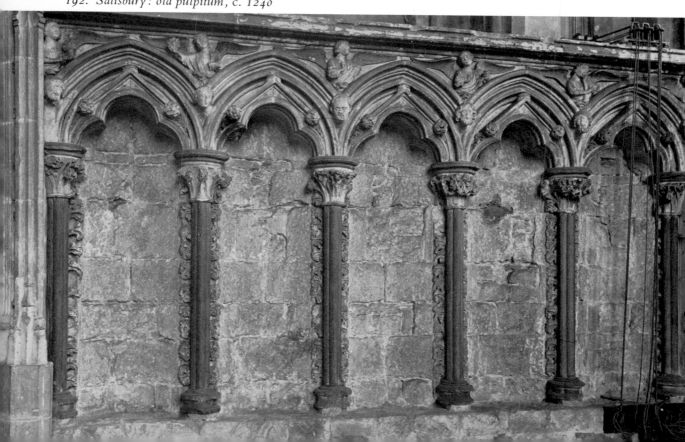

193. Chester: refectory pulpit, c. 1260   *194. Southwell: doorway of chapter house, c. 1295*

was developed at Chichester about 1335, and was united with further elaboration of the gable by William Hurley at Ely in 1336–48. His procedure was to surmount the range of arcading with a second storey of cusped and crocketed tabernacles. At Gloucester between 1337 and 1350 another scheme had been reached by reversal of the Ely design, the tabernacles being above the seats, with a higher range of tracery ending in horizontal cresting. The Ely design was further elaborated about 1370 at Lincoln, almost certainly by William and Hugh Herland the king's carpenters, Hurley's successors; their style is clearly seen in the architectural details of canopies, pinnacles and blind tracery. The rich tabernacle-work then produced was adopted at York and at Chester about 1390, and some time after 1400 at Carlisle. Meanwhile the less popular horizontal design had appeared at Hereford, *c.* 1380, and increasingly played a part as a motive in tabernacle design at Norwich, *c.* 1420, and the stalls made by William Brownfleet of Ripon for his own minster, 1489–94, and for the churches of Manchester, *c.* 1508, and Beverley, 1520. A purely horizontal scheme again appears at Bristol, also made about 1520, and in the Renaissance stalls of Cartmel and King's College, Cambridge; the triumph of this type under classic influence was complete at new St. Paul's by 1697, and in the choir woodwork of Canterbury Cathedral, made between

195. St. Albans: base of shrine, perhaps 1302–08   *196. Rochester: chapter house doorway, c. 1340*

1675 and 1706 and now destroyed. But the final achievement of the Gothic tabernacled design was reserved for Durham, where in 1665 the Restoration bishop, John Cosin, contributed the splendid stalls and font-cover which still exist. These are the only major survivals of post-Reformation fittings in the Gothic cathedrals, but there are many smaller objects of interest of the period 1550–1850 still to be seen, which could only be described in a separate volume.

Naturally the cathedrals differ in richness; some have treasures of all kinds, as Canterbury; others, like Rochester, have comparatively (but only comparatively) little to offer. In some the architecture is the main attraction; in others there is a great variety of decorative arts. Canterbury and York are pre-eminent for their glass, and others specially distinguished in this respect are Exeter, Gloucester and Wells; Winchester, which has a large collection of fragments in its west window; Lincoln, with some notable early remains; and Carlisle, where the tracery of the great east window contains some of the richest coloured glass still extant. Canterbury is also famous for wall-paintings, and should be equally noted for its panel-paintings. Winchester, St. Albans and Chichester also contain important wall-paintings, and at

Norwich are the remains of a late fourteenth-century painted retable. Lovers of bells will hearken to Great Paul in London, Great Peter in York (a mediaeval bell recast in 1845) and above all to Great Tom of Oxford, brought from Oseney Abbey when the see was moved to Christ Church.

In a category distinct from the decoration, fittings and furniture, stand chantries and monuments. Generally speaking they do not form an integral part of the structure, though there are exceptions, such as William of Wykeham's chantry at Winchester, which forms a constructional part of the nave arcade. In other cases, as at Bristol, tomb recesses in the walls form part of the ornamental design of the building. The chantries and canopied tombs are frequently of great architectural interest, as they seem often to have served as opportunities for modelling to scale features of fresh design. Experiments in vaulting which could be carried out on a small scale as applied ornament were the basis for much of the later development of the stellar, reticulated and fan vaults. And in spite of the destruction wrought at the Reformation and since, the cathedrals (with Westminster Abbey) hold the important examples of our monuments and tombs of all kinds, from the Norman period to the twentieth century.

197. St. Albans: tomb of Duke Humphrey of Gloucester, c. 1440–50

198. Winchester: Beaufort (right) and Waynflete chapels, c. 1445 and c. 1485

199, 200. Winchester: vaults of (top) Waynflete's chapel, c. 1485; and Wykeham's chapel, c. 1395, by William Wynford

This is not the place for a discussion of cathedral services and music, but a few remarks from the historical point of view may not be amiss. The distinctive feature of cathedral services, in common with those of other collegiate churches, is that they are not primarily aimed at the lay worshipper. They are an end subsisting in themselves, and as thoroughly 'impractical' as the expenditure of many thousands of pounds upon the building and upkeep of the fabrics. Except where a part of the nave has always been parochial, the custom of having a nave altar with congregational services has no traditional authority, and has no part in the heritage of the cathedral. If this is to be regarded as a falling away from the ancient purity of cathedral worship, there is compensation in the increased and increasing regard for the best music. After centuries of neglect, the great English composers of Tudor, Elizabethan and Stuart times have been revived, not as mere antiquarianism, but for the splendour of their music on its own merits.

Certain cathedrals have special fame as musical centres, notably the 'Three Choirs' of Gloucester, Hereford and Worcester. At the end of the Middle Ages several others were particularly important for their choir-schools, and the famous composers who were organists or choir-masters: Lincoln, London and Wells were all notable in this way, and are again musically notable in the twentieth century. But it would be invidious to single out any cathedrals for praise, where the standard of all is high, and has been so enormously raised within the memory of many now living. From being the land without music, England has rapidly recovered its singing voice, with the cathedrals in the lead. As for instrumental music, there were cathedral orchestras in the Middle Ages, if we accept the evidence of the gallery in the nave at Exeter, and the angels playing upon divers instruments in the Gloucester vault. Great organs have always been found in the English cathedral, since the building of that which in the tenth century at Winchester had four hundred pipes, and required seventy men to blow and four hands to play.

Music is the art most closely associated with the cathedrals in the public mind; it is too often forgotten that the cathedral is the embodiment of architecture and its highest expression. That it was also the cause and at the same time the repository of many of the supreme flights of genius in sculpture and painting can be forgotten only too easily, on account of the destruction wrought in the past four centuries. But it is singular that the cathedral should have evoked so little response from English writers. With the exception of a number of passing references in the poetry of the Romantics, mostly of a generalized character, our literature seems to be almost unmarked by the existence of the great churches in our midst. Probably the longest, as well as the finest, passage directly inspired by an English cathedral is the description of St. Hugh's church at Lincoln in the Latin poem on his life written soon after 1220. Amounting to 133 lines, the description not only reaches a high level as literature, but is founded on close observation of detail.

Modern authors have used cathedrals as the setting for dramatic action, but it can hardly be said that the building itself has appealed to their imaginations. Much more attention has, perhaps naturally, been given to the psychology of the cathedral close as a type of society. As often happens, the shortcomings of a way of life have been dwelt upon, and to many who have not lived in a cathedral city the phrase 'atmosphere of the Close' conveys an impression of snobbery, servility and petty bickering. Naturally these qualities do exist, as in other societies, but they are not the only qualities. A fact commonly overlooked by critics of ecclesiasticism is that high office necessarily calls for administrative capacity. In the nature of things this cannot always, if ever, be linked with other-worldly saintship. But, among that hierarchy of bishop, dean, canons, vicars and minor officials that makes up any given Close, there is commonly a saint, an artist, a historian or a man of letters: or even all at once. And if not to produce, at least to find a niche for such people, is still as it always has been one of the clearest justifications of the English cathedrals.

Saints are born and not made, but there is a special sense in which the whole of English culture is owed to the cathedrals. The origin of all our education is found in the cathedral school. Some sixty years ago the late A. F. Leach showed that in the Dark and Middle Ages instruction was in the hands, not of the monks, but of the secular clergy. Where the monks maintained schools, it was as the successors of earlier bodies of secular clergy dispossessed in the great monastic movement of late Saxon England. In general, these monastic schools were at the monastic cathedrals; and at the secular cathedrals the schools pursued their steady course without interruption. The whole of the English school system without exception can be traced back, step by step, to the grammar school of Canterbury Cathedral, first mentioned in AD 631. Other cathedral schools which were certainly in existence in the Saxon period were at Rochester, at Winchester and St. Peter's School at York. There is no reason to doubt that similar schools existed at the remaining cathedrals and greater minsters, and soon after the Norman Conquest there is evidence of many: at Salisbury, Lincoln, Wells, St. Paul's in London, Southwell and Ripon; and at the monastic cathedrals of Carlisle, Norwich and Worcester. And so it is that whatever there may be of learning and letters in this country is owed directly or indirectly to the English cathedral.

The work begun by the cathedral schools was carried a stage further by the cathedral libraries. Canterbury, York, Durham and Peterborough were especially famous for their large collections of books, and Hereford still keeps its chained library, reminding us of the extreme value of books when every copy had to be laboriously written by hand. Our first book-collector on a grand scale, Richard of Bury, was a fourteenth-century bishop of Durham. Nowadays perhaps few people would think a cathedral a likely place for a library to be; still fewer would dream of going to a cathedral library for purposes of study. Yet all our cathedrals are equipped with libraries, some of them still of very great importance for the rare works, both manuscript and printed, in their possession. Outmoded by the modern public libraries for reference and loan, the older institutions have in some cases fallen on evil days, and have but rarely been used even by scholars. Lately their value has been realized, and they are being assisted by the far-seeing Pilgrim Trust to re-equip themselves. Several libraries have become associated with new universities, as at Canterbury, Exeter and York. Once again the cathedral library is taking its place as a vital element of English life.

Last, but possibly the greatest of the benefits conferred by the ancient cathedrals, is their function as regional centres: centres of culture, and centres of affection. We have seen how they came into being, each as a focus for the spiritual life of an early kingdom or province. As their number has grown, in accordance with the growth of population, smaller and more precisely defined districts have been provided with such a focus. Every one of them is the spiritual hearth and home of a group of people, the centre of a special devotion and a personal loyalty. According to ties of birth, descent or domicile, each of us feels one cathedral to be particularly his own. Between all there is a healthy and friendly rivalry. And this particular love is not exclusive: the special affection for one can be heightened by a proper appreciation of all. To each of us belongs our own dear minster: but the heritage of all of us is the English cathedral.

Appendix – Some problems and definitions

In a text intended mainly for the general reader it has been impossible to consider in adequate detail a number of relevant problems. As far as possible these are dealt with here in chronological order:

1   *The Romanesque style*   In architectural history the word 'Romanesque' is properly used (see standard dictionaries) of the whole period between the end of the Classical and the opening of the Gothic – from the sixth to the twelfth century. As the name suggests, it embraces all forms derived from the Roman yet not classical, and this sense is clear and logical. Confusion has been introduced by recent art historians who have subdivided the pre-Gothic styles and appropriated Romanesque only to the last of these (*c.* AD 1000–1200). It is to be hoped that this misleading usage will be abandoned.

    It is desirable in Britain to avoid the term as far as possible, using the traditional epithets Saxon and Norman which are explicit and (apart from the overlap of *c.* 1050–1100) chronologically distinctive.

2   *Types of architecture*   In much of the standard literature reference is made to the 'architecture' of monastic orders, of secular cathedrals and of collegiate churches; to military, civil and domestic architecture, as though these were distinct and mutually exclusive. It cannot be too strongly emphasized that architecture was a unity and lay altogether in the hands of the same skilled masters. There was no such thing as 'Benedictine,' 'Cluniac,' 'Cistercian' or 'collegiate' *architecture*; different programmes imposed varying sets of conditions upon the designers. It is perfectly true that the general character of, for instance, ecclesiastical buildings differs from that of the civil or military, but any given style of architecture inevitably comprehends all types of work. The many mediaeval architects whose names and careers are known are found working for patrons of diverse interests. For them the same man might design, to meet distinct demands, churches, abbeys, guildhalls, houses, castles, bridges, memorials and works of decorative art.

3   *English monastic cathedrals*   Outside England the concepts 'cathedral' and 'monastery' were normally exclusive of one another. The ideal of monasticism lay in (at

least relative) withdrawal from the world; the cathedral was the supreme meeting-place for great congregations drawn from the worldly laity. Its ('secular') clergy maintained the regular services on behalf of the world.

The English phenomenon of the monastic cathedral was due in the first place to an exceptional campaign of church reform during the second half of the tenth century. Establishments of secular priests were converted, under heavy pressure, into Benedictine monasteries. Among the great churches thus turned into priories were the cathedrals of Winchester and Worcester as well as several later to achieve cathedral rank: Bath, Ely and Peterborough. Notwithstanding this reform, the Norman hierarchy a hundred years later regarded the clergy of the Saxon minsters as intolerably slack, and imposed monasticism on a fresh crop of churches including Canterbury, Durham, Norwich and Rochester.

Tension usually developed between the bishop and the body of monks at a monastic cathedral, and the struggle was resolved in various ways. Explicit dichotomy occurred in the cases of the co-equal cathedrals of Bath and Wells, and Coventry and Lichfield. Episcopal attempts to found new non-monastic cathedrals were foiled at Canterbury and at Worcester. At Durham the palatine bishop was effectively in control; at Ely, Norwich, Rochester and Winchester the division of powers remained unresolved. Even in these instances the force of episcopal patronage was sufficient to overcome the reluctance of the monks, and bishop and prior worked in harmony so far as the cathedral fabric was concerned.

4   *Polygonal east ends*   Polygonal apses have an ancient history in church architecture, but in the English mediaeval period they form a special case derived from the apsidal plans of monastic churches. These were continental in origin and were generally rejected in favour of square east fronts in the course of the twelfth century. The polygonal apse appeared on a large scale at Lincoln in St. Hugh's cathedral begun in 1192, but this was destroyed before the completion of the Angel Choir in 1280. A distinct origin must be sought for the polygonal terminations which appear suddenly in the first half of the fourteenth century. These are all unaisled versions of the type established by the Sainte Chapelle in Paris (*c.* 1241–48), itself derived in plan from the royal chapel of St. Germain-en-Laye of 1238. Yet this plan had been decisively rejected in favour of the English front at St. Stephen's Chapel in the Palace of Westminster, begun in 1292.

The reintroduction of the polygon is very possibly due to a personal preference on the part of Walter Langton, bishop of Coventry and Lichfield 1296–1321 and a frequent visitor to the continent on official business. The Lady Chapel at Lichfield, though not built until *c.* 1320–36, was probably designed rather earlier, and may have been directly inspired by the project for Notre Dame at Huy in Belgium, begun in 1311. This would account for the imitative building of a chapel with polygonal apse in the lower ward of Kenilworth Castle between 1313 and 1322. Later in the fourteenth century similar apses were given to the king's chapel of St. George in Windsor Castle (*c.* 1350–56), to the great parish church of St. Michael at Coventry, and to the sanctuary aisles of St. Werburgh's (now the cathedral) at Chester. The polygonal Lady Chapel at Wells, though almost contemporary with that at Lichfield, is of very different type and is probably related to polygonal chapter-houses (see below).

5 *The polygonal chapter-house* The paradox that England, where the apse was rejected, should adopt the central plan for the chapter-house, has caused frequent comment. As with the apse, the circular or polygonal plan has roots going far back to classical and to early Christian architecture. The immediate sources, however, were undoubtedly the Rotunda of the Holy Sepulchre at Jerusalem, and its derivative the Dome of the Rock (A D 688–91), regarded by crusaders and pilgrims as the Temple. The Rotunda, after its rebuilding in 1048, was of 20 bays; the Dome of the Rock of 16, set within an outer octagon and having an intermediate octagonal colonnade of 24 openings. There was thus a choice of precedents, simplified by halving, for dividing a centrally planned building into ten, eight or twelve bays.

The first known English building of this kind was Wulfric's rotunda (1050) at St. Augustine's, Canterbury. This was octagonal outside, circular within, and had an inner rotunda of eight bays. It may have owed something to the rotunda of St. Bénigne at Dijon, of 1001–18, derived from the Holy Sepulchre. But at Dijon there were three concentric colonnades, of eight, sixteen and twenty-four bays, and it did not form an octagon externally. It seems more probable that Wulfric's work was directly inspired by pilgrims' reports of the new rotunda in Jerusalem just completed, and conflated with the octagonal exterior of 'the Temple', which Christian pilgrims could then see from distant viewpoints only. It must be remembered that the outside of the rotunda of the Sepulchre was inaccessible and more or less invisible.

At Worcester Cathedral the Norman apse was built above a crypt begun in 1084. This crypt still exists and is particularly interesting because in it a synod was held in 1092, soon after its completion. Because of this quasi-capitular use it has been suggested that the half-polygon formed by the internal apse on plan was the source for the later circular chapter-house. This is most unlikely on architectural grounds, for the low groined vaulting of the many small compartments of the crypt bears no real resemblance to the spacious and lofty chapter-house, whose ribbed vault is supported by a single pillar. We should rather regard the Worcester chapter-house as an independent introduction of the rotunda due to direct information from Palestine. The leaders of the First Crusade had in 1099, shortly after the capture of Jerusalem, held a council in the Dome of the Rock, and must have been impressed by such a meeting place. At Worcester the employment of a central column was an ingenious structural solution produced by a master without any knowledge of domes. The large diameter of 56 feet implies a setting-out circle of 60 feet (possibly Norman feet, i.e. 58′ 7½″), substituted for the '66' feet of the Dome of the Rock, just a cricket-pitch across.

The development from the Worcester circle, divided into ten bays, to the slightly larger decagon at Lincoln built in *c.* 1220–35 is perfectly clear. The diameter of 59 feet is evidence for the use of the modern English foot to provide a notional setting-out of 60 feet. But the concept of centralized space extended beyond the chapter-house to include polygons such as the six-sided porch of St Mary Redcliffe (*c.* 1325), the octagon at Ely designed in 1322, and the great circular Round Table with a diameter of 200 feet begun in Windsor Castle in 1344. This could hardly have been meant to be roofed, but was evidently an open arena for the holding of tournaments by an order of 'Arthurian' knights, forerunning the Order of the Garter. The idea of the Heavenly Jerusalem with its circular plan (mirrored in the actual circular city of Bagdad built in A D 762–67) and of the dome as a symbol of the firmament may not merely have been combined with one another, but in the case of central-pillar buildings also with the northern mythological ash-tree Yggdrasil supporting the heavens. However vague such symbolic ideas might be, they would help to explain the force of the English tradition.

As has been suggested above, the Wells Lady Chapel probably belongs to the same family of buildings. In a general sense suggested by the immediately preceding octagon of the chapter-house, it nevertheless represents a deliberate attempt to eliminate the central pier. The curious domical ribbed vault can be seen as an experiment devized to realize this programme. The example of the unsupported (wooden) vault of the York chapter-house (58 feet in span) must have become known about 1300, and this stone vault at Wells had been designed not later than 1310 and perhaps some years earlier.

6   *The Central Tower*   Norman churches were commonly designed with central towers of importance, and this fashion was brought over to England. Since the central tower was relatively uncommon in northern France beyond Normandy, development was mainly insular. Influence from the central tower of the abbey of Fécamp on the Norman coast is, however, possible in regard to the Lincoln tower designed after the collapse of 1237. Another important tower, now lost, was that at York built over the immense crossing of the Norman cathedral in *c.* 1234–51. This, described as 'a bell-tower lofty and delectable to see' in the midst of the church, fell in 1407 in a storm, apparently weakened by the work of underpinning with the enlarged crossing-arches begun about 1395. Its quite exceptional size would have given opportunity for full development of turretted angles and ranges of three rather than two windows, set in blind arcading. If so, this tower was probably the main influence underlying the new Lincoln tower of 1238 and thus fundamental for later English design.

A point of general interest is raised by the loss of the great York tower. We know that other towers of considerable importance fell during the Middle Ages, but most of these were Norman. After the Reformation various towers were demolished or fell, as at Bury St. Edmunds (two), Malmesbury, Oseney and Waltham Abbeys. All the free-standing belfries except those of Chichester Cathedral and Evesham Abbey were sacrificed at one time or another. Yet the losses of significant Gothic towers may well be relatively slight. Among the cathedrals we know that the western tower of Hereford fell in 1786, but views of it survive. Among greater churches outside the cathedrals we have records also of the central tower of Whitby Abbey (fell 1830) and the western tower at St. John's Abbey, Chester (fell 1881). It is striking that the only non-cathedral Gothic central tower of notable quality is that at Howden. Where monastic towers exist they are mostly late and of a single stage: Christchurch, Malvern, Milton, Pershore, Sherborne; or are early survivals: New Shoreham, Tewkesbury, Wimborne, and the gate-tower at Bury. Other non-central towers of importance survive, as at Fountains and Wymondham. It seems that losses of first-class Gothic towers are few and that most of the story of their development is still available.

It is unfortunate that, while most of the towers can be closely dated, documentation is scanty precisely for several of great significance in the first half of the four-teenth century. Accurate dates can be assigned to the upper stage at Lincoln (1306–11) and to Wells in its original form (1315–22). But much is obscure regarding the works at Lichfield, Hereford, Peterborough and Salisbury. Of these Peterborough (now an accurate rebuild of 1883–86) is manifestly the latest, having reticulated tracery and transoms, but no Perpendicular detail (design c. 1335–40?). This Gothic tower may have been undertaken as a precautionary measure prompted by the collapse of the Norman central tower at Ely in 1322.

The three central towers of Lichfield, Hereford and Salisbury may best be considered in that order, as it corresponds to a development from the simple to the complex. At this highest level of design it may be regarded as certain that the architects involved were aware, not only of other works in progress, but also of major designs already set down on parchment. At Hereford we know that there had been a conference of mason-architects in respect of the adequacy of the old founda-tions, and such a meeting would afford opportunity for every master present to carry away at least a mental picture of the designs.

When Lichfield was visited by two Irish friars in March 1323 the cathedral already had two or more very high stone 'towers' (*turribus lapideis sive campanilibus altissimis*). Undoubtedly *turris* here means or includes a spire, and the probable implication is that all three towers and spires were then complete or nearly so. (The north-west spire is now a rebuilding, perhaps of c. 1522–33, the central spire a restoration after the Civil War in 1661–69.) Normal procedure would indicate completion of the central tower first, and this agrees with the absence of ball-flower ornament, profusely employed on the western towers and spires above the level of the front. On the other hand, the design of the central tower cannot be put earlier than c. 1300.

Although the ball-flower was used as an enrichment over a very long period, the date of its profuse employment centred mainly on the reign of Edward II (1307–27), continuing in some parts rather later. The principal first-class work with a close dating is the south nave aisle at Gloucester built within the years 1319–29. Other approximately dated instances of profuse ball-flower are the north aisle of Ludlow Church, Shropshire (c. 1317) and a build at Weobley, Herefordshire, consecrated in 1325. In round figures, then, the Lichfield central tower was built about 1300–10, and the western towers in 1310–20.

At Hereford two towers were built in this period. The central tower survives but that built over the western bay of the Norman nave fell in 1786. Engravings show that, like the central tower, it was heavily encrusted with ball-flower. The crucial document is a papal bull of 1320 answering petitions of 1319 from the Dean and Chapter. A superstructure had been built upon the ancient foundation, deemed firm and steady in the judgment of masons or architects skilled in their art (*cementariorum seu architectorum qui in arte sua reputabantur periti*) and more than 20,000 marks (say £14,000; in 1973 probably worth at least £4,000,000) had been spent. The foundation had, all the same, proved weak and deficient and such ruin was threatened that it could not be averted, again according to the judgment of architects of repute, unless the fabric were renewed from the foundations.

What part of the cathedral constituted this dangerous superstructure, and was it in fact taken down and rebuilt? The western tower was built upon the Norman front and it is manifest from engravings that this was certainly not rebuilt after 1320. Though this tower did eventually collapse in 1786, it cannot well be the dangerous structure reported in 1319. Presumably the problem concerned the central tower: but was it the tower that survives, or a predecessor? There is sufficient evidence that extensive repairs were carried out around the crossing to suggest that the existing tower was kept up and therefore goes back to a date before 1319. Stylistic evidence on the whole tends to confirm this.

The main factor is again the prolific use of ball-flower which is also found on a group of tombs in the cathedral including that of Bishop Richard Swinfield who died on 15 March 1317. This monument is a later insertion in the wall of the north-east transept, itself stylistically of about 1300 or slightly later. The structural work does not employ ball-flower. It seems reasonably certain that the date of c. 1295–1300 proposed by Mr. George Marshall for the start of the central tower must be too early. Firstly, the design should follow that of Lichfield; secondly, the serious deformation reported in 1319 would be likely to follow quickly upon completion of such a tower built on old crossing-arches. Provisionally the date must be put at c. 1315.

The 'epicentre' of ball-flower ornament seems to have been Hereford or some-where not far away, and its use in profusion at Salisbury may well have been later. The general character of the tower appears decidedly later and approaches towards the Perpendicular in composition, but there is still no specific mark of the new style. A date much later than 1340 for the design would be virtually impossible; one earlier than 1320 unlikely. The fact that the Chapter in July 1334 appointed a new architect, Richard (Davy) of Farleigh, notable as being already in charge of works at Bath and Reading Abbeys, has always appeared to mark the inception of this extraordinary undertaking. There are, however, several difficulties:

(a) The contract of appointment refers to a predecessor, Robert the mason, as still alive. This must have been the *Robertus cementarius* who had charge for 25 years and whose obit was kept on 17 August yearly. This suggests that Master Robert must have been a man of importance in his own right. He is not likely to have become master before 1312, since in the previous year a Salisbury master named William de Schoverville was paid £1 for visiting Exeter Cathedral to give advice. Robert's period of responsibility may have stretched from c. 1312–15 until c. 1337–40, and in that case Farleigh was brought in as a junior colleague or perhaps as a specialist in construction.

(b) The profuse use of ball-flower throughout the work, even though at a distance from Hereford and Gloucester, favours design some years earlier than 1334.

(c) The architectonic aspects of the design indicate strong influence from the Lincoln tower completed in 1311 as well as the more obvious assimilation of detail from Lichfield and Hereford. There is also an extremely close stylistic affinity with the central tower of Pershore Abbey, which looks like a reduced copy of the lower stage only. The Pershore details are certainly later than those at Salisbury and suggest a date not long before the onset of Perpendicular, probably c. 1330–35. This in turn indicates that the Salisbury drawings had been made some years earlier still.

To sum up, the design of the Salisbury steeple must probably be put back into the period of Master Robert, but not before completion (*c.* 1318) of the Hereford tower. It is likely that the structural problems at Hereford were kept in mind and that exceptional precautions were taken at Salisbury. Design within the decade 1320–30 seems to accommodate all the factors. The spire was probably finished before 1387.

7   *The Mitred Abbeys*   It was pointed out above, in connection with the greater towers, that in that field the losses to Gothic architecture have probably been less than might be imagined. This is regrettably not the case with other features, and there is reason to think that the mitred abbeys in particular were a class of buildings almost as influential as the cathedrals. Out of twenty-seven only thirteen survive in use or as substantial ruins. Of the lost fourteen at least nine (Abingdon, Battle, Bury, Canterbury St. Augustine, Evesham, Ramsey, Reading, Winchcombe and Hyde) were architecturally outstanding. Though plans have mostly been recovered, our knowledge is inadequate and a campaign of research is required to correlate surviving fragments of detail with churches and other extant buildings that belonged to each abbey or came within its sphere of influence. From those mitred abbeys that have come down to us it is obvious that Westminster and the three now cathedrals, Malmesbury, Selby and Tewkesbury are of cardinal importance. The disappearance of Henry II's church at Waltham is probably the greatest single loss in British architectural history. Built between 1177 and 1242 it was the contemporary of Wells Cathedral and could have shown the exact state of early Gothic style under the royal masters.

While it is fruitless to mourn the glories of these buildings almost altogether lost, it is worth considering the contributions made to our knowledge of style by those that survive. Most of them provide a great deal of information on regional varieties of Norman style, but several are far more important for displaying the individual styles of the fourteenth century: Malmesbury, Selby and Tewkesbury. Croyland, in the aisle that was left as parish church, is a Perpendicular fragment of unique interest. At Evesham the free-standing bell-tower gives a clue to yet another local style of the end of the Middle Ages.

Historical and descriptive notes on each cathedral

In these notes the thirty-one cathedrals are arranged alphabetically. Each note contains a statement of the main facts about the see and foundation; dimensions of the building; the chief building dates; and, where known, the architects' names. The dimensions are external, except the heights to vault or ceiling; authorities differ as to dimensions, but the figures given are believed to be approximately correct. Plan dimensions include buttresses; the width is given across the main transept (eastern transept in the case of Canterbury). Destroyed parts of the buildings are in *italics*; '(F)' indicates that fragments are visible.

The names of architects given are those of the master craftsmen, where these are known from documentary sources; names in square brackets indicate strong stylistic evidence. The dates are the *floruit* of each artist, not those of his connection with the individual building. Where no date is given, the evidence is limited to the particular work in question. Dates of building known from documentary evidence are given thus: 1501–39. When the start or finish of work is known, it is shown 1501–, or –1539; where the date is known to lie within a given period, it is shown in parentheses: (1501–39). Uncertain dates are shown thus: *c.* 1500; *c.* 1501–39, the double date indicating a rather higher degree of probability.

The ground plans of each cathedral are all reproduced to a uniform scale of 100 feet to one inch.

218

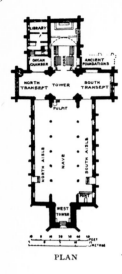

PLAN

BANGOR *(St. Deiniol)*

See: *c.* 525; refounded 1092
Foundation: Secular Canons
Dimensions: length 236 feet; width 115 feet; tower 60 feet

Building dates		Architects
c. 1075–	*Rebuilding* (F)	
1291–*c.* 1350	Transepts; nave aisle walls	
1471–1496	Restoration	
(1496–1500)	Choir	
1509–1532	Nave; west tower	
1866–1875	Restoration	Sir George Gilbert Scott

BATH *(St. Peter and St. Paul)*

See: removed from Wells 1090; Bath and Glastonbury 1192; Bath and Wells 1218
Foundation: Nunnery 676; Secular Canons *c.* 775; Benedictine Monks *c.* 970–1539.
Dimensions: length 225 feet; width 142 feet; height 75 feet; tower 162 feet.

Building dates		Architects
c. 1090–1120	*Romanesque church* (F)	
(1248–64)	*Lady Chapel*	
1324–	*Extensive repairs*	Richard Farleigh (1332–63)
c. 1420	*Bubwith's chantry chapel*	
1501–39	Present cathedral	Robert Vertue (1475–d. 1506); and William Vertue (1500–d. 1527)
1515–	Prior Bird's chantry	William Vertue; John Molton (1524–d. 1547)
1833–35	Restoration	George Philip Manners
1864–73	Nave and transept vaults	Sir George Gilbert Scott
1895–1901	West front restored	Sir Thomas Graham Jackson
1925–26	Cloister	Sir Thomas Graham Jackson

BRISTOL *(St. Augustine; now Holy Trinity)*

See: 1542; united to Gloucester 1836; revived 1897.
Foundation: Augustinian Regular Canons 1140–1538; a Mitred Abbey 1332–41.
Dimensions: length 338 feet; width 137 feet; height 52 feet; tower 136 feet.

Building dates		*Architects*
1140–48	*Original church* (F); gateway to Abbot's lodging	
c. 1154–64	Chapter-house; great gateway (lower part)	
c. 1220–30	Elder Lady Chapel	('L.', sculptor)
c. 1280	East end and window of Elder Lady Chapel	
c. 1311–40	Choir; Berkeley and Newton Chapels	
c. 1320	East window	
(1428–73)	Transepts	
c. 1466–71	Central tower	
(1480–1515)	Transept window	
(1481–1526)	Gatehouse over great gateway	
c. 1515–25	Cloisters; stalls; south transept vault	
1868–88	Nave and western towers	George Edmund Street
1888–93	Restoration	J. L. Pearson
1899–1905	Reredos and choir screen	J. L. Pearson

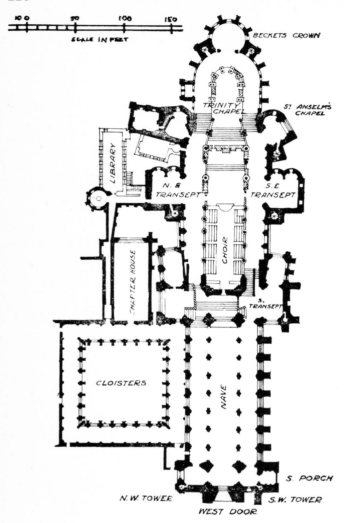

SCALE IN FEET

BECKETS CROWN

TRINITY CHAPEL

ST ANSELM'S CHAPEL

LIBRARY

N.E TRANSEPT

S.E TRANSEPT

CHOIR

CHAPTER HOUSE

S. TRANSEPT

CLOISTERS

NAVE

S. PORCH

N.W. TOWER

S.W. TOWER

WEST DOOR

CANTERBURY *(Christ Church)*

See: 597.

Foundation: Secular Canons 597; Benedictine Monks 1070–1539.

Pilgrimage: Thomas Becket, abp. 1162–70, can. 1172, tr. 1220.

Dimensions: length 547 feet; width 171 feet; height (nave) 80 feet; tower 235 feet.

Building dates		*Architects*
1070–77	*Lanfranc's church* (F)	
c. 1096–1107	*Choir; east transepts* (F); crypt	
1175–78	Choir	Wm. of Sens (1174–d. 1180)
1179–84	Trinity Chapel and corona	William Englishman (1175–d. 1214)
1236–38	*Cloister* (F)	
1304–20	Screens of choir; chapter-house (lower part)	[Thomas of Canterbury (1324–35)]
1336	Window of St. Anselm's Chapel	

1341–43	Infirmary table-hall	
c. 1363–	Black Prince's chantry in crypt	? John Box (1333–d. c. 1375)
c. 1372–77	Crypt Lady Chapel	? John Box
1379–1405	Nave and south transept	Henry Yeveley (1353–d. 1400)
1397–1414	Cloisters	Henry Yeveley, Stephen Lote
c. 1400–12	Chapter-house (upper part)	Stephen Lote (1381–d. 1417)
c. 1410	West face of pulpitum	Stephen Lote
1410–39	St. Michael's Chapel	Stephen Lote
c. 1420	South transept vault	
1423–34	South-west tower	Thomas Mapilton (1408–d. 1438)
c. 1440	Henry IV's Chantry	
1448–55	North transept and Lady Chapel	Richard Beke (1409–d. 1458)
1449–68	Tabernacles round south-west tower	Richard Beke
c. 1468	Lady Chapel vault	
1493–97	Central tower and strainer arches in crossing	John Wastell (1485–1515)
c. 1505	Tower vault	[John Wastell]
c. 1515–20	Christ Church gate	? John Wastell
1834–41	North-west tower	George Austin
1904–12	Restoration of towers	W. D. Caröe

CARLISLE *(Holy Trinity)*

See: 1133.
Foundation: Secular Canons 1092; Augustinian Regular Canons 1123–1540.
Dimensions: length 239 feet; width 141 feet; height 72 feet; tower 110 feet.

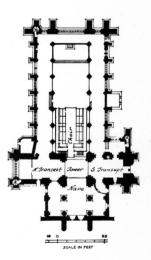

Building dates		*Architects*
(1092–1123)	Nave; south transept	
(1245–92)	Choir, aisles and arcading	
1293–1322	Choir, piers and east bay	? Ivo de Raghton (1317–38)
(1363–95)	Upper walls of choir	? John Lewyn (1364–d. c. 1398)
(1400–19)	North transept; tower; stalls	
(1484–1507)	Fratry	
1527	Gatehouse	
1853–70	Restoration	Ewan Christian

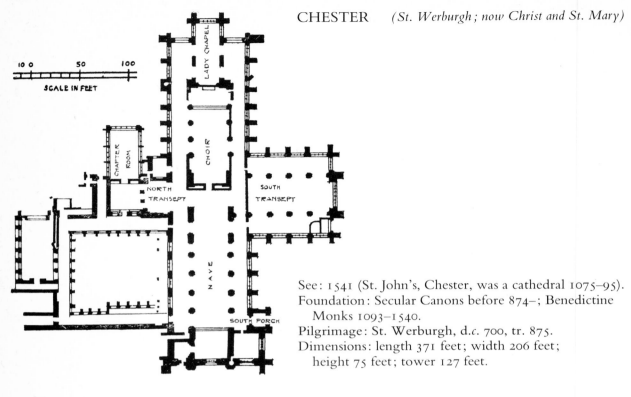

CHESTER   *(St. Werburgh; now Christ and St. Mary)*

10 0   50   100

SCALE IN FEET

LADY CHAPEL

CHOIR

CHAPTER ROOM

NORTH TRANSEPT

SOUTH TRANSEPT

NAVE

SOUTH PORCH

See: 1541 (St. John's, Chester, was a cathedral 1075–95).
Foundation: Secular Canons before 874–; Benedictine
    Monks 1093–1540.
Pilgrimage: St. Werburgh, d.*c.* 700, tr. 875.
Dimensions: length 371 feet; width 206 feet;
    height 75 feet; tower 127 feet.

Building dates		*Architects*
1093–1140	North transept; north-west tower	
1194–1211	*Choir*	
c. 1230–50	Chapter-house vestibule	
c. 1249–65	Chapter-house and refectory	
(1265–90)	Lady Chapel	
c. 1283–1315	Choir	Richard Lenginour (1272–1314)
c. 1323–75	Nave (part); south transept (part)	? Nicholas de Derneford (1316–1331)
c. 1390	Stalls	
(1485–92)	Nave, north arcade	? William Rediche (1461–d. 1495)
(1493–1537)	Central tower; south transept; porch	? Seth Derwall (1495–1525)
1508–37	South-west tower	? Seth Derwall and George Derwall (1525–37)
(*c.* 1500–30)	Cloisters	? Seth Derwall
1868–72	Restoration	Sir G. G. Scott
1939	Refectory restored	Frederick Herbert Crossley

CHICHESTER *(Holy Trinity)*

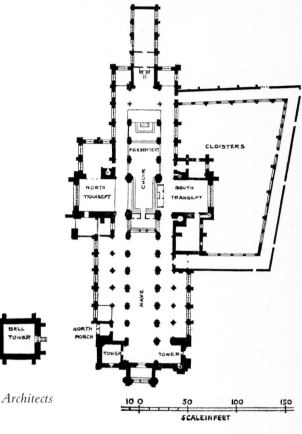

See: (at Selsey 709); removed to Chichester 1075.
Foundation: Secular Canons.
Pilgrimage: St. Richard (Wych) of Chichester,
    can. 1262, tr. 1276.
Dimensions: length 408 feet; width 157 feet;
    height 61 feet; spire 277 feet.

Building dates		*Architects*
1088–1108	Presbytery	
1114–23	East nave	
(1123–48)	West nave; south-west tower	
1187–99	Retrochoir; recasing and vaulting	? Walter of Coventry
(1215–25)	South-west tower (upper stage)	
(c. 1225–50)	South chapels and north-east chapels of nave	
c. 1244–47	Central tower	
(c. 1250–75)	North-west chapels of nave; west porch	
(1288–1304)	Lady Chapel, eastern bays	
(1305–37)	South transept remodelled	
(1391–1402)	Spire completed	John Mason (c. 1348–1403)
1396–c. 1403	Vicars' Hall	John Mason
c. 1405–10	Pulpitum	? Walter Walton (1383–d. 1418)
c. 1410–40	Campanile	Walter Walton
(c. 1400–1500)	Cloisters	? William Wynford
1861–66	Central tower and spire rebuilt	Sir G. G. Scott
1899–1901	North-west tower	J. L. Pearson

DURHAM *(St. Mary and St. Cuthbert; now Christ and St. Mary)*

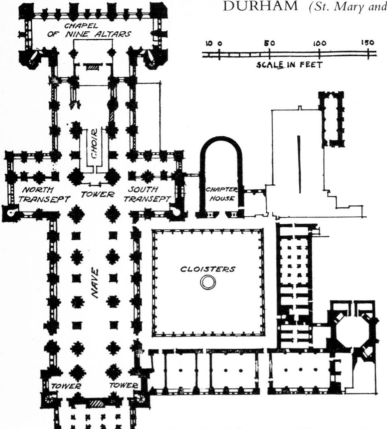

See: (Lindisfarne 635; Chester-le-Street 883); removed to Durham 997.
Foundation: Celtic Monks 995; Secular Canons?; Benedictine Monks 1093–1540.
Pilgrimage: St. Cuthbert, d. 687, tr. 995, 1104.
Dimensions: length 502 feet; width 192 feet; height 74 feet; tower 218 feet.

Building dates		Architects
1093–99	Choir	
1099–1128	Nave	
1128–33	Nave vault	
1133–40	Chapter-house	
c. 1170–75	Galilee	Richard Wolveston (1170– d. c. 1182)
c. 1220	West towers (upper stages)	
1242–80	Chapel of Nine Altars	Richard Farnham (1242–47)
c. 1341	West window	? Roger Mason (1337)
1366–71	Kitchen	John Lewyn (1364–d. c. 1398)

1375–80	Reredos (Neville screen)	? Henry Yeveley (1353–d. 1400) and John Lewyn
1390–1418	Cloisters	John Lewyn; Thomas Mapilton (1408–d. 1438)
1465–75	Central tower (lower stage)	? Thomas Barton (1447–c. 1475)
c. 1483–90	Central tower (upper stage)	John Bell, junior (1478–88)
c. 1510–20	Spire begun	Christopher Scune (1505–21)
1795–97	Alterations	James Wyatt (1746–1813)
1895	Chapter-house restored	Hodgson Fowler

ELY *(St. Peter and St. Etheldreda; now Holy Trinity)*

See: 1109.
Foundation: Benedictine Nuns 673; Benedictine Monks 970–1540.
Pilgrimage: St. Etheldreda, d. 679.
Dimensions: length 537 feet; width 199 feet; height 86 feet; western tower 215 feet.

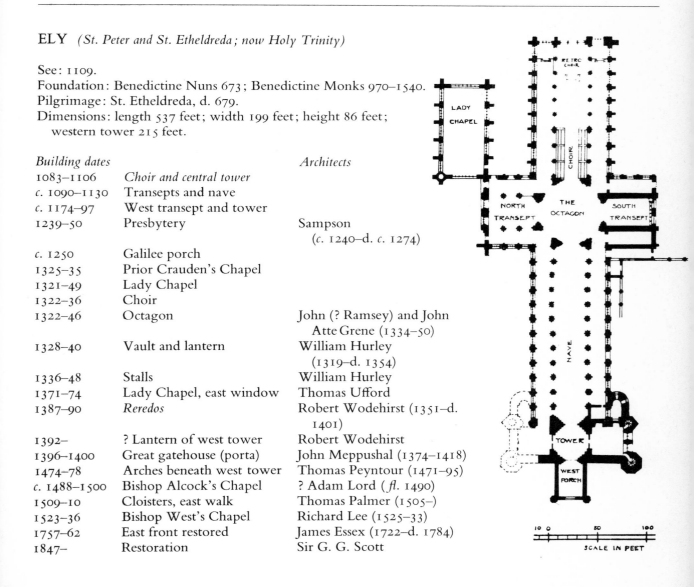

Building dates		*Architects*
1083–1106	*Choir and central tower*	
c. 1090–1130	Transepts and nave	
c. 1174–97	West transept and tower	
1239–50	Presbytery	Sampson (c. 1240–d. c. 1274)
c. 1250	Galilee porch	
1325–35	Prior Crauden's Chapel	
1321–49	Lady Chapel	
1322–36	Choir	
1322–46	Octagon	John (? Ramsey) and John Atte Grene (1334–50)
1328–40	Vault and lantern	William Hurley (1319–d. 1354)
1336–48	Stalls	William Hurley
1371–74	Lady Chapel, east window	Thomas Ufford
1387–90	*Reredos*	Robert Wodehirst (1351–d. 1401)
1392–	? Lantern of west tower	Robert Wodehirst
1396–1400	Great gatehouse (porta)	John Meppushal (1374–1418)
1474–78	Arches beneath west tower	Thomas Peyntour (1471–95)
c. 1488–1500	Bishop Alcock's Chapel	? Adam Lord (*fl.* 1490)
1509–10	Cloisters, east walk	Thomas Palmer (1505–)
1523–36	Bishop West's Chapel	Richard Lee (1525–33)
1757–62	East front restored	James Essex (1722–d. 1784)
1847–	Restoration	Sir G. G. Scott

EXETER *(St. Peter)*

See: (Crediton 909); removed to Exeter 1049.
Foundation: Benedictine Monks ?–1003 and 1019–49; Secular Canons 1050–.
Dimensions: length 409 feet; width 158 feet; height 69 feet; towers 130 feet.

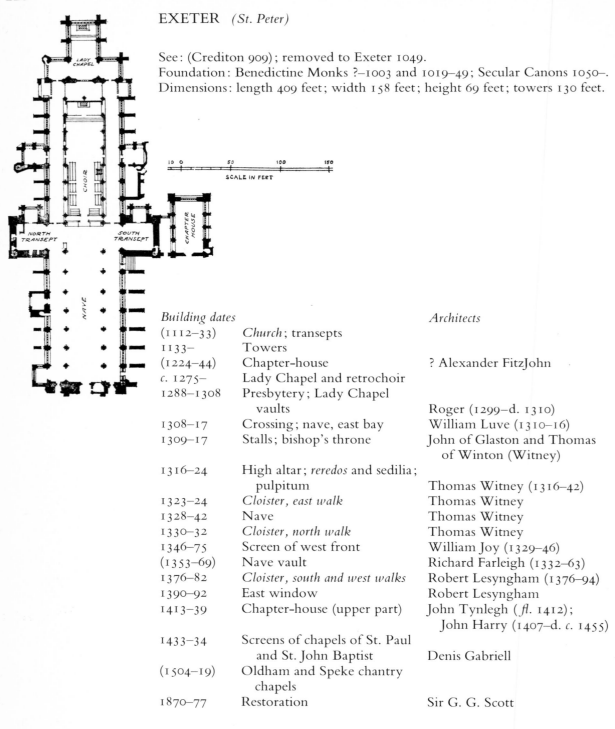

SCALE IN FEET

Building dates		*Architects*
(1112–33)	*Church*; transepts	
1133–	Towers	
(1224–44)	Chapter-house	? Alexander FitzJohn
c. 1275–	Lady Chapel and retrochoir	
1288–1308	Presbytery; Lady Chapel vaults	Roger (1299–d. 1310)
1308–17	Crossing; nave, east bay	William Luve (1310–16)
1309–17	Stalls; bishop's throne	John of Glaston and Thomas of Winton (Witney)
1316–24	High altar; *reredos* and sedilia; pulpitum	Thomas Witney (1316–42)
1323–24	*Cloister, east walk*	Thomas Witney
1328–42	Nave	Thomas Witney
1330–32	*Cloister, north walk*	Thomas Witney
1346–75	Screen of west front	William Joy (1329–46)
(1353–69)	Nave vault	Richard Farleigh (1332–63)
1376–82	*Cloister, south and west walks*	Robert Lesyngham (1376–94)
1390–92	East window	Robert Lesyngham
1413–39	Chapter-house (upper part)	John Tynlegh (*fl.* 1412); John Harry (1407–d. c. 1455)
1433–34	Screens of chapels of St. Paul and St. John Baptist	Denis Gabriell
(1504–19)	Oldham and Speke chantry chapels	
1870–77	Restoration	Sir G. G. Scott

GLOUCESTER *(St. Peter; now Holy Trinity)*

See: 1541; united with Bristol 1836; separated 1897.
Foundation: Benedictine Monks and Nuns 681; Secular Priests 823;
    Benedictine Monks 1022–1539.
Pilgrimage: King Edward II, d. 1327
Dimensions: length 425 feet; width 154 feet; height (choir) 86 feet;
    tower 225 feet.

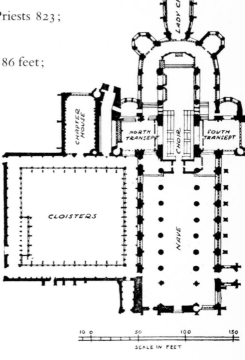

Building Dates		*Architects*
1089–1100	Crypt and choir	
c. 1120–60	Nave	
–1222	*Central tower* (F)	
1242–45	Nave vault	? John of Gloucester (1245–d. 1260)
1242–*c.* 1260	*South-west tower*	
(1318–29)	Nave, south aisle	?Martin of Sponebed (*c.* 1320)
(1331–37)	South transept remodelled	
(1337–67)	Choir remodelled; stalls	[William Ramsey (1325–d. 1349)]
1368–74	North transept remodelled	[Robert Lesyngham (1376–94)]
c. 1370–77	Cloister, six south bays east walk	[Robert Lesyngham]
(1381–1412)	Cloisters completed	
(1421–37)	West front and two bays; south porch	
1450–60	Central tower	? John Hobbs (1455–75)
(1457–83)	Lady Chapel	? John Hobbs
1847–	Restoration	F. S. Waller
1853–	Restoration	Sir G. G. Scott

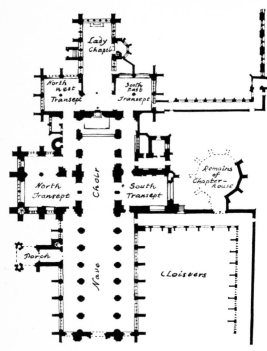

SCALE IN FEET

HEREFORD *(St. Mary and St. Ethelbert)*

See: 676.
Foundation: Secular Canons.
Pilgrimages: St. Ethelbert, King and Martyr,
    d. 794; St. Thomas Cantilupe, bp 1275–82,
    tr. 1287, can. 1330.
Dimensions: length 344 feet; width 177 feet;
    height 64 feet; tower 165 feet.

Building Dates		*Architects*
1079–1110	Choir; south transept (part)	
c. 1100–45	Nave and transepts	
c. 1190	Vestibule of Lady Chapel	
1217–25	Lady Chapel	
c. 1235–40	Choir clerestory and vault	
1250–68	North transept; inner north porch	
c. 1290–94	Aisle walls	Hugh Mason (*fl.* 1291)
c. 1315	Central tower	
1359–70	*Chapter-house* (F)	John of Evesham; Thomas Cambridge
c. 1400	South transept vault	
1412–18	Cloister (part)	Thomas Denyar (1406–16)
c. 1470	Bishop Stanbury's chantry chapel	
1490–1500	Bishop Audley's chantry; vicars' cloister	
c. 1520–30	Outer north porch; Bishop's cloister	
1786–96	Repairs and alterations	James Wyatt (1746–1813)
1841–52	Restoration	L. N. & N. J. Cottingham
1902–08	West front	J. Oldrid Scott

LICHFIELD *(St. Mary and St. Chad)*

See: 669 (Archbishopric 787–803); removed to Chester 1075;
   to Coventry 1095; Coventry and Lichfield 1148; Lichfield
   and Coventry 1539; Lichfield 1836.
Foundation: Secular Canons.
Pilgrimage: St. Chad, d. 672.
Dimensions: length 397 feet; width 177 feet; height 57 feet;
   central spire 258 feet.

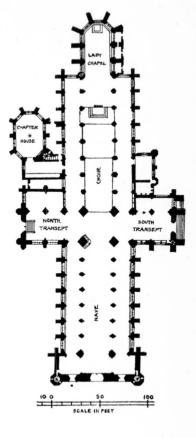

Building Dates		Architects
1195–1208	Choir arcades and crossing	
c. 1220–40	Transepts	Thomas (*c.* 1230–50)
c. 1239–49	Chapter-house and vestibule	Thomas
c. 1265–93	Nave; west front (lower part)	? William FitzThomas
		(*c.* 1250–65) and Thomas
		Wallace (*c.* 1265–80)
(1294–1320)	West front (upper part)	? Nicholas of Eyton
c. 1300–20	Central tower and W. spires	
c. 1320–36	Lady Chapel	William of Eyton (1322–36)
1337–50	Presbytery	William Ramsey (1325–d. 1349)
1385–	? Spires completed	Gilbert Mason
? 1522–33	N.W. Spire rebuilt	
1661–69	General restoration	Sir William Wilson (1641–d.
		1710)
1788–90	Alterations	James Wyatt (1746–1813)
1856–84	Restoration	Sir G. G. Scott & J. O. Scott

LINCOLN *(St. Mary)*

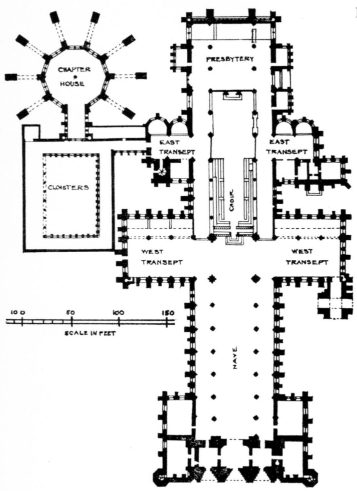

See: (Lindsey 678; removed to Dorchester, Oxon, 958); Lincoln 1073.
Foundation: Secular Canons.
Pilgrimages: St. Hugh of Avalon, bp 1186–1200, can. 1220, tr. 1280; 'Little'
   St. Hugh, martyr, d. 1255.
Dimensions: length 512 feet; width 251 feet; height 82 feet; tower 271 feet.

Building Dates		Architects
1074–92	Centre of west front	
c. 1142–46	West doorways; west towers (lower parts)	
1192–1210	Choir and east transept	(Geoffrey de Noyers); Richard Mason (*fl. c.* 1195)

c. 1215–30	Great transept	? Michael (*fl. c.* 1210–30)
c. 1220–35	Chapter-house	Alexander (1235–57)
c. 1225–53	Nave; west front; Galilee	Alexander
1238–55	Central tower (lower part)	Alexander
1256–80	Angel choir	Simon of Thirsk (*c.* 1260–90)
1295–1305	Cloisters	? Richard of Stow
1307–11	Central tower (upper part)	Richard of Stow (*c.* 1275–1311)
c. 1335–40	South transept gable with 'Bishop's Eye'	
c. 1360–75	Statues over west door, etc.	
c. 1363–72	Stalls	
? *c.* 1370–1400	West towers (upper parts)	? Geoffrey (*fl.* 1359)
c. 1475	Bishop Fleming's chantry chapel	
c. 1493	Bishop Russell's chantry chapel	
c. 1548	Bishop Longland's chantry chapel	? William Kitchin (1528–59)
1762–65	Restoration	James Essex (1722–d. 1784)
1922–32	Restoration	R. S. Godfrey

LLANDAFF *(St. Peter and St. Paul)*

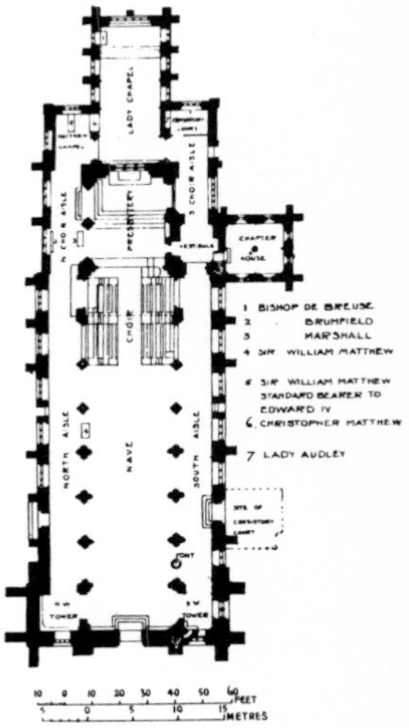

See *c.* 545; refounded 1107
Foundation: Secular Canons
Dimensions: length 268 feet; width 90 feet; spire 195 feet.

Building Dates		*Architects*
1120–1133	*Rebuilding* (F)	
1193–1229	Choir; nave; west front	
1244–1265	Chapter-house	
1266–1287	Lady Chapel	
1315–1360	Presbytery remodelled	
c. 1375	Aisle walls, choir and nave	
c. 1485–1500	North-west tower	? William Hart (1490–1526)
1734	*'Italian Temple' church*	John Wood of Bath
1859–1869	Restoration; south-west tower	John Prichard

PLAN

LONDON *(St. Paul)*

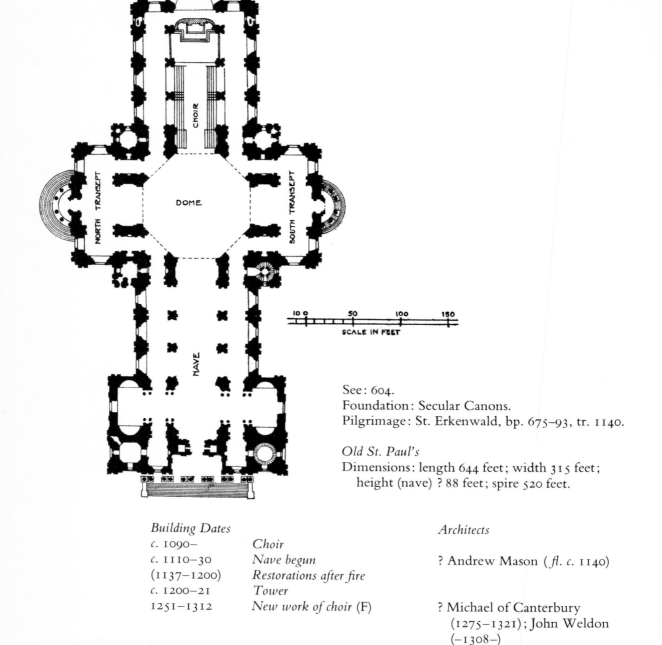

See: 604.
Foundation: Secular Canons.
Pilgrimage: St. Erkenwald, bp. 675–93, tr. 1140.

Old St. Paul's
Dimensions: length 644 feet; width 315 feet;
 height (nave) ? 88 feet; spire 520 feet.

Building Dates		*Architects*
c. 1090–	*Choir*	
c. 1110–30	*Nave begun*	? Andrew Mason (*fl. c.* 1140)
(1137–1200)	*Restorations after fire*	
c. 1200–21	*Tower*	
1251–1312	*New work of choir* (F)	? Michael of Canterbury (1275–1321); John Weldon (–1308–)
1256–	*Transepts*	
1332–	*Chapter-house and cloister* (F)	William Ramsey (1325–d. 1349)

1374–78	*Tomb of John of Gaunt*	Henry Yeveley (1353–d. 1400)
1382–87	*South transept front*	Henry Yeveley
1388–	*? Pulpitum*	Henry Yeveley
1631–40	*West portico ; refacing*	Inigo Jones (1573–d. 1651)
(1686)	Demolition completed	

New St. Paul's

Dimensions: length 510 feet; width 280 feet; height 89 feet; dome to top of cross 366 feet.

| *Building Dates* | | *Architect* |
| 1675–1710 | (Completion to top of lantern) | Sir Christopher Wren (1632–d. 1723) |

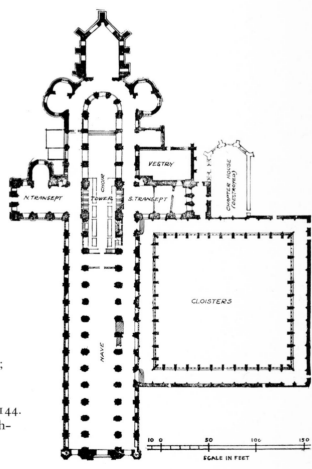

NORWICH *(Holy Trinity)*

See: (Dunwich 631; Elmham 673; Thetford 1070); removed to Norwich 1094.
Foundation: Benedictine Monks 1095–1539.
Pilgrimage: St. William of Norwich, martyr, d. 1144.
Dimensions: length 481 feet (inclusive of thirteenth-century Lady Chapel); width 190 feet; height 83 feet; spire 320 feet.

Building Dates		*Architects*
1096–1120	Choir and transepts	
c. 1121–45	Nave and tower	
1171–73	Completion after fire	
1289–1303	*Chapter-house* (F)	Richard (? Curteys/Ramsey) (1285–90)
1297–1318	Cloister, east walk	John Ramsey (1304–39)
1299–1325	Windows of north nave aisle	John Ramsey
1316–25	Carnary Chapel	John Ramsey
1318–30	St. Ethelbert gate	William Ramsey (1325–d. 1349)
1324–30	Cloister, south walk	William Ramsey
1344–47	Cloister, west walk	
c. 1362–69	Presbytery clerestory	Robert Wodehirst (1351–d. 1401)
1385–1415	Cloister, north walk	Robert Wodehirst
1416–25	Erpingham gate	James Woderofe (1415–51)
1416–30	Cloister, north and west vaults	James Woderofe
1426–50	West front; inserted windows	? James Woderofe
c. 1464–72	Nave vault; spire	Robert Everard (1440–85)
c. 1472–99	Presbytery vault; flying buttresses	Robert Everard
c. 1501–36	Catton screen; Nykke's chantry; transept vaults	
1830–40	Restoration	Anthony Salvin & Edward Blore
1930–32	War Memorial Chapel	Sir Charles Nicholson

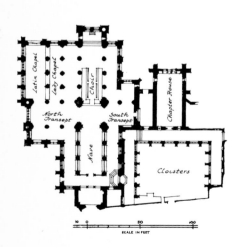

OXFORD *(St. Frideswide; now Christ Church)*

See: (in Oseney Abbey 1542); removed to Christ Church 1546.
Foundation: Nuns 727–1049; Secular Canons 1049–1111; Augustinian Regular Canons 1111–1524.
Pilgrimage: St. Frideswide, d. 735?; tr. 1181, 1289.
Dimensions: length 187 feet; width 111 feet; height 44 feet; spire 144 feet.

Building Dates		Architects
1158–80	Church; tower (lower stage)	
c. 1220–50	Tower (upper stage and spire); chapter-house; Lady Chapel	
c. 1350–55	Latin Chapel	
(1478–1503)	Choir vault; cloisters	? William Orchard (1468–d. 1504)
1525–29	Hall and Tom Quad	John Lebons (1506–37) and Henry Redman (1495–d. 1528)
1869–	Restoration	Sir G. G. Scott
1886	Western porch	G. F. Bodley

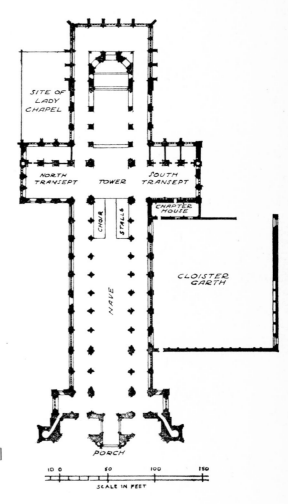

PETERBOROUGH
(St. Peter; now St. Peter, St. Paul and St. Andrew)

See: 1541.
Foundation: Benedictine Monks 654–870; 972–1539.
Pilgrimage: St. Oswald, King and Martyr, d. 641.
Dimensions: length 481 feet; width 206 feet;
    height 81 feet; tower 143 feet.

Building Dates		Architects
1117–c. 1155	Choir and transept	
c. 1155–75	Nave	
c. 1177–93	West transept	
c. 1193–1230	West front	
c. 1220–60	*South Cloister* (F)	
1272–86	*Lady Chapel* (F)	
c. 1335	Central tower	
c. 1375	Galilee porch	
c. 1475	*Cloisters* (F)	? John Kilham (1473–88)
c. 1496–1508	New building	[John Wastell (1485–1515)]
1827–32	Restoration	Edward Blore
1883–86	Central tower rebuilt	J. L. Pearson

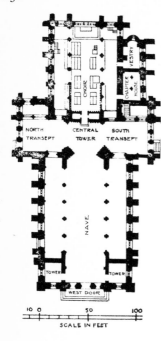

RIPON *(St. Peter and St. Wilfrid)*

See: 1836.
Foundation: Celtic Monks 657–664; Benedictine Monks 664–948;
    Secular Canons before 1066–
Dimensions: length 297 feet; width 156 feet; height 64 feet;
    towers 121 feet.

Building Dates		*Architects*
(c. 1175–81)	Transepts; *nave* (F)	? Arthur Mason (*fl. c.* 1190)
c. 1230–40	West front and towers	
(1288–97)	East end of choir	
c. 1460	Central tower	
c. 1482	Choir, two west bays of south side; pulpitum	
1489–94	Stalls	William Brownfleet (1489–1523)
1502–22	Nave	Christopher Scune (1505–21)
1861–69	Restoration	Sir G. G. Scott

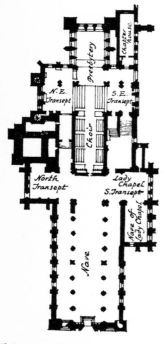

ROCHESTER *(St. Andrew; now Christ and St. Mary)*

See: 604.
Foundation: Secular Canons 604–1076; Benedictine Monks 1076–1540.
Pilgrimage: St. William of Perth, d. 1201.
Dimensions: length 324 feet; width 146 feet; height 55 feet; spire 156 feet.

Building Dates		*Architects*
(1077–1108)	Church (F) including crypt; north tower	
c. 1115–30	Nave	
c. 1150–60	West front	
c. 1200–27	Presbytery; east transept; choir	? Richard Mason
c. 1240–55	North transept	
c. 1280–	South transept; nave, two east bays	
(1319–52)	Chapter-house doorway; central tower	
c. 1470	West window	
c. 1490	Nave clerestory	
c. 1500–12	Lady Chapel	? John Birch
1825–	Restoration	Lewis Nockalls Cottingham
1871–	Restoration	Sir G. G. Scott
1892–	Restoration	J. L. Pearson

ST. ALBANS *(St. Alban)*

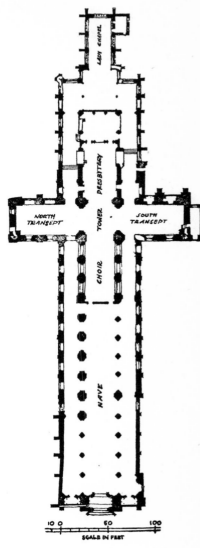

See: 1878.
Foundation: Benedictine Monks 793–1539.
Pilgrimage: St. Alban and St. Amphibalus, d. 303?
Dimensions: length 550 feet; width 191 feet; height 70 feet;
    tower 144 feet.

Building Dates		*Architects*
1077–1115	Norman church and tower	Robert Mason
1195–1214	West front (part)	Hugh Goldcliff
1214–35	West front completed; west bays of nave	
1235–*c.* 1290	Presbytery	
(1260–1326)	Ante-chapel	
c. 1302–08	Shrine of St. Alban	
(1308–26)	Lady Chapel	? William Boyden
1314–	Stalls	Geoffrey Carpenter
1324–27	Nave, five bays south side	Henry Wy
c. 1360–80	Great gatehouse; nave screen	? Henry Yeveley (1353–d. 1400)
(1447)	Tomb of Humphrey Duke of Gloucester	? John Wolvey (1428–d. 1462)
(1476–84)	Reredos	
(1492–1521)	Abbot Ramryge's chantry	
1856–77	Restoration	Sir G. G. Scott
1879–85	Fronts rebuilt; nave restored	Lord Grimthorpe

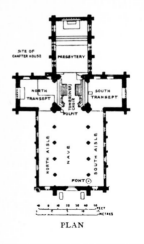

PLAN

ST. ASAPH *(St. Asaph)*

See *c.* 560; refounded 1143.
Foundation: Secular Canons
Dimensions: length 195 feet; width 125 feet; tower 93 feet.

Building Dates		Architects
1284–1352	Rebuilding	
1391–1392	Central tower	Robert Fagan (1391–1414)
1471–1495	Restoration	
c. 1475–1490	Stalls	
c. 1780	Choir rebuilt	
1867–1875	Restoration	Sir George Gilbert Scott

PLAN

ST. DAVIDS *(St. Andrew; now St. David of Wales)*

See: *c.* 550; refounded 1115.
Foundation: Secular Canons.
Pilgrimage: St. David, d. *c.* 601; can. 1120.
Dimensions: length 313 feet; width 144 feet; tower 125 feet.

Building Dates		Architects
1180–(1198)	Nave and west front	
1221–	Presbytery and east crossing	
1248–	Retrochoir	
1296–(1328)	Lady Chapel, etc.	
1324–1347	Rood Screen	
1328–1347	East end altered; Tower (middle stage)	
c. 1470	Stalls	
(1472–1509)	Nave roof	
1509–1522	Central tower (upper stage); Trinity Chapel, fan vault	
1846–	Restoration	
1862–1878	Restoration	Sir George Gilbert Scott

SALISBURY *(St. Mary)*

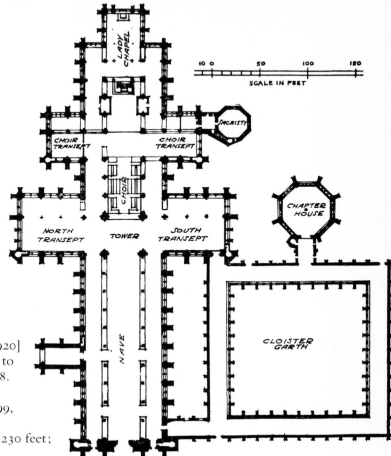

See: (Sherborne 705; Ramsbury [920]
    and Sherborne 1058); removed to
    Old Sarum *c.* 1075; Salisbury 1228.
Foundation: Secular Canons.
Pilgrimage: St. Osmund, bp 1078–99,
    can. 1457.
Dimensions: length 473 feet; width 230 feet;
    height 84 feet; spire 404 feet.

Building Dates		Architects
1220–25	Lady Chapel	(Elias of Dereham); Nicholas of Ely
1225–37	Choir	(Elias of Dereham); Nicholas of Ely
1237–58	Great transept; nave	(Elias of Dereham); Nicholas of Ely
c. 1258–66	West front	Richard Mason (1267)
c. 1263–84	Cloister	Richard Mason
c. 1275–	Chapter-house	Richard Mason
1320–*c.* 1380	Tower and spire	Robert Mason (*c.* 1315–40) and Richard Farleigh (1332–63)
c. 1388–95	? Strainer arches in east transepts	Nicholas Portland
c. 1415–23	? Strainer arches beneath tower	Robert Wayte

1479–	Crossing-vault	Henry Stevens
1787–93	Alterations	James Wyatt (1746–1813)
1863–	Restoration	Sir G. G. Scott

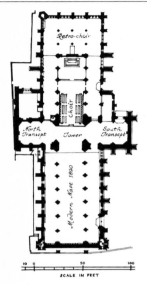

SCALE IN FEET

SOUTHWARK *(St. Mary; now St. Saviour and St. Peter)*

See: 1905.
Foundation: Nuns ?; Secular Canons 852; Augustinian Regular Canons 1106–1539.
Dimensions: length 262 feet; width 130 feet; height 55 feet; tower 163 feet.

Building Dates		Architects
c. 1213–35	Choir and retrochoir	? Richard Mason (1208)
c. 1273–	Transepts; *nave*	
c. 1380–90	*West front*; tower (lower stage)	? Henry Yeveley (1353–d. 1400)
c. 1430–45	South transept altered	
c. 1520	Reredos; tower (top stage)	? Thomas Berty (1501–d. 1555)
1822–35	Restoration	George Gwilt
1889–97	Nave	Sir Arthur Blomfield

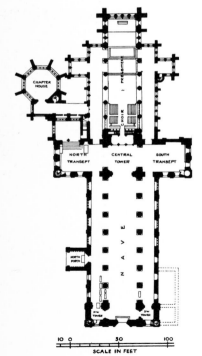

SCALE IN FEET

SOUTHWELL *(St. Mary)*

See: 1884.
Foundation: Secular Canons.
Dimensions: length 318 feet; width 137 feet; height 50 feet; tower 105 feet.

Building Dates		Architects
(1108–50)	Transept and nave	
1234–50	Eastern arm	
c. 1293–1300	Chapter-house	
c. 1320–35	Pulpitum	? Ivo de Raghton
c. 1450	West window	
1851–	Restoration	Ewan Christian

WELLS *(St. Andrew)*

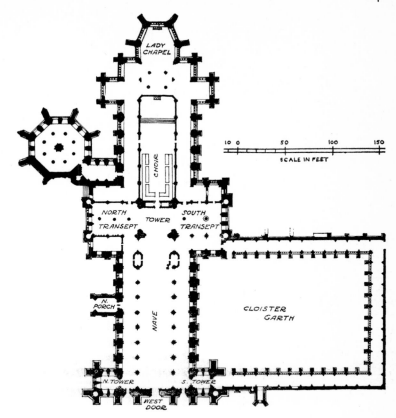

See: 909; removed to Bath 1090; Bath and Wells 1218.
Foundation: Secular Canons.
Dimensions: length 415 feet; width 153 feet; height (choir) 73 feet; tower 182 feet.

Building Dates		Architects
c. 1175–	Choir	
(1192–*c.* 1230)	Transept; nave; north porch	Adam Lock (d. 1229)
c. 1230–60	West front	Thomas Norreys (1229–49)
c. 1255–86	Undercroft of chapter-house	
c. 1286–1306	Chapter-house	
c. 1310–19	Lady Chapel	? Thomas Witney (1316–42)
c. 1315–22	Central tower	? Thomas Witney
c. 1329–45	Retrochoir; choir reconstructed	William Joy (1329–46)
c. 1338–55	'St. Andrew's Arches' under tower	? William Joy
1365–95	South-west tower	William Wynford (1360–1403)

c. 1425–35	North-west tower	
c. 1420–1508	Cloisters (*c.* 1420–24 E. walk (7½ bays); 1425–32 Library over; 1433–57 E. walk (5 bays and angle) and Library over, S. walk (1 bay); *c.* 1460–65 W. walk, N. end; 1465–70 W. walk, completed and S. walk (1 bay); 1490–1508 S. walk (except end bays).	William Smyth William Atwood (1490–1507)
1439–50	Central tower altered	
c. 1475–90	Crossing vault; Sugar's Chapel	William Smyth (*c.* 1460–d. 1490)
1477–88	*Cloister Lady Chapel* (F)	William Smyth
1842–57	Choir and pulpitum altered	Benjamin Ferrey & Anthony Salvin

WINCHESTER
(SS Peter, Paul, Amphibalus and Swithun; now Holy Trinity)

See: (Dorchester, Oxon. 635); removed to
   Winchester 662.
Foundation: Secular Canons 662;
   Benedictine Monks 963–1540.
Pilgrimage: St. Swithun, bp 852–62, tr. 971,
   1093, 1150.
Dimensions: length 554 feet; width 231 feet;
   height 78 feet; tower 140 feet.

Building Dates		*Architects*
1079–93	Crypt; transepts	Hugh Mason (1086)
c. 1108–20	Tower and north and south bays adjoining	
1202–*c.* 1235	Retrochoir and Lady Chapel	Richard (1208); ? Stephen
1308–10	Stalls	William Lyngwode
c. 1315–60	Presbytery	Thomas Witney (1315–42)
c. 1360–	West front with two bays of north aisle and one bay of south aisle	
1394–*c.* 1450	Nave; Wykeham's Chapel	William Wynford (1360–d.1405); Robert Hulle (1400–d. 1442)

c. 1475–85	Reredos	? Walter Nicholl
c. 1490–1500	Lady Chapel: eastern bay and vault	
c. 1520–32	Presbytery: aisles, screens and clerestory; Fox's chantry	Thomas Berty (1501–d. 1555)
1635–40	*Screen* (F); wooden vault of crossing	Inigo Jones (1573–d. 1651)
1905–12	Restoration	Sir Thomas Graham Jackson

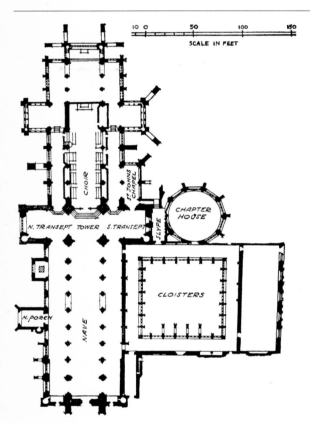

WORCESTER *(Christ and St. Mary)*

See: 680.

Foundation: Secular Canons 680; Benedictine Monks c. 970–1539.

Pilgrimages: St. Oswald, bp. 961–92; St. Wulstan, bp. 1062–95, can. 1203.

Dimensions: length 425 feet; width 147 feet; height 68 feet; tower 196 feet.

Building Dates		*Architects*
1084–92	Crypt	
c. 1120	Chapter-house	
c. 1175	Nave, two western bays	
1224–c. 1269	Choir and retrochoir	Alexander Mason
1317–24	Nave, five east bays on north	William of Shockerwick (*fl.* 1316)
c. 1360–74	Nave, two bays on north and seven on south; tower	John Clyve (1362–92)

1375–95	Vaults of nave and crossing; west front; north porch; east cloister	John Clyve
1386–92	Chapter-house: door, windows, buttresses; vault altered	John Clyve
1404–32	North and south cloisters	
1435–38	West cloister	John Chapman
1502–04	Prince Arthur's chantry chapel	
1857–69	Restoration	W. A. Perkins
1870–74	Restoration	Sir G. G. Scott

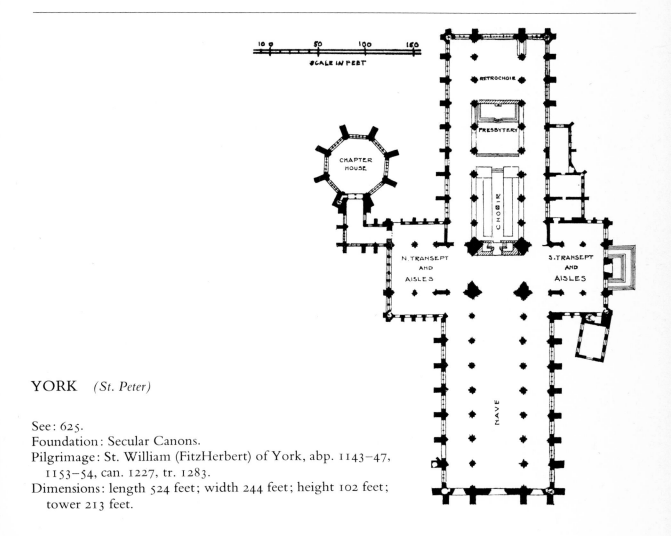

YORK *(St. Peter)*

See: 625.

Foundation: Secular Canons.

Pilgrimage: St. William (FitzHerbert) of York, abp. 1143–47, 1153–54, can. 1227, tr. 1283.

Dimensions: length 524 feet; width 244 feet; height 102 feet; tower 213 feet.

Building Dates		Architects
(1154–81)	Crypt	
c. 1225–34	North transept	
c. 1230–41	South transept	
c. 1265–;		
1286–96	Chapter-house	
1291–1345	Nave; west front	Simon Mason (1301–d. 1322)
c. 1330–38	West window, etc.	Ivo de Raghton (1317–38)
1354–70	*Nave vault* (wood)	Philip Lincoln (1346–75)
1361–72	Lady Chapel: four bays	William Hoton (1351–68);
		Robert Patrington (1369–85)
c. 1385–1400	Choir: five west bays	Hugh Hedon (1394–1408)
1408–23	Central tower	William Colchester (1395–d. 1420)
1432–56	South-west tower	Thomas Pak (1420–41)
1470–74	North-west tower; completion of central tower	William Hyndeley (1466–d. 1505)
1475–1500?	Rood screen	William Hyndeley
1802–11	West front restored	William Shout
1829–42	Choir and nave restored	Sir Robert Smirke
1875–80	South transept restored	George Edmund Street
1887–1911	Restoration	G. F. Bodley

The Descent of Architectural Features

The following tables and charts are intended to show at a glance the historical growth of various types of certain architectural features. In every case the date given approximates to that of design, not necessarily that of construction.

RIBBED VAULTS

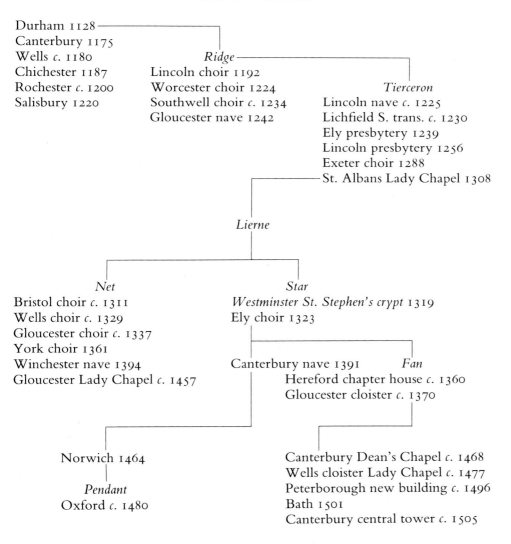

Durham 1128
Canterbury 1175
Wells *c.* 1180
Chichester 1187
Rochester *c.* 1200
Salisbury 1220

Ridge
Lincoln choir 1192
Worcester choir 1224
Southwell choir *c.* 1234
Gloucester nave 1242

Tierceron
Lincoln nave *c.* 1225
Lichfield S. trans. *c.* 1230
Ely presbytery 1239
Lincoln presbytery 1256
Exeter choir 1288
St. Albans Lady Chapel 1308

Lierne

Net
Bristol choir *c.* 1311
Wells choir *c.* 1329
Gloucester choir *c.* 1337
York choir 1361
Winchester nave 1394
Gloucester Lady Chapel *c.* 1457

Star
Westminster St. Stephen's crypt 1319
Ely choir 1323

Canterbury nave 1391   *Fan*
Hereford chapter house *c.* 1360
Gloucester cloister *c.* 1370

Norwich 1464

Pendant
Oxford *c.* 1480

Canterbury Dean's Chapel *c.* 1468
Wells cloister Lady Chapel *c.* 1477
Peterborough new building *c.* 1496
Bath 1501
Canterbury central tower *c.* 1505

GOTHIC EAST FRONTS

Flush	*Projection*	
(Square across aisles)	High East Chapel:	Low East Chapel: Old Sarum *c.* 1115
	Oxford *c.* 1160	
		Chichester 1187
		Hereford *c.* 1190
	Rochester *c.* 1200	
		Winchester 1202
	Worcester 1224	Southwark *c.* 1220
	Southwell *c.* 1234	Salisbury 1220
Ely 1239		*Westminster* 1220
Durham 1242		Norwich 1245
Old St. Paul's 1251		Chester *c.* 1265
Lincoln 1256		Exeter *c.* 1275
Ripon 1288		St. Albans *c.* 1308
Carlisle 1293	Bristol *c.* 1311	Wells *c.* 1310
	Lichfield *c.* 1320	
York 1361		
		Gloucester *c.* 1457
Bath 1501		

Note: Canterbury is in a class by itself, in no way resembling any other cathedral in its eastern termination. Peterborough has a square series of *low* eastern chapels.

WEST FRONTS

No towers	*Towers on Aisle Axes*	*Towers outside Aisles*
	Lincoln *c.* 1074	
	Chester *c.* 1100	
Hereford *c.* 1100[1]	Durham *c.* 1100	
	Chichester *c.* 1125	
	Southwell *c.* 1130	
Rochester *c.* 1150		Old St. Paul's *c.* 1130
Worcester *c.* 1175		(Ely *c.* 1174)[2]
		Peterborough *c.* 1177
		St. Albans *c.* 1195
		Wells *c.* 1230
		(Ripon *c.* 1230)[3]
Salisbury *c.* 1258		(Lincoln W. transept *c.* 1230)
	Lichfield *c.* 1280	
	York 1291	
Exeter 1328		
Winchester *c.* 1360		
	Canterbury 1379	
Gloucester *c.* 1421		
Norwich 1426		
Bath 1501		

The place of the type with outside towers was taken by the horizontal porch-range or screen front, as below.

Screen Fronts and Welcoming Porches

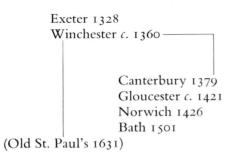

Exeter 1328
Winchester *c.* 1360

Canterbury 1379
Gloucester *c.* 1421
Norwich 1426
Bath 1501

(Old St. Paul's 1631)

[1] Hereford had a single western tower, not at first planned.
[2] Ely has a single tower, with a projecting western transept.
[3] Ripon had no aisles, but a broad nave with three western doors between the towers.

GREAT TOWERS

The number of windows in the main stage is shown in brackets.

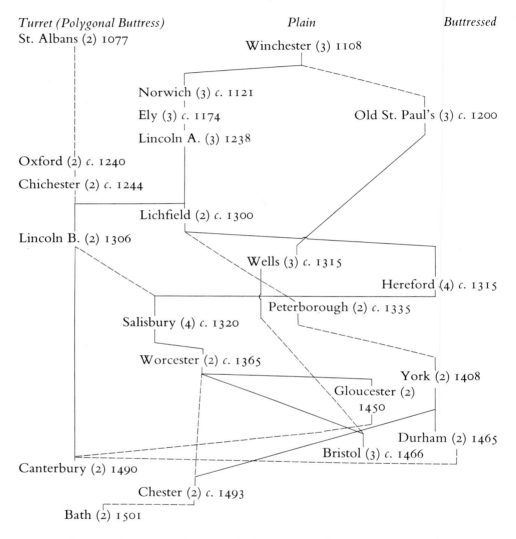

Turret (Polygonal Buttress)   *Plain*   *Buttressed*

St. Albans (2) 1077

Winchester (3) 1108

Norwich (3) *c.* 1121

Ely (3) *c.* 1174

Old St. Paul's (3) *c.* 1200

Lincoln A. (3) 1238

Oxford (2) *c.* 1240

Chichester (2) *c.* 1244

Lichfield (2) *c.* 1300

Lincoln B. (2) 1306

Wells (3) *c.* 1315

Hereford (4) *c.* 1315

Peterborough (2) *c.* 1335

Salisbury (4) *c.* 1320

Worcester (2) *c.* 1365

York (2) 1408

Gloucester (2) 1450

Durham (2) 1465

Bristol (3) *c.* 1466

Canterbury (2) 1490

Chester (2) *c.* 1493

Bath (2) 1501

Note: Influences from outside the cathedral group of towers were strong in some cases, notably at Bath. The later towers are eclectic and not precisely classifiable.

POLYGONAL CHAPTER-HOUSES

The number of sides (or bays) is shown in brackets.

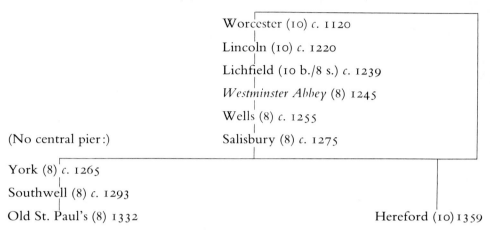

Worcester (10) *c.* 1120

Lincoln (10) *c.* 1220

Lichfield (10 b./8 s.) *c.* 1239

Westminster Abbey (8) 1245

Wells (8) *c.* 1255

(No central pier:)   Salisbury (8) *c.* 1275

York (8) *c.* 1265

Southwell (8) *c.* 1293

Old St. Paul's (8) 1332   Hereford (10) 1359

CLOISTERS

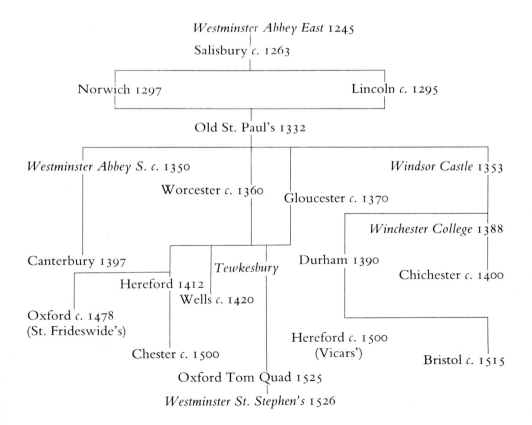

Westminster Abbey East 1245

Salisbury *c.* 1263

Norwich 1297   Lincoln *c.* 1295

Old St. Paul's 1332

Westminster Abbey S. c. 1350   *Windsor Castle* 1353

Worcester *c.* 1360

Gloucester *c.* 1370

Winchester College 1388

Canterbury 1397   *Tewkesbury*   Durham 1390

Hereford 1412   Chichester *c.* 1400

Wells *c.* 1420

Oxford *c.* 1478
(St. Frideswide's)

Chester *c.* 1500   Hereford *c.* 1500
                      (Vicars')   Bristol *c.* 1515

Oxford Tom Quad 1525

Westminster St. Stephen's 1526

Glossary

This short glossary is intended to cover only the essential technical senses of words used in the text; for detailed definitions and diagrams reference should be made to one of the standard glossaries of architecture, such as T. D. Atkinson: *A Glossary of Terms used in English Architecture* (6th ed., 1946).

Abbey A monastery under the governance of an abbot, aided by a lieutenant known as the prior (see Priory).

Ball-Flower A characteristic enrichment of the early fourteenth century, consisting of a globular ball carved with the appearance of an outer skin pierced and folded back in petals.

Bay The vertical compartment between two columns, roof-trusses, buttresses, etc.

Cathedral A church in which a bishop has his throne.

Centering Temporary wooden framework used to support an arch or vault during construction.

Chapter-House A room provided for the meetings of the chapter (of canons or monks) forming the governing body of a cathedral.

Choir Structurally, that part of a church in which the singers have their place; often, though inaccurately, used of the eastern arm. (See Presbytery, Sanctuary.)

Clerestory An upper range of windows.

Crocket A projection, usually of hooked form, from the edges of spires, pinnacles, canopies, etc.

Cusp A pointed projection from the inner surface of an arch, formed by two arcs of small radius.

Diocese The territorial area under the jurisdiction of a bishop.

Fan-Vault A vault whose ribs are spaced at equal angles and have the same curvature.

Flamboyant Flame-shaped tracery, invented in England in the fourteenth century, but mainly used on the Continent during the Middle Ages.

Four-Centred Arch A pointed arch struck from four centres, so that the two upper arcs are of greater radius than those at the springings.

Hall-Church   A church whose aisles are all of the same height and which consequently has neither triforium nor clerestory.

Hammer-Beam   A horizontal cantilever projecting as a bracket in certain roof-trusses.

Hammer-Post   A vertical post supported upon the free end of a hammer-beam.

Lady Chapel   A chapel containing an altar dedicated to the Blessed Virgin Mary; in England often placed beyond the east end of the sanctuary.

Lancet   A tall narrow window with a pointed untraceried head, common from *c*. 1150 to *c*. 1250.

Lantern   A tower with windows admitting light into the church; also, a polygonal top stage of a tower.

Lierne   A vault-rib which does not start from the springing and is not a ridge-rib.

Misericord   A hinged tip-up seat with its edge widened to form a support for its occupants when standing during the services. The under side, exposed when the seat is tipped up, was usually decorated with carving of a symbolic or grotesque character.

Nave   The body of a church, normally to west of the sanctuary, transept and choir.

Ogee   A curve of S-form.

Presbytery   That part of a church reserved for the priests; usually the eastern arm, or the area between the choir and the high altar.

Priory   A monastery under the governance of a prior, but subject to the jurisdiction of the abbot of a superior house elsewhere, or to the bishop in the case of a monastic cathedral.

Pulpitum   A screen at the west end of the choir, and the gallery or loft supported by it, on which the organ was commonly placed.

Retrochoir   Generally that part of the eastern arm lying behind the high altar; sometimes used of an ambulatory lying between the sanctuary and an eastern Lady Chapel.

Ridge-Rib   A horizontal vault-rib running along the crown of a vault.

Rose   A circular window composed of tracery.

Sanctuary   The part of a church containing the high altar; normally in the eastern arm.

Sedilia   Canopied seats in the presbytery for the clergy.

See   The jurisdiction committed to a bishop.

Severy   A bay or compartment, especially of a vault.

Springing   The level bed from which an arch begins.

Stalls   Canopied seats in the choir for the members of a chapter or monastery.

Tierceron   An intermediate vault-rib starting from the springing.

Tracery   Ornamental patternwork pierced through the head of a window; (blind tracery) imitations of tracery not pierced but worked on walls and other surfaces as decoration.

Transept   The cross-arm of a cruciform church, normally running in a north–south direction; each arm of this separately.

Triforium   The intermediate level between a main arcade and a clerestory, corresponding to the aisle roofs and often occupied by a pierced arcading.

Bibliographical note

This includes only a few of the most useful modern books on the subject; others will be found in the list of Abbreviations which follows. An extensive classified bibliography will be found in the author's *Gothic England* (2nd edition, revised, 1948) and a select bibliography with a discussion of historical literature on the cathedrals in *English Cathedrals: A Reader's Guide,* published for the National Book League by the Cambridge University Press (1951). For building in the Middle Ages see L. F. Salzman, *Building in England down to 1540* (1952; enlarged edition 1967); D. Knoop & G. P. Jones, *The Mediaeval Mason* (1933; 3rd edition, revised, 1967); John Harvey, *The Gothic World* (1950; paperback 1969), and *The Master Builders* (1971). On the subject of mediaeval designers see John Harvey, *The Mediaeval Architect* (1972), and for careers of individual master craftsmen mentioned, *English Mediaeval Architects* (1954). The Latin historical sources for the history of the cathedrals down to 1307 are now conveniently accessible in O. Lehmann-Brockhaus, *Schriftquellen zur Kunst in England* (Munich, 1955).

Atkinson, T. D., *English and Welsh Cathedrals,* 1912
Bell, E., ed., *Bell's Cathedral Series*
Bond, F., *The Cathedrals of England and Wales,* 1912
Builder, The, *Cathedrals of England and Wales,* 1894
Bumpus, T. F., *The Cathedrals of England and Wales,* 1929
Cranage, D. H. S., *Cathedrals and how they were built,* 1948
Ditchfield, P. H., *The Cathedrals of Great Britain,* 1931
Pevsner, N., (In *The Buildings of England,* 1951–)
Prior, E. S., *The Cathedral Builders in England,* 1905
Thompson, A. H., *The Cathedral Churches of England,* 1925

Abbreviations used in the notes

A   *Archaeologia* (Society of Antiquaries of London)

AA   *Archaeologia AEliana* (Newcastle upon Tyne)

AB   *Art Bulletin* (The College Art Association of America)

Addleshaw 1954   G. W. O. Addleshaw, *The Development of the Parochial System from Charlemagne (768–814) to Urban II (1088–1099).* (St. Anthony's Hall Publications, no. 6, 1954)

AJ   *Archaeological Journal* (Royal Archaeological Institute)

Allen 1932   F. J. Allen, *The Great Church Towers of England* (Cambridge U. P., 1932)

ANJ   *The Antiquaries Journal* (Society of Antiquaries of London)

Batsford & Fry 1934   H. Batsford & C. Fry, *The Cathedrals of England* (Batsford, 1934, etc.)

Batsford & Fry 1940   —— ——, *The Greater English Church of the Middle Ages* (Batsford, 1940)

Benson 1956   H. Benson, 'Church Orientations and Patronal Festivals', in ANJ, XXXVI, 1956, 205–13

Bilson 1895   J. Bilson, 'On the discovery of some Remains of the Chapter-house of Beverley Minster', in A, LIV, 1895, 425–32

Bilson 1922   ——, 'Durham Cathedral and the Chronology of its Vaults', in AJ, LXXIX, 1922, 101

BMA   *The Burlington Magazine*

Bock 1962   H. Bock, *Der Decorated Style* (Heidelberg, Winter, 1962)

Bond 1906   F. Bond, *Gothic Architecture in England* (Batsford, 1906)

Bond 1913   ——, *An Introduction to English Church Architecture,* 2 vols. (London, Oxford U. P., 1913)

Braunfels 1972   W. Braunfels, *Monasteries of Western Europe* (Thames & Hudson, 1972)

Briggs 1952   M. S. Briggs, *Goths and Vandals* (Constable, 1952)

Burne 1958   R. V. H. Burne, *Chester Cathedral* (S.P.C.K., 1958)

Cave 1948   C. J. P. Cave, *Roof Bosses in Medieval Churches* (Cambridge U. P., 1948)

Clapham 1952   A. Clapham, *Whitby Abbey: Official Guidebook* (H. M. S. O., 1952)

Cobb 1942   G. Cobb, *The Old Churches of London* (Batsford, 1942; 3rd ed., 1948)

Cockerell 1846   C. R. Cockerell, 'William of Wykeham', in *Proceedings of the Archaeological Institute at Winchester in 1845* (Longman, 1846)

Conant 1959   K. J. Conant, *Carolingian and Romanesque Architecture 800 to 1200* (Harmondsworth, Penguin, 1959; 2nd ed., 1966)

Conant 1963   ——, 'Medieval Academy Excavations at Cluny, ix: Systematic Dimensions in the Buildings', in S, XXXVIII, 1963, 1–45

Cook 1947   G. H. Cook, *Mediaeval Chantries and Chantry Chapels* (Phoenix House, 1947)

Cook 1955   ——, *Old St. Paul's Cathedral* (Phoenix House, 1955)

Cook 1959   ——, *English Collegiate Churches of the Middle Ages* (Phoenix House, 1959)

Cordingley 1933   R. A. Cordingley, 'Norman Decoration in Durham Cathedral', in AA, 4th Series, X, 1933

Cordingley 1955   ——, 'Cathedral Innovations – James Wyatt, Architect at Durham Cathedral, 1795–97', in TAMS, New Series, III, 1955, 31–55

CPL   *Calendar of Papal Letters*

Creswell 1958   K. A. C. Creswell, *A Short Account of Early Muslim Architecture* (Harmondsworth, Penguin, 1958)

Creswell 1969   ——, *Early Muslim Architecture,* vol. I, 2nd ed. (Oxford, Clarendon Press, 1969)

Crossley 1935   F. H. Crossley, *The English Abbey* (Batsford, 1935)

CYS   Canterbury and York Society (publications)

Davis 1962   R. H. C. Davis, 'Brixworth and Clofesho', in JBAA, 3rd Series, XXV, 1962, 71

Dimock 1860   J. F. Dimock, *Metrical Life of St Hugh, Bishop of Lincoln* (Lincoln, W. & B. Brooke, 1860)

Doursther 1840   H. Doursther, *Dictionnaire Universel des Poids et Mesures* (1840; reprint Amsterdam, Meridian, 1965)

Drinkwater 1956   N. Drinkwater, 'Hereford Cathedral: the Chapter House', in AJ, CXII, 1956, 61–74

Edwards 1949   K. Edwards, *The English Secular Cathedrals in the Middle Ages* (Manchester U. P., 1949)

Esposito 1960   M. Esposito, *Itinerarium Symonis Semeonis ab Hybernia ad Terram Sanctam* (Dublin, Institute for Advanced Studies, 1960)

Evans 1938   J. Evans, *The Romanesque Architecture of the Order of Cluny* (Cambridge U. P., 1938)

Evans 1950   ——, *Cluniac Art of the Romanesque Period* (Cambridge U. P., 1950)

Frankl 1945   P. Frankl, 'The Secret of the Mediaeval Masons', in AB, XXVII, 1945

Frankl 1960   ——, *The Gothic: Literary Sources and Interpretations . . .* (Princeton, N. J., Princeton U. P., 1960)

Franklin 1958   J. Franklin, *The Cathedrals of Italy* (Batsford, 1958)

Gardner 1952   A. Gardner, *The Lincoln Angels* (Lincoln Minster Pamphlets, 1st Series, No. 6, 1952)

Gilyard-Beer 1958   R. Gilyard-Beer, *Abbeys – An Introduction to the Religious Houses of England and Wales* (H. M. S. O., 1958)

Goodwin 1971   G. Goodwin, *A History of Ottoman Architecture* (Thames & Hudson, 1971)

Graham 1947   R. Graham, 'An Appeal about 1175 for the Building Fund of St Paul's Cathedral Church', in JBAA, 3rd Series, X, 1945–47, 73–6

Hart 1863   W. H. Hart, ed., *Historia et Cartularium Monasterii Sancti Petri Gloucestriae,* 3 vols. (Rolls Series, 1863–7)

Harvey &c 1910   W. Harvey, W. R. Lethaby & others, *The Church of the Nativity at Bethlehem* (Byzantine Research Fund, 1910)

Harvey 1935   ——, *Structural Survey of the Church of the Nativity at Bethlehem* (London, Oxford U. P., 1935)

Harvey & Harvey 1938   W. Harvey & J. H. Harvey, 'Recent Discoveries at the Church of the Nativity, Bethlehem', in A, LXXXVII, 1938, 7–17

Harvey 1949   J. H. Harvey, *Dublin: a Study in Environment* (Batsford, 1949; revised ed., S. R. Publishers, 1972)

Harvey 1950   ——, *The Gothic World 1100–1600: a Survey of Architecture and Art* (Batsford, 1950; paperback, Harper Colophon, 1969)

Harvey 1954   ——, *English Mediaeval Architects: a Biographical Dictionary down to 1550* (Batsford, 1954)

Harvey 1957   ——, 'The Masons of Westminster Abbey', in AJ, CXIII, 1957, 82–101

Harvey 1957 (2)   ——, *The Cathedrals of Spain* (Batsford, 1957)

Harvey 1958   ——, 'Had Winchester Cathedral a central Spire?', in WCR, No. 27, 1958, 9–13

Harvey 1961   ——, 'The Architects of St George's Chapel', I, in RSG, IV, No. 2, 1961, 48–55

Harvey 1962   ——, 'The Origin of the Perpendicular Style', in E. M. Jope, ed., *Studies in Building History* (Odhams, "1961"), 1962, 134–65

Harvey 1968   ——, 'The Origins of Gothic Architecture: Some Further Thoughts', in ANJ, XLVIII, part i, 1968, 87–99

Harvey 1969   ——, 'The Tracing Floor in York Minster', in RYM, XL for 1968, 1969, 9–13

Harvey 1969 (2)   ——, *William Worcestre: Itineraries* (Latin text with English translation, Oxford Medieval Texts, 1969)

Harvey 1971   ——, *The Master Builders* (Thames & Hudson, 1971)

Harvey 1971 (2)   ——, 'Richard II and York', in F. R. H. du Boulay & C. M. Barron, edd., *The Reign of Richard II* (Athlone Press, 1971), 202–17

Harvey 1972   ——, *The Mediaeval Architect* (Wayland, 1972)

Harvey 1972 (2)   ——, *Conservation of Buildings* (John Baker, 1972)

Hayter 1970   W. Hayter, *William of Wykeham – Patron of the Arts* (Chatto & Windus, 1970)

Heyman 1966   J. Heyman, 'The Stone Skeleton', in IJSS, II, 1966, 249–79

Hill 1948   J. W. F. Hill, *Medieval Lincoln* (Cambridge U. P., 1948)

Hills 1871   G. M. Hills, 'The Architectural History of Hereford Cathedral', in JBAA, XXVII, 1871, 46–84, 496–513

HKW   *The History of the King's Works,* ed. H. M. Colvin (H. M. S. O., 1963)

Howgrave-Graham 1948   R. P. Howgrave-Graham, 'Westminster Abbey, the sequence and dates of the transepts and nave', in JBAA, 3rd Series, XI, 1948, 60–78

Howgrave-Graham 1959   ——, *The Cathedrals of France* (Batsford, 1959)

Idries Shah 1964   Sayed Idries Shah, *The Sufis* (1964; Cape paperback, 1971)

IJSS   *International Journal of Solids Structures*

Innocent 1916   C. F. Innocent, *The Development of English Building Construction* (1916; Newton Abbot, David & Charles, 1971)

Jackson & Fletcher 1961   E. D. C. Jackson & E. G. M. Fletcher, 'Excavations at Brixworth, 1958', in JBAA, 3rd Series, XXIV, 1961, 1–15

JBAA   *Journal* of the British Archaeological Association

Kendrick 1898   A. F. Kendrick, *The Cathedral Church of Lincoln* (Bell, 1899)

Knoop & Jones 1933   D. Knoop & G. P. Jones, *The Mediaeval Mason* (Manchester U. P., 1933; revised 1967)

Lang 1956   J. Lang, *Rebuilding St Paul's after the Great Fire of London* (Oxford U. P., 1956)

Leach 1899   A. F. Leach, *A History of Winchester College* (Duckworth, 1899)

Leach 1910   ——, 'Schools', in *Encyclopaedia Britannica,* 11th ed., 1910, vol. 24, 359–72

Lethaby 1906   W. R. Lethaby, *Westminster Abbey and the Kings' Craftsmen* (Duckworth, 1906)

Lethaby 1925   ——, *Westminster Abbey Re-examined* (Duckworth, 1925)

MA   *Mediaeval Archaeology* (Society for Medieval Archaeology)

Malden 1944   R. H. Malden, *The Growth, Building and Work of a Cathedral Church* (Oxford U. P., 1944)

Marshall 1951   G. Marshall, *Hereford Cathedral: its Evolution and Growth* (Worcester, Littlebury, 1951)

Menéndez Pidal 1941   R. Menéndez Pidal, *Poesía árabe y poesía europea* (Buenos Aires, Espasa Calpe, 1941)

Nicholson 1937   C. B. Nicholson, *England's Greater Churches* (Batsford, 1937; 3rd ed., 1949)

Oswald 1939   A. Oswald, 'Canterbury Cathedral – the Nave and its Designer', in BMA, LXXV, 1939, 221–8

Panofsky 1946   E. Panofsky, *Abbot Suger on the Abbey Church of St-Denis* (Princeton, N. J., Princeton U. P., 1946)

Parker 1858   J. H. Parker, *The Medieval Architecture of Chester* (J. H. & J. Parker, 1858)

Parker 1871   ——, 'On the English Origin of Gothic Architecture', in A, XLIII, 1871, 73

Pevsner 1945   N. Pevsner, *The Leaves of Southwell* (Harmondsworth, Penguin, 1945)

Prior 1900   E. S. Prior, *A History of Gothic Art in England* (Bell, 1900)

RCC   *Report* of the Friends of Canterbury Cathedral

Remnant 1969   G. L. Remnant, *A Catalogue of Misericords in Great Britain* (Oxford, Clarendon Press, 1969)

Rigold 1963   S. E. Rigold, 'The Anglian Cathedral of North Elmham, Norfolk', in MA, VI–VII, 1962–63, 67–108

RSG   *Report* of the Society of the Friends of St George's . . . Chapel, Windsor Castle

RYM   *Report* of the Friends of York Minster

S   *Speculum* – A Journal of Mediaeval Studies (Mediaeval Academy of America)

Salzman 1952   L. F. Salzman, *Building in England down to 1540* (Oxford, Clarendon Press, 1952; revised, 1967)

Saxl 1946   F. Saxl, 'Lincoln Cathedral: the Eleventh-century Design for the West Front', in AJ, CIII, 1946, 105

Shelby 1961   L. R. Shelby, 'Medieval Masons' Tools: The Level and Plumb Rule', in TAC, II, 1961, 127–30

Shelby 1965   ——, 'Medieval Masons' Tools, ii: Compass and Square', in TAC, VI, 1965, 236–48

Smith 1943   R. A. L. Smith, *Canterbury Cathedral Priory: a study in monastic administration* (Cambridge U. P., 1943)

Stone 1955   L. Stone, *Sculpture in Britain: the Middle Ages* (Harmondsworth, Penguin, 1955)

TAMS   *Transactions* of the Ancient Monuments Society

Tanner & Clapham 1933   L. E. Tanner & A. W. Clapham, 'Recent Discoveries in the Nave of Westminster Abbey', in A, LXXXIII, 1933, 227–36

Taylor & Taylor 1965   H. M. Taylor & J. Taylor, *Anglo-Saxon Architecture* (Cambridge U. P., 1965)

Urry 1965   W. Urry, 'Cardinal Morton and the Angel Steeple', in RCC, No. 38, 1965, 18–24, 29

Vallance 1947   A. Vallance, *Greater English Church Screens* (Batsford, 1947)

Vallery-Radot 1928   J. Vallery-Radot, *L'Eglise de la Trinité de Fécamp* (Paris, H. Laurens, 1928)

VCH   *Victoria County History*

WCR   *Winchester Cathedral Record* (Friends of Winchester Cathedral)

Webb 1956   G. Webb, *Architecture in Britain: the Middle Ages* (Harmondsworth, Penguin, 1956)

Zarnecki 1953   G. Zarnecki, *Later English Romanesque Sculpture, 1140–1210* (Tiranti, 1953)

Zarnecki 1963   ——, *Romanesque Sculpture at Lincoln Cathedral* (Lincoln Minster Pamphlets, 2nd Series, No. 2, 1963)

Zarnecki 1972   ——, *The Monastic Achievement* (Thames & Hudson, 1972)

Notes to the text

References are given only for matters of importance not readily discoverable in the works mentioned in the Bibliographical Note (above, page 254).

page INTRODUCTION

19 Cathedrals – the best short introduction to the subject is Malden 1944; for the greater churches generally see Batsford & Fry 1940; Nicholson 1937; Crossley 1935; Gilyard-Beer 1958; Cook 1959. The parish-church cathedrals are included in Batsford & Fry 1934. Westminster Abbey – the classic studies are still Lethaby 1906 and Lethaby 1925, but cf Howgrave-Graham 1948, Harvey 1957
Secular cathedrals – Edwards 1949

20 Monastic cathedrals – Smith 1943
Cathedrals of Henry VIII – for a typical case see Burne 1958
Coventry – for the old cathedral see B. Hobley and M. W. Lambert in *Transactions* of the Birmingham and Warwickshire Archaeological Society, vol. 84, 1971, 45–139

21 Confucius – *Analects,* VII, xx
European cathedrals – Harvey 1950, Harvey 1957 (2), Franklin 1958, Howgrave-Graham 1959

24 Gothic sources – Harvey 1968; Harvey 1972, 46–52, 155–7

28 Monastic cathedrals – cf Braunfels 1972, 153–74; Zarnecki 1972

30 Spain – Harvey 1957 (2)

36 Restoration – Briggs 1952; cf Harvey 1972 (2), 173–80

37 English Gothic progress – Heyman 1966, 250

CHAPTER ONE

38 Organization – Knoop & Jones 1933, chapter 1; Architect – Harvey 1972

39 Early cathedrals – Conant 1959, 8

40 Parishes – Addleshaw 1954

41 Norman Westminster Abbey – Tanner & Clapham 1933
Coutances – Harvey 1972, 59–60

42 Collaboration – Harvey 1972, 57, 73–4, 78; Santiago – for an English version see Harvey 1972, 232–6

45 Abingdon Abbey – Salzman 1952, 244–5; St Denis – Panofsky 1946, 94–7
46 Great churches – Conant 1959
47 Cluny – ibid, 142
    Barbastro – Menéndez Pidal 1941, 33–5
49 Area of supports – Conant 1959, 96; Prior 1900, 98, 107–9
50 St Mary Aldermary – Cobb 1942, 73 note; cf Harvey 1972, figs. 49, 50

CHAPTER TWO

52 Spires – see Chapter III (pp. 77–80) and notes thereto
    Honorius of Autun – for extracts in translation, see Harvey 1972, 225–7
    Proportion – Conant 1963
53 Sufis – Idries Shah 1964, 174, 190, 372, 399
    Milan Cathedral – Cockerell 1846, 33–7; Frankl 1945; Secrecy – Harvey 1972, 102–4
54 Organization – ibid, 137–50 'Constitutions' – for a complete modernized text see Harvey 1972, 191–207
56 Canterbury – ibid, 210
57 Education of architects – ibid, 87–100
58 Sculpture – Harvey 1954, 324
59 Construction – Innocent 1916; cf Harvey 1972 (2)
    Measures – Doursther 1840
60 Orientation – Benson 1956
61 Tracing house – Harvey 1972, 114–16
    Foundation stones – Salzman 1952, 87, 380–1; Tools – ibid, 330–48; Shelby 1961; Shelby 1965
62 Bench work – Cordingley 1933; Scaffolding and plant – Innocent 1916, 125–6; Salzman 1952, 318–29; Harvey 1950, 15–18
63 Building season – Harvey 1962, 154 note 10; Salzman 1952, 58–60, 226–7
    Impressment – Knoop & Jones 1933, 80–5
    Centering – Salzman 1952, 320–1; Harvey 1972, 106–7; Leadwork – Salzman 1952, 262–6
64 Holidays – Knoop & Jones 1933, 106–8; Salzman 1952, 78–80

CHAPTER THREE

72 Bethlehem – Harvey &c 1910; Harvey 1935; Harvey & Harvey 1938
74 Square chevet – Bond 1913, i, 126–32; Polygonal chapter-houses – Bilston 1895; Prior 1900, 318–20
79 Durham spire – Cordingley 1955, 47–9; Winchester – Harvey 1958
80 Lübeck – altarpiece of the Nikolaikirche at Reval (Tallinn), by Hermen Rode
    Areas – Prior 1900, 33–5
    Piers – ibid, 98, 108
82 Appeals – Graham 1947
83 Tracing floors – Harvey 1962, 164; Harvey 1969; Harvey 1971, 33; Harvey 1972, 98, 114–16

CHAPTER FOUR

87 Saxon churches – Taylor & Taylor 1965
    North Elmham – Webb 1956, 20–1; Rigold 1963; Brixworth – Jackson &
    Fletcher 1961; Davis 1962
88 Arculf – Harvey &c 1910, 57–8
    Mosques – Cresswell 1969; Creswell 1958; Goodwin 1971
94 Grid plan – Conant 1963; Harvey 1972, 122
96 Raoul Glaber – Migne, *Patrologia Latina*, CXLII, col. 710

CHAPTER FIVE

98   Cluniac art – Evans 1938; Evans 1950
113 Rochester – Zarnecki 1953, 39, 59
114 Lincoln – Saxl 1946; Zarnecki 1963
     Chesterton – G. K. Chesterton, *A Miscellany of Men* (1912), 208–13

CHAPTER SIX

118 Durham – Bilson 1922
120 Dublin – Harvey 1949, 103; Canterbury – Harvey 1972, 210–15
124 Lincoln – Bond 1906, 109–13; cf Parker 1871; Kendrick 1898, 14–18; Hill
     1948, 113
130 Worcestre – Harvey 1969 (2)

CHAPTER SEVEN

141 Sedding – *Transactions* of the St. Paul's Ecclesiological Society, I, 44; Naturalistic
     forms – Pevsner 1945; Stone 1955, 138–41
143 Lincoln angels – Gardner 1952
147 Thomas Witney – Harvey 1972, 133–6; Exeter – for date of 1288 see Harvey
     1969 (2), 117
155 Weldon – CYS, VII, 91–3
157 Raghton – Harvey 1972, 79–80
158 Lichfield spires – Esposito 1960, 24–5
165 English influence on Germany – Bock 1962

CHAPTER EIGHT

171 Perpendicular – Harvey 1962
175 Hereford chapter-house – Drinkwater 1956
177 Welcoming porch – cf Harvey 1961, 51
181 Wykeham's works – Hayter 1970
182 Canterbury and Westminster – Oswald 1939
188 Somerset towers – Allen 1932
195 Canterbury, Bell Harry tower – Urry 1965

CHAPTER NINE

199 St Paul's – Cook 1955, 81–4; Lang 1956
200 Church restorers – cf Harvey 1972 (2), 174–7

201 Roof-bosses – Cave 1948
     Misericords – Remnant 1969
     Screens – Vallance 1947
205 Chantries – Cook 1947
207 St. Hugh – Dimock 1860, 32–7; this architectural section of the poem is translated in Harvey 1972, 236–9
208 Schools – Leach 1899, 9–17; Leach 1910, 361–8

APPENDIX

210 Monastic cathedrals – Braunfels 1972
211 Huy – Harvey 1950, 89; fig. 169; Windsor – Harvey 1961, 52; fig. 1
212 Dome of the Rock – Creswell 1958, 17–34; Canterbury – Webb 1956, 17–18; fig. 9; Dijon – Conant 1959, 84–7; fig. 27
     Heavenly Jerusalem – Honorius of Autun in Migne, *Patrologia Latina*, CLXXII, cap xli (translation in Harvey 1972, 227); Creswell 1958, 161–73; figs. 31–3; cf Frankl 1960, 179–93; Central pillar – Frankl 1960, 170
213 Fécamp – Vallery-Radot 1928, 72–4; 39, 79; York – CPL 1404–15, 137–8; Harvey 1971 (2) 207–14
     Whitby – Clapham 1952, 6; plate facing 8; Chester – Parker 1858, St. John's Church, plates facing 1, 8
214 Lichfield – Esposito 1960, 24–5; VCH, *Staffordshire*, III, 149–50, 157–9
     Gloucester – Hart 1863, I, 44–5; Hereford – CPL 1305–42, 196
215 Date of tower – Marshall 1951, 102–7
216 Waltham – HKW, I, 88; fig. 16

Index

Architects and artists are listed separately after the main index. Numerals in *italics* are principal references; those in **heavy type** refer to the figure numbers of illustrations or (with **p.**) to the pages on which line-blocks occur.

INDEX OF ARCHITECTS AND ARTISTS

Business
and
Preservation

by Raynor M. Warner,
Sibyl McCormac Groff
and Ranne P. Warner
with Sandi Weiss

editor: Frank Stella

**A survey of
business conservation
of buildings and
neighborhoods**

Business
and
Preservation

An INFORM Book

INFORM is a nonprofit, tax-exempt organization, established in 1973, which conducts research on the impact of American corporations on the environment, employees, and consumers. INFORM publishes books, condensed reports, and newsletters. These seek to clarify and define the nature of some of today's most serious corporate social problems. They describe and evaluate programs and practices that industries could adopt to improve future social performance. INFORM's program is supported by subscriptions and contributions from foundations, corporations, financial institutions, universities, government agencies, and concerned individuals.

This project is supported by a grant from the National Endowment for the Arts in Washington, D.C., a federal agency.

Cover photograph: Tom Crane, Haverford, Pennsylvania. Courtesy of Architectural Resources Cambridge, Inc.

All photographs unless otherwise credited were provided by the company profiled.

INFORM
25 Broad Street
New York, N.Y. 10004
212/425-3550

ISBN 0-918780-07-1 (hardcover)
ISBN 0-918780-08-X (paperback)

Library of Congress #77-90918

Produced for INFORM by the Publishing Center for Cultural Resources, New York City. Manufactured in the United States of America.

Contents

This book could not have been written ten years ago, and it would not have been written five years ago. It expresses a truth become tolerable. By the time it goes into its second printing, what is now tolerable may have become self-evident. We are so quick to adapt to changed circumstances that we may not recognize how much has changed and how rapidly. The peril is that, having adapted, we may fail to see that the tide of events still swells, and that what has become easy is already insufficient.

Therefore, it may be well to note why urban and industrial preservation is beginning to seem a necessary response to economic reality, and also why it has not been so in past decades. Recycling buildings may be as much an expression of the 1980s as disposable clothing and planned obsolescence were of the 1950s and 1960s. We are no more pious than our predecessors; we are responding to a different normalcy. Let us review the record and then ask whether mere adaptation to the obtrusive present is enough to prepare us for the future.

I was born while the nation was keeping cool with Coolidge. Construction costs had been constant for fifty years. A building could be put up for the same dollars in 1926 as in 1876. There was no need to explain in 1926 what kind of dollars you were spending. For half a century, "nominal" dollars had equaled "real dollars" for houses or factories. Indeed, inflation for all goods and services averaged less than one-half percent per year for forty years until World War I. That was my father's experience.

My grandfather had learned economics during a long deflationary boom during which most of the downtown area in my hometown was built. St. Paul, Minnesota, like Chicago and most other places built around railroad depots, tripled its size in the 1880s, while construction costs declined steadily. Logs jammed the rivers on the way to the mills, wheat glutted the elevators, labor was cheap, and there were plenty of eager replacements coming ashore. Land? Some land was still $2 an acre along James J. Hill's shiny new rails. (Most was more, but still very cheap by present standards.)

Although Frederick Jackson Turner told us that the frontier was closing in 1893, more land was homesteaded after that date than before it, and the frontier could be defined as the edge of the unused, plentiful and cheap. The common experience of my parents and grandparents was profusion and steady prices. On the micro-economic level, there were privation and hard work, bleached bones on the prairie, and squalor in the immigrant slums, but speaking in macro-economic terms (as we are wont to do in short introductions like this) there was plenty for Cal to be cool about.

The Depression came as an abrupt deflationary shock. Bond holders in corporations which stayed solvent made fortunes, but as the NRA told us, the rest of the nation suffered from glut: too much unemployed labor, and too many goods. The War of 1941 produced a recovery from that Depression. Its shortages were perceived as sufficiently abnormal to permit those at home a little easy heroism in self-denial. Profusion was still our natural setting, and we feared a post-war depression because we did not know what to do with profusion. Wartime self-restraint was an economic necessity because government expenditure, financed by debt and taxes, accompanied a program of government employment on a scale which made the WPA seem trifling. The money, of course, went for what might be called single-purpose goods, more quickly depreciable than usual, and the work was perilous but (again speaking from the perspective of macro-economics) we had always been an unusually wasteful people, and we were just wasting more than usual.

After the War, there was no Depression, but there was, after a while, a second amazingly profusive aberration in our economic history: the capital glut which seemed to condition the normalcy of the middle classes of my generation. Our parents and grandparents grew up with cheap labor and steady prices. We grew up with the cheapest capital in the history of American capitalism. The postwar boom had such enormous momentum that a businessman selling stock could sell a dollar of current earnings (and, of course, the hope of capital gains) to a new shareholder for twice as much in 1958 as he could in 1948, and five years later, buyers of common stock on the New York Stock Exchange were willing to pay twice as much—again—for a dollar of current earnings.

During the 1950s, the large corporations were still paying rates of interest for borrowed money less than a third of those prevailing today.* That meant, of course, that even though construction costs had begun to escalate in the late 1920s, it was easy to take in partners (new equity owners) for the purpose of building new plants. It is possible, although the figures are slippery, that the decline of the cost of capital just about offset the increase of the cost of construction between 1926 and 1966.

What has all this to do with this book? The discovery of preservation is natural to my generation because we live in a time of steadily rising costs and expensive capital. We owe our predecessors some graceful acknowledgment that their normalcy is no longer accessible to us. We are, therefore, free to adapt to circumstances which have now prevailed long enough for them to become normalcy to us.

There are examples in this book of action which anticipates necessity by so wide a space as to be remarkable. Why remarkable? A businessman operating to protect his shareholders cannot go too far ahead of what appears likely to be required of him lest he be caught by changes of economic climate or of governmental requirements which turn a good plan into an embarrassing anachronism.

Yet, the only greater danger than planning too far in advance is refusing to plan far enough. As the corporate managers described in this book looked about at the inventory of buildings which they could include in their plans, they had to make computations about alternative ways of housing their plants. They knew what an existing building would cost, and they could get respectable estimates of what conversion would cost. All they could know about new facilities was that they would go up in cost the longer their construction was delayed.

Computations produced more preservation, I'll bet, than sentiment did. And having written more books and articles about architectural history than I like to count, and having given more lectures about historic

---

*Computing the effect of money cost, of interest, upon construction is a dicey business. But if one could imagine zero interest cost—a Swiss instance, perhaps—that would differ from the 12 percent construction loans of 1974 atop what we *now* think to be an underlying inflation rate of 6 percent and differ again from 5 percent construction loans atop a 3 percent inflation rate of earlier years.

buildings than I can remember, I am fully prepared to put my faith in computation as the better hope for the future than moral suasion or aesthetic admonition.

When it makes economic sense to reuse an existing plant, there is presented an opportunity to do the job well. When among one's choices for reuse there are ugly buildings and handsome buildings, at nearly the same price, one will be likely to use a handsome one, as several case studies in this book demonstrate. Solving an aesthetic and economic puzzle simultaneously is fun, like Chinese checkers. And there are good reasons for doing so.

There are very few corporate managers who are indifferent to the multiple constituencies who surround them: stockholders, workers, customers, bankers, suppliers, and journalists. When the economics are close to right, it is pleasant to have something good to report.

Businessmen occupy places of power quite briefly, and they know it. The long progression up the corporate Jungle Gym consumes decades, for most people, and when the summit is reached, the person who becomes boss looks about to make a mark while he may; and for interesting ways to make that mark. This is as true in a corporation as it was in the feudality or the Renaissance church, in Pharaoh's Egypt, or in any People's Republic. And throughout human society, a sound economic decision may be to create something beautiful, or save something beautiful, which may be associated with the boss for many years. It may be his best way of proclaiming his survival as well as his taste.

I do not mean to discredit this impulse. It is hardly derogatory to classify anyone with Lorenzo de'Medici, Urban II, Cheops, the Earl of Carlisle, Louis XIV, or Pericles. What this book adds to the earnest work of architectural historians, and to the education which has refined the taste of those who hold economic power, is a series of examples of sound business arguments for the cause of old buildings.

There are, of course, less numerical arguments to be made. We could speak of used buildings as constructed natural resources, to be regarded with as much, or even more, reverence as natural resources. We would emphasize the fact that the environment for most people is an urban environment, not a bucolic or sylvan one. Bombed-out and brutalized neighborhoods are inhabited by more people than bosky dells, and we should use public policy to make it easier, not harder, for the individual local choices of businessmen to serve these people.

Finally, I must express a personal apprehension which I cannot support with any elaborate statistical base. The largest unknown cost of future construction is energy or, to be more precise, oil. We have adjusted to a large single price increase in oil and are adjusting to the syphoning off of consumer disposal income from industrial countries toward producing countries. But there are good economists who say that we are growing more slowly, as an economy, than in the past.

Slower growth coupled with intractable unemployment (possibly oc-casioned by the gap between the requirements of high technology and the attainments of popular education, possibly by deeper causes related to the nature of human services actually required by modern, mechanized society) constitute heavy weights on a society already burdened by a need to buy much of its energy from others. An economy which has an oil leak, out of which flows consumer purchasing power, *and* which grows slowly, cannot afford waste.

This book suggests that we are beginning to learn how to diminish our waste of old buildings: to return our empty bottles. We are going to have to learn these lessons and a lot more. The corporate managers who created these test cases can take satisfaction in having led the way through what was desirable in the present toward what will be necessary in the future.

Roger G. Kennedy
Vice President
The Ford Foundation

Acknowledgments

The authors and editor of this INFORM study would like to express their gratitude to the scores of friends, advisors, preservationists, community leaders, and businesspeople whose cooperation helped make the project possible. We are particularly indebted to INFORM's director, Joanna Underwood, for her attention, support, and enthusiasm. We'd also like to thank Jean Halloran, INFORM's editorial director, for her dedication to the task of completing this book, as well as for the confidence she showed in us, and the fresh perspective and thoughtful analysis she brought to the review of our efforts.

We would like to express our appreciation to Garry Tanner for his research efforts, particularly in the area of residential revitalization; to Michael Friedman for his research on Bird & Son, Tremont Nail, and Harbridge House; and to copyeditor Dan Smullyan for his patient contribution to making our text more lucid. Special thanks to typists Mary Ferguson, Bob Szwed, John Klingberg, and Marsha Archer, both for their care in creating the comprehensible from the chaotic, and for their editorial suggestions and comments. We are grateful for the help of Sheron Milliner, Dick Griffin, and Nancy Stella for preparing the glossary and footnotes; and beyond these specific contributions, we deeply appreciate the moral support of the entire INFORM staff.

The authors and editor would like to express their appreciation to the members of the advisory board: especially to Roger Webb, President of Architectural Heritage Foundation in Boston who, along with providing expert guidance, also donated office space to carry out much of the research and writing; to Martin Cleary, Vice President, Teachers Insurance and Annuity Association; to Professor James Marston Fitch of the Columbia University School of Architecture; to Ronald Lee Fleming, Executive Director of Vision, Inc.; to Dun Gifford, a real estate developer in Boston; to Roger Lang, Director of Restoration and Renovation Services, Perry, Dean, Stahl and Rogers; to Theodore H. M. Prudon, restoration architect (whose analysis and advice were especially helpful), Ezra D. Ehrencrantz & Associates; to Lynda Simmons, Vice President, Phipps Houses; and to Arthur Ziegler, President, Pittsburgh History and Landmarks Foundation.

Many others assisted this study in a variety of ways. We are particularly grateful to Gideon Chagy, Vice President, Business Committee for the Arts; Robertson Collins, Board member, National Trust for Historic Preservation; and Kip Forbes, Editor, *19th Century* magazine, for their advice and assistance. Special thanks for help in the area of residential revitalization must go to Stephen Allen, Program Specialist, Urban Reinvestment Task Force; Jim Cook, Director, Neighborhood Housing Services of Jamaica; Robert Corletta, President, National Center for Urban Ethnic Affairs; and Helen Murray, Redlining Reinvestment Specialist, National Training and Information Center.

We'd also like to thank the staff of the National Trust; especially, Jess Barnett, John Frisbee, Richard Haupt, Russell Keune, Michael Leventhal, Pat Martin, J. E. Moody, and Tom Slade.

Architectural Heritage's staff deserve credit for their assistance and support. Special thanks to Andrew Burns, F. Aldrich Edwards, and Patricia Swygert. For their assistance and advice we'd also like to thank AIA staff members, Mark Maves and Maurice Payne.

Many local preservationists and friends helped us with information about their projects and also with generous hospitality as we visited their cities and towns. We are especially indebted to: Leopold Adler II, Chip and Amanda Allen, Kenneth Anderson, Robert Berner, Peter Brink, Chris Carson, Henry Cauthen, Jr., John W. Cheek, Stephanie Churchill, Dana Crawford, Karen and Fred Diamond, Carl Feiss, Jack Finglass, Junius Fishburne, John Flowers, Richard Freeman, James W. Garrison, Sam Gowan, Rick and Margaret Green, Dorothy Hall, Kay and Bill James, William Kelso, Judy Kitchen, Ruth La Compte, Truett Latimer, Weiming Lu, Bruce and Jill MacDougale, Elaine Mayo, Langdon Morris, Nancy Negley, Deborah Neu, Susan and John Owens, John Parry, Boone and Cathy Powell, Martha Robinson, Alicia Rudolph, Nadine Russell, Janet Seapker, David Sherman, Nancy Shirk, Joseph Stettinius, José and Yvonne Tacoronte, Michele and Dennis Walters, Mary and Vernon Weston, Jay Williams and family, Joe Williams, J. Reid Williamson, Merrill Wilson, and Samuel Wilson. To any whom we may have missed, our apologies and thanks as well.

We would like to thank the National Endowment for the Arts, the Rockefeller Family Fund, the Chase Manhattan Bank, the Ford Foundation, and the J. M. Kaplan Fund for their most generous support which, over the past two years, has enabled us to proceed with this work. We are also grateful to Penntech Papers for its donation of the paper on which this book is printed.

Introduction

The United States has historically been a country endowed with natural resources in such abundance as to inspire profligacy. Land, energy, water, minerals, timber: all of these have been used, until very recently, with little regard for their supply. When converted to other forms—when hauled, hammered, bolted, and transformed to create buildings—we generally ceased thinking of these items as resources at all. Buildings became products, to be used until other products—less worn, more stylish, or better located—were constructed.

Nevertheless, over the decades America's buildings have become extraordinary storehouses of our natural resources, of wood, stone, mortar, and steel, as well as of the energy used to assemble them. At the same time, they have become repositories of cultural and social resources. Human effort, imagination, and creativity are embodied in everything from simply and functionally designed homes to ornately decorated public edifices. Our social structure is embodied in buildings from county courthouses to downtown storefronts. Buildings are the physical shells which have formed neighborhoods, shaped social contacts, and molded patterns of doing business to such a degree that to alter them today tears our economic and social fabric.

Today, we are gradually coming to realize the value and importance of our physical, social, and cultural resources. With many of our prime forests cut down, the highest quality iron reserves mined, and most accessible oil fields pumped dry, raw-material costs are rising. With the vast waves of immigration over and the sons and daughters of immigrants demanding a better standard of living, the era of cheap labor has passed. And with the migration of millions of people from rural areas to megalopolis, particularly to its mass-produced suburbs, much of the former character and identity of neighborhoods has been lost.

These trends have led some groups, individuals, and businesses—including the 71 businesses profiled in this study—to a new appreciation of old buildings, and thus to work for their preservation. Some companies have recycled buildings, others have worked to renew neighborhoods and older business districts, and still others have made donations to projects working toward these ends, as well as to more traditional historic-preservation activities. The case studies presented in this book provide useful examples for other businesses interested in building and community preservation, and for citizens groups interested in obtaining support for these causes.

Appreciation of the worth of old buildings is by no means universal, however. Indeed, for most of this century, countervailing social and economic forces have held sway. Older cities and towns have been steadily losing businesses and population. In twenty years, New York, Chicago, Pittsburgh, Philadelphia, Boston, and Detroit's share of the top 500 companies has decreased from 250 to 140.[1] Between 1968 and 1978, New York City will have lost 111 of the nation's top 1,100 corporations, though its suburbs will have gained 60.[2] As businesses left cities, so did jobs. New York City lost

650,000 jobs between 1969 and 1976.[3] Detroit's workforce has declined by 26 percent in the last five years.[4] The loss of jobs has meant the escalation of unemployment and welfare costs, as well as the lethal combination of a shrinking tax base and rising taxes: in short, a climate increasingly hazardous to both businesses and communities.

Because of such losses, older neighborhoods and commercial districts in both cities and towns, as well as important older buildings, have increasingly stood underutilized, their very existence threatened. New York City in mid-1977 had upwards of 10,000 abandoned buildings.[5] Its Chrysler Building, an Art Deco landmark, will be only 50 percent occupied by January 1, 1978. The Prudential Building in downtown Buffalo, a masterpiece of early skyscraper construction, can find no business tenants. Similar situations exist across the country.

The suburbs, to which many city dwellers chose to pick up and flee, are now beginning to face problems similar to those their residents hoped they had left behind: crime, rising real estate prices and taxes, and in some places, aging housing stock. Building moratoriums and more stringent zoning laws have created a scarcity of land for new construction. Both the remaining open land and the existing housing stock in urban and suburban areas are resources which are requiring increasingly careful use and preservation.

Until the last fifteen years, just a few preservation groups scattered around the U.S. had much interest in saving old buildings. Their interest was focused on the historic, aesthetic, or architectural significance of a structure. The number of such groups has grown as the threat to such buildings has grown. In 1966, there were 2,500 preservation groups; as of mid-1977, there were over 6,000. Battles have been waged to save New York City's Grand Central Station; and others are underway across the country. Preservation groups are fighting to save South Hall, a National Register landmark on the campus of the University of Wisconsin, River Falls; and the Harvey House in Barstow, California, a turn-of-the-century grand hotel built in the Spanish style.

Added to the voices of these historic-preservation organizations have been those—especially since the sixties—of community groups and government agencies concerned about deteriorating or abandoned urban housing in once sound neighborhoods. Brooklyn's Bedford Stuyvesant Restoration Corporation and Rochester's WEDGE have been actively involved in improving their neighborhoods for about ten years. In 1965, the federal government created the Department of Housing and Urban Development to deal with these issues.

The Bicentennial has helped too, bringing increased awareness of America's heritage.

Yet private industry in this country, which has perhaps the largest impact on real estate, has been slow in developing an interest in using old buildings or in seeing the need to support their continued use. American corporations, through direct ownership, control approximately $650 billion in domestic real property assets.* This does not include property controlled through leasing or other influences, nor does it include property owned or leased by smaller business institutions. Until recently, much of the business community believed that preservation was regressive. While building the *new* was seen as progressive and good for business image, rebuilding the *old* was not.

The climate established by political, legal, social, and economic forces did not favor the widespread preservation and reuse of buildings, especially by business. Tax incentives were provided for demolishing an old structure and building a new one in its place. Banks regarded older buildings and neighborhoods not as challenges but as high risks. Government renewal programs of the 1950s cleared vast areas of built-on land for new buildings, many of which were never built. Public and government opinion took little account of the uniqueness or economic value of older buildings, or of their contribution to the scale, identity, and visual richness of the environment.

If preservation is to become widespread, the participation and support of private industry will be essential. Data on the corporate involvement is sparse, but what indicators there are suggest possible new trends. Figures on the total extent of current recycling of old buildings by companies for their own business purposes—as headquarters, plants, or offices—are not available. However, a few recent developments point to increased activity. Each year, the McGraw-Hill Information Systems Company publishes the *Dodge Manual for Building Construction and Pricing Scheduling*. In its 1977 issue, a special section was included for the first time on "remodeling and renovation," referring to it as a "popular segment of the construction industry."[6] *Buildings* magazine, a publication for the construction and building management industries, publishes a special issue on "modernization" each year. For the past few years, it has surveyed its readers to determine the size of this growing market. Although the magazine's survey includes both private- and public-sector work, the total modernization market for 1976 was estimated at $10 billion, up $2 billion from the previous year.[7] Of this figure, more than 50 percent was attributable to commercial-business expenditures.

Because business-sponsored neighborhood revitalization is an even newer phenomenon, meaningful figures on the overall corporate contribution to such projects are even less readily available.

The level of business's involvement in preservation activities presents a mixed picture. A study carried out by the Business Committee for the Arts, a nonprofit organization established in 1967 to promote business support for the arts, indicated that arts support increased overall from $144 million to $221 million between 1973 and 1976, but that preservation's share of these contributions slipped from 5 percent in 1973 to 3 percent in 1976.[8]

*Howard Stevenson of the Harvard Graduate School of Business Administration faculty is currently preparing a paper on corporate investments in real estate. He places total corporate ownership of real estate at 18 percent of total corporate assets, based on historical costs (actual past costs). The most recent figures, as published in U.S. Bureau of Census, *Statistical Abstract of the United States 1976,* Washington, D.C., indicate that active corporate assets are currently $3.6 trillion.

Perhaps, over the coming decade, of sheer necessity, the business sector will increasingly turn to reusing buildings and to rebuilding the neighborhoods and communities around them. At present, however, substantive information about what businesses have already attempted and achieved in these fields could greatly extend industry's overall awareness of preservation as an alternative. It could help to define the problems and benefits that have accrued to both the companies and communities involved, as well as to the broader rural and urban environment. While business efforts around the U.S. may only undertake preservation on a building by building or block by block basis, what, after all, are cities and towns physically, but aggregations of buildings and blocks?

The INFORM Study   INFORM has sought to fill the existing information gap on business involvement in preservation. In two years of research, several hundred projects across the country were identified. The projects profiled illustrate the ways in which business has either made use of existing buildings or given support to others for their preservation. These projects involve preservation by profit-oriented, privately and publicly owned commercial, industrial, and service organizations of old buildings, industrial facilities, neighborhoods, and commercial districts. Some of the buildings rebuilt and reused were of architectural and historic significance; others had purely economic, social, and ecological values.

A total of 71 of the projects best exemplifying the range of efforts and the kinds of experience business has had in this field were selected for examination in some detail. Companies whose primary line of business is development were excluded, in order to highlight the potential for involvement of businesses of all types. These 71 project profiles make up the bulk of this report. They are presented in three separate chapters by project type:

• *Building Recycling*—discussing the adaptive reuse of old buildings for new business purposes; continued use of significant buildings for extended business life; and the combination of new and old buildings for image and efficiency.

• *Community Revitalization*—presenting some of the ways business has participated in breathing new life into residential neighbor- hoods; highlighting several business development and support efforts to create new economic vitality in older commercial areas.

• *General Preservation Support*—discussing the variety of ways in which business has contributed to the preservation of historic buildings and sites.

Each case study begins with a brief summary highlighting the project's most important aspects. Following the summary are discussions of: the sequence of events leading up to the company's decision to become involved in the project; the project execution; the costs involved; the problems encountered in the work itself and in dealings with community groups or government agencies, if these problems arose; the short-term and long-term benefits obtained; and a brief description of the company involved. At the end of each case study, at least one contact at the company and sometimes other contacts at related preservation or community groups are noted, should further information on the work be of interest to the reader.

The 71 companies profiled include international industrial giants, such as Exxon, R. J. Reynolds Industries, and General Mills, as well as small specialty firms like Hitchcock Chair of Riverton, Connecticut, or Pinaire Lithographing of Louisville, Kentucky. They represent a broad range of business activity: there are heavy manufacturing firms, oil companies, public utilities, consumer-oriented industries, banks, insurance companies, and service companies. Each firm had different reasons for embarking on its project: a need for space; a desire to help improve the value and quality of its city or town, the neighborhood surrounding its plant or headquarters; a special cultural or aesthetic interest in seeing a valuable old structure have continued life; or a request for assistance by a local preservation or community organization.

In addition to the 71 case studies, 71 company projects are listed and described briefly in the Appendix.

The portrait of resource reuse contained in these pages reveals the considerable ingenuity, planning, and skills that businesses have recently begun to devote to preservation. It suggests the tremendous potential value that such activity offers to companies and to communities, as well as to the nation's rural and urban environments.

These cases should certainly inspire a closer, more serious look at preservation possibilities by the still many thousands of businesses and corporations that continue to stampede for increasingly expensive and scarce "new turf," remaining oblivious to a resource now too valuable to ignore. The range of problems and benefits accruing to the firms profiled here should assist other companies plan projects of their own.

Benefits   The projects profiled in this study suggest that many economic, aesthetic, and public-relations benefits have accrued to the companies involved.

Economics.   The recycling and continued use of existing buildings can usually be justified on economic grounds alone. The shell of an office or factory building, including the foundation, supporting structure, and outer enclosure, represents a substantial cost in construction dollars and time. The cost of demolition and new construction, both from a dollars-and-cents and an energy standpoint, is often high. While there are no universal rules, INFORM found that at most of the seventeen reuse projects profiled, the costs ran from 30 percent to 40 percent less than replacement new construction. Lawyers Co-operative, a Rochester publishing company, spent about $15 per square foot to convert a nineteenth-century mill complex to office space. This represented a considerable saving over the approximately $45-per-square-foot cost of similar new construction. Adaptive reuse exceeded the cost of new construction in only three of seventeen cases.

Construction time, as well as cost, depends on the scope of work required, the number and extent of changes from the original, the number of unforeseen problems, and the skill of the architects and contractors executing the work. An accurate restoration of a historic building, even if only the exterior, costs a great deal of time and money. Skilled labor is expensive, and repair and reproduction of intricate detail takes time. The exact duplication of the Hotel Utah's exterior terra cotta and the recreation of the atmosphere in its turn-of-the-century public rooms cost $40,000 per room and took three years. Most business recycling projects, however, need not require such major restoration work.

Based on the projects studied by INFORM, operating costs in recycled buildings average no higher than in new construction. Operable windows, thick masonry walls, high ceilings, and proper orientation, often characteristics of older structures, actually made some of the buildings more efficient in warm weather, although some were less efficient during the winter heating months. Heating costs were substantially higher for Connecticut Savings Bank's Cheshire branch, located in an old mansion, than they would have been in a comparable new building. This occurred because the branch did not wish to replace the old windows and interfere with the building's appearance. Loose, poorly sealed windows often need to be tightened. To be truly energy efficient, many must be replaced with dual-pane insulating glass or covered with storm windows. New insulation, of course, is a necessity in most recycling projects, since many older buildings are poorly insulated. In general, however, with the addition of proper insulation and modern heating and other mechanical systems, old buildings can be as economical to operate as new ones.

One final advantage to a company's recycling an older building can be good employee relations and retention of a trained workforce. Levi Strauss' renovation of its Mission District plant in San Francisco enabled many employees to stay on who would not have been able to commute had the compay decided to move to a suburban location.

Where a corporation is reusing a building for its own business purposes, the economic advantages accrue mainly to the firm itself. However, where business supports community revitalization, cost and time savings most directly benefit community residents and governments. In most such cases, homes and local businesses can be occupied more quickly, and dislocation problems are usually not as severe as they would be if the areas were totally razed and built over. Dislocation of residents proved to be a problem in only two of the thirteen residential-revitalization cases studied. Underutilized or abandoned buildings, often defaulting in their tax obligations, are returned to tax-paying status without an appreciable increase in the cost of city services. The Brooklyn Union Gas Company has helped buyers obtain financing to purchase and renovate abandoned houses and storefronts in several sections of Brooklyn with just this effect.

The companies who participated in residential-revitalization projects often benefited directly as well, as in the case of South Shore Bank in Chicago. After three years of working with residents of its deteriorating service area to improve housing, stabilize business, and increase public understanding of banking services, the bank reversed a seven-year decline in deposits and recorded a 25 percent increase. Other companies studied hoped to register indirect gains by improving the quality of life in their city or neighborhood. Tasty Baking is hoping to accomplish exactly this by supporting a program to renovate and sell (at a slight loss) houses in the Philadelphia neighborhood in which it is located.

Even if a company does not undertake an entire building or community revitalization and simply makes a donation to preservation activities, it can and usually does accrue some financial benefit through tax write-offs. Only two of the companies studied were actually willing to indicate the amount of such benefits. One of them, Union Camp, realized a $26,000 tax deduction for its donation of the Tower Hill Plantation to the National Trust for Historic Preservation.

Aesthetics. Aesthetic benefits, while more difficult to categorize, also accrue to company employees and society at large. A look at any American city or town today affirms that new construction, often standardized to reduce cost, tends to produce a bland similarity of spaces and appearance. Several companies, on the other hand, have noted that recycling buildings is good for employee morale and has brought a favorable response from the community. Employees of Digital Equipment Corporation like the option of designing their own office space in a former textile-mill complex. SEDCO's conversion of an old school in Dallas to corporate offices has brought the company acclaim from local historical and architectural groups.

New additions can harmonize with older buildings through the use of modern materials, techniques, and details. In the six such cases profiled, an effort was made to develop stylistically compatible new designs. Older residential areas often contain architectural diamonds in the rough, like Brooklyn Union's brownstones in Brooklyn or Lakewood Bank's Dallas project which contained prairie-style homes inspired and in one case designed by Frank Lloyd Wright.

Landmark industrial, community, or residential buildings are an invaluable part of the past. The twenty companies profiled in the "general support" section realized the importance of preserving this legacy. Hercules, a chemical company, donated $50,000 to help restore the Grand Opera House in Wilmington, Delaware. Its contribution encouraged other businesses to donate funds and helped bring the century-old Grand back to productive use.

Company Public Relations. Probably the most consistently cited benefit among all of the projects surveyed is that of enhanced image.

Preservation activities can provide a sophisticated advertising
vehicle whereby awareness of both the company and its products is
increased. Older buildings usually reflect quality, stability, and
continuity in the community. This may, in fact, be one major reason
why 11 of the 29 recycled-building cases surveyed involved the
conversion of older buildings by banks. The First New Haven
National Bank's renovation of an eighteenth-century house as its
Westbrook branch brought the bank extensive local publicity. In
addition, new accounts and deposits in the branch exceeded
projections. The experience was similar for the Connecticut Savings
Bank, which turned another eighteenth-century house into one
of its branches.

On the other hand, recycled buildings need not project a
conservative image or rely on nostalgia for acceptance. With much
of modern architecture resulting in look-alike anonymity, the
unique identity an old building provides is often a positive business
benefit in itself. McGraw-Hill is pleased with both the location and
individuality of its Publications Company's Western Regions Office
located in a converted ice cream factory. Although the company is
only a tenant, the building was renamed the McGraw-Hill Building.

Support of community revitalization also brings public-relations
benefits. Most such projects have resulted in extensive local
publicity. Some have brought industry recognition, and state and
national attention as well. Frederic Rider, the Brooklyn Union
official in charge of the company's residential-redevelopment
activities, has been interviewed by newspapers across the country.
Trend Publications received the 1976 Annual Governor's Award in
the Arts for its conversion of an old cigar factory in Tampa, Florida,
into a commercial center.

Similarly, business donations can produce image and public-
relations benefits. The contribution of money, property, materials,
and services to preservation efforts has done so in seventeen of
twenty cases. Bird & Son was praised by former Vice President
Rockefeller, cited in the *Congressional Record*, and recognized by the
Bicentennial Commission for its matching-grants awards to preservation groups.

Problems   In the 71 cases in this survey INFORM found three
general problem areas to be associated with business-sponsored
preservation activities: problems in obtaining adequate capital,
uncertainties and delays resulting from the unconventional nature
of the projects, and employee apprehensiveness about recycling and
revitalizing. These problems relate largely to recycling buildings
and revitalizing neighborhoods, and do not apply to charitable
contributions to preservation. While preservation groups are
frequently hard pressed to raise money, the giving of donations does
not involve many problems for companies. The problems found were
real enough, but in most cases not insoluble. As preservation
projects proliferate, construction problems will lessen and financial
backing should become easier to obtain. If commercial and

residential revitalization projects are successful, apprehension should decrease.

Availability of Capital. The novel and—for now—somewhat uncommon nature of many preservation projects leads to greater technical and financial uncertainty than is generally encountered in new construction. Difficulties in obtaining mortgages and loans because of banks' perceptions of greater risk were found to cause delays and/or to require changes in the plans of 9 of 22 community-revitalization projects. The more ambitious the project, the more prevalent the problem seemed to be. The Jefferson Company's $20 million project to redevelop the neglected Minneapolis river front was delayed nearly three years while the company searched for bank financing. The company finally obtained partial financing, and was able to proceed with the first phase of the project.

Uncertainties in Construction. Contractors and architects are often hesitant to provide firm bids and guaranteed completion dates on recycling projects. Structural problems, initially hidden from view, are at times exposed as work progresses, resulting in extensive delays and/or cost overruns. Replacing the existing plumbing in Cleveland's Cuyahoga Building, an unexpected part of the renovation of the structure, resulted in a $300,000 overrun in the Sohio case. Obtaining variances for zoning or code violations can also cause delays and cost money.

Such uncertainities could, of course, be reduced by employing architects and contractors with previous experience in recycling, and by thoroughly inspecting a building before making a reuse decision. Nevertheless, there is no way to eliminate all risks involved.

Community, Employee, and Management Apprehension. Employees and management alike often have not been exposed to the good qualities of recycled buildings. Managers of public companies are also reluctant to invest in properties that might not appear profitable to stockholders. In addition, communities and sometimes, ironically, preservation groups are hesitant to allow a business to reuse a historic building for fear that the use might destroy the landmark's original character. Many Philadelphians resisted Design Research's efforts to convert an old mansion to its Philadelphia branch, until local efforts to find an alternate use failed.

Similar reservations exist within neighborhoods and commercial districts. Some residents fear the heavy hand of business support; ostensibly, control might outweigh the benefits of revitalization. General Mills' Stevens Court project in Minneapolis, which purchases and renovates small apartment buildings and rents them to local residents, initially encountered fear of company control and the evils of the company town among some Minneapolis residents.

Public Sector Policies and Programs   Government recognition of the need to support preservation is increasing, and on several levels, efforts are beginning to be made to encourage the recycling of old buildings for commercial, business, and residential use. On the federal level, diverse regulations, programs, and tax policies are being reviewed. On the state and local levels, a reevaluation is taking place of building codes, zoning ordinances, and property taxes which affect business decisions about reusing old buildings.

Federal. Federal support for preservation has been evolving slowly since the beginning of the century. The first piece of preservation legislation passed was the Antiquities Act of 1906, which provided for the protection of historic and prehistoric sites on federal lands and for the designation of national monuments. In 1916, the National Park Service was created as a bureau of the Department of the Interior. (The Department of the Interior still supplies most federal support for historic-preservation activities.) However, it was not until passage of the Historic Sites Act of 1935 that a national policy for preserving historic sites, buildings, and objects for public use was established. Under this Act, the Historic American Buildings Survey (HABS), originally established under the Works Progress Administration in 1933, became a permanent body recording the country's architectural heritage. (In 1969, the Historic American Engineering Record [HAER] was set up to supplement the HABS by recording and documenting industrial buildings and engineering artifacts, such as bridges.) The National Historic Landmarks Program, which identifies, lists, and maintains nationally important properties, also evolved from the 1935 Act.

In 1966, another major piece of legislation was passed, the National Historic Preservation Act (NHPA). The NHPA expanded the kinds of property eligible for federal notice, and officially created the National Register of Historic Places. Besides properties of national significance, the Register was to include districts, sites, buildings, and objects of state and local significance. Published biennially, the Register serves as the primary catalog of significant historic properties in the United States. Although only approximately 20 percent complete, it contains more than 12,000 entries. The NHPA also established a matching-grants program for survey, acquisition, and restoration of historic properties. These funds are administered by the National Park Service and allocated in each state by a State Historic Preservation Officer appointed by the Governor. Still another provision of the NHPA created the Advisory Council on Historic Preservation to advise the federal government on preservation matters, to coordinate federal, state, and local programs, as well as public and private preservation activities, and to insure that federal funds are not used to the detriment of historic properties.

In 1969, Congress passed the National Environmental Policy Act (NEPA), which included preservation of historic and cultural assets as a major goal. A section of the NEPA requires that Environmental Impact Statements (EIS) be prepared for federal actions that may significantly affect the quality of the environment. In May, 1971, a presidential directive, Executive Order 11593, was issued to encourage federal agencies to support the preservation of federally owned historic properties and to assure that federal plans and programs contribute to preserving and enhancing historic properties even when they are not under federal ownership.*

Since its inception in 1949, the National Trust for Historic Preservation has been one of the key organizations in the preservation field. It was chartered by Congress as a private, nonprofit organization to promote preservation through educational, technical, service, and advisory programs. The Trust administers small grants and revolving loan funds, and maintains and leases historic buildings. Although not equipped with any regulatory powers, the organization has provided leadership, and serves as a valuable information clearing house, producing a variety of publications on preservation subjects. The work of the Trust is funded by federal support, by the dues of its 115,000 members, and by private contributions. Recently, in an attempt to stimulate corporate awareness and support for preservation, the Trust created a Corporate Associates Program, which has enlisted more than 100 corporate members at a minimum annual membership fee of $1,000. The National Trust has a current budget of $5.8 million.

Federal preservation regulations only partially protect historic properties from direct federal or federally assisted intervention, and they do not apply at all to private-sector action. For example, properties listed in or eligible for listing in the National Register of Historic Places are only guaranteed review if threatened with destruction by a federally financed project. Even then, they are only assured a delay to permit Advisory Council review and recommendations. Protection from totally private intervention is provided only if a local landmark or historic-district ordinance assures it.

There are some federal programs and policies that may be used by business to obtain financial assistance for building reuse. These include a variety of grants, loans, and tax incentives. As indicated above, businesses using or supporting properties included in or eligible for inclusion in the National Register may obtain National Park Service matching grants for acquisition and restoration under the National Historic Preservation Act of 1966. Matching grants provide a maximum of 50 percent of project funds. Approximately 3,000 projects have received grant aid to date. Funding for the grants increased from $2 million in 1967 to $40 million for fiscal 1978. Authorizations of $100 million for fiscal 1978 and 1979, and $150 million for fiscal 1980 and 1981, have already been made, but may not be fully funded. The Land and Water Conservation Act, passed in 1976, authorized the creation of the National Historic Preservation Fund, which distributes monies the government receives from off-shore oil leases and mineral rights. One of the companies studied by INFORM, Harbridge House, Inc., with corporate headquarters in a nineteenth-century mansion in Boston's Back Bay historic district, applied for a $73,000 grant of this

*A more complete description of this Executive Order can be found in *A Guide to Federal Programs*, published in 1974 by the National Trust for Historic Preservation and updated in 1976.

type in 1976 to restore its facade. Park Service allocations to Massachusetts were not sufficient to finance the project at that time.

Other federal funding programs that may be applicable to business preservation projects include low-interest loans and grants-in-aid under the Department of Agriculture, the Commerce Department's Economic Development Administration (EDA), the Small Business Administration (SBA), and the Department of Housing and Urban Development (HUD). The Department of Agriculture programs are primarily directed toward private business development in rural areas and would include renovation projects if they reinforce employment. The EDA's programs are directed at improving employment through state and local public-works projects, especially in high-unemployment and redevelopment areas.

In 1976, the EDA-administered Local Capital Development and Investment Program channeled $3.2 billion into state and local public-works projects, including preservation efforts. Current efforts are underway to extend the Program and increase its preservation-related application.

Preservation work is more labor intensive than new construction. Kenneth Tapman, legal counsel for the Advisory Council on Historic Preservation, testified before the House Subcommittee on Economic Development in February, 1977, that "50 percent more jobs [per $1 million spent were] produced by restoration and renovation than by new construction."[9] This finding could increase EDA funding for preservation in the future.

The Small Business Administration (SBA) administers several loan programs and offers loan guarantees that can assist commercial revitalization and reuse of older buildings. Section 502 of the Small Business Investment Act of 1958, as amended, authorizes the SBA to "make loans to state and local development companies for use in assisting specific small businesses . . . to construct, modernize or expand their plants."[10] The Lowell Development and Financial Corporation, a local Massachusetts development company discussed in this study, was established under SBA guidelines. In September, 1976, the SBA initiated a neighborhood-revitalization program to expand the "502" concept in urban areas. Old Town Mall in Baltimore was the first neighborhood commercial-revitalization project to receive substantial assistance from the SBA's Section 502 lending program. More than eighty stores built in the 1800s on Baltimore's East Side were redeveloped under a renovation/preservation theme. The SBA loaned approximately $2 million to businesses to purchase and renovate these buildings. Urban-renewal funds and private investment completed the coalition. The project has been so successful that the City of Baltimore has expanded the concept to apply to a dozen other neighborhoods.

The Department of Housing and Urban Development (HUD) has several programs designed to assist the commercial and residential revitalization of city buildings. Under Section 312 of the National Housing Act of 1964, loans for repairs and improvements are available to bring privately owned property up to current building-code standards. More than $80 million is budgeted in fiscal 1977 for the rehabilitation-loan program.

Under Title I of the Housing and Community Development Act of 1974, a number of HUD categorical grant programs were replaced. Money is now given directly to communities in the form of Community Development Block Grants. Funding for the Block Grant program amounts to $3.15 billion in 1977. These funds can be spent on the rehabilitation of commercial properties as part of a total neighborhood-rehabilitation program. The community can also transfer the funds to local development corporations for commercial rehabilitation. The money may be used to acquire and rehabilitate older buildings, provide low-interest loans or grants for renovation, and finance preservation planning. In addition, Community Development Block Grants can be used to obtain National Park Service matching restoration grants.

The Tax Reform Act of 1976 offered increased tax incentives to businesses renovating and reusing landmark buildings. Section 2124 of this Act permits a five-year amortization of certain owner-incurred expenses resulting from the rehabilitation of a qualified depreciable property. Such property must be listed in the National Register or be designated significant by state or local statute (subject to approval by the Secretary of the Interior). The Act disallows a deduction for demolition and the undepreciated costs of such a property, and if the property is still demolished, it disallows accelerated depreciation for any new structures built on that site. A business or developer which buys a historic property to renovate and preserve, even if it is adapted for new use, may be able to take accelerated depreciation if renovations meet standards specified by the Secretary of the Interior.

The first rehabilitation to be approved under the 1976 Act may be the new corporate headquarters for the Schlegel Corporation, to be located in a converted historic house in Rochester, New York.*

State and Local. Most state and local regulations and programs that apply to preservation deal specifically with building renovation and reuse. In the area of corporate donations to preservation activities, however, the Commonwealth of Pennsylvania allows a charitable deduction up to a total of 89.5 cents on every $1. Since Pennsylvania's law became effective in March, 1977, the Tasty Baking Company has taken such deductions for its contribution to the Allegheny West Community Development Project, an effort to improve the neighborhood adjacent to the company's plant.

State and local registers and historic districts also provide a degree of protection for buildings designated as important. Boston's regulations require city approval of any exterior alteration or any change of use that conflicts with current residential zoning for buildings in its historic districts.

Some states provide funds for preservation projects. The State of Washington has authorized $1.7 million for preservation grants

*The news of this corporate adaptive use came too late to include here as a complete case study, but a short description and a source for further information can be found in the Appendix.

between 1975 and 1979. These funds are allocated through local governments for properties on both the state and National Registers. (State-registered properties receive preference.) Money is provided for code-requirement improvements, structural stabilization, and documented restoration. Matching grants up to a 50 pecent maximum are available for work on privately owned buildings. Publicly owned buildings are eligible for grants of up to 100 percent of costs.*

Building codes can either aid or complicate rehabilitation projects. While codes have traditionally been locally determined and enforced, there is a trend today toward uniform statewide application. The Basic Building Code published by the Building Officials and Code, International (BOCA) and the Uniform Building Code are widely used as models for these regulations. When an old building is recycled for a new use, it must meet current code standards. Because such standards are usually written explicitly for new construction, they are often difficult to comply with in recycling. An amendment to the BOCA Code, Section 318.0, dealing with special historic buildings and districts, may help to alleviate this problem. It specifies that in designated historic structures, certified architects and engineers may vary established code regulations if their designs meet the basic tenets of health, safety, and welfare. Although there are still difficulties in defining a "historic building" and in determining adequate and enforceable performance standards for life-safety compliance, code problems previously confronted in converting old buildings to new uses may be less serious in the future.

Local zoning ordinances regulate density, height and bulk limitations, and land use. Residential, commercial, industrial, recreation and entertainment, and historic districts are but a few of the typical uses zoned by most municipalities. Although a large aggregation of historic buildings may promote the establishment of special historic districts, many historic buildings and others worthy of preservation are located in other parts of town. Local landmark or historic commissions and planning organizations are usually responsible for identifying and protecting these structures.

There are two major zoning issues that affect business reuse and revitalization of older buildings and areas. First, if a building with recycling potential is located in a district defined for a use other than that proposed in the recycling, a zoning variance may be required. For example, large, late-nineteenth-century homes in established residential districts often cannot be affordably maintained as residences. Some alternative use must be found, or the buildings will have to be demolished. Businesses such as small publishers, law firms, insurance agencies, and banks may be able to efficiently reuse these structures if zoning variances are permitted. While there are no guarantees that variances will be obtainable, in the cases researched by INFORM, no examples were found where change-of-use presented a difficult zoning-variance problem. In fact,

*Further information about state preservation programs can be found in *A Guide to State Programs*, published by the National Trust for Historic Preservation in 1972 and revised in 1976.

some local regulatory bodies appear to be encouraging this activity. In Savannah, the Morris Newspaper Corporation has adapted a historic house for its offices with strong support from the city. As public awareness of recycling projects is increased, business reuse of buildings in non-business zones is likely to become more common.

The second zoning issue affecting business reuse of old buildings and areas is more complicated. Many important buildings are located in neighborhoods that are zoned for greater density than the old buildings provide. Although they have historic and social value, and there are strong reasons for their retention, under the philosophy of "highest and best use," these landmarks are often not able to justify their existence economically. More profitable structures can be built to the maximum allowable density level. In larger cities like New York and Chicago, a concept known as Transfer of Development Rights (TDR) has been developed to deal with this problem.* TDR refers to the transfer of developable density from one site to another. The owner of a historic building may sell the extra density rights currently unused at the site to increase occupancy levels on another piece of property. The proceeds can then be applied to the old building's maintenance and support. TDR can help historic buildings to survive even if they are not fulfilling the highest and most profitable use allowable for the site. The same concept is also being applied to open-space areas. None of the projects in the INFORM study utilized this conservation tool, but it will undoubtedly be applied in larger cities in the future.

Property taxes can also hinder preservation. Local property taxes are often assessed on the potential value of a site, rather than on the actual economic value generated. This policy obviously discourages preservation of old buildings, since the owner must pay the same high taxes on the old structure as he would have to pay if a new, higher-revenue-producing building were located on the site. However, such policies can backfire. In recent years, economic realities have restricted the amount of new construction possible. Older, underutilized buildings have often been razed for potential new development that never took place, leaving the city's fiscal burdens not reduced, but exacerbated.

Some cities and states have introduced tax abatements and other incentives to attempt to encourage building reuse and commercial and neighborhood revitalization. New York City has several abatement programs to promote residential and commercial rehabilitation. Section J-51-2.5 of New York City's Administrative Code was originally implemented in 1955 to encourage owners of multiple-unit dwellings to bring their properties up to building-code requirements. As of January, 1976, it provides up to a twelve-year exemption from any increase in assessed valuation and an abatement of property taxes up to 90 percent of the cost of rehabilitating a residential or commercial building for residential use.

A concept known as tax increment financing has been established

---

*This concept is presented in detail by John J. Costonis, in his book, *Space Adrift*, published by the National Trust for Historic Preservation.

in several cities to promote neighborhood or district revitalization. Sacramento, California, was the first city to adopt the concept in an effort to restore economic vitality to Old Sacramento, its historic business center. Tax increment financing attempts to encourage private rehabilitation efforts by freezing the existing property-tax levels in a renewal area. In this way, owners are not penalized by higher taxes for improving their properties, a common disincentive to rehabilitation. As investment and improvement take place in the area, some increases are made in the property valuation, but the increment is set aside in a special city fund, to be reinvested only in the area. Bonds, secured by the increment, are also sold to support extensive improvements like new street lighting, sidewalks, and landscaping. Through this approach, the whole area may be rapidly renewed, benefiting both the private and public sectors.

While public and private support of preservation has been slow to develop, advances are gradually being made. Perhaps with an increased public awareness that preservation is more than just the exact restoration of historic structures, government and business alike will come to agree with James Biddle, President of the National Trust, who said:

Progress doesn't always have to be something new. Progress is taking the best advantage of the assets you have. Preservation is progress.[11]

Footnotes

1. Michael Sterne, "Corporate Moves: New York Region Holds Its Own," *New York Times*, 21 August 1977, sec. 11 (Long Island Weekly), p. 8.
2. *Ibid*. p. 1.
3. INFORM interview with Frank Corbin, Deputy Director, Economic Development Administration, New York City, August, 1977.
4. Gurney Breckenfeld, "It's Up to the Cities to Save Themselves," *Fortune*, March, 1977, p. 195.
5. Urban Homesteading Assistance Board, *Urban Homesteading Assistance Board Annual Report*, (New York: Urban Homesteading Assistance Board, 1976).
6. McGraw-Hill Information Systems and Wood and Tower, Inc., *Dodge Manual for Building Construction and Pricing Scheduling*, (New York: McGraw-Hill, 1976), p. 1.
7. "More is Better: Strong Modernization Market Continues," *Buildings*, 1976, p. 56.
8. Business Committee for the Arts, *Business Support of the Arts—1976*, (New York: Business Committee for the Arts, 1976).
9. "EDA Funding Reviewed," *Preservation News*, March, 1977, pp. 1, 12.
10. *U.S. Small Business Administration Loans to Local Development Companies*, (Washing--ton, D.C.: U.S. Small Business Administration, n.d.).
11. Alan Otten, "Politics & People—Spare that Building," *Wall Street Journal*, 8 January 1976.

Restoration, renovation, rehabilitation, remodeling, retrofitting; all involve saving and extending the useful life of an existing building. Recycling, as this activity is called, includes: *adaptive reuse*, converting an existing building from its originally intended (or currently defined) purpose to a new one; *continued use*, consciously extending the useful life of important older buildings for the purpose originally intended; and *new additions*, adding compatible new construction onto older structures, or building new structures which "fit" within an established historic context.

Adaptive Reuse INFORM has examined seventeen recycling projects in the adaptive-reuse category. Among the leading practitioners of this form of recycling are banks. Five cases deal with historic houses which have been turned into bank branches, such as the Victorian residence of a former cattle baron in Sacramento, converted into a San Diego Federal branch. Other kinds of businesses met their own divergent space needs through the adaptation of a variety of structures. Three cases involve townhouses now serving as distinctive office spaces. Morris Newspaper's offices, for example, are located in one of Savannah's ten oldest buildings. Two cases involve vintage homes which were successfully converted to retail space. One of them, Design Research's Philadelphia store, is actually a city-registered landmark. Three conversions involve old industrial buildings made into office space: an ice cream factory converted into McGraw-Hill Publications' Western Regions Office; a textile mill used by Digital Equipment Corporation to meet its office and production needs; and a factory complex reused as the home offices of Lawyers Co-operative. The remaining four cases involve conversion of a school building, a hotel, a nondescript storefront, and a courthouse to commercial or office space.

In almost every case, the exteriors of the buildings have been rehabilitated or maintained in their original state, while the interiors have been adapted to fit the new use. In many projects, the interior adaptation has also attempted to respect the original design, including the restoration and incorporation of important decorative elements and original room configurations.

Companies and financial institutions that have decided to adaptively reuse old buildings give a variety of reasons for their decision. In thirteen of the seventeen cases profiled by INFORM, the firms wanted and believed they received enhanced public images. This was particularly important to the First New Haven National Bank, which was moving into a new market in Westbrook, Connecticut. However, it seemed to be equally important to a firm like Lawyers Co-operative, a law publisher long established in Rochester.

Economic considerations were another strong reason given for recycling. Space in an adapted older structure is often less expensive than that acquired through new construction. This was true for Digital in Maynard, Massachusetts, which obtained office and manufacturing space for $15 per square foot as opposed to the $25 to $30 per square foot it would have had to pay for new construction; and for Wachovia Bank, where recycling proved to be 20 percent cheaper than new construction. Costs varied according to the degree of renovation, the nature of the business, the availability of materials, and regional pay scales. Among the cases studied by INFORM, the per-square-foot cost of renovation ranged from a low of $15 in the Lawyers Co-operative and Digital cases to a high of $110 in the San Diego Federal Savings and Loan case. Adaptive reuse was reported to be as much as two-thirds less expensive than new construction. In only three cases—San Diego Federal, Design Research, and Commonwealth Bank and Trust—did the cost of rehabilitation exceed the estimated cost of new construction designed for similar use.

Location was also often a key factor in the decision to reuse existing buildings. The study includes nine cases of companies who were looking for a new location for a branch or other facility in an established area. They found that construction of a new building would generally necessitate demolition of an existing structure. Demolition is often expensive, and the approvals required are not easily obtained. Thus, the adaptive reuse of structures already existing in good locations became a logical alternative. Connecticut Savings Bank found a location for its Cheshire branch in a badly neglected old house on a main commercial street. Instead of demolishing the building, the bank restored the exterior and renovated the interior, turning the old home into a productive branch and helping maintain the character of the area.

INFORM also profiled six cases of companies which were established in an area and needed to expand their facilities. Building on adjacent sites often proved to be the most feasible plan. Harbridge House, a Boston-based consulting firm, purchased a house adjacent to its Back Bay offices (also located in old houses), and is using it for additional office space. The reused houses provide the cheapest office space of any of the company's locations.

In almost every building-recycling project studied by INFORM, aesthetic considerations played a significant role. Often the force behind the project was a concerned executive to whom aesthetics were important. This top-level individual often had participated in local preservation and community activities. While companies tend to stress economic or "image enhancement" grounds as justification for their projects, aesthetics and that special interest of a high-level official seemed to have triggered the initial consideration and study of reuse as an option in almost every case. One example is Morris Newspaper's President Charles Morris. A Trustee of Historic Savannah, Morris wanted a historic building to house his offices in that city.

Although not a major motivating factor, five of the companies INFORM studied felt that reusing older buildings resulted in improved employee morale. The employees of Digital Equipment Corporation like the option they have of personalizing their office space in the company's converted textile mill.

The problems encountered in adaptive reuse varied according to the nature of the building and the purpose for which it was to be renovated. Among the problems cited, technical difficulties were most common, but they were reported by only four of the seventeen companies studied. For example, the National Bank of the Commonwealth, in converting the Indiana County Courthouse to bank offices, found that the thickness of the building's walls limited floor-plan designs and created difficulties in installing heating and air-conditioning systems.

Continued Use   INFORM has also profiled the efforts of six businesses to continue to use significant old buildings. Continued use, while not requiring as extensive alteration as adaptive reuse, can still at times involve major rehabilitation.

Just as with adaptive reuse projects, businesses decide to continue to use existing buildings primarily for economic and aesthetic reasons. Most of the examples of continued use studied by INFORM involve company-owned buildings. The companies, including nail producers, banks, chair manufacturers, lumber companies, and clothing manufacturers, have made major investments in buildings, and over the years have reduced the debts on them. Property taxes are usually low as well, since the assessed valuation is in most cases less than for comparable new buildings.

A comparison of costs for renovation versus new construction reveals that renovation is often the cheaper alternative. This was true in almost all the cases studied by INFORM, and was specifically cited by two companies as a reason for continued use. According to its architects, Alamo National Bank got a $30 million bargain from a $5 million renovation.

A further reason for continuing to use an old building is that good public and employee relations often result. All six companies received favorable publicity and recognition for their efforts. Levi Strauss was praised by the Mayor of San Francisco for renovating and preserving its 71-year-old clothing factory located in the city's Mission District. The company's employees had roots in the neighborhood, and needed to be near homes and children. Many would have found it difficult to commute to a suburban location since they did not own automobiles.

Several companies, through association with a particular building, had achieved an image and identity which they did not want to alter. The Hitchcock Chair Company is located in the same building as the original nineteenth-century "manufactory." Hitchcock's President John T. Kenney revived both the process and the building more than eighty years after the original company ceased operations.

One company, Sohio, cited energy conservation as a factor motivating its commitment to lease 40,000 of the Cuyahoga Building's 63,000 square feet. According to the company, renovation and continued use saved the energy that would have been expended in demolition and new construction, as well as that used in the production of building materials.

Finally, aesthetic considerations played a role in the decision to continue to use five buildings. Three projects are even tourist attractions, providing a source of additional revenue. Tremont Nail's nineteenth-century nail factory attracts many customers to the company's gift shop.

None of the companies studied encountered major internal difficulties in their continued-use projects. The original buildings were structurally sound and accommodated the space and functional needs of the businesses and residents involved. Mechanical and life-safety systems could usually be upgraded at a lower cost than would have been required if they were being built from scratch. Alamo National Bank redesigned and enlarged the service area in its San Antonio headquarters, but only had to refurbish rather than totally replace the electrical and mechanical systems.

Where problems did occur, they were generally the result of some external factor, such as location, rather than the nature of the building itself. Most older buildings are located in dense, central-city areas. At projects in Cleveland and San Francisco, this created difficulties with employee and customer accessibility, parking, and security. Other problems connected with continued-use projects were unique to the individual situation, like the inconvenience Pope & Talbot's renovation efforts caused residents of historic homes in Port Gamble. Port Gamble is a company lumbering town in the State of Washington. Residents have been badgered by over-eager tourists wanting to see the interiors of their restored homes.

New Additions Often, a business will want to remain or locate in an old building whose present size and condition fails to suit its needs; or, it may want to locate in a historic area with explicit design restrictions. The result in many cases has been to pick another location and start over. However, as an alternative, some companies have undertaken construction of compatible new additions and enlargements. While the benefits of such efforts are obvious—demolition or abandonment of the older building is often avoided, and the economic stability and well-being of the area is maintained—the designing of new additions in order to "fit" within an established historic context is a controversial subject. Among the points of debate are: the degree of alteration of historic structures which should be permitted; the elements that constitute compatible design; and the extent to which cost and functional considerations should be allowed to take precedence over historical accuracy and aesthetics. Given the many design restrictions placed on older areas, the scarcity of prime building land, and the faltering economic vitality of many existing "downtowns," the need for harmonious combinations of new and old buildings is a growing and important concern.

The six projects in this category studied by INFORM all involve new intervention which has attempted to respect older surroundings. They include hotels, insurance-company offices, banks, and department-store complexes. The six cases illustrate three basic design approaches:

1. *Recreation*—copying the design of the past with today's materials and labor; exemplified by Charleston Associates and Deseret Management. Critics claim that this approach is anachronistic, lacks originality, and may deceive the untrained observer into believing that the new is actually not new. Many others, however, see no problems with recreation.

2. *Tokenism*—incorporating an artifact or piece of the old building as a historic symbol within new construction; exemplified by Zions Cooperative and Penn Mutual. There is some controversy over this approach too, since all but a small part of the original building is lost. Furthermore, tokenism generally creates sculptures of portions of buildings never intended for that purpose. However, the alternative is often complete destruction.

3. *Compatible contemporary additions*—building in today's idiom, but relating the new building to adjacent older buildings through design elements such as scale, proportion, configuration, pattern, materials, color, and texture; exemplified by the Boston Five Cents Savings Bank

and the Bank of California. This approach, clearly the most challenging to architects, also involves the most subjective judgments. What is good compatible contemporary architecture? How can compatibility be measured? Should it be measured? Does striving for compatibility stifle creativity and originality? Will it yield a bland environment containing stripped-down contemporary copies of historic counterparts?

For these questions, all well worth considering, there are no concrete answers. However, the City of Savannah has made an attempt at creating some measurable standards for evaluating new development within historic areas. Its findings, published in a *Historic Preservation Plan*, include sixteen criteria by which to judge the relationship between new and old buildings:

Height	Relationship of color
Proportion of buildings' front facades	Relationship of architectural details
Proportion of openings within that facade	Relationship of roof shapes
Rhythm of solids to voids in front facades	Walls of continuity
Rhythm of spacing of buildings on streets	Relationship of landscaping
Rhythm of entrance and/or	Ground cover
porch projections	Scale
Relationship of materials	Directional expression
Relationship of textures	of front elevation[1]

Most business decisions concerning whether or not to construct a new building that is sympathetic to its historic surroundings are not made on a strictly economic basis. Accommodating the craftsmanship and detail which characterize older buildings can be a costly and time-consuming proposition. Quality in architecture, as in most other things, costs money. It is almost impossible to devise any tangible scale of measurement for the business benefits derived. Deseret Management decided on an addition which was an exact replica of the old Hotel Utah at a cost of about $40,000 per room, much more than a modern addition would have cost. Indeed, it appears that several of these projects were undertaken because companies feared the negative consequences of not doing so, rather than because any positive economic benefit was to be gained. In two cases, Penn Mutual and Zions Cooperative, pressure from local preservation groups saved at least part of the original historic structures.

While economics are usually a secondary consideration in creating compatible new additions, Salt Lake City has gained special economic benefits from the Zions Cooperative and Deseret Management projects. The city has become a center of restoration expertise, and its architects and craftsmen have assisted in other projects around the country.

The companies studied by INFORM cited costs and delays as the major difficulties associated with the construction of new additions. These seemed to correlate with the degree of compatibility of recreation the company desired. The Bank of California's attention to detail, careful workmanship, and unique design brought the cost of building a new addition to its old banking hall to $90 per square foot, a relatively high figure. The exact duplication of terra cotta exteriors and the recreation of turn-of-the-century-style public spaces helped delay the opening of the Hotel Utah's new addition for about a year. Technical difficulties, including the use of unfamiliar building material, such as the terra cotta at the Hotel Utah, arose in four projects, but in all instances were overcome.

An additional problem arose after completion in three cases. Public reaction to the new addition and to the philosophy behind it was divided, and the projects became the focus of controversy among architecture critics.

Footnotes

1. *Historic Preservation Plan for the Central Area General Neighborhood Renewal Area, Savannah, Georgia,* (Washington, D.C.: U.S. Department of Housing and Urban Development, n.d.), pp. 12-18.

*Commonwealth Bank and
Trust Company*

Adaptive Reuse

Summary Commonwealth Bank and
Trust Company purchased the historic
Squire Hays Homestead in Williamsport, Pennsylvania, to save it from
demolition, and relocated and renovated it for use as a branch office
which opened in 1975. The branch has
been very successful; the renovation
provided a unique way of establishing
the bank in a new market.

Background In 1973, the construction of Robert Hall Village, a shopping-center complex, threatened
the demolition of the Squire Hays
Homestead, one of the oldest surviving
structures in Lycoming County. The
Homestead, standing in the middle of
the complex's proposed parking lot, was
scheduled to be torn down. Commonwealth Bank and Trust, under President Glenn Fenstermacher, had
decided to locate a branch in Williamsport and was looking for a
way to promote itself in a new community. The bank thought the Squire
Hays Homestead would serve both
these ends.

The Squire Hays Homestead was
built in 1806 by John Hays to replace a
log house, the original home of the
Hays family. Constructed entirely of
stone and wood from the surrounding
countryside, the house was originally
two stories, with two doors on the first
floor. After the Civil War, a two-story
addition was made, and in 1885, a
porch was added to the front of the
house.

Execution The house was moved
across the road from its original site,
an effort requiring considerable time
and patience; and its architecture and
history were researched with the help
of the Lycoming County Historical
Society and Museum. The restoration
architect, Richard Merrill Sweitzer,
A.I.A., returned the exterior of the
house to its post-Civil War appearance,
removing the 1885 porch. He added
drive-in banking windows, custom
built to blend in with the original bay
windows, and a vault extension covered
with stone taken from the foundation of
another vintage building that had been
demolished.

The house has seven rooms. On the
first floor, in what was the kitchen/
dining area, a wall was removed to
make more room for the bank manager's office and bank lobby. Other
rooms are used for banking and office
space. Two were set aside as period
rooms, and another as a meeting room.
The period rooms were furnished with
colonial pieces from the Lycoming
County Museum, and with other items
of special interest from the early 1800s.
The offices are furnished with antique
office furniture where possible. Objects
and documents were supplied by the
people of Lycoming County; some of
these donations are now being collected
and placed in a *Memory Book* by the
bank. In addition, the bank was instrumental in having the home placed
on the Pennsylvania Inventory of Historic Places in 1974.

Costs While Commonwealth Bank
and Trust indicated that the costs of
renovating this building were higher
than those for building a new branch, it
would not release any specific financial
figures.

Problems The major cause for concern during the course of the renovation was the initial relocation. Due to
the extreme age of the stone building,
the move across the street required
great care, and as a result took many
months. It was, nevertheless, completed without incident.

**Squire Hays Homestead being moved to
its new location.**

Benefits The restoration has generated much favorable publicity for the bank, which also uses the Squire Hays Homestead in its advertising. Squire Hays Homestead hand-cast coins and metal plates are given away for new accounts over $50.

The renovation and the branch's excellent location, near a prime traffic area, both contributed to its success. The community's economy has benefited from the jobs and tax revenues created by the new addition, as well as from the preservation of a part of its heritage. The Squire Hays branch was a stop on the Christmas, 1976, Williamsport tour of Historic Homes.

The Company In 1965, Commonwealth Bank and Trust was formed by the merger of the Tioga County Savings and Trust Company, the First National Bank of Galeton, the First National Bank of Lawrenceville, and the Farmer's and Trader's National Bank of Westfield. Commonwealth serves a five-county area, and has seventeen branches besides its home office in Muncy, Pennsylvania. The bank employs 189 people and had assets of $152 million as of 1976.

Other Preservation Activities. Commonwealth Bank and Trust has recently renovated its branch office in Renovo, Pennsylvania. The building, in continuous use as a bank since the turn of the century, has marble floors and rich woodwork.

For further information contact:
Linda S. Williams
Marketing Assistant
Commonwealth Bank and Trust
Company
61 Main Street
Wellsboro, Pennsylvania 19601

The renovated farmhouse, now a branch office of the Commonwealth Bank and Trust Co.

Connecticut Savings Bank

Summary In December, 1973, the Connecticut Savings Bank opened its Cheshire branch office in the historic Governor Foote House on South Main Street. Built in 1769, the house is a superb example of colonial Connecticut architecture and an important component of historic Cheshire. In return for this contribution to preservation, the bank has received business benefits, as well as much local and even national public acclaim. Bank President Paul Johnson states: "business growth in the new branch is far above projected expectations and better than any other branch in our system."[1] He believes that the building is responsible for much of the branch's popularity.

Background In 1973, the bank was looking for a site in Cheshire for a new branch office. The Governor Foote House was ideally suited to its needs; it was on the main commercial street, but had enough adjacent land to accommodate a drive-in window and bank parking. In recent years, however, the Foote House had been neglected by its owner and, according to local historian, Dr. Robert Craig, was in a "deplorable state."[2] The three-story frame house retains many of its original clapboards still held in place with hand-crafted nails. It also has many of its original shutters.

The house was the birthplace of Samuel Augustus Foote who served both in Congress and as the Governor of Connecticut. It remained a residence until the end of the nineteenth century, when it became a private girls' school Its eighteenth-century interiors were altered at that time to accommodate its function as a school. Later, the house was converted back into a residence, and was the home of a former journalist with the *Cheshire Herald*. It is still one of the finest and best-preserved examples of early colonial architecture in the Cheshire area.

On Cheshire's South Main Street, as on the main streets of many older towns, residential and commercial development have been intertwined. South Main Street is zoned for commercial use on one side and for residential use on the other. The Foote House is on the residential side. However, the residential zoning permitted banks to establish branches in the area, subject to approval by the town's Planning and Zoning Board. Recently, the property directly across the street was scheduled to be the new location of a fast-food restaurant. While local residents blocked this change, future growth was bound to pose further threats. Just up the street from the Foote House, one of the large older homes was gutted by fire, and has since been converted to office use. Dr. Craig feared that the Foote House was in such a state of disrepair that it would soon be razed for another gas station. He evaluates the bank's use of the building and site: "Either the bank made it a 'taxpayer' or the old shack was going to fall down."[3] Two letters published in the

Cheshire Herald—and in part, reprinted here—illustrate the diversity of opinion concerning the bank's proposed reuse. One, by an Assistant Commissioner in the state Department of Environmental Protection, praised the bank's plan. The other, by a freshman at Southern Connecticut State College in New Haven, took an opposing view.

One of the most environmentally sound actions which a bank could take in Cheshire has now been started by CSB. The purchase and renovation of an existing historic structure, i.e., the Foote house in Cheshire, for a branch bank, is a significant action. It has no disturbing effect on open space land as a new structure would; it has the character of the community as a base in its architecture, and it improves a building which was becoming a blight to the town.

Other financial institutions which operate in Cheshire should note as a sound example the action of CSB.[4]

In my opinion the Clinton Branch Bank [a previous renovation by CSB] was tastelessly put together and permanently ruined. I do not know the historical background of the house, as on the outside there was no sign or plaque containing its history, but we can be sure it is not as historically significant as our Foote House. The outside of this house (which isn't even one half the size of the Foote House) had evidences of being at one time a fairly nice looking home. But with all the new fixtures and shutters bolted to the structure, its Colonial charm was somehow lost. . . . What I am trying to say to the bank is this: I hope they realize that restoration means more than just redoing the outside appearance of something, it means taking time and care to fix things and not just tear out and replace them. And it means taking this care in both the outside and inside. They are equally important aspects to consider when undertaking such an important project as the Foote House, and can not be taken lightly.[5]

Execution The bank, in fact, did restore the exterior of the Foote House to its original state, and managed to retain many key features of the interior, while accommodating modern banking needs. The original exterior clapboards were hand sanded and then stained a brownish grey, and the shutters were restored and stained a dark brown. The roof was re-shingled with cedar shingles, and the modern double

The Governor Foote House before restoration. Bank President Paul Johnson escorts visitors.

The same building after restoration. (Interdesign)

front door was replaced with an authentic eighteenth-century single door found in Newport, Rhode Island. In the interior, the first floor was opened up to produce a more convenient banking space. Those partitions which were removed were mostly nineteenth-century additions. The central fireplace was left exposed in the middle of the open space, acting as a divider for banking activities and as the focal point of the interior. Because much of the original interior finish was missing, new wood trim, appropriate to the original period of the house, was used, and even the tellers' counters were paneled. Modern flooring on the ground level was replaced with wide oak floorboards salvaged from another period house in Durham, Connecticut. The second floor, used as office space, was generally refurbished without any structural alteration.

The building is equipped with all the conveniences and security of a completely new facility: a computer system links the branch to all records stored in the main office; and a modern vault facility, with eighteen-inch-thick walls to meet Federal Deposit Insurance Corporation requirements, has been incorporated in a new addition to the rear of the house. The renovated building contains 3,800 square feet of usable space; the ground floor is used for customer banking needs, and the second floor for office suites. A parking lot, accommodating 24 cars, has been designed at the rear of the building, and is hidden from the main street by landscaping. The drive-in window is separate from the building, and utilizes an automated TV teller system. The cost of this convenience is greater than an integrated drive-up system, but the unit helps preserve the character of the house. Frederick Biebesheimer and Jonathan Isleib of Interdesign, Inc., were responsible for the conversion design and restoration.

Lighting and mechanical systems sometimes cause problems in renovation projects where preservation of an original character is desired. Modern

Plan of first floor illustrating arrangement of main banking activities. (Interdesign)

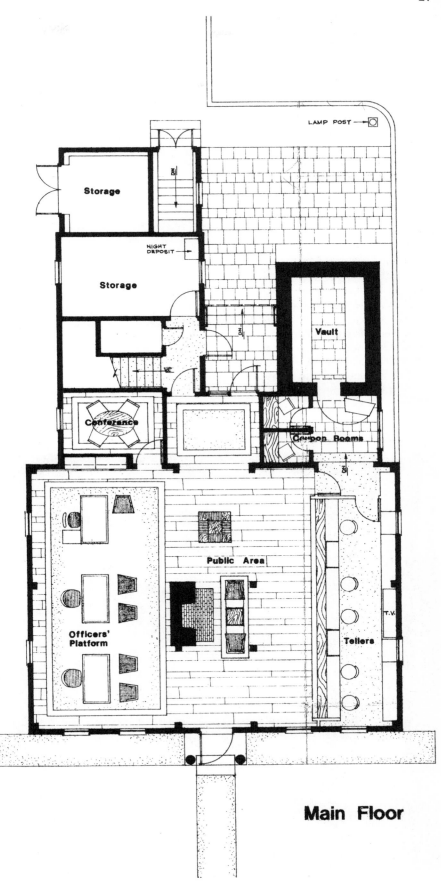

Main Floor

banking needs and local code requirements prohibited the use of period oil lamps, and modern fluorescent fixtures were not in keeping with eighteenth-century design. Interdesign chose recessed incandescent lighting which unobtrusively provides adequate light for the workspace and enhances architectural detail. A completely new gas-fired, ducted heating system and electric central air conditioning have been installed. The seven-and-a-half-ton air-handling unit is located in the basement, and ground-level heating and cooling is provided by registers in the floor. For the upper level, the ducts are brought up vertically to the attic and then branch out and blow down to condition the rooms below. This solution eliminated any exposed ducts or dropped ceilings. New plumbing and wiring were also installed. According to Interdesign, there were no specific building-code or structural problems. The construction took six months.

Costs The bank paid approximately $65,000 for the house. Interdesign puts the renovation cost at $147,000, and the mechanical and electrical work at $43,000, for a total project cost, excluding furnishings and bank equipment, of approximately $255,000, or $35 per square foot for the total 5,600 square feet.

Operating costs for heating/ventilation and air conditioning average about $650 per month, according to Branch Manager, Carol Oesterlin.[6] This is approximately 11 cents per square foot per month. No storm windows were used because the designers felt that they would detract from the original character of the windows. Heating the house is thus somewhat more expensive than it would otherwise be.

Benefits The benefits accrued to the town of Cheshire have been discussed. The business benefits to the bank are important. According to Mrs. Oesterlin, "Customers are mentioning what a fine job we did with the restoration all the time. For many of them it would appear to be the main reason they come in."[7] The three-year projected deposits for the branch were estimated at $14 million. Actual deposits have been $15.4 million. Bank President Paul Johnson attributes most of this increase to the restoration. The bank has received widespread favorable publicity for the project, including an article in the National Trust's April, 1976, *Preservation News*.

The central chimney and fireplace divide the banking floor into the teller and office areas. (Charles M. Pratt)

The Company The Connecticut Savings Bank was chartered in 1857, and is today the fourth largest savings institution in the state. Assets rose from $505 million in 1975 to $586 million in 1976. Fifteen branch offices serve New Haven and its surrounding communities. Several are in older buildings.

Other Preservation Activities. The bank's main office in New Haven is located in a Greek-temple-like structure built in 1907. This building has been fully restored by the bank and Interdesign. The exterior marble was water cleaned; the old barrel-vaulted, coffered ceiling was uncovered and restored (it had been hidden behind a lowered ceiling for many years); and new lighting and mechanical systems were introduced. The bank has linked this older building to a new administrative building on an adjacent piece of land. Although joining a classical temple—meant to be seen from all sides—to anything is a difficult problem, the resulting solution of a neutral black "hyphen" between the two buildings is quite effective. The bank received a plaque from the New Haven Preservation Trust declaring the temple building a historic landmark.

For further information contact:
Paul Johnson
President and Chief Executive
Officer
Connecticut Savings Bank
47 Church Street
New Haven, Connecticut 06510

Footnotes
1. INFORM interview with Paul Johnson, President, Chief Executive Officer, Connecticut Savings Bank, May, 1976.
2. INFORM interview with Dr. Robert Craig, Historian, March, 1977.
3. *Ibid.*
4. Carroll J. Hughes, "A Bank Plans For Restoring Foote House: The Case For It," *Cheshire Herald*, 2 November 1972, p. 21.
5. Donald Menzies, "A Bank Plans For Restoring Foote House: The Case Against It," *Cheshire Herald*, 2 November 1972, p. 21.
6. INFORM interview with Carol Oesterlin, Manager, Connecticut Savings Bank, Cheshire branch, May, 1976.
7. *Ibid.*

The barrel-vaulted interior of the bank's restored main office.

Summary In October, 1975, Design Research, a retail chain specializing in contemporary furnishings, fabrics, and accessories, opened its eleventh store in the historic Van Rensselaer Mansion on Philadelphia's Rittenhouse Square. Prior to the company's adaptive reuse, the building—once the home of one of the city's wealthiest and most prominent families—was unoccupied and threatened with demolition because it was an unprofitable structure on a very valuable piece of urban real estate. Design Research has a twenty-year lease on the 17,000 square feet of space in the Van Rensselaer Mansion. It pays more than $130,000 per year to use the building, and has spent more than $1.2 million on the adaptation/renovation. Design Research's reuse scheme, resulting in the removal of most of the original interior to achieve more efficient selling space, generated considerable public controversy. Although the project has not been a financial success to date, the company still feels it was worthwhile and may reuse other buildings in the future.

Background The Van Rensselaer Mansion was built in 1897 for Sara Drexel Fell, a member of the wealthy Drexel family, which owned most of the property around Rittenhouse Square. After the death of her husband, John R. Fell, Sara married Alexander Van Rensselaer, and her mansion has been known ever since by the Van Rensselaer name.*

The three-story building, designed in the Renaissance Revival style by the Boston architectural firm of Peabody and Stearns, possesses an exterior of finely carved granite. A two-story, pavilion-like wing is joined on the north side. The central feature of the interior is a stained-glass, domed

*Information on the history of this building has come from a student paper by Hava J. Gelblum titled "1801-1803 Walnut St.— Past & Present," which was written on December 1, 1975 for Art History 446 at the University of Pennsylvania.

skylight which is visible from the first floor through a semicircular three-story space. The major living/entertaining rooms were on the first floor, including a grand dining room in the wing. This room has been named the Pope's Room because of the framed, painted portraits of religious leaders which are affixed to the ceiling. The second floor contained the primary sleeping quarters, and the third floor was for guests and servants. Kitchen and storage facilities were located in the basement.

The Van Rensselaer Mansion was owned and used by the family until the 1940s, when it was sold to the Penn Athletic Club. In 1964, the Club was forced to sell because of declining membership and high maintenance costs. However, the Presbyterian Ministers Fund, an insurance company for the clergy, bought the property and leased it to the Club until 1972. After

The Van Rensselaer Mansion.

The stained glass, domed skylight in its new setting. (Tom Crane)

32

the Club left, the Fund was unable to find a new tenant, and the building remained empty for the next two years. The Presbyterian Ministers Fund reportedly contemplated demolishing the structure.

In 1973, Design Research Chairman Peter Sprague and President Phillip Doub were looking for a location in Philadelphia for a branch store. The Van Rensselaer Mansion was of immediate interest. Although the building's interior was in need of refurbishing, Rittenhouse Square was a fashionable location, close to some of Philadelphia's finest stores, and an established and growing residential neighborhood. The Van Rensselaer Mansion is a city landmark, and Sprague and Doub believed that its image

would help the store. Design Research has several other stores located in older buildings. The two men had also "fallen in love"[1] with the Mansion, and were interested in its preservation. Design Research's architects, Architectural Resources Cambridge, Inc., examined the building and developed preliminary plans. In January, 1974, the company signed a twenty-year lease with the Presbyterian Ministers Fund.

The architects—Architectural Resources Cambridge, Inc.—created four selling floors from three. Cut-outs and two-story spaces provide a flow of space and view from one floor to the next. (Architectural Resources Cambridge, Inc.)

Execution Because the Mansion is a registered Philadelphia landmark, no exterior alterations could be made. All reuse plans had to be reviewed by the Philadelphia Historical Commission. The residential interiors were elegant, but their formality and organization restricted flexible use. To transform the old home into a workable store displaying and selling contemporary furnishings and accessories, the three existing floors in the main part of the house were removed, and four new floors were created. This produced slightly over 11,000 square feet of sales space. The old ceiling heights had been nine, seventeen, and eleven feet; the new ones are eight-and-a-half feet. Two-story spaces were strategically located to visually connect one floor to the next

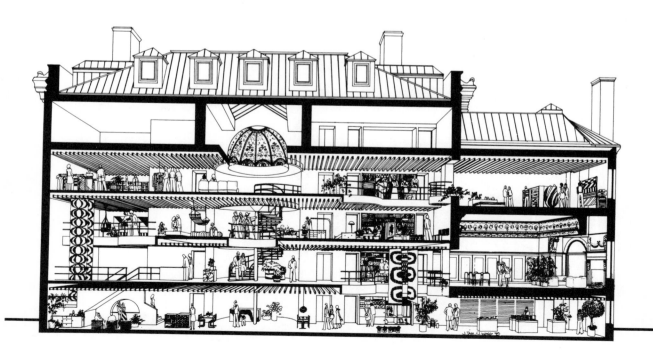

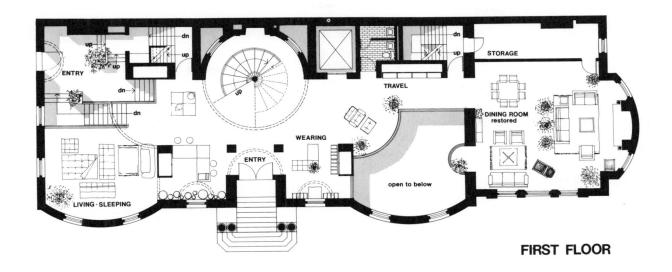

FIRST FLOOR

Floor plan of Design Research's
Philadelphia store. Floor area is divided
by product line. (Architectural Resources Cambridge, Inc.)

(below)

Philadelphia's design restrictions permitted no alteration of the building's
exterior. (Architectural Resources
Cambridge, Inc.)

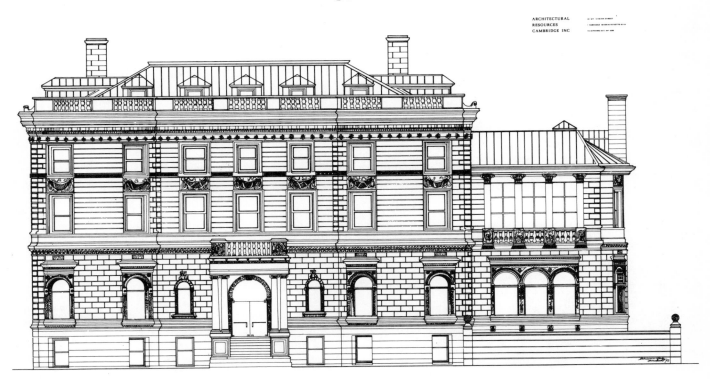

and create a sense of open space. Because much of Design Research's business is the result of impulse-buying, the open flow of light, space, and view is important to the store's marketing efforts. The new interior has white walls, quarry-tile and brightly colored, carpeted floors, and wood slatted ceilings. The latter were used to hide ducts and wires and to display hanging merchandise. The original interior was symmetrically organized around the central three-story space, emphasized by the stained-glass dome. To promote customer circulation, a new spiral staircase was introduced in this space.

After some discussions with the Philadelphia Historical Commission and others, Design Research and its

architects agreed to preserve the stained-glass dome, the marble fireplace and flanking stained-glass windows in the entry hall, and the Pope's Room, complete with painted ceiling, and ornate plaster and wood detailing. The Historical Commission approved the company's decision to cut a new entry into one of the basement windows on Walnut Street to meet building/fire-code egress requirements. The renovation took 21 months to complete from the date the lease arrangements were made.

Costs The cost for adapting the space exceeded $1.2 million, or $107 per square foot for 11,200 square feet of selling space. (There are approximately 17,000 gross square feet in the building.) The Presbyterian Ministers Fund loaned Design Research $600,000 of the renovation cost at 9¼ percent interest for twenty years. The annual rent for the twenty-year lease is $64,500, bringing the total annual cost to the company, including debt service, to $130,500, or $11.65 per square foot leased. This compares to a $7.45-per-square-foot average cost for all other Design Research stores. Fixture costs for Design Research stores average a maximum $5 per square foot.

Former dining room of the Van Rensselaer Mansion. (Tom Crane)

Problems Design Research's reuse of the Van Rensselaer Mansion produced two major problems. First, the design plans, specifically the major alteration of the interiors, generated considerable public controversy. When the company submitted its plans to the city in spring, 1974, it met with opposition from the Preservation Committee of the Philadelphia Chapter of the American Institute of Architects, the Philadelphia Historical Commission, and other groups. An article by *Philadelphia Inquirer* architecture critic Thomas Hine referred to Design Research's plans to preserve and reuse the building as: "a sweet and sour kind of recycling . . . battle that's not yet finished."[2] Because of the controversy and required approvals, it took Design Research until the following winter before actual renovations could begin. Opposition continued in June, 1974. Three high school students wrote a letter to Mayor Rizzo protesting the company's plans: "You're the only one left," they wrote. "Please can't you do something to prevent the gutting?"[3] While the city did not want to discourage Design Research from coming to Philadelphia, nor to thwart the company's efforts to try to inject life into the old building, the Mayor could not ignore the controversy. He directed the appropriate city agencies, primarily the Historical Commission, to determine the proper action to take to ensure that the significant interiors were preserved.

The Committee for the Mansion, a group of concerned citizens headed by Roy Warren West, developed an alternative proposal. They suggested that the building be used as a residence for Philadelphia's mayors. The cost to restore the Mansion for this use was placed at $2 million, which was to be raised from private sources. Mayor Rizzo had just spent a considerable sum on his house in the suburbs, so the Committee's proposal may not have received strong city support, but Design Research realized that its plans were in jeopardy. The company offered to swallow its losses—approximately $30,000 at that time—and according to President Phillip Doub, "step aside and assign the lease to any qualified person or company who can use the building without changes."[4]

No qualified person or company came up with the necessary funding, and Design Research moved ahead with its plans. According to Susan Becher, Manager of the Philadelphia store after it opened in October, 1975, "We probably converted about 40 percent of the negative opinions after they saw the finished results. About 85 percent of the people coming in have a positive reaction."[5] Nevertheless, Dr. George Thomas, an architectural professor at Drexel University and a historical consultant for the American Institute of Architects' Preservation Committee, believes that the gutted house will be worthless and unusable in twenty years. "The slick-shick banal modern interior will be dated then,"[6] he says.

The project faces an additional difficulty. According to company owner and Chairman Sprague:

The Philadelphia store is our least profitable store. We could have done four conventional 6,500 square foot mall stores for the same price. Economically, it probably did not make much sense.[7]

The location is good, but it may not be good enough. Sprague indicates that Design Research's presence in the area has lured several competitors to nearby shops. Philadelphia may just not be ready to absorb so much contemporary merchandise. Judy Kasameyer, a resident, says, "Philadelphia is a conservative city. The downtown stores are all hurting because Philadelphians either shop in the suburbs or in New York."[8]

Some of the high-cost problems obviously fall on the building's shoulders; some of the poor business performance may also. According to Susan Becher, "the formality of the building may be its biggest problem. It doesn't feel like a store. It is almost too elegant . . . a sort of museum quality."[9] Peter Sprague feels that people may see the building, be intimidated by it, and "be afraid to come in."[10] Although there are signs in the windows and banners of Marimekko fabric hanging outside, it is not easy to recognize the Mansion as a store.

Benefits In spite of its problems, the Design Research reuse of the Van Rensselaer Mansion has resulted in some significant benefits. The store's design has been widely praised by the public and by many preservationists. In the *Art* column of the *Philadelphia Inquirer*, Thomas Hine wrote:

In an earlier column we complained about plans to gut the building, destroying some truly eccentric and irreplaceable domed spaces and fireplaces.

But the building plans which do involve rebuilding of nearly the entire interior, now propose to preserve intact the building's one outstanding room, its ceiling lined with medallions of the Doges of Venice*, and they increase the dramatic impact of an existing glass dome.

Most importantly, though, Design Research has a 20-year lease. Thus at least one stately house on the Square will be around for another two decades.

Like many of the properties on the Square, this one is owned by an institution which has neither the money nor the inclination to preserve the atmosphere of the city. Fortunately, a tenant was found who does.[11]

The project has also been written about in architectural and interior-design publications. An editorial accompanying an extensive article on the recycling in the April, 1976, issue of *Interiors* stated:

The new Design Research store in Philadelphia, housed in the old Van Rensselaer mansion, is a superb example of how to use today's materials, products and techniques—with a respect equal to that held for the space itself.[12]

In response to criticism of the building's modern interior, Colin Smith of Architectural Resources Cambridge, Inc., the architects for the project, says:

It is a normal part of the design cycle which reflects society's tasks and aspirations at any given point in our history—for better or for worse. An honest design needs to be concerned about that. Being dated in twenty years often leads to being fashionable in

*Medallions in the Pope's Room had been mistakenly identified as portraits of the Doges of Venice.

another twenty, and so the process goes.[13]

An editorial in the National Trust's *Preservation News* examined the alternatives:

If Design Research had not been permitted to adapt the building, it may have become another parking lot and the visual quality of that corner of Rittenhouse Square lost forever. Today the building stands, an example of realistic preservation.[14]

Employees like the store, as do most shoppers. Maggie Mayer, Assistant Store Manager in Philadelphia, says, "This is our most beautiful store . . . I love the contrasts of contemporary furnishings in an old building."[15]

The Company Design Research, Inc., a retailer of contemporary furnishings, fabrics, and accessories, with eleven branch stores located in Massachusetts, Connecticut, New York, Pennsylvania, and California, was founded in Cambridge, Massachusetts, by architect Benjamin Thompson in 1953. Its first store was in a converted house. As business grew, Thompson and his architectural firm designed a modern concrete and glass shop in Cambridge's Harvard Square. The New York and San Francisco branches are in adaptively reused older buildings. The company is privately held, and no financial figures are available.

For further information contact:

Peter Sprague
Chairman
Design Research, Inc.
2 Campanelli Drive
Braintree, Massachusetts 02184

Colin Smith
Architectural Resources Cambridge, Inc.
102 Mt. Auburn Street
Cambridge, Massachusetts 02138

Footnotes

1. INFORM interview with Peter Sprague, Chairman, Design Research, May, 1977.
2. Thomas Hine, "Playing Cupid Proved Trust-Worthy," *Philadelphia Inquirer*, 3 March 1974.
3. Nessa Forman, "Update: . . . On the Fate of a Mansion," *Sunday Bulletin* (Philadelphia), 18 August 1974, sec. 5, p. 8.
4. Nessa Forman, "Mansion Eyed As Home for Philadelphia Mayors," *Sunday Bulletin* (Philadelphia), 8 September 1974, sec. 1, p. 30.
5. INFORM interview with Susan Becher, Manager, Design Research, Philadelphia branch, May, 1977.
6. Peg Harris, "Store Fits Midcity Mansion to Its Design," *Philadelphia Daily News*, 9 October 1975, p. 28.
7. INFORM interview with Peter Sprague, Chairman, Design Research, May, 1977.
8. INFORM interview with Judy Kasameyer, Philadelphia resident, May, 1977.
9. INFORM interview with Susan Becher, Manager, Design Research, Philadelphia branch, May, 1977.
10. INFORM interview with Peter Sprague, Chairman, Design Research, May, 1977.
11. Thomas Hine, "New Building Ruins a Scene, and That's on the Square," *Philadelphia Inquirer*. 5 May 1974.
12. "Editorial," *Interiors*, April, 1976.
13. INFORM interview with Colin Smith, architect, Architectural Resources Cambridge, Inc., July, 1977.
14. "Editorial: The Enemy Within," *Preservation News*, October, 1976.
15. INFORM interview with Maggie Mayer, Assistant Manager, Design Research, Philadelphia branch, May, 1977.

Digital Equipment Corporation

Summary A rambling nineteenth-century mill complex in Maynard, Massachusetts, is currently being recycled for use by the Digital Equipment Corporation as corporate offices, design and engineering facilities, and a manufacturing center. The buildings, dating from the 1860s, have proved to be easily adaptable to today's needs and inexpensive to renovate. Kenneth Olsen, President of the company, explained the primary reason for Digital's location in the old mill as "cheap space."[1] Other less tangible reasons, relating to the emotional and psychological benefits of working in these surroundings, were summed up in the statement of one of the company's oldest and most loyal employees: "If they moved me to a *new* building, I don't know if I would stay."[2]

Background Maynard is a typical small New England town that grew up around a textile mill. In the beginning, it was just a few small houses for the mill workers. Later, retail shops and public buildings were added. The mill itself was the economic and social hub of the town. In 1871, Maynard was incorporated, and began to function as a separate entity. Its name was taken from the man who had developed it from a sparsely settled farming district to a prosperous, bustling manufacturing center: Amory Maynard, founder of the mill. Residents of Maynard are descended from the many nationalities who came to work in the mill in search of a "better life."

The American Woolen Company ran the mill at one point. It installed a dynamo system to produce electric power for the mill and also sold electric power to the town to light the streets. Except for a brief period during the Great Depression, the mill and the town flourished. However, with the introduction of synthetic cloth materials in the 1940s, the textile industry underwent a dramatic transformation. In 1950, the American Woolen Company closed down permanently, leaving the mill and the town to deteriorate together.

This clock tower was once the focal point of Maynard's nineteenth-century woolen mill complex. Today it serves the same function for a new industry.

The 1950s and 1960s in Massachusetts and other New England states represent a period of great change. The textile industry was moving south, and the technology and service industries were in their infancy. In 1953, a group of businessmen purchased the mill and formed Maynard Industries. Their plan was to provide leaseable space for many of these growing new firms. In 1957, the Digital Equipment Corporation—then just an idea—purchased a lease for 8,500 square feet of space in the mill. By 1974, it would own and occupy the entire complex.

Execution An article in *Business Week* calls the company's base in Maynard "one of the world's most incongruous high-technology plants, a 1 million sq. ft. Civil War woolen mill that turned out blankets for the Union Army."[3]

There are more than twenty individual buildings in the mill complex, dating from the 1860s through more recent times. Most are joined together to form, in effect, a horizontal highrise, permitting separate departments to function in their own buildings or floors, but allowing easy interdepartmental communication. Administration, research, and engineering take place in the smaller buildings,

while the larger ones are used for production.

Like most mill construction, the individual buildings are long, low, and shallow with many window openings. The construction is heavy-timber framing with brick-masonry supporting walls. The column spacing and deep floor beams create large, flexible interior spaces with high ceilings. The load capacity of the floors in the mill complex ranges from 50 pounds per square foot to 200 pounds per square foot. This inconsistency makes using the buildings for manufacturing and production more complicated, since the floor-load requirement for such use is 150 pounds per square foot. Office and engineering use, however, are easily accommodated. Differential settlement over the years has created a noticeable sloping of floors in most buildings, but there is no indication of structural deficiency.

The mill was built along the banks of the Assabet River, and waterpower is still available today for a number of Digital's needs, the most recent, a cooling source for the air-conditioning system.

According to Digital's published *General Guidelines for Mill Renovation,* the company is not renovating the entire mill at once, but instead, as natural moves occur, renovations are made to improve the space. Nevertheless, with over a million square feet to work with, and the company's rapid expansion, a full-time renovation operation is necessary. To do this, Digital primarily uses an in-house team of designers, engineers, and carpenters. Even the renovation materials, like partitions and duct work, are made in the company shop. Outside contractors are brought in for specialized tasks when needed.

The renovation plan is simple and efficient. As a floor becomes ready for renovation, all existing partitions, walls, lighting, and mechanical systems are removed. The brick walls and wood ceilings are sandblasted. The old wood floors are sanded and sealed. In certain areas, floor coverings are used and experimentation with different types of floor coverings is now being conducted to determine an inexpensive but efficient way to reduce noise-level problems. The old windows are replaced with dual-pane insulating glass, and new wiring, plumbing, heating, and air-conditioning systems are installed.

"Open office" planning is employed on each floor. Low partitioned enclosures allow light and ventilation to enter the space freely through the many windows. According to the Digital *Renovation Guidelines*:

Fundamentally, the Mill has the potential for an ideal working environment because of its general layout, high ceilings, open areas, and expanse of windows. We must realize this potential and not try to panel it or otherwise build within it on the basis of a non-descript modern building.[4]

Heating, ventilating, plumbing, and electrical systems run unobstructed and exposed in the high ceiling space. This minimizes the cost of installation and makes alterations and repairs easier and cheaper. Bright colored partitions and pipes, as well as individual personal decoration such as plants and pictures, add life and an informal atmosphere.

According to the company, there have been no major building-code problems which have caused it to alter its reuse plans. Sprinklers are incorporated in all spaces, and fire- and smoke-detection equipment is also used. Stairs—some of them winding—are of original wood construction, but are located in nonflammable enclosures.

Renovation designer Pat McCormick has provided a "kit of parts"—a variety of layouts, partition types, and color schemes—to be used in all future space alterations. Hired to work on Digital's staff, she has participated in this renovation process from 1975 to 1977. Ms. McCormick is particularly interested in the psychological effects of working environments on workers. She describes how her kit is used: "Managers and department personnel are like kids with a tinker toy set . . . moving the parts around to shape their own environments."[5]

Other than the installation of the new windows, few changes have been made in the exterior of the buildings. Because the complex is so large, and because it is industrial in character, changes can take place without altering the overall visual integrity or impact of the architecture. For example, rooftop mechanical equipment has been added to some buildings, but blends with all the other stacks and appendages to avoid being visually disturbing. Research is currently being conducted to evaluate the benefits of utilizing roof-mounted solar collectors to produce hot water for hygienic and industrial use. The addition of these collectors should not detract from the overall appearance of the mill complex.

Costs The exact price Digital paid for the mill is unknown. A stock transfer in exchange for mill assets was made in 1974. The previous owners had paid approximately $200,000 for the complex in 1953. All financing for the renovation work comes from within the company. Depreciation is computed on a straight-line basis over 33 years.

Digital estimates the cost of renovating the mill, including the purchase price, at approximately $15 per square foot ($5.50 per square foot for renovation, $5.50 per square foot for "fit up," and $4.00 per square foot for amortization). According to its real estate people, comparable new construction, for the same purpose, costs, conservatively, $25 to $30 per square foot. Thus, the renovated space costs 40 percent to 50 percent less. In addition, renovated space can be occupied in less than three months, while it takes anywhere from one-and-a-half to two years to complete a new building.

The mill complex containing more than a million square feet.

Interior of the mill after renovation.

Problems The difficulties arising from Digital's association with the mill have been primarily external problems for the town of Maynard. The demand on services and the traffic and parking problems have been significant. A new sewage-treatment facility had to be built, and the company's use of the town water supply has reduced the pressure to a trickle during peak-consumption periods. New roads are contemplated to ease the traffic burden, and the police force has had to be increased to control the 6,000 cars going in and out of town each day. Maynard currently has a population of 9,901, with approximately 10 percent of its residents employed by Digital. This figure represents only about 15 percent of the 7,000 employees working in the Maynard facilities, meaning that over 5,000 people commute to the town every workday. Needless to say, traffic congestion could easily consume Maynard's microscopic 5.2-square-mile area if proper planning is not carried out. Digital is working on this problem in cooperation with local and state government planners.

Another problem resulting specifically from the renovation of the mill buildings is excessive internal noise. Old mill buildings, unless expensively adapted by adding new concrete floors or sound insulation in the ceilings, are going to be noisy. Digital has hired acoustical consultants to try to find a solution.

Benefits The primary benefit to the company is the lower cost of space. Although maintenance and security costs are higher, the overall cost of operating the mill is less than similar new construction. This is primarily due to lower real estate taxes on the existing facility. The costs for lighting and power are roughly the same as in a new building, but efforts to encourage user-controlled lighting should help reduce electrical-energy consumption in the future. While heating the space is more expensive, due to the perimeter exposed, the high ceilings, and the many windows, cooling costs can be reduced because windows may be opened to introduce outside ventilation.

Functionally, the mill provides a great degree of internal flexibility.

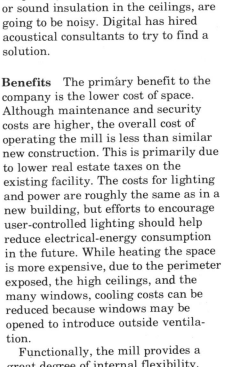

Alterations are quickly, easily, and inexpensively made. The goal of the renovation is to provide an efficient and pleasant working environment in the shortest possible time. Parts and components are designed to permit future changes in even a shorter period of time.

The feeling of participation and pride in working in an unusual but pleasant environment has improved employee morale at Digital. Librarian Karen Feingold refers to a "sense of history" and an "informal atmosphere"[6] when describing the mill and her experience working in it. Her library space has recently been refurbished and it rivals many a public library in its pleasant reading environment. Mary Jane Forbes, Assistant to Vice President Gordon Bell, describes Digital's employees as "individuals"[7] operating, in large part, on their own initiative. According to Ms. Forbes, the mill is a perfect environment for this kind of creative work.

Gordon Bell, Vice President, Engineering, has been in the mill for fifteen years. In addition to his engineering responsibilities, he has taken on the job of "landlord of the mill." Wearing this hat, he is responsible for all the space allocations and renovations of the structure. His goals are to reduce the mean time that it takes a particular department to move to a new location within the mill; and to increase the mean time between moves by making the space adaptable to growth and change. According to Bell, the mill has performed very well in helping to realize these goals.

The location, within an easy commute from a number of residential communities, helps provide an available and contented company work force, free from many of the problems that plague a more densely urban working population.

Some Maynard residents are critical of the impact of Digital on the town, primarily because of the traffic congestion problems, but others seem to take it in stride. Ralph Sheridan, the 78-year-old President of the Maynard Historical Society, was born and raised in the town, as was his father. Every member of his family has worked in the mill at some time. When asked about the image of the old mill in the town, Sheridan concludes:

I believe most of us who have worked in it and looked at it all our lives see a great deal of beauty in the mill. They don't build buildings like that today! Just look at that clock tower and at some of the interesting ways that they used bricks. It is an asset to the town.[8]

The Company The Digital Equipment Corporation designs, sells, and services computers and other items and systems using digital techniques. For the year ending June 30, 1977, the company had revenues of $1.1 billion, an increase of 49.5 percent over the previous year's revenues of $736 million. Over the same period, net income rose 47.5 percent from $73.4 million to $108.4 million. Digital's products are used worldwide in a variety of applications and programs, including scientific research, computation, communications, education, data analysis, industrial-control systems, and medical-systems instrumentation. The company employs over 19,000 people, and occupies more than 3 million square feet of floor space in fourteen plants throughout the world. In Massachusetts alone, it employs more than 11,000 people and is located in six communities across the state.

Because of its extremely rapid growth, Digital has had difficulty meeting space needs quickly. It has reused a variety of existing buildings: an old armory building, storefronts on mainstreets, and even more modern facilities recently vacated by RCA in Marlboro, Massachusetts. In each case, the primary reasons for reusing the existing buildings were the location, the employment picture, and the economic viability (the costs and time considerations). The armory is located in Springfield, Massachusetts, and is situated in the middle of a ghetto. It has proved to be a "great success," according to President Olsen. "Ninety-five percent of the people we hired were unemployed."[9] The former RCA plant was simply an irresistible bargain. Digital was able to acquire the 730,000-square-foot building for $12.8 million or approximately $17 per square foot. This is less than half of what it would have cost to build the same facility new. Furthermore, the building took a fraction of the time to prepare for use.

For further information, contact: Gordon Bell Vice President Digital Equipment Corporation 146 Main Street Maynard, Massachusetts 01754

Footnotes

1. INFORM interview with Kenneth Olsen, President, Digital Equipment Corporation, September, 1976.
2. INFORM interview with employee, Digital Equipment Corporation, May, 1976.
3. "Mini Computers Challenge the Big Machines," *Business Week,* April 26, 1976, p. 63.
4. Memorandum: *General Guidelines on Mill Renovation,* from Gordon Bell and Al Sharon, Digital Equipment Corporation executives, November 11, 1974.
5. INFORM interview with Pat McCormick, Designer, Digital Equipment Corporation, September, 1976.
6. INFORM interview with Karen Feingold, Librarian, Digital Equipment Corporation, April, 1976.
7. INFORM interview with Mary Jane Forbes, Assistant to Vice President, Engineering, Digital Equipment Corporation, April, 1976.
8. INFORM interview with Ralph Sheridan, President, Maynard Historical Society, January, 1977.
9. Lawrence Collins, "A Critical Look At Massachusetts," *Boston Sunday Globe,* 30 November 1975, pp. 64-65.

Feldmann's Phase 2

Summary Between 1969 and 1972, C. J. Feldmann, owner and manager of a retail clothing operation in Des Moines, Iowa, purchased and renovated two late-nineteenth-century mansions for use as fashion shops. He wanted to preserve these older homes and provide an intimate sales space in a central-city location, adjacent to downtown but without its traffic and parking problems; a space different from the large commercial floor areas common to most present-day retail establishments. While the location and space have cost him some additional expense in maintaining security, the distinctive atmosphere has proved attractive to customers, giving him a competitive edge in a very tough market. The cost of the renovations averaged approximately $22 per square foot (including the price of the land and buildings) and compares favorably to $40 per square foot for comparable new construction in the area.

Background The Feldmann family has been in the retailing business since 1887. In 1952, C. J. "Pete" Feldmann entered the business, and between that year and 1969, his shops expanded to shopping centers, first in Minnesota and later in Des Moines. In 1969, Feldmann wanted to get away from the gigantism of the shopping center and move back to the central-city area. He purchased number 1915 Grand Avenue in Des Moines for $200,000—"essentially the price of the land,"[1] says Feldmann—and began to restore it for use as a store.

The house was the former Finkbine mansion, a three-story stone and brick structure, built in 1895. The Finkbines had been in the construction, lumber, and hardware business in Des Moines during the last century (State Senator Robert Finkbine personally supervised the construction of the Iowa state capitol in the late 1870s). The Finkbines spared no expense in building their home. Eclectic in style, it possesses many neo-classic and Romanesque details and was decorated with beveled glass windows and handsomely carved wooden interiors. Architecturally, it was a museum piece worth preserving.

In 1972, Feldmann also purchased the Polk family home across the street. Constructed in the early 1880s for Mr. and Mrs. Jefferson Polk, this home was known as Herndon Hall, after Mrs. Polk's maiden name, and was designed by a celebrated architect of the day, T. A. Roberts of Newark, New Jersey. An example of the Victorian style of architecture, it contains a massive central staircase, nine large fireplaces, stained glass, beautiful rare-wood interior paneling, frescoed plaster ceilings, and a large ballroom on the third floor. Mr. Polk was a leading Des Moines citizen during the latter half of the nineteenth century, and participated in the founding of the Equitable Life Insurance Company of Iowa, the Des Moines Waterworks, a steam-railway company, and the Interurban Electric Railway Company.

Although originally located in a residential area, both of these fine homes are now adjacent to the downtown commercial district. They most recently served as offices for small insurance and printing companies. The land itself is valuable, but when it was acquired by Feldmann, the buildings had been appraised at next to nothing because local lending institutions were not familiar with evaluating old buildings for potential new uses. In fact, when Feldmann bought the Finkbine mansion, the building had a negative value of $5,000, the cost of demolition. Feldmann wanted to expand his fashion line but preferred not to build carbon-copy "boxes" in the suburbs to house it. He explained his reasons for buying and renovating the old houses:

I believe for a city to be healthy, it has to have a central area that is healthy. The land is valuable, but business traditionally does not look on buildings of this age as worth being restored. . . We didn't try to create museums. We attempted to take a landmark and make out of it a living thing for this generation.[2]

Execution The Finkbine mansion contains approximately 10,000 square feet and the Polk house about 15,000. Feldmann started out doing a pure restoration of the Finkbine mansion, but soon found this impractical for modern retail use because of the expense and functional requirements. Accordingly, he changed his efforts to preservation and compatible modernization.

Both renovations included new wiring and lighting. Previous tenants had installed fluorescent fixtures but Feldmann had them removed and replaced with antique fixtures and more compatible modern lighting. Smoke and heat alarm systems were also installed to comply with the local building code. A code variance had to be obtained to avoid installing sprinklers which would have ruined the beautiful old ceilings and woodwork. The Des Moines Board of Review granted this variance provided that the smoke and heat alarm system were substituted. The third floor in the Polk house only had one means of egress, so Feldmann had to have another set of stairs constructed. An interior staircase was installed unobtrusively. Central air conditioning was not feasible because of the number of small rooms and because a duct system would have destroyed the woodwork and ceilings. For these reasons, individual window units are used. Woodwork was restored and refinished, and rooms were repainted and covered with new wallpaper where appropriate. Other renovations included the surfacing of outside parking areas and minor landscaping.

In most cases, old buildings are adapted to fit new uses by altering the interiors to meet new functional needs. In this case, the use has been adapted to fit the old building and is actually enhanced by it. Clothing is displayed in the existing residential rooms and is hung from the woodwork. The stairs are also used as a progressive display case for merchandise.

The Polk mansion's opulent exterior is depicted in an early photograph.

The original floor plans show large rooms radiating from a central stairhall and chimney.

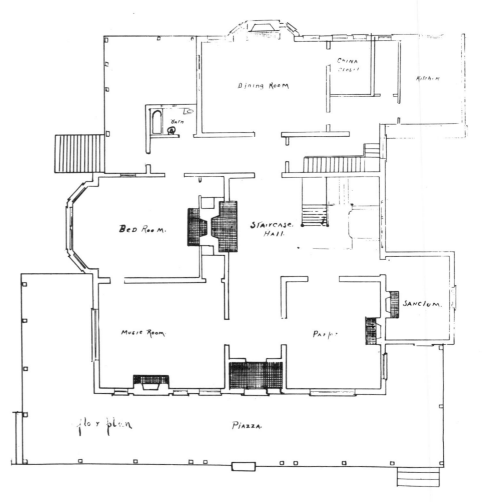

Costs Feldmann paid $200,000 for the Finkbine mansion and land, and spent approximately $60,000 for renovation, for a total of $260,000 or approximately $26 per square foot for the 10,000 square-foot house. The building was valued at a negative $5,000, so essentially it was thrown in for the price of the land. The Polk mansion was appraised at zero value, and Feldmann paid $175,000 for the land with the building included. While no figures are available on the specific renovation costs, Feldmann says that he has spent about $290,000 total to date on Herndon Hall. This would put renovations at approximately $115,000. Prorated over the total 15,000 square feet, the cost for building and land is about $20 per square foot. According to Feldmann, new construction in the area costs about $40 per square

foot, and one would be hard pressed to call it comparable. The Polk mansion was again appraised in January, 1977, for $525,000: land, $266,500; building $258,500.

Problems The primary reason for Feldmann's selection and use of the old homes was the different kind of sales space they offered. A variety of small spaces would provide a more personal shopping experience. Unfortunately, these kinds of spaces require more personnel to supply the same degree of service as conventional retail stores. They also require a greater attention to security. A large number of small spaces with plenty of places to hide is an ideal environment for shoplifting. To overcome this problem, Feldmann has had to hire more personnel and install an electronic tag security system.

In 1976, because of financial difficulties, Feldmann sold the Finkbine mansion for $370,000. While the new owners—a construction company—were primarily interested in the land, which was adjacent to their corporate headquarters, they have preserved the building and are using it for additional office space. Although he feels that his decision to reuse the old houses was a good one, Feldmann is concerned by the high cost of doing business in them and by the lack of financial support for old buildings provided by local financial institutions. As lenders become aware of the potential value in the reuse of old buildings, the latter problem may be reduced.

Benefits From a business standpoint, Feldmann feels that the old buildings enabled him to maintain his position in a glutted market. In the last five years, the number of retail clothing stores in Des Moines has grown from 47 to more than 198. Feldmann has been able to hold his position in this fragmented market, and the old houses have provided unique display areas.

Feldmann has also received a great deal of publicity for his preservation and restoration efforts. The Iowa Antique Association presented him with a brass plaque inscribed: "In appreciation for the restoration of Herndon Hall."[3] In 1977, the State Historical Department of Iowa recommended that Herndon Hall be included in the National Register of Historic Places. At present, the application is pending.

The Company Feldmann's Phase 2 is a privately held family business. No financial figures are available.

For further information contact:
C. J. Feldmann
President
Feldmann's Phase 2
2000 Grand Avenue
Des Moines, Iowa 50309

Footnotes

1. INFORM interview with C. J. Feldmann, President, Feldmann's Phase 2, March, 1977.
2. Patricia Cooney, "The Restoration of Two Mansions," *Des Moines Tribune*, 25 May 1973, p. 17.
3. *Ibid.*

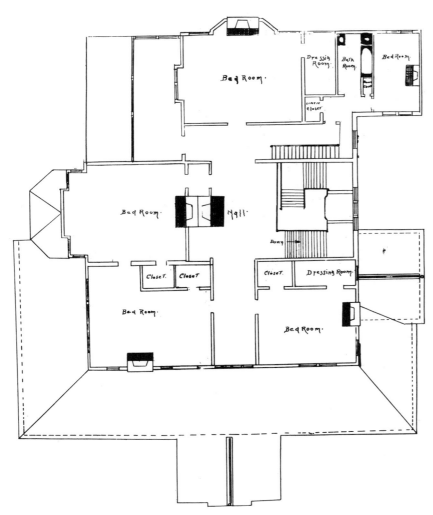

Summary On December 7, 1974, the historic 1750s Redfield House became the 24th office of the First New Haven National Bank. The house, located in the small Connecticut shoreline town of Westbrook, is a classic example of mid-eighteenth-century house design. It had been occupied but severely neglected for many years. Deterioration was so extensive that almost no one thought the building could be saved, much less reused as a functioning bank branch. The cost to adapt the building was $146,000, or $36 per square foot.

Background The bank had decided to locate a branch office in Westbrook back in the early 1970s, and in 1972 bought the Redfield property. It was an excellent location, situated near the center of town on the old Post Road. The bank originally planned to raze the old two-story frame house, with its steeply pitched gabled roof, and "build a small, efficient and architecturally attractive branch that would provide full service commercial banking in a hometown environment."[1] A delay in plans for the next two years saved the building.

In 1972, Assistant Vice President Bruce D. Stuckey was placed in charge of planning and coordinating the construction of new branches. He, a designer friend, Tim Rosenham, and architect Al Davis had experience with residential restoration and thought that the old Redfield House could be used as the new Westbrook branch. Bank officers were skeptical; the building was in very bad condition, and they believed that it would cost too much to restore and adapt. A professional engineering firm was hired by Mr. Stuckey to examine the feasibility of reusing the structure; the study found the building to be structurally unsound, and concluded that commercial use would require complete reconstruction. Bruce Stuckey still had his doubts; he felt that the engineering firm was not familiar with restoration practices. He convinced his superiors that: 1. the building was potentially useful as a branch; 2. it would be less expensive to restore this building than to build a new one on the same site; 3. saving the structure would be appreciated by the community and would greatly enhance the bank's hometown image. Doubts about the practicality of the project turned to increased support and enthusiasm as the work progressed.

Execution The exterior of the building was restored to its original state. The masonry foundation was repointed as was the central chimney. The roof was re-shingled with cedar shakes; the clapboarding was repaired—or where necessary replaced—and stained a dark brown. The original windows were repaired, and the paneled front door was recreated. A new addition, executed in a compatible but contemporary design, was built at the rear of the building. The addition, not visible from the street, houses the new vault. A driveway circles the building, accommodating drive-up service. Parking is in the rear.

In the interior of the house, the walls of the main rooms on the first floor were removed, creating a large space for banking/teller service. The original central chimney and fireplaces act as a pivot point, dividing the space and directing the flow of customer movement to the tellers' counter on one side or to a town historical-society display of local community crafts or historical objects on the other. To further open up the space and to provide an education in eighteenth-century framing and masonry techniques, the upper-story flooring has been removed exposing the structural skeleton and allowing a view up to the peak of the gabled roof. A staircase built in front of the central chimney permits access to a small catwalk on the second floor from which it is possible to look down on the mortised and numbered framing members. (When houses like this were originally constructed, timbers were numbered with Roman numerals to assist in assembly.) This catwalk leads to an employee kitchen/lounge/conference area on the second story of the new rear addition. The entire main banking area is lighted by fluorescent lighting suspended from the gabled roof. All new plumbing, wiring, heating, and air-conditioning systems have been installed.

Costs According to the bank, the cost of the restoration and adaptation was $146,000, or $36 per square foot, for the completed job (including banking equipment, furniture, signs, and landscaping).

Problems The major problems came initially in trying to convince bank executives of the desirability of restoring an old building that engineers deemed beyond repair. The structure proved to be sound.

Benefits Benefits were realized by the bank, the town of Westbrook, and the nearby communities. The bank got a new branch office at approximately 75 percent of the cost of new construction. According to Bruce Stuckey:

The Westbrook branch before renovation. (James Meehan)

The Westbrook branch after renovation. (James Meehan)

We have paid as much as $90 per square foot in the past for our branches and my estimates for new construction in Westbrook came in at about $47 per square foot. We completed our project for $36 per square foot and held extras to less than 2 percent realizing a savings of about $25,000.[2]

Articles in local newspapers and periodicals publicized the restoration and probably served to increase support and patronage for the bank. New accounts and deposits have exceeded expectations. In addition, a very good example of mid-eighteenth-century architecture has been preserved and reincorporated into the economy of the town.

A most important business benefit was the resulting enthusiasm among the branch's staff. Mr. Christopher Soulias, the Manager of the bank, is extremely proud of his "new" old building and says it is a "hometown bank with a hometown way of looking at things."[3] Bruce Stuckey is equally pleased: "As a result of Chris's competence and enthusiasm, the branch has been a complete success for us."[4]

The Company   Founded in 1792, the First New Haven National Bank is today the eighth largest bank in the State of Connecticut. Assets increased from $327 million in 1975 to $357 million in 1976. Thirty branches, most of new construction, are located primarily in New Haven County.

For further information contact:
Bruce D. Stuckey
Assistant Vice President
The First New Haven National Bank
One Church Street
New Haven, Connecticut 06502

Footnotes

1. The First New Haven National Bank, *The Redfield House and the First New Haven National Bank* (brochure distributed at Westbrook branch's opening, The First New Haven National Bank, December 7, 1974), p. 1.
2. INFORM interview with Bruce D. Stuckey, Assistant Vice President, The First New Haven National Bank, May, 1976.
3. INFORM interview with Christopher Soulias, Manager, Westbrook branch, The First New Haven National Bank, May, 1976.
4. INFORM interview with Bruce D. Stuckey, Assistant Vice President, The First New Haven National Bank, May, 1976.

The interior space has been opened exposing the timber framing and central chimney. Banking activities take place on the ground floor. (James Meehan)

An extension was added on the rear of the building housing the vault and offices. Parking is accommodated in the rear, hidden from the street.

Harbridge House, Inc.

Summary Harbridge House, Inc., an international consulting firm, has its Boston home offices in "the finest surviving mansion of those originally fronting on the Public Garden."[1] The original structure, completed in 1861, was one of the first houses erected in the Back Bay after it was reclaimed from the Charles River by land-filling begun in 1857. Harbridge House bought the building in 1967. According to Harry Hague, one of the founders of the company: "It is by far the cheapest cost-per-square-foot space to occupy of our offices anywhere in the world; and it provides the best of all possible images . . . of stability, durability, and tradition."[2] The cost for Harbridge House's 46,000-square-foot Back Bay office complex was just under $1 million.

Background In the early 1960s, Harbridge House had outgrown its Back Bay headquarters and was looking for room to expand. When numbers 10 and 11 Arlington Street came up for sale, the company bought these attached nineteenth-century rowhouses and set up operations there. In 1967, Harbridge House purchased the former mansion of the J. Montgomery Sears family, number 12 Arlington Street, which the Sears had combined with number 1 Commonwealth Avenue, just around the corner, in 1893.

Number 12 Arlington Street is a five-story building, faced with brownstone, and crowned with a mansard roof. Typical of the Second Empire style of architecture, it was designed by Boston architect Arthur Gilman, who helped design the Old Boston City Hall.

The building is located in the Back Bay Historic District which was listed in the National Register of Historic Places in 1973. Boston's strict municipal regulations for historic districts require approval of any change of use that conflicts with current residential zoning, and of any exterior alteration of a building.

The interiors of number 12 Arlington Street, although not protected by historic-district restrictions, are of superb architectural quality. There is lavishly carved hardwood detail throughout the main two floors, along with ornate plaster moldings, medallions, and cornices. When number 12 Arlington was combined with number 1 Commonwealth in 1893, two huge rooms, one on the first floor and one on the second, were created. Architectural details suggest that these rooms served as a music room and formal dining room, respectively; there is also a large ballroom over the kitchen. These large rooms, with exceptionally high ceilings—twelve to fourteen feet—and elaborate detail, make conversion to office space especially difficult: division into smaller spaces would destroy the proportions and detail of the rooms, and the high columns represent a large amount of unusable space. City zoning regulations affecting change of use were not a problem. The building had previously been owned and occupied by the Ursuline religious order so that precedent for a change from residential to institutional/office use had already been established.

A former elegant parlor now a conference room.

Execution No single plan guided the renovation work at Harbridge House's number 12 Arlington Street location. Mr. Hague set forth the basic guidelines for the work: the architectural integrity of the first two floors of the building was to be respected and restored, but the upper three floors could be rearranged to suit the firm's particular needs. The exterior of the building remained in its original state.*

The main foyer of the building was carpeted; walls were repainted with original colors; and woodwork was restored on the first two floors. These floors serve as reception, conference, library, and office facilities. Above the second floor, little if any major work was done except for general painting and cleanup; the upper three floors are used for offices. Existing heating, plumbing, and electrical systems were retained. In numbers 10 and 11 Arlington Street more extensive renovation has taken place, with new wiring and other services installed, but the basic room layouts have remained the same.

In 1977, Harbridge House retained the architectural firm of Perry, Dean, Stahl and Rogers to devise more specific and efficient space/renovation plans for all the buildings.

*In 1976, the company applied to the Massachusetts Historical Commission, under the National Park Service's Historic Preservation Grants Program, for matching funds for exterior restoration of the building, but the application was turned down due to the Commission's lack of funds at that time.

Costs The total cost of acquiring and renovating the three structures has thus far been just under $1 million, or $21 per square foot. More money will be spent to improve the buildings following the recommendations of the architects, but comparable new-construction costs in the same location would probably be more than double the total costs to date.

Problems The existing steam heating system at number 12 has created zoning-control difficulties. In order to maintain a comfortable temperature on the lower floors, the upper floors must be very hot. According to a company official, it is not surprising to find air conditioners in use during the winter on the top floors. Conditions might be improved by upgrading the current heating system to provide separate zoning on each floor.

Space and staff circulation also pose problems. Small rooms impair the traffic flow between offices. Proper planning may improve this situation.

Benefits The primary benefits to Harbridge House from re-using these former residences are the desirable location and the exceptionally inexpensive cost of space. A secondary advantage to the company is the pride officers and employees take in the buildings and the image they present.

The Company Harbridge House, founded in 1950 by three Harvard Business School faculty members, is a management consulting organization. With offices in five U.S. cities and three European countries, it provides a range of services including: socioeconomic studies, management consulting, organization and management development, and systems training. Harbridge House is a subsidiary of the Allstate Insurance Company, Inc. It would not make available any company financial information.

For further information contact:
Kristin L. Servison
Assistant Manager, Personnel and Administrative Services
Harbridge House, Inc.
11 Arlington Street
Boston, Massachusetts 02116

Footnotes

1. Nancy Smith, "Architectural Notes, 12 Arlington Street, Boston (unpublished paper presented to the Boston chapter of the Victorian Society, n.d.), p. 1.
2. INFORM interview with Harry Hague, member, Board of Directors, Harbridge House, May, 1976.

Number 12 Arlington Street, and numbers 10 and 11 next door, the headquarters of Harbridge House in Boston. These Second-Empire-style buildings were once grand city residences.

The Lawyers Co-operative Publishing Co.

Summary   In 1971, Lawyers Co-operative, located in a vintage mill complex in downtown Rochester, needed additional space for its expanded operations. The company, one of the nation's leading law publishers, asked its architects, Handler/Grosso, to determine whether it would be practical to recycle the existing structures. The architects' feasibility study showed that renovating the 125,000 square feet of the existing buildings would cost approximately $15 per square foot as compared to $45 per square foot for demolition and new construction. Completed in one year, the Lawyers Co-operative recycling, the first major rehabilitation project in downtown Rochester, has served as an instructive example. The success of the first project inspired Lawyers Co-operative to recycle another building in the complex, as well as to create a new park adjacent to its headquarters.

Background   Lawyers Co-operative is located in six brick buildings along the Genesee River. In 1901, the company occupied the Aqueduct Building, the oldest structure in the complex, a former shoe factory dating from about 1880. As business increased, Lawyers Co-operative gradually expanded to the adjacent buildings: a warehouse dating from 1890; a smaller pre-1900 industrial building; and a 1950 addition to the 1880s mill. Two other buildings, yet to be renovated, complete the complex. Floor space for the four renovated buildings measures approximately 125,000 square feet.

Through the years, the company continued to grow. In 1965, it also leased additional space outside the complex to house administrative offices, and two years later, it expanded into suburban Rochester, adding a new manufacturing plant for printing and binding. In 1971, management asked Handler/Grosso, architects, to study the feasibility of recycling their historic building complex to meet their space requirements.

Execution   Handler/Grosso found the buildings to be structurally sound and in excellent condition, and concluded that renovation would be economically feasible. The company decided to proceed.

The recycling of the buildings took one year, and was done in stages so that production would not be disrupted. The exterior masonry was cleaned, using dry grit, and waterproofed—except where ivy-covered—with a silicone coating. Some of the finer architectural details, the brick-arched floors, cast-iron columns, and wrought-iron beams, typical of nineteenth-century mill construction, were left exposed. Many interior walls were cleaned, highlighting the brick. Windows were replaced, and air conditioning was installed throughout the complex. All new heating, wiring, and plumbing systems were added. The newly retrofitted buildings now serve as administrative and editorial offices. All manufacturing previously done in the complex has been transferred to the suburban Rochester facility.

Interior with exposed and painted original brickwork.

The crowning feat of the renovation was the construction of an Italianate tower, topped by a statue of Mercury 163 feet above street level, on an existing elevator shaft. A familiar landmark, the 21-foot, 700-pound copper-plated statue, dating from 1881, had been atop the nearby Peerless Tobacco Works. It had been kept in storage by the City of Rochester since Peerless's demolition in 1950.

Relying on this experience, the company has recently retrofitted another smaller building in its complex and is now leasing the space. Handler/Grosso revitalized the 1890 structure, exposing the brickwork, installing new plumbing, heating, air-conditioning and electric systems, as well as new windows, a new elevator, and an acoustical ceiling. This renovation took ten months.

Adjacent to its buildings, along the Genesee River, Lawyers Co-operative created a pleasant public park. Designed by Carol R. Johnson and Associates, the park effectively links the complex with the rest of downtown, and provides increased green space for Rochester's citizens.

Costs The cost of recycling the vintage buildings was much lower than the cost of new construction: about $15 per square foot as compared to about $45 per square foot. Handler/Grosso provided a breakdown on the comparative costs (see below).

The renovation cost an estimated $1.8 million. Development of the park cost about $250,000.

Problems The temperature of the condensate from the steam used to heat the renovated buildings had to be lowered before it was returned to the city's sewers. To solve this problem, condensate-cooling pipes were installed below the sidewalks. In winter, the pipes serve to melt the abundant snow, while at the same time lowering the condensate temperature.

Benefits Richard Handler, of Handler/Grosso, enthusiastically assessed the results of the rehabilitation:

At a cost of less than one-half of a new building, this office building provides functional area equal to any new building with the elements of charm and historic continuity for the company as well as historic significance for the community.[1]

In addition to the cost savings, rehabilitation, unlike new construction, made it unnecessary for the company to reshuffle its operations and employees. The newly decorated, bright, and spacious interiors also enhance the working environment. Employees take pride in their offices and in Mercury, a Rochester landmark for years.

The new park is popular with both employees and city residents; it has even led to the establishment of a bocce league among the employees. In addition, some local citizens have telephoned the company to express their appreciation. The company has received a good deal of favorable publicity in local newspapers and magazines.

Following the Lawyers Co-operative example, other businesses have chosen to remain and retrofit rather than flee to the suburbs. Rochester Telephone Company has recently completed a new mini-park, and Handler/Grosso is renovating a vintage former Federal Building (c.1890) as the City Hall.

In June, 1975, Handler/Grosso received a Design Award from the Rochester Chapter of the American Institute of Architects for the Mercury statue and tower. The Award read, "Chosen for its imaginative contribution to the city of a meaningful landmark and its sensitive relationship to existing buildings."[2]

The Company The Lawyers Co-operative Publishing Company, the second largest publisher of law books and related materials in the country, was founded in 1882. Its publications include legal text and reference books, and *Case and Comment*, a magazine for lawyers. In 1964, Lawyers Co-operative acquired the Research Institute of America, which publishes information on business management, including security and tax matters, training, automation, and economics. Lawyers Co-operative is privately held, and no financial figures are available.

For further information contact:
Thomas Ryan
Facilities Planner
The Lawyers Co-operative
Publishing Co.
Aqueduct Building
Rochester, N.Y. 14603

Architects/Engineers:
Handler/Grosso
2209 Monroe Avenue
Rochester, N.Y. 14618

Footnotes

1. Written communication from Richard Handler, partner, Handler/Grosso, to INFORM, February, 1977.
2. Sally Walsh, "Eight Buildings Cited in Design Awards," *Rochester Democrat & Chronicle*, 20 June 1975, p. 15C.

	Retrofitting		*New*
land value	$ 300,000		$ 300,000
value of existing shell	1,250,000		—
cost to demolish	—		100,000
total square foot need	125,000		125,000
renovation costs, including:	1,800,000	new construction costs, including:	6,250,000
mechanical systems	700,000		700,000
floor finish	150,000		150,000
window replacement	100,000		—
time for renovation	1 year	time for new construction	1½ years

The recycled Lawyers Cooperative buildings.

Summary   Since 1971, McGraw-Hill Publications, a subsidiary of McGraw-Hill, Inc., a large and diversified international publishing and communications company, has operated its U.S. Western Regions office from a 1920s ice cream factory located in the heart of the downtown San Francisco business district. Although the company leases only about one-half of the 65,000-square-foot space, it has renovated the structure to meet its specific needs, as well as to provide additional space for subleasing. These subleases help offset the cost of building improvements. They also allow a measure of security for future expansion. Including the cost of improvements, the cost to McGraw-Hill for the master lease is approximately 50 percent of what it would be for comparable space in one of the area's new high-rise office buildings. In addition, the company is not just a name on a large lobby directory, but the principal tenant in a unique building.

Background   Since 1912, McGraw-Hill has had offices in San Francisco in several locations; in 1970, the Publications Company was once again looking for new space. Thomas Carmody, a Vice President in charge of its Western Regions office, is confined to a wheelchair. His primary requirements for new space were that it be free of architectural barriers and be accessible to the handicapped, unlike so many of the new buildings he had worked in or looked at. In addition, business required that the office be located in the central downtown district. After examining buildings in the area, Carmody found:

In many of these new office buildings, designed for the most modern of conveniences, I have to enter the building like a "piece of baggage" from the service alley and up the freight elevator. I cannot negotiate the many steps and escalators that are often the only means of gaining access to the building and to such amenities as plazas and commercial mall areas . . . the main selling attractions of most of these newer buildings.[1]

One day, Ron Kaufman, a local developer, asked Carmody to look at the recently renovated Fibreboard Headquarters Building at 55 Francisco Street. This fifty-year-old corrugated-box plant had been converted into offices for the Fibreboard Corporation (see Appendix) and additional leaseable space for other tenants. Carmody and representatives from the company's Real Estate and General Services Division in New York visited the Fibreboard conversion and liked what they saw. The only problem was that the location was not quite right; it was a few blocks away from the desired area.

Kaufman then found the old Foremost Ice Cream Factory, built in the 1920s, in just the right location for McGraw-Hill. He approached Carmody and the New York staff with a proposal to sign a master lease for 24,000 square feet of this space and to spend a considerable sum of money improving the building's interior and exterior. Foremost had made some mechanical improvements, including the installation of air conditioning, but the part that McGraw-Hill would lease was virtually "raw space" and required all new finishes. Windows had to be replaced, and in the eyes of the company, the exterior needed some modernization. Carmody and his staff were less than enthusiastic about space in the new high rises they had visited, but the idea of recycling an old ice cream factory for their new offices excited them. According to Carmody, "This was a project that we all felt we were taking an active part in creating, and the entire staff is very proud of the results."[2]

A new front unifies two old industrial buildings now the San Francisco offices of McGraw-Hill. (Cine Kersha Photography)

Execution The building contains approximately 65,000 square feet: four floors of 12,000 square feet each, 5,000 square feet on the roof, including a penthouse of about 1,000 square feet, and approximately 12,000 square feet of street-level commercial space. McGraw-Hill leased 24,000 square feet, of which 12,000 was subleased to other tenants. The lease extended for twenty years with a termination clause available to McGraw-Hill after ten.

Although McGraw-Hill was to spend a sizable sum of its own money improving the space and the exterior, the lease arrangements were financially beneficial to the company. The building owner pays for all taxes, utilities, and maintenance. This arrangement results in the space costing McGraw-Hill approximately 50 percent of what it would cost in a new building, excluding the cost of improvements, and about 75 percent after these costs are included. In addition, if the owner receives higher rent from other tenants in the future, which can be attributable to McGraw-Hill's improvements, the company receives a percentage of the rent increase as a reduction in its rent. Although McGraw-Hill had to absorb most of the 20 percent tax increase due to exterior improvements, it was able to recoup this added expense from the other tenants in the building.

Actually, the ice cream factory was not one building, but two separate structures attached to each other. There is a difference in floor levels of from three to three-and-a-half feet. This could have been a formidable architectural barrier, but Carmody's conversion design circumvented this problem by utilizing a system of ramps. Other design features specifically for the handicapped included: wider door openings to accommodate wheelchairs, grip bars, elevator controls which can be reached from a sitting position, and toilet facilities specifically designed to accommodate the handicapped. A special parking spot was included on the ground level to permit Mr. Carmody to enter the building conveniently from his car.

McGraw-Hill's staff designed the office interiors, which involved some partitioning of the open industrial space and refurbishing of existing offices. The exterior of the buildings was unified by installing new matching operable windows, and spandrel and column coverings. In addition, a roof terrace, with a trellis designed to equalize the height of the roof lines, was built, providing employees with an outdoor space for relaxation. A small covered kitchen area was installed on the roof to provide refreshments.

Other tenants rent office and banking space in the building, but McGraw-Hill positioned its logo over the entry doors, making the structure, in effect, the McGraw-Hill Building, an identifiable address in the city.

Costs The company did not disclose the exact lease rate per square foot in its building, but it did indicate that the cost to McGraw-Hill is below the average $12-per-square-foot market rate for comparable space in new office buildings in the area.

According to Lou Gallo, General Manager-Real Estate for the company, McGraw-Hill spent approximately $415,000 for the improvements on the building. Of this, about $240,000 went for exterior alterations; the balance was used for interior renovations of the company's own space, tenant space, elevators and lobby, and the new penthouse garden. Since occupying the building in 1971, McGraw-Hill has spent another $50,000 on additional improvements. This equals a total investment of about $19 per square foot for the 24,000 square feet leased by McGraw-Hill, to be amortized over twenty years.

No figures are available on operating costs, but according to Lou Gallo, the 425 Battery Street building is "very efficient to operate and comparable to offices in newer buildings."³

Problems In the original proposal, the additional space that McGraw-Hill was to sublease was to provide enough income above expenses to offset the cost of the exterior improvements. Because the space was made available during a very soft office market—there was a glut of new office buildings in downtown San Francisco at that time—it did not rent as quickly as expected. The building took two years to fully lease, and this delay increased McGraw-Hill's total cost.

Benefits Even with this additional cost, the company's decision to lease space in an older renovated building has provided it with excellent space at a cost lower than that in new office construction. Space could be shaped to suit McGraw-Hill's requirements, and the location conforms well to the company's needs. Employees are proud of the new home they helped to design. Mr. Carmody says:

*It is like a little oasis in a high rise forest and we feel like we are special people. It has been a profitable venture for McGraw-Hill, and we have our own building with our own name on it. We are not just one of the many hundreds of tenants in someone else's monument.*⁴

The Company McGraw-Hill, Inc., is a diversified communications company, which publishes business, trade, and educational publications for national and international markets. The company also produces audio-visual materials and owns four television stations in the United States. Its regional offices are located across the United States and around the world. The company's total operating revenue for 1976 was $590 million, up from 1975 operating revenues of $536 million. Net income rose from $33 million in 1975 to $40.4 million in 1976.

For further information contact:
Thomas H. Carmody
Vice President, Western Regions
McGraw-Hill Publications
425 Battery Street
San Francisco, California 94111

Footnotes

1. INFORM interview with Thomas Carmody, Vice President, Western Regions, McGraw-Hill Publications, August, 1975.
2. *Ibid.*
3. INFORM interview with Lou Gallo, Jr., General Manager, Real Estate, McGraw-Hill, Inc., August, 1975.
4. INFORM interview with Thomas Carmody, Vice President, Western Regions, McGraw-Hill Publications, August, 1975.

Summary The Morris Newspaper Corporation decided to locate its corporate headquarters in a historic Federal-style house in the heart of the financial district in Savannah, Georgia. Under Charles H. Morris, President and former publisher of the *Savannah Morning News and Evening Press*, who founded the firm in 1970, Morris Newspaper expanded rapidly. By 1971, it was faced with finding a new location for its headquarters. Mr. Morris gives his reasons for choosing to renovate an old building:

Our direction was influenced through my interest in Savannah for more than a decade, and through my activities as a Trustee of Historic Savannah. We decided to look for a historic building that might meet our corporate space needs and my interest in Savannah's past.[1]

The renovation of the 8,000-square-foot structure cost approximately $30 per square foot.

Background The Oliver Sturges House was built in 1813 facing Reynold's Square. It is among the ten oldest buildings in Savannah and is both architecturally and historically significant. The site on which the building stands was included in the plans drawn up by General Oglethorpe when he first laid out the town of Savannah in 1733. Oglethorpe designed the street patterns around the squares that Savannah is famous for today. The Sturges House site was originally reserved for the Christ Church, and a parsonage was built on it shortly after 1733. When John Wesley came to Savannah from England in 1736, he lived in this parsonage for almost two years. It was here that he was said to have experienced his second conversion which led to the development of Methodism.

The parsonage occupied the site until after the Revolutionary War, when it was leveled in the great fire of 1796. Shortly thereafter, Oliver Sturges and a partner bought the lot from the church, and the two men built their houses on it. In 1816, Oliver Sturges helped form the Steam Boat Company of Georgia and later the Steam Ship Company of Savannah, which commissioned the construction of a 320-ton steam vessel that would make the first

The corporate offices of the Morris Newspaper chain are now located in the old Oliver Sturges House on the site where John Wesley once lived and preached. (Richard Meeks)

trans-Atlantic steam crossing. It is believed that many of the plans for the historic voyage of the S.S. Savannah took shape in meetings held in the Oliver Sturges House.

Originally, the brick house consisted of two stories over a semi-basement. An octagonal boardroom was added to the rear in 1819, and its interior detail reflects the increasing affluence of its owner. The moldings and plasterwork are more ornate than in any room in the original house. A third story was added sometime between 1850 and 1860. This addition is especially evident in the exterior because of the change in brick color. The brick was probably imported from Pennsylvania or Baltimore and was laid in a Flemish bond. The house had several other owners after Sturges, and during the twentieth century, became a boarding house and rapidly deteriorated. Threatened with destruction, it was purchased in 1964 by the Historic Savannah Foundation.

The Historic Savannah Foundation was established in 1955 to foster the preservation of Savannah's historic townscape. To accomplish this task, the Foundation operates and maintains historic properties; supports a revolving redevelopment fund which acquires endangered properties and resells them for restoration; and conducts an educational program to acquaint people with the importance of preserving Savannah's historic buildings. The revolving redevelopment fund owned the Sturges House for six years before Charles Morris offered to purchase and restore the structure for use as his company's offices. His offer was accepted, and construction began in fall, 1971.

The building stood empty and rundown for many years until the Historic Savannah Foundation, Inc., purchased it for resale to a buyer who would restore it.

Execution   Morris hired architects Robert Gunn and Eric Meyerhoff to execute the restoration and conversion. Historian Walter Hartridge provided research to guide the restoration. All of the rooms on the first two floors were returned to their original configuration, and the original heart-pine floors were restored. Moldings and other plaster details were measured and photographed, and replicas were made where necessary with castings from the remaining original segments. All the original mantelpieces were restored except for one in the octagonal board-room which had to be replaced with a replica. The variety of colors used on the first two floors came from the group of "Historic Savannah" colors developed by Ann Osteen, a restoration consultant. The rooms on these restored floors are used for offices for Mr. Morris, Mr. William B. Hill, Vice President, and their secretaries. The boardroom is used as a conference room, and there is a library on the second floor.

The third floor, which has been converted to general office space, is decorated in contemporary style. In the basement, the original kitchen of the house, the floor was lowered to provide adequate headroom, and the stone-rubble masonry was left exposed in the new offices that were created there. This rubble was originally ballast from some of the many merchant ships that sailed in and out of Savannah, and was used in building many of the city's old foundations and walls. All masonry had to be repointed with new mortar, and in some cases, where severe bowing had occurred, reinforcement was necessary. Heavy turnbuckles were used to pull the walls back to their proper position. Reinforcing rods had already been used on the upper levels to stabilize the house after the earthquake that jolted Savannah in the 1890s.

All new plumbing and wiring was installed. Heating and cooling are supplied electrically, and duct work has been concealed in walls and between floors. Work was completed in September, 1973.

Costs   The total usable area in the converted building is approximately 8,000 square feet. Renovations cost about $250,000 or roughly $30 per square foot. This figure is roughly equivalent to the cost of comparable new construction at the time.

Problems   The company experienced difficulties in matching the moldings and other plaster details, and old doors. In digging out the basement to create additional office space, workmen had to go below the original foundation and below the sewer line. Additional foundation reinforcing was necessary, and as a precaution, a pump has been installed to handle any potential sewage overflow.

Benefits   The major benefits to the company have been in the area of corporate image. When the building was dedicated, more than 3,000 people lined up to visit it. It has received many awards, including a special Award of Merit from the Georgia Land Development Association. The building has been recorded by the Historic American Buildings Survey and is in the National Register of Historic Places.

The Company   Morris Newspaper Corporation owns fifteen newspapers in Florida, Georgia, Tennessee, Kansas, New York, and California. It has eight employees in the Savannah offices. Since Morris is a privately held company, financial figures were not available.

For further information contact:
Charles H. Morris
President
Morris Newspaper Corporation
27 Abercorn Street
Savannah, Georgia 31401

Footnotes

1. "Preserving the Past While Growing into the Future," *Provident Review*, May 14, 1977, p. 12.

Summary In 1973, the National Bank of the Commonwealth signed a fifty-year lease with the County of Indiana, Pennsylvania, for use of the historic Indiana County Courthouse. The building, which dates back to the 1870s, had been vacant since the construction of a new courthouse in 1970. The bank needed space to house executive offices and central support facilities for its growing fourteen-branch network. It agreed to restore the exterior of the building as a part of the bargain. This restoration and interior renovation cost $500,000. The bank pays the County a monthly rent of $1,000 for the 12,500 square feet of usable space, less than half the cost of comparable space in the area's new buildings.

Background The county courthouse has played an important role in American history. It was not just the legal and political center of the community, but often the social center, as well. In addition to functioning as a repository of county records of all kinds, from titles and deeds to birth, marriage, and death certificates, the courthouse was the place where licenses were issued, taxes were collected, and ballots were counted. These activities generated a stream of daily visitors, as did the courtroom hearings themselves.

Architecturally, county courthouses usually reflect the dignity and prominence that their function dictates. The three-story Indiana County Courthouse is no exception. Designed in 1870 by architect James W. Drum, the structure:

is a magnificent example of the Second Empire Style. Because the building received its impetus from the New Louvre in Paris, a contemporary structure, it was considered an example of the then "modern movement." The style was prominent in domestic architecture from the 1850's through government and commercial structures during the period of Grant's Administration.... The simple rectangular form with its mansard roof, and Renaissance moldings, lintels and columns, is distinguished by a large clock tower that rises above and dominates the structure. The simplicity of the form is reinforced by the combination of materials. The use of brick and stone recalls the Georgian tradition and contributes to the building's stately appearance, while the cast iron capitals on the stone columns exemplify the beginning of industrial architectural components.[1]

In 1970, Drum's building stopped serving its original purpose. County offices were moved to new, more spacious quarters. The old building stood abandoned and neglected for the next three years. The peeling paint, rotted and missing woodwork, and age-soiled masonry soon turned a once distinguished landmark into an eyesore. In 1973, the National Bank of the Commonwealth needed to expand its central office facilities in the town of Indiana. The vacant courthouse stood just across the street from the bank's existing offices, and a Vice President suggested moving into the old building. Edward B. Bennett, Jr., President of the bank, liked and personally championed the proposal.

Execution In early 1973, the bank entered into a fifty-year preservation lease agreement with Indiana County. The agreement stipulated that the bank would pay a monthly rent of $1,000, and would finance the restoration of the exterior of the building and all interior improvements and maintenance. Ownership would remain in public hands with the County responsible for paying the property tax. An escalator clause allows the County to increase the annual rent if taxes increase. The primary concern during the restoration was maintaining the architectural integrity of the century-old structure, while providing a pleasant work area for bank officers and staff. Work began in spring, 1973. The exterior was sand-blasted to clean the surface, and the masonry was re-pointed and sealed to retard future deterioration. Rotted and missing decorative detail was replaced, and all detail, including the cupola dome, was refinished. The four-faced clock in the tower was also restored and put in working order.

The first two floors of the interior were completely refurbished: walls replastered and painted; marble floors and woodwork refinished; new lighting and heating systems installed; and offices carpeted and finished. Although the interior was redesigned to accommodate modern office functions, according to Bob Wagner, the bank's Marketing Director, "much of the old interior remains; we couldn't knock down the walls even if we wanted to."[2] Approximately fifty people work in the building. The architect for the restoration/renovation was William E. Kerr, A.I.A. of Pittsburgh, and the contractor was Pevarnik Brothers of Latrobe, Pennsylvania. The courtyard was totally relandscaped by Raymond Blanchard, Enterprises.

Costs   The cost for the restoration and renovation was $500,000. The bank also pays the County a monthly rental of $1,000 and all maintenance and operating expenses, which average $15,000 per year. The $500,000, amortized over the fifty-year lease period, amounts to $10,000 per year, making the total annual payment approximately $37,000, or equivalent to $3 per square foot. This compared to $7 to $8 per square foot for comparable space in new buildings in the area in 1976.

Problems   Because of the thickness of the interior and exterior walls, floor-plan options were limited, and the installation of the heating/air-conditioning system was unusually difficult.

Benefits   The community benefited by the preservation of a publicly owned landmark, and county income was increased through the rent payments. In the words of Bob Wagner, "What had become an eyesore was transformed into an attractive center-of-town focal point all are proud of, and the lease agreement has turned a county liability into an asset."[3] The County was also relieved of the maintenance costs on the building and spared the eventual expense of demolition. The building is now included in both the Pennsylvania Register of Historic Sites and Landmarks and the National Register of Historic Places.

The bank benefited by the addition of much-needed office space at a reasonable cost. According to the President of the bank, Edward Bennett: "We've been delighted with it. It is built like a fort and works well for our needs. Although it can't be measured, the restoration has had a very positive effect on our business. On opening day more than 4,000 people came through, and we have had many letters of praise from people we don't even know."[4] The bank opens its large hall for community art and cultural affairs.

In 1975, the bank was presented one of twenty Business in the Arts Awards sponsored by the Business Committee for the Arts and *Esquire* magazine. The Pennsylvania Federation of Garden Clubs has twice honored the bank with statewide awards, and the Pittsburgh Chapter of the American Institute of Architects cited the project as the best reclamation effort in the Pittsburgh area completed within the past five years.

The Company   The National Bank of the Commonwealth serves approximately 200,000 people in five western Pennsylvania counties, including: Cambria, Clearfield, Indiana, Jefferson, and Westmoreland. It has fourteen full-service offices and two drive-in facilities located in twelve towns. Assets rose from $138 million in 1975 to $161 million in 1976. Net income increased from $944,600 in 1975 to $1.13 million in 1976

For further information contact:
Robert Wagner
Marketing Director
National Bank of the
Commonwealth
P.O. Box 400
Indiana, Pennsylvania 15701

Footnotes

1. Edward B. Bennett, Jr., "Pennsylvania Register of Historic Sites and Landmarks and Museum Commission Nomination Form," December 17, 1973, p. 3.
2. INFORM interview with Robert Wagner, Marketing Director, National Bank of the Commonwealth, June, 1977.
3. *Ibid.*
4. INFORM interview with Edward B. Bennett, Jr., President, National Bank of the Commonwealth, June, 1977.

Summary In 1968, the Pfaltzgraff Company, a stoneware manufacturer and a division of the Susquehanna Broadcasting Company, purchased the mid-Victorian Lebach House on East Market Street in York, Pennsylvania. The house, located in York's historic center, has been completely restored and adapted for use as the company's offices. The renovation cost $73,000, or $42 per square foot.

Background The Lebach House derives its name from its second owners, Joseph and Jacob Lebach, who purchased it in 1867. Thought to have been constructed in the mid-1850s, the house functioned as a single-family residence until sometime between 1867 and 1883, when a two-story addition facing the street was made, converting it to multi-family use. Between 1883 and 1900, several rooms were added to the rear of the house.

The two-story, mid-Victorian structure is laid in Flemish Bond brickwork. The window lintels are rococo, a more elaborate style than the austere Greek Revival architecture in vogue during the earlier part of the nineteenth century. The ornamental ironwork over each of the doorways was cast at York's Variety Iron Works, a foundry which has served York since the time of the Civil War.

The house, continuously owned by the Lebach family for almost a hundred years, underwent some striking changes in this century. In 1940, it became a retail store called the Fabric Shop, selling yard goods and women's apparel. In 1955, Sophia and Bella Lebach, descendants of Jacob and Joseph, opened a gift shop and mail-order caramel business in the original section of the house. This business continued until Pfaltzgraff's purchase of the property in 1968.

Pfaltzgraff's reasons for recycling the Lebach House were both pragmatic and social; it needed additional space and wanted to help preserve the area's historic architecture. Specifically, the project would provide: additional studio space for the company's growing Product Development staff; a design workshop and modeling studio; and an adequate showroom for company products. It would also serve to enhance the appearance of the house and that of the neighborhood.

Execution Planning and design work for the Lebach House project, as with all company renovation efforts, was executed by Pfaltzgraff's own design staff. Maurice G. Mountain, Design Director, was responsible for developing the plans. He was assisted by C. William Dize, A.I.A., an outside advisor.

Initially, the company found the rooms to be small and awkwardly arranged. The house had been neglected; and the elements had not been kind: the roof leaked, and much of the interior had been destroyed by water damage. One of the later additions had settled unevenly, and according to Maurice Mountain, "Listed so badly that it made you feel dizzy."[1] This addition was removed, but others were reused, including one that originally had been an outhouse. Where the brick walls needed structural reinforcement, steel tie-rods were inserted through the building at the second-floor level and fastened on the outside with retaining plates to hold the brick in place.

In redesigning the interior, Mountain sketched out several alternative floor arrangements to suit the needs of the Product Development staff. The final selection was made on the basis of efficiency of traffic patterns and space requirements. Non-structural interior walls were removed and replaced to conform to the new plans. Completely new plumbing, heating, and electrical systems were installed. Window-unit air conditioners were used on the first floor since there was no room for a central ducted system. However, a central system was used on the second floor where ducts could be concealed in the attic.

The building's exterior was restored to its original state. Paint was removed from the brickwork by sandblasting. Later porch additions on the rear were also removed. The old roof was replaced, and the windows, wood trim, and shutters were restored. Some window openings which had been enlarged over the years were returned to their original size and configuration. All renovation and restoration was executed by Harold Hogg, the general contractor. The grounds were landscaped with new shrubbery and brick-paved walks by Burns & Longwell, landscape architects, and Shiloh Nurseries, landscape contractors.

Approximately twenty employees use the building's 1,700-square-foot space. The project took approximately nine months from conceptual planning to actual occupancy.

Costs The total restoration and re-cycling of the Lebach House cost the company $73,000, including $48,000 for construction and exterior restora-tion; $19,000 for interior decoration, furnishings, and finishing; and $6,000 for landscaping. The company pur-chased the house and land for $32,500 in 1968.

Problems Pfaltzgraff described the following difficulties encountered in undertaking this project:.

Our organization is not structured to undertake this type of project on a full-time basis. It was necessary to proceed with normal work activities in addition to this project. Original design of the house was conceived in another era and was not easily changed to include the modern accommodations needed or the specialized functions that were planned to be performed.[2]

A few specific problems were encoun-tered in trying to meet standards established by the Pennsylvania De-partment of Labor and Industry. All plans for renovations and new con-struction of office and industrial facilities must receive the Depart-ment's approval prior to implementa-tion. Fire-safety requirements, such as two second-floor exits, door swings, and approved doorknobs, locks, and other safety hardware, were problems. An existing fire escape solved the second-floor exit problem. Doors were rehung to swing in the direction of the exit ways, and a compromise was reached eliminating the necessity of installing the new safety hardware. This hardware is not in keeping with the style and scale of older buildings, and the company wanted to reuse the origi-nal period knobs and locks instead of the approved modern ones. The com-promise solution was to fix the old locks in the open position and install auto-matic door closers, keeping the doors shut by pressure rather than by locking.

The rear of the Lebach House before restoration. (Maurice Mountain, Jr.)

Exterior of the house after cleaning and repointing. (Maurice Mountain, Jr.)

Benefits In addition to providing a functional and pleasant place to work, the recycled Labach House is close to Susquehanna's corporate headquarters and convenient for all employees. Cleared land in the area, large enough to accommodate a new building, is nonexistent. Reusing an existing structure permitted occupancy at a reasonable cost in a short period of time.

Improvement of the surrounding area is another significant plus. The neighborhood has been enhanced, and according to the company, "an otherwise unproductive building has been turned into a center for creative productivity."[3] As a result of the success of this project, the company is currently renovating several other old buildings in the area, including a warehouse and two nineteenth-century residences, for use as additional office space.

The Company The Pfaltzgraff Company, a division of the Susquehanna Broadcasting Company, has been manufacturing stoneware products in York since 1811. These nationally distributed products, with designs in early American and country patterns, are used for cooking and serving food, as well as for decorative purposes. Susquehanna Broadcasting is a privately owned company, and financial information is not available.

Other Preservation Activities. Susquehanna Broadcasting, through the efforts of its President, Louis J. Appell, and some of its management personnel, has also been involved in many preservation projects in York, including the maintenance of the historic Bonham House, owned and operated by the York County Historical Society. This house/museum is located between the Lebach House and Susquehanna's corporate headquarters, a new structure designed to relate to the surrounding historic architecture. In addition, Susquehanna employees have contributed time and talent to the proposed reuse of two movie theaters as a performing arts center, and to the continuing use of York's major downtown hotel.

For further information contact:
Louis J. Appel, Jr.
President
Susquehanna Broadcasting
Company
P.O. Box 2026
York, Pennsylvania 17405

Footnotes

1. INFORM interview with Maurice Mountain, Design Director, The Pfaltzgraff Co., June, 1977.
2. Written communication from Dawn D. Russo, Executive Secretary, Susquehanna Broadcasting Company, to INFORM, February 25, 1977.
3. *Ibid.*

Summary   On December 31, 1973, the San Diego Federal Savings and Loan Association opened its branch offices in Sacramento, California, in a Victorian mansion, the Heilbron House. Excellent central location, distinct individuality and high visibility, and a desire to preserve an important part of Sacramento's heritage, all contributed to San Diego Federal's decision to purchase and adaptively restore the 1881 structure. The cost for the project was $851,000, or approximately $110 per square foot, including the land.

Background   In 1880, August Heilbron, a German immigrant who became one of California's leading cattle breeders, commissioned Nathaniel Dudley Goodell, a distinguished eastern architect, to design and build a house. Goodell had recently completed a beautiful mansion for a Sacramento businessman, Albert Gallatin; this mansion later served as the official residence for California governors. Today it is a state-maintained museum.

The Heilbron House was designed as a compact but beautifully detailed Victorian residence complete with a rich bracketed cornice and high mansard roof. Symmetrical bay windows on the front facade frame an entrance portico supported by Corinthian columns. The entire first floor rests on a basement foundation setting it eight feet off the ground. This was done as a precaution against Sacramento River floods, a frequent occurrence at that time. High ceilings on the first two floors, together with this eight-foot base, give the building a soaring and stately presence. All window openings are decorated with richly carved and detailed wood trim. An ornamental grand front stair, with turned balusters and contoured railings, reinforces the elegant entrance. An ornamental iron fence encircles the property.

In the interior, before its conversion, the basement contained servant quarters, storage rooms, and a summer kitchen. The first floor was the entertaining area and consisted of two formal parlors, the dining room, library, kitchen, and pantry. The master bedroom and bath were on the second floor in addition to other bedrooms and a nursery. The top mansard floor contained other sleeping quarters and a large water tank which maintained water pressure for the bathroom fixtures below. On the main floors, carved plaster moldings and ceiling ornamentations together with hand-rubbed woodwork provided rich interior detail. Five marble-manteled fireplaces furnished warmth on winter days. The Heilbron House was ready for occupancy in 1881 and cost $10,000 to build.

The Heilbron family lived in the house until 1953. It was then sold and converted to a restaurant which operated until 1971. Gordon C. Luce, President and Chief Executive Officer of San Diego Federal, had served as head of the state's Business and Transportation Agency in Sacramento from 1967 to 1969. During that time, he had eaten many times in the restaurant in the Heilbron House. When San Diego Federal was granted a branch office in downtown Sacramento in the early 1970s, Luce and the bank's Board of Directors purchased the Heilbron House to preserve it and create from it a new and distinctive business address in the city. According to Luce:

We wanted a site where we could build something that would stand alone. A place that would stand for building homes, adding to them, and refurbishing them. . . . We looked at the "Mall," but everything had a feeling of sameness.

We purchased this grand old Victorian home because of its historical significance and determined at the outset to maintain its grace and charm in the conversion to a financial institution. Our goal–in addition to providing an efficient savings and loan institution–is to preserve the building so its heritage can be enjoyed by the entire community.[1]

Execution The architectural firm of William C. Krommenhoek and Associates and interior designer Brenda Mason were responsible for the restoration/conversion. The exterior of the house remains essentially unchanged and has been carefully restored by the architects. Missing or deteriorated woodwork has been duplicated or repaired, and the exterior has been repainted. A Victorian-style gazebo was designed to provide drive-up window service and is located on a landscaped piece of property adjacent to the house.

In the interior, steel reinforcing provides additional support for the house's new use as a savings and loan office. The basic integrity of the main rooms has been retained, but walls had to be opened up to accommodate the banking facilities. Plaster detail has been carefully preserved, and, in many cases was reinstalled after the steel was in place. Three of the five marble fireplaces have been retained as well as the grand staircase. Antiques, period fabrics, and wall coverings mix with more contemporary office furnishings and equipment. Private loan offices and other administrative functions are located on the second floor. The total area used for business purposes is 7,748 square feet, resulting in an efficiency factor comparable to new construction.

Cost The purchase price for the land and building was $225,000. About $626,000 more was spent on the restoration and conversion, including all fixtures and furnishings. The $80 cost per square foot for renovation, according to the company, is comparable to the cost of constructing and furnishing a new branch-office.

Benefits Chief Executive Officer Gordon Luce evaluates the project:

We believe that restoration of handsome historic landmarks such as these by the private sector is in the interest of the communities we serve and, at the same time, makes good business sense.[2]

The Sacramento community deposited more than $9 million in new savings in that office during the first year alone. During the first week of the bank's operations in the Heilbron House more than 6,000 visitors came to see the results.

Many special commendations from a variety of sources have been given to San Diego Federal for its restoration of the Heilbron House, including: the California Historical Society, the California State Assembly, the Sacramento Board of Supervisors, the Sacramento Old City Association, and the Sacramento Chapter of the American Association of University Women.

The Company San Diego Federal Savings and Loan is the oldest federally chartered savings and loan association in the state of California, dating from 1885. It had branches in 48 locations around the state and total assets of more than $1.3 billion as of 1976.

Other Preservation Activities. Following the successful results of the Heilbron House restoration and the favorable public response to it, San Diego Federal recently undertook another conversion, this time of the historic Los Altos, California, train depot into its 26th branch office. This early-1900s structure was the hub of the Los Altos community and played an important part in California transportation history.

For further information contact:
Nancy A. Peterson
Assistant Vice President, Public Affairs
San Diego Federal Savings and Loan
600 B Street
San Diego, California 92183

The former Heilbron House, now the San Diego Federal Sacramento branch.

Footnotes

1. Paul Mapes, "Old Mansion: Wall-to-Wall Memory At New S and L Office," *Sacramento Union*, 8 January 1974.
2. San Diego Federal Savings and Loan Association, "San Diego Federal Savings Will Restore and Preserve the Old Los Altos Station as its Newest Savings and Loan Office," *News from San Diego Federal*, May, 1975, pp. 1-2.

Summary SEDCO, Inc., a major international offshore-drilling, pipeline-construction, and engineering company, has corporate offices in an 1888 "Texas Victorian" school. Reputed to be the first brick school built in Dallas, the Cumberland Hill School was up for sale in the 1960s, and almost everyone expected that it would soon be razed for new development.[1] However, William P. Clements, Jr., SEDCO's Chairman of the Board, liked the building; his relatives had taught there, and he thought its uniqueness and location gave it commercial potential. In 1969, Clements purchased the property and convinced SEDCO to renovate it. The total cost of purchase and renovation was more than $2.5 million, or approximately $64 per square foot.

The Cumberland Hill School after SEDCO's renovation. (Burson, Hendricks & Walls, Architects)

Background The Cumberland Hill School once served an affluent Dallas community. The original building was constructed in a square configuration with four classrooms on each floor rotating about a central stair space in pinwheel fashion. Through the years, the neighborhood changed, becoming a melting pot of immigrant nationalities, and so did the school. Wings were added increasing the number of classrooms to meet the growing student population. The early additions conformed to the style of the original structure, employing the same "Dallas Stiff Mud" brick, a light buff-colored brick native to the area. In 1919, however, a square section was added to the north end of the school using different brick and different construction techniques.

As the neighborhood became more heavily commercial, enrollment declined, and in 1959, the building became a vocational training school. In 1961, the school board put the building

up for sale, but it was not sold until 1969, when William P. Clements, Jr., made an offer of nearly $1.4 million.

The Cumberland Hill School site was ripe for redevelopment. It was located on a major artery in the central business district and was near the new Fairmont Hotel. Although Clements was determined to save the building, he had no specific use in mind when he purchased it. One early idea was to convert it into a boutique shopping complex, but Clements felt that if it were good enough for that use, it might also be good for SEDCO's own offices. At that time, that company's Dallas headquarters was spread out over three floors of the First National Bank Building, and it was in the process of looking for a home of its own. The young architectural team of Rodger Burson and James Hendricks—now Burson, Hendricks, and Walls—was hired to explore the possibilities of renovating the sound but neglected school building.

Execution According to James Hendricks:

Until we saw the old picture of the original building, we didn't fully realize what was wrong with the building we had. It was that flat roof. We sketched the building with a pitched roof and cupola and it was right. The parapet had destroyed what was a beautiful building. The building had deteriorated each time it was remodeled and enlarged.[2]

The architects set out to unify and restore the original character of the old school while adapting it to serve the functions of a contemporary office building. They did not plan a pure

School before renovation and recreation of pitched roof. (Burson, Hendricks & Walls, Architects)

On-site parking is accommodated and extensive landscaping creates a park-like setting. (Burson, Hendricks & Walls, Architects)

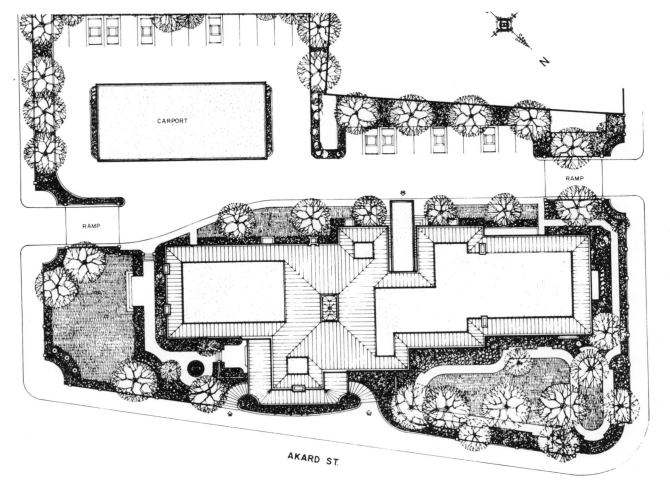

restoration, but rather attempted to recreate the "spirit" of the original.

The two-story structure, which also has a basement, was constructed with brick supporting walls and wood framing. Its total gross area is 40,000 square feet. In the renovation, all exterior masonry walls were saved, and new windows, porches, and entrances were installed. A new steel roof structure was superimposed on the existing flat roof to accommodate the recreated pewter-finish sheet-metal pitched roof and cupola. The entire facade is painted yellow ochre, the color of the original Dallas Stiff Mud bricks. Painting was necessary to waterproof the exterior, as well as to unify the various additions which had used different color brick. The window and door trim is white, while the railings and porch columns are black iron.

To level the original wood floors, which had settled unevenly over the years, steel beams were installed under all wood floor joists, and a concrete topping was poured on the existing floors. The floor loads were carried directly by the masonry supporting walls; additional structural reinforcing was only necessary where the original masonry had been punctured for openings.* The foundation was in excellent condition and rested directly on solid rock.

All interior masonry walls, as well as some interior details, were retained in the renovation. Also saved were a few of the old school's wooden doors, complete with initials carved by mischievous students. The interior was completely redone in a Victorian manner, including wood paneling, and new stairs, ceilings, and floors. Some of the brick walls were left exposed, and old globe and chain lighting fixtures from Dallas Hall at Southern Methodist University were reused. A 45-foot-high central space, opening into the cupola above, contains a reception area and the grand staircase. An elevator was added. Waiting rooms, executive offices, general office and office-pool areas, and a dining facility in the basement fill the remaining space.

New plumbing and wiring, and a new two-duct heating, ventilating, and

*According to architect Larry Walls, several unreinforced openings were discovered after plaster was removed during demolition.[3]

air-conditioning system were installed throughout the building. Mixing boxes, blending the hot and cold air, and individual thermostat controls are located in each office. The original ceiling heights, 15 feet floor to floor, were lowered in some areas to accommodate the mechanical system, but never below the existing window heights. In the executive offices, the high ceilings were retained, and the heating, ventilation, and air-conditioning were designed to feed from below, through the floor.

The site was completely landscaped with new brick retaining walls, ornamental iron fencing, walkways, drives, and parking facilities. It contains a rich variety of plants which make it a green oasis in downtown Dallas.

The post-renovation ratio of 38,000 net square feet of usable space to 40,000 gross square feet in the building provides approximately a 95 percent efficiency factor, better than in most new construction. Renovations were completed in only eleven months through the use of a "fastrack" system of design and construction. Under this system, demolition and construction begins before all plans have been completed. Interior demolition began as soon as measured drawings and demolition plans were executed. Design and working drawings followed, and many of the drawings were actually completed on the site during construction. A number of the tradesmen who worked on the project had actually studied in the building when it was a vocational school. According to architect Larry Walls: "They took great pride in the place."[4] The efficiency of the operation was also improved by the use of a construction-management company, Earl L. Jones & Associates.

Costs The land was purchased outright by Mr. Clements in 1969 for $1.36 million. Disregarding the value of the building, this is equal to approximately $20 per square foot for the one-and-a-half acre site. The cost of the renovation, excluding landscaping and furnishings, was about $1.2 million for the entire 40,000-square foot structure or $30 per square foot. This is comparable to the cost of new construction in the area in 1971. Operating costs are not available.

Benefits SEDCO has improved its corporate image through its reuse of the Cumberland Hill School. William P. Clements, Jr. describes the renovation's effects:

SEDCO will identify with this building as we could never do with just another modern glass-walled building. Everyone in town will be aware of this building, and know it's the SEDCO building.[5]

In 1971, SEDCO was awarded an official historical marker by the Texas State Historical Survey Committee. The company also received top honors from the Texas Society of Architects and an Award of Merit from the American Association for State and Local History. The latter award, given for the year 1971, cited the SEDCO conversion as a "handsome and functional building and a richer legacy to Dallas almost certainly than a new structure could have been."[6]

The more than ninety employees who use the building also find it an efficient and pleasant environment. One functional benefit was the reduced noise level due to the high ceilings.

The Company Founded in 1947 by William P. Clements, Jr., as an oil-drilling contractor, SEDCO over the years has expanded from land drilling to offshore drilling, pipeline construction, manufacturing, research, and consulting. SEDCO's sales increased from $229 million in 1975 to $337 million in 1976. Net income for 1976 was $44 million, up from 1975's figure of $37.5 million. Within the last five years, the company has more than tripled its income. However, offshore drilling is a volatile and unpredictable industry, and SEDCO is currently working on diversification projects, such as floating production facilities and deep-ocean mining.

Growth and expansion since 1971 have caused SEDCO to seek more space for its Dallas operations. While the Cumberland Hill School still serves as corporate headquarters, the company is developing the land immediately behind it. An eight-story, 130,000-square-foot concrete and glass office building is now under construction, and another thirteen-story tower is planned. SEDCO will occupy about 50 percent of the space in the new eight-story tower and will lease the rest. The new buildings provide a background for the old school and will be related to it through similar landscaping. Other than a concern for scale, no attempt has been made to relate the new with the old via materials or architectural design. Burson, Hendricks, and Walls are also the architects for this complex.

For further information contact:
Edwin J. Smith, Jr.
Manager, Insurance Department
SEDCO, Inc.
Cumberland Hill
1901 North Akard
Dallas, Texas 75201

Footnotes

1. Dorothie Erwin, "Victorian Flavor: Old Cumberland School to be Office," *Dallas Morning News*, 23 May 1970, section AA.
2. *Ibid.*
3. INFORM interview with Larry Walls, architect, Burson, Hendricks and Walls, March, 1977.
4. *Ibid.*
5. Erwin, *op. cit.*
6. "Dallas-Based Firm Preserves Historic School," *History News*, September, 1972, p. 188.

Executive office after renovation. (Burson, Hendricks & Walls, Architects)

Major structural walls were retained, and former classroom spaces were subdivided for office use. (Burson, Hendricks & Walls, Architects)

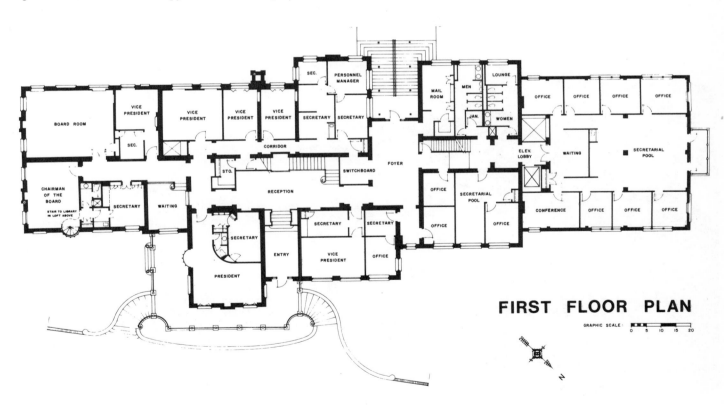

FIRST FLOOR PLAN

Summary   In January, 1965, the U.S. National Bank of Oregon opened a branch office in the vintage United States Hotel in Jacksonville, a gold rush boom town gone bust. Ironically, the town's decline had produced the unexpected benefit of preserving much of its original nineteenth-century flavor. In the early 1960s, a local group, seeing the value of maintaining and capitalizing on Jacksonville's history, purchased the hotel and sought federal funds to renovate other existing buildings. The hotel, completed in 1880, was the keystone in this effort. The bank agreed to prepay $25,000—covering the first ten years of its lease—for 2,300 square feet of space in the old building. In 1965, it paid approximately $76,000, or $33 per square foot, to remodel the space. In addition, the hotel's owners renovated the building to meet minimal building-code standards at a cost of more than $100,000. Although the town ultimately rejected federal urban-renewal financing, reuse of the hotel encouraged additional renovations, and Jacksonville is becoming a popular tourist attraction.

Background   In 1851, Jacksonville was a bustling boom town; gold had been discovered in the area, and the town's population of 1,200 residents was prosperous and proud. But the mother lode soon ran out, and the economy shifted to agriculture. A more serious decline began in 1883, when the railroad bypassed Jacksonville, putting it off the beaten track. By the early 1960s, the population had dropped to less than 1,000. However, the decline had unexpected advantages; Jacksonville remained almost perfectly preserved, reflecting much of the physical character of the gold rush days. For this reason, in 1964, the town was declared a National Historic Landmark.

The United States Hotel, completed in 1880, quickly became an important part of the community. This two-story Western-style brick building includes a wooden porch and balcony. President Rutherford B. Hayes stayed in it in 1881. The hotel remained in operation until 1915 when the town took ownership because of tax arrears. It served as a museum until 1949. The hotel was used intermittently by local groups but continued to deteriorate, and in the early 1960s the town condemned it.

Jacksonville Properties for Historic Preservation, led by Robertson Collins, a local businessman and currently a trustee of the National Trust for Historic Preservation, was formed in 1963 to explore ways to save the vintage hotel. The group learned that the U.S. National Bank of Oregon was planning to open a branch office in Jacksonville. Aware that the bank had several branch offices in historic buildings, the group asked it to lease ground-floor space in the old hotel. The bank agreed, and signed a twenty-year lease. It also prepaid $25,000, its rent for ten years, which enabled Jacksonville Properties for Historic Preservation to obtain additional financing.

In 1964, the federal Urban Renewal Administration conducted engineering studies for an extensive urban-renewal project to renovate and restore the buildings in Jacksonville's core area. This project would have restored the entire district and capitalized on the town's historic character to attract tourists. The hotel's reuse and the efforts of Jacksonville Properties for Historic Preservation were important factors in obtaining federal attention.

The former United States Hotel now houses the Jacksonville branch of the U.S. National Bank of Oregon. (Graphics West Photo)

Execution The two-story brick building needed a great deal of work. Jacksonville Properties for Historic Preservation reconstructed the wooden porch, installed a new roof, and added steel supporting columns, concealed in the original brick of the exterior walls. The brick was repointed, and new plumbing, wiring, air conditioning, and fire-protection equipment were also installed. These renovations were required to bring the building up to current building codes and to keep it from further deterioration.

The bank hired architect Walter Pappas, A.I.A., general contractor Jack Batzer, and interior decorator Lila Colwell, A.I.D., to recreate an authentic nineteenth-century interior. "More than 16,000 man hours of research were done to provide a decor of the 1850s for the Jacksonville Branch, and the result is one of the most unique banking institutions on the West Coast."[1] Burlap wall coverings and custom-reproduced wallpaper cover the walls. Eight branch chandeliers with glass shades were reproduced from old sketches. Oak teller cages were duplicated from period ones. The furnishings include gold scales from 1840, yew wood chairs (c. 1840), a wall clock (c. 1876), antique inkwells, and brass spitoons. In addition, the bank contributed to the renovation of the ballroom, on the second floor, which is leased for social events, and distributed a free brochure describing Jacksonville's historic buildings.

Costs The total cost for renovating the building to bring it up to code requirements was well over $100,000. It was paid by the owners, Jacksonville Properties For Historic Preservation. The bank's cost for remodeling its 2,300 square feet of space is itemized as follows:*

General Construction	$38,500
Counters and Tellers' fixtures	20,000
Office Furniture	5,000
Vault Door and Night Depository	6,500
Alarm	1,500
Miscellaneous	4,500
TOTAL:	$76,000

*These costs are twelve years old; comparable work today would be much more expensive.

The hotel's recycled interior. (Graphics West Photo)

Problems The reuse of the United States Hotel was to be a catalyst for a large-scale renewal effort. However, according to a spokesman for Jacksonville Properties for Historic Preservation, Jacksonville citizens rejected the urban-renewal project in a local referendum, out of fear of federal intervention.[2]

Benefits Because of a well conceived public relations campaign for the opening of the Jacksonville branch, the bank has been featured in numerous Oregon newspapers, including the *Portland Oregonian* and the *Ashland Daily Tidings*, as well as in the *Western Banker*, the *Pacific Banker & Business*, and *Sunset* magazines.

In addition to saving and reusing the old hotel, the bank's decision to locate in Jacksonville became the catalyst for the renovation of other historic buildings in the town. These efforts are gradually turning the town into a popular tourist attraction. In 1976, the Jacksonville Museum attracted almost 86,000 visitors.

The bank has also provided mortgages for the revitalization of residential areas and other historic buildings. The town now has grown to 2,000, but further expansion is presently restricted due to a sewer moratorium. The assessed valuation of the town has increased from $2.7 million in 1965 to $22 million in 1976.

The Company The U.S. National Bank of Oregon is a wholly owned subsidiary of U.S. Bancorp, which provides financial services. U.S. Bancorp had assets of $3.1 billion in 1975 and of $3.3 billion in 1976. For the same period, net income rose 18 percent, from about $25 million to $29.6 million. The U.S. National Bank of Oregon has 150 offices throughout Oregon.

For further information contact:
James W. Parry
Assistant Vice President
Bank Properties Division
United States National
Bank of Oregon
P.O. Box 4412
Portland, Oregon 97208

Footnotes

1. "A Modern Bank Steps into the Past," *Medford Mail Tribune*, 17 January 1965, sec. B, p. 1.
2. INFORM interview with official, Jacksonville Properties for Historic Preservation, August, 1977.

Summary In 1974, the Wachovia Bank and Trust Company, a leading North Carolina bank, recycled a storefront dating from 1918 for use as a branch office in downtown Chapel Hill. Although not an individually significant structure, this building was an integral part of the small-town streetscape, and was protected by city ordinances. The bank's recycling effort won it considerable praise and a number of awards. The 3,300-square-foot project cost $140,000, 20 percent less than the cost of new construction, and took about one year to complete.

Background In 1972, the Wachovia Bank and Trust Company requested permission to locate a branch office on Franklin Street, a major artery of downtown Chapel Hill, home of the main campus of the University of North Carolina. Since Chapel Hill's small-town character is considered a valuable asset and is regulated and protected by city ordinances, there was great reluctance on the part of many residents to welcome a modern bank facility to Franklin Street. In 1972, the City of Chapel Hill had barred the construction of a six-story bank building proposed by one of Wachovia's competitors.

When Wachovia received approval to establish an office, it sent Lloyd Abbott, the Chief Facilities Officer of its General Services Department, to Chapel Hill to seek guidance on a building design from the Planning Board and city Appearance Commission. The Appearance Commission approved the bank's suggestion of a contemporary building, but one in harmony with the unique atmosphere of Franklin Street. The solution was to recycle the interior of an existing building, converting it into a modern banking facility, while preserving the original exterior facade to maintain continuity with the surrounding area. The building chosen had been used for several purposes since its construction in 1918. It housed, at one time, an electrical-appliance company, at another, a university cafeteria.

Execution Wachovia hired John D. Latimer and Associates of Durham, North Carolina, and Roger C. Clark of the North Carolina State University School of Design to furnish the architectural design. Two problems immediately arose: eliminating the tunnel-like effect caused by windowless interior walls, and preserving the continuous street-scape design. The building's exterior featured a brick flat arch, previously covered by aluminum siding, which ran along under the roof line and linked the structure to nearby storefronts. According to architect Clark, "We saw Franklin Street as a kind of brick wall that really should be saved."[1]

The original facade was retained, but does not function as the entrance to the building. Instead, the flat arch opens on a second facade made of white stucco and grey tinted glass set off by black window frames. A glass door to the bank is located there. Two structural bays behind the original facade were removed, and the roof was cut back so that the area in front of the new entrance is opened to the sky. Glass was installed above the stucco wall over the door, and the interior ceiling of the bank slopes dramatically to meet the top of the glass. This introduces natural light into the building.

The entrance to the bank on Franklin Street was specifically designed with pedestrians in mind. The night deposit box and Teller II, an automated banking service, both have been set in white stucco in the facade itself. This effect is explained:

[The] night deposit box has become an integral part of the design, reaching out from the new in one corner to touch the old, "marrying" the two as architect Clark puts it.[2]

The inside of the 3,300-square-foot bank is like any other modern bank facility, with teller counters to one side and customer counters on the other. Bank officers' desks are in the rear. There is no drive-in window, since the bank is downtown and is readily accessible to pedestrians.

Wachovia's Chapel Hill branch. (Jim Thornton)

Costs The work on the building took one year to complete and cost the Wachovia Bank and Trust Company $140,000—$16,000 for architectural fees and $124,000 for general construction—or approximately $42 per square foot. This includes the cost of the vault, but not of other banking equipment.

According to the company, recycling represented a 20 percent savings over the cost of new construction.

Benefits The Wachovia Bank Building provides architectural continuity with the rest of Franklin Street, which chiefly consists of smaller buildings, the University Methodist Church, and part of the campus of the University of North Carolina.

Charles H. Wartman, the bank's Manager, says that after being in the building for a year, "The employees love to work there because it's so light and airy."[3] He couldn't directly attribute new deposits to the appearance of the building, but indicated that the bank is doing well.

Wachovia's building received high praise from the American Institute of Architects' South Atlantic Regional Convention, in Savannah, Georgia, in 1974, as "a fine example of recycling which appropriately blends with its surroundings."[4] The Chapel Hill Appearance Commission also awarded it a Certificate of Commendation. The bank has been featured in articles in several magazines and newspapers, including the *Raleigh News-Observer* and *Architecture Plus* magazine.

The Company Founded in 1879, the Wachovia Bank merged in 1911 with the Wachovia Loan and Trust Company to create the Wachovia Bank and Trust Company. Wachovia is an English version of the name *Wachau* which the Moravians, who acquired the land in 1753, applied to the area around Piedmont, North Carolina. The bank currently has 186 offices throughout North Carolina. Wachovia ranked 33rd among the nation's banks, with $2.85 billion in deposits, $3.5 billion in assets, and $30 million in earnings for the year ending December 31, 1976.

For further information contact:
Tonya Widemon
Writer, Public Relations
Wachovia Bank and Trust Co.
P.O. Box 3099
Winston-Salem, North Carolina
27102

Footnotes

1. Ernie Wood, "A Small Town Streetscape Saved," *Raleigh News-Observer*, 29 September 1974, p. 5-V.
2. *Ibid.*
3. *Ibid.*
4. *Ibid.*

The branch's modern interior. (Jim Thornton)

Zions First National Bank

Summary   In 1974, Zions National Bank moved its Heber City, Utah, branch into the Abram Hatch House, which was built about 1892 for a prominent local religious, civic, and business leader. Early in 1972, the bank had rejected a remodeling plan for the building as too expensive, and had considered razing the structure or moving it to another location so that a new branch could be constructed on the site. In summer, 1972, after a Historic American Buildings Survey team study of the house, the bank reevaluated its earlier scheme and decided to execute an "adaptive restoration." It would retain the character of the house and much of its interior design, while at the same time, converting the 4,100 square feet of space to accommodate a modern commercial operation. According to Don Bingham, the project's architect, costs were comparable to other new branch offices constructed during this time.

The Abram Hatch House. (Busath Photography)

Background   Abram Hatch was sent to Heber City by Brigham Young in 1867 to establish himself as community and religious leader. He also built and operated a store, and was responsible for the construction of several other buildings in town. Among them was a fine residence, built in the early 1890s to accommodate his family and his official functions. Only the best native materials and craftsmen were used in construction. The walls of the house are light, salmon-colored, trimmed sandstone quarried outside of Heber City, and the elaborately shaped roof is shingled in red cedar. The large, 50-foot by 64-foot, one-and-a-half-story structure features a symmetrical facade decorated with delicate spindled and carved wood. Although the neighborhood where the house is located was residential in the 1890s, it is today part of Heber City's central business district.

The Hatch family occupied the house until the 1930s. After that, there were several other owners, but except for a few modifications to convert it into apartments, the building remained essentially in its original state.

The local office of the Zions First National Bank had outgrown its facility in the early 1970s, and was looking at possible sites for a new building. The Hatch House site was considered most desirable. A remodeling plan was explored in early 1972, but the bank believed that it would be too costly an alternative, and it was rejected. Thought was then given to moving the old house to another site to make room for a new building.

In summer, 1972, a team from the Historic American Buildings Survey completely documented the Hatch House and studied its history. The bank was encouraged and impressed by this survey and reevaluated its former decision. That fall, at the urging of President Roy W. Simmons and with the encouragement of the Utah Historical Society, the bank decided to adaptively reuse and preserve the structure.

Execution The adaptive-reuse plan was coordinated by Don Bingham, an architect with Montmorency, Hayes and Talbot, Architects, Inc., of Salt Lake City. Minimum repair was required on the exterior stone work. The addition on the rear was removed, returning the building to its original configuration, and some of the stone from this addition was reused to reconstruct a window in one of the bays, which had been enlarged at some point to make a doorway. A new cedar-shingle roof was installed, and all the wood trim and porches were refurbished, retaining as much of the original detail as possible. Sam Moss, of the Perce-Young Construction Company and job foreman for the project, utilized old photographs of the building to duplicate the carvings and turnings. New dowels, spindles, and other elements were reconstructed to exactly match their missing or deteriorated counterparts, and all wood trim was repainted. The site was also redesigned to accommodate new driveways, walkways, and landscaping. A drive-in facility utilizes one of the bay windows, fitted with bullet-resistant glass, as a view station connected to remote units by underground pneumatic tubes.

The rooms on the main floor have been adapted to accommodate banking needs. The parlor, sitting room, and central stair hall were opened up by the removal of several interior walls, creating a large public banking area. Where these walls were structurally supporting, steel and concrete columns have been installed to carry the loads. Teller counters, designed and built by Fetzer's, Inc., of Salt Lake City to match the woodwork of the house, have been placed in this space. Modern recessed incandescent lighting and restored chandeliers provide illumination. The bank vault now occupies the former two first-floor bedrooms. Eighteen-inch, reinforced, concrete walls, ceilings, and floor, together with the original sandstone outer walls of the house, form a secure "box" for the vault. The additional load is supported on concrete piers from the basement grade below.

The rooms on the other side of the hall have not been altered, and serve as conference and office space. A small elevator has been installed at the rear of the hall. The rooms on the second floor, used for lounge space, toilets, storage, and future offices, remain essentially in their original configuration.

All surfaces in the building have been repainted or refinished. The original Brigham Oak graining—a method of painting the surface to look like oak-grained wood—has been duplicated on woodwork throughout the main floor. All the brass door knobs, locks, and hinges were removed, repolished, and replaced.

New mechanical systems were installed in the unused attic and enlarged basement crawl spaces, and all plumbing and wiring has been replaced.

Costs According to the architect, the project costs were comparable to those for new branch offices constructed during the same period. Operating costs are also comparable to those of new construction. The bank did not disclose cost figures.

Benefits The bank is proud of its Heber City office and claims that business has exceeded expectations. The location is excellent, and the adaptation of the historic building has generated much public goodwill. Several local publications have written articles about it. In 1974, the Hatch House was included in the National Register of Historic Places.

The Company Zions First National Bank was founded in 1873 by Brigham Young. Originally known as Zion's Savings Bank and Trust, it was Utah's first state-chartered savings bank. The bank is now held by Zions Utah Bancorporation, a holding company which had total assets of $798.2 million in 1976. Zions First National Bank has 42 branch offices throughout the State of Utah.

For further information contact:
Clair Norton
Branch Manager
Zions First National Bank
81 East Center Street
Heber City, Utah 84032

Don Bingham, A.I.A.
Montmorency, Hayes and Talbot, Architects, Inc.
2398 West North Temple Street
Salt Lake City, Utah 84116

Several interior walls were removed to provide space for banking use. Teller counters were designed to match the house's woodwork. (Busath Photography)

Summary In January, 1975, the Alamo National Bank began the recycling of its existing 23-story, 1930s landmark building in downtown San Antonio. The bank's decision to stay and renovate was based on several considerations, including the inexpensive space and prime location the building would provide, and the position of the building in the historic fabric of the city. The remodeling cost $5 million, or $38 per square foot, and according to one of the project's architects, Chris Carson, "We could afford to do it because the building was already here. If you replaced this building today, you'd have to spend upwards of $25 million to $30 million."[1] The project was completed fourteen months later in February, 1976.

Background The 23-story tower was built in 1930 at a cost of $2.5 million. It was designed by the Chicago architectural firm of Graham, Anderson, Probst and White. (The firm also designed Chicago's landmark Wrigley Building.) The tower was designed in the Art Deco style, clad in earth-tone brick masonry, and decorated with terra cotta and bronze. The bank has continuously occupied four floors, leasing the remaining nineteen for other office use. Such original materials as travertine floors, marble wainscoting, solid brass and bronze fittings, and a grand lobby which soars to forty feet, "made the bank a landmark in San Antonio,"[2] states William Flannery, Alamo National's Chairman of the Board.

Functional needs, additional customer services, and the bank's growth all required expansion in 1975. About 35,000 square feet of additional space was needed. The tower's location on San Antonio's main commercial thoroughfare as well as its distinctive aesthetic character were both important factors in the bank's decision to remodel.

Execution The bank decided that all contracts for the remodeling work would go to San Antonio firms to keep the money in the city. Accordingly, Ford, Powell and Carson Architects and Planners, Inc., of San Antonio, designed the recycling plan to accommodate new functional and space requirements, while blending the changes with the existing character and materials of the building. The Bartlett Locke, Jr., Construction Company was the general contractor and worked with consulting engineers Fred T. Goetting and Associates, and W. E. Simpson Company, Inc. Orville Carr and Associates, in conjunction with the architects, was responsible for the interior design.

The first eight floors, designed to accommodate banking needs, received the major alterations, but the electrical and mechanical systems and the windows were refurbished throughout the entire building. On the main banking floor, at street level, the mezzanine area was enlarged, and the service area was redesigned. A large spiral staircase, enclosed by a glass-and-bronze handrail, was built surrounding a three-story center well to connect the new mezzanine area with the main banking floor and the safe-deposit area on the lower level. New teller paying/receiving counters have been installed between existing columns on the main level, and are sheathed in bronze and marble. The most dramatic visual change has been the addition of a Tiffany-like lighted ceiling consisting of five-foot-square bronze coffers containing a grid of bronze light diffusers.

The accounting, bookkeeping, and administrative offices, as well as community rooms, a boardroom, and a new employees' snack bar are located on floors three through seven. These floors are designed on the open-plan office concept, featuring flexible work stations, acoustic screens, and new lighting systems.

To conserve energy, save money, and update the existing wood-frame double-sash windows in the building, a bronze-glazed, snap-on aluminum frame was applied directly over the existing wood frames. The 1,100 windows are all operable, and can be cleaned from the inside. The cost was approximately $300,000, or approximately $270 per window. According to Bradford R. Breuer, a Vice President at Alamo National, "What we have done is to remodel to meet all existing building codes. In essence, we've built a new building without 'building a new building.'"[3]

On the exterior, new bronze-tinted glass panels were installed at street level to provide an easy view of banking activities. These windows also create a spacious atmosphere in the bank's lobby. The walk-in front of the building has been paved with brick in a herringbone pattern, and trees in recessed plant wells have been included.

The Alamo National Building. (Zintgraff Photographers)

80

Costs The renovation cost $5 million, or according to a report by the architects, about $38 per square foot for the 85,000 square feet renovated. This is well below the $70 per square foot cost for comparable new construction. Architect Chris Carson says that the "Alamo Bank got a $25 million bargain in usable space out of a $5 million investment in repair and renovation."[4] (see graph.)

Problems During the recycling, the bank temporarily located movable banking facilities in a former furniture building across the street, while the vaults and other fixed items remained in the old structure. This resulted in some inconveniences during the fourteen months of construction.

Benefits The bank was able to consolidate specific service departments, which previously were scattered throughout the building and even in other buildings. This has resulted in a more efficient operation. The renovation extended the life of the building at least another forty years and offered space to the bank at a great savings.

The bank has received much praise and attention for the recycling. Texas Governor Dolph Briscoe was present at the dedication ceremonies and congratulated all who made the project possible. Richard Teniente, Mayor Pro Tem of San Antonio, also at the reopening ceremonies, congratulated the bank for setting a good example for downtown revitalization. A local editorial stated:

Key to the center of the city is the community's financial structure and the major banks are the hub of that structure. Alamo National's upgrading is visible encouragement to a new wave of downtown interest at a time when San Antonio's heart is being examined with a keener interest than usual. Major investment by any institution and particularly by a major bank is important because it helps buoy the kind of momentum needed to stimulate other investment for renewal.[5]

The remodeled main banking floor. (Zintgraff Photographers)

The Company Founded in 1891, the Alamo National Bank is the third largest bank in San Antonio. Its assets declined from $334 million in 1975 to $326 million in 1976.

For further information contact:
Bradford R. Breuer
Vice President
Alamo National Bank
Saint Mary's at Commerce
P.O. Box 900
San Antonio, Texas 78293

Footnotes

1. Deborah Weser, "Bank Completes Renovation Plan," *San Antonio Express News* 29 February 1976.
2. Morris Willson, "Face Lift Plans Related," *San Antonio Light*, 21 January 1975.
3. "Alamo National to Open," *San Antonio Light*, 22 February 1976, p. 24C.
4. Weser, *op. cit.*, p. 4-G.
5. "Editorial: Alamo National's Forward Steps Help Encourage More Renewal," *San Antonio Express*, 23 January 1975, p. 18A.

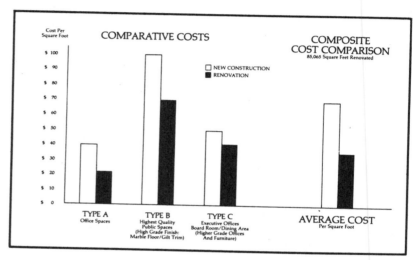

Architect's comparison of recycling costs and typical new construction. (Architectural Recycling, Ford, Powell, and Carson, Architects and Planners)

Summary The Hitchcock Chair Company has revived production of Hitchcock furniture, following nineteenth-century practices, and has even utilized the historic 1826 factory in Riverton, Connecticut, where until 1849, Lambert Hitchcock maintained his "Chair and Cabinet Furniture Manufactory." Since beginning the endeavor in 1946, John T. Kenney, owner of the present company, has built this furniture-making concern into a profitable and flourishing business. The Hitchcock Chair Company has also used an 1830 Gothic Revival church as a museum exhibiting Lambert Hitchcock's wares. Because of the company's efforts, jobs, a measure of prosperity, and an increasing number of tourists have been attracted to the picturesque town of Riverton, in northwestern Connecticut.

Background Lambert Hitchcock was born on May 28, 1795, in Cheshire, Connecticut. After an apprenticeship to a local cabinetmaker, Hitchcock set off for the northwestern part of the state in 1818. He settled in a tiny community at the fork of the Farmington River, because it possessed abundant waterpower and trees.

Hitchcock's business, producing chair parts with a saw and lathe, must have prospered, because a new brick factory employing about 100 people was completed in 1826. This three-story structure still has its original weathervane and cupola. Some of Hitchcock's "fancy" chairs resembled country versions of chairs appearing in Hepplewhite and Sheraton's pattern books, while others of his chairs resembled Duncan Phyfe's. The chairs were made in different styles, such as "pillow" and "bolster," and had seats of rush, cane or wood.

An article describes Hitchcock's "manufactory":

The chairs were assembled in the factory, often called the "works," as well as in the homes, in a kind of family manner. Men did all the woodworking: sawing, turning, bending, shaping, and "driving-up" parts into frames. Then children rubbed on a priming coat of red paint so that a patina similar to Duncan Phyfe's real rosewood was obtained when black paint was grained over it. Several variations of graining were used. . . . Women did most of the ornamenting. They stripped fine lines with quills; brushed gold bands on the front of the legs: cut stencil designs out of the best available paper and laid them on tacky surfaces . . . . With bare fingers or a piece of velvet they rubbed the varicolored powders through the open stencil pattern. The finished product was then varnished all over.[1]

Hitchcock chairs wholesaled for from 40 cents to $3 for the top of the line. For a few years, the business flourished, and these chairs were sent all over the eastern United States. But in 1829, a cash squeeze, due to late customer payments, forced Hitchcock to declare bankruptcy, although the manufactory was able to continue operations under trustees. Hitchcock resolved his financial crisis with help from his brother-in-law, Arba Alford, and the two formed a new partnership, "Hitchcock, Alford & Co." They expanded their furniture production lines to include chests, tables, and mirrors, as sales increased in the growing Western market. The partnership grew; they bought a nearby factory in 1839, and stepped up production to 40,000 items a year. In 1844, Hitchcock and Alford leased another factory in Unionville, whose location on a canal gave access to additional markets. Unfortunately, four years later, the railroad replaced the canal system as the primary means of shipping goods. Since none of their manufactories were near railroads, the business was doomed. In 1849, the company was dissolved, and Hitchcock's former partner and his brother created the A. & A. Alford Company, which continued the manufactory in Hitchcocks-ville. In 1852, Lambert Hitchcock died; in 1865, the town's name was changed to Riverton.

Production of Hitchcock-style chairs ceased in 1864, when the Alfords sold the factory to a producer of ivory-tipped wooden pocket rulers, which continued operations until 1901. The factory was used for various purposes during the following years until finally, it was abandoned. The windows were blocked up, and the site of the manufactory of Hitchcock chairs seemed doomed to decay.

Execution In spring, 1946, while on a fishing trip, John T. Kenney of West Hartford noted the boarded-up Hitchcock Chair factory and a state marker describing Lambert Hitchcock's manufactory. Although he was a shoe salesman with little expertise in furniture, Kenney decided to revive the old factory and make furniture reproductions in the Hitchcock style. He leased the factory from its owners for $300 a year with an option to buy it for $10,000 after two years. On October 17, 1946, the Hitchcock Chair Company again became operational with Kenney serving as President and Treasurer and his woodworking colleague, Richard Coombs, acting as Vice President and Assistant Treasurer. Working capital amounted to about $25,000. For two and a half years, they worked retrofitting the old factory and researching Hitchcock's furniture-making techniques. With assets of $375.63, the team finally obtained a $7,000 bank loan in March, 1949.

Since then, the Hitchcock Chair Company has prospered by creating reproductions of "fancy furniture" for a growing market. Today, its seven retail stores in Connecticut, Massachusetts, and New York gross over $15 million. The product line has been expanded to include bookcases, chests, mirrors, tables, and benches. However, Hitchcock-style chairs are still the biggest seller. They are handcrafted in thirty different standard colors and designs, as well as in limited editions. Production is carried on in the original factory and two modern plants. The present company employs about 150 people, who rotate their jobs in order to become familiar with various aspects of furniture making. Production techniques used at the restored factory are virtually the same as in Lambert Hitchcock's time. Automation is utilized only in the production of individual chair parts. According to G. Stafford Broughton, Hitchcock Vice President, "On a single lathe today, we get 1,200 to 1,600 turnings. The best a skilled craftsman could turn out on a lathe in the old days was about 120 pieces."[2] Approximately 3,000 chairs a week are produced at the factory. In Hitchcock's time, about 30,000 a year were turned out.

Tourists can visit the factory, observe the craftsmen at work, and hear them describe their tasks: turning a leg, rushing a seat, or applying stencils on the furniture. More than one-half of the Hitchcock factory is now a retail store, where pieces can often be bought at a discount.

Kenney has also reused the Old Union Church in the town as a museum. A short walk from the Hitchcock Factory, this Gothic Revival church was built with the assistance of Lambert Hitchcock, and it was there that he was married. Antique pieces of Hitchcock furniture and vintage woodworking tools provide an appropriate setting for the study of Hitchcock's life and work. About 30,000 visitors tour the museum each year. There is no charge.

Costs The company did not release figures on the cost of the retrofitting. However, it did release the following figures on the Hitchcock Museum:

Cost of purchase	$30,000
Renovation	$50,000
Annual Operating Costs	$50,000

Benefits The Hitchcock Chair Company, having profitably adapted nineteenth-century furniture techniques to twentieth-century requirements, is today providing jobs and increased tourism, thus improving the local economy. In addition, the company has expanded its business ventures in the town of Riverton and further helped to preserve the character of this New England village by purchasing and renovating eight vintage houses which it leases as antique, dress, and clock shops and a restaurant.

The Company The Hitchcock Chair Company is privately held. No financial figures are available.

For further information contact:
Thomas Glennon
President
Hitchcock Chair Company
Riverton, Connecticut 06065

Ellen Glennon
Director
Hitchcock Museum
Riverton, Connecticut 06065

Sue White
Vice President
Advantage Associates
60 Washington Street
Hartford, Connecticut 06106

Footnotes

1. "Lambert Hitchcock of Hitchcocks-ville, Connecticut," *Bulletin of the Antiquarian and Landmarks Society, Inc., of Connecticut,* July, 1966, p. 3.
2. Virginia Bohlin, "Hitchcock: Some Day These Products Will Be Antiques," *Boston Sunday Globe* (New England), 20 February 1977, p. 53.

The restored old Hitchcock Chair Factory.

Summary From 1968 to 1970, Levi Strauss & Co., the famous maker of blue jeans, completely renovated its wood-frame Valencia Street manufacturing plant, built in 1906. The cost of this renovation was $1 million. The plant now serves not only the company, but the community as well: its cafeteria is being used after hours as a center for community meetings and also as a classroom where the company's Spanish- and Chinese-speaking employees may study English. Using company land near the plant, Levi Strauss also made improvements of value to the community. It helped renovate a rundown playgound located directly in front of the plant. It also built an employee parking lot which is used as a basketball court after hours by neighborhood residents.

Background Levi Strauss opened the Valencia Street factory, a three-story timber-frame structure, shortly after the San Francisco earthquake in 1906. It has been producing blue jeans there ever since. The 83,000-square-foot plant is located in the Mission District of San Francisco, once a suburban area but now part of the deteriorating inner city. Levi Strauss is one of the area's major employers, drawing almost 350 workers from the surrounding neighborhoods.

By the late 1960s, the plant was becoming a burden to the company; it was old, unattractive, and almost obsolete. Levi Strauss considered moving to an industrial area in South San Francisco, ten miles from its present location. However, an informal survey of employee reaction found that most people working at the plant had very close ties with the neighborhood. Many employees didn't own cars, and either walked or took the bus to work each morning. Many female employees especially needed to be near their homes and children.

Levi Strauss is a major participant in the JOBs (Just One Break) program of the National Alliance of Businessmen, a program intended to help individuals who are having trouble finding employment on their own. According to the company, its awareness of local job-related problems made it reluctant to disrupt the lives of its employees, or to make the inner-city job situation any worse.

Furthermore, although most of its factories are located outside California, the company wanted to maintain a plant in San Francisco, the city where Levi Strauss opened his first store in 1850.

Execution In late 1967, Levi Strauss asked architect Howard A. Friedman, F.A.I.A., to improve the looks and efficiency of the Valencia Street plant. The plan proposed by Friedman and his staff, in addition to consisting of a general renovation, included construction of a Western-style porch to run the length of the front of the building, giving it the look of an old hotel.

Renovation work began on the first floor in 1968, under general contractors Maloney and O'Hare. It proceeded one floor at a time until the work was completed in 1970. In this way, the company was able to keep the plant in full operation throughout the renovation.

The major construction work included erecting a series of stair towers at the four corners of the building. After these were finished, all interior stairs were removed. The interior was then altered to accommodate the conveniences of a modern plant, including air conditioning. New washrooms were added, and the sewing operation was consolidated from three floors to one. Hardwood floors were refinished, but the old timber structure was found to have stood up well. The exterior required little work: the building was painted bright white and yellow, and the Western-style front porch, once erected, was furnished with benches and checker tables.

The first floor of the refurbished factory contains the company's administrative offices, a warehouse, and the shipping department. The second floor is the location of all manufacturing facilities which produce Levi's denim and corduroy jeans. The third floor houses several staff operations moved from the company's downtown office building, including research and development, a product-testing laboratory, an experimental sewing factory, and the styling and design department, as well as a cafeteria dining room. The latter is made available to neighborhood and civic groups for meetings and banquets, and also serves employees as an after-work classroom where English is taught.

After the renovation was completed, Levi Strauss had to decide what to do with the land surrounding the factory. In front was a playground which had fallen into disuse and disrepair. After consulting the San Francisco Recreation and Parks Department and community leaders to determine the best use for the land, the company decided to restore this playground. It had a mini-park built that was designed by Howard Friedman. The City of San Francisco agreed to contribute shrubbery and landscaping as well as the services of a park director. On additional company land, since many plant employees needed parking facilities, a parking lot was constructed. It is used after hours as a basketball court for neighborhood youth.

Costs The renovation of the Valencia Street factory cost Levi Strauss & Co. almost $1 million.

Benefits The newly renovated plant has been praised by community residents and even by commuters. San Francisco Planning Director Allan

Jacobs wrote to Levi Strauss: "I hope that others will follow your example in staying in San Francisco and in doing such tasteful rehabilitation of fine old properties."[1] Mayor Joseph Alioto said that the remodeled plant "gives testimony to the recognition by a leading corporate manufacturer of the problems of the neighboring community and participation in the solution."[2]

The Company In 1850, Levi Strauss, a Bavarian dry-goods merchant, arrived in San Francisco with a roll of canvas tent material. Discovering gold miners' need for good-quality, tough-wearing pants, he asked a local tailor to make several pairs of pants from his tent material. These were sold almost immediately, and the miners wanted more of "Levi's Pants." Strauss opened a shop in San Francisco, and began to produce waist-high overalls in the canvas material, and sometime later, in denim.

Today Levi Strauss & Co. produces a variety of clothes. In 1976, it had sales of $1.2 billion, up from 1975 sales of $1.01 billion. Income rose from $64.7 million in 1975 to $104.8 million in 1976.

Several pairs of Levi Strauss's original canvas jeans are now in the Smithsonian Institution, part of its Americana collection.

For further information contact:
Elise Rychlewski
Assistant Director, History Room,
Public Relations Department
Levi Strauss & Co.
2 Embarcadero Center
San Francisco, California 94106

Footnotes

1. Walter A. Hass, Jr., "Levi's Old/New Pants Factory," *Historic Preservation* (Washington, D.C.: Preservation Press, National Trust for Historic Preservation, n.d.), p. 17.
2. *Ibid.*, p. 14.

The renovated 1906 factory.

Summary Pope & Talbot, one of the country's oldest forest-products companies, has restored most of the buildings in the town of Port Gamble, Washington, where it has operated continuously since it was founded in 1853. The company has renovated about thirty residential and commercial buildings since the late 1960s at a cost of about $250,000. Port Gamble is a living, working company town, a historic community, and a unique example of preservation.

Background During the heyday of the gold rush, in the 1850s, Andrew J. Pope and Captain William C. Talbot left Maine and migrated west to make their fortunes. When they got to California, they put their lumber backgrounds to good use, and developed a thriving wood-products business tied directly to the gold boom. Shortly thereafter, Captain Talbot set off for Puget Sound to find timberlands and a sawmill site. He chose Port Gamble, and in 1853, Pope & Talbot built a sawmill there. This sawmill, which has been modernized several times, is still processing lumber, and has the distinction of being the oldest continuously operating sawmill in North America.

As business grew, so did Port Gamble. Houses were built for the employees, and a few shops were constructed to service their needs. Port Gamble, with a population of about 250, is still a company town today. All 35 buildings are owned by Pope & Talbot and rented to its employees. About 35 percent of the Port Gamble plant's 225 employees live there.

Although the buildings were maintained through the years, the mostly Victorian-style edifices suffered heavy wear and tear. In the 1960s, the company had to decide whether to restore or demolish the existing buildings.

Pope & Talbot President Guy Pope, his wife, and several other company officials realized that Port Gamble provided a unique example of a living and working historic community. Furthermore, the mostly Victorian architecture (several buildings are copies of New England prototypes) was of widespread interest. Lumber processed from the company's timberlands was utilized in the original construction of the buildings.

Restoration of the town seemed an appropriate way to commemorate the company's 125th anniversary and the Bicentennial. Management also decided to collect all records and historical documents spread around the company's offices in the Pacific Northwest and to establish an archives in Port Gamble.

Execution Renovation began in 1969. Since the interiors had been modernized and maintained, exteriors were the central focus. Many of the houses were scraped and painted their original colors. Among the popular colors are: mustard, light grey, white and dark red. Where necessary, woodwork was replaced by company carpenters. To date, five houses, two commercial buildings, and St. Paul's Church have been restored to their original condition. One of the houses, the Gothic Revival Thompson House (c. 1859), is the oldest continuously occupied house in the state. Another, the Walker Ames House, was built in 1887 as the manager's residence, and is an excellent example of the Queen Anne shingle style. About fifteen years ago, previous tenants

Port Gamble homes restored by Pope & Talbot.

completely renewed the rich interior, which includes fine handcrafted woodwork, stained glass, and a fireplace still boasting its original tiles. The wooden, two-story General Store (c. 1853) originally served as a trading post. The store now houses the newly collected company archives in its basement, as well as the Port Gamble Historic Museum. The Museum's exhibits and artifacts depict the past, present, and future of Pope & Talbot and the lumber business in the Pacific Northwest. The restored Romanesque Revival St. Paul's Episcopal Church (c. 1870) is a copy of the Congregational Church in East Machias, Maine. Also repainted was the Masonic Temple (c. 1870), the oldest masonic temple in the state.

The improvements to the town continue. Recently, about twenty workmen's row houses, dating from the turn of the century, have been renovated and repainted, and the chimneys on the town's buildings are being repaired where necessary.

The streetscape of Port Gamble has been improved by placing electric and telephone lines underground and installing reproductions of turn-of-the-century gas streetlights.

Pope & Talbot has prepared a promotional pamphlet called *Port Gamble—America's Oldest Continuously Operating Forest Products Community* which describes the town's historic structures. Although tourists may walk around and identify the various historic sites, none of the houses are open to the public.

Costs The company has spent about $250,000 on the renovation and improvements to Port Gamble. These funds have been generated internally.

Problems The increasing flow of tourists has caused some problems for town residents. They complain of eager visitors ringing their bells and wanting to see the interiors of their houses. Some tourists complain about the lack of restaurants, although the company has provided picnic facilities.

The Port Gamble church, designed after a church in Maine.

Benefits Pope & Talbot's efforts have resulted in better employee relations. According to the company, residents take great pride in their unique town. The project has also generated favorable publicity; Port Gamble has been the subject of articles in such publications as *Sunset* magazine, the *Christian Science Monitor*, the *New York Times*, *Progressive Architecture*, and the *Seattle Times* as well as other regional newspapers. An increasing number of visitors to the nearby Olympic Mountains, a prime tourist attraction, are now stopping at Port Gamble. The Port Gamble Historic Museum, opened in July, 1976, has been another attraction. The company reports that the number of tourists doubled between 1976 and 1977.

The Company Pope & Talbot has manufacturing operations in Oregon, Washington, and British Columbia. The company had revenues of $94.3 million in 1976 and a net income of $3.6 million. The revenues reflect a 35 percent increase over 1975 sales of $69.4 million. However, the net income for 1976 was down from a 1975 figure of $3.99 million, primarily due to losses on a discontinued operation. Sales break down as follows: lumber, 59.2 percent; pulp chips, 12.4 percent; specialty plywood, 12.3 percent; logs and timber, 8.1 percent; veneer, 4.3 percent; and other, 3.7 percent.

For further information contact:
Holly R. Hutchins
Director
Corporate Communications
Pope & Talbot, Inc.
P.O. Box 8171
Portland, Oregon 97207

Summary In September, 1976, the Engineering Department of the Standard Oil Company of Ohio (Sohio) moved into the 83-year-old Cuyahoga Building on Superior Avenue and Public Square in downtown Cleveland. This historic landmark, designed by Daniel H. Burnham, is one of the few remaining examples of the Chicago skyscraper school of architecture. In 1976, the building was renovated by its owners, Broadview Management (a subsidiary of the Broadview Savings and Loan Company) and private interests. Sohio is the largest tenant. It has leased 40,000 of the building's 63,000 square feet for seven years at an annual cost of $7 per square foot. The desirable location, plus Sohio's confidence that the structure could be successfully and comfortably renovated to accommodate its engineering staff were the major reasons behind the decision to rent the space.

Background Sohio, founded by John D. Rockefeller and located in Cleveland since 1870, has its headquarters in the Midland Building, a Classical Revival structure built in 1929. By 1976, the company had outgrown its space in the Midland Building and sought additional office space in the nearby Cuyahoga Building. Built in 1893, the Cuyahoga was developed by two of Cleveland's most prominent business leaders, Myron T. Herrick and James Parmalee. Herrick was a banker and statesman, a Governor of Ohio, an advisor to President William McKinley, and an Ambassador to France. Parmalee was Herrick's business partner.

The eight-story Cuyahoga Building was designed by Daniel H. Burnham, and was the first steel-frame structure in Cleveland. Burnham was one of the leading architects at the turn of the century. Among his other credits were the World's Columbian Exposition in Chicago in 1893 and the Western Reserve Building (see Higbee) in Cleveland, where he also developed a plan of wide vistas, malls, and a spacious center of municipal and office buildings for the downtown area.

The Cuyahoga Building is faced with brown brick and has a sandstone and terra cotta trim. Stylistically, it contains neo-classical elements such as horizontal divisions clearly defining the base, middle, and top portions of the building. Romanesque arches are interspersed between three-part, projecting bay windows, and these features are grouped in vertical strips that correspond to the dimensions of the structural-steel supports. The central entrance on Superior Avenue is a two-story archway surrounded with terra cotta ornamentation. The archway contains a delicate, lace-like iron grillwork above the doors. According to the National Register Nomination Form for the building:

As an urban design element it [the Cuyahoga Building] effectively complements the Romanesque facade of the Society National Bank, also by Burnham and Root [Burnham's partner], on the north side of the Public Square, and the Romanesque Cleveland Arcade in the middle of the same block on Superior.[1]

All three buildings are in the National Register of Historic Places.

In 1904, the Williamson Building, an eighteen-story structure designed by George B. Post, was erected next to the Cuyahoga Building. In 1944, the two buildings were joined and connected by an arcade and stairway. The Cuyahoga Building had been vacant since 1967, when it was purchased in 1971 by the Broadview Savings and Loan Company and private interests who also own the Williamson Building. No renovations were planned until 1973. That year, Richard Kortier, President of Broadview Management and Vice President of Broadview Savings, who had just joined the firm, contacted several contractors. He recognized the demand for additional office space in the Public Square area, and felt that the Cuyahoga Building had excellent renovation potential.

The restored Cuyahoga Building. The Williamson Building is on the right. (Broadview Management Corporation)

88

Execution Kortier hired Drake Construction, a firm experienced in renovation, as the general contractors; and Myron Manders, of Bialosky and Manders, as the supervising architect. According to architect Manders, the objective of the renovation was "to preserve the historical richness of the exterior and to provide modern usable interior office space."[2] The business objective was to extend the building's useful and profitable life, while upgrading an area where the owners have additional property investments. To accomplish these objectives a "backward plan" was developed, which first determined the cash flow the renovated building could generate, and then decided what renovation work this cash flow would support. Commonly, developers first determine the cost of the renovation work, and then decide whether the market will accept the rents required. If net revenues do not provide an adequate return on investment, then a new renovation scheme must be developed. Leonard Nyman, Secretary-Treasurer of Drake Construction, states, "Why waste the cost of designing the building twice? A six-month delay when inflation is 10 percent can be pretty costly."[3]

The owners determined that an acceptable return on the building's rents after conversion could be achieved if $1.5 million were invested in renovation work and amortized over fifteen years. A six-month schedule was established. All subcontractors bidding on the job knew that there was a $400-a-day penalty for each day over the schedule. This approach matched the renovation work and the money available. It also rigidly budgeted and conserved time.

The building's interior was gutted, and new mechanical, plumbing, and electrical systems, as well as new elevators, were installed. A new steam/hot-water heating and cooling system was installed which has lowered energy costs by 25 percent.

The exterior was cleaned by sandblasting; the masonry was repointed; and all the wood window frames were covered with baked-enamel, aluminum frames and operable sashes that matched the originals. One-eighth-inch insulating glass was used in the new windows. The public lobby was restored to its original 1890s decor. The owners plan to restore the street-level retail space to its original style in 1978.

Work began on April 1, 1976, and by August, 1976, the Sohio Engineering Department moved into four of its five 8,000-square-foot floors. The Sohio facilities include an engineering library, a computer terminal area, reception and meeting rooms, and offices.

By September, 1977, all retail space on the ground level had been rented, and the building's owners were negotiating with interested tenants for the available top two floors at rents of $8.50 per square foot. The owners pay all taxes, operating expenses, and debt service for the building, but tenants are required to pay a proportionate share of all increases in taxes and operating costs. Tenants finished individual spaces to their own specifications.

Costs The cost for renovation of the total 63,000 square feet was $1.8 million or $28.50 per square foot. An additional $300,000 expenditure over the original $1.5 million budget was required to replace the plumbing system, which was found to be inadequate during renovation. Renovation costs were financed with a $1.8 million mortgage payable over fifteen years at a 10 percent interest rate. When the building is fully leased, tenant income will cover all building operating expenses and debt service. It will also provide the owners with a 6 percent return on their investment.

Sohio pays approximately $7 per square foot for 40,000 square feet of space, and has spent nearly $25,000 making improvements of its own. This rent compares to about $10 per square foot for space in new buildings in the area.

Main entrance to Cuyahoga Building. Archway has elaborate terra cotta ornamentation with iron filagree screen. (Broadview Management Corporation)

Problems Although the renovation proceeded nearly on schedule, when the mechanical and structural systems were exposed, it was found that the existing plumbing could not be reused. The pipes had to be replaced at a cost of nearly $300,000.

Benefits Broadview Management has brought a vacant, unprofitable building back to life and is receiving a reasonable return on its investment. According to Richard Kortier, "I wish we had ten more floors on Public Square like those in the 63,000-square-foot Cuyahoga Building. Public Square office space will be at a premium."[4]

Sohio, because of this recycling effort, has been able to gain the additional office space it needed close to its home offices. John Graham, Engineering Manager for the company, says:

We looked at a number of potential office sites before we selected the Cuyahoga Building. We were certain it could be modernized nicely and we were pleased with its proximity to the Midland building and the departments we serve. We've got the best of both worlds, the inside is as attractive and comfortable as any new building in the city, and the outside retains the character of an era that was exciting in Cleveland's history. Recycling soundly constructed older buildings, especially of a landmark like this one, is a form of energy conservation one should not overlook.[5]

The Company Standard Oil of Ohio, a diversified oil company, became independent in 1911 when the original Standard Oil Company was broken up. Today, Sohio's products include gasoline and other petroleum products, plastics, chemicals, and fertilizers. The company also has holdings in uranium, motels, and the food-service industry. Sohio's sales rose from a figure of $2.5 billion in 1975 to a figure of $2.9 billion in 1976. Net income increased from $126.5 million to $136.9 million over the same period.

For further information contact:
Samuel B. Baker
Public Affairs Associate
The Standard Oil Company of Ohio
Midland Building
Cleveland, Ohio 44115

Richard G. Kortier
President
Broadview Management Company
320 Williamson Building
Cleveland, Ohio 44114

Footnotes

1. "National Register of Historic Places, Inventory, Nomination Form" 10-300 (Washington, D.C.: U.S. Department of the Interior, National Park Service, December 31, 1974), sec. 6.
2. Gene Bluhm, "Restoring the Grandeur of the Past . . . the Cuyahoga Building," *Properties*, September, 1976, p. 90.
3. *Ibid*., p. 92.
4. *Ibid*., p. 97.
5. Standard Oil Company of Ohio, *Sohio News Service*, September 13, 1976, pp. 2-3.

Summary The Tremont Nail Company, dating from the early nineteenth century, is reputed to be the country's oldest nail manufacturer. Located in Wareham, Massachusetts, it is one of only three cut-nail manufacturers in America today. The company's factory complex, composed of nine nineteenth-century buildings, has been in continuous operation since 1848, when the main factory building was erected. The National Register of Historic Places' nominating form describes the complex:

Architecturally, the original factory building . . . and the other nineteenth and early twentieth century buildings comprise a significant industrial complex. Industrially, the nineteenth century processes which are still used to produce cut nails . . . illustrate well the human skill oriented processes of manufacture which characterize nineteenth century production.[1]

The Tremont Nail Factory has been listed in the National Register of Historic Places since October, 1976.

Background Tremont Nail was established in 1819 in Tremont, a suburb of Wareham, Massachusetts. In 1848, the company moved into buildings previously owned by the Parker Mills Nail Company in Wareham. It has been continuously operating there ever since. Seven out of the nine buildings in the complex are still used in the cut-nail manufacturing process.

The main factory building, located on the Wankinco River and originally powered by a waterwheel, is a large, shingled, rectangular structure. The original building is 240 feet long and 90 feet wide; an extension at the rear measures 50 feet by 50 feet. The factory's medium-pitched, ridged, green-shingled roof is topped by a wooden cupola. Sash windows line the facade of the building, and are supplemented in the two-story rear addition by smaller-paned windows.

The interior of the main building is an open area filled with machinery. Its walls and ceiling are constructed of unfinished lumber. Situated in the center of the room is the original brick tempering forge, which with the help of pot-bellied stoves, heats the building in winter.

Other buildings, all dating from about 1900, include a clapboard office building built in the Federal style, two workers houses, and three sheds. Two nineteenth-century shingle buildings, the store and the carpenter's shop, complete the complex.

Cut nails differ from wire nails in having four distinct sides and blunt tips. These features prevent chipping and splitting when working with cinderblock or concrete, and provide greater holding power. The production of cut nails is an intricate process. After being blasted with shot to remove rust and scale, sheets of steel are cut into strips whose width is determined by the size of the nail to be produced. The strips are then fed by hand into a nail-cutting machine, run by a wood and canvas belt-pulley system, which cuts and heads the nail with one stroke.

Actual production is carried out by highly skilled workmen, including a master mechanic and a nail maker. It takes years of experience to learn the process of nail making:

A good operator can produce 4,000-5,000 pounds of nails a day from his battery of four nail machines. But the key man is the "nailer" who fine tunes the machines, grinds the blades and sets the dies that determine the shape and quality of the nails.[2]

Today, there are only three nail makers at Tremont, and no one in training. The skill is not being passed along, and in fact, nail-cutting machines are no longer being produced.

The cut-nail business is closely tied to the housing market. Originally used for the installation of hardwood flooring, cut nails were very much in demand. However, with the increased use of automatic nailing machines which use wire nails, the market for the cut flooring nail is declining. Apart from flooring and masonry, cut nails are used in boat building, foundry work, the restoration of older houses, and for decoration.

In 1969, the company celebrated its 150th birthday. Efficiency has enabled the factory to operate today almost as it did during the Civil War. Recently, the price of wire nails has risen to equal that of cut nails, which should help Tremont Nail remain competitive.

Execution The continued use of the old factory complex has not presented any unusual maintenance problems. The main factory building, where most of the production takes place, is a sturdy structure. The company has recently replaced the wooden-shake roof with asphalt tile, and the roof itself is replaced every 25 to 30 years. The trim on the buildings is painted every 3 years.

Recently, to make way for machinery, several roof supports were removed. Several months later the roof began to sag in that area. To remedy this, Tremont Nail replaced the supports using cut-down telephone poles.

The buildings have also at times been hit hard by hurricanes, resulting in water damage from the nearby Wankinco River. Once, in 1938, the entire roof was ripped off. The company replaced the roof, but apart from that, continued functioning as usual.

In the past, Tremont Nail sponsored tours of its factory during the summer months, since Wareham's seaside location attracts tourists to the area. However, due to the lack of space, and safety considerations, the tours have been discontinued for the present.

Costs The new steel-shot cleaning system (see "Problems") cost Tremont Nail nearly a quarter of a million dollars. Other figures were not available.

Problems Although structurally sound, the building was not designed with twentieth-century safety regulations in mind. Tremont Nail has had particular difficulty meeting new health regulations established by the Occupational Safety and Health Administration (OSHA), which sets ambient noise levels and other safety standards. To solve some of these problems, the company requires workers to wear goggles and ear-protection devices specified by OSHA regulations.

In addition, the company has instituted a new method of cleaning the sheet steel. Previously, the metal was cleaned by dipping it in hot sulphuric acid, which was then discharged into the nearby Wankinco River. Now, due to Environmental Protection Agency regulations, the steel is cleaned by bombarding it with steel shot, a non-polluting method. This effort has brought Tremont Nail a citation from the Massachusetts Pollution Control Agency.

Benefits Continued use of the old factory complex has generated considerable publicity. James Kenyon, Jr., President of Tremont Nail, estimates that from 1971 to 1976, there were fifteen to twenty unsolicited articles about the company. Most recently, Tremont Nail was featured in a report by CBS news, inspired by a 1976 front-page story in the *Wall Street Journal*. This exposure has helped the company a great deal, especially in the do-it-yourself market. According to Kenyon:

When I first came here, I'm not sure the old buildings helped our image, but now I'd say that they surely do. . . . Some people say we're a backwoods company, but our product is good and people know that.[3]

Kenyon believes that the old buildings signify reliability and friendly, personal service to Tremont's customers.

The Company In 1973, sales for this privately held company reached a record $2 million, and afterwards, decreased to $1.5 million. In 1976, sales rose to $1.65 million, and 1977's projected sales are back to the $2 million mark.

Other Preservation Activities. In 1969, Tremont Nail redesigned its nineteenth-century cooper's shop, which originally manufactured the kegs in which the cut nails were shipped, as an "Old Fashioned Country Store." The store sells peanut butter, pot-bellied stoves, oil lamps, nail kegs, and sassafras. It features antiques and cut-nail jewelry, along with a regular display of cut nails.

For further information contact:
James Kenyon, Jr.
President
Tremont Nail Company
21 Elm Street
Wareham, Massachusetts 02571

Footnotes

1. Andrea M. Gilmore and Christine Boulding, "National Register of Historic Places, Inventory, Nomination Form," 10-300 (U.S. Department of the Interior, National Park Service, July, 1976), p. 3.
2. Richard Martin, "Old Plant Bangs Out Old-Fashioned Nails and Tries to Stay Old," *Wall Street Journal*, 17 May 1976, p. 1.
3. *Ibid.*, p. 19.

Tremont Nail's nineteenth-century main factory building.

Summary By the 1960s, the Bank of California had outgrown its landmark, Corinthian-columned, classic banking hall located in the heart of San Francisco's financial district. The first major building constructed after the earthquake of 1906, this structure is considered one of the city's prime examples of Classical Revival architecture. The bank's Board of Directors considered razing the structure to build a more lucrative new building, but, instead, decided to build a new tower addition which would complement and enhance the existing banking hall. The resulting design has received widespread praise for its response to the older building. The restoration and new construction cost more than $22 million.

Background The Bank of California opened its doors in San Francisco on July 5, 1864. By 1867, it occupied the site of its present main office at 400 California Street. Outgrowing this facility by 1905, the bank demolished the building to build a new one, and, by January, 1906, had moved to temporary quarters nearby. On April 18, 1906, a massive earthquake and subsequent fire left San Francisco in ruins. Almost 500 blocks of the city, including the financial, wholesale, and retail districts, were destroyed. Within six weeks, as the city began its rebuilding efforts, the bank received authorization to begin work on its new building. By September, 1908, the new building, 112 feet long, 80 feet wide, and with 60-foot ceilings, was completed and occupied.

In the 1950s, the bank expanded and added branch offices up and down the Pacific Coast. By the 1960s, it was a $1 billion institution with 48 offices. The bank had long since outgrown its classic headquarters, and its staff was spread out in offices in adjacent buildings. A new building was clearly needed. Although some consideration was given to the financial benefits of razing the existing landmark and building a large, leasable office building on the site, the directors decided otherwise. Instead, a new tower addition would be built incorporating the old building. President Charles De Bretteville explained the bank's decision:

The new 314-foot tower is approximately four times the height of the old building, but relates to it in scale and detail. (Ted Mahieu)

94

The endeavor of the Bank was to uphold the architectural traditions that have helped San Francisco earn a worldwide reputation for beauty. As a bank with roots in the earliest San Francisco and the West, we felt an obligation to ourselves and the city to preserve our historic building, the first major structure after the 1906 earthquake.[1]

Execution   After several years of research by bank personnel and the San Francisco architectural team of Anshen and Allen, a design attempting to integrate the old and new was developed. The old banking hall would be completely preserved and remodeled, including restoration of exterior and interior detail and incorporation of new electrical and mechanical systems. A new skyscraper, related in proportion, line, and detail would be built next to the older temple-like structure, adding over 240,000 square feet of floor space. To retain the unity and prominence of the original, powerfully symmetrical building, the new tower is set back ten feet from the property line; it is asymmetrical in design and appears to be growing out of the wall of the original building. The interiors are linked by interconnecting lobby passageways.

Although the new tower is 314 feet tall, or approximately four times the height of the old building, it produces a visual and proportional harmony without overpowering the smaller structure. To contrast and set off the banking hall's monumental form with its tall portico, strongly vertical entrance, and enclosure of columns, the tower has a broad, low horizontal entrance with a good deal of glass.

The decorative reeds or fluting of the tower's precast concrete facade match the fluting of the original Corinthian columns and the curved granite cornices of the old building. The original color scheme of light grey granite and dark bronze grills is also repeated on the new tower.

The established setbacks from public streets, the desired setback for the entry, and the height constraint required a daring and relatively expensive design to create the necessary usable floor area to make the project economically feasible. The new building is cantilevered up to 30 feet over the banking hall gaining more than 3,100 square feet of usable space per floor (82 percent of the total floor space). Additional space was created by sinking the new building three levels below ground to a depth of 54 feet below the sidewalk; 45 feet below the high-water tide level of San Francisco Bay and 40 feet below the existing water table. In order to accomplish this, a unique foundation was constructed. A 2-foot-thick concrete wall was poured 80 feet deep—four times deeper than normal for local foundations—around the entire site, and an 8-foot thick concrete mat was poured at the bottom. This formed a floating raft-like foundation. The project was completed in December, 1968, six years after its inception.

Costs   Approximately $2.8 million, or $140 per square foot, was spent on the restoration and remodeling of the banking hall. The new headquarters tower cost $19.7 million, or $90 per square foot. Together, the two buildings have a gross floor area of 300,000 square feet.

Problems   Time and expense were the major difficulties involved in this project. The high quality, compatible detail, and careful workmanship specified by the architects and client were costly and time-consuming. Unlike many standard curtain-wall facades that can be purchased virtually prefabricated and affixed to steel frames, the precast fluted spandrels had to be custom-designed and custom-made. The unusual foundation and cantilevering necessary to satisfy the building's space needs also required additional expense and time.

Benefits   The bank has received praise for its efforts to preserve the old building and to design the tower in a compatible manner. In a report, *The Preservation of Landmarks in San Francisco*, published by the San Francisco Department of City Planning, the success of this project was affirmed: "These efforts substantially support the goal of the city having character and depth in its physical environment."[2]

The Company   The Bank of California ranks 39th among the banks in the United States. It was the first incorporated commercial bank in the West, and, through a unique national charter, it is the only tri-state bank in the country. A wholly owned subsidiary of BanCal Tri-State Corporation, the bank provides services throughout the world. The parent company had assets of about $3 billion in 1976, compared with 1975's assets of $3.1 billion. Net income declined from $3.3 million in 1975 to $2.7 million in 1976.

For further information contact:
Diana Fedorchak
Director of Public Relations
The Bank of California
400 California Street
San Francisco, California 94145

Footnotes

1. The Bank of California, *400 California Street . . . A Century Plus Five*, n.d., p. 66.
2. *Ibid.*, p. 94.

The Boston Five Cents Savings Bank

Summary In 1966, the Boston Five Cents Savings Bank held an architectural design competition for a new addition to its 1920s, eight-story neoclassic headquarters on School Street in Boston's central business district. The design problem was not only to functionally and aesthetically complement the existing bank building, but also to relate the new addition to Boston's historic urban core. To the east, stood the Old South Meeting House, an important landmark built in 1729; to the north, was the Old Corner Book Store, recently restored with financial support from the Boston Globe (see Appendix); and to the west, was the Old Boston City Hall, a nineteenth-century landmark. Further complicating the design task, a proposed street realignment by the Boston Redevelopment Authority would create a new triangular public "square" and a wedge-shaped redevelopment site adjacent to the bank. Kallmann & McKinnell, architects of Boston's new City Hall, won the competition. As evaluated by the jury, their design, a contemporary, glass and concrete, colonnaded structure, "handsomely related to the square, the church, and the other existing buildings."[1] The 45,000-square-foot addition was completed in 1967. The bank spent $3.3 million on its construction; it contributed another $96,000 for the design and construction of the triangular plaza.

Background The Boston Redevelopment Authority (BRA) is Boston's planning and renewal agency. It has made innovative efforts to improve the city and encourage new development within an overall framework that consciously respects existing historic architecture.

In the mid-1960s, the BRA proposed a realignment of School Street to ease traffic flow through the central business district. This project would create two triangular pieces of land: one, to be left open as a public plaza, and the other, to be privately developed. The plaza, in the historic heart of the city, was to open up and set off two important landmarks on Boston's Freedom Trail: the Old Corner Book Store, one of the city's oldest buildings, built in

The public plaza in front of the new building. (Ezra Stoller © ESTO.)

1718, and the Old South Meeting House, where the Boston Tea Party was planned, built in 1729. The plaza was also designed to offer the pedestrian a stopping place along Washington Street, the main shopping street in town.

The developable triangular plot abutted the Boston Five Cents Savings Bank building on its east side, and contained 9,350 gross square feet of buildable land. Before the BRA could implement its realignment/plaza plans, it had to find a buyer for this land. The bank had been contemplating expansion and saw the odd-shaped building plot as a way to reorient its main entrance from School Street toward Washington Street to capitalize on the heavier pedestrian traffic flow. Constructing an addition to the present building would also permit uninterrupted service and allow future expansion in the same location.

The existing bank building, neoclassical in design, was constructed in the 1920s. It contains: a colonnaded base, the former banking hall, a middle section of offices with paired windows corresponding to the column spacing, and a crowning, broad cornice. Pilasters on the corners extend the height of the building and define the outer edges.

(on facing page)
The new building's fan-like form opens out to the street, the public plaza, and the historic buildings that surround it. (Ezra Stoller © ESTO.)

(below)
Competition drawing of the new addition, the bank, and the Old South Meeting House. (Kallmann, McKinnell & Wood, Architects, Inc.)

Execution   Robert M. Morgan, then Chairman of the bank, had also served as Chairman of the Government Center Commission, which had redeveloped an extensive portion of Boston's downtown area. He had been closely involved with the process of selecting and working with the architects for the new City Hall.* He believed that an architectural competition would result in the best possible design for the new bank addition. Four architectural firms were invited to participate; the design competition proposal read as follows:

Though not large or complex, the new building must satisfy conditions that are unusual, difficult, perhaps contradictory. Clearly both BRA and the Bank are concerned about the exterior

*Morgan was later responsible for putting together the financial support to back the adaptive reuse of the Old Boston City Hall for office use.

NORTH   ELEVATION

manifestation of the building and the treatment of its setting, and therefore the combination of plaza and facade should be of major concern to the designer. In addition the Bank, as client, has a real business function to perform that requires a noble interior space, so there is the opportunity to fuse the expression of the inside with the outside. Yet the conditions are stringent: to come to terms with colonial tradition while extending a building conceived in a quite anti-colonial spirit and scale, and to cope with a site whose distorted and curtailed form is the byproduct of a traffic adjustment.[2]

The BRA required:

[that] the new building facade on the open space be throughout at least as high as the ridge of Old South, 65 feet above its street . . . also . . . a setback along the curve frontage such that the sidewalk of the new building will be at least 12 feet wide throughout.[3]

The selection jury consisted of: Pietro Belluschi, F.A.I.A., G. Holmes Perkins, F.A.I.A., both distinguished architects, and bank Chairman Robert Morgan.

The winner, Kallmann & McKinnell, was selected from drawings and models. Their design was praised for its impressive, interestingly lighted banking room, and the relationship of this structure to the street. The jury stated that:

the visual and operational relation to the old bank is so outstandingly handled that this feature, uniting the old and the new, could be made a major asset in the operation of the Bank. The exterior with its simple colonnade is handsomely related to the square, the Church, and the other existing building.[4]

The corner, wedge-shaped site dictated the basic fan form of the new contemporary addition. Large radiating beams and columns placed outside the building enclosure free the interior space, providing internal flexibility, and create a covered walkway adjacent to the sidewalk. The spacing of the exterior columns echoes the column and window configuration of the old building. The glass skin, set back seven feet from these columns, encourages views both into the building and out from within. From almost all points inside, one can see the Old South

Church, the Old Corner Book Store, and the new plaza. In this way, the plaza becomes an "urban living room" with the new and the old buildings forming its perimeter furnishings.

In keeping with the spirit of the old, as well as with BRA restrictions, the height of the new addition is approximately the same as the ridge height of Old South Church. The addition also is capped by a wide cornice similar to that of the original bank building. The predominantly concrete addition is also compatible in color with the earlier structure's grey limestone.

In the interior, the new building's four stories match the floor levels of the original building. The decoration is contemporary, with granite finishes used throughout on the street level. Fluorescent strip lighting follows the radiating beams, emphasizing the fan-like form.

Costs The total cost for the building's 45,000 square feet was $3.3 million, or approximately $73 per square foot. The bank also contributed $96,000 to the design and construction of the public plaza in front of the new building in lieu of, and exceeding, the city's requirement that 1 percent of the cost of construction for all new buildings be donated for public art.

Problems The only difficulty encountered was the relatively high cost of construction. Much of it was the result of the extensive granite interior finishes and other furnishings specifically requested by the client, not the building's basic design.

Benefits Boston received a new public space and a new building that complements the landmarks surrounding it. The bank's image was enhanced, and in 1975, it received the Harleston Parker Award of the Boston Society of Architects for excellence in architectural design. The building has been praised by several architectural publications, as well as several books on Boston landmarks.

The Company The Boston Five Cents Savings Bank, founded in 1854, has long been one of New England's largest mutual savings banks. It has fourteen offices throughout Boston. Total assets increased from $899 million in 1975 to $964 million in 1976.

For further information contact:
John Vernon
Manager, Purchasing Department
Boston Five Cents Savings Bank
10 School Street
Boston, Massachusetts 02108

Footnotes

1. Pietro Belluschi, Robert M.Morgan, G. Holmes Perkins, Chairman, "Report of Jury: The Boston Five Cents Savings Bank," (mimeographed, The Boston Five Cents Savings Bank, September 14, 1966), p. 2.
2. The Boston Five Cents Savings Bank, "Competition to Select an Architect for a Proposal to Redevelop a Parcel at School and Washington Streets in Boston" (mimeographed, The Boston Five Cents Savings Bank, June, 1966), pp. 2-3.
3. *Ibid.*, p. 2.
4. Belluschi, Morgan, Perkins, *op. cit.*, p. 2.

Charleston Associates

Summary   In October, 1970, the Mills Hyatt House opened its doors as Charleston's "newest-oldest" hotel. The 240-bedroom luxury hotel is a finely executed reproduction of the original Mills House, an 1853 hotel built on the same site. Charleston Associates, a limited partnership, purchased the old building in 1968 with the idea of restoring it. This plan was scrapped, however, when architectural consultants found the structure unsafe. Instead, an alternative plan to faithfully recreate the older building in an enlarged version was adopted. The new hotel cost $5.8 million to construct and furnish. Today, this hotel, managed by the Hyatt Corporation, serves an important business and preservation role in historic Charleston's core.

Background   The oldest portion of the original Mills House was constructed on the site by silversmith John Paul Grimke before 1791. The property became a hotel in 1801. Otis Mills, a New Englander, came to Charleston in the 1820s and made a fortune in the grain business. He invested his earnings in real estate, and bought and leased the hotel in 1836. Mills took over the operation of the hotel himself in 1852, renovating and enlarging the structure. According to some reports, it was the finest building in Charleston, with both running water and steam heat. Samuel Gaillard Stoney, a Charleston historian, described the building as representing the "apex of Charleston's Victorian style."[1] Distinguished guests such as General Robert E. Lee, Stephen A. Douglas, and President Theodore Roosevelt are reported to have lodged in the hotel.

During this century, the hotel changed owners and names several times, and in 1954, it became known as the St. John Hotel. Active overnight business was on the decline in the 1960s, and the St. John became a residential hotel. The Baptist College of Charleston even leased it for temporary dormitory space in 1965. Although still an elegant building, the years were taking their toll, when in 1967, Richard H. Jenrette, a New York investment banker, became interested in the structure. He saw the possibilities of a renovated hotel as an integral part of Charleston's restored historic district. After discussing the building with several Charleston friends, including Frances Edmunds, Director of the Historic Charleston Foundation, Jenrette took an option on the building. He became full owner in 1968.

Richard H. Jenrette is a partner in the New York City-based investment banking firm of Donaldson, Lufkin and Jenrette. Although he was not able to interest representatives of the finan-

The Mills-Hyatt House. (Al Satterwhite)

cial community in the Mills House project, he did secure interim financing from the Ford Foundation and put together a limited partnership, called Charleston Associates, to syndicate interested investors.

Jenrette hired architectural consultants to study the feasibility of renovating the old hotel. The building was found to be structurally unsound: pilings would have to be placed under it and this could not be accomplished without razing the present structure. A plan was proposed to reconstruct the old hotel on the same site but in an enlarged version that would make it economically feasible.

Execution   The original five-story hotel contained 150 rooms. The new seven-story version would contain 240 rooms, but be only ten feet taller than the original because ceiling heights would be reduced. The architectural firm of Curtis and Davis, with offices in New York, New Orleans, and London, was retained to carry out the reconstruction. This firm was responsible for the design of the new Royal Orleans Hotel, in the French Quarter of New Orleans, the model for the new Mills House concept. Simons, Lapham, Mitchell and Small, a Charleston architectural firm, was retained as consultants on the design's historical appropriateness.

Before the reconstruction could take place, Jenrette had to secure the endorsement of the local historic-preservation groups. The hotel site was in the Historic Charleston downtown district, and any new construction had to conform with the character of the surrounding buildings. Both the Historic Charleston Foundation and the Preservation Society of Charleston gave approval.

Construction began in summer, 1968, and took about sixteen months to complete. The exterior walls of the old Mills House were made of brick with a stuccoed cement facing. The new exterior walls are made of concrete block, faced with brick, and covered with

stucco to exactly duplicate the old surface. The new windows exactly match the old; even the pediment detail has been recast in fiberglass from molds made from the original building. The antique iron grillwork on the Meeting Street facade was salvaged from the building and reused on the new Meeting Street facade. A copy made from a mold of this original ironwork has been installed on the Queen Street side as well. Although originally there was never such a detail on the Queen Street facade, it was believed that its placement there would help provide visual relief from the essentially solid wall of windows. Roof cornices and bracket details were also exactly duplicated. The general contractor was Ruscon Construction Company of Charleston.

A new one-story wing on the rear south side of the building has been added. This accommodates a restaurant and kitchen on the ground level and a swimming pool and sun deck on top. Flagstones, preserved from old Charleston sidewalks dating back to the late 1790s, have been reused in front of the hotel. A replica of a formal nineteenth-century Charleston garden with a cast-iron fountain is situated on the south side of the building. Both the new wing and the garden are shielded from the street by an arcaded gallery. The garden provides a pleasant view from the restaurant and main lobby/lounge area. The landscape architect was Loutrel Briggs of Charleston.

In the interior, the original ceiling heights of the first two floors have been retained, but on the upper floors, the ceilings were lowered to keep the overall building height as low as possible. An attempt was made to duplicate the detail and atmosphere of the lobby and the two main rooms on the first floor. One room serves as a cocktail lounge and the other as the main waiting lounge. The front two rooms on the second floor, also duplicates of the original rooms, are now used for large group meetings and social events. Hand-molded, decorative pediments, medallions, friezes, and cornices—all representing a nearly lost art—were executed on these first two floors by A. Lewis Keyser of High Point, North Carolina, and Clarence Ketner, an associate.

A period chandelier from Belle

Meade, a plantation in Nashville, Tennessee, now hangs in the main registration lobby. An English Regency zebrawood table serves as a center table in the lobby. Georgian mirrors, Greek Revival sofas, Chippendale chairs, antique Chinese vases, and much more help to give this recreated "old hotel" an authentic feeling. The New England Society has even loaned a portrait of Otis Mills, which now hangs in the hotel parlor. Anthony Hail, A.I.D., an interior designer from San Francisco, was responsible for the furnishings and interior decoration. He was assisted by John Dickenson, A.I.D., also of San Francisco, and H. Chambers and Company, decorators from Baltimore. Mr. Hail had earlier assisted in the restoration of the White House.

The average room rate is $39 per day, and occupancy has averaged 85 percent. In the spring, during the tourist season, the hotel is virtually 100 percent filled.

Costs   The total project cost was approximately $6 million: land, $150,000; construction, $4 million; furnishings, $1 million; and initial year operating expenses, $600,000. The total construction cost prorated per room was $20,000 in 1969/1970—quite low when compared to industry standards, and even low when compared to adaptive-reuse hotel conversions like the Stanford Court in San Francisco, which cost $22,344 per room in 1972. Mills Hyatt's low cost is primarily attributable to the location. According to Mr. Jenrette, "Charleston's building costs were quite low at that time."[2]

Problems When the hotel first opened, there were a few lean years. Jenrette and other partners in Charleston Associates had to invest an additional $600,000 to keep the hotel afloat. "This is a common problem with new hotels,"[3] claims Jenrette. Today, the hotel is enjoying a better cash flow.

Setting up the management and the financing presented more problems. Jenrette and Charleston Associates were not in the hotel business, and had to secure a qualified management team to operate the hotel. At first, Hotel Corporation of America (HCA) agreed to do it, a key factor in Jenrette's decision to go through with the project. However, this was not a period of great financial stability, and HCA withdrew during the planning stages. After approaching a few other hotel companies, Jenrette was finally able to interest the Hyatt Corporation, which was beginning to receive national acclaim for its Hyatt Regency in Atlanta. Although the Mills House did not have breathtaking open spaces like the Regency, it had a historic atmosphere and an excellent location. Hyatt recognized these qualities as valuable business assets.

Mortgage rates were very high at the time. The four-year Ford Foundation loan was for interim financing only. It was high-risk money at 12 percent interest. Because of the difficulty in securing a management contract and the negative cash-flow picture during the first few years of operations, it was difficult to interest permanent lenders at a favorable interest rate. After several other temporary loans, Charleston Associates was finally able to obtain longer-term financing from Aetna Business Credit, and the Washington Mutual Savings and Loan in Seattle, Washington.

There were many technical problems in executing the reconstruction, but all were surmountable because skilled designers and craftsmen were utilized.

Another, more controversial problem involves the philosophy of recreating images of the past rather than building in today's idiom. Many believe that it is deceptive to disguise a modern building in antique trappings. For this reason, the Mills Hyatt House has received some criticism from architects and architectural critics.

Benefits The success of this project as a popular and profitable hotel has helped to improve Charleston's economic base. The Mills Hyatt House is the largest private employer in the city's downtown area. It has received local and national press coverage and praise for the quality of its reproduction and for its compatibility within the local historic context.

The Company Charleston Associates was formed specifically for the purchase of the Mills House. No financial information is available.

For further information contact:
Richard H. Jenrette
Donaldson, Lufkin & Jenrette, Inc.
140 Broadway
New York, New York 10004

Footnotes

1. "Hope For A Hotel," *Preservation Progress*, January, 1968, p. 6.
2. INFORM interview with Richard H. Jenrette, partner, Charleston Associates, May, 1977.
3. *Ibid.*

The new lobby and public meeting rooms emulate the grand rooms in the old building. (Al Satterwhite)

Summary In 1973, Deseret Management Corporation, a profit-oriented branch of the Church of Jesus Christ of Latter Day Saints (Mormons), decided to renovate the Hotel Utah, which it owns, and to build a new 160-room addition. The 1911 building, an example of the "Grand Hotel" style of architecture, is rich in classical ornamentation both inside and out. In the renovated and new portions of the structure, the company chose to meticulously duplicate the terra cotta facade and decoration of the original. Deseret spent approximately $40,000 per room on the project.

Background The opulent Classical Revival Hotel Utah, designed by architects John Parkinson and Edwin Bergstrom of Los Angeles, was opened in the heart of Salt Lake City in 1911. The gleaming, white glazed-brick and terra cotta facade boasts many decorative embellishments, such as festoons, lions' heads, and medallions, all made of terra cotta by the firm of Gladding, McBean & Co. of Lincoln, California. Terra cotta was a popular building material in this country from about 1880 to 1930, before other materials and technologies replaced it. It was durable, and particularly resistant to fire and weather.

The ten-story hotel reflects the richness of the era in which it was built. In the lobby, grey marble columns with composite capitals support cornices filled with decorative plaster motifs. The latter are highlighted with gold leaf. Delicate iron railings adorn the balcony overlooking the elegant lobby. The lobby is crowned by a leaded, blue and green stained-glass interior skylight designed in geometric patterns. Guest rooms are spacious. In 1911, *Hotel Monthly*, a trade publication, heralded this new, luxurious hotel:

No other hotel anywhere in the world has a more interesting or beautiful setting, or more self-contained features for the pleasure and comfort of the guests, than the new Hotel Utah.[1]

The Hotel Utah is located across from the ten-acre Temple Square and the Gothic Revival Mormon Temple, with its renowned Tabernacle Choir and landscaped gardens. It is near the Utah State Capitol, Brigham Young's residence, the Beehive House, the shopping mall of the recently expanded Zions Cooperative Mercantile Institution (see profile), and the new $20 million Salt Palace convention and sports center.

In recent years, however, in spite of the hotel's prime location, and the fact that it has been well maintained—it was modernized in 1967—occupancy levels declined because of competition from outlying motels and general lack of interest in the downtown area.

In 1973, a feasibility study was undertaken by the firm of Harris, Kerr, Forster & Co. and Robert A. Fowler Associated Architects of Salt Lake City to determine the future of the hotel. Since Deseret Management respected the architecture of the old building, it never seriously considered demolition or construction of a non-compatible modern addition. But based on the study, the company decided to renovate the hotel, both inside and out, and to add the 160-room extension that was to replicate exactly the exterior of the original building.

Execution Work began on the Hotel Utah in March, 1974; it was completed in mid-1977. The hotel remained open during the entire construction period. The architects, Robert A. Fowler and Edward Joe Ruben of Robert A. Fowler Associated Architects, planned the new wing and restored the facade using the original architectural plans and drawings. In addition, the original drawings and molds for the terra cotta were located at Gladding, McBean & Co. in Lincoln, California.

The interior of the original hotel was completely renovated. The richly ornamented lobby was cleaned and repainted. All new wiring, new plumbing, and a heat-pump heating/air-conditioning system were installed. The kitchen was modernized, and all of the hotel's bedrooms and 100 bathrooms were refurbished. Heinz Janders of San Francisco was the interior designer and decorator for both the renovation and the new addition.

In the 160-room addition, Janders attempted to coordinate the ambiance and style of the new public rooms with the old hotel. The new ballroom is designed in the Victorian style and has damask curtains, a red and gold pat-

The new addition and the old Hotel Utah.

terned carpet, and Belgian crystal chandeliers. New consoles (ornamental brackets), beneath the ceiling cornice which extends around the ballroom, were duplicated from existing consoles in the vintage hotel and reproduced in plaster. Wood panels around this room were hand grained as in the old hotel. The ballroom's 15,000 square feet can accommodate 1,200 people for banquets and 1,800 for receptions.

The new addition includes a 10,000-square-foot exhibit hall to attract the convention and corporate trade, and a new roof restaurant.

Terra Cotta. One of the most interesting aspects of the construction of the new addition and the restoration of the old facade involves the duplication and installation of the terra cotta. When the old facade was cleaned, using hot water and detergent, the terra cotta was found to have held up quite well. It was in much better condition than the wooden sashes, metal trim, roofing, and cast iron, which had to be replaced or reworked.

The architects solicited bids for both terra cotta and precast concrete substitutes to be used in building the new addition and in replacing lost details in the old facade. The production contract was awarded to Gladding, McBean & Co., the firm that had done the original terra cotta work for the hotel. (The precast concrete bid was nearly $200,000 higher and was not guaranteed.) The installation contract went to Earl Child Masonry of Salt Lake City.

Even for a master mason, the installation of the terra cotta was a monumental undertaking. Child said that this job was "the biggest challenge I've ever had in the masonry business."[2] Installation techniques had changed since 1911; then, the terra cotta was put in place first, and backing brick was laid, tying it into the clay-tile interior wall; today with the development of concrete-block unit construction, the procedure is reversed. The terra cotta facing units were tied to the concrete-block wall with stainless steel wires and dowels. The cavity between the terra cotta and the concrete-block wall was then reinforced and filled in with a concrete grout consisting of three-eighths-inch rock, sand, and cement. This could only be accomplished four inches at a time. An earlier attempt at pumping in the grout indicated that the terra cotta units shifted too much. It was therefore necessary to pour the grout gently from coal buckets, and then pack it into the cavity by hand.

The actual installation was not the only problem; once the 12,000 terra cotta units were received from Gladding, McBean, Child had to organize them into 400 different configurations. Still another challenge was lifting and placing the terra cotta units on the new addition. The lions' heads weighed 425 pounds each, and the festoons 500 pounds each. According to Child:

There was not a craftsman on the job who wasn't challenged. For example, if the terra cotta was not in line, the craftsman had to stay with it until it was set. Thus, on every piece of terra cotta, the mason had to make his own decision when it was set well enough for him to let it go. However, just when the mason would become familiar with the setting process for one shape of terra cotta unit, it would be time to use a different type unit requiring different work procedures.[3]

In addition to increasing the capacity of the hotel, Deseret has made a concerted effort in the last three years to attract more tourist and convention business. The present marketing staff promotes the hotel through such devices as trade luncheons and advertising in trade-convention and airline publications. The annual budget for national advertising is $30,000.

The opulent lobby of the original hotel.

Costs Deseret would not release figures on the total cost of the renovation, addition, and refurbishing. However, the company estimated the cost of the project at about $40,000 per room. Judging from the quality of the work, as reflected in the replacement and duplication of the terra cotta and the hand-crafted decorations, it could be easily estimated that this was a multi-million-dollar undertaking.

The financing was generated internally by Deseret. The company is presently considering converting some of its short-term obligations into long-term debt.

Problems Stuart G. Cross, Executive Vice President and Managing Director of the Hotel Utah, said in an interview that the main problem experienced was the difficulty in carrying on an efficient hotel operation in the midst of construction. Occupancy was down, while staff were maintained, a combination which cut profits and increased costs. In addition, construction took a year longer than planned.

Benefits Occupancy levels are running at about 60 percent of new capacity. Before the restoration/addition, the old hotel—with fewer rooms—was running at roughly the same percentage. As a result of the new addition and the advertising campaigns, conventioneers now account for 35 percent of the guests, as opposed to 20 percent before renovation.

The restoration/re-creation work on Hotel Utah has been featured in many publications, such as *Hotel & Motel Management*. The new terra cotta techniques have brought additional publicity in *Masonry* and the *International Union of Brick Layers and Allied Craftsmen Journal*.

Because of the success of this and other complex and extensive projects, like Zions Cooperative Mercantile Institution, Salt Lake City is gaining a wide reputation for quality workmanship in restoration techniques. Its architects and craftsmen have assisted in projects across the country, including the Wilmington, Delaware, Grand Opera House (see Hercules).

The Company The Deseret Management Corporation, owner of the Hotel Utah, is a holding company of the Church of Jesus Christ of Latter Day Saints. This profit-oriented division of the Mormon Church includes among its operations bookstores, farms, and TV and radio stations. Deseret is privately owned; no financial figures are available.

For further information contact:
Stuart G. Cross
Executive Vice President and Managing Director
Hotel Utah
Main at South Temple
Salt Lake City, Utah 84111

Footnotes

1. *Hotel Monthly*, November, 1911, p. 36.
2. "The Enduring Elegance of Masonry," *Masonry*, March, 1977, p. 7.
3. *Ibid.*, p.26.

Summary In mid-1974, Penn Mutual Life Insurance Company re-erected a four-story Egyptian Revival marble facade on its original site on Walnut Street in Philadelphia. The company incorporated this historic artifact, designed in 1835, as part of the facade of its new 21-story, $22 million, office-building addition facing Independence Hall. Penn Mutual spent several hundred thousand dollars to save and reuse the facade. In 1977, the company received an American Institute of Architects Honor Award for the new building.

Background When the Pennsylvania Fire Insurance Company expanded in 1902, it duplicated the facade of its original building, forming a unified front. The original or eastern half, designed by John Haviland and erected in 1838, is a fine example of the Egyptian Revival style popular in this country during the 1830s. The western half, a replica of the Haviland design, was created in 1902 by architect Theophilus P. Chandler. Chandler united the two fronts with a crowning cornice featuring a hawk relief of the Egyptian god Horus, and the Pennsylvania Fire Insurance Company name carved in Vermont marble. John Haviland was an architect of some renown, having designed many of the nation's well-known prisons. Among his buildings are the Tombs in New York, state penitentiaries in New Jersey, Missouri, and Rhode Island, and the U.S. Mint in Philadelphia.

By 1970, Penn Mutual, which had owned the property for many years, was contemplating expansion of its adjacent facilities. The original Penn Mutual Building, a ten-story structure on the western corner of the block, had been erected in 1913. A nineteen-story addition had been built to the east in 1931. Penn Mutual and its architects, Mitchell/Giurgola Architects of Philadelphia and New York, proposed a scheme for a new 21-story, 440,000-square-foot addition that would abut the 1931 structure. The Haviland/Chandler Egyptian Revival building would have to be demolished to accommodate this plan. Local opposition to the demolition encouraged Penn Mutual to incorporate the old facade in the new design. Because of the historic context, the new design proposals had to be submitted to both the Philadelphia Historical Commission—which until 1970 had included Penn Mutual's Chairman—and the Philadelphia Art Commission for review and approval. The Historical Commission regretted the demolition of the old building, but commended the retention of the facade.

The old facade was one of the two remaining examples of Egyptian-influenced design in Philadelphia, a city once believed to have had the largest number of Egyptian Revival buildings in America. This stylistic treatment incorporates decorative Egyptian motifs like papyrus leaves, bundled reeds, and bird forms.

Execution According to the architects: "The new building relates in mass to the existing office structure and completes a symmetrical backdrop for Independence Hall on axis with the Mall."[1] The eastern facade includes a poured-in-place concrete screen which shades the glass on that side. This screen also carries one-half of the load of the seventy-foot framing trusses which extend to the concrete service core on the west. These large span trusses create a totally column-free and flexible office space, and match floor levels with the existing 1931 structure. The south facade consists of double-pane, insulating, reflective glass, and the north facade is of similar grey-tinted glass. The north facade provides a neutral backdrop for Independence Hall and the Mall which face it. Glass-walled elevators on this face carry visitors up to a public observation deck and a 10,000-square-foot exhibit hall on the top level of the building. The Egyptian Revival facade was designed into the north facade as a free-standing sculptural screen marking the entrance to the building and creating a transition between the human scale of the street, and the high-rise tower to the rear.

Thomas Hine, writing in the *Philadelphia Inquirer*, describes the building: "It is a both-and building—both steel structure and concrete structure, both historic preservation and new development, both background and assertion."[2]

The project took three-and-a-half years to complete. In April, 1971, the Albert Cosenza Co., Philadelphia stone specialists, began dismantling the old facade. Some 400 blocks of Vermont marble, weighing as much as 1,000 pounds each, were numbered and stored for reconstruction. In August, 1974, the facade was returned to its original position in a new role, that of public art.

Costs Although local newspapers have written that the preservation and reuse of the Egyptian Revival facade cost Penn Mutual $130,000, Geoffrey Irvine, Staff Engineer with the company indicates that the cost was considerably more.[3] The exact figure is difficult to itemize. Besides dismantling, storing, and re-erecting the facade, a new reinforced concrete backup wall and foundation had to be designed and built to support it. Engineering, architectural, and construction fees for the facade were included in the overall $22 million cost for the new addition. These expenditures fulfilled Philadelphia's required public art contribution. This statute stipulates that 1 percent of total construction costs, for any new construction or renovation project on redevelopment property, be spent to purchase public art for the city.

Problems There were no specific problems directly related to reusing the facade, other than some of the technical difficulties encountered in the actual dismantling and re-erection. Although most public reaction to the project has been positive, some architectural critics feel that Penn Mutual has been given too much praise. They would rather have seen the old building kept intact than become a sculpture.[4]

Benefits According to Romaldo Giurgola, one of the principals in the architectural firm, "The Egyptian Revival facade allows Penn Mutual and the city to retain an original example of great architecture of the past as well as maintain a cultural heritage of another generation."[5] The Philadelphia Art Commission termed the preservation of the Haviland/Chandler facade "a great teaching example of combining modern building with historic and traditional landmarks."[6] The project received much praise in the press. Nessa Forman, writing in the Art column of the *Sunday Bulletin*, said: "Penn Mutual deserves kudos for its preservation approach. The facade, when all is said and done, is the only part of the building worth saving."[7] Paul Goldberger, of the *New York Times*, stated that the inclusion of the Egyptian Revival facade is:

a brilliant design decision—not in terms of preservation, for the old building was hardly preserved, but in terms of its meaning for urban architecture. For the thin elegant facade is a reminder that even real building fronts often serve a stage-set role. The relationship between this one and the glass and concrete tower is a comfortable one and, as an added bonus, the space behind the false front—that is, between the old facade and the new building—is full of dramatic tension and excitement.[8]

Original facade and new addition from ground level. (Rollin R. La France)

(below)
The original facade forms a free-standing sculpture screen. (Rollin R. La France)

(on facing page)
Penn Mutual tower with preserved facade at lower left. (Rollin R. La France)

In 1977, the American Institute of Architects selected the new Penn Mutual Tower as one of eleven recipients of its "Top Building Projects—Honor Awards" for new buildings. The Award's jury commented:

This office tower addition to an older area in Philadelphia sensitively retains the remnants of the original . . . facades integrating them with the new high rise structures behind them. Broken massing and window penetrations recall, at a different scale, the previous architectural endeavors. The complementary use of color and materials, in conjunction with the scale, provides a sensitive addition to the historic area.[9]

The Company Penn Mutual, Pennsylvania's largest insurance company, was founded in Philadelphia in 1847. It offers a variety of life insurance plans, pension programs, and other financial services for individuals, families, and business and professional groups. More than 1,900 people are employed in the Philadelphia office.

Penn Mutual is the seventeenth largest insurance company in the nation in terms of assets. Assets rose from $2.9 billion in 1975 to $3.07 billion in 1976. Net investment income increased from $168.5 million to $179.5 million over the same period.

Other Preservation Activities. Penn Mutual also preserved two original marble fireplaces from the Haviland/Chandler building. One of these has been donated to the Philadelphia Museum of Art.

In 1818, architect John Haviland made what was our nation's first attempt at restoration by a master craftsman. He reproduced some paneling for use in Independence Hall's assembly room, copying the designs of the paneling in Congress Hall. In 1963, historians discovered the original designs for the Independence Hall paneling, and the Haviland additions were removed and stored in a National Park Service warehouse. They were to be discarded in 1973, when Penn Mutual offered to install them in the exhibit space on top of its new tower.

In addition, the company, together with other Philadelphia corporations, contributed $100,000—which brought federal matching funds—to refurbish the subway station at Fifth and Market Streets.

For further information contact:
William A. Burbaum
Media Relations Manager
The Penn Mutual Life Insurance Company
Independence Square
Philadelphia, Pennsylvania 19172

Footnotes

1. INFORM interview with Mitchell/Giurgola, Architects, May, 1977.
2. Thomas Hine, "Penn Mutual Building: View Changes the Face," *Philadelphia Inquirer*, 28 February 1975, p. 1-B.
3. INFORM interview with Geoffrey Irvine, Staff Engineer, Penn Mutual Life Insurance Company, May, 1977.
4. Hine, *op. cit.*
5. *Downtown Record*, 4 March 1971.
6. The Penn Mutual Life Insurance Company, "Penn Mutual Tower's Unique Egyptian Facade," (Background Information Sheet, The Penn Mutual Life Insurance Company, n.d.).
7. Nessa Forman, "On the Survival of a Facade," *Sunday Bulletin* (Philadelphia), 18 August 1974.
8. Paul Goldberger, "Innovative Firm Puts Its Imprint on Philadelphia," *New York Times*, 6 May 1976.
9. American Institute of Architects, *Press Release*, May 13, 1977.

Summary Zions Cooperative Mercantile Institution (ZCMI), reputed to be America's first department store, was founded in 1868 in Salt Lake City, Utah. Brigham Young, the pioneer Mormon leader, conceived of the store as a community-owned establishment which could sell goods "as low as they can be sold, and let the profits be divided among the people at large."[1] In 1976, in conjunction with Zions Securities Corporation, this expanding operation completed construction of a 2 million-square-foot ZCMI Center, claimed by the company to be "the only downtown covered supermall in Western America and the largest of its kind in the nation."[2] The contemporary facade of this new multi-use complex incorporates the classically ornate cast-iron front of the former store, commemorating ZCMI's heritage, and pleasing local preservationists who fought for its retention.

Background More than twenty years ago, ZCMI realized it needed to expand its downtown store. Initial plans called for expansion into the basement and first three floors of an adjacent, new office building erected to house the Utah office of the Kennecott Copper Corporation. However, difficulties arose in aligning the floors of the old buildings with the floors of the new one. In addition, fire protection, heating, and air conditioning presented obstacles. The plan was scrapped, and the company decided instead to acquire property and expand south of the store. This plan called for dismantling the present store and constructing a completely new facility. A feasibility study determined that a new downtown shopping mall might encompass most or all of the ten-acre block in which the store was located. The planning, study, acquisition, and execution took almost twenty years.

The new ZCMI Center utilizes approximately 75 percent of the ten-acre block. During construction, ZCMI continued operations in its old building, while the surrounding property was demolished and rebuilt to the new design. Original plans did not provide for the preservation of the old store's cast-iron front. However, as word of ZCMI's intentions spread, a movement started within the community to save it. Actually, this front was a combination of three separate facades. The center portion had been completed in May, 1876, the south section in April, 1880, and the north section in April, 1892. The center and south sections were cast-iron, while the north section was wood covered with molded sheet metal to approximate the design of the cast iron. The facade is a three-tiered composition of neoclassical design incorporating Corinthianesque columns supporting slightly arched lintels and

The restored facade incorporated in the new mall.

crowned with a triangular pediment. The cast-iron construction was based on a technique developed in the mid-1800s by New York architect James Bogardus to achieve the effect of carved stone.

Without ZCMI's knowledge or support, a local organization was formed to develop a preservation publicity program. Postage-meter-stamp ads and other printed materials stated "ZCMI's Main Street Facade Is Irreplaceable! Help Save It!" ZCMI architects, after some coaxing, decided to retain the old facade and incorporate it into the new design. At first, only the two cast-iron portions were to be used, but it was finally decided to save the entire front.

Execution According to Steven T. Baird, a local architect hired by ZCMI to oversee the restoration project:

This is the first time a cast iron facade has been restored and we had to relearn an old craft. We simply went back to the original system used and put it to the test.[3]

Hand-carved wood patterns were made locally from the pieces removed from the two cast-iron sections, and new parts were cast for the north section. Each column consists of approximately 140 pieces. When the original front was disassembled, every piece was cleaned and marked for reassembly. The restored front was fastened to a special steel framework and inserted in an exterior wall of the new shopping mall. It is used as a display feature or free-standing sculptural grille. The new wall has been recessed approximately sixteen feet, leaving a space between it and the old facade. At night, lighting behind the old facade produces an interesting play of shadows. A ceiling surface has been constructed between the old front and the new wall. It is covered with pressed sheet metal similar to that used on many ceilings in the old store. The entire facade has been given a 23-carat gold-leaf finish emphasizing its jewel-like quality. Alfred A. Lippold, the painting contractor, has worked on many restorations in the Salt Lake area, including the Beehive House and the Hotel Utah (see Deseret Management). Mr. Lippold estimates that his gold-leaf work will last at least thirty years.

State Brass, the Rummel Pattern Company, and the Metals Manufacturing Company, all in the Salt Lake area, executed the ZCMI restoration.

Costs The company states that it has spent in excess of $500,000 for the restoration and installation of the cast-iron front. Cost figures for construction of the new 2-million-square-foot complex were not available.

Problems According to Wendell E. Adams, a Vice President of the company, "The major problems have been those of economics, engineering, architectural design and more than a small element of public relations finesse."[4] The gold-leaf finish, of course, contributed significantly to the high cost, as did the recreation of one section in cast iron. Additional architectural and engineering costs resulted from the extra design work involved in adapting the new facade to receive the old one, and in making the entire construction safe and stable.

Benefits According to Wendell Adams,

The real benefits of this restoration are several. First it is a beautiful building with a combination of the very modern along with a delightful retention of our nostalgic heritage. It has delighted those who were vocal for saving the front and has pleased the rest of the community who had not given much priority to the problem of worrying about the past. All concerned, both within and outside the company, are delighted with this beautiful solution to a special problem.[5]

Although the company did not consider this when the decision was made to restore the facade, much new business has been brought to the "restoration industry" in Utah. Salt Lake City has now built a reputation for quality craftsmanship in metals restoration and replication. New processes involving the recasting of original designs in aluminum are being implemented. As a result, hundreds of thousands of dollars in new business are expected to come to Utah. Since the ZCMI project architect Steven Baird has developed a special skill in cast-iron restoration and has been called on to work on a number of other cast-iron restorations including the Wilmington Opera House (see Hercules) in Wilmington, Delaware.

The Company Net sales for the company in 1976 were $82 million, an increase of 19 percent, over a comparable 1975 figure of $68.7 million. Net income for each year was about the same, $2.9 million. In addition to its new facilities in the ZCMI Center, the company has operations in five other locations in and around Salt Lake City.

For further information contact:
Wendell E. Adams
Vice President—Director
Personnel & Services
Zions Cooperative Mercantile
Institution
15 South Main Street
Salt Lake City, Utah 84137

Footnotes

1. Zions Cooperative Mercantile Institution, *ZCMI: Pioneering Still* (Advertising brochure, Salt Lake City: Zions Cooperative Mercantile Institution, 1976), p.2.
2. *Ibid.*
3. R. Scott Henderson, "Shopping the ZCMI Center," *Utah Holiday*, 18 October 1976, p. 47.
4. Letter from Mr. Wendell E. Adams, Vice President, Director, Personnel and Services, ZCMI, to INFORM, February 14, 1977, p. 3.
5. *Ibid.*

A persistent national problem since the late 1940s has been the slow deterioration of urban neighborhoods. Ironically, a series of decisions by government and business appear to have inadvertently stimulated the process. The Housing Act of 1949, which poured massive amounts of federal money into America's cities, often produced ill-conceived and ineffective urban-renewal efforts. In many cases, these resulted in the leveling of sound but deteriorating housing stock, and the destruction of poor, but sometimes still viable neighborhoods. The programs created monolithic apartment complexes like Pruitt-Igoe in St. Louis. Pruitt-Igoe suffered from such low occupancy and high crime rates that much of it has already been demolished. Federal programs also subsidized an extensive highway system which bisected cities or bypassed them entirely while speeding the flight of the middle class to the suburbs. Mass transit was neglected; inner-city crime increased; downtown commercial areas declined; and business sought more secure and less expensive locations outside the city. Redlining by banks and unrealistic insurance premiums often made staying in the city impossible even for those who wished to do so. Cities lost jobs and population, and became increasingly polarized between the very rich and the very poor.

In the 1960s, the equation began to change. Riots, which shook cities to their foundations, brought a reexamination of priorities. Urban pioneers, like Jane Jacobs, championed the scale and diversity of city neighborhoods and opposed massive urban renewal.

In the early 1970s, suburbanites began to discover that they shared some of the cities' problems. Suburban crime was increasing; real estate prices and taxes were rising. At the same time, the energy crisis made suburban life more expensive and less convenient.

Even so, the attraction of the suburbs remains strong. In recent years, businesses have participated in and often led the flight from the cities. Between 1969 and 1976, New York City lost 650,000 jobs.[1] It is projected that by the end of 1978, only 127 of the nation's 1,100 largest companies will be headquartered in New York City, as opposed to the 238 that were there in 1968.[2] Of the companies that remained in the cities in the early 1970s, many prepared to leave if the prognosis grew much worse. Some businesses, however, perhaps because, like the utilities, they had little choice about their location or because they felt their present location had valuable advantages, chose to face urban problems head on. A few tried—on a limited scale—to save existing housing, preserve sound neighborhoods, and restore downtown commercial areas.

Residential Revitalization   INFORM has examined thirteen companies which have attempted some form of housing and neighborhood redevelopment projects, twelve in deteriorating urban areas and a thirteenth in a relatively healthy suburb. Among them are five banks, three food manufacturers, one insurance company, a utility, and a consortium of businesses and foundations. These companies have supplied money and expertise, formed development banks, and joined local residents and activists to fight urban decay.

In twelve of the thirteen cases studied, INFORM found that the company's location was a key reason for undertaking the venture. Connecticut Mutual encouraged formation of a community organization to improve conditions in Asylum Hill, the Hartford neighborhood in which its headquarters are located. The company also provides short-term home-improvement loans at low interest rates to employees of local firms and of the City of Hartford who wish to move to Asylum Hill. In Minneapolis, General Mills' former home city, the company has joined a local developer to renovate the deteriorating Stevens Square area, and upgrade housing while keeping rents within reach of community residents.

In seven of the cases INFORM studied, business participants received favorable publicity as a result of their efforts. Brooklyn Union's financial support, advertising, and leverage with local banks have helped renovation projects throughout Brooklyn. The company has received an award for its advertising from the American Gas Association, and Frederic Rider, the company Vice President directing the "Cinderella" projects, has been interviewed by national publications.

Six projects have brought an economic return to their sponsors. The South Shore National Bank has successfully increased its assets as a result of helping its blighted Chicago service area return to economic health. The bank's management undertook a variety of programs, including special high-risk loans to local residents, the organization and support of renovation projects within the community, and the education of local residents about banking operations and services.

Five companies reported that their efforts, which concentrated mainly on improving the housing stock, have brought increased commercial interest to the project areas. Better city services and increased job opportunities have resulted in three cases. As a community organizes and improves, the backing of an important company can make city officials become more receptive to its requests. This occurred in both the Connecticut Mutual case and the Tasty Baking project. Real estate values increased in nine of the cases profiled.

Helping neighborhoods can be good for employee morale too. In two cases, companies reported that employees appreciated attempts to improve the areas in which they worked. In the Connecticut Mutual case, a direct benefit to company employees was inexpensive housing.

A final motivating factor may have been tax benefits obtained through contributions of money, materials, facilities, or employee time. Although the companies surveyed usually did not divulge tax benefits gained from their efforts, at least one company, Tasty Baking, reported that it took special tax deductions related to its neighborhood-rehabilitation efforts.

Urban revitalization is no simple matter; needless to say, the thirteen companies studied by INFORM experienced many problems in the course of their projects. Five were plagued by escalating costs. In the General Mills case, a dispute over the company's use of nonunion labor brought the threat of a national boycott of its products by the AFL-CIO. General Mills capitulated, but the cost to its Stevens Court project in Minneapolis destroyed any hopes of an economic return for the company, and increased rents 25 percent to 40 percent. Three projects suffered from bureaucratic delays. Ralston Purina's project, a three-phased program, was scheduled to be completed in five years. It is now in its second phase, nine years after inception. The primary problem has been the slowness of federal approvals and cash commitments.

In three cases, local organizations have overextended themselves, forcing both reorganization and cutbacks. ACTION-Housing, a community group supported by 21 major businesses in Pittsburgh, tried to fill a cash-flow gap left by government and other large lenders, and subsequently found itself with a number of debtors who could not repay their loans. The organization, in turn, could not repay the businesses who had provided the money for the loan program. Today, ACTION-Housing is in the process of trying to change its funding from loans to grants.

Dislocation of community residents was cited as a problem in only two cases. However, most of the revitalization programs studied by INFORM are in their early stages, and dislocation may become a greater problem in the future. In the Lakewood Bank case, a zoning change and the renovation and reconversion of older multiple-unit housing back to single-family homes forced relocation of former residents.

A wide variety of government programs affect neighborhood revitalization. Many have been tried as vehicles of support, some successfully, some not.* The federally sponsored Neighborhood Housing Services (NHS) program has been among the most successful. Conceived in Pittsburgh in 1968, the NHS is a partnership of local residents, government, banks, and businesses, which: helps residents of deteriorating areas comply with building- and health-code standards; provides counseling; obtains commitments from local banks to make loans to credit-worthy applicants; offers financial rehabilitation assistance through a high-risk loan fund; supplies technical help and supervises renovation work; educates residents about home maintenance; and obtains city cooperation in improving public facilities. The NHS-Jamaica, located in New York City's Borough of Queens and actively supported by Citibank, is helping stabilize and improve the Baisley Park section through just such a program. An NHS in Philadelphia is assisting Tasty Baking and the Allegheny West Community Development Project improve that part of the city.

The success of the NHS resulted in the establishment of the Urban Reinvestment Task Force in 1974 to promote the NHS idea nationally. The Task Force includes representatives of the Federal Home Loan Bank, the Department of Housing and Urban Development, the Federal Deposit Insurance Corporation, the Federal Reserve System, and the Comptroller of the Currency. It provides counseling to interested local groups who wish to establish an NHS, and commits dollars—usually between $50,000 and $100,000 depending on the size of the project and the area—for the creation of a high-risk revolving fund. Today, there are fifty NHS's, operational or in the planning stage, around the country. HUD funding for the Task Force amounted to $5 million in 1977.

The Housing and Community Development Act of 1974 (which replaced the urban-renewal grants, Model Cities, and other diverse federal programs) authorizes Community Development Block Grants to cities and towns for a wide variety of programs, including neighborhood revitalization. These Block Grants allow a greater autonomy to local government than the old urban-renewal grants, which were earmarked for specific projects.

The Home Mortgage Disclosure Act of 1975 requires all federally chartered and insured financial institutions to report their lending

*For further information on local programs consult: *Neighborhood Preservation*, published by the U.S. Department of Housing and Urban Development in 1975; *Neighborhood Conservation*, published by the National Endowment for the Arts in 1975; *Neighborhood Reinvestment*, published by the National Center for Urban Ethnic Affairs in 1977; and *A Guide to Federal Programs for Historic Preservation*, published by the National Trust for Historic Preservation in 1974, with a supplement in 1976.

practices by census tract, making it simpler to monitor redlining. These institutions must include information on the type of unit receiving loans, and on the kind of loan: first-mortgage, refinancing, or home-improvement. However, no information on the number of rejections, or the income, age, race, or sex of the borrowers is required.

The Carter administration has established a task force to study neighborhood revitalization and the creation of an urban-development bank, which would encourage both commercial and residential development in cities.

A HUD-proposed $1.2 billion "action grants" program, according to HUD Secretary Patricia Harris, "will stimulate new and increased private investment in cities of greatest need."[3] The program would furnish such cities with extra money over a three-year period for the purpose of attracting private investment to inner-city neighborhoods. At present, the proposal is tied up in interdepartmental jurisdictional disputes and a Senate-House conference committee.

The National Neighborhood Policy Act, also as yet unpassed, would create a National Commission on Neighborhoods, composed of at least one-third neighborhood representatives, to analyze government and business activities, as well as investment patterns in neighborhoods. It is scheduled for reintroduction before Congress in the near future.

Numerous regulations affect neighborhood revitalization on the state and local level. Lending-practice disclosure requirements, which augment the Federal Home Mortgage Disclosure Act by requiring information on the number of rejections, are in effect in several states, including Illinois and California. However, many rejections never reach a formal written stage, and some opponents of redlining believe that banks should be required to undertake an affirmative-action plan to solicit loans in inner-city areas as they do in the suburbs. This would make disclosure statistics more significant. New York City also provides a number of incentives for neighborhood revitalization, such as section J-51-2.5 of the Administrative Code of the City of New York, which provides tax incentives for recycling residential and commercial buildings for residential use. This directive provides up to a twelve-year exemption on increases in assessed valuation and an abatement of property taxes of up to 90 percent of the cost of rehabilitation for such renovations.

Commercial Redevelopment   The causes of commercial decline are the same as those affecting residential neighborhoods. For various reasons, a number of businesses have decided to become involved in large-scale commercial-redevelopment projects in older downtown areas. INFORM has studied nine such projects, ranging in scope from Bethlehem Steel's financing of a $40,000 planning study on how to revitalize downtown Bethlehem, to the Higbee Company's projected $100 million project to rebuild a seven-acre section of Cleveland's river front. Eight of the nine projects involve the renovation and usually the reuse of older buildings in a way which capitalizes on their uniqueness and character (the ninth involves a historic village). Many of these projects rely on "nostalgia" or the contrast between restored exteriors and adapted interiors to attract customers or tenants. The vintage structures are solidly built, often with greater attention to detail than contemporary buildings. Their high quality is frequently a strong selling point.

The companies profiled represent diverse sectors of American business. They include banks, department stores, bus lines, heavy industry, and communications companies. All are medium to large corporations with the staying power to see through innovative and large-scale projects. None of them is primarily a developer, although five have formed special development subsidiaries. While most of the projects studied are ventures undertaken by individual companies, one is supported by a consortium of ten local financial institutions which have united to help redevelop downtown Lowell, Massachusetts, in cooperation with local, state, and federal programs. All efforts are directed toward turning downtown Lowell into a vital commercial area, preserving and capitalizing on its nineteenth-century industrial character.

Four cases involve redevelopment in large cities, two deal with small cities, and two more are being carried out in small towns. Four companies are trying to redevelop waterfront areas.

The goal of all but one of the projects studied is to revitalize downtown business areas which have suffered decline. The most prevalent reason for undertaking such projects was a concern on the part of the business for its home community. Seven of the projects are in the cities where the company itself is headquartered. Textron, a diversified manufacturing company located in Providence, for example, has undertaken a $46 million redevelopment in downtown Providence, including renovation of the Union Station and Biltmore Hotel.

Six projects were at least partly prompted by a desire for income or savings from leasing or using commercial or office space. In rehabilitating an old cigar factory in a Hispanic area of Tampa, Trend, a magazine publisher, created space for its own offices. It also provided space for a restaurant, specialty shops, and for vendors in a weekend Nostalgia Market.

Three projects, including Higbee's, stemmed from a particular personal interest in the community on the part of a member of management. Higbee's Chairman Herbert Strawbridge, as head of a major Cleveland department store, felt that his company had a substantial stake in the city's future and should try to reverse the pattern of decay in the downtown area. Higbee's Settlers' Landing project is the result.

Although all the companies received press coverage for their efforts, four specifically referred to the public relations benefits they have gained. Trend Publications received Florida's Annual Governor's Award in the Arts for its Tampa project.

Many factors influenced the success of the various projects, including location; the unique character of the architecture and its convertibility; the mix of new uses; the size of the project; its marketability; the availability and cost of financing; the ability to attract public dollars and support; and the depth and staying power of the developer.

The projects studied have met with varying degrees of success. Five have brought increased commercial interest in the redeveloped areas. In Corning, New York, for example, a 15 percent vacancy rate on Main Street has been eliminated due to the efforts of the Corning Glass-sponsored Market Street Restoration Program. The Program encourages store owners to renovate their facades in keeping with the town's nineteenth-century character and provides free designs to those wishing to participate. The Program also attempts to encourage tourists to visit the town and promotes preservation activities.

In five cases, commercial redevelopment has helped attract government funding, leading to joint public-private revitalization efforts. Commitments of $350,000 from ten Lowell-area financial institutions, and plans for a $2 million private bond issue to fund commercial renovation, helped attract $26 million in combined local, state, and federal commitments to revitalize that city's downtown area.

Although many of these nine projects are still in progress, four have already resulted in a return on investment for the companies involved. Inland Steel's project in Washington, D.C., has adapted an old foundry and constructed a new building in keeping with the nineteenth-century surroundings. Inland's buildings now house a restaurant and shopping arcade in what was formerly a neglected industrial property.

The most common problem INFORM found in these projects was a lower return on investment than anticipated. This seemed to be at least partly the result of the relative newness of the concept of commercial redevelopment. Many large and small businesses, as well as lenders, have adopted a "wait and see" attitude, leading to low occupancy rates, high turnover, and inadequate capital. Progress in leasing in both the Higbee and Trend projects has been slower than anticipated. Trend's cigar-factory renovation has been hindered by its inability to attract larger numbers of shoppers to an inner-city location isolated from Tampa's other shopping areas. Four firms have had to alter plans and extend schedules to accommodate cash-flow difficulties. The Jefferson Company's difficulties in finding tenants and long-term financing caused a three-year interval between the announcement of its project and the actual start of construction.

Inconvenient locations have hampered success in two cases, and structural and technical problems have created difficulties for two others.

Footnotes

1. INFORM interview with Frank Corbin, Deputy Director, Economic Development Administration, New York City, August, 1977.
2. Michael Sterne, "Corporate Moves: New York Region Holds Its Own," *New York Times*, 21 August 1977, sec. 11 (Long Island Weekly), p. 1.
3. "An Erosion of Aid to the Cities," *Business Week*, August 15, 1977, p. 36.

Residential Revitalization

Summary The Allegheny Council to Improve Our Neighborhoods, or ACTION-Housing, Inc., was established in the late 1950s. Its aim was to revitalize Pittsburgh's housing and neighborhoods and to help achieve this goal, ACTION-Housing established a revolving loan fund, called the Pittsburgh Development Fund (PDF). The Fund provided intermediate equity capital, and/or seed money, for the construction of privately or federally financed housing for moderate-income families. The PDF was terminated in 1976, but its successor, known as the ACTION-Housing Development Fund, is supported by grants from major corporations and foundations in Pittsburgh. It will become active in 1978. During the fourteen years of its existence, the PDF had accumulated more than $1.2 million from 24 companies, and had made loans of $4.1 million. The initial funds were turned over four times, assisting creation of more than 3,000 units of new and rehabilitated housing. Rehabilitation, as a tool for neighborhood renewal, accounted for 13 percent of the PDF's work.

Background In 1957, the Allegheny Conference on Community Development, a leading Pittsburgh nonprofit business and civic group, sponsored a study to determine Pittsburgh's and Allegheny County's housing needs. Based on the study's recommendations, ACTION-Housing, Inc., was formed. It was designed to provide encouragement, consultation, and economic support to those wishing to initiate private development of new and rehabilitated moderate-income housing. Its area of operation included some of Pittsburgh's most deteriorated neighborhoods.

Execution ACTION-Housing quickly discovered that many qualified but underfinanced private developers could not obtain the funds to initiate much-needed housing development. Private developers needed money at reasonable rates early in the development process. However, short-term loans were expensive, if they could be obtained at all. To deal with this problem, ACTION-Housing created the Pittsburgh Development Fund (PDF), a revolving loan fund designed to provide short-term loans at market rates. As the loans were repaid—usually after construction financing was secured—the money would once again become available to other borrowers.

The PDF's goals were set forth as follows:

1. Involving the business community as an active partner in improving Pittsburgh's housing stock.

2. Providing initial short-term financing to builders and others, either for the construction of new housing, or for the modernization of older houses and neighborhoods, thus speeding regeneration.

3. Providing large-scale demonstrations of new housing materials, design, technology, and production.

4. Acquiring land available only upon total cash purchase for resale in whole or in part to developers, thereby also acting as a "land bank."

Action-Housing reviewed these concepts with three Mellon Foundations which subsequently made grants of $350,000 to establish the Fund. The grants, however, were made conditional on the PDF's receipt of additional major financial support from local business and industrial interests. If no such support was forthcoming, the entire proposal was to be abandoned. The group approached the Westinghouse Electric Corporation, Jones and Laughlin Steel Corporation, and the United States Steel Corporation, the three largest private employers in Pittsburgh. It was estimated that one out of every six houses in Allegheny County was occupied by an employee of one of these three firms.

The three giant corporations, together with many other Pittsburgh businesses, supported the PDF through grants and loans. The Fund initially sought $2 million, but it was activated after $1.4 million was raised. Grants initially accounted for about 12 percent of the total, while the balance was made up of loans, a concept encouraged by ACTION-Housing because of its businesslike approach and its value as a model to other cities. The loan subscriptions ranged from $10,000 to $250,000, and returned 4 percent interest to the subscribers if the money was used by a private developer. For the developers, the loans resembled a line of credit at a bank. They were made at the prevailing interest rate, and the difference between this rate and the 4 percent due the subscribers was used to meet the PDF's administrative costs. To encourage reuse of financial resources, loans to developers were not to exceed five years.

The PDF specifically implemented its objectives by:

1. Lending up to:
   a. 90 percent of the cost of the raw land;
   b. 70 percent of the cost of land improvements, streets, and utilities; and
   c. 70 percent of equity capital on completed developments for a short term (five years).

2. Requiring repayment of loans at the going rate of interest on a completed-unit basis.

3. Supplying a land-bank program for builders, holding land until needed for timely construction.

4. Providing preliminary site planning and architectural study.

5. Acquiring large tracts of land for cash to assure lowest cost and economic large-scale development.

6. Avoiding excess interest, bonuses, or service charges for land and land improvements, permitting a reasonable relationship of land to total dwelling cost.

7. Reviewing the builder's architectural planning. Sales and rental prices are similarly subject to prior agreement and review to assure reflection of cost savings to the consumer.

8. Providing the builder with public-oriented aid and support in zoning, planning, financing, and general community problems.

9. Providing aid and guidance in formulating advertising and sales programs.

10. Serving as a conduit between government and builder; business and builder; and consumer and builder.[1]

The rehabilitation of Cora Street, a typical example of a neighborhood-improvement project executed with the PDF's assistance, was described in a case-study ACTION-Housing publication:

Cora Street . . . lies in the very heart of the poorest area of Brushton, classified as a poverty neighborhood by the Mayor's Committee on Human Resources of the Federal Office of Economic Opportunity. However, Cora Street happens to be outside that portion of Homewood-Brushton designated an official urban renewal district. . . .

The Cora Street houses acquired for rehabilitation were 22 single-family, two-story row houses more than 60 years old, ten located on one side of the street, twelve directly opposite on the other side. . . . The row dwellings are small and compact and the relative isolation and nondescript character of the street together with its location in one of the poorest areas of the city make it a difficult candidate for any kind of improvement. One realtor in the area said of it: "It is a sore spot, a cancerous spot; you name it and it takes place in that area."

This difficulty was one of the motivations for ACTION-Housing. . . . Slums are never pleasant or congenial places, and facing them realistically in the form of Cora Street made for a more widely applicable demonstration program. . . . As Mr. Loshbough [Executive Director of ACTION-Housing] has observed: "If rehabilitation can be carried out successfully here, it can be done anywhere."

The 22 Cora Street brick row houses purchased by ACTION-Housing each contained a living room, two bedrooms, a kitchen, bathroom and basement. Their condition varied considerably.

In order to bring such a project into being, considerable funds are needed.

Not only must fiscal soundness and integrity be demonstrated to FHA when applying for mortgage insurance, but ACTION-Housing had to risk hand money (amounting to $6,000), fees for preliminary work by the architect, a real estate commission, legal fees, and ultimately one third (in excess of $70,000) of the purchase and construction costs in a participation construction loan with the lender. Except for the construction loan participation, this is called in the trade "front money," and without ACTION-Housing's Development Fund to provide it, the program could not have proceeded.

ACTION-Housing obtained 100% financing of the final mortgage under the Demonstration Program of Section 233 of the Housing Act of 1961, as amended in 1965 pursuant to Section 221 (d) (3). As a result, all of the "front money" the organization expended in the project development could be returned to its Development Fund. In addition, the Fund served, together with Mellon Bank, to provide all the interim financing required until completion of construction when federal funds (FNMA) provided the permanent mortgage at 3% interest rate. The Cora Street rehabilitation was carried out without other subsidy except for a foundation grant for landscaping.[2]

Unfortunately, the corporate loan program had to be discontinued in 1976 due to difficulties in making interest payments on time (see "Problems," below). The ACTION-Housing Development Fund, which is replacing the terminated PDF, will operate only on grants.

Costs The total value of the ACTION-Housing Development Fund today is $133,164, of which 22 percent has been contributed by businesses. Administration costs approximately $15,000 per year depending on the Fund's activity. The administrative staff consists of three to five paid employees and seven volunteer Finance Committee Members.

The Pittsburgh Development Fund provided loans for the rehabilitation of 22 brick row houses on Cora Street. (John L. Alexandrowicz)

Problems In 1976, the original Pittsburgh Development Fund was terminated, and a new fund was established. The business loan-subscription program had not been successful. The reasons stem from the difficulties in promptly paying off interest to the corporations. Most of the housing projects were subsidized through inadequately financed government programs. The PDF tried to offset cash-flow problems by making operating loans to the projects. However, by trying to keep the projects afloat when the government did not, it utilized income that should have been used for interest payments to note holders. When it became apparent that the funding structure was not going to improve, the PDF's cash assets were liquidated, and a new fund, called the ACTION-Housing Development Fund, was established. This Fund is supported entirely from grants. The process of lending money to private developers has not changed, and the requirements and goals are the same. Interest collected on the loans will be completely returned to the Fund. Corporations, previously offering loans, have been encouraged to convert their contributions into outright grants. Staff is currently reviewing proposals for use of the new Fund, and anticipates that it will become active during 1978.

Benefits Corporate participation in the revolving loan program has helped create more than 3,000 units of new and rehabilitated housing in Pittsburgh.

Companies Participating Companies Participating in the Pittsburgh Development Fund were:

Note Holders

Allegheny Ludlum Steel Corp.
The Alcoa Foundation
Columbia Gas of Pennsylvania
Consolidated Coal Company
Duquesne Light Company
Koppers Foundation
The Levinson Steel Company
Mine Safety Appliances Company, Charitable Trust
The Peoples Natural Gas Co.
Pittsburgh Coke and Chemical Co.

Rockwell Manufacturing Co.
United States Steel Corp.
Western Pennsylvania National Bank
Westinghouse Air Brake Company
Westinghouse Electric Corp.
Edwin L. Wiegand Company

Grantors

Commonwealth Trust Company
Crane Company
Equitable Gas Company
Jones & Laughlin Steel Corporation
Mellon National Bank and Trust Company
Pittsburgh National Bank
The Pittsburgh Plate Glass Foundation
Retail Merchants Association
The Union National Bank of Pittsburgh
West Penn Power Company

Companies Making Grants to the ACTION-Housing Development Fund are:

The Alcoa Foundation	$ 57,374
Columbia Gas of Pennsylvania	5,737
Consolidated Coal Company	5,737
The Hillman Foundation	8,606
Koppers Foundation	28,688
Mine Safety Appliance Co., Charitable Trust	9,254
The Peoples Natural Gas Company	14,344
Edwin L. Wiegand Company	3,424
Total Grants	$133,164

For further information contact:
Sally Mizerak
Director
Education & Community Affairs
ACTION-Housing, Inc.
Number Two Gateway Center
Pittsburgh, Pennsylvania 15222

Footnotes

1. ACTION-Housing, Inc., "The Pittsburgh Development Fund of ACTION-Housing, Inc.," (mimeographed, ACTION-Housing, Inc., n.d.), pp. 5-7.
2. Arthur P. Ziegler, Jr., *Cora Street: A Pioneering Demonstration in Rehabilitating Aging but Structurally Sound Housing,* (Pittsburgh: ACTION-Housing, Inc., 1969), pp. 9-10.

Cora Street after renovation. (Mark Perrott)

Summary In January, 1975, based on a company task-force recommendation, the Bank of America, the major subsidiary of BankAmerica Corporation, created the City Improvement and Restoration Program (CIRP) to seek out financing opportunities to assist community-revitalization efforts in the State of California. The CIRP's five-man staff advises municipalities on funding sources, including city bonds, tax revenues, Community Development Block Grant funds, and federal revenue-sharing monies, as well as on the availability of the bank's own loans. The CIRP's monies also support home-improvement loans at below the market interest.

In order to further improve California cities, the CIRP announced the formation in 1977 of a second subsidiary to revitalize housing stock. This new subsidiary, Bank of America City Improvement and Restoration Program Corporation (BACIRP), will purchase and rehabilitate abandoned properties and offer them for sale. East Oakland was chosen as its first target area.

Background In 1973, the Bank of America became concerned about the impact of massive suburbanization on urban neighborhoods and business districts located in its home state of California. It was particularly interested in the metropolitan areas of San Francisco and Los Angeles, which house about two-thirds of the state's population. Many districts had seen declining personal income, business, and residential values, and were experiencing financial disinvestment.

In 1974, BankAmerica's President A. W. Clausen appointed a task force to collect data and to formulate a role for the bank in urban revitalization. Communities in the state were analyzed to determine their revitalization needs and to define appropriate banking services which could assist them. Four areas required immediate attention: "rehabilitation of existing housing stock, mortgage financing of older homes, construction of low-cost and senior citizen housing, and open space acquisition."[1]

Execution In 1975, the City Improvement and Restoration Program (CIRP) was created to actualize the bank's commitment to urban revitalization. The supervisory committee, composed of senior management, was headed by K. S. Smeby, Senior Vice President, Administration. The committee evaluates proposed projects, provides expertise in structuring them, and monitors their progress. The CIRP adopted a package of plans, each to be tested before wide implementation.

Under CIRP's auspices the following programs have been established:

Victorian Period Homes—Purchase and Restoration, San Francisco. In February, 1975, the Bank of America became involved in the restoration of ten Victorian homes in San Francisco's Western Addition. The unoccupied homes were previously owned by the San Francisco Redevelopment Agency. These were to be removed from the site of a redevelopment project. The Agency paid the relocation costs. It is coordinating rehabilitation plans, specifications, and code-requirement approval with the city and with the bank's Appraisal Department. The Bank of America allocated $500,000 for mortgages and restoration. A total of $350,000 has been loaned thus far, under flexible terms, to seven homeowners renovating these houses.

Community Development Program. This CIRP-backed Program assists municipalities in obtaining and administering government monies for housing rehabilitation. Under this Program, the bank makes loans to homeowners in areas designated by the cooperating city or county. Federal Community Development Block Grant funds deposited by the participating government provide collateral enabling the bank to lend money at interest rates below the prevailing market rate. Loans amounted to over $1 million in 1976. The housing-stock rehabilitated has ranged from 25 to 100 years old. The CIRP administers the loans in cooperation with 3 counties and 22 cities.

The Community Development Program calls for a clear separation of duties between the bank and the city.

The bank performs its customary credit evaluation of the applicant; then the city evaluates an applicant with community preservation and development objectives in mind. If the city decides the loan should be made in spite of the applicant's lack of qualifications for normal credit consideration, it directs the bank to do so. All loans are secured by a non-interest-bearing deposit account in which the city places a share of its Community Development funds.

Since the deposit account is non-interest-bearing, the bank is relieved of all but 3 percent of the amount it ordinarily pays for using Federal-Reserve-administered funds in support of public agency projects. Thus, the effective rate to the borrower can be as low as 3.75 percent when supported by a 100 percent deposit from the city.

Residential Assistance Program, San Francisco. In San Francisco, the BankAmerica Investment Securities Division, the CIRP, the county, and the city are cooperating to develop a city-financed housing-rehabilitation program which would offer loans at below current interest rates.

In November, 1976, the City and County of San Francisco sold bonds to capitalize the Residential Assistance Program, a rehabilitation loan fund. The Bank of America has made a

Victorian house restored with Bank of America's help. (Sirlin Studios)

House in process of restoration. (Sirlin Studios)

commitment to bid for up to $20 million in rehabilitation-assistance bonds over a five-year period, and has already purchased $2.5 million of these bonds, the entire initial offering. As security for the bonds, the city pledged the accumulated proceeds from rehabilitation-loan payments, the deeds of trust it receives when making rehabilitation loans, and a bad-debt reserve established from the sale of the bonds.

A temporary roadblock in implementing the Residential Assistance Program was removed when the state appellate court ruled favorably on the constitutionality of public loans from a municipality to individuals. An Internal Revenue Service ruling on taxation of the interest income earned by financial institutions on bonds issued by a municipality is pending.

Although the Program is not yet operational due to city administrative delays, Residential Assistance loans will be made to all qualified property owners in certain target areas. They will cover minimum building code-enforcement work, minor building violations, or obsolescence of plumbing, wiring and other mechanical systems. The Program will provide up to $17,500 per unit, with a maximum indebtedness of 90 percent of after-rehabilitation value. The loans will be repaid over a period of twenty years, or three-fourths of the economic life of a building, whichever is less. The interest rate to borrowers depends on the interest rate on city bonds on the date of purchase. If the Internal Revenue Service decides that a bank's income from the purchase of city bonds is tax free, interest charges to the city can be reduced, and loans to property owners can be made at below market rates. The average life of a Residential Assistance loan is expected to be eight to ten years.

Applicants unqualified under conventional lending standards are eligible for hardship loans of up to $3,500 per building. These interest-free loans will cover code-enforcement repairs, and will carry a lien against the property, with no repayments due until sale or transfer to a new owner, or after twenty years.

BankAmerica City Improvement and Restoration Program. After receiving approval from the Federal Reserve Board in January, 1977, the BankAmerica City Improvement and Restoration Program (BACIRP) began to purchase vacant single-family homes in a declining area in the eastern part of Oakland, California. Upon completion of rehabilitation work by local contractors, the properties will be sold through local real estate brokers. The moderately priced homes will be sold to low- and middle-income, credit-worthy applicants.

A. W. Clausen, President of BankAmerica Corporation, explained that the new subsidiary will operate "essentially at a break-even level." He added, "No profits will accrue to BankAmerica Corp."[2] Any profits that are made will be used for expansion of the Program. The BACIRP is capitalized with $150,000 for operating expenses and $150,000 for a revolving line of credit. Based on the level of success here and on Federal Reserve approval, the bank will consider expanding this Program to other California cities. Since the BACIRP is in its infancy, details on its activities and results are not yet available. The bank states that because of the efforts of speculators and problems dealing with foreclosed HUD properties, real estate prices in Oakland had escalated before the bank got clearance for the BACIRP. The bank is delaying implementation of the proposed Program since many houses in the targeted area are being independently renovated.

Before the CIRP was established, the bank had undertaken the following revitalization projects:

Rehabilitation, Chico. The Bank of America, through its Chico, California, branch, committed $102,000 in 1973 to the Chico Housing Improvement Program (CHIP) for rehabilitation of senior-citizen and low-income dwellings. The bank loans were earmarked for the purchase of building materials for homeowners to make limited renovations of their residences. The CHIP also received $22,000 from federal revenue-sharing funds to cover its operating costs and to create a high-risk loan pool.

The CHIP is sponsored by the bank, the city, and California State University, Chico. Its seven-member Board of Directors is composed of local citizens, including a loan officer of the Chico branch of the Bank of America. Thus far, 32 homes have been rehabilitated using loans made at market interest rates and loans from the city's high-risk loan pool.

To stretch the available funds, the CHIP organized a system of free labor. Chico State University students, the University's Industrial Technology Department, and Vista Volunteers have provided free assistance to low-income and disabled homeowners, but homeowners themselves have been expected to participate as fully as possible.

The CHIP distributes information about home improvements, and advises homeowners of the sources of financial assistance. The improvements made under its auspices are limited to structural corrections, such as wiring, roofing, foundations, and plumbing.

Neighborhood Rehabilitation, Berkeley. In 1974, Bank of America Vice President Leo Sullivan helped the City of Berkeley, California, plan and develop a pilot program to assist individual homeowners in the rehabilitation of some fifty-year-old housing stock.

Berkeley established a Municipal Loan Pool with $550,000 in city funds. The Pool is administered by a loan committee, which is assisted by the Manager of the bank's Berkeley branch. The committee reviews home-improvement-loan applications from homeowners who are normally unqualified for conventional mortgages. The loans cover code-enforcement repairs, the elimination of substandard conditions, and room additions.

The city provides the cost estimate, counsels the homeowner in applying for an improvement loan, and supplies community services to the residents of the target area. To date, loans amounting to $350,000 have been made. The average loan has been about $8,000. There have been no defaults.

Costs Operating budgets for the CIRP are funded annually through the bank's Urban Affairs Department. The Program's current staff includes the department head, two officers, a research assistant, and a secretary. The CIRP relies very heavily on existing bank personnel and resources to meet its objectives. Its loan totals are carried under appropriate existing loan categories. Since they are not segregated from other bank resources, a breakdown of Program costs is not available.

Problems Two programs supported by the Bank of America have not yet been implemented as of mid-1977. The Residential Assistance Program is not yet underway, in part because of City of San Francisco administrative delays. The BACIRP has had difficulties obtaining foreclosed HUD properties. Real estate prices in Oakland have also risen faster than the bank anticipated.

Benefits The Bank of America is deeply involved in California's economy, and its prosperity depends on the health of the state. It feels that its economic self-interest is directly served by preserving the soundness of neighborhoods. The bank also maintains goodwill by helping communities with neighborhood revitalization.

The Company The Bank of America, the major subsidiary of BankAmerica Corporation, is the largest commercial bank in the world and the largest savings institution in the country. Branch offices in California number over 1,060. Net interest income of the holding company was $1.61 billion in 1976, up 7.5 percent from $1.50 billion in the previous fiscal year. Net income rose 11.2 percent from $302.8 million in 1975 to $336.8 million in 1976.

Other Preservation Activities/Trust for Public Land. The Trust for Public Land (TPL), a San Francisco-based nonprofit organization, works to preserve open-space areas for public use. Its primary effort involves locating and purchasing land parcels around the United States that are suitable for recreation or conservation. TPL holds them until they can be purchased by an already interested government agency or until the TPL can find an appropriate purchaser and work out resale and land conservation terms.

Since 1973, the Bank of America has annually committed a $10 million credit line to this organization. The TPL's other contributed support comes from foundations and individuals. The "TPL's method of acquisition offers tax benefits to the seller and substantial cash savings to the acquiring city or other agency."[3] In the past four years, the TPL has arranged and accomplished transfer of 33 properties in seven states totaling over 10,000 acres, and saved public agencies approximately $4 million.[4]

The TPL also sponsors the National Urban Land Program, whose purpose is to create land trust/conservancies in urban centers. Unused city lots are obtained and turned over to residents to be cultivated for vegetable gardens or planted with grass and trees for use as public parks. Some parcels are placed in a land bank for future use.

A Bank of America specialist in land appraisal and acquisition began assisting the TPL with this Program in January, 1976. Other corporations, private individuals, and lending institutions have made donations to it of land parcels with an estimated total value of $110,000.

Beaudry Street House, Los Angeles. In 1975, the Bank of America financed the relocation of Beaudry Street House in Los Angeles. The house was moved from the site of a bank data-processing center to Heritage Square, a public park for landmark homes dating from the period 1860 to 1910. The Bank of America Foundation also donated $30,000 to construct a permanent foundation for the house.

For further information contact:
James S. Young
City Improvement Coordinator
Kyhl S. Smeby
Senior Vice-President, Administration
City Improvement and Restoration Program
Bank of America
Bank of America World Headquarters
Suite 2135
555 California Street
San Francisco, California 94104

Footnotes

1. Bank of America, *The Community and the Bank: A Report on 1975 Social Policy Activities* (San Francisco: Bank of America, 1975), p. 9.
2. "Bank America Plans Unit to Buy, Restore Urban-Area Housing," *Wall Street Journal*, 10 November 1976.
3. Bank of America, "City Improvement and Restoration Program, Information Packet," (mimeographed, Bank of America, February, 1977), p. 8.
4. *Ibid.*

Summary In 1966, the Brooklyn Union Gas Company joined the "Back to Brooklyn" movement, an effort by Brooklyn businesses and residents to arrest the urban decay beginning to encompass downtown Brooklyn. Realizing its stake in the stability of its market, Brooklyn Union initiated the Cinderella Program to encourage renovation rather than demolition of sound housing. The company purchased and renovated a dilapidated and abandoned brownstone at 211 Berkeley Place in Park Slope. This restoration, named Cinderella I, was to demonstrate that brownstone renovation was economically feasible, and was made the focal point of an extensive advertising campaign to involve middle-income families in brownstone renovation in downtown Brooklyn.

The success of Cinderella I has led to other renovations. Brooklyn Union selects projects in marginal areas, which are carried out by a local contractor or community group, and are financed by a local bank. These sites are then given the Cinderella designation, and Brooklyn Union supplies the renovated site with improvements, such as gas lights and patio furniture, and publicity. To date, the company has spent $400,000 on the program, which now includes fifteen projects around the borough.

Background Brooklyn was New York City's first suburb. In the nineteenth and early twentieth century, many wealthy Manhattanites, in search of a more residential atmosphere, moved to Brooklyn Heights, Cobble Hill, Boerum Hill, Park Slope, and other affluent brownstone communities. Most of the brownstones in Brooklyn are well built and beautifully designed. Many are Victorian in style, with three or four floors, large rooms, sliding wooden doors, stained glass, decorative plaster moldings, high ceilings, and parquet floors.

During the 1940s, the racial composition of downtown Brooklyn began to change. Middle-income families were emigrating to the borough's newly developed outlying areas and to Queens and Long Island. Absentee landlords neglected their buildings, and many were abandoned; businesses closed, and banks refused new mortgages. The downtown communities rapidly deteriorated. Neighborhoods which had been home to the wealthy one hundred years before had badly decayed by the mid-1960s.

These changes worried Brooklyn Union, whose headquarters has been located in Brooklyn Heights since its founding in 1895. Brooklyn Union, unlike many corporations, could not move to a more affluent area. Its

investments—gas pipelines—lie beneath the surface of every Brooklyn street. Frederic H. J. Rider, Assistant Vice President for Public Relations at Brooklyn Union, and coordinator of the Cinderella Program, summarized the situation:

Our future growth hinges on the future of our service area. It's that simple. We realized years ago that the everyday problems of our business are a part of a much larger social problem. The only way to help our own situation was to try to pump some life and money back into Brooklyn neighborhoods before the entire borough becomes a ghetto.[1]

Brooklyn Union was determined to try to encourage a return of middle-income people who had moved to the suburbs during the previous decades. With more money in circulation, old businesses would remain, and new ones would move into the area, bolstering the downtown economy. It hoped that the renovation project at 211 Berkeley Place would be a catalyst for economic renewal.

Execution In 1966, Brooklyn Union purchased an abandoned mid-nineteenth-century brownstone at 211 Berkeley Place with the intention of filming its transformation from an eyesore into an elegant residence. The work on Cinderella I, as the project was called, began in 1966 under architect Edwin B. Taylor, with the Dover Construction Company acting as general contractors. The renovation took one year to complete. A local interior decorator, Evelyn Ortner, herself a brownstone enthusiast, designed the interiors and selected the furnishings.

The brownstone was converted into two duplex apartments. This necessitated some redesign of its 4,000-square-foot interior. A basement kitchen was reused as a laundry room, and a bathroom in the master bedroom was removed to create more space. The renovation utilized the best talents and materials available. All woodwork and plasterwork were restored. The house was furnished with a combination of contemporary and Victorian furniture in an attempt to maintain, within practical limits, the house's original flavor. Brooklyn Union purchased the abandoned brownstone for $15,000 and

Cinderella project: before.

renovated it for $50,000, for a total cost of $65,000, or $16.25 per square foot. After the renovation, the house was opened to the public for one year, and 4,000 people visited it. It was later sold for $63,000.

In 1972, Brooklyn Union became involved in a project that was to become Cinderella II. During that year, Everett Ortner, founder of the Park Slope Betterment Committee, and President of Back to the City, Inc., asked Brooklyn Union's help in renovating several abandoned brownstones on a Prospect Place block which Frederic Rider has called "the worst block in Brooklyn."[2] In addition to the abandoned and neglected brownstones, there were three abandoned storefronts on the other side of the street. Brooklyn Union felt these stores would make ideal renovation projects, since they had been abandoned for over twenty years and had become a haven for drug addicts and other unwanted elements in the neighborhood.

The company purchased the three stores for $10,000, and sold them to Asen Brothers and Lester Brooks, builders and contractors, who renovated them as residences at a cost of between $35,000 and $38,000 per store. Brooklyn Union repaved the backyards, supplied gravel for the patios, and provided gas lights and gas barbecue grills. The company also purchased interior furnishings for these "colonial townhouses" from Abraham & Strauss, Brooklyn's largest downtown department store. Financing for the renovation was obtained from the Greater New York Savings Bank, which paid for one-half of the promotional campaign for Cinderella II. Asen Brothers sold the first two townhouses for $45,000 and $48,000. The last house was re-purchased by Brooklyn Union and opened to visitors for one year; it was later resold for $65,000. Brooklyn Union has shown a continuing interest in this block, donating gas lights and advising people who wish to renovate properties on it.

In 1975, the Bedford Stuyvesant Restoration Corporation renovated five adjoining apartment buildings in the Bedford Stuyvesant section of Brooklyn. The organization asked Brooklyn Union's assistance in cleaning up the vacant and trash-filled lot between the buildings, which had been gutted by fire. Brooklyn Union spent $25,000 in cleaning out the lot and renovating it as a brick-paved, gas-lit central courtyard. The five-building restoration was designated Cinderella III.

Later in 1975, a two-story brownstone at 93 Prospect Place became Cinderella IV. The partially renovated building had been abandoned after several mishaps, and after an adjoining store was torn down, leaving a vacant lot between it and an abandoned supermarket. Brooklyn Union financed the renovation, with Mara Management Corporation acting as general contractors. The supermarket became a branch of Brooklyn Union and the brownstone became the company's Brownstone Information Center. The vacant lot became a gaslit, brick-paved courtyard, complete with fountain. The Center provides information on local bank mortgages, local electricians, contractors, and all aspects of home renovation to Brooklyn residents and those who wish to move there. Recently, the Center began compiling and distributing a community calendar and newsletter.

Cinderella V is being undertaken by John Melvin Associates in 1977, and is perhaps the most strategically important project thus far in the Program. It is located on St. Felix Street, near the Brooklyn Academy of Music which draws thousands of people to downtown Brooklyn each year. Ten abandoned houses on St. Felix Street are slated for renovation by the end of the year; six have already been completed under the Cinderella name. Financing for the construction was obtained from the Williamsburg Savings Bank, whose banking headquarters are around the corner. Brooklyn Union is supplying decorative shrubbery, trees, and gas lights for the street.

While Cinderellas VI through XV have not yet been completed, Brooklyn Union has sought to become involved in every Brooklyn community. Several of these projects are located in some of the borough's most deteriorated areas, and most are being carried out by neighborhood-improvement organizations. In East New York, for example, 27 homes are being renovated by the city's Small Home Improvements Program; in Sunset Park, a local developer is converting a factory into 10 apartment units. The most recent project, the old Cathedral Club on Flatbush Avenue, is being renovated by a Haitian Society. In 1978, the company plans to begin several projects in Woodside, Queens, part of its service area.

Brooklyn Union's main contribution to these renovations has been its exten-

Cinderella project: after. The old stores were converted into town-houses.

sive advertising of each project. To date, full-page ads have been run in 170 major newspapers across the country. This advertising, of course, creates good publicity for the company; but it also often helps the individual project gain credibility, particularly with local lenders. In addition to its advertisements, Brooklyn Union sponsors films outlining the renovation process, and promoting brownstones in Brooklyn. The films are distributed free to interested community groups. Titles have included: *My, My Brooklyn, Cinderella of Prospect Place, Brownstone Brooklyn, To Brooklyn with Love from Geraldine Fitzgerald*. The company plans an upcoming film that will deal with the first four Cinderella projects, and hopes to sponsor one film each year in the future. Brooklyn Union also sponsors the annual Brownstone Fair and Promenade Art Show held every October. In 1976, 25,000 people turned out for the event. In addition, the company holds Brownstone seminars at its main office, explaining the history of the Program and the advantages of brownstone living.

Costs In addition to advertising expenditures, Brooklyn Union Gas spent $400,000 on Cinderellas I through IV. The costs included: the purchase price of the house on Berkeley Place, $15,000, and the cost of renovation, $50,000; the purchase price of the three stores on Prospect Place, $10,000; and the creation of the courtyard in Cinderella III, $25,000. Information on other specific costs was not available. Brooklyn Union plans to allocate $70,000 a year to the Cinderella Program, as well as a substantial amount for advertising. For accounting purposes, the company's expenditures have thus far been considered part of operating expenses, and amount to approximately 1/2 cent per meter per month.

Problems The greatest problem facing Brooklyn Union, or anyone interested in renovating in the downtown area, is financing. Banks often judge a house solely on the area in which it is located, not the soundness of the structure itself, or the purchaser's ability to pay. This "redlining" has made it very difficult to finance houses in some neighborhoods. However, due to the efforts of Brooklyn Union Gas and Frederic Rider, several local banks have provided mortgage money.

Benefits According to a Brooklyn Union official, the company's sales have increased because of the new customers attracted to Brooklyn,[3] and the company has gained a good deal of favorable publicity. One of the company's Cinderella ads won an award from the American Gas Association for the best advertisement by a utility in 1976. Company Assistant Vice President for Public Relations Frederic Rider was recently interviewed for an article scheduled to appear in 22 major newspapers across the country. The success of the Program has also solidified the company's commitment to Brooklyn (it had contemplated a move to Queens).

Brooklyn Union feels its Program has been much more successful in changing the attitudes and climate of downtown Brooklyn than could have been anticipated:

We simply wanted to demonstrate ... what could be done with a hammer, some paint and imagination. We had no idea that we were starting a boom, let alone a renaissance. To our great delight we discovered that improvement in a community is far more contagious than deterioration.[4]

Property values have risen since the Program began. Two years after the completion of Cinderella I, twenty new families had moved into Berkeley Place, and in the past decade, the values of some of the houses have risen from $15,000 to $90,000.

Since the inception of the Cinderella Program, the communities in the downtown area have begun to take a serious interest in renovation, and Brooklyn Union is being approached by many organizations who wish to have their project given the Cinderella des-

ignation. One example of Cinderella's impact is a dry-cleaning store located around the corner from Cinderella IV. The owners had just about given up trying to survive the surrounding decay, but Brooklyn Union's efforts prompted them to stay and modernize. The store has been renamed the Cinderella Cleaners.

The Cinderella Program has helped inspire house tours of the various neighborhoods, and has helped attract new business and craftsmen to the area. It has also aided the growth of the Victorian Society and the Back to the City movement, which are now nationwide organizations.

The Company Brooklyn Union Gas has been located on Court and Montague Streets in Brooklyn Heights since its founding in 1895. The company today distributes natural gas to an estimated 4 million people in the boroughs of Brooklyn, Queens, and Staten Island. Revenues rose from $267 million in 1975 to $312 million in 1976. Net income increased from $17.8 million to $18.6 million over the same period. Revenues break down as follows: 59 percent residences with gas heating, 22 percent other residences, 16 percent commercial and industrial, and 2 percent temperature-control heating.

For further information contact:
Frederic Rider
Assistant Vice President for Public Relations
Alan Smith
Manager of Public Relations and Advertising
Alfred Jennings
Community Relations Supervisor
The Brooklyn Union Gas Company
195 Montague Street
Brooklyn, New York 11201

Footnotes

1. "Brooklyn Union's Cinderella Luring People Back to the City," *Gas Line*, 1976, vol. 2, no. 2, p. 14.
2. INFORM interview with F. H. J. Rider, Assistant Vice President for Public Relations, The Brooklyn Union Gas Company, June, 1977.
3. *Ibid.*
4. *Gas Line, op. cit.*, p. 14.

Summary Chemical Bank, one of New York City's major financial institutions, has played a vital role in the rehabilitation of a badly deteriorated tenement on Manhattan's Lower East Side. Residents of East 11th Street, assisted by local housing activists, acquired an abandoned, city-owned building at address 519, and set out to rehabilitate it themselves; a concept known as "sweat equity." The project also included the installation of a solar collection system to heat domestic hot water and a two-kilowatt windmill to partially meet power needs. The bank, through its Urban Affairs Department, provided loans for seed money to cover architectural, legal, and developmental costs, as well as bridge loans to relieve cash-flow problems which occurred during the reconstruction process. The East 11th Street rehabilitation was part of a diverse program of inner-city projects supported by Chemical Bank.

Background Policy for all the bank's social-action programs is determined by the Urban Affairs Advisory Committee, which is composed of senior management from its major departments. After a study of inner-city needs and possible strategies, the Committee, under Chairman Norborne Berkeley, Jr., Chemical's President, established the Urban Affairs Department in 1971. According to the bank:

The reality underlying this thinking is that Chemical's success as a business depends on the health of the markets it serves. If New York and other urban centers crumble under the impact of problems like slum housing, crime, drug abuse, poor education and unemployment, the bank's business and the quality of its employees will also erode.[1]

Chemical's Urban Housing Unit, a division of the Urban Affairs Department, administers a $100 million allocation of credit for use in low- and moderate-income housing and community development projects. Juan Villaneuva, a former administrator in the New York City Housing and Development Administration, was hired in May, 1975, to head the Unit, and he has been liaison to the East 11th Street Housing Movement.

Number 519 East 11th Street was built in the first decade of the twentieth century. The five-story brick building is functional in design, with the exception of brick window decoration, two intricate cornices at the roofline, and sculpted masks and cherubs.

Throughout the first half of the century, it served as a tenement for Italian, Ukrainian, Polish, and Jewish immigrants. In the 1960s, poor blacks and Puerto Ricans moved in. "I couldn't believe the conditions," said Robert Nazario, who helped organize the tenants several years ago. "Junkies were using the roof as a shooting gallery."[2] The residents were prey to constant criminal activity, and the children had no place to play other than streets heaped with rotting garbage and debris.

By spring, 1972, thirteen fires had ravaged 519 East 11th Street, finally driving the tenants out. When the building was abandoned by its owner, the city took possession because of property tax arrears.

Abandonment is the end of the line for most tenement buildings, and in 1972, it looked as if 519 would be counted among them.* Demolition for safety reasons seemed certain.

*According to the Urban Homesteading Assistance Board, approximately 150,000 units in 10,000 buildings were abandoned in New York City by 1976, and an average of two or three buildings are added to this number each day.[3]

Execution In August, 1973, a group of low-income neighborhood residents, supported by professional housing activists from Interfaith Adopt-a-Building, a church-supported, non-profit organization, asked the city if it could supply them with a suitable building for renovation and occupation. Many of the residents had no high school education, little command of English, and little work experience. The city's Department of Real Estate, which had jurisdiction over a large stock of abandoned buildings acquired from landlords delinquent in paying property taxes, sold number 519 to the group for $1,800.

The group—by this point constituted as the East 11th Street Housing Movement—negotiated a $177,494 loan with the New York City Housing and Development Administration (HDA) through the "sweat equity" portion of the now-defunct Municipal Loan Program. The terms of the loan called for a thirty-year renovation mortgage at 7 1/2 percent interest.

Instead of a substantial downpayment to purchase already renovated apartment units, future residents were required to contribute their "sweat," doing most of the **rehabilitation** work themselves.

Interior of 519 East 11th Street in the process of rehabilitation. (East 11th Street Housing Movement)

In winter, 1974, Interfaith Adopt-a-Building received a $20,000 "seed money" loan from Chemical Bank's Urban Affairs Department to cover the architectural, legal, and developmental (cost estimating, construction supervision, loan packaging) costs of its projects, including 519 East 11th Street.

The Office of Cooperative Conversion of the city's Housing and Development Administration has a range of programs which use the sweat-equity concept. At 519, the Sweat Equity Training Program was employed. The fifty members of the Movement were paid $3 per hour, using federal Comprehensive Employment and Training Act (CETA) Funds, to carry out all aspects of the rehabilitation except electrical wiring. Partial supervision and some tools were provided by union and nonunion tradesmen. The tradesmen were paid a total of $2,000. Each member of the Movement worked a forty-hour week, of which eight hours were unpaid as sweat equity on the project. The Office of Cooperative Conversion estimates that 6,758 sweat-equity hours over a period of one-and-a-half years were invested in the building. This amounts to a savings of $20,274.

Renovation work began in spring, 1974. The interior of the building was cleared of debris and gutted of all interior fixtures. Entirely new interior walls, floors, plumbing, and wiring were installed; and windows, doors, ceilings, and 300 beams were replaced.

Cash-flow difficulties arose soon after the loan closing in October, 1974. Renovations were funded after the need was verified by city inspectors, but Municipal Loan Program allocations were too slow to satisfy creditors who supplied the homesteaders with materials. These delays endangered the project's credit standing. The HDA, which administered the Municipal Loan Program, routinely took between six and eight weeks to process checks. Michael Freedberg, director of the East 11th Street project, could see that he needed some kind of short-term financing to cover the costs between allocations, so he again turned to Chemical's Urban Affairs Department for help. The bank provided a "bridge" loan of $5,000, with ninety-day repayment terms, using the group's vouchers, backed by the city, as security. On five subsequent occasions, bridge loans were made, each of about $5,000.

More recently, the problem has been cost overruns, a result of inflation, financing delays, and unforeseen reconstruction problems. The Hayden Foundation supplied a grant of $15,000 to cover the overruns.

The rehabilitation of 519 East 11th Street was completed in March, 1977, and the building was inspected by the New York City Office of Housing Rehabilitation, a department of the Housing and Development Administration. All eleven apartments and two storefronts have been renovated. The eleven families moved in while the work was still in progress, and pay $42 per room, per month. This income covers the mortgage, operational costs, and maintenance.

Currently, Michael Freedberg is supervising three more sweat-equity rehabilitation projects in adjacent buildings on East 11th Street. Chemical Bank is providing seed money for two of them.

Energy. Under the supervision of architect Travis Price, a member of the Movement, three types of energy-conservation measures were employed in the rehabilitated building. These included: extra insulation, a solar collector, and a windmill. Refitting the entire building with the highest grade of insulation plus the installation of storm windows cost about $11,000. The solar collector was financed by a $43,000 grant from the federal Community Services Administration. Installed on the roof, it heats and circulates hot water through pipes to a heat exchanger and storage tank in the basement. The system consists of thirty glass-covered solar collecting units, which have the capacity to supply 80 percent of the building's hot-water needs. A two-kilowatt windmill, designed and installed under a $13,622 grant from the Community Services Administration, is also located on the roof. It generates enough electricity to operate twenty 100-watt lightbulbs when it is operating at full capacity.

The solar hot water system and effective use of insulation have cut the BTU requirements of the building by 70 percent (20 percent through the use of the solar hot water system and 50 percent through effective insulation). The annual energy bill for a building this size would be about $8,000 to $9,000. The savings achieved by this lower energy use is about $5,600.

Costs Doug Ades, Vice President of Chemical's Urban Affairs Department, estimated the cost of new apartment construction to be between $35,000 and $45,000 per unit.[4] Commercial costs for a gut rehabilitation similar to the one at 519 East 11th Street are over $25,000 per unit. With sweat equity, rehabilitation of the East 11th Street project cost $13,657 per unit.

Problems Initial difficulties at 519 East 11th Street stemmed largely from the project's innovative nature. Residents had no experience in construction and little overall work experience. This caused organizational problems. There was a high turnover in workers as well. About half the original members of the cooperative dropped out in the early stages.

The city's administrative practices are slow and cumbersome. Individuals or groups applying for the right to homestead on city properties have frequently run into a wall of bureaucratic red tape, and have become discouraged from following through. The level of discouragement rose here appreciably during periods when city-committed assistance was delayed and work could not proceed.

Benefits The initiative and persistence of the East 11th Street Movement, the assistance of Chemical Bank, and other public and private agencies have helped turn around a block in the process of complete deterioration. The 519 project, though delayed by the inexperience of its work force and municipal red tape, has created a viable residential property.

Efficient insulation and innovative energy systems have reduced operating costs substantially for the building's residents and brought extensive publicity. The building was the focus of a series of tours by business leaders conducted by several environmental groups.

The 519 project also illustrates the benefits of sweat equity. Lower rehabilitation costs make sweat equity an affordable method of housing the poor without long-term subsidy. No other program can do this. "Adequate subsidies," the Urban Homesteading Assistance Board points out, "simply do not exist to align these extremely high costs of new construction and commercial rehabilitation with the income of the poor."[5] Robert Schur, Executive Director of the Association of Neighborhood Housing Developers and former Deputy Commissioner of the New York City Housing and Development Administration, adds, "Anything below luxury housing is not do-able, economically."[6]

Community residents gained job skills while working on the rehabilitation, which increased their employment potential. The expertise gained on the project is currently being used to help three other buildings on the block follow the same sweat equity process.

The financial community and the neighborhood also benefit from the sweat-equity program. Chemical Bank has demonstrated that supporting housing cooperatives in a poor, minority community, as it did on East 11th Street, is a practical step which strengthens the urban environment in which the bank operates. Over the years, the revitalized community should be a regular customer for the bank's financial services. Goodwill has been generated in the community; a very visible process of community stabilization has begun, and from the bank's point of view, a pool of potential depositors has been created there.

After a period of ten years, during which property taxes are abated, the once-abandoned buildings are returned to the city tax rolls. Furthermore, the $6,000 cost of demolition is avoided. People who at one time were consumers of city social services become taxpaying citizens through job training and placement.

Exterior view of 519 East 11th Street after renovation. (Richard Griffin)

The Company Chemical Bank, the major subsidiary of Chemical New York Corporation, is the sixth largest bank in the United States. It has about 220 branches in the New York area. In 1976, revenues for the holding company amounted to $577 million with a net income of $92.6 million. Comparable figures for 1975 were $645.4 million and $95.9 million.

Other Preservation Activities/Branch 139, Bedford Stuyvesant. In 1967, Chemical opened a branch in the newly renovated Sheffield House, headquarters of the Bedford-Stuyvesant Restoration Corporation. The area was in very bad condition, but had a 28 percent rate of owner-occupancy— much higher than similar areas in either Harlem or the South Bronx— and many of its houses were solidly built brownstones. The work of the Bedford-Stuyvesant Restoration Corporation has reassured the bank that its commitment is secure. Restoration, as it is called, has developed housing, encouraged industry to settle in the area, and has established both for-profit and nonprofit businesses.

Street Banking. Chemical set up the first street-banking unit in Harlem in 1969 to deliver financial services to individuals and organizations who have not routinely used them: in many cases, people who are just beginning to raise themselves and their communities out of poverty and require project funding on an interim basis. Today, the program has been expanded to several other inner-city areas, including the East Village and the Lower East Side. The street bankers make daily visits to residents, businesses, government organizations, schools, day-care centers, and health facilities to familiarize the community with various banking services, such as checking and savings accounts, loan programs, and payroll management.

The Urban Homesteading Assistance Board. The Urban Homesteading Assistance Board is the city-wide organization established by the Cathedral of St. John the Divine in 1975 to help urban homesteaders successfully manage the process of rehabilitating abandoned buildings. The Board has tried to fill the gap left by city agencies which were forced to cut back their efforts due to budget restraints.

Chemical Bank, Bankers Trust, Morgan Guaranty, Chase Manhattan, and Manufacturers Hanover Trust made grants to the organization totaling $56,900. Most of this funding went to individual buildings or to programs with which the Board is involved.

Interfaith Adopt-a-Building. Adopt-a-Building is the Lower East Side church-supported community organization which established the East 11th Street Housing Movement. Adopt-a-Building has served as an intermediary between tenant groups and the legal system, the financial community, and real estate interests.

Chemical has been closely involved with Adopt-a-Building since 1969. The bank has provided the following grants for the East 11th Street project: in 1972, $2,500 for general support; in 1974, $5,000 to establish professional bookkeeping procedures; in 1975, $2,500 for administration, $5,000 for general support, and a $15,000 loan; and in 1976, $1,000 for general support. Chemical's staff has also contributed its financial and technical expertise.

For further information contact:
Barbara Fiorito
Vice President for Urban Affairs
Chemical Bank
20 Pine Street
New York, New York 10005

Michael Freedberg
East 11th Street Housing Movement
519 East 11th Street
New York, New York 10003

Footnotes

1. Chemical Bank Corporation, *Banking on New York*, (New York: Chemical Bank Corporation, 1976), p. 3.
2. Jim Kaplan, "When Tenants Take Over," *New York Sunday News Magazine*, 19 March 1976, p. 40.
3. Urban Homesteading Assistance Board, *Urban Homesteading Assistance Board Annual Report*, (New York: Urban Homesteading Assistance Board, 1976).
4. INFORM interview with Douglas Ades, Vice President, Urban Affairs Department, Chemical Bank, May, 1977.
5. Urban Homesteading Board, *op. cit.*, p. 2.
6. INFORM interview with Robert Schur, Executive Director, Association of Neighborhood Housing Developers, May, 1977.

Summary In 1972, in an effort to diversify its holdings and increase cash flow, Chicago Bridge and Iron (CBI), a leading fabricator of heavy-gauge-steel industrial storage facilities, purchased Fairlington, a 340-acre apartment development in Arlington, Va. That same year, CBI formed a real estate subsidiary, CBI-Fairmac, to manage these developments and recycle the Fairlington complex as 3,439 condominium townhouse and apartment units.

Although the Fairlington conversion experienced early losses as costs exceeded initial selling prices, it has subsequently proven to be extremely profitable. Built in 1942, the complex is just fifteen minutes from Washington, D.C., one of the strongest residential markets in the country. The units were constructed of top-quality materials and have been well maintained, providing a solid base for the renovation work. Because CBI purchased the existing buildings and land at an initial cost of $15,000 per unit,[1] it is able to invest up to $21,000 per unit in renovation work and still maintain a 14 percent pre-tax profit margin.[2]

Fairlington villages are a series of small clusters, many of which surround small parks. (Eduardo E. Latour)

Background Fairlington was built in the early 1940s for Pentagon executives who came to Washington after the U.S. entry into World War II. President Roosevelt commissioned the 3,439-unit project and allowed Houston architect Kenneth Franzheim his pick of skilled workers and scarce building materials. A generous budget, allowing an average cost of $10,300 per unit, permitted the installation of slate roofing, heavy hardwood doors, plaster walls, and brick and stone exteriors.

Franzheim also employed advanced planning techniques. Instead of a grid design, units were clustered in a variety of patterns, predominantly around private courtyards. Although there is a basic regularity to the overall design, the architect varied rooflines and entranceways, alternating long rows of houses with short ones and juxtaposing groups of units against each other. With only ten units per acre, there was ample room for large lawns and scattered trees. Built in a neo-Georgian style, with small porches and colonial-style windows and shutters, the units were clustered in a series of seven villages.

After the War, the government sold the complex to two Texas businessmen, who operated it as rental units from 1947 to 1959. In 1959, the Texans dissolved their partnership by flipping a coin. One retained the ownership of

Fairlington, worth an estimated $15 million and the other took the $4 million the project had in the bank. Leland Fikes, the winner, became sole owner of the complex and named one of his executives, Walter J. Hodges, General Manager. Fikes died in 1966, and two years later, his estate sold Fairlington to Hartford Fire Insurance. Hodges and another executive, J. D. Lee, became minority stockholders. In 1972, Hartford Fire, now part of ITT, sold the project to Chicago Bridge and Iron.

CBI's purchase was based on an appraisal of Fairlington as a rental project. In its cost analysis, the company allocated $15,000 per unit for building and land: a $51.6 million initial investment. A subsidiary, CBI-Fairmac, was formed with Hodges as President and Lee as Executive Vice President and Treasurer.

Under Hodges' management, Fairlington had been well maintained, and a sense of community spirit had been created. However, after thirty years, bathrooms and kitchens needed modern fixtures and appliances; exteriors needed a face-lift; and there was substantial underutilized space in the basements of all the units. Hodges believed that to obtain the greatest financial return from the modernization, the units should be renovated in phases and sold as condominiums.

Execution Since 1972, the Fairlington condominium conversion has been developed in phases by villages. Each village contains over 300 townhouse and apartment units. Existing tenants in a section under renovation are given ninety-day notices to vacate, and if they desire, can move to other rental units in the project.

In the conversion, each unit is renovated as follows:

• All mechanical systems are replaced, including wiring and plumbing, and individual gas-fired heating and cooling units are installed. (Originally, the buildings were heated with steam from large boiler units located in each village. Technical obsolescence of these systems made it impossible to reuse them.)

• Kitchens and baths are totally refurbished with new appliances, fixtures, tile, vanities, and cabinets.

• Slate roofs are insulated, and double-glazed windows are installed to reduce energy consumption.

• Tunnels which originally connected all units are sealed off, and the basements are finished to create recreation rooms, dens, baths, and laundries. This adds an average of 500 square feet of living space to each unit.

• Exterior masonry is cleaned and repointed; flashing and downspouts are replaced; all exterior trim is repainted; and new door and window hardware is installed.

• Exterior amenities are created through landscaping and the addition of fenced patios and decks.

All electrical lines are being placed underground, and colonial-style fixtures are being substituted for light poles. Parking areas are being expanded, sidewalks and streets are being repaired and resurfaced, and storm-drainage systems are being enlarged to handle the increased runoff. Extensive recreational facilities are also being provided. Each village has its own Olympic-sized swimming pool (and children's wading pool), bathhouse, paddle-tennis courts, tennis courts, basketball courts, and children's play area.

After conversion, most villages contain a selection of ten models ranging from 712 square feet to 2,145 square feet. The smallest models are on one floor and have one bedroom, while larger houses have three bedrooms, three baths, and a den. The most popular model, which accounts for 60 percent of the total complex, is a 1,500-square-foot triplex with two bedrooms, two baths, and a den. The smallest units in the project are priced as low as $38,500, while the most expensive reach $70,000. Financing plans have been arranged which allow down payments as low as 5 percent of the purchase price.

A low-key sales strategy has been adopted. Salespeople are paid straight salaries, and prospective buyers are encouraged to tour the grounds and models unescorted. In Village I, existing tenants bought 73 percent of the townhouses, while in Village II, the figure was down to 62 percent. As the purchase prices have risen, less than 50 percent of the former tenants have been able to purchase the renovated units. The average Fairlington homeowner has an annual income of $32,000.[3]

The development has a good reputation, and 45 percent of its sales come from referrals. Community activities, such as art shows and house tours, also provide useful marketing tools. Fairlington has an annual advertising and promotion budget of $475,000, with 55 percent allotted to newspapers, 40 percent to television, and 5 percent to radio.[4]

By mid-1977, 2,750 units had been completed and sold. At a production rate of 25 units per week, the remaining 700 units were expected to be complete by the end of 1977, and the total project sold out by early 1978.

Costs To cover the costs of the renovation, the project's $17 million five-year loan was refinanced to $24 million at a half percentage point over prime. As the condominiums are sold, the company pays 115 percent of the money it has borrowed on each unit, gradually reducing the principle on the entire loan. Other funds for the renovation program are provided from cash generated by condominium sales.

In 1976, the company spent about $21,000 to renovate each unit and the surrounding grounds. The budget for an average unit breaks down as follows:[5]

Construction costs		$17,000
Permits	$ 400	
Plumbing	3,200	
Electrical	1,600	
Heating/air conditioning	1,100	
Ventilation	1,100	
Insulation/weatherproofing	150	
Masonry	350	
Cleaning	250	
Finishing costs:		
Lower bath/laundry	1,200	
Upper bath	860	
Kitchen	2,200	
Bedrooms/hallway	900	
Living and dining room	1,090	
Basement	1,900	
Patio/fencing	700	
Site improvements, including landscaping and recreational facilities	2,000	
Construction field overhead	2,000	
Total Renovation Costs/ average unit.		$21,000
Other costs per unit average:		
Land and existing unit	$15,000	
Warranty work and customer service	400	
Sales and marketing	3,000	
Financing and closing cost	3,200	
Administrative overhead	1,200	
Subtotal/other costs		$22,800
TOTAL Cost/Average Unit		$43,800

According to Hodges, since 1972, the average purchase price has risen from $36,000 to $51,000 per unit, allowing CBI-Fairmac a $7,200 pre-tax profit or a 14 percent pre-tax margin on each sale.[6]

Problems Cost controls have been developed through bitter experience. Since contractors were uncertain about the extent of renovation the units required most submitted high bids to protect themselves. Hodges first tried to control renovation costs by forming his own construction operation. However, his crews were inexperienced, and a few trained men had to teach and supervise a work force that eventually grew to 700. The in-house construction firm produced less than one house per day. In the first two years, renovation costs averaged $20,000 per unit. Total unit costs reached $41,000, and the cost of borrowing money shot up. The average price of the first 400 sales was only $36,000 resulting in a $5,000 loss per unit and a $2 million reduction in working capital in 1973.[7]

In order to increase efficiency and lower unit costs, Hodges radically altered his operation in 1974. The Fairlington Construction Company was disbanded, and the most skilled and industrious workers were asked to form their own independent subcontracting firms to work on a piecework basis. With the best workers receiving the highest wages and overtime, production jumped from less than one house a day to three and then to over four. Improved cost control and better accounting systems also helped reduce renovation costs by 25 percent.

In addition to construction problems, Hodges faced problems with Arlington County officials. In 1972, Virginia's condominium law and much of the county building code were not applicable to renovation work. Extensive meetings with county officials were required to establish guidelines for the construction work and the sales program.

Other problems were encountered in coordinating the construction activities with tenant relocation. Those rental units which were not ready to be renovated were hard to keep occupied. In some cases, tenants failed to receive adequate information about construction schedules. They tended to move out in anticipation of the renovation work, reducing the project's annual income.

Benefits After overcoming the initial construction management and pricing problems, Fairlington has become a major financial success for CBI. Due to the constant turnover of government personnel, the Washington, D.C., area has represented an exceptionally strong housing market during the 1970s. The price of houses has increased steadily along with the market demand. CBI-Fairmac will continue its management contract to maintain the condominium project for the new owners, and will receive brokerage commissions for the resale of condominiums.

The project has won many awards, including the first in a new category created in 1974 by the local chapter of the National Association of Home Builders: Revitalization of Community and Excellence in Restoration.

The Fairlington conversion has created construction jobs for the Arlington community, and has resulted in 3,439 units of modern housing at prices nearly 25 percent less than competitive new construction in the area. The Fairlington units retail at approximately $34 per square foot, compared with an estimated $45 per square foot cost for similar new housing.[8]

The Company Chicago Bridge and Iron Company (CBI) is a leading fabricator of heavy-gauge steel-plate structures. It was founded in 1889, and is headquartered in Oak Brook, Illinois. CBI owns a 92 percent interest in CBI-Fairmac, with the remaining 8 percent held by the subsidiary's two top officers, Walter Hodges and J. D. Lee.

Net income for the parent company increased 36 percent in 1976 to nearly $56 million, or $5.73 per share on total sales of $577 million. Corresponding figures for 1975 were $41 million and $564 million. CBI-Fairmac contributed about 50 cents per share, or $4.86 million, to CBI's net earnings in 1976, approximately 9 percent of the parent company's net income.

For further information contact:
Walter J. Hodges
President
CBI-Fairmac Corporation
3118 South Abington Street
Arlington, Virginia 22206

Footnotes

1. Michael Robinson, "Is This the Hottest Condo Conversion in the Country?," *House & Home*, August, 1975, p. 51.
2. Robinson, *op. cit.,* p. 51, updated by INFORM interview with W. J. Hodges, President, CBI-Fairmac Corporation, May, 1977.
3. INFORM interview with W. J. Hodges, President, CBI-Fairmac Corporation, May, 1977.
4. Robinson, *op. cit.,* p. 53.
5. Robinson, *op. cit.,* updated by INFORM interview with W. J. Hodges, President, CBI-Fairmac Corporation, May, 1977.
6. INFORM interview with W. J. Hodges, President, CBI-Fairmac Corporation, May, 1977.
7. Robinson, *op. cit.,* p. 51.
8. John Sower, "Financing and Developing Large Commercial Preservation Projects," *Economic Benefits of Preserving Old Buildings* (Washington, D.C.: Preservation Press, National Trust for Historic Preservation, 1976), p. 137.

Summary In response to the turmoil of the late 1960s, New York's Citibank assigned several of its officers the task of improving banking services and community relations in inner-city neighborhoods. One of these officers, Norman Hunte, was assigned to Jamaica, Queens. In the early 1970s, he was alarmed by the accelerating deterioration of the area and worked closely with local neighborhood groups to stabilize it. Residents of Baisley Park, a section of Jamaica, were concerned about their degenerating neighborhood and the lack of financial commitment by the local banks. They organized, and together with Hunte, rallied community, financial, and government support, resulting in the formation of a Neighborhood Housing Services (NHS) in Jamaica in 1974. NHS-Jamaica, part of a growing national movement, is a nonprofit organization which counsels neighborhood residents on financial and housing matters, stimulates lending by financial institutions in neighborhoods showing early signs of deterioration, and establishes a high-risk loan pool for home-improvement loans. Hunte serves as Treasurer of NHS-Jamaica and is on the organization's Board of Directors. With his encouragement, as well as that of other interested bankers, financial institutions in Jamaica have committed over $1.2 million in conventional home-improvement and mortgage loans.

Background In the early 1970s, Jamaica was experiencing the classic problems of urban decay: absentee ownership was increasing; more and more houses were being abandoned or poorly maintained; and there was a growing inability among homeowners to obtain mortgages and home-improvement loans.

Several local organizations were formed to deal with these problems, including Baisley Neighbors in Housing, a group which helped tenants with problems caused by absentee landlords and tried to persuade banks to grant loans and mortgages. Some residents of Baisley Park (population 8,200) also sought advice from Norman Hunte and Sherman Brown, Hunte's counterpart at Chase Manhattan Bank.

Norman Hunte, Assistant Vice President for the Street Banking Unit at Citibank, has a long history of community involvement, especially in Jamaica. In 1968, he recognized a growing juvenile crime problem, at least partially brought on by high teenage unemployment, and instituted a summer employment program, backed by Citibank, among gang members. Beginning in 1972, Hunte worked from a storefront office, counseling residents of South Queens, the section of the borough in which Jamaica is located, in all aspects of financial management.

Because of his long experience, Hunte was asked by Citibank to head its Street Banking Unit in 1973 in its first location, South Jamaica. The Street Banking Unit makes consumer loans to people who are turned down at the bank's branches. In 1976, it made 521 loans to 3 percent of those who applied. It provides financial assistance to independent businesses, and assists people in getting professional help with social problems, such as compulsive gambling.

Hunte and Sherman Brown urged community leaders, the Office of Jamacia Planning and Development, and other financial institutions to establish an organization to seek solutions. At their urging, Citibank helped finance a visit to Pittsburgh by about ten Baisley Park residents in 1973. These residents went to investigate NHS-Pittsburgh, the first Neighborhood Housing Services in the nation, formed in 1968.

NHS-Pittsburgh, located in a section known as the Central North Side, was established through the efforts of interested residents and public officials, who sought and finally obtained the financial backing of local banks. The Central North Side (population 7,900; 46.5 percent black) underwent significant disinvestment and decline during the 1960s. Its turn-of-the-century row houses, 23 percent owner-occupied, were in need of major renovation. However, financing from the city's banks was not forthcoming. NHS-Pittsburgh, still in operation today, provides financial assistance through a high-risk revolving loan fund; obtains the backing of banks to grant loans; helps residents comply with building- and health-code standards; supervises all contracted rehabilitation work; establishes a maintenance program; offers financial and home-repair counseling; and plans neighborhood capital improvements. By 1974, over 350 homes had been renovated using loans from the high-risk revolving loan fund. With 80 percent of the housing in the area brought up to code, property values gradually increased. The success of NHS-Pittsburgh has provided an example for other neighborhoods; almost forty other cities have developed programs based on the Pittsburgh model.

The staff of NHS-Pittsburgh pinpointed four elements of critical importance to the formation of NHS-Jamaica:

1. A target area of residents who wish to preserve their home and community.

2. A firm commitment from the financial industry to make all bankable loans for the target area, and to pay for the administrative cost of an NHS office.

3. Availability of a revolving loan fund for non-bankable loans within the target area.

4. City support to ensure enforcement of minimal code compliance and improvement of public services.[1]

Baisley Park, a predominantly black neighborhood, needed the program and seemed to offer a good chance for success. Of its 2,100 dwellings, 1,650 were one- and two-family homes, with 67 percent owner-occupied, a relatively high level. About half the housing was built prior to 1939, but much of the rest was of comparatively recent construction: 28 percent between 1940 and 1959, and 21 percent since 1960. The average price of a house was about $20,000. Many homes had flower gardens and well-tended yards, and the area had shaded streets, a park, a pond, and several playgrounds. Its community leaders were active and capable.

However, there were some alarming developments too. Absentee ownership of housing increased from 26 percent to 33 percent between 1960 and 1970. Only 51 percent of the residents remained in the same house between 1965 and 1970, compared to 64 percent between 1955 and 1960. Vacant properties were becoming a problem: eleven houses and eight commercial buildings were burned out, sealed, or abandoned by 1970, further discouraging residents from making repairs. Mortgages and home-improvement loans were hard to obtain, and the quality of public services was diminishing.

LAND USE

SINGLE AND TWO FAMILY DETACHED

SINGLE FAMILY ATTACHED

THREE AND FOUR FAMILY

RETAIL

VACANT LAND

INSTITUTIONAL

OPEN SPACE

Execution In 1974, after a year devoted to preliminary research and securing financial support, NHS-Jamaica was formed. A Board of Directors was chosen from among the active community and business participants. Sherman Brown of Chase Manhattan was elected President of the NHS-Jamaica Board. Norman Hunte became a Board member and the organization's Treasurer. To assure local control of the Board, eight of its fifteen members are community residents.

Hunte and Brown approached many financial institutions before they successfully managed to obtain enough firm commitments to finance NHS-Jamaica's operating expenses. In addition to the financial backing of their own banks—Citibank, $10,000 and Chase Manhattan, $12,500—they received contributions from Bankers Trust, $4,000, Manufacturers Hanover Trust, $2,500, the First Federal Savings and Loan Association, $1,000, and The Savings Bank Association, $20,000. Whenever possible, NHS-Jamaica tried to get a multi-year commitment from these institutions.

Some of the above financial institutions also contributed office equipment, supplies, meeting rooms, funds for special summer projects, clerical assistance, accounting services, salaried community workers, and legal planning advice.

In September, 1974, the Board of NHS-Jamaica hired James Cook to direct the program. Cook, who left a position as Associate Director of NHS-Pittsburgh to come to Jamaica, hired two additional staff members: an Assistant Director, and an Administrative Assistant/Secretary. NHS-Jamaica then became operational.

While temporary headquarters were set up in the Office of Planning in Jamaica, Cook convinced the Board that to more fully understand the needs and problems of the target area's residents, the NHS-Jamaica office should be located in Baisley Park. NHS-Jamaica bought a dilapidated house in Baisley Park for $5,000, and renovated it for $16,000. In summer, 1975, the house became the organization's headquarters.

Cook spoke to community groups about NHS-Jamaica and distributed flyers describing its services. Hunte and Brown helped secure commitments from Citibank, Chase, and other local financial institutions to make conventional home-improvement and mortgage loans to all qualified applicants. Since the inception of NHS-Jamaica, financial institutions have made loans totaling over $1.2 million. The organization aims for a three-to-one ratio of conventional loans to high-risk loans.

Through its contacts with city officials, NHS-Jamaica also attempts to improve the quality of community services, such as garbage removal and street maintenance, in Baisley Park.

NHS-Jamaica has four principal programs:

The High Risk Revolving Loan Fund. This Fund makes long-term, low-interest loans to high-risk homeowners for home improvements to meet minimal building-code standards. In 1975, it received grants from the following foundations: The Rockefeller Brothers Fund, $60,000; The Taconic Foundation, $25,000; the New York Community Trust, $10,000; and the Klingenstein Foundation, $10,000. In addition, an $85,000 matching fund was established by the Urban Reinvestment Task Force, which is made up of representatives of the federal financial regulatory agencies and the Secretary of the U.S. Department of Housing and Urban Development. The Task Force's main objective is to further the establishment of the NHS nationally.

A loan committee, composed of three local residents and two representatives of the business community, reviews each application, approves loans, and sets interest rates and monthly payments based on the applicant's ability to pay. Interest rates are flexible, ranging from 0 percent to 8 percent, with the average loan made at 3 percent. Repayment terms run from five to fifteen years, depending on the borrower's ability to pay.

After guiding the applicant through the qualifying stage, NHS-Jamaica's staff examine the property and secure the services of a reputable contractor; explain the process; monitor the progress of the renovation; and provide follow-up services.

Between the inception of the program in 1975 and April, 1977, 68 high-risk loans for home improvements were approved, representing a total outlay of $150,000. These loans averaged $2,900, with a $5,000 ceiling. The average recipient has resided in Baisley Park for over ten years and is employed. Senior citizens on pensions and Social Security received 25 percent of the loans.

The following case helps illustrate the program:

Mr. P, 39, single and disabled, lived with his 74-year-old, widowed mother in a single-family home. Together they received Social Security and Supplemental Security Income, amounting to $406.16 per month. They had no mortgage, a small savings account, and monthly housing expenses which permitted no financial flexibility. A year before the implementation of NHS, their converted boiler ceased to function. Mr. P contacted various public agencies for assistance, but was refused. After reading a news article describing the NHS program, Mr. P applied for a loan. Within five days a High Risk Loan was granted to cover the cost of replacing the boiler and repairing the heating system, at a rate and term suited to Mr. P's ability to repay. Encouraged, he applied $500 in personal savings toward the cost of repairs.[2]

To date, Cook has been satisfied with the results of the High Risk Revolving Loan Fund. There have been no foreclosures or write-offs. By monitoring the loans and carefully selecting the recipients, Cook and his staff are able to keep abreast of delinquencies.

Financial Counseling. The NHS has found that stabilizing the finances of individual families helps stabilize the overall community. The staff, aided by Hunte and Brown, either assist applicants with debt consolidation and credit counseling, or refer them to the proper community service agency. Currently, between 35 and 50 people per month take advantage of this counseling service.

NHS-Jamaica offered an example of a Baisley Park resident who has come to them for aid:

Mr. C, 63, had four dependents and was recently married. He was the owner of a two-family home with a mortgage from a savings and loan association. Laid off from his job as a trucker, he was unable to secure another job because of heart trouble, age, and tension. He supported his family on unemployment benefits until they ran out; mortgage payments fell behind, and eventually Mr. C was foreclosed by the savings and loan association. He approached NHS-Jamaica, which contacted the savings and loan association and negotiated a delay of the foreclosure action. The staff helped Mr. C untangle his financial problems, and helped secure part-time work for both Mr. C and his wife. The organization also provided financing to bring the mortgage up to date, and contracted to have repairs made on the property.[3]

Home Maintenance Education. The NHS recognizes that preventive maintenance is the most cost-effective form of neighborhood conservation. NHS-Jamaica, in cooperation with the Queens branch of the New York Urban League, which also provides facilities, and York College's Division of Adult and Continuing Education, initiated a Home Maintenance Training Program to teach community residents basic techniques in carpentry, plumbing, and electrical wiring. Some students of the Program have been put to work rehabilitating a foreclosed property obtained from HUD. An additional course has been developed to train community youths to do minor home repairs for older residents.

The original home maintenance course has increased from one to three sessions per week, and is of twelve weeks duration. An advanced course has been added to meet growing demand. The Program is partly financed by a $32,000 grant from the Urban Reinvestment Task Force. About 150 community residents have taken advantage of this Program.

Urban Homesteading. About fifty properties in Baisley Park have been the subject of foreclosure by the Federal Housing Administration (FHA). Since 1976, Cook has been negotiating with FHA and city officials to establish an urban-homesteading program in the neighborhood, which would be partially financed under Section 312 of the Federal Housing Act of 1964, and administered by the city's Housing and Development Administration (HDA).

Baisley Park streetscape. (Neighborhood Housing Services—Jamaica)

Debris-filled yards. Neighborhood Housing Services—Jamaica tries to deal with deterioration before it becomes widespread. (Neighborhood Housing Services—Jamaica)

Under Section 312, loans at 3 percent interest, and up to a maximum of $3,450, would be available to homeowners who wish to renovate. The staff of NHS-Jamaica have been counseling several potential homesteaders.

NHS-Jamaica studies estimate that renovation of each house will cost about $10,000. Since urban homesteaders do not receive clear title to a property for three years, banks will not grant conventional loans. Therefore, Cook hopes to finance the approximate $6,550 differential between Section 312's maximum loan and the cost of renovation through NHS-Jamaica's High Risk Revolving Loan Fund. With the assistance of the project's staff, two urban homesteaders have already obtained contractors for renovation. However, construction is being delayed until the HDA gives clearance to the renovation. Cook is optimistic that the program will soon be operational.

Costs NHS-Jamaica's budget for 1976 was $54,254, of which $45,374 was used to pay salaries and fringe benefits for the staff of three. Operating expenses, including office rental, repair, and maintenance, supplies, utilities, insurance, legal expenses, credit membership, printing costs, and travel, totaled $8,880. The budget for 1977 is $60,000 and is subject to monthly review by the Board.

Citibank commits $10,000 per year toward the project's operating expenses and has a three-year renewable commitment. The bank also donates administrative services, such as Hunte's time and expertise. Donations by financial institutions pay all operating costs. In 1975, foundation grants, totaling $125,000, and an $85,000 grant from the federal Urban Reinvestment Task Force served the High Risk Revolving Loan Fund.

Problems An increased work load and a limited budget have strained NHS-Jamaica's resources. Cook and his staff also feel that New York City government should become more directly involved in Baisley Park by upgrading services and enforcing building-code standards for single-family units.

Benefits Financial support of NHS-Jamaica has proven to be a sensible and profitable business investment. As indicated above, lending institutions have made $1.2 million in conventional home-improvement loans in the area since the project's inception in 1975. About 250 homes have been renovated using bank loans and the High Risk Revolving Loan Fund.

Since the average value of homes in Baisley Park has increased, more property tax revenues will be coming to the city. Home values now range from $20,000 to $35,000, up from a $20,000 average. Another sign of the community's improving economics is that for the first time in seven years, a new house is being built.

Through the help of Norman Hunte, Citibank has gained new customers, increased visibility, and goodwill from the residents of Baisley Park. NHS-Jamaica and Citibank have been featured in numerous articles in the *New York Times*, the *New York Post*, and the *New York Daily News*.

The Company Citibank, the largest bank in New York and the second largest in the world, is part of the holding company, Citicorp. Citibank has about 270 branch offices in the New York metropolitan area.

The holding company's net interest income for 1976 amounted to $1.78 billion, an increase of 10.5 percent over 1975's $1.61 billion. Net income for the same period rose 15 percent from $349.9 million to $401.4 million.

Other Preservation Activities/Bedford-Stuyvesant Restoration Corporation. Citibank has provided $50,000 in operating capital for 1976 to the Bedford-Stuyvesant Restoration Corporation. Bedford-Stuyvesant, a section of Brooklyn, is one of the largest and poorest black communities in the nation. The bank's president, William I. Spencer, has led fund-raising efforts for the Restoration Corporation.

Economic Development Center. Citibank also assists New Yorkers through its Economic Development Center (EDC), established in 1971. The EDC makes loans in three kinds of situations:

1. To minority entrepreneurs for help in purchasing, expanding, or starting a business.

2. To businesses that may not be minority-owned, but will create or increase employment for New Yorkers.

3. To nonprofit groups and firms whose activities result in a measurable improvement of the environment.[3]

To these businesses, Citibank provides technical assistance in the form of financial counseling and sales analysis, and if necessary, refers the businesses to other agencies.

South Street Seaport. Citibank pledged a five-year, $100,000 grant to the South Street Seaport Museum in 1976, to be used for the renovation and maintenance of piers 15 and 16. The two piers are at the center of the Seaport, which today is a popular shopping and sightseeing attraction, as well as a reminder of the Port of New York's history.

For further information contact:
Norman Hunte
Assistant Vice President, Urban Community Affairs
Citibank
399 Park Avenue
New York, New York 10022

James Cook
Director
NHS-Jamaica
152-13 118th Avenue
Jamaica, New York 11434

Footnotes

1. Neighborhood Housing Services of Jamaica, Inc., *Neighborhood Housing Services of Jamaica, Inc., First Annual Report*, (New York: Neighborhood Housing Services of Jamaica, Inc., May 31, 1976), pp. 3-4.
2. *Ibid.*, p. 11.
3. *Ibid.*, p. 12.

Summary In 1971, the multi-billion-dollar Connecticut Mutual Life Insurance Co., concerned by the deterioration of Asylum Hill, its home area just west of downtown Hartford, encouraged other local businesses to undertake a study of the Hill's problems and needs. In 1972, the study resulted in the formation of Asylum Hill, Inc., a nonprofit organization which attempts to improve the neighborhood and attract employees of local companies to live as well as work there. As a further incentive to promote owner-occupancy in Asylum Hill, in summer, 1975, Connecticut Mutual Life created a $150,000 revolving loan pool through which its employees and the employees of the nearby St. Francis Hospital could obtain short-term loans to purchase and renovate houses at a 6 percent interest rate, well below the going market rate. The company hired the Connecticut Housing Investment Fund (CHIF), a nonprofit organization which specializes in assisting families in purchasing homes, to screen and counsel applicants and arrange financing. So far, thirteen families have taken advantage of the program. In March, 1977, Connecticut Mutual lowered the interest rate to 3 percent and extended these benefits to city employees and employees of the other major contributors to Asylum Hill, Inc.

Background Connecticut Mutual has maintained its headquarters in Asylum Hill since 1926. At the turn of the century, the streets were lined with large late-Victorian houses, and the residents included Hartford's most successful businessmen and citizens (Mark Twain once live there). But, as in many other inner-city neighborhoods, the flight to the suburbs had taken its toll. Crime and deteriorating houses were becoming major problems. The population, which today consists mostly of students, the elderly, transient younger people, and welfare recipients, is racially mixed: approximately 50 percent white, 30 percent black, and 20 percent Hispanic.

The area is a mixture of modern office buildings, Victorian and more modern houses, and older apartment buildings. The housing stock is about one-third one- and two-family residences and two-thirds four-family dwellings or apartments. Many period houses were demolished in order to build apartments. However, many of the Victorian-style houses which remain possess fine architectural details and such decorative amenities as stained-glass windows and magnificent interior woodwork.

More than 25,000 people work in Asylum Hill, though just 9,000 live there; Connecticut Mutual itself has 1,400 workers in its home office.

Connecticut Housing Investment Fund. The Connecticut Housing Investment Fund (CHIF), which administers the revolving loan pool, is a nonprofit organization founded in 1965 to promote open housing in the Hartford suburbs. Headquartered in Hartford and funded by corporate, foundation, and individual contributions, its operations have expanded into broader areas of housing needs as well as other locations. It now has offices in Waterbury, Stamford, and New Haven. The CHIF's operations include engaging in service contracts with many corporations to assist relocated employees in finding adequate housing, and arranging second mortgages for home buyers who cannot meet all the financial requirements for the purchase of a house. The CHIF also provides free advice on real estate, credit, mortgages, and renovation to prospective home buyers. In February, 1975, the CHIF created a Back to the City Program which encourages and counsels middle-income families contemplating buying houses in Hartford. It helped 64 families relocate there in 1975 and 1976.

Execution

Asylum Hill, Inc. Connecticut Mutual's management recognized the problems and potential of Asylum Hill in 1971. The company, supported by its corporate neighbors, Aetna Life and Casualty, the Hartford Insurance Group, and the Society for Savings, initiated a fact-finding study of Asylum Hill's needs and problems, outlined a plan of action, and sought additional local backing. As a result of this study, Asylum Hill, Inc., was founded in February, 1972. Its initial budget of $118,000 included provision for a full-time director. By 1976, the budget had expanded to $144,000.*

The first priority of this nonprofit, neighborhood-improvement association was to stabilize the area to attract potential home buyers. Since crime was a major concern, high-intensity streetlights were installed with the aid of the city, and citizen and canine patrols were established. In addition, traffic patterns were changed by creating one-way streets and cul-de-sacs to decrease traffic flow through the neighborhood. To strengthen community spirit and attract middle-class interest, Asylum Hill, Inc., sponsors an annual Octoberfest, an outdoor festival including arts and crafts displays, entertainment, food, and walking tours of the area. Asylum Hill, Inc., also fosters the establishment of civic organizations. Several organizations—West Hill Organization, Central Asylum Hill Association, Laurel Gardens and Sigourney Square Civic Association—have been formed. Their programs include: social events for children and adults; zoning and code-enforcement courses at a local educational institution; summer musical programs in the park; lawn-care advice; an annual plant sale; and gardening plots on some

*The major contributors in 1976 were:

Aetna Life & Casualty	$55,000
The Hartford Insurance Group	36,650
Connecticut Mutual Life	23,000
Society For Savings	23,000
Hartford Home Savings & Loan	2,000
Veeder Industries	1,750
Mechanics Savings Bank	1,350
Connecticut Bank & Trust	600
St. Joseph Cathedral	500
State Bank for Savings	260
Total	$144,110

140

of Aetna's property. Asylum Hill, Inc., coordinates these diverse activities, serves as a resource center, and publishes a local newspaper, *The Hill Ink*, distributed free to area residents.

Establishment of Revolving Loan Pool.
Connecticut Mutual realized that for the neighborhood to improve further, more middle-income people had to move there. In 1975, the company created a $150,000 revolving loan fund, as an incentive enabling potential home buyers to purchase and renovate houses. The interest charge was first set at 6 percent, well below the prevailing market price; and later, in March, 1977, it was lowered to 3 percent, about one-third the market rate. The average cost of a house in the area is $20,000 to $30,000, with renovation costing $10,000 to $15,000. The average short-term loan is about $45,000, including purchase price and renovation, and has a duration of about six months. Once renovation is completed, the owner obtains a conventional long-term mortgage and repays the interim loan. There is usually no difficulty in securing a long-term mortgage.

Connecticut Mutual hired the CHIF to administer the program in October, 1975. The CHIF screens and counsels potential home buyers, and arranges a short-term loan when a house is selected. Fees for its services range from $50 to $350 per case depending on staff time and final disposition. The CHIF also assists in arranging permanent mortgages from local banks when rehabilitation is completed.

Connecticut Mutual is responsible for the promotion of the program. In summer, 1975, the company began a detailed promotional campaign on Asylum Hill, consisting of articles in its house publications and local newspapers, slide shows and dinners for interested employees, and walking tours of the area.

Another objective was outlined by Connecticut Mutual's President, Edward B. Bates:

We not only hope to stimulate interest in buying homes but also hope to stimulate interest in similar action programs by other companies in the area.[1]

In April, 1976, Aetna Life & Casualty

Company established a revolving low-interest, short-term loan fund. The Connecticut Bank and Trust Company is also providing mortgages to employees with interest rates below those of the prevailing market. In another section of Hartford, Trinity College, Hartford Hospital, and the Institute of Living have recently announced similar programs for their employees.

Since the inception of Connecticut Mutual's revolving loan pool, about 13 families have taken advantage of the loan program, and 52 families have moved to the area.

In order to increase participation and expand the pool of eligible borrowers, Connecticut Mutual lowered the interest rate on its loans to 3 percent and extended borrowing privileges to all city employees and employees of the

other major contributors to Asylum Hill, Inc. (Aetna Life & Casualty, the Hartford Insurance Group, and the Society for Savings). Jill Diskan of the CHIF reports that since the interest rate was lowered, inquiries have increased from 12 to 35 per month. In this period, twelve houses have been sold through the CHIF, with six buyers utilizing Connecticut Mutual's revolving pool.

A house in Asylum Hill, before renovation with Connecticut Mutual's help.

Costs Connecticut Mutual contributed $150,000 to create the short-term revolving fund. When this amount is committed, Connecticut Mutual has indicated its intent to contribute more. In addition, the company pays the CHIF for its administration of the program, and Connecticut Mutual employees help promote it. Figures for these costs are not available. In 1976, the company's annual contribution to Asylum Hill, Inc., was $23,000.

Problems Connecticut Mutual says that there are no existing problems. However, it anticipates the displacement of local residents and escalating real estate prices within the foreseeable future.

Benefits Because of the publicity on Asylum Hill, real estate prices have increased 10 percent since the inception of the program in late 1972. Although this is not a significant increase, it represents a reversal of the 10 percent annual decrease in property values prior to the program's inception, and indicates that Asylum Hill's real estate is stabilizing. The number of local real estate agents has increased from one to four since Connecticut Mutual became involved in the community.

In mid-1976, a Neighborhood Housing Services (see Citibank) was established in the Sigourney Square section of Asylum Hill. In its first year, it made about forty home loans.

In another sign of Asylum Hill's changing character, a private developer recently purchased property near Connecticut Mutual's headquarters and plans to build a childcare center there. This facility, scheduled for completion in fall, 1977, will accommodate 100 children.

Connecticut Mutual has created good will among its employees, and also has influenced other corporations to establish similar loan programs. Mrs. Lurayn Haines, the second Connecticut Mutual employee to relocate there stated:

I like cities. I plan to stay with the company so I figured why not live close to it? ... And let's face it, the price is a bargain.[2]

In March, 1977, the company received the CHIF's second annual Corporate Responsibility in Housing Award. The citation stated:

This year we honor Connecticut Mutual Life Insurance Company for its creative approach to employee housing needs, an approach which also emphasizes corporate involvement in the community. ... Connecticut Mutual Life's is an excellent example to the corporate and business community. It provides a stimulus for others to begin thinking about corporate responsibility in satisfying employee housing needs and to define the corporate role in the neighborhood, community, and region in which offices are located.[3]

The Company Connecticut Mutual, founded in 1846, is the oldest life insurance company in Connecticut and the sixth oldest in the United States. Principally a life insurance company, its product line also includes guaranteed, variable, and accumulation annuity plans, individual pension and profit-sharing plans, and disability-income plans. Connecticut Mutual ranked tenth among American mutual companies, with assets of $3.95 billion in 1976, up from 1975's figure of $3.67 billion. Net investment income also rose from $198 million in 1975 to $212 million in 1976.

For further information contact:
Terry M. D'Italia
Associate Consultant, Communications Division
Connecticut Mutual Life Insurance Company
140 Garden Street
Hartford, Connecticut 06115

Jill Diskan
Director
Back to the City
Connecticut Home Improvement Fund
121 Tremont Street
Hartford, Connecticut 06105

Jack D. Middleton
Executive Director
Asylum Hill, Inc.
121 Sigourney Street
Hartford, Connecticut 06105

Footnotes

1. "Housing Owner Plan Signed," *Hartford Times*, 16 October 1975.
2. Terry D'Italia, "Collins Considers Asylum Hill Home," *CML News*, 15 April 1976.
3. Connecticut Housing Investment Fund, *Second Annual Connecticut Housing Investment Fund Corporate Social Responsibility in Housing Award and the 10 Plus 3 Anniversary of Connecticut Housing Investment Fund, Dinner Program*, (Hartford: Connecticut Housing Investment Fund, March 2, 1977), p. 1.

Summary Eastman Kodak has long taken an active interest in the well being of Rochester, its home community. In 1968, the company, in response to requests for help from WEDGE, a local community action group, became involved in the effort to revitalize Brown Square, a rapidly deteriorating area adjacent to company headquarters. Kodak contributed $150,000 to build a new neighborhood park. Kodak and other local businesses are contributing personnel, money, and ideas to help revitalize the neighborhood. These donations, together with the efforts of local community groups, are improving the Brown Square area.

Background In the early 1800s, Matthew and Francis Brown developed a millrace along the Genesee Falls, utilizing its water to generate power. This area became one of the first industrial sections in Rochester. The Browns built their homes and designed a park—later deeded to the city— adjacent to the falls and the mill. The area became known as Brown Square.

Through the years, the composition of the neighborhood which grew up in this 216-acre area changed. The number of buildings run by absentee landlords increased; junkyards flourished; a railroad track bisected the area; businesses were left vacant; and buildings decayed.

However, there are still many houses—mostly single-family units dating from the nineteenth and twentieth centuries—that are well maintained or at least structurally sound. The neighborhood has many tree-lined streets, well-maintained yards, and a strong community spirit.

Brown Square's population of about 1,100 people is approximately 55 percent white, primarily of Italian extraction; 29 percent Hispanic, and 16 percent black. Of the Italians, 90 percent are homeowners and 29 percent are retired. However, overall less than 35 percent of the households are owner-occupied. Unemployment fluctuates, but as of mid-1977, it was high.

In 1967, the City of Rochester requested U.S. Department of Housing and Urban Development (HUD) sponsorship of an urban-renewal plan for Brown Square. But this project did not materialize due to lack of federal funding. Since help from HUD was not forthcoming, parishioners of nearby downtown churches decided to mobilize the residents of the area to try to improve their own living conditions. They enlisted a local resident, Mrs. Jenette Major, to organize the community. As a result of these initiatives, WEDGE, a neighborhood action group dedicated to improving the physical surroundings and fostering economic growth in Brown Square, was founded in 1967.

Award-winning house in the "Fix-Up '76" Program.

Execution In 1968, when WEDGE decided to open an operations office, it approached its corporate neighbor, Eastman Kodak, for a loan to purchase a building. Kodak agreed to supply the money if WEDGE would apply to the Community Chest for membership as a social agency and for operating funds. Both requests were made and granted, and Kodak donated the money WEDGE needed to buy the building.

Between 1968 and 1973, WEDGE organized meetings and social events to unify the neighborhood, and solicited residents' suggestions for improving the area. Based on these suggestions and on the research of Gruen Associates, a professional planning firm whose work on the project was underwritten by Kodak, a master plan, Total Community Renewal in Brown Square, was conceived.

Following the plan, in June, 1973, WEDGE set up the Brown Square Development Corporation (BSDC). The BSDC has four main objectives:

1. Providing for the construction of new housing and community facilities, the renovation of existing housing, and the creation of a viable urban service center.

2. Fostering private and public investment in Brown Square.

3. Encouraging orderly land development.

4. Assembling technical assistance from individuals and organizations for redeveloping Brown Square.[1]

The fourteen-member BSDC Board of Directors draws on all fields of expertise in the Rochester area. Three Board members are from WEDGE, two from businesses in Brown Square; two from its churches; two from industry; and five from Rochester's legal, financial, accounting, real estate, and construction sectors. Kodak presently has two employees on the Board. A member of WEDGE must serve as Chairman or Vice Chairman. There is a full-time Director. The 1977 BSDC budget is about $56,000, entirely raised from private sources, including Kodak. The company also donates in-kind services.

Since the BSDC's inception, its staff and Board members, along with local residents, have conducted several surveys. An exploratory economic analysis examined possible reuses of existing commercial, industrial, and residental structures. A diagnostic family survey collected information on area households and computerized it for future use. Property maps were prepared in detail. A structural-qualifications survey examined the existing housing stock and recommended needed repairs. In a sample section, more detailed inspections and cost estimates for repairs were made.

In late 1976, another Kodak employee, who is a BSDC Board Member, surveyed existing and required community service agencies in the Brown Square area in an attempt to centralize the agencies in one location.

Based on these surveys, the BSDC is currently considering several projects:

1. Setting up a revolving fund for buying and rehabilitating houses, which would allow houses to be rented with an option to buy.

2. Establishing a Neighborhood Housing Services agency (see Citibank and Tasty Baking). However, to qualify for this program, the area must cover one square mile. The Brown Square area is too small, so the BSDC is considering broadening its base to include the adjacent Edgerton area.

3. Building about 120 single-family rental units, to be financed by developers and local banks and managed by the BSDC.

In 1976, the BSDC, WEDGE, and the American Jewish Society for Service, a New York-based organization, sponsored FIX-UP '76, a seven-week summer project in which twelve young people, aged 16 to 21, from all over the country, donated their services along with the Director of the American Jewish Society for Service, his wife, and two of the Society's camp counselors to renovate and repaint about 25 Brown Square houses. Materials were paid for through a $5,000 donation from Rochester's Department of Community Development, the BSDC, and WEDGE.

The BSDC and WEDGE publicized the project. Members from both groups then selected the houses that would be renovated. Kodak provided two employees to teach basic repair skills and supervise the project. Residents of the houses selected chose the colors for repainting, and the young workers repaired gutters and roofs, and painted the houses inside and out. According to Charles Fitzgibbon of Kodak, a great sense of camaraderie developed between the summer work group and the local residents. Their efforts resulted in additional home improvements by other area residents.[2]

The BSDC has also been instrumental in removing the junkyards which were numerous in the neighborhood. In 1974, at the BSDC's urging, the zoning was changed from commercial to residential on the 67 acres where the yards were located. A court order required the removal of the last remaining yard by June, 1977.

In 1976, the BSDC obtained funding for improving the commercial area on Lyell Avenue. Storefronts are now being rehabilitated, and more parking space and better street lighting are being added under Rochester's Community Development Block Grant Program. In June, 1976, a neighborhood newsletter, the *Brown Square News*, began to be published. It appears quarterly and is available to area residents at no cost.

In 1976, the BSDC initiated an awards program for property improvements in the area. Six awards were given each year, in 1976 and 1977, for residential, commercial, and industrial improvements, as well as for the best compatible new construction.

In keeping with the spirit of the Brown brothers' park, established in the 1820s, Kodak announced, in summer, 1976, plans for construction of a new Brown Square Bicentennial Park. Kodak contributed $150,000 with the City of Rochester adding another $75,000. Design services were contributed by the architectural firm of Joe Y Ko. The 4.2-acre park, completed in summer, 1977, includes an open meadow, walkways, bocce courts, a fountain plaza, picnic facilities, and gardens as well as a late-nineteenth-century freight station that will be adaptively reused for park offices, maintenance services, and public facilities.

Costs Kodak did not provide a breakdown of its financial contribution to Brown Square. However, the company contributed $150,000 to rebuild Brown Square Park. Kodak employees have also donated time and technical assistance to the BSDC.

Problems Publicity on Brown Square has made absentee landlords seek higher prices for their real estate. There is also a problem with neighborhood continuity, since many of Brown Square's residents are elderly. Homes in the area are difficult to sell, and the heirs of deceased residents often must rent to transients who sometimes fail to maintain the property.

Benefits The Brown Square neighborhood is improving. Many houses have been and are being renovated. Community stability has been reinforced by the BSDC and WEDGE, which provide avenues for local citizens to obtain information and assistance on financial and housing needs.

Revitalization efforts have increased commercial interest in Brown Square. A foundry is being converted into a restaurant, and a cast-iron commercial structure is being renovated to accommodate specialty stores. A local public broadcasting station has relocated in the area and built new headquarters on land donated by Kodak.

The Company Kodak, the world's largest producer of photographic products, had sales of $5.4 billion for fiscal 1976, representing a 10 percent increase over the 1975 figure of $4.9 billion. For the comparable period, net income rose 6 percent from $613.7 million to $650.6 million. Sales are broken down as follows: photographic equipment, U.S. and Canadian, 50 percent; international, 31 percent; chemicals, 19 percent. Kodak is also an important producer of plastics and man-made fibers.

Other Preservation Activities. Hospitals, medical and musical schools, and other educational institutions, not only in Rochester, but also in Europe and other parts of the United States, have been the beneficiaries of Kodak's contributions. Kodak's preservation support in Rochester includes:

1. Contributions to the establishment of the independent International Museum of Photography at George Eastman's fifty-room, early-twentieth-century mansion.

2. Donations to finance the restoration of George Eastman's birthplace. The 1854 Greek Revival house was moved from its former location in upstate New York and relocated on the property of Eastman's later home in Rochester.

3. A $1.7 million donation, in 1971, to renovate the Eastman Theatre, dating from 1922, reputed to be one of the finest theaters acoustically in the world.

4. Contributions to the Landmark Society of Western New York.

Kodak also spent about $30 million to update its own facilities and landscape them. As part of the program, the company has incorporated several old factory buildings into its corporate headquarters. This required creating a uniform facade and remodeling the interior.

For further information contact:
Charles Fitzgibbon
Director of State and Local Affairs
Eastman Kodak Company
343 State Street
Rochester, New York 14650

Robert J. Ferraro
Director
Brown Square Development Corporation
507 North Plymouth Avenue
Rochester, New York 14608

Footnotes

1. "Brown Square Development Corporation," *Brown Square News,* June, 1976.
2. INFORM interview with Charles Fitzgibbon, Director, State and Local Affairs, Eastman Kodak Company, December, 1976.

Summary In July, 1974, General Mills announced its intention to help reverse the process of physical deterioration and economic downslide in its home city of Minneapolis. Its plan was to purchase, renovate, and revitalize a fifty-block residential neighborhood, known as Stevens Square, located in a sound but rapidly deteriorating section of the city. For this purpose, General Mills formed a profit-making subsidiary with an established local real estate developer called Stevens Court, Inc. The project utilized community residents and local subcontractors, wherever possible. In October, 1975, the company was threatened with a national boycott of its products by the AFL-CIO because it was paying nonunion wages and using nonunion construction personnel at Stevens Court. The union's demands were subsequently met, but the original profit-making goals and the rent structure of the renovated units had to be greatly altered.

Background In 1958, General Mills moved to a new suburban office complex in Golden Valley, west of downtown Minneapolis. The reasons cited for the move were: the physical inadequacies of its downtown building, including overcrowding, limited meeting space, lack of room for expansion, and inefficient office layouts; and the traffic, parking, and congestion problems employees experienced coming to work downtown. The company felt that only a new building, in a suburban location, designed specifically for its needs could overcome these shortcomings.

Nevertheless, showing a continued interest in and allegiance to its home city, General Mills has continued to contribute to education, the arts, and civic activities in Minneapolis. Its foundation dispenses more than $3 million in grants annually.

General Mills believed that it could accomplish more for Minneapolis through normal profit-oriented business activities than through traditional channels of civic support. As a result, in 1974, it decided to form a for-profit subsidiary to renovate a fifty-block residential neighborhood in the Stevens Square area, a few blocks from the downtown Minneapolis central business district. In the initial press conference describing General Mills' involvement in Stevens Court, Inc., Cyrus Johnson, Vice President for Social Action, said:

I believe that doing what is in society's interest can and should be profitable. I believe that a company that attempts to improve its city and its society is entitled to a profit. We have to lay the idea to rest that social responsibility is incompatible with profit. We have to begin to seek out new areas of activity where there is a happy confluence of profit and principle.[1]

Execution In its regular consumer-products business, General Mills has grown by developing new products in areas of existing company expertise. In areas where it has no prior experience, growth is usually achieved through merger with or acquisition of successful companies. Possessing no internal residential real estate experience, General Mills selected as its partner in the venture Jim Larson, who had been working in the Stevens Square area for over eight years. Larson had already renovated approximately 85 apartment units in the area and was eager to do more, should financing become available.

Jim Larson and his staff were made responsible for selecting, purchasing, renovating, renting, maintaining, and managing all properties developed by the company. General Mills acted as the "banker" for the Stevens Court real estate development enterprise, but with more control and personal involvement in the operation and outcome than is customary for one acting in that capacity.

Initially, Stevens Court, Inc., planned to buy about 1,000 apartment units within a fifty-block area, approximately 40 percent of the apartments in the Stevens Square neighborhood. General Mills selected Stevens Square because improvement would not require total demolition of the existing housing stock. The buildings were sound, renewable brick structures dating from the early 1900s and the resident population was committed to improving conditions.

After renovations, rents were to range from $125 to $127 per month, only $10 to $15 per month higher than pre-renovation rents. New plumbing, wiring, appliances, bathrooms and kitchens, walls, ceilings, and the refinishing of hardwood floors and original woodwork were to be included in the work. This resulted in roughly a $3,000-per-unit expenditure for renovation in addition to a $6,000 per-unit acquisition cost. Neighborhood residents were to provide labor for the project, and if possible, subcontractors and suppliers were also to have local affiliations. Almost all construction work was to be done by nonunion crews.

The neighborhood population mix—

approximately 60 percent elderly and 40 percent young, working, and students—was to remain the same. A key feature of the proposal was that Larson's organization would establish permanent residence in Steven's Square and play an important role in the neighborhood's social and political life, as well as in the construction and maintenance of the renovated apartments. According to the plan, Stevens Court, Inc., would help residents find jobs, and participate in health-care programs. It would also facilitate communication in the neighborhood through close contact between staff and residents, build information kiosks, and perhaps hire a protection agency to supplement the local police force.

In the three years since General Mills' involvement began, 457 units have been purchased and 300 have been renovated. Jim Larson reports that property values have not escalated, and he can still acquire distressed or abandoned buildings for around $6,000 per unit.

Costs Initially, General Mills invested just under $400,000 for a 51 percent interest in Stevens Court, Inc. Jim Larson and his partner owned the remaining 49 percent. By early 1975, General Mills owned 65 percent of the operation, while Larson owned the remaining 35 percent.

Although Stevens Court, Inc., was established as a profit-making venture, all profits for the first ten years were expected to be reinvested in additional buildings and further improvements. After ten years, General Mills anticipated a return on its investment of 5 percent to 10 percent, a rate substantially below that required on the parent company's other new capital expenditures. As Cyrus Johnson points out: "It is very important for the public to know that in a strict financial sense, General Mills could make better investments. But, socially, we seriously doubt we could."[2]

Problems At first, some Stevens Square residents were suspicious that General Mills might be out to milk the community for exorbitant profits, or to gain title to large tracts of land for future speculation or development. Father Greg Welch of St. Stephen's Roman Catholic Church, located in the neighborhood, stated:

This is an exciting pilot project in renovation of present housing by a private institution. But it will be a huge gathering of land in a single given area under single ownership and that kind of power says "danger."[3]

Charlie Ellis, a 27-year-old seminary student who lives in the area, commented that he has:

more confidence in Larson and Waage [a partner] than in General Mills. Big money is big money. I'm suspicious of it. I agree that it's important for corporations to be involved in neighborhood renovation. But they can't forget that residents must have some sense of control over their destiny.[4]

Stevens Square neighborhood and two buildings renovated by Stevens Court, Inc.

In October, 1975, after about 200 apartments had been purchased and renovations had been underway for sixteen months, the project ran into difficulty with the unions. The members of the buildings trades unions and their parent organization, the AFL-CIO, threatened to stage a national boycott of General Mills' products unless the company discontinued involvement in the Stevens Court renovations or complied with union labor rates and restrictions on all the work performed. According to the company, the unions were upset because Stevens Court, Inc., was using nonunion workers to carry out the renovations, and paying them less than union scale.

General Mills presented its case in "A Message to the Twin Cities Community," published in the *Minneapolis Tribune* on October 1, 1975. In this message, the company threatened to discontinue its efforts unless a mutually satisfactory agreement could be reached with the unions. However, General Mills did not wish to abandon the people and property of Stevens Court, nor its new concept of corporate community involvement. As a result, it finally agreed to the union demands and replaced nonunion workers with card-carrying crews under union subcontractors and at union wage scales. The boycott threat was dropped, but twenty area residents employed in the renovation work had to be let go.*

*Since that time, the unions claimed that General Mills was still using nonunion workers for some operations.

Dan Gustafson, President of the Minneapolis Building and Construction Trades Union Council, claims that the union was concerned about the undercutting of the union wage scale, not about the hiring of non-card-carrying residents. Gustafson also suggested that if General Mills was truly concerned with helping the city, it could have "put the $3 million it gives annually through its foundation into the Stevens Court project, hired union workers, and really made some impact on unemployment as well as housing."[5] He added that if General Mills had remained in the city, instead of moving to the suburbs, "it would have kept its money where its mouth is."[6] Gustafson cited the Honeywell Corporation as an example of a company concerned with the revitalization of the city.**

**Honeywell has stayed in its downtown location and has contributed to the city's employment base as well as to the neighborhood surrounding its plant. Through its neighborhood-improvement program, the company purchases rundown properties, rehabilitates them, and resells them to community residents at or below cost.

Buildings owned by Stevens Court, Inc., and possible future acquisitions (as of October, 1976).

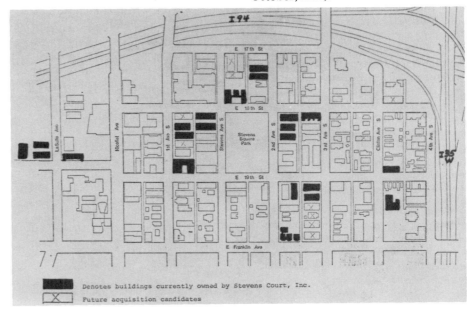

Denotes buildings currently owned by Stevens Court, Inc.

Future acquisition candidates

During renovation.

After renovation.

As of mid-1977, almost two years after the threatened boycott, Stevens Court, Inc., is still in business. However, any potential profits for General Mills or Jim Larson are virtually gone. According to Larson, General Mills' contribution must now be considered totally philanthropic. Due to the increased cost of labor, building materials, energy, and taxes, renovation costs as well as rents have increased considerably over the original estimates. "An apartment that formerly rented for from $150 to $175 had to be raised to $210 to $220,"[7] says Larson.

Benefits As a result of General Mills' efforts, 300 units have been upgraded in an important central-city residential area. This neighborhood, which had started to decline, is receiving renewed attention from local citizens' groups and the city government. City services have increased, and street and park improvements have been made. Finally, according to the company, the renovation of buildings in Stevens Square has helped increase community spirit and pride.

The Stevens Square Community Organization (SSCO), a group of residents from the area, stated:

We are confident that this General Mills interest [in the restoration and rehabilitation of sound existing structures] is compatible with the interests of the neighborhood, and that rents will continue to remain within the realm of current residents' ability to live here.[8]

A representative of the SSCO said:

In the past, American corporations have not been responsive to the needs of the communities they affect. If General Mills does indeed operate as they have described, it will be a welcome change. The S.S.C.O. hopes the company will respond to this challenge.[9]

Eight months after General Mills began its involvement in the revitalization of the area, John McNamara, another member of SSCO who lives in a rehabilitated apartment, said:

Our neighborhood is beginning to form a strong image. . . . I think we're well on our way to becoming a stable, viable community.[10]

The Company In 1886, C. C. Washburn built his first flour mill on the banks of the Mississippi in Minneapolis, forming the Washburn Crosby Company. In 1921, the company created a food authority, Betty Crocker, to represent its expanding line of food products, and in 1923, it introduced Wheaties. In 1928, several leading milling companies merged with the Washburn Crosby Company to form General Mills, Inc. The first product introduced by this new corporation was Bisquick, the nation's first prepared cake mix. Since that time, General Mills has grown and expanded its operations until today it is a large, diversified, international company. In 1976, sales increased to $2.9 billion, up from a 1975 figure of $2.3 billion. Net income rose from $76.2 million in 1975 to $117 million in 1976. General Mills employs more than 52,000 people; 3,600 of these in the Minneapolis area.

For further information contact:
Cyrus Johnson
Vice President for Social Action
General Mills, Inc.
9200 Wayzata Boulevard
Minneapolis, Minnesota 55440

Footnotes

1. General Mills, Inc., "Press Conference for Stevens Court Project," *News Release*, July 25, 1974, p. 3.
2. *Ibid.*, p. 4.
3. Ron Ostman, "Stevens Renovations Will Hold Closed Meetings," *The Paper*, 2 October 1974.
4. Terry Wolkerstorfer, "General Mills Backing Renovation," *Minneapolis Star*, 26 July 1974.
5. INFORM interview with Dan Gustafson, President, Minneapolis Building and Construction Trades Union Council, November, 1976.
6. *Ibid.*
7. INFORM interview with Jim Larson, President, Stevens Court, Inc., November, 1976.
8. Bill Grimberg and Doug Madson, "Stevens Square Residents Testing Selves, General Mills," *Common Ground*, November, 1974, p. 30.
9. *Ibid.*
10. Carol Matlack, "For-profit Rehab: Can Investors Save Neighborhoods," *Common Ground*, Summer, 1975.

Summary In 1972, Lakewood Bank and Trust Company of Dallas, Texas, established a $1 million loan fund to finance the purchase and renovation of the homes along Swiss Avenue, a deteriorating section of Old East Dallas, its home area. Lakewood Bank made additional loan commitments of $1 million each in 1974 and 1975 to renovate homes in the Hollywood Heights and Belmont Extension areas of Old East Dallas. Expanding its involvement, the bank announced a $2 million loan program in September, 1976, in cooperation with the Federal National Mortgage Association to provide financing for the purchase and renovation of single-family owner-occupied homes in Munger Place. These programs have helped check the spread of urban blight in Old East Dallas.

Background Lakewood Bank and Trust is located four miles from Dallas's center in Old East Dallas, which was one of the first sections of the city to be developed. Most of the homes were built between 1890 and 1940, when the area was the residence of the city's political and cultural elite. Many homes, especially the older ones in the Munger Place and Swiss Avenue sections, are large and well built, reflecting a wide range of architectural styles.

The homes along Swiss Avenue, dating from 1905 to 1925, are slightly newer and more luxurious than those in Munger Place. The architecture is mixed: Spanish-style and Classical Revival houses, interspersed with some examples of the "prairie style," including one designed by Frank Lloyd Wright. The latter style, characterized by low horizontal roof lines, overhanging eaves, and massive porch columns, was created in the 1890s by Wright, and remained popular through the early twentieth century.

Many homes in the Hollywood Heights and Belmont Extension areas are less than 45 years old. Those in Hollywood Heights are two-story brick structures, designed in the Tudor style, with steep pitched roofs and decorative stone, brick, and stained-glass detail. Most homes in this area were built in the 1930s and are single-family units. The sixty-square-block area is 90 per-cent owner-occupied and has 600 homes. The Belmont Extension area, located northwest of Lakewood Bank, is composed of one-, two-, and three-story wooden-frame structures. The architecture is largely mixed; many homes are built in the cottage style, with front porches and dormers in the attic. Apartment houses and two-family brick buildings are interspersed with the smaller dwellings. There are 550 homes in the fifty-square-block area. While the houses in Hollywood Heights and the Belmont Extension are not as large as those on Swiss Avenue or Munger Place, they are newer and have been better maintained. The average house in Hollywood Heights and the Belmont Extension "as is" is worth between $20,000 and $25,000.

Most of the homes in the ten-square-block Munger Place area are in great need of repair. They sell for about $20,000 "as is," and require $35,000 to $40,000 to recondition. Rotting wood needs to be replaced; the house must be painted inside and out; siding replaced; and new plumbing, heating, and electrical systems installed.

The homes on Swiss Avenue were carefully maintained until the mid-1950s, when many residents began leaving for the newly developed suburbs. In response to this outward flow of homeowners, the City of Dallas rezoned the 2,000 homes in Old East Dallas for multi-family use in 1965. Many old homes were converted into boarding houses; some were divided into apartments; and two structures were demolished to make way for more lucrative high-rise construction. The predominantly owner-occupied (75 percent) area became 80 percent renter-occupied. Absentee landlords allowed their buildings to decay, while waiting for developers to purchase their properties for demolition and new construction. Rents were cheaper in these dilapidated boarding houses, attracting a more transient population. Crime increased. Those attempting to maintain their homes found it difficult to obtain home-improvement loans for major repairs. Nevertheless, a few older families were determined to maintain their homes in spite of the deteriorating conditions.

In 1971, the residents of Swiss Avenue and other parts of Old East Dallas decided to do something about the encroaching decay. They formed a small group and sought advice from neighboring districts, the National Trust for Historic Preservation, the State Historic Preservation Officer, the Texas Historical Commission, and Jacob Morrison, author of *Historic Preservation Law*. Acting on what they learned, the group incorporated as the Historic Preservation League in 1973. The Historic Preservation League learned from the Urban Design Division of the Dallas City Planning Department that further demolition could be prevented by having Swiss Avenue designated a historic district. However, to obtain this designation for the neighborhood, the League needed the support of local residents, owners, businesses, and financial institutions.

After much effort and many slide presentations, the League won its battle, and in September, 1973, Swiss Avenue was designated a historic district, under the landmark ordinance of the City of Dallas. That same year, after Swiss Avenue's redesignation and rezoning for single-family use, the National Trust awarded an $800 matching grant to help the League pay legal fees accumulated in the fight against construction of a high-rise apartment complex in the district.

Execution The concern of Swiss Avenue's residents, the neighborhood's designation as a historic district, and the soundness of many of the buildings greatly facilitated revitalization. In 1972, Lakewood Bank and Trust, concerned by the swift decline of the neighborhood which was the source of almost all of its business, made a commitment to lend $1 million for the purchase and renovation of 200 homes on Swiss Avenue. This innovative gesture provided needed financing which had been nonexistent during the years of decline.

Target areas for loans were chosen by bank officials and community leaders. Special departments were created at the bank for processing the loans and securing second mortgages, since Lakewood is a commercial bank and normally does not handle many such transactions. The loan program itself is directed by the bank's Senior Vice President for Community Affairs, Artie Barnett, who is also on the Historic Preservation League's Advisory Board. Each new program was announced at a gathering of interested citizens and the news media.

The mortgage loans furnished by Lakewood finance 80 percent of the cost of a house (90 percent with Prime Mortgage Insurance). These conventional loans extend for twenty years, with an interest rate of 9¼ percent. Loans are made on the condition that the homes will be owner-occupied and improved to meet city safety regulations. Since the establishment of the $1 million loan fund, financing on Swiss Avenue has become comparatively easy to obtain. Approximately one year after Lakewood's successful involvement with the neighborhood, ninety homes had been renovated. In 1973, ten financial institutions also became interested in supplying mortgage loans in the area at terms of 8¾ percent for 25 years. In 1974, Swiss Avenue was listed in the National Register of Historic Places.

In 1974 and 1975, Lakewood made two commitments of $1 million each in the Belmont Extension and Hollywood Heights areas for similar loan programs. Seventy-five conventional loans, totaling $2 million, have been made.

In September, 1976, Lakewood Bank and Trust initiated a $1 million Munger Place mortgage loan fund, and with an additional $1 million from the Federal National Mortgage Association (FNMA), succeeded in making available $2 million in funds for purchase and renovation. This is the first instance of the FNMA's involvement with only one local bank.

The Historic Preservation League has also established a revolving fund to buy homes in Munger Place and resell them through local realtors. So far 22 homes have been bought by the League. In addition, the League is trying to obtain historic-district status for Munger Place. Following Lakewood's lead, other banks have begun making loans in the area.

In the one year the program has been in effect, almost 30 percent of the 200 houses in Munger Place have been renovated, and thirty loans totaling $900,000 have been made by Lakewood. Though progress is being made, it will take three to five years before the revitalization of Munger Place reaches a level comparable to that of Swiss Avenue. In the five years that Lakewood has been financing these two high-risk projects, there has not been one foreclosure.

Lakewood is now planning to establish a $5 million loan fund to further encourage residential and commercial redevelopment in Junius Heights and other sections of Old East Dallas. The bank also helped finance a Historic Preservation League booklet entitled, *Buying a Home in Historic Old East Dallas.*

Costs Over the past two years, Lakewood Bank and Trust has spent approximately $50,000 on the revitalization of Old East Dallas. This amount includes the cost of opinion surveys, public relations, and luncheons for community leaders. Lakewood feels that the income from new loans, as well as new business generated from the public relations surrounding the programs, offset the costs.

Problems In some cases, it was necessary to help relocate families when multi-family dwellings were sold by their owners.

Benefits Since the beginning of the Swiss Avenue loan fund and related projects, real estate values in the area have skyrocketed. Homes along Swiss Avenue have doubled and even tripled in value. One home, which was purchased for $28,000, was resold after renovation for $239,000. With minor repairs and some home improvements, the prices of homes in Hollywood Heights and the Belmont Extension increased from between $20,000 and $25,000 to between $30,000 and $35,000. In Munger Place, unrenovated homes that were sold "as is" for $12,000 before the neighboring Swiss Avenue renovations are now sold for $20,000.

Lakewood Bank and Trust has benefited from the neighborhood stabilization and improved economic base of its prime market. In addition, its involvement with the revitalization effort has brought much publicity, and as a result, new business. In 1976, Lakewood received an award from the Dallas Chapter of the American Institute of Architects for the work in Old East Dallas. This Citation of Honor was presented by Downing Thomas, Chapter President, who said of the renovations:

Lakewood's significant contribution made in the revitalization and environmental improvement of the East Dallas area can be measured in terms of rising property values, new construction, historic restoration, influx of new families and above all increased community pride.[1]

The community has benefited from these renovations as well. Decay has been checked in the project areas, and the tax base has been increased, resulting in more city services, such as street improvements and new parks.

The Company Lakewood Bank and Trust began serving the Dallas area in 1941. Since then, it has expanded throughout Dallas and North Texas. Its assets for 1976 were $119.3 million, as compared with $99.9 million in 1975. Net income for 1976 was $1.01 million versus $.7 million in 1975.

Other Preservation Activities
Lakewood is currently the major participant in a home-improvement loan pool involving five other financial institutions. The project is intended to help low- and moderate-income families, and is guaranteed by the City of Dallas.

For further information contact:
A. L. Artie Barnett
Senior Vice President
Lakewood Bank and Trust Company
Gaston and LaVista Streets
P.O. Box 140000
Dallas, Texas 75214

Virginia Savage Talkington
Chairman of the Historic Dallas Fund
Historic Preservation League
5600 Swiss Avenue
Dallas, Texas 75214

House in Old East Dallas before renovation.

The same house after renovation.

Footnotes

1. Lakewood Bank and Trust Company, *Lakewood Bank and Trust Company Annual Report* (Dallas: Lakewood Bank and Trust Company, 1976), p. 4.

Summary In 1968, Ralston Purina, a leading producer of consumer food products and animal feeds, set up a wholly owned subsidiary, the LaSalle Park Redevelopment Corporation, to redevelop a 140-acre area of blighted urban real estate adjacent to its St. Louis corporate headquarters complex, Checkerboard Square. The program sought to create a self-sufficient, balanced community of residential, commercial, and industrial inhabitants. Originally, the company planned a great deal more new construction than rehabilitation of older structures, but pressure from local preservationists has resulted in something of a change in emphasis. Governmental delays have caused actual construction and rehabilitation to proceed much more slowly than expected. However, this unique project is the first renewal plan of its type and magnitude to involve federal, state, and local government programs, as well as the participation of a major industrial corporation. Ralston Purina has already invested nearly $2 million in the project, and expects to spend at least another $1.5 million before its completion.

Background Pierre Laclede founded St. Louis in 1764, setting up his fur-trading operations along the Mississippi near the spot where the famous Gateway Arch is located today. The LaSalle Park area is situated southwest of the Arch. It was first settled by Laclede's French followers; later inhabitants came from Germany, Ireland, Italy, and other European countries. At the turn of the century, a Lebanese population settled there. The Lebanese church, St. Raymond's Catholic Church, has since then been a symbol of neighborhood identity and cohesiveness. Even after many of the Lebanese moved away from the area, they continued to return to the church in its old quarters, a converted four-family brick flat. Today, persistent fund-raising efforts by the congregation have financed a new church building which has become the harbinger of the neighborhood's renewal.

The LaSalle Park area has always been a white working-class neighborhood. However, since World War II, many businesses have moved out. (Even Ralston Purina contemplated relocating its operations to the suburbs.) Houses have been neglected, abandoned, and vandalized, and most of the more successful residents have moved away, leaving primarily the poor.

The same range of problems as was afflicting this aging neighborhood was occurring in other parts of St. Louis, and by the early 1950s, the city was faced with a need for major urban renewal. Its initial reaction, like that of many other cities, was to wipe away the blight and start anew. Throughout the city, the nineteenth-century housing stock—primarily low-rise units on small lots or row houses—was demolished. Utilizing government funds, new medium-rise apartment buildings were constructed with the hope of attracting a racially and economically mixed population. But, because the whites, who were more mobile, continued to flee the city, the new projects soon became almost totally occupied by poor blacks.

A much publicized St. Louis public-housing project—Pruitt-Igoe—which attempted to provide housing on a large scale, failed, and in fact, this failure became a valuable lesson to renewal planners in many U.S. cities. Completed in 1954, Pruitt-Igoe consisted of 33 eleven-story block buildings containing 2,762 units. The design of the buildings on large, open, unprotected sites, and their unsatisfactory layout and poor construction led to safety hazards and deterioration so severe that many of the buildings have already been abandoned and demolished.

In the LaSalle Park area, the city's efforts at selective clearance resulted in land parcels too small to make total redevelopment feasible. This further detracted from the appearance and safety of the neighborhood, creating

Exterior view of the first home being completely rehabilitated by Ralston Purina Company's LaSalle Park Redevelopment Corporation. Resurfacing of streets and sidewalks has not yet been completed.

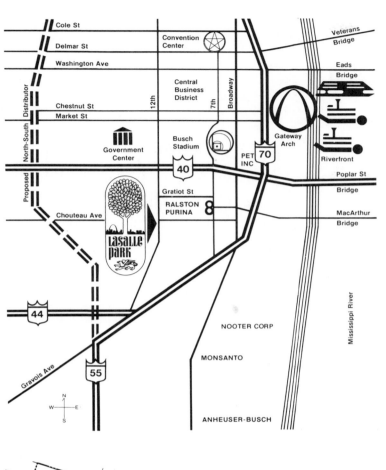

vacant lots full of debris and empty buildings ripe for vandalism and crime.

In 1968, Mayor Alfonso J. Cervantes asked for Ralston Purina's participation in an effort to renew the LaSalle Park area. He hoped that the participation of a major corporation would "spur other St. Louis firms to invest in the commercial and residential future of the city."[1]

Ralston's Chairman R. Hal Dean accepted the Mayor's challenge, and obtained approval from the company's Board of Directors to assume leadership responsibility for the redevelopment project. The company agreed to donate up to $2 million, in effect, the amount the city required to obtain federal funds for the revitalization. Once this commitment was made, Ralston Purina contracted well-respected planning and architectural firms to ensure that the project would not suffer the same problems as earlier city renewal efforts.

In October, 1969, one year after the

LaSalle Park adjacent to Ralston Purina's Checkerboard Square complex in St. Louis.

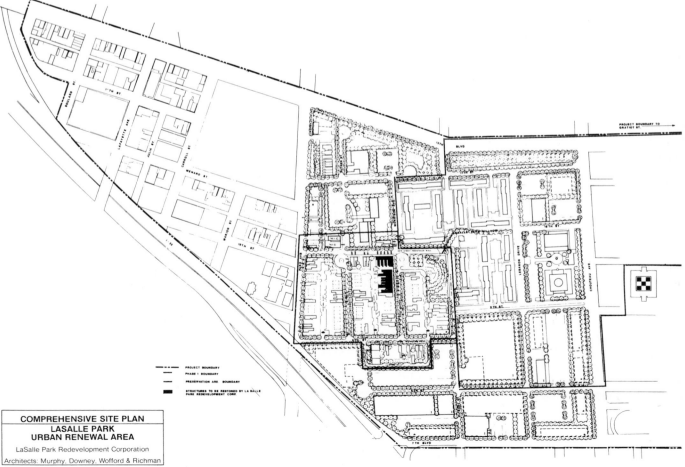

COMPREHENSIVE SITE PLAN
LASALLE PARK
URBAN RENEWAL AREA
LaSalle Park Redevelopment Corporation
Architects: Murphy, Downey, Wofford & Richman

154

Numbered buildings are to be preserved. Broken lines indicate proposed new housing.

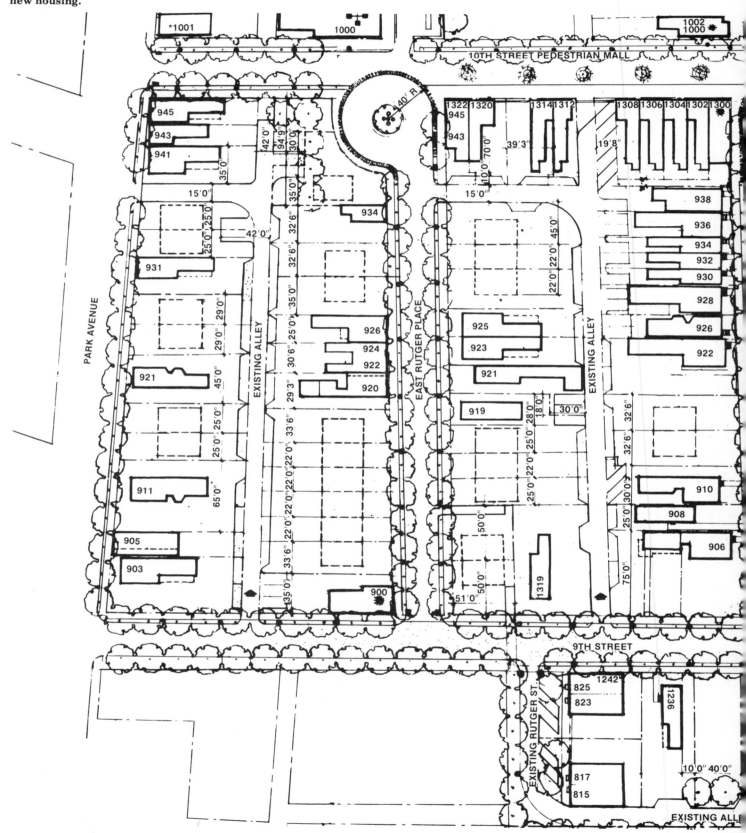

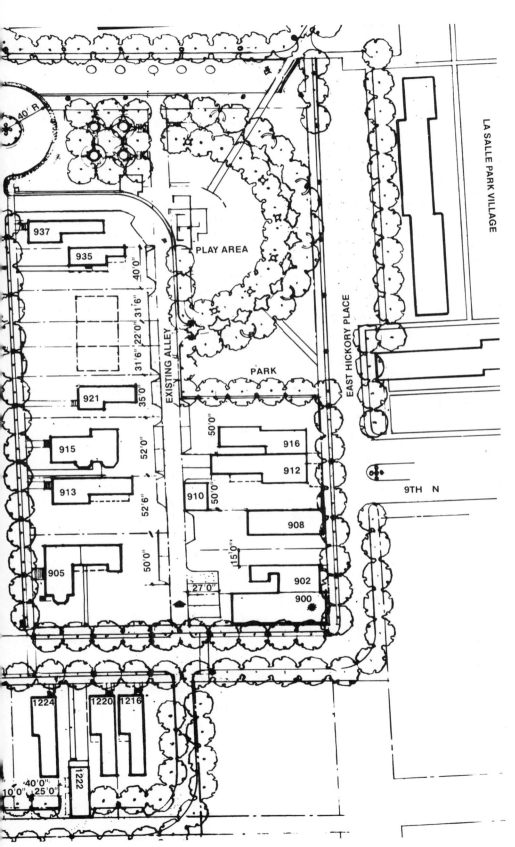

Mayor approached Ralston Purina, the company announced its redevelopment plan, a $30 million proposal to create a "newtown-intown."[2] The plan had to be approved by city and federal agencies, but it was designed to be implemented by the LaSalle Park Redevelopment Corporation, a subsidiary of Ralston Purina. While the company would supply personnel for this new subsidiary, as well as financial and legal management services, new construction and renovation was to be financed by a variety of federal programs. In 1969, it was estimated that the project—to be completed in three phases—would take about five years. The work in each phase consisted of the following:

Phase I
- Construction of 9 acres of new residential development, including 148 townhouse apartment units
- Construction of 2 acres of commercial development
- Construction of 6 acres of light industrial development
- Allocation of 3 acres for the new St. Raymond's Church complex
- Reservation of 24 acres for Ralston Purina's use

Phase II & III
- Development of the balance of the renewal area for:
  200 new townhouses
  400 apartments for the elderly
  rehabilitation of a small number of selected residential structures
- Development of additional commercial and industrial facilities
- Retention of all existing churches, social, and recreational facilities.

According to the St. Louis Land Clearance for Redevelopment Authority, the city's overall urban-renewal agency, all but 75 of LaSalle Park's 875 residences were in substandard condition as of 1969. There were 450 families and 200 single residents in the area. The total LaSalle Park project called for more than 1,500 new or rehabilitated housing units.

The proposal also called for tax incentives provided by the Missouri Urban Redevelopment Act to encourage additional commercial and light industrial development. Local institutions established in LaSalle Park would be preserved, and land would be set aside for their expansion.

Execution

Phase I. The project progressed gradually from proposal to dedication:

In February, 1971—sixteen months after the initial announcement, following much work with the planners, residents, and city agencies, a plan for "about 700 low rise dwelling units"[3] was submitted to the St. Louis Board of Aldermen and the U.S. Department of Housing and Urban Development (HUD).

In May, 1972—two-and-a-half years after the initial announcement, and after much planning, the company announced the approval of Phase I, involving demolition of buildings and new construction in 44 acres of the LaSalle Park urban-renewal area, by the St. Louis Land Clearance for Redevelopment Authority. Ralston Purina was also selected to develop the balance of the 140-acre area, pending the availability of federal and local funding.* The housing would be financed under the "Turnkey I" federal homeowner-opportunity program for low-and moderate-income families. In accordance with this program, Ralston Purina would sell the completed residences to the St. Louis Housing Authority which, in turn, would be reimbursed by federal funds.

In February, 1974—nineteen months later—Ralston Purina announced that the federal government had finally reserved funds for the construction of the 148 garden apartment and townhouse units in the initial phase of the project.

In April, 1975—ten months later—the official ground-breaking ceremony took place for 16 two-story buildings containing 30 two-bedroom units, 78 three-bedroom units, and 40 four-bedroom units. The St. Louis Housing Authority anticipated that the average rental would range from $115 to $130 per month, with the average gross income of residents between $6,000 and $10,000. The first units would be available for occupancy within twelve months.

Finally, in September, 1976—another seventeen months later—the dedication ceremonies were held. The new housing is now fully occupied.

*Five months earlier, in January, 1972, the federal government made $4 million available to the city to start the project.

By mid-1977, the LaSalle Park Redevelopment Corporation was working on Phase II and Phase III of its project. This was more than nine years after the project, which was originally scheduled to take a total of only five years, was conceived. But during the nine years, the corporation had learned a great deal about working with a neighborhood, a city and its many agencies, and about dealing with the complex, slow-moving federal bureaucracy.

Ralston Purina also learned how to work with local public-interest groups concerned with specific causes like the preservation of old buildings. The City of St. Louis and its Land Clearance for Redevelopment Authority (LCRA) had paid little attention to the architectural value of the many buildings they were eliminating in the name of renewal, and this strategy was not initially questioned by Purina. A 1971 "Architectural Survey of LaSalle Park" carried out by Heritage/St. Louis, a local preservation organization, indicated that about eight buildings still standing at that time could be considered "most significant architecturally." Another approximately ninety buildings in the area could be considered "architecturally significant," and another approximately 160 buildings were labeled as being of "some architectural interest for the neighborhood."[4] Among these buildings were seven houses in the St. John Nepomuk District which had been included in the National Register. As of 1975, when the ground breaking commenced on LaSalle Park Village, as the new construction in Phase I was called, almost ninety buildings in all three categories had been demolished.

Local preservationists were understandably disturbed. Carolyn Toft, now preservation planner of the Landmarks Association of St. Louis, Inc., had few kind words for the project in its early days, claiming that LCRA, the city, and the company were anything but sensitive to the opportunities for reusing existing buildings. However, since federal funds were being used to complete the project, the local agencies were required to justify the removal of historic buildings to obtain full funding. Ms. Toft notified the Advisory Council on Historic Preservation that

preservation was being completely ignored, and the Council sent the City of St. Louis a letter requesting compliance.

Later, Ms. Toft was appointed the Historic Preservation Officer for the St. Louis Community Development Agency, a body established in 1974 to administer Community Development Block Grants made by HUD. In this position, she worked with the city and Ralston Purina to draft a $2 million Community Development Block Grant funding program which included preservation as a key element of the development strategy. The program insured the preservation and renovation of architecturally important buildings still remaining in the Phase II and Phase III sections of the project.

Working closely with community groups, Ralston Purina redirected its plan for the residential development in Phase II. The company will invest over $500,000 to rehabilitate 13 of the 57 architecturally significant structures remaining in a three-block, six-acre parcel. It will offer them for sale to area families "at cost" and, if necessary, at a slight loss. According to Fred H. Perabo, Manager of the Ralston Purina Real Estate Division and President of the LaSalle Park Redevelopment Corporation, "Our investment is designed as a catalyst to demonstrate the possibilities in the area and will hopefully encourage other citizens to buy and renovate the remaining homes."[5]

The remaining houses in Phase II are being offered at cost to families who will renovate them. By mid-1977, over 70 percent of these had been sold, and buyers had expressed interest in Phase III houses. Renovation guidelines have been established to insure that the architectural integrity of the nineteenth-century buildings is preserved. Once the renovation work is complete, additional new housing will be built. A pedestrian mall, period lighting fixtures, a small park, and off-street parking for each dwelling are also planned for the area. New utility lines will be installed below ground.

In addition, the company has donated the historic Lucy Dolusic House to the Landmarks Association. The group will restore the exterior and sell the house to a family who will renovate the interior. Ralston Purina has also

New townhouse apartments.

donated $2,500 to the Landmarks Association for a revolving fund which will be used in the restoration.

Costs It is estimated that over $30 million in new investment, from both public and private sources, will be required to complete the LaSalle Park project. By 1977, nearly $12 million had been invested in Phase I, and renovation work in Phase II was underway. By mid-1977, Ralston Purina's share of this investment included:

Direct Contributions

• $1.2 million—a cash contribution to the City of St. Louis to help the city meet a $2 million goal enabling it to obtain $4 million in federal funds for the urban-renewal program. Ralston Purina's money was used for land acquisition, clearance, feasibility studies, and street improvements.*

• $500,000—an estimated amount spent on surveys, studies, reports, and staff time.

Additional Investment (Most of this money will be recovered as the project is completed.)

• $700,000—the cost of the land purchased from the LCRA for Phase I. Of the 44 acres purchased, the firm will retain 24 for its own expansion needs; 12 have been developed and sold for the new housing and the new church; and the remaining acres are to be developed for commercial and light industrial use.

• $750,000 to $1 million—required to purchase the remaining acreage in Phase II and III.

• $500,000—required to restore and renovate the thirteen houses in the Phase II preservation area. These houses will be sold at cost.

Problems The most significant problem for this corporation posed by participating in neighborhood renewal projects involving local, state, and federal programs has been the long time period necessary for the review and

*Since the inception of Phase I, the urban-renewal programs have been replaced by a program of Community Development Block Grants which no longer require the city to supply funds to obtain federal money.

approval mechanism to work. This has required more staff time than was anticipated and has increased Ralston Purina's costs.

Benefits LaSalle Park Redevelopment Corporation's President Fred Perabo described the benefits to Ralston Purina:

We have purchased property for our own use; the area has improved aesthetically, as well as from a safety standpoint; and our own investment in the area has been strengthened. A public relations "profit" has resulted.[6]

Chairman R. Hal Dean also gave an assessment of the project:

Now we can see that a once dying neighborhood has become a vital community, a place where people can live, work and prosper.[7]

Ralston's officer in charge of corporate social responsibility, John P. Bard, added:

The management of our company has gained credibility in the social responsibility arena. . . . As far as conclusions go, I believe that large corporations should and must seek ways to support efforts to improve our cities. Taking an active role can be more important, and more productive, than simply a dollar investment. A corporation can and should become a part of the community in which it operates. Clearly there are risks, but well conceived approaches and programs can be rewarding.[8]

In 1975, *Business and Society Review* awarded Ralston Purina recognition for improving urban life. The company was one of 13 winners selected from 45 applicants for a Corporate Responsibility Awards Program.

The company, city, and developer all learned that urban re-development requires—and benefits from—a respect for, and use of existing older buildings as well as the construction of new ones.

The Company Established in 1894 in a small feed store along the St. Louis Mississippi Riverfront, Ralston Purina has grown into the largest producer of commercial feeds for livestock and poultry in the world. Sales rose from $3.15 billion in 1975 to $3.39 billion in 1976. Net income in 1976 was $83 million, a decline from 1975's $99.5 million. Ralston Purina is also a leading producer of pet foods and consumer food products, such as cereals. Its corporate symbol, the Checkerboard, and its products are known throughout the world.

For further information contact:
Fred H. Perabo
President, LaSalle Park Redevelopment Corporation
Ralston Purina Company
Checkerboard Square
St. Louis, Missouri 63188

Footnotes

1. Ralston Purina Company, *News from Checkerboard Square*, October 31, 1969, p. 3.
2. *Ibid.*, p. 1.
3. Ralston Purina Company, *News from Checkerboard Square*, February 25, 1971, p. 1.
4. "Architectural Survey of LaSalle Park Area, St. Louis," (unpublished survey conducted by Heritage/St. Louis, May 7, 1971).
5. INFORM interview with Fred H. Perabo, Manager, Ralston Purina Real Estate Division; President, LaSalle Park Redevelopment Corporation, January 25, 1977.
6. *Ibid.*
7. Ralston Purina Company, *News from Checkerboard Square*, September 26, 1976.
8. INFORM interview with John P. Bard, officer, Corporate Responsibility, Ralston Purina Company, May, 1977.

Summary In 1972, the former management of the South Shore National
Bank decided to turn its back on its
inner-city neighborhood and relocate in
downtown Chicago. Area residents
fought the move and in a landmark
decision, the Comptroller of the U.S.
Currency thwarted the bank's management. Local groups then approached Ronald Grzywinski, a banker
and student of urban problems who had
studied the possibilities and methods of
setting up a neighborhood-development bank. He took over the bank
in August, 1973, aided by a recent
Federal Reserve ruling that allowed a
bank holding company to establish a
subsidiary that is both profit- and
community-oriented. Under the new
management, whose primary investment objective is neighborhood revitalization, depositors have been attracted to the bank; close cooperation
has been established with community
organizations, and some of the housing
and commercial buildings have been
partially rehabilitated. Both the bank's
assets and the housing stock are appreciating.

Background South Shore (population 80,000), a turn-of-the-century area
of broad, tree-lined streets, is located
along Lake Michigan only fifteen minutes from Chicago's central downtown
"Loop." The housing stock is diversified and includes early-twentieth-
century mansions, large tracts of red-
brick two-story middle-income residences, stucco and brick homes built by
the affluent Irish in the 1920s and
1930s, and numerous bungalows dating from the same period. The area also
possesses pockets of high-density
walk-up rental buildings with six to
thirty flats. Modern high-rise apartments line the lakefront. Although
more than 75 percent of the dwellings
are rental units, more than 75 percent
of the geographic area is covered by
single-family, owner-occupied houses.
South Shore has three commercial
strips.

Like many other urban areas in
recent years, South Shore was a victim
of the flight to the suburbs and a
changing neighborhood population. A
stable middle-class neighborhood
rapidly deteriorated. Absentee landlords neglected buildings or abandoned
them outright. Chicago's generous

grace period for nonpayment of property taxes—ten years—aggravated the
situation. Federal Housing Administration loans were foreclosed, accelerating the demise of sound housing;
and businesses fled the area. In 1960,
only 1 percent of the residents were
black. By 1970, 88 percent of the
former residents had left the neighborhood, and it was 77 percent black.

The management of South Shore
National Bank, the area's major financial institution, saw deposits steadily
decrease from $72 million in 1967 to
$47.8 million in 1972. In the same
period, the bank's assets dropped from
$78 million to $54.8 million. Management made little effort to relate to the
community and its problems, and the
general level of banking services declined. The building itself became dirty
and unkempt.

In 1972, the bank announced that it
would move to a new location in the
Loop. However, before it could do so, it
had to get the approval of the Comptroller of the Currency of the United
States. The South Shore Commission, a
local citizens' group, rallied and fought
the bank's plan to abandon the neighborhood. In a landmark decision the
Comptroller ruled:

*South Shore National Bank has failed
to show persuasive reason at this time
for abandoning its present service area
and leaving the South Shore community without a strong, established and
adequately capitalized commercial
bank.*[1]

Following the decision, the South
Shore Commission sought buyers for
the bank. The Commission approached
Ronald Grzywinski of nearby Hyde
Park, former President of the Hyde
Park Bank and Trust Company.
Grzywinski and his associates, Mary
Houghton and Milton Davis, had previously implemented progressive
neighborhood-development financing,
such as loans to minority businesses. In
1972, Grzywinski had just completed a
three-year study at the Adlai Stevenson Institute and Center for Community Change. His research had convinced him that neighborhood banks
should be the catalyst for neighborhood
revitalization. Using a substantial pool
of capital, knowledge of the social and
economic conditions in their areas, and

locally trained personnel, neighborhood banks could profitably help stem
the wave of decay. Grzywinski thought
that:

*A true development bank should be an
innovative institution which continuously infuses capital, long-term credit,
and technical assistance into social and
economic improvement projects. It
should possess the capacity to initiate
development projects when other ini-
tiators are unavailable.*[2]

Up to this time, commercial banks
were legally able only to render financial services. However, the Federal
Reserve had recently decided that
banks could establish holding companies with community-oriented subsidiaries whose prime objective would
be high-risk development. These subsidiaries would invest in and assist
lower-income areas. Highly profitable,
middle-income-oriented activities
would be explicitly excluded. As a
result, in 1972, Grzywinski and his
colleagues formed the Illinois Neighborhood Development Corporation
(INDC). After reviewing the financial statements of the South Shore
National Bank and conferring with
neighborhood residents, INDC proceeded to raise $3.2 million for acquisi-
tion of the bank. Nearly $1 million
came from selling stock units of
$160,000 each to six investors: foun-
dations, individuals, and churches in
the Chicago area. The remaining $2.2
million was obtained from a loan made
by the American National Bank,
located in Chicago's Loop.

Execution In August, 1973, the Illinois Neighborhood Development Corporation officially acquired the South Shore National Bank. The new management team, Ronald Grzywinski, Milton Davis, and Mary Houghton, wanted to restore the image of the bank both figuratively and literally. To assure continuity and improve morale, former employees of the bank were retained. Salaries were reviewed and raised, and the banking hall and exterior were refurbished. Mary Houghton describes the transformation that took place:

[At first] I was ashamed to say that I worked there, it was grubby and depressing. . . . People had been saying the bank must be in trouble, any place that looked as lousy as this one had to be in trouble. Then we fixed up the place and people began saying the bank must be doing real well, and that meant South Shore was doing better because not only were we staying here, but we looked prosperous.[3]

The new management team spent a good deal of time in the lobby, talking to present and potential customers over coffee. They went to neighborhood meetings to find out residents' wants and needs, to attract customers, and to restore the image of the bank. These efforts paid off. Deposits increased from $40.6 million to $48.1 million between 1973 and 1976.

The new management strengthened the organization of the bank and increased the staff. The Conventional Loan Divison, which administers business and personal loans and mortgages for those customers who meet credit requirements, made loans totaling $26.1 million in 1976. The percentage of the bank's portfolio loaned to the community increased from 25 percent to 33 percent, the latter being a much higher figure than at other Chicago banks. At the end of 1976, mortgage loans totaling $8.5 million were outstanding, an 18 percent increase over the previous year. Of this amount, $1.6 million was committed to seventy single-family and condominium mortgages in the South Shore community.

South Shore's most visionary banking innovation was the establishment of the Neighborhood Development Center (NDC). This profit-oriented di-

Two typical houses in Chicago's South Shore area.

vision screens and administers loans and mortgages to high-risk applicants, assists neighborhood residents who need special banking services, and helps implement revitalization projects in the community. The Center is financed by development deposits—minimum $1,000—from outside the South Shore neighborhood. While these depositors receive the same interest rates that other banks pay, South Shore makes it clear that a large portion of the revenues from such deposits will be used to improve the neighborhood and help borrowers who cannot meet conventional banking standards.

The NDC, headed by Mary Houghton, made $2.9 million in loans in 1976. These break down as follows:

New Development Loans: 1976[4]

Type of Loan

Small Business	$ 582,964
Community Organizations	115,689
Mortgage	1,416,065
Education	246,518
Home Improvement	321,835
Development/Personal	245,734
Total	$2,928,805

Of the NDC's mortgage and home improvement loans, 54 percent went for the purchase or renovation of properties in the South Shore community.

NDC deposits increased from less than $3 million in 1974 to nearly $8 million at the end of 1976. Additional NDC funds accounted for one-third of the total increase in the bank's deposits for 1976. Although the NDC is profit-oriented, margins are not as great as those of conventional divisions. This is due in part to the great expenditure of staff time high-risk loans require. The NDC funds are subject to separate audit.

The NDC provides other services for the community: it publishes a newsletter, *The Bread Rapper*, that tells of the bank's activities and gives consumer advice. It sponsors conferences on various aspects of banking that provide a better understanding of financial matters. The NDC also publishes a pamphlet, *Guide to Banking Services*, which familiarizes customers with banking practices.

Besides its financial commitments to South Shore, the staff of the NDC devotes much of its time to developing,

and sometimes supporting, new projects with residents and local groups. To formalize this working relationship with the community, a nineteen-member Resident Advisory Board has been established, consisting of representatives of the nine local councils and other community organizations. Meetings of the Board are held bimonthly.

The Resident Advisory Board has been instrumental in creating the South Shore Area Development Corporation, whose objective is attracting business to the area. This independent nonprofit organization administers Small Business Administration (SBA) loans of up to $500,000 at 6⅝ percent interest for periods of up to 25 years. One of only a few such organizations in the country, the Development Corporation, in its first year, granted one loan for $275,000. As of mid-1977, two additional loans were under review.

At the end of 1976, the Resident Advisory Board also was responsible for the establishment of the South Shore Community Trust which will solicit and administer funds for commercial and rehabilitation pursuits. The Trust hopes eventually to distribute revenue to nonprofit organizations.

In addition to those projects already mentioned, South Shore Bank has been involved with and encouraged several other community organizations. The South Shore Block Club Coalition for United Action is rehabilitating nine postwar abandoned houses which it obtained from HUD. The bank's staff has lent its expertise. The project is utilizing a $30,000 Model Cities Administration grant.

Another neighborhood group is attempting to rescue a turn-of-the-century Spanish-style country club and golf course, which has been neglected since being taken over by the Chicago Park District. In cooperation with the Resident Advisory Board and the Neighborhood Development Center, this group is exploring different ways to make the club—now designated the South Shore Center—viable.

In the future, the bank plans to establish profitable development subsidiaries to rehabilitate multi-unit buildings and improve the area's commercial districts. It also wants to set up a nonprofit subsidiary to seek government and foundation funding for com-

munity service organizations.

The bank also sponsors a street-side banker who works in one of the most deprived parts of the community, known as Parkside, attempting to discover the needs of the area's people and to familiarize potential customers with the bank's services. This bank representative, whose salary is paid by a foundation, has been responsible for soliciting and processing several home-improvement loans. Commenting on his job, the street-side banker says:

At first we really weren't trusted, but lately that's changed. In one month we made seven home improvement loans; we've applied for a grant to landscape three empty lots as parks.[5]

Costs The INDC paid $3.2 million to purchase South Shore National Bank.

Problems Mary Houghton states:

The major problems are to run a profitable bank in an urban area with high transiency and a low-income segment while also pulling off neighborhood revitalization. The bank was moderately profitable in 1976, will hopefully improve on that performance in 1977, but it is a difficult management task.[6]

Benefits Between 1974 and 1976, the average single-family dwelling in South Shore has appreciated about 18 percent, from $22,500 to $26,500. Furthermore, because of the bank's efforts, developers and other banking institutions are investing in the area. Assisted by bank financing, the South Shore Villa, an older apartment building, has been renovated to provide 39 condominium units. Renewal Effort Service Corporation (RESCORP), a consortium of sixty Chicago savings and loan associations, rehabilitated 148 units in five apartment buildings. All the apartments have been rented. Since RESCORP found this undertaking profitable, it is currently renovating 154 additional apartments in six buildings. Commercial confidence is increasing: Walgreen's, a drugstore chain, is renovating one store and adding to another. Jewel Company, a supermarket chain, is planning to build a new 44,000-square-foot store, its second largest in the Chicago area. A letter written by Edwin W. Booth, Executive Director of the Cummins Engine Foundation and a member of the Board of the Illinois Neighborhood Development Corporation, clearly states the accomplishments and hopes of the South Shore National Bank:

The South Shore National Bank is an important experiment whose implications reach well beyond Chicago's South Shore Community. . . . It is beginning to show that neighborhood redevelopment can also be a source of superior profit performance. If successful, the Bank should set new performance standards, helping other financial institutions recognize that their own self-interests can best be served by similar actions.[7]

The Company Between 1975 and 1976, South Shore National Bank's assets rose from just under $42 million to over $54 million. Operating income rose over the same period from over $3.5 million to more than $4 million.

The Neighborhood Development Center audit for 1976 showed $66,953 in income, up from $29,292 the year before. Expenses also rose from $154,978 to $184,093.

For further information contact:
Mary Houghton
Vice President
South Shore National Bank of Chicago
71st and Jeffrey Boulevard
Chicago, Illinois 60649

Footnotes

1. South Shore National Bank of Chicago, *The Rebuilding of an American Neighborhood*, (Chicago: South Shore National Bank of Chicago, n.d.).
2. "Memorandum: Bank Companies as Neighborhood Development Corporation" from Ronald Grzywinski, Chairman of the Board, South Shore National Bank of Chicago, January 30, 1976, p. 3.
3. Judith Barnard, "Money Matters," *Chicago*, February, 1977, p. 100.
4. South Shore National Bank of Chicago, *1976 Annual Report and Neighborhood Development Audit* (Chicago: South Shore National Bank of Chicago, 1976), p. 23.
5. Barnard, *op. cit.*, p.104.
6. Letter from Mary Houghton, Vice President, South Shore National Bank of Chicago, to INFORM, July 11, 1977.
7. South Shore National Bank, *1976 Annual Report*, p.3.

Summary In May, 1968, Paul R. Kaiser, President and Chairman of the Board of the Tasty Baking Company, started considering ways to arrest the urban decay beginning to afflict the neighborhoods adjacent to the company's Hunting Park Avenue headquarters in North Philadelphia. After meetings with a City Councilman, an expert on urban renewal, the head of a local industrial real estate firm, and a group of community leaders, it became apparent to Mr. Kaiser that there was little chance of government support to help stop the deterioration of the Allegheny West area. He decided, with the approval of the company's Board of Directors, to involve the Tasty Baking Company in improving conditions in the surrounding neighborhoods. This resulted in the establishment of the Allegheny West Community Development Project (AWCDP), a nonprofit organization.

Since its inception in 1968, the Project has rehabilitated 55 abandoned "shell" buildings, and now plans to rehabilitate approximately 50 each year. The AWCDP has been involved in every phase of community life, from assisting home buyers in obtaining mortgages and home improvement loans to supporting day-care centers, schools, neighborhood groups, and block associations. To date, Tasty Baking has spent $933,627 on the AWCDP. Other corporations have followed Tasty's example by contributing funds. The company itself, committed to its Allegheny West location, will spend $3 million to expand its own facilities there.

Background After the decision was made to create the AWCDP, the area from the industrial complex along Hunting Park Avenue on the north to Clearfield Street on the south, and between 22nd Street and Ridge Avenue on the east and west respectively—was surveyed by the Jackson Cross Company, a Philadelphia industrial real estate firm. The area covers a total of ten city blocks north and south and six city blocks east and west. The survey examined the overall conditions there and particularly assessed the state of the exterior of the houses.

Allegheny West is almost purely residential, with the exception of some industrial facilities at the north end. It has a population of about 23,000, and approximately 6,300 single-family two-story row houses, which were built between 1900 and 1925. The housing quality of Allegheny West is erratic, with blocks of well-kept homes next to blocks riddled with poorly kept or boarded-up and abandoned houses. Most of the once numerous corner stores have been abandoned, and many yards are littered with broken glass and trash. The decay is even more extensive in the southern section, a tightly packed area with seemingly endless blocks of row houses; only two playgrounds, one playing field, and one park serve a population more than 43 percent of which is nineteen years of age or younger.

Prior to 1960, Allegheny West was what is commonly called a community in transition. Though it was not far from slum areas of the core city, south of Lehigh Avenue, it had been able to maintain its stability. Many of its residents were of Irish and Italian descent, 15 percent and 13 percent respectively, and there was a large community of eastern European Jews. Of the homes there, 83 percent were owner-occupied. However, during the decade of the 1960s, Allegheny West experienced a traumatic ethnic and socio-economic shift. By 1970, only 74 percent of its homes were owner-occupied (still far above Philadelphia's average of 60 percent). The neighborhood had gone from a middle-class/working-class area to working-class and poor. Unemployment had risen from 5 percent to 7.2 percent. The percentage of families below poverty level (16 percent) and the percentage receiving public welfare assistance (40 percent) in 1970, were both above the city's average. Of children under nineteen, 94 percent were black. Older buildings were abandoned, but rarely demolished. Overcrowding became a problem, since average family size grew, and little addition or improvement had been made to the existing housing stock since 1960.

Apparently, migration to Allegheny West was occurring from the slum areas to the south, and was beginning to bring its characteristic problems. Crimes against persons and property were increasing, and small industries were moving out of the area due to vandalism and the higher cost of security. The average level of education dropped to below the high school level, and the number of welfare recipients continued to increase. In 1960, more than one-third of the working force held white collar or professional jobs; by 1970, white collar workers constituted less than one-quarter of the jobholders. While the percentage of blue collar workers remained constant at 45 percent, that of unskilled laborers rose from 18 percent to 32 percent. It was after these changes in the character of the area that the Allegheny West Community Development Project came into being.

Tasty Baking Company came to the Allegheny West area in 1923. In that year, the company, which was rapidly expanding, left its original Philadelphia plant on Sedgely Avenue to move to its present facility at 2801 Hunting Park Avenue, a six-story structure covering approximately three-and-a-half acres and housing 1,900 of Tasty Baking Company's 2,200 employees. One of the reasons for the move in 1923 was the readily available labor supply in the surrounding residential areas of East Falls, Roxborough, and Allegheny West. Allegheny West alone supplied almost one-half of the work force.

Tasty Baking undertook the AWCDP with two goals in mind: the first was to preserve the equity of its stockholders, including 80 percent of the company's employees who take advantage of a stock-purchase plan; the second was to help serve and preserve the community of Allegheny West.

Execution For six months in 1968, exploratory meetings were held between Mr. Kaiser, local community leaders, and company employees examining the interdependence of the community and company. Mr. Kaiser first announced that a community-controlled organization would be formed by Tasty Baking with the task of improving a target neighborhood. This concept was abandoned before the project began, however, when Tasty Baking decided it was important to maintain initial control over the AWCDP and to take advantage of favorable tax deductions.

In 1968, the AWCDP was formed with the Greater Philadelphia Foundation, the nonprofit affiliate of the Greater Philadelphia Chamber of Commerce, acting as the vehicle for the renewal effort until the AWCDP became more familiar with the local community organizations. The goal of the AWCDP was to improve and renovate all derelict housing in Allegheny West as a way of "assisting community maintenance and improvement." Mr. Kaiser explained, "Tasty Baking's interest is primarily housing, although we realize the importance of education and jobs."[1] The company wished to boost real estate values and to attract home buyers to the area. Tasty committed $40,000 a year for three years, which was used to hire the AWCDP staff: a director and secretary housed in an office in the Tasty plant. There are now five full-time staff members: the Project Director, Phillip Price, who is a lawyer; a technical advisor, a former builder with teaching experience in architectural design and construction; an executive secretary; a secretary-bookkeeper; and a neighborhood representative. In 1969, the AWCDP began to assist those community organizations already in existence—the Adelphos Civic Association and the R-A-H Civic Association (Ridge Avenue, Allegheny Avenue and Hunting Park Association)—by providing financial, legal, and technical help where needed so that the residents could determine the Project's ultimate course of action. Although its primary interest is housing, more than 25 percent of staff time is devoted to individual counseling and assisting with the organization of community groups. From 1968 to 1977, Tasty spent a total of $933,627 (see table). At present, the AWCDP's Board of Directors consists of seven local businessmen, including Tasty's Chairman, Paul Kaiser, three community residents, and a member of the Philadelphia City Council.

Housing. Since late 1970, the AWCDP has rehabilitated more than 55 "shell" houses as single-family residences.

Rehabilitation work began slowly, since the Project Director had little experience in housing. It took nine months to work out a satisfactory mortgaging agreement with the Philadelphia National Bank, and one year for the first house to be rehabilitated and sold. In 1970, a technical advisor was hired to supervise all rehabilitation work. He decided that each house should be completely redesigned according to modern standards, with all structural faults corrected. Additional rooms and closets were to be added where necessary; plumbing, electrical, and heating systems revamped; all doors and windows replaced; a modern kitchen with new appliances installed—in most instances donated by co-sponsor, Sears, Roebuck and Company; the exterior of each house painted or sided; and the buyer given a guaranteed roof. The AWCDP has employed local labor so far, and most repairs of defects, however minor, are made by the Project for three years after sale.

The average purchase price for a shell is $600. The rehabilitation cost for a typical 1,240-square-foot three-bedroom row house is $13,900 or $11.20 per square foot. A new building with exactly the same facilities and square footage would cost twice as much: approximately $27,170, or $22 a square foot. The renovated house includes wall-to-wall carpeting, a washer-dryer, a full bath, a stove, and a refrigerator.

The AWCDP sells each house at a loss—the present average loss is $4,000—under a 25-year mortgage provided by an installment sale. For the first three years, the Project has title to the house and thereby retains the risk of loss. If a family defaults in the first three years, they are evicted and the property resold. Mortgages are obtained from four commercial banks: the Philadelphia National Bank, Fidelity Bank, Girard Bank, and Central Penn National Bank. From the Project's inception, there have only been three foreclosures after the 3-year period. The monthly payments include settlement costs, water and sewer rents, insurance, and real estate taxes.[2] The homes are usually sold quickly upon referral of applicants by community leaders, and their availability is publicized by word of mouth and poster advertising throughout Allegheny West.

House renovated by Allegheny West Community Development Project.

Decaying row house in Allegheny West.

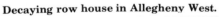

In April, 1970, the AWCDP began Operation Facelift, which offered free advice about home maintenance and improvement in the form of Service Bulletins and other literature. The initial mailing brought responses from about 1,000 area households, about one in six. Anyone responding to it became a member of the "Development Team," and was sent a membership card, entitling him or her to discounts on home-maintenance supplies from five retail stores in the area, free advice on any home-improvement problem, Service Bulletins, and information about community matters. The Service Bulletins prepared for the members of the Development Team dealt with topics like roofing, plumbing, electrical work, painting and paneling, ceiling and floor tiles, and prices and contractors. All Bulletins were eventually consolidated into the *Allegheny West Community Handbook*, which has had two separate editions, and has been distributed to more than 2,500 households in the area.

In 1972, the AWCDP began the "Merit Award" program, which recognizes efforts made at home improvement by individuals either with or without the Project's help. By the end of the year, over 120 homeowners received these awards. They have encouraged increased neighborhood involvement and boosted residents' morale. Beginning in 1973, the Project also made available a team of mechanics to do home-remodeling work at a substantial savings.

Because of the AWCDP's success, in 1976, a Neighborhood Housing Services (NHS) unit was established in Allegheny West. NHS is a national program designed to help maintain and renew inner-city areas. Under the leaderhsip of Executive Director Julia Robinson and President Donald McGill, the NHS-Allegheny West has provided a source of private conventional loans for mortgages and home improvement, and helped obtain improved city services for the area. The local NHS is financed by approximately thirty banks as well as by a grant from the William Penn Foundation.

Education. The AWCDP has supplied assistance to several educational and child-care institutions. It provided the money to purchase juice and cookies for one year for twenty pre-school children at the day-care center located in the Berean Baptist Church. After that year, a Tasty employee and the head of a foundation took over the responsibility. The Project helped the center obtain a use certificate from the Philadelphia Zoning Board of Adjustment, so the center could receive regular medical and technical assistance from the city. In addition, it supervised renovation of the basement area which is used for the child-care center. Funds for the work came from members of Berean Baptist Church.

The AWCDP also supervised and coordinated the incorporation of an organization called Black Interested Parents, Inc. Under this incorporated structure, a group of working mothers became eligible to receive funds for operation of a pre-school child-care center. The AWCDP acted as negotiator for the John Greenleaf Whittier Elementary School in its effort to obtain financial support from the Philadelphia National Bank for what is now the Philadelphia National Bank-Whittier Reading Improvement Center. Finally, Tasty personnel donate several hours each week to the Thomas May Pierce School to tutor elementary school students in math and reading.

Jobs. Tasty and other local large industries have attempted to aid area residents by giving them preference in job consideration. In addition, Tasty and The Budd Company have instituted summer-job programs for teenagers to work on community improvements. At the end of each summer, the participating teenagers, working under the supervision of Tasty employees, receive certificates for "outstanding support to the community," signed by company Chairman Kaiser.

Community Affairs. The AWCDP has helped the local groups in their fight against the sources of problems in their respective neighborhoods. On several occasions, from 1969 to 1975, Phillip Price, the Director of the AWCDP, successfully represented R-A-H and Adelphos, local community organizations, at Liquor Control Board hearings; in 1974, he assisted community groups in their fight to have a long-time and very profitable State Liquor Store removed from its present site, 300 feet away from an elementary school.

In 1970, the AWCDP requested additional street lighting from the city to deter street crime. This request led to the allocation for lighting of over $48,000. That same year, the Project helped coordinate the efforts of the Ringgold Square Improvement Committee, and donated $3,628 to turn a run-down lot in the center of 61 houses into a park. Work on the park began in spring, 1970; co-sponsor, Morris, Wheeler & Co., Inc., donated steel railing for it, and Tasty Baking arranged the donation, from a paving contractor, of materials and labor to repair the broken surfacing tiles. The city cooperated by providing the labor to do the remaining work. Phillip Price provides general legal services to the community, while the Project's builder provides architectural services.

In 1973, the AWCDP was the subject of an in-depth study conducted by the Institute for Environmental Studies of the University of Pennsylvania for the U.S. Department of Housing and Urban Development. The Project was selected as a unique example of a privately financed neighborhood conservation effort.

The study focuses on two main questions: "the actual and potential impact of the AWCDP on the Allegheny West area, and the immediate causes of decay and abandonment in the neighborhoods where these problems are in their early stages."[3]

A voluminous account of the inception of the AWCDP, Tasty Baking Company's part in it, and its progress up through 1972, the study describes the economic changes that have shaken Allegheny West, the structure of the AWCDP, and the real estate market and its impact on the housing quality and economics of the area. It found that though whites are moving out of the area, many black residents and small businessmen are optimistic about the change taking place within their neighborhoods.

The interviewers also found that only 35 percent of area residents had heard of the work that Tasty Baking was doing, and that even fewer people recognized the AWCDP's activities. A quarter of those interviewed had heard of Operation Facelift, and three-quarters of those who knew of Tasty's housing activities described them as very helpful. In the ensuing five years, both the visibility and effectiveness of the AWCDP have increased dramatically.

Costs   In addition to the $933,627, donated by Tasty Baking to the AWCDP from the time of its inception in 1968 through 1976, the company planned to contribute another $300,000 in 1977. Tasty's annual allocation of $40,000 constituted the Project's entire operating budget until September, 1970, when Mr. Kaiser began meeting with heads of other locally based corporations to obtain funds for the coming years. Eight other firms are now contributing regularly and account for between 10 percent and 20 percent of all contributions made in any one year.

Beyond Paul Kaiser's involvement, other Tasty Baking employees have worked with the Project since its inception: the Treasurer, Controller, Assistant Treasurer, Art Director, Public Relations Manager, and Personnel Director. Tasty has also provided office space, as well as telephones, duplicating facilities, and stationery to the AWCDP.

Problems   The AWCDP has found major problems in reeducating some residents of Allegheny West. Many people did not know or understand and had to be instructed in how to maintain their newly renovated homes. The AWCDP also devoted much time helping existing community groups become better organized to increase their effectiveness in dealing with the city.

Approximately 15 percent of the new residents in the renovated homes default within the initial three-year period. Some of these people have refused to move, at times resulting in complicated legal battles.

Many new residents have also had problems adjusting to their new homes. The first renovated structure was sold to a minister in 1970, who made the home available to a needy family. This family had several children, and had previously lived in a one-room apartment. After several months of living in their new home, the family moved back to their apartment; coping with a full-size house was too drastic a change.

Benefits   Federal and state tax benefits are available to contributors to the AWCDP. Since the latter part of 1968, the Commonwealth of Pennsylvania has granted tax credits under the Neighborhood Assistance Act to corporations which spend money on improving impoverished neighborhoods. This Act has provided corporate contributors with credits against corporate net reserve taxes of up to 50 percent of monies donated to the Project.

The combined federal and state tax situation is encouraging. Prior to March 19, 1977, approximately 77 cents out of every corporate dollar contributed to the AWCDP was deductible against income for federal or state tax purposes. Since March 19, 1977, for "special program priorities," of which the AWCDP is one, the Commonwealth grants a tax credit of 70 percent. Each contributing company can now deduct 89½ cents of every dollar given.

If a company doing business in Pennsylvania earns more than $25,000, and contributes $10,000 under the recently liberalized Neighborhood Assistance Act, tax credits reduce the actual cash outlay as follows:

Contribution to The Allegheny West Foundation	$10,000
Less State and Federal Income Taxes (9½ percent—Corporate Net Income Tax Rate—of $10,000 and 48 percent of remainder—$9,050, respectively)	5,294
Net Cost before Credit	4,706
Pennsylvania Tax Credit (70 percent) $7,000	
Less Federal Income Tax (48 percent of $7,000) 3,360	
Net Credit After Taxes	3,640
Net Cost of Contribution	1,066

Tasty's leverage in the business community has greatly aided the AWCDP in dealing with local merchants, contractors, and financial institutions, as well as in obtaining increased services from the city. The Project has attracted more and better medical services to the area; several doctors have opened practices there.

Due to Tasty's efforts, many corporations have joined the AWCDP's war on deterioration. The success of the Project has confirmed the company's decision to remain in Allegheny West and continue to upgrade the area. As a natural outgrowth of this policy, Tasty recently purchased a large vacant industrial building and the surrounding land for $1 million and will spend $1.8 million to improve the complex for additional corporate facilities.

The AWCDP should, in time, realize its intention of rehabilitating all derelict property in Allegheny West. Although in the beginning, the rate of abandonment was very high, abandonment has ceased in recent years. Private investment, in the form of small-scale speculation and investor interest, is now reappearing. In 1970, a shell property sold for $350; today it sells for over $2,600. The AWCDP's managers estimate that a continuation of the current rate of rehabilitation of fifty houses a year, coupled with the vital program of the Neighborhood Housing Services, and the addition of new large-scale employers to the area, will in four years bring about a takeover by the private real estate sector. At that point, the stabilization of Allegheny West will be a fact.

The Company The Tasty Baking Company was founded in Philadelphia in 1914 by Phillip J. Baur, a baker, and Herbert C. Morris, a salesman. The first product was a pre-sliced and iced individually wrapped cake, a revolutionary item at a time when almost all cake was baked at home. The product caught on, and Tasty Baking expanded. In the 1930s, it introduced rectangular fruit pies that further increased sales. In 1965, Tasty Baking started diversifying into other product lines: toys, graphic arts, and cookies. The main baking plant is located in North Philadelphia, and houses 1,900 of the company's 2,200 employees.

Total sales were $157.4 million in 1976, up from $146.2 million in 1975; the earnings for 1976 were $6.66 million, up from $6.45 million the previous year.

An excerpt from the company's 1976 Annual Report reflects Tasty's concern about social issues:

In the area of social responsibility, our neighborhood approach to urban renewal, begun in 1968, has come of age. It is now receiving community development funds from the City of Philadelphia. To us, this is compelling evidence that government agrees the best way to halt inner city decay is through projects similar to our three-way Allegheny West partnership among business, government, and the citizens themselves.[4]

Other Preservation Activities. At the Franklin Institute's new Science Park, Tasty Baking has reconstructed two row houses, one deteriorated and one rehabilitated, to show what the AWCDP, in cooperation with the residents of the area and local government, has accomplished. A film and illustrative material accompany the exhibit and show the process and cost of rehabilitation.

For further information contact:
Phillip Price, Jr.
Secretary and Director
The Allegheny West Foundation
2801 Hunting Park Avenue
Philadelphia, Pennsylvania 19129

Footnotes

1. Institute for Environmental Studies, University of Pennsylvnia, "The Allegheny West Community Development Project: An Experiment in Privately Financed Neighborhood Conservation," (mimeographed, prepared for the U.S. Department of Housing and Urban Development, 1973), chap. 3, p. 12.
2. Allegheny West Community Development Project, *A Unique Approach to Urban Development*, (Philadelphia: Allegheny West Community Development Project, n.d.), pp. 5–6.
3. Institute for Environmental Studies, *op. cit.*, chap. 1, p. 2.
4. Tasty Baking Company, *Tasty Baking Company 1976 Annual Report* (Philadelphia: Tasty Baking Company, 1976), p. 3.

Cash Contributions to Allegheny West Community Development Project
1969–1976

1968–1969

Tasty Baking Company		$ 37,200.

1970

Tasty Baking Company		$ 54,028.*
Cassidy/Richlar, Inc.	$ 1,667	
Morris, Wheeler & Co., Inc.	3,333.	
Penn Fishing Tackle Mfg. Co.	833.	
Rosenau Brothers, Inc. (Foundation)	1,000.	
Sears, Roebuck & Co.	6,667	
Steel Heddle Mfg. Co.	500.	
Other		$ 14,000.
Total		$ 68,028.

*$3,000. of this amount was from Tasty Baking Company's Foundation.

1971

Tasty Baking Company		$ 42,873.
Crown Printing Company	$ 50.	
Penn Fishing Tackle Mfg. Co.	2,500.	
The Pep Boys—Manny, Moe & Jack	500.	
Philadelphia Electric Company	5,000.	
Rosenau Brothers, Inc. (Foundation)	3,000.	
Other		$ 11,050.
Total		$ 53,923.

1972
Tasty Baking Company $120,792.

Helen D. G. Beatty Trust $ 1,500.
The Budd Company   1,000.
Container Corporation of America Foundation   1,000.
Morris, Wheeler & Co., Inc.   10,000.
Penn Fishing Tackle Mfg. Co.   2,500.
Philadelphia Electric Company   10,000.
Rosenau Brothers, Inc. (Foundation)   500.
Sears, Roebuck & Co.   7,000.
Strauss Foundation   1,000.
    Other $ 34,500.
    Total $155,292.

1973
Tasty Baking Company $107,550.

Helen D. G. Beatty Trust $ 1,000.
The Budd Company   1,500.
Container Corporation of America Foundation   1,000.
Philadelphia Electric Company   10,000.
Philadelphia National Bank   1,500.
Rosenau Brothers, Inc. (Foundation)   1,000.
Strauss Foundation   1,500.
    Other $ 17,500.
    Total $125,050.

1974
Tasty Baking Company $147,500.

Container Corporation of America $ 1,000.
The Fidelity Bank   500.
Girard Bank   500.
Morris, Wheeler & Co., Inc.   5,000.
Penn Fishing Tackle Mfg. Co.   2,500.
Philadelphia Electric Company   10,000.
Royal Electric Supply Co.   1,000.
Steel Heddle Mfg. Co.   500.
    Other $ 21,000.
    Total $168,500.

1975
Tasty Baking Company $202,500.

Alexander & Alexander, Inc. $ 100.
The Budd Company   6,000.
Container Corporation of America   1,500.
Morris, Wheeler & Co., Inc.   5,000.
Philadelphia Electric Company   10,000.
Steel Heddle Mfg. Co.   8,000.
Van Tents, Inc.   100.
    Other $ 30,700.
    Total $233,200.

1976
Tasty Baking Company $221,184

The Fidelity Bank $ 200.
The Budd Company   8,000.
F.M.C. Corporation (Foundation)   750.
Van Tents Inc.   100.
Steel Heddle Mfg. Co.   10,000.
    Other $ 19,050.
    Total $240,234.

American Broadcasting Companies, Inc.

Commercial Redevelopment

Summary In July, 1974, American Broadcasting Companies, Inc. (ABC), acquired the Historic Towne of Smithville in southern New Jersey for $8 million. This historic village complex contains restaurants, shops, and a museum village. ABC's purchase was the first instance of a publicly held company's buying a historic village. To date, ABC has spent $1.5 million to renovate the Towne.

Background A rambling stagecoach inn, whose original section dates from about 1787, was the nucleus for the development of the flourishing Historic Towne of Smithville complex. In 1949, Mr. and Mrs. Fred Noyes purchased this rundown historic inn, and renovated it, establishing a restaurant. Through the years, they moved additional vintage buildings from southern New Jersey to the thirty-acre site, and renovated these structures as restaurants and shops. New compatible buildings were constructed as Smithville became an increasingly popular tourist attraction.

In recent years, the Noyeses had been developing a separate Living Village as part of the Historic Towne, again utilizing historic New Jersey buildings from the late eighteenth and nineteenth centuries. Several structures were renovated and furnished with authentic period pieces. Now known as the Old Village, this is an additional attraction of the Towne which also provides theater, concerts, lectures, and craft shows.

Several years ago, wanting more leisure time, the Noyeses decided to sell the Historic Towne.

Execution ABC was approached by a broker, and purchased the Historic Towne of Smithville from the Noyeses in July, 1974, for $8 million, to be paid over a four- to five-year period.

After the purchase by ABC, Mr. and Mrs. Noyes stayed with the operation until they retired in November, 1975. During the transition period, ABC invested about $1.5 million to complete the Old Village. All 33 buildings were renovated, including private houses, a fire house, a blacksmith shop, and Liederkranz Hall, a social hall. The houses are appropriately furnished with authentic period pieces. The completely landscaped Village, depicting life in a typical southern New Jersey community from the 1820s to 1850s, was opened to the public in spring, 1975. Today, each house has a resident artisan demonstrating local crafts, such as glass blowing, wood carving, weaving, spinning, apple-doll making, leathercraft, and pottery.

Although the Historic Towne of Smithville is less profitable than ABC's television operations, television, radio, and press promotion in the contiguous Delaware Valley area is expected to increase margins.

Costs To date, ABC has spent a total of more than $9.5 million for the purchase and renovation of Historic Smithville.

Benefits Besides being profitable, the Historic Towne of Smithville is an asset to other divisions of ABC. In January, 1976, ABC televised a two-hour Bicentennial show utilizing various historic sites throughout the country, including the Towne. This of course served to publicize the Smithville venture as well.

Historic Smithville employs about 800 people in the summer and 350 in the winter. With ABC's advertising and promotional help, receipts at the Old Village have tripled.

The Company American Broadcasting Companies, Inc., is an entertainment conglomerate whose operations include television and radio networks, theaters, and special-attraction parks. In 1954, Leonard Golden, the founder of ABC and currently its Chairman, helped finance California's Disneyland, and in the same year, ABC bought Silver Springs, Florida, a special-attraction park. Through the years, it has expanded this property to include not only subtropical and underwater features, but also an Early American Museum featuring displays of horse-drawn vehicles and cars. In 1957, ABC purchased another Florida entertainment park, Weeki Wachee, where young women costumed as mermaids perform in an underwater amphitheater. These two wholly owned theme parks have been highly profitable. However, a wildlife park in Largo, Maryland, has proven less successful.

In 1976, ABC's revenues amounted to $1.3 billion, representing an 18 percent increase over 1975's $1.1 billion. Net income rose from $17 million to $71.4 million over the same period. With increased profit margins, earnings per share improved to $4.05 in 1976, versus 99 cents the year before.

For further information contact:
Michael Winter
Director of Marketing
American Broadcasting Companies, Inc.
1330 Avenue of the Americas
New York, NY 10019

Frank Lyons
President and General Manager
Historic Towne of Smithville
Rte. 9
Smithville, NJ 08201

The Smithville Inn (c. 1787), the nucleus of Historic Smithville.

Bethlehem Steel Corporation

Summary Bethlehem Steel, the second largest steel producer in the country, has taken an active role in preservation causes, particularly in its hometown of Bethlehem, Pennsylvania. The company has been a major contributor to Historic Bethlehem, Inc. (HBI), a voluntary nonprofit community organization founded in 1964 to preserve and restore Bethlehem's eighteenth-century Moravian community. In 1975, its support for HBI included a donation of $100,000 in Lehigh Valley Industrial Park Bonds plus $50,000 in accumulated interest. The following year, it sponsored a study by the Urban Land Institute on the redevelopment of downtown Bethlehem's commercial area, which is adjacent to Historic Bethlehem. Implementation of a redevelopment program for this commercial area began in 1977.

Background Bethlehem, Pennsylvania was founded in 1741 by a group of German-speaking Protestants known as Moravians. By 1747, the town had 32 industries in operation and a variety of businesses, trades, and crafts fostered by the hard-working Moravians. This wealth of economic activity made the town almost self-sufficient. But the nineteenth century brought some drastic changes to Bethlehem. New technologies made most of the early industries outmoded, and the buildings which had housed them were either torn down or put to new uses.

By the twentieth century, only a few buildings of historic importance remained. These were surrounded by an automobile junkyard. When the few remnants were threatened by a flood in the mid-1960s, it became clear that decisive action would have to be taken, or they would be lost.

Execution Flood-control measures were instituted, and the citizens of Bethlehem rallied to save what was left of the colonial industrial area; Historic Bethlehem, Inc., was founded in 1964. Bethlehem Steel donated $125,000 at the new organization's inception to help pay for administrative expenses and archeological surveys. Assisted by Bethlehem Steel and other individuals and businesses, HBI has expanded rapidly. To date, five buildings have either been restored or totally reconstructed. In addition, five sites of historic value have been identified, and parts of the foundations of four former structures have been located.

The first building restored by HBI was the Tannery, built in 1761. The structure had been an industrial facility until 1873, when it was converted to tenement housing, and later, to a laundry. The restoration, begun in 1971 and completed at a cost of $250,000, has provided HBI with its main exhibit area, including displays on tanning, spinning, weaving, and pottery. The reconstruction of the Spring House, a log structure whose prototype had been built in 1764, was completed in 1971 at a cost of $43,000. In 1972, HBI restored the 1762 Waterworks. It was intact but required extensive interior and exterior improvements which took four years and $125,000 to accomplish. HBI also restored the Goundie House, built by a prosperous brewer in 1810. The house, opened in 1976, contains a museum shop and several period rooms, including a kitchen. In 1976, HBI also made structural improvements costing $23,000 on the Grist Miller's House, a 1782 building with an 1832 brick addition.

HBI has located and surveyed the sites of many of the other buildings in the colonial industrial complex, including the Bark Shed and Oil Mill. The organization conducts walking tours of the area with guides often dressed in eighteenth-century Moravian fashions.

In 1975, Bethlehem Steel donated $100,000 in Lehigh Valley Industrial Park Bonds to HBI. These bonds, which had been issued in 1963 to finance construction of buildings and support facilities for the industrial park, paid 5 percent interest annually and matured in March, 1975. Instead of redeeming the bonds, Bethlehem Steel, in an innovative gesture of support, donated them to HBI. HBI also received the accumulated interest on the bonds—amounting to $50,000—which Bethlehem Steel had not collected through the years. HBI's budget in 1977 was $119,000.

Many Bethlehem Steel employees, including high-level management officials, have been and continue to be active in HBI.

Study on the Revitalization of the Downtown Business District. In spring, 1976, Bethlehem Steel financed a $40,000 study of ways to revitalize and redevelop downtown Bethlehem. The published study was conducted by the Urban Land Institute, an independent Washington-based research group established in 1936 to examine land-use trends and to help identify the best and most efficient development methods.

Due to suburban competition, the Bethlehem Plaza Mall, a new shopping center, was finding it difficult to attract department stores, and leasing was proceeding slowly. The Urban Land Institute's study suggested that downtown Bethlehem would benefit more from taking into account the tourism inspired by HBI's colonial industrial area than from the addition of large shopping and office areas. The study found that many of the stores along Main Street were of Victorian vintage. It emphasized utilizing their unique nature to attract business, and suggested developing specialty stores, such as ice cream parlors, antique stores, and craft shops, rather than large supermarket complexes. A mall-like atmosphere would be encouraged by two large pedestrian walkways lined with benches and trees. Each store owner would be responsible for his own frontage, but each structure would have to conform to standards set by the city to maintain a unity of atmosphere. This would create a Main Street more effectively linked to the adjacent HBI industrial area. The restoration would also attract shoppers and tourists to the Bethlehem Plaza Mall through development of a "hinge block" at the end of Main Street. This link to the new mall would contain a variety of sites of interest, including the restored colonial Sun Inn, and a new performing arts center and garage.

The Sun Inn, a colonial inn built in 1758, would be both a tourist attraction—"George Washington slept here"—and a functioning inn. The proposed 450-seat performing arts center would help the area attract business. A parking facility, which opened in December, 1976, is located adjacent to the Bethlehem Plaza Mall, and shops between the garage and the mall serve as a link between performing-arts patrons and mall shoppers.

In order to implement the Urban Land Institute's proposals, the study suggested the formation of the Committee for Center City Greater Bethlehem (CGB), a nonprofit corporation. This organization, composed of concerned citizens and a staff executive, would help identify community problems, serve as a catalyst in spurring community action, provide nonpartisan leadership to projects undertaken, and secure cooperation from city or state government agencies. The CGB would require an annual budget of $125,000 and would need a five-year pledge commitment to ensure its effectiveness.

Hotel Bethlehem. In response to the Urban Land Institute's study, Bethlehem Steel is also currently investigating the possibility of further improving the Hotel Bethlehem, of which it is part owner. The Hotel has been a main tourist attraction and convention center since its construction in 1921. The company has renovated and improved parts of the building over the years: in 1963, the exterior was completely renovated at a cost of $300,000; in 1966, a parking garage was added; the Continental Dining Room was completed in 1969; and the interior was refurbished in 1973.

Costs In addition to its initial $125,000 donation and the $150,000 in Lehigh Valley Park Bonds and interest, Bethlehem Steel supports HBI fund-raising campaigns. It also paid for the Urban Land Institute's $40,000 study. The company has made additional expenditures on renovations and improvements of the Hotel Bethlehem. But the figures on its costs in this area were not available, nor was information on tax benefits gained by Bethlehem Steel through its donations to HBI.

Benefits Bethlehem Steel's donations to HBI have allowed the organization to renovate or reconstruct the Tannery, Goundie House, the Waterworks, Spring House, and the Grist Miller's House, helping make the complex a major local tourist attraction, and bringing economic benefits to the City of Bethlehem. According to Dennis Scholl, an official of the Bethlehem Chamber of Commerce, HBI's restorations and reconstructions attract about 20,000 visitors per year.[1]

The implementation of the Urban Land Institute's study could help revitalize downtown Bethlehem's commercial area. The expansion of HBI and the development of downtown Bethlehem may draw more people to the area and could increase business for the Hotel Bethlehem and other commercial establishments. The company's contributions are also an important factor in generating goodwill in its home city.

The Company Bethlehem Steel is the second largest steel maker in the United States, processing 15 percent of the nation's raw steel. Its turn-of-the-century Bethlehem facility is the largest structural-steel-producing plant in the country. Bethlehem Steel is also the principal employer in the Lehigh Valley, employing almost 20,000 people from Bethlehem and the surrounding area.

In 1976, company revenues were $5.3 billion, a 5.5 percent increase over the previous year's $5.03 billion. However, net income declined 30.6 percent from $242 million in 1975 to $168 million in 1976. Bethlehem Steel's principal markets are: construction, 22 percent; transportation, 29.5 percent; service centers and processors, 20 percent; machinery, 10.2 percent; and other, 18 percent.

Other Preservation Activities. Bethlehem Steel contributed $30,000 for the renovation and relocation of the Johnstown Flood Museum, commemorating one of the country's worst natural disasters, which took place in 1889.

The company has also donated funds for the re-creation of a historic oil boom town, Gladys City, Texas. This town became famous in January, 1901, when two men made a strike which produced twice as much oil as all the wells in Pennsylvania. It was here that four major oil companies, Mobil, Exxon, Gulf, and Texaco, began. The museum-city, now open to the public, includes clapboard houses of the 1880s, oil derricks, wooden tanks, and oil-field-equipment display areas. Future plans call for relocating an existing monument and museum to the re-creation site.

In addition, Bethlehem Steel has donated a steel door to cover the mouth of a pre-Civil War Underground Railway tunnel at the Orchard Street Church in Baltimore, Maryland, used to aid slaves from the South to reach the free North. The church, built in 1828, is a major part of the historic section of Baltimore, and its restoration is a local Bicentennial effort. The company also helped produce "The Underground Tunnel," an audio-visual presentation on the tunnel and its history.

For further information contact:
J. V. Robertson
Manager of Community Affairs
Bethlehem Steel Corporation
Martin Tower
Bethlehem, Pennsylvania 18016

(on facing page)
An 1810 house, restored by Historic Bethlehem, Inc. (Historic Bethlehem, Inc.)

(below on facing page)
The Tannery (c. 1761). (Historic Bethlehem, Inc.)

Footnotes

1. INFORM interview with Dennis Scholl, Director of Convention and Visitors Bureau, Bethlehem Area Chamber of Commerce, September, 1977.

Corning Glass Works

Summary In Corning, New York, Corning Glass Works is contributing to urban revitalization by providing the leadership and financial support to help restore and preserve the original nineteenth-century character of a four-block downtown commercial street. Market Street's basically sound buildings suffered from neglect and disfiguration over many years. In 1972 they were, further, hit by a devastating flood. That same year, to help reverse the fortunes of the area, the Market Street Restoration Program was developed with seed money from the Corning Glass Works Foundation. A team of professional consultants conducted studies to map out appropriate restoration and revitalization plans. These plans were coordinated with major urban-renewal plans developed in 1970 for an eight-square-block area directly east of Market Street.

In 1974, the Market Street Restoration Agency, a private, nonprofit corporation, fully supported by grants from the Corning Glass Works Foundation, was established to assist local businesses in revitalizing the street. So far, more than 75 percent of the store owners on Market Street have participated in the Program. Corning Glass has contributed close to $3 million to the Market Street project and to area urban renewal over the past five years. The company's reasons are clear: to support the community in which its employees live and work; and to make the town a more desirable environment which will attract and keep good employees.

Background The town of Corning is located on the banks of the Chemung River in a beautiful valley in Steuben County. It is near both the recreation and resort area of the Finger Lakes and the intersection of Routes 15, 17, and 81, major east-west and north-south traffic arteries in western New York State. This central location and the existence of the Corning Glass Center and Museum, which contains one of the finest glass collections in the world, have helped make Corning the third largest tourist site in the state: it attracts more than 750,000 people a year. Until recently, however, most tourists only passed through the town on their way to the Glass Center.

The Corning Glass Works has been headquartered in Corning since 1868, and it is the largest employer in the area.

Downtown Corning's Market Street is a typical American "Main Street," a four-block commercial street with an assortment of two- and three-story structures built between 1880 and 1910. Like many older downtown commercial districts across the country, Market Street has suffered from the growth of the suburbs and a loss of business to surrounding shopping centers.

Market Street store owners initially resisted this loss of business by trying to "modernize" their stores with new facades and larger, more contemporary signs. But these efforts failed to attract customers, and many merchants were forced to close down and move out.

In 1970, an urban-renewal plan, financed in part by the Corning Glass Works Foundation, and coordinated by James Sheaffer, Executive Director of the Corning Urban Renewal Agency, was developed for an eight-square-block downtown area. Geddes, Brecher, Qualls, and Cunningham, architects and urban design consultants from Princeton, New Jersey, and Philadelphia, Pennsylvania, were hired to conduct studies and develop the renewal plans. They were assisted by Davis A. Chiodo, an architect and Manager of Product and Business Development for the Corning Glass Works. The studies resulted in proposals for a new city hall, a new public library, a new civic center/ice rink, a new 125-room hotel, and residential and commercial complexes. Market Street was to become a pedestrian retail/commercial mall.

The idea of restoring Market Street to its turn-of-the-century character did not arise from the urban renewal plans. It came later in 1971 and 1972 when Thomas S. Buechner, President of the Corning Glass Works Foundation, began to promote the idea, perhaps partially inspired by the efforts in the late 1960s of two women from the local historical society, Virginia Wright and Jean Wozinski, who had tried to interest Market Street merchants in restoring their buildings. Buechner had been the Director of the Brooklyn Museum prior to joining Corning as President of Steuben Glass and Chairman of the Foundation's Board of Trustees. He convinced many local merchants and the Corning Urban Renewal Agency of the business benefits of restoring and maintaining the scale and unified style of architecture along Market Street.

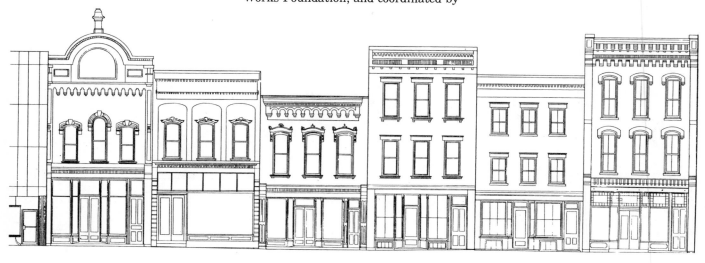

Market Street in Corning, New York consists of four blocks of two-, three-, and four-story commercial buildings dating from the turn of the century. (Corning Glass Foundation)

Facades along Corning's Main Street. (Market Street Restoration Agency)

Execution A Restoration Committee was established which included Buechner, Sheaffer, Chiodo, Mayor Joseph J. Nasser, and eighteen other Corning citizens. Geddes, Brecher, Qualls, and Cunningham suggested that John Milner and the National Heritage Corporation, a firm specializing in restoration architecture, be retained to study and plan the Market Street Restoration Program. A seed grant from the Corning Glass Works Foundation would support the project in the planning stage. The Program's objectives were:

1. To reestablish Market Street as a unique commercial center.

2. To establish within an attractive environment a downtown that reflects the quality of life in the community; the quality of its people, organizations, business, and industry.

3. To preserve structures that possess a rare uniformity of architectural style and character as a downtown attraction for the thousands of visitors who annually tour the Corning Glass Center and other area attractions.[1]

The overall plan dealt with such issues as: traffic and pedestrian flow, parking, improved lighting and signs, and landscaping, as well as building rehabilitation. Rehabilitation guidelines, shaped by the local historical society's extensive research of old photographs of Market Street, were published and distributed to insure appropriate facade treatment. Facades were to be restored to their original design where possible or to new designs that would harmonize with the scale of the building, the configuration of windows and doors, and the nature and color of the predominant building material.* The Program aimed at re-establishing the small, pleasant scale of a nineteenth-century shopping street, and at developing a "sense of a special unified space."[2] In addition to the rehabilitation guidelines, sign guidelines and

design recommendations for public-space developments were also set forth.

Although the Restoration Program was conceived in 1972, it did not get into full swing until 1974. A major disaster hindered restoration progress, although in the long run, it may have stimulated greater citizen participation and support. Hurricane Agnes struck Corning in the summer of 1972, and the Chemung River flooded the town. More than 60 percent of it was under water. The Corning Glass Works, the state government, and the federal government all pitched in to help Corning recover. Local residents united behind an effort to rebuild the town and preserve its remaining heritage.

Corning Glass Works played an active as well as supportive role in the revitalization of Market Street. The company owned several buildings on the street and took the lead by rehabilitating a nineteenth-century mill turned recreation center to house its offices and archives. Corning Glass also renovated the first floor of the old Baron Steuben Hotel as a series of shops, while the second floor served as a temporary home for the Rockwell-Corning Museum, a collection of art of the American West; other floors will provide office space. In addition to company and town activities, public funds in the form of a HUD "open space grant" of $500,000 provided new brick sidewalks and trees for the street.

In 1974, the Market Street Restoration Agency was established to coordinate rehabilitation of storefronts on the street and to oversee the entire revitalization effort. This private, non-profit organization is being directed by Norman Mintz, who was trained in Columbia University's Historic Preservation Program. Mintz's task has demanded diplomatic as well as design skills. He has had to convince some store owners that their new aluminum and plastic fronts were "inappropriate." Not all merchants agree that restoration, rather than modernization, is best. "It is as much an education job as it is a design job,"[3] says Mintz. Mintz and his wife, Melanie, have also been working with schools in the area to create an awareness of architecture and to introduce students to the benefits of preserving old buildings.

Since 1974, about 25 percent of the buildings along Market Street have been rehabilitated, and over 75 percent of the merchants and landlords have participated in the Program in some way. The Market Street Restoration Agency provides free design plans and working drawings, but does not fund the actual costs of rehabilitation. These costs are paid by the store owners, and range from $250 to $4,500. "The most important thing to remember," says Mintz, "is that we are not trying to create a Disneyland of cute recreations of somebody's concept of the past. We are just trying to design new storefronts that respect the design of the original buildings."[4] As a result, not all storefronts or signs are in the Victorian style; contemporary designs that harmonize with the character of the original architecture are also used.

Norman Mintz has also been responsible for promoting Market Street. He works closely with the Market Street Association (MSA), a merchants' organization, coordinating radio and newspaper advertising under the MSA logo, and creating special events to attract local residents and some of the more than 750,000 tourists who visit the Corning Glass Center each year. In June, 1976, a summer festival celebrating the town's rebuilding efforts and the nation's Bicentennial brought more than 50,000 people to Market Street.

___

* Prior to the restoration concept, the Corning Glass Works had contributed to the modern "cover-ups" on two of these old storefronts. The company produced a glass-ceramic wall panel material that had been tested on a store and a bank along Market Street.

Costs The Corning Glass Works, through its Foundation, has provided more than $250,000 for the revitalization of Market Street since the idea was first conceived. Approximately $100,000 of this was spent on the initial studies and plans. The balance has supported the Market Street Restoration Agency whose budget is about $60,000 per year.

Since 1970, the company has also contributed about $2.8 million more to the overall urban-renewal effort in downtown Corning. Of this, $128,000 was used for the initial planning studies; $144,000 paid for the architectural fees for the new city hall and firehouse; $500,000 helped build the ice skating rink; and $1.6 million was used to design and build the new Corning Public Library. The company has also donated $31,232 to fund restoration/conversion studies for the old city hall, a Victorian brick structure vacated when the new city hall was completed. Plans are now under consideration to reuse the old building to house the Rockwell Corning Museum, featuring a superb collection of Western American art on loan from Mr. and Mrs. Robert Rockwell of Corning.

Problems According to George Douglas, Director of Community Affairs for the company, Corning Glass Works is "the largest company with its World Headquarters in a town this small in the United States."[5] This presents problems both for the company and for the town; while the company could take a more active role to speed the Market Street revitalization project, it feels that a democratic process is more desirable. Of course, the effort may take more time to produce visible results.

Contemporary storefronts are compatible in design, materials, color, and signs with the original buildings. (Kellogg Studio)

Benefits Since Corning Glass has acted as a catalyst for the revitalization of downtown Corning, its private capital has helped to attract public capital. More than $7 million has gone into the renewal program from state and federal sources, more than doubling the company's contribution.

Market Street itself has been a widely touted success. All stores on the street are now occupied as compared to a 15 percent vacancy rate in 1974. The scale of Market Street has been maintained and has strongly influenced the kind of new architecture in the renewal area. Norman Mintz has been asked to speak in many parts of the country, and the Market Street Restoration Program has been a model for other commercial-district revitalization programs. A recent article on the rebirth of Corning states: "These accomplishments . . . cast a whole new light on how urbane our outlying communities could end up being."[6]

Besides seeing its community environment improve, Corning Glass has also received its share of favorable publicity for its efforts and has developed community goodwill. According to Urban Renewal Director Jim Sheaffer: "The high quality of the product is definitely related to the fact that the Corning Glass Works is in Corning, New York."[7]

The Company Corning Glass Works, an international producer of glass, glass-ceramic, and related products, was established in 1851 and has been located in Corning, New York, since 1868. The company has offices, plants, and subsidiary and associated companies in 25 countries. Corning's net sales for 1976 were $1.02 billion, up from 1975's $938.9 million. The company's net income in 1976 was $83.7 million, the highest in its history, more than double 1975's $31.1 million.

Other Preservation Activities. The Corning Glass Works Foundation, incorporated in 1952, has usually supported projects in areas where the parent company has plants, although some programs have been national and international in scope. Preservation grants in the past five years have included donations for: the restoration of the Old Slater Mill and Museum expansion, Pawtucket, Rhode Island; the restoration of the Patterson Inn, Corning, New York; the creation of a storefront museum for the Corning-Painted Post, New York, Historical Society; the restoration of City Square and historic homes, Bradford, Pennsylvania; the downtown restoration project, Greenville, Ohio; the conversion of old theater buildings to performing arts centers in Elmira, New York, Providence, Rhode Island, and Louisville, Kentucky; the renovation of the Martins Mill (covered) Bridge, Greencastle, Pennsylvania; general support for the Historic Homes Foundation, Louisville, Kentucky; and co-sponsorship of a New York State preservation conference.

For further information contact:
Norman Mintz
Project Director
Market Street Restoration Agency
2 West Market Street
Corning, New York 14830

Footnotes

1. *Market Street Restored*, (Corning, New York: City of Corning, n.d.).
2. *Ibid.*
3. INFORM interview with Norman Mintz, Project Director, Market Street Restoration Agency, February, 1977.
4. *Ibid.*
5. INFORM interview with George Douglas, Director, Community Affairs, Corning Glass Works, April, 1977.
6. "The Home Towns Come Back," *Architectural Record*, December, 1976.
7. INFORM interview with Jim Sheaffer, Executive Director, Corning Urban Renewal Agency, February, 1977.

Summary   In 1973, Higbee's, a Cleveland department store, formed a real estate subsidiary, the Higbee Development Corporation, to redevelop a 6.9-acre site in downtown Cleveland. The redevelopment project combines the recycling of existing buildings with new construction in an area along the Cuyahoga River called Settlers' Landing. Modeled after Ghirardelli Square in San Francisco, the project will contain retail shops, restaurants, entertainment facilities, a hotel, and office buildings. Work is proceeding in stages. By mid-1977, the company had converted a former trucking terminal into a contemporary discotheque and restaurant, renovated the historic Western Reserve Building as modern office space, and adapted a former hemp mill as office space for architects, artisans, and other professionals. To date, Higbee's has invested almost $7 million in the project. Although progress has been slower than anticipated, the company has been recognized in the community for its pioneering work in saving the historically important river front. Its efforts have encouraged additional investment and interest in the area.

Background   Historians believe that Moses Cleaveland—the city's founder—and his band of surveyors first landed at the Settlers' Landing site in 1796. The city was orginally named Cleaveland, but the Ohio legislature changed the spelling to Cleveland in 1831. With the opening of the Ohio Canal, the city, located at the mouth of the Cuyahoga River on Lake Erie, prospered as a shipping and warehouse center. Later, after the railroads were built, it became an industrial center.

Cleveland experienced tremendous growth during the last half of the nineteenth century. Its population increased from 17,000 in 1850 to 361,000 in 1900. Today the Cleveland metropolitan area has 2 million residents. Until 1900, the financial and commercial center of the city remained compact, clustered on either side of Superior Street, which stretches along the river front surrounding Settlers' Landing. In the late nineteenth century, great industrialists, such as Samuel Mather and John D. Rockefeller, built high-rise office buildings and massive warehouses in the area.

By the turn of the century, downtown Cleveland was suffering from increasing congestion, and water and air pollution. At about that time, the configuration of downtown was substantially altered by Chicago architect Daniel Burnham. Burnham's plan emphasized the Public Square as the central point of the city. By creating wide boulevards, he oriented future commercial development toward the east, away from the river front. As a result, during the last seventy years, the river front and the surrounding commercial areas have been increasingly underutilized, abandoned, or destroyed.

In recent decades, as in other major urban areas, pollution, increased crime, and racial conflicts stifled new investment. In the late 1960s, the Cuyahoga River became famous when the surface sludge spontaneously caught fire. As head of a major downtown department store with a substantial stake in the central-city's vitality, Higbee's Chairman, Herbert Strawbridge, decided to help reverse downtown deterioration.

Execution   Strawbridge felt that the river front, the birthplace of the city, was the appropriate place to begin. At the time, a local businessman was attempting to convert the area into an auto junkyard. In late 1972, Higbee's acquired four acres at the western end of Superior Street along the Cuyahoga River; and in July, 1973, the Higbee Development Corporation was formed to revitalize the property.

The acreage includes approximately 600 feet of river front and encompasses all the land to West Ninth Street, stretching from the Superior Viaduct Bridge to St. Clair. The company owns all the real estate in the parcel, except for two large warehouse buildings near St. Clair, which are owned by the International Seaway Trading Company. A railway track of the Pennsylvania Railroad crosses the property and is actively used. The Western Reserve Building, erected in 1891 and 1892 by wealthy industrialist Samuel Mather and designed by Chicago architect Daniel H. Burnham, is the most important building on the site. Located on a triangular plot at the corner of West Ninth and Superior, the building is one of three Burnham structures in Cleveland, and the one most characteristic of the Chicago style of architecture. It is eight stories tall, made of brick, and has a series of irregularly spaced bays on the exterior with a simple curved, corbelled-brick cornice, similar to Burnham's Chicago masterpiece, the Monadnock Building. The exterior walls are masonry load-bearing, and interior supports are cast and wrought iron. The floors are supported by tiled arches. From the elaborately paneled offices on the top floor of the Western Reserve, Mather conducted his diverse business operations, which included United States Steel, American Ship Building, and iron-ore and coal-mining interests, as well as many educational and philanthropic activities.

Other buildings on the site include a former truck-loading terminal, a warehouse building near the river front, and a row of warehouse structures on West Ninth Street. One of the latter group has an ornamental cast-iron facade only 25 feet wide. The remainder of the hillside site is open space, intersected by railroad tracks and the Old River Road. Two important structures have been lost in recent years. A fire in 1974 destroyed the National Furniture Warehouse, a building adjacent to the Western Reserve on West Ninth Street which had excellent renovation potential. The Bethel Hotel (1870), built by wealthy Cleveland families as a hotel for sailors, was determined to be structurally unsound and demolished in late 1975.

On July 3, 1973, Higbee's announced that it would commit $17 million to redevelop the four-acre parcel (later increased to nearly seven acres). Although the property was then overgrown with weeds and littered with debris, company Chairman Herbert Strawbridge saw the river front with its barges, mechanical bridges, and industrial structures as a unique setting for an imaginative development similar to San Francisco's Ghirardelli Square. Higbee's helped develop several suburban shopping centers, and Strawbridge decided that the company should become the developer for Settlers' Landing in order to control the project and effectively manage the risks.

He hired Lawrence Halprin & Associates, the San Francisco urban planners who had worked on Ghirardelli Square, to prepare the development scheme. Gruen and Gruen Plus Associates of San Francisco was retained to conduct the sociological and economic feasibility studies.

As a first step, the property was cleared of weeds and debris. The City of Cleveland placed markers on the river front noting the place where Moses Cleaveland first landed and the spot where Lorenzo Carter built the first cabin. Throughout 1973 and 1974, Halprin's firm planned a development concept for the site. However, as work progressed, it became clear that completion of the entire project would take five to ten years. In addition, for the effort to be successful, local residents would have to rediscover and use the river front area. The likelihood of this happening was increased by implementation of an extensive pollution-control program for the Cuyahoga River.

In early 1975, Higbee's decided to create immediate visibility for the project by converting a vacant trucking terminal on the lower portion of the site into a discotheque. On June 13, 1975, 55 days after the start of construction, Cleaveland Crate and Trucking Company opened for business. The discotheque featured an automated bar and disc jockey stand in the cab of a diesel truck. Cleaveland Crate and Trucking was initially a huge success, attracting large crowds of young professionals. Although its popularity soon waned (see "Problems"), the endeavor demonstrated that a sizable market existed for river-front entertainment activities.

Halprin finished his development plan for the entire project in summer, 1975. His strategy was to create a constituency for river-front businesses by building in a captive market, the office workers who would eat, drink, and shop in the complex; and by providing enough excitement and unique attractions to bring local citizens and tourists into the area both day and night. Renovation of the Western Reserve Building as a modern office facility was to be the keystone of the project. In addition, new ten- to twelve-story office buildings with retail shops on the street level were to be built, providing the commercial anchor for the total development. These office buildings would incorporate the facades of the existing warehouse structures on West Ninth Street. A small luxury hotel was planned for a site near St. Clair Street, while the upper portion of the property was to be nearly covered by a multi-level, glass-enclosed walkway extending over the railroad track and containing a variety of shops and restaurants. A park, including a boat dock offering excursion rides, and a museum were to be located on the river front. The museum would house a local collection of Salvador Dali's paintings, the largest single, privately owned collection of the artist's work. The plan provided for 1,500 parking spaces on three levels below the glass-enclosed walkway.

Although the Halprin scheme was visually exciting, its price tag of nearly $70 million was not. The total project was too large for Higbee's to assume at once. In addition, the amount of income-producing property under the plan was too small to support the investment required to create the large open spaces and parking facilities. In order to manage the risks involved, the company decided to complete the development in phases. Because of its historical and architectural importance, the Western Reserve Building was to be renovated first. This work could be completed with internally generated funds, and would not require additional borrowing. Work began in fall, 1975.

Restoration of the Western Reserve's exterior included the re-creation of the original arched doorway with cast concrete. After World War II, the exterior had been modernized, and the original carved pink-sandstone arch had been defaced and covered with imitation marble. Pollution had badly discolored the brick building, and windows were broken and rotted. Exterior brick was cleaned by sandblasting, and repointed. Windows were replaced with new bronze-colored aluminum ones. New brick sidewalks were installed, along with cast-iron street lamps.

The "modernization" work of the late 1940s had also obliterated the ornate Italian-marble main lobby. Except for the impressive cast-iron staircase—with marble treads and ornamental cast-iron risers—and the elaborately paneled offices of Samuel Mather, there was little interior detail left in the building. Modern lighting, wiring, plumbing, heating, air conditioning, life-safety systems, fluorescent lighting in new dropped ceilings, and new automatic elevators have been installed. The new lobby, a series of domed vaults covered with brick tiles, was developed from research of period designs. Heavy steel and leaded-glass gates of a spider-web design were installed for first-floor retail and restaurant tenants. Additional space was created for restrooms, fire stairs, and heating and air-conditioning ducts by filling in a light well at the north end of the building. Two sections of the site were graded and hard surfaced, providing 104 parking spaces.

On September 3, 1976, restoration work on the Western Reserve was completed, and shortly thereafter, the building's first tenant, Parker B. Advertising moved in. Seven of the eight floors—approximately 52,500 net leasable square feet—were converted to modern office space, but the leasing program has moved slowly. By July, 1977, the building was 28 percent leased with five tenants occupying

Exterior of the Western Reserve Building restored in 1976.

15,950 feet. The largest single tenant, United Airlines, occupies 4,000 square feet. Samuel Mather's office on the top floor will be restored when a tenant is found for the entire floor. Rents range from $9 to $10 per square foot, which is competitive with prime downtown office space.

Also available for lease are 9,300 square feet on the street and basement levels designed for use as a rathskeller and restaurant, and an additional 900 square feet adjacent to the main door on the street level which is suitable for retail use.

During 1976, as work on the Western Reserve Building was being completed,

Aerial view of downtown Cleveland showing boundaries of the Settlers' Landing development.

Higbee's explored a variety of ambitious development proposals for the second phase of the project:

1. *A high-rise office building with a large single tenant.* Higbee's tried to persuade a large Cleveland industrial company to locate its corporate headquarters in Settlers' Landing and co-develop a major high-rise office building of 650,000 to 850,000 square feet along West Ninth Street.

2. *A series of smaller office buildings.* Major tenants were sought to pre-lease a series of smaller multi-tenant office buildings ranging in size from 200,000 to 400,000 square feet to be built along West Ninth Street.

3. *Condominium apartments and townhouses.* A series of river-front condominium units was designed. However, cost estimates dictated selling prices of $165,000 to $300,000 per unit.

4. *A retail/restaurant/entertainment complex.* A local architectural firm, Hoag-Wismar, which had also worked on the Western Reserve Building, prepared a plan for 100,000 square feet of restaurant and retail space in a series of buildings clustered along the river front. The structures would be historically accurate replicas of early nineteenth-century buildings.

By early 1977, however, having found no market support for these large-scale development proposals, Higbee's decided that a slower, more cautious approach would be appropriate until the Western Reserve Building was fully leased. Still, the company was anxious to preserve the project's momentum. It decided that another building, a former hemp-rope mill, could be renovated and profitably rented to architects, artisans, and similar professionals. Although architecturally undistinguished, the three-story brick building—actually a series of three buildings—had a good view of the river and was structurally sound. During spring and summer, 1977, a local architectural firm, Todd-Schmidt, was retained to prepare conceptual plans for renovating the building. The

exterior was sandblasted, windows were enlarged on the upper floors, and a new interior staircase was added. New plumbing, electrical wiring, air conditioning, and life-safety systems were installed. Interior spaces were left with exposed beams and brick walls. By mid-summer, 1977, approximately two-thirds of the 20,000 square feet had been leased to architects, a weaver, an opera company, and a furniture maker. Only space on the third floor and in the old boxcar shed was still vacant. Depending on tenant improvements, rents range from $4 to $6 per square foot.

Before the end of 1977, Higbee's plans to remodel the Cleaveland Crate and Trucking Company, placing more emphasis on the food business. It will upgrade and expand the lunch and dinner menus, increase the size of the cocktail lounge, and change the disco entertainment to a lower-key format. Cini, Grissom, restaurant consultants, have been retained to help Higbee's develop this new concept.

Costs In July, 1973, Higbee's committed $17 million to redevelop the four acres of the Settlers' Landing project. Since that time, the project has increased to nearly seven acres, and a development plan has been devised which if implemented could cost $100 million. By mid-1977, the company's investment totaled approximately $7 million. The costs break down as follows:

Acquisition (nearly seven acres and eight structures)	$2,500,000
Renovation of the Western Reserve	3,360,000
Cleaveland Crate and Trucking Company	675,000
Renovation of the Riverview Building	225,000
Fees, operating costs, parking	125,000
	$6,885,000

There are no mortgages or long-term debts held against the property. Funds for the project's first phase have been provided from Higbee's regular business operations. Since only a small percentage of the total project is complete and rented, the current income has yet to provide the company with a return on its investment.

Problems Creating a commercial base to support the retail, restaurant, and entertainment complex originally envisioned for Settlers' Landing has been a major barrier frustrating the project's progress. Renovation of the Western Reserve Building was the first attempt to establish such a base, but the work was completed without a major anchor tenant. The leasing of the building to smaller tenants has been slow, since many firms have been reluctant to move into a nearly empty building several blocks from downtown shopping, restaurants, and other office buildings. In addition, because there are few offices in the area, it has been difficult to attract ground-floor retail tenants and a restaurant.

Although Higbee's spent nearly $56 per square foot to restore the Western Reserve Building, the work has prompted controversy. Some local architectural critics and preservationists have questioned whether the building's historic or architectural value warrants such lavish treatment. The lobby's brick-veneer domes, alcoves, and arches have been characterized as "early wine cellar," and criticized as "corny" and "inappropriate."[1] Although the exterior brick has been sealed against further deterioration the surface is badly pitted from earlier sandblasting.

Progress has also been slowed by the loss of two major buildings. The National Furniture Warehouse Building, which was destroyed by fire in 1974, could have been converted into office space complementing the Western Reserve and providing a larger nucleus for the project. Demolition of the Bethel Hotel left the Western Reserve isolated on the site. Financing for new construction is not available.

Efforts to build the entertainment segment of Settlers' Landing have been similarly hampered. The Cleaveland Crate and Trucking Company's initial success was based on the fact that it was the first discotheque in Cleveland. The idea was soon copied in suburban locations, and the initial clientele declined as people were attracted to competing discos closer to their homes. In six months, gross sales fell off sharply, and the less profitable restaurant business became more important. Higbee's now plans to upgrade and expand the restaurant facilities to attract a higher-income clientele.

As of mid-1977, the future of the Dali Museum is uncertain, since the donation of the artist's work is in doubt. Finally, if Higbee's is to complete its land holdings within the Settlers' Landing project, it must still purchase the two International Seaway Buildings sometime in the future.

Benefits   Although after four years, the company has yet to achieve a financial return on its investment in Settlers' Landing, the project is becoming a catalyst for further development. Diagonally across Superior Street from the Western Reserve Building, the State of Ohio is building a 600,000-square-foot building which will bring 2,000 office workers a day into the area. Standard Oil of Ohio has also recently announced plans to erect a new high-rise headquarters office building behind the Terminal Tower near Settlers' Landing.

In May, 1977, a study by the Cleveland Landmarks Commission recommended revitalization of the Warehouse District, a more than fifty-acre area which surrounds Settlers' Landing and includes numerous landmark buildings. Adjacent to Settlers' Landing, on the river front along the Old River Road, enterprising entrepreneurs are opening a variety of shops in old warehouses. The stores offer high-quality gifts, antiques, gourmet kitchenware, and furniture. Another developer is converting a former power station located across the Cuyahoga River from the project into an entertainment complex and a series of shops.

Higbee's regards Settlers' Landing as both a business venture and part of its social responsibility to downtown Cleveland. As a result of its leadership, other companies are also making commitments to the downtown area. In May, 1977, Higbee's along with Chessie System, TRW, Eaton, Cleveland Stadium Company, the Stouffer Corporation, and E. J. O'Neill agreed to purchase the Sheraton-Cleveland Hotel on the Public Square. This once grand hotel will receive a $10 million renovation, and will be operated by Stouffer.

The Company   Founded in 1860 by two Ohio entrepreneurs, John G. Hower and Edwin C. Higbee, the Higbee Company has grown from a small retail clothing store to a large independent department-store chain. It operates 25 stores throughout northern Ohio, as well as women's specialty shops and shoe stores. In 1976, the company's total income reached $173 million, up 5.3 percent from the 1975 figure of $164.3 million. Net income for 1976 dropped 15.2 percent to $3.5 million from the previous year's $4.1 million. Assets at the beginning of 1977 totaled $118 million. The company has 5,700 full-time employees and 1,500 seasonal staff. The stock is closely held by under 3,000 shareholders and is traded on the over-the-counter market.

Settlers' Landing is the only project of the Higbee Development Corporation. However, Higbee's has investments in several suburban shopping malls, and owns a 117-acre farm in Summit County, Ohio, which was purchased as a potential development site for a shopping center.

For further information contact:
Herbert Strawbridge
Chairman
The Higbee Company
Public Square
Cleveland, Ohio 44113

Footnotes

1. Jim Wood, "A Vote Against Reserve Building," *Sunday Plain-Dealer* (Cleveland), 14 November 1976, sec. 5, p. 2.

The Inland Steel Company

Summary In 1970, Inland Steel, the sixth largest steel producer in the United States, created the Inland Steel Development Corporation (ISDC), a wholly owned subsidiary. The ISDC has recently developed several preservation-related projects. Work began on the Foundry, a modern commercial complex in Washington, D.C. which includes an old foundry, in 1970. A second project, initiated in 1973, was the conversion into apartments of the old Cairo Hotel built in 1894 and still the tallest private building in Washington. Renovation of the Foundry building cost $1.3 million, while the Cairo project cost $4.3 million. Both projects have helped revitalize the areas in which they are located, and brought additional economic benefits to the company.

The Foundry Complex

Background According to Inland Steel, the ISDC is committed to urban revitalization, emphasizing high-quality commercial and residential development as a means of bringing people and business back to the cities. The Washington area is also a lucrative real estate market.

Inland's Foundry project was initiated in Georgetown, a historic section of Washington established in the early eighteenth century. The community possesses a large and well-preserved supply of eighteenth- and nineteenth-century buildings.

Although there have always been some blighted and unsightly areas, especially along the river front, much of Georgetown has remained an exclusive residential community for Washington's wealthy. Today, it contains an active retail district of fine shops, restaurants, and entertainment facilities.

The Progressive Citizens Association of Georgetown, a group of residents who became interested in preservation in the 1940s, worked diligently to maintain the community's architectural heritage. Because of its efforts, Congress passed a bill in 1950 requiring that all building and demolition permits for the area be submitted for review to a committee of architects appointed by the Fine Arts Commission of Washington, D.C. Shortly thereafter, Historic Georgetown, Inc., was formed and has served as a citizen-based catalyst for a variety of preservation projects, including the restoration of the old Chesapeake and Ohio Canal which runs through Georgetown.

In 1970, the developers of Canal Square, a shopping and office complex incorporating new design with renovated and adapted nineteenth-century industrial buildings along the edge of the Canal, approached Inland Steel. They proposed to co-develop twelve acres of underutilized industrial property lying between the Canal and the Potomac River. The ISDC hired an architectural firm from Berkeley, California, ELS Design Group, and the Real Estate Research Corporation from Chicago to study the feasibility of the project from both the design and marketing standpoints.

Execution In fall, 1970, the ISDC purchased seven of the available twelve acres. The company's plan, later known as Georgetown Harbor, encompassed property from the Chesapeake and Ohio Canal south to the Potomac, and included offices, shops, restaurants, a luxury inn, a conference center, recreational facilities, and public spaces. The Canal Square developers became minority stockholders (they were later completely bought out), and the group's architect, Arthur Cotton Moore, became involved with the planning and design.

Moore had successfully mixed new construction with historic preservation in the Canal Square project a few blocks from the Inland site. Besides being a respected architect, he was a resident of Georgetown, which would make him extremely valuable in implementing the ISDC's plan within the regulations imposed by the preservation-oriented Georgetown community. The ISDC hired both ELS and Moore to work cooperatively on designing the first building. Another design firm, Sasaki Associates of Watertown, Massachusetts, was hired to work on landscaping and to design a public plaza along the Canal. Washington architect Vlastimil Koubek prepared the construction documents and supervised the work. Tishman Construction Company was the Construction Manager.

The total project was to be developed in three major phases. The first, begun in 1970, included construction of a building containing offices, shops, and restaurants directly south of the Canal, and rehabilitation of an existing building. The undeveloped site contained a two-story brick building used as office space, an auto repair shop, and a storage building, as well as a former foundry which had been used to produce arms and implements during the Civil War. The office and storage buildings were not of significant economic or architectural value and were demolished. However, the Foundry, built in the 1850s, was a fine example of early Georgetown industrial architecture. Moore and ELS urged the ISDC to save the structure and incorporate it into the design of the new complex.

The reuse of the Foundry required considerable effort and expense. The

two-and-a-half story, 88-foot long building was raised from its foundation, and large steel beams were placed under the main supporting walls. To facilitate excavation work for a new underground garage, the building was rolled on rails off the site. Once the initial construction work was complete, it was rolled to its present location, where the exterior was restored, a new roof, skylight, and windows were installed, and the brick masonry, previously covered with aluminum paint, was cleaned and repaired. The original interior had been completely altered over the building's life and contained nothing worth preserving. It has been completely redesigned to accommodate a two-level restaurant and bar.

This act of preservation helped mute some of the local criticism of the new development. Nevertheless, the Fine

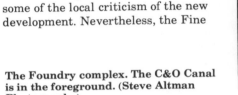

The Foundry complex. The C&O Canal is in the foreground. (Steve Altman Photography)

Arts Committee initially did not approve the plans for the complex. The community was concerned that the development would increase traffic congestion in an already car-crowded Georgetown, that the new building proposed for the site would not fit within the traditional Georgetown architecture of small, residential brick buildings, and that public access to and use of the Canal would be curtailed.

·To help alleviate the traffic-congestion problem, a 300-car parking garage was designed under the new building. The basic form and facade of the new building was designed to relate to its existing context. The exterior cladding is brick in keeping with the older surrounding architecture. Current zoning allowed a structure up to six stories or ninety feet tall on the site. The new design called for six stories, but an actual height of only about sixty feet. The height was minimized by stepping back some of the upper floors, producing outdoor landscaped terraces overlooking the Canal.

Five of the new building's levels are above ground. One is mostly below grade, but is partially visible because the site slopes to the south. A retail shopping mall occupies the ground level and one level below. It is connected by an interior "piazza" containing a reflecting pool and grand staircase. The five upper floors are leased as offices. Elevators to all levels are accessible from the piazza.

The building is cut back along the canal edge creating a public plaza. The ISDC rents a strip of land along the Canal from the National Park Service, and has spent more than $50,000 landscaping and improving the canal-front area.

Both the new building and the placement of the Foundry respect Georgetown's historic form. Their facades establish a building line related to the street edge, just as the traditional rowhouses do on many of the community's streets. On the uppermost floors, the new building's facade is sloped back, reminiscent of the pitched-gable roofs of the early Federal-style houses. The Foundry's small scale and pitched roof also help to reduce the mass of the new building behind it.

Costs   Inland Steel spent $135,000 to move the Foundry. Restoration of the building's masonry cost approximately $60,000, while the new roof and other work cost $50,000. The ISDC spent an additional $1 million for restaurant fixtures and finishes, bringing the total cost for the Foundry reuse, including new landscaping, to $1.3 million. The cost for the remaining 366,000 square feet of the complex was about $12 million, or equivalent to $33 per square foot.

Problems   The only significant difficulties encountered were those involving design approvals by the Fine Arts Commission and objections from the community. After considerable negotiation, the project was able to move forward.

Benefits   A portion of the Canal has been improved and made more accessible to the public through the Company's efforts. A blighted section of Georgetown has been refurbished and returned to active, revenue-producing use. New business has been attracted to the area. The office floors are fully leased, and the retail space is 90 percent rented. According to William Marlin, writing in the February, 1977, *Architectural Record*:

Because the new building in town, even for the most suspicious, is fitting in very well, offering a spritely mix of activities, going about its business in a polite pleasant fashion, and (the real test) showing respect for its elders . . . the new neighbor on Thomas Jefferson Street has not only accommodated the history of Georgetown, it is making some.[1]

The Cairo Hotel

Background   In 1894, Thomas Franklin Schneider designed and built the Cairo Hotel, the first steel-framed skyscraper in Washington, D.C. His 156-foot, thirteen-story building was and still is taller than any other privately owned building in the capital. The brick- and stone-clad structure is eclectic in style, with classical, Romanesque, and Art Nouveau elements. Many called it:

"Schneider's Folly" because they were convinced that its steel frame, a novelty at the time, would never hold all that stone and brick in place. One neighbor moved out of his house and into a hotel and tried to make Schneider pick up the bill—until the building passed the wind tests.[2]

Fearing that the city might soon be filled with skyscrapers like New York and Chicago, Congress passed a law in 1910 limiting all buildings in Washington to a height of 130 feet, 26 feet less than the Cairo. This law is still in effect today.

The building, located east of the Dupont Circle area of Washington, remained an elegant residential hotel well into the twentieth century. In its heyday, it contained a restaurant, ballroom, drugstore, billiard room, bowling alley, bakery, and a rooftop tropical garden. The Schneider family owned the Cairo until the 1950s when the old hotel was finally sold, and served as a transient residence until it was boarded up in 1972.

Execution   Inland Steel purchased the property in 1973, and then converted it into apartments utilizing the Federal Housing Administration's (FHA) 221 d (4) Program. Under this Program, upon completion of a project, permanent financing was available for up to 90 percent of the renewed property's FHA-appraised value for forty years at 7 percent interest. Market rents could be charged in the renovated building. The ISDC raised equity capital by forming a limited partnership with a syndicate of high-income individuals.[3] The cost of construction was financed through another of the parent company's subsidiaries, Inland Steel Finance Company.

The entry to the Cairo after renovation.

Arthur Cotton Moore was selected as the architect for the renovation. His design converted 350 small hotel rooms and several larger public areas—a total of 130,000 square feet of space—into 162 apartments and eight two-story townhouse units.

The hotel's exterior was cleaned and preserved, and new windows were installed. A contemporary front door, echoing but not imitating the style of the original, provides a transition to the modern contrasting interior.

Very little has been saved of the old hotel's lush interior decoration. The lobby's original marble fountains, mosaic tiles, richly carved plasterwork, and elegant Victorian furnishings have all been removed. Only a few traces of plaster detail remain. The high ceilings are still there, but the rooms in the new apartments are quite small, resulting in very different proportional relationships. The new rooms are contemporary, with rough-cut cedar used to replace the original window casings and baseboards. At least one wall in each apartment is exposed brick. Many of the apartments still retain the original ornamental fireplaces, and a few have niches and balconies from the grand public function rooms that were partitioned to accommodate the renovation scheme.

The alteration which made the project financially feasible was Moore's decision to remove the roof from the original back lobby and east ballroom.[4] This left an open well or atrium in the middle of the building, allowing light and ventilation into the interior, and creating garden spaces for townhouse units. The completed two-story townhouses utilize the old basement level as their first floor, and open on to the atrium.

Efficiency apartments rent for $240 to $291 per month; one-bedroom units for $315 to $375; two-bedroom units for $430 to $493; and townhouses for $500 to $555. All utilities are included.

Costs Inland purchased the building for $500,000, and spent $3.8 million on the renovation. The resulting cost per square foot was approximately $33, or an average of $25,000 per unit.

Problems During the construction, some of the clay-tile, arched floor supports were found to be defective and had to be replaced with steel-reinforced concrete. This delayed the project's completion and increased total costs. A decision to install an all-electric system for cooking and heating caused additional problems. Between 1972 and 1976, while the building was being renovated, the cost of electricity in Washington more than tripled. The Cairo's electric bill increased from $52,000 to $150,000, drastically altering the original operating expense projections. Both problems resulted in rents substantially above those initially planned and reduced the level of the return.

Benefits In addition to the preservation benefits from saving the Cairo and returning it to the tax rolls, the area in which it is located has received an economic boost. Business has improved for local merchants, and property values are rising.

The Company Inland Steel is engaged in the production, fabrication, and sale of steel and related products, as well as the mining of iron ore, coal, and limestone. Inland's net sales in 1976 were over $2.6 billion, an increase from a 1975 figure of $2.1 billion. Net income rose from $83.3 million to $104 million over the same period. In addition to Inland Steel Development Corporation's real estate development activities, Inland has subsidiaries engaged in the design and production of mobile homes and prefabricated housing units, and the development, construction, and management of commercial and residential real estate, including government-assisted housing.

Other Preservation Activities. The ISDC has also converted the 75-year-old Woodley apartment building in northwest Washington into 73 condominium units.

For further information contact:
Paul H. Upchurch
Vice President and General Manager
Inland Steel Development
Corporation
1055 Thomas Jefferson Street, N.W.
Washington, D.C. 20007

Footnotes

1. William Marlin, "Georgetown's Nice New Neighbor," *Architectural Record*, February, 1977, p. 95.
2. Sarah Booth Conroy, "Moving in Where Legend Leaves Off," *Washington Post*, 11 April 1976, p. H3.
3. John Sower, "Financing and Developing Large Commercial Preservation Project," *Economic Benefits of Preserving Old Buildings,* (Washington, D.C.: Preservation Press, The National Trust for Historic Preservation, 1976), p. 136.
4. Conroy, *op. cit.*, p. H1.

The Jefferson Company

Summary In summer, 1977, the Jefferson Company, the third largest bus line in the United States, began renovation work on St. Anthony Main, a multi-use development located on the east bank of the Mississippi River near downtown Minneapolis. When complete, the project, which covers almost two city blocks, will contain nearly 200,000 square feet of space. Its ten buildings will house retail stores, restaurants, a theater and entertainment complex, apartments, and perhaps a luxury inn. New construction may also be added. The first phase, scheduled for completion by fall, 1977, involves renovation of a 40,000-square-foot former mattress factory to accommodate three restaurants and 11,000 square feet of specialty stores. Jefferson's investment in this initial phase totals approximately $3.1 million, including all land and building acquisition costs. Although the project has moved more slowly than anticipated, when it becomes operational, it is expected to be an important catalyst in the revitalization of the long-neglected Minneapolis river front.

Background The St. Anthony Main development consists of nearly two square blocks on the site where Minneapolis was first settled in 1838. St. Anthony, as the town was originally called, merged with Minneapolis in 1374. The river front was developed primarily as an industrial center. However, as industries along the river declined, the area deteriorated and became increasingly inaccessible.

In recent years, several comprehensive plans have been proposed for reclaiming all 200 acres of the river front and three river islands, and reusing them as a public park. Approximately $7 million in federal, state, and local funds have been committed for the first phase of the work which covers a

St. Anthony Main Street project prior to renovation work in early 1977. The Pillsbury A mill is in the background. (Minneapolis Star)

Salisbury Mattress Factory

Upton Block

Limestone Building

Pracna Restaurant

S.E. Main St.

20-acre area on the river's east bank surrounding the St. Anthony Main project. South East Main Street, which runs in front of the project, was to be recobbled, new landscaping and lighting fixtures were to be added, and an observation deck was to be built by summer, 1978. Future plans call for open air facilities for the performing arts, hiking trails, a recreated waterfall, and a river-front museum across from the St. Anthony Main project.

The prime mover behind the St. Anthony Main project is Louis Zelle, President of both the Jefferson Company and the firm's real estate development subsidiary, the MTS Company. A civic-minded businessman, Zelle has previously served on the building committees for the Guthrie Theater for the Performing Arts and the Orchestra Hall in Minneapolis and as Chairman of the Minnesota State Arts Council.

The total St. Anthony Main site contains about 180,000 square feet of land and ten buildings, some of which have been in the Zelle family since 1900. The oldest building on the site, the Upton Block was built of light-colored brick in 1854 by the Upton Brothers as their general store. The offices and newsroom of the first Minneapolis newspaper, the *Minnesota Republican*, were upstairs in this building. The Limestone Building next to the Upton Block served as municipal offices for St. Anthony's mayor and housed the town's fire department. In 1879, the Union Iron Works Foundry was added behind the two buildings. Next to this complex is an 1898 Victorian commercial building, which is the only building in the project not owned by the Jefferson Company. In 1974, the latter structure was converted into a restaurant and bar called Pracna-on-Main, which has been very successful, averaging about a thousand meals a day. Above the Pracna on the same block is the three-story Truman Building, a 1918 industrial building. A one-story structure formerly used as the bus company's gas station is next door.

In addition, the site contains the Salisbury Mattress Factory, which is actually six buildings. The rear section was built in three parts in 1860 and 1880 as a warehouse for nearby flour mills. The main building, erected in 1906, was also a warehouse, and has the same heavy timber construction as the Butler Building, a downtown Minneapolis warehouse that has been recycled into a retail and office complex. The Mattress Factory complex includes an 1898 warehouse and a turn-of-the-century foundry.

Execution   In April, 1974, the Jefferson Company announced plans to redevelop 200,000 square feet of existing building space, and add over 800,000 square feet of new construction in order to create an extensive multi-use complex on the two-block St. Anthony Main site. The project was to include 424 apartments and condominiums, 171,000 square feet of office space, and 180,000 square feet of commercial, retail, and entertainment space. In addition, the plan called for construction of a new hotel on the nearby Pillsbury A Mill property.

In announcing these preliminary plans, Zelle expressed determination to involve the people of Minneapolis in the project: "The project is being designed for people. We want people's help in putting it together."[1] Throughout the planning stages, Zelle has actively sought advice from local preservation and community groups, including the Riverfront Advisory Council and the Heritage Preservation Commission.

Zelle hired Benjamin Thompson of Cambridge, Massachusetts, architect for Boston's Faneuil Hall Market interiors, to prepare the master plan and architectural drawings for the project. However, money became very tight during the recession of 1974 and 1975,

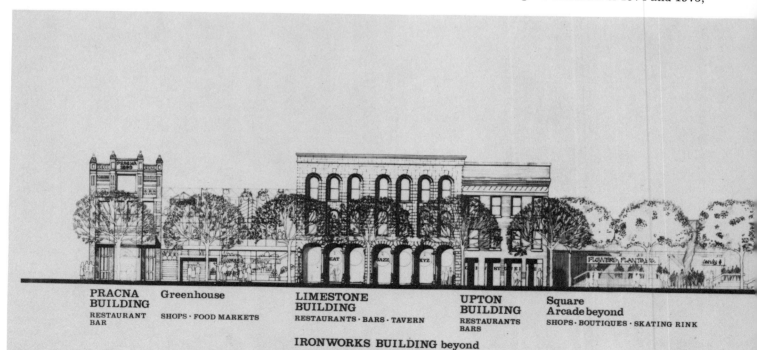

PRACNA BUILDING
RESTAURANT BAR

Greenhouse
SHOPS · FOOD MARKETS

LIMESTONE BUILDING
RESTAURANTS · BARS · TAVERN

IRONWORKS BUILDING beyond
RESTAURANT · BAR

UPTON BUILDING
RESTAURANTS BARS

Square
Arcade beyond
SHOPS · BOUTIQUES · SKATING RINK

and Zelle could not find the necessary long-term financing to start construction. In addition, it took longer than expected to secure tenants for the complex. As a result, construction was delayed until spring, 1977, when the project's first phase received a $1.2 million long-term mortgage commitment from the locally based Northwestern National Life Insurance Company.

The original master plan was reworked several times, and by 1977, the total project was scaled down considerably. The revised design called for little new construction, emphasizing instead the reuse of existing buildings. The section of the Salisbury Mattress Factory facing Main Street, known as Salisbury A, was selected for renovation in the project's initial phase. Conversion of this 40,000 square-foot building into space for restaurant and retail use could be accomplished at a reasonable cost.

Major tenants in the Salisbury A building will be three restaurants occupying 20,000 square feet of the total 31,000 net leasable square feet. The remaining 11,000 square feet on the

first and second floors will contain retail shops offering specialty clothing, jewelry, foods, and plants. A store offering quality home furnishings and gourmet cookware is being sought for the first floor.

Interior renovation work includes exposing and cleaning brick walls and heavy timber supports, refinishing wood floors, and installing new electrical and plumbing systems throughout the building. A new energy-conserving heat-pump system has also been installed to supply heating, cooling, and ventilation with separate controls for each tenant. Tenants will finish individual shops to their own specifications.

The exterior brick will be cleaned, and new windows will be installed. A covered deck is to be built around the exterior on the ground level, and an outdoor courtyard will be created between the buildings. A new entrance way and elevator will be built on 2nd Avenue S.E. where the A building joins the back wing, known as the B and C buildings. Automobile access to 2nd Avenue S.E. will be limited, and the street will be landscaped.

Commercial tenants in the Salisbury A building will pay rents based on a percentage of sales above a required minimum. In addition to this base rental rate, each tenant will pay a pro-rata share of common operating costs: heat, air conditioning, electricity, security, garbage removal, maintenance of common areas, and real estate taxes. An additional fee will be assessed for advertising and marketing. Minimum rentals in the Salisbury A will start at $8 per square foot.

The B and C buildings will be converted when additional long-term financing is obtained. Final plans for these buildings have not been established, but at least one floor is to house an open market area with a series of small shops offering foods and specialty items. Renovation work will be similar to that in the A building.

Development plans for other buildings in the St. Anthony Main complex are uncertain. The warehouse next to the Salisbury buildings may be recycled as either a luxury inn with sixty rooms, facilities for small meetings, a cocktail lounge, and a gourmet restaurant, or as rental apartments. In the

Architectural rendering of the completely renovated St. Anthony Main Street project. (Benjamin Thompson Associates)

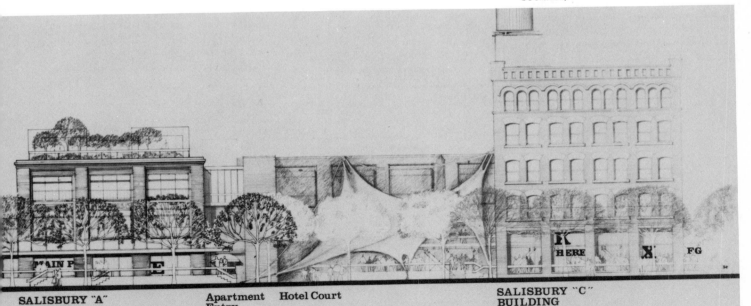

SALISBURY "A" BUILDING
SHOPS·
PENTHOUSE APARTMENTS ABOVE

Apartment Entry

Hotel Court
RESTAURANT

SALISBURY "C" BUILDING
HOTEL · RESTAURANT · TAVERN
PENTHOUSE APARTMENTS ABOVE

next block, a theater and entertainment complex is contemplated for the Upton, Limestone, and Foundry buildings. Condominium apartments have been discussed for the Truman Building, where the addition of two new floors to the existing three floors could create nine to twelve large luxury units ranging in size from 3,500 to 5,500 square feet. Prices for the units would start at $150,000. Additional new townhouses with a garden court are also under consideration for a site in front of the Truman Building. Zelle feels strongly that the project needs a residential base. Future development projects will proceed as financing becomes available and market demand dictates.

Costs   By mid-1977, the Jefferson Company had invested approximately $1.5 million to acquire land for the project other than that already held by the Zelle family. Total renovation costs for the Salisbury A Building, including fees, interest, overhead, and tenant improvements, but not land and acquisition costs, are $1.6 million. Construction financing has been provided by a local bank. In addition, a $1.2 million mortgage has been secured from the Northwestern National Life Insurance Company at 10 percent interest. Total costs for the project are estimated at $20 million. However, since the development plans are not final, these estimates are no more than guesses.

Problems   The inability to find long-term financing for the project and the difficulty in finding retail and restaurant leases delayed the start of construction for nearly three years, from 1974 when the project was announced, until 1977. Completion of the total project may require as much as ten years. In addition, the initial construction cost estimates were greater than could be justified economically, and architectural plans had to be revised accordingly.

There has been some deterioration in the foundation of the Upton Block buildings. If these problems are excessive, renovation of the structures may not be justifiable economically.

Although the project is centrally positioned between the downtown Minneapolis business district and the University of Minnesota campus, it is not within walking distance of either, particularly in harsh Minnesota winters. Nevertheless, the initial success of the Pracna restaurant has demonstrated that the river-front area has unique appeal. Whether enough people will come to the area to support the St. Anthony Main project remains to be seen.

Minneapolis is a car-oriented community, and additional parking must be provided to assure the project's completion and long-term success. There is surface parking on the Jefferson property for 150 cars, adequate only for the Salisbury A building. The city has discussed building a parking ramp on property adjoining the project, but as yet no appropriations have been made.

Benefits   Since the St. Anthony Main project was not yet operational by mid-1977, the company has yet to achieve a financial return. However, initial leasing activity indicates that in the long term, the development should be profitable. For the citizens of Minneapolis, the project will be the first major commercial investment on the river front in recent years. If successful, it will bring economic and social vitality to this important natural amenity. For Louis Zelle, completion of the project will mean the rebirth of an area where his family started in business over 125 years ago.

The Company   The Jefferson Company was founded in 1922 by Louis Zelle's father, Edgar Zelle. Peter Rauen, Zelle's great grandfather, started a dry-goods store on the east bank of the Mississippi near St. Anthony Main in the 1850s. Except for Greyhound's 40 percent interest in Jefferson Bus Lines, the major subsidiary of the Jefferson Company, the firm is privately held. As a result, no data on total sales, income, or assets is available.

The MTS Company, a wholly owned subsidiary of the Jefferson Company headquartered in Minneapolis, is the developer of the St. Anthony Main project. The company has real estate holdings on the interstate highway in Owatonna, and other properties in Albert Lea and downtown Rochester, Minnesota, as well as in Bethany, Missouri. It also owns hotels in Owatonna and Albert Lea.

Other Preservation Activities. In September, 1976, the Jefferson Company announced it would develop the First Street Depot in downtown Rochester, Minnesota, as a retail, restaurant, and entertainment complex at an estimated cost of $785,000. The Victorian-style building, formerly the Chicago-Northwestern railway depot and freight house, is now a company bus station. By mid-1977, Jefferson was still seeking a new location for the bus terminal and a liquor license for the restaurant. Benjamin Thompson Associates is the project architect.

For further information contact:
Louis Zelle
President
The Jefferson Company
1206 Currie Avenue
Minneapolis, Minnesota 55403

Footnotes

1. The Jefferson Company, *News Release*, April 26, 1974.

Lowell Development and Financial Corporation

Summary The Lowell Development and Financial Corporation (LDFC) is a consortium of financial institutions in the greater Lowell, Massachusetts, area that have joined together to promote the development and expansion of business activities and organizations through rehabilitation and restoration of the city's historic central business district. The LDFC provides low-cost loans to encourage building owners and tenants to renovate and restore their properties in harmony with the State Heritage Park and the proposed Urban National Cultural Park. Established in December, 1975, the LDFC has accumulated more than $350,000 which it lends at 4 percent to 5½ percent for this purpose, and it expects to raise a total of $2 million over the next three years. The program is acting as a catalyst for local, state, and federal programs to help revitalize Lowell's central business district.

Lowell's Division of Planning and Development provides free design service to local businesses who want to rehabilitate the facades of their buildings. Photo of Kimball Sign Building before renovation. (Lowell Division of Planning and Development)

Design suggestions for the same building by Lowell's Division of Planning and Development. (Lowell Division of Planning and Development)

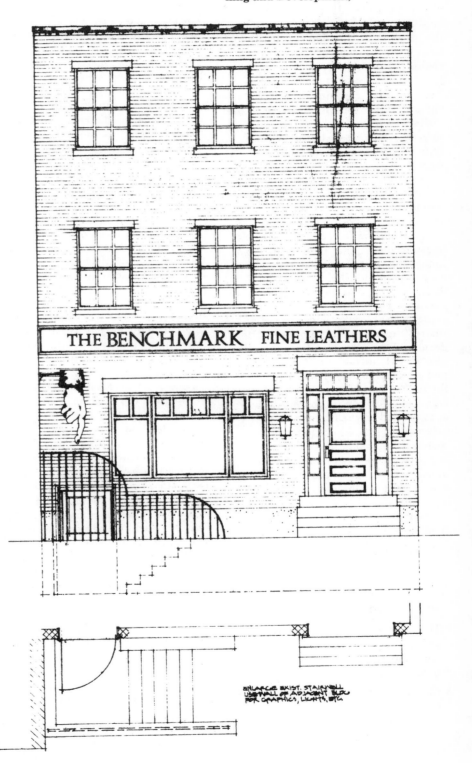

THE BENCHMARK   FINE LEATHERS

Background Lowell, located on the Merrimack River thirty miles north-west of Boston, was founded in 1822. It was one of the first planned industrial communities in the United States, and today is known as the birthplace of the American Industrial Revolution. The city had the abundant waterpower and access to cheap transportation ideal for the growing textile industry. By 1850, Lowell was the largest cotton textile center in the country; thousands of immigrants settled there to staff the "mile of mills" that lined the Merrimack. This prosperity lasted until the 1920s, when the New England textile industry started to collapse. At that time, the industry moved south leaving workers and mills behind.

As with many other New England towns, the departure of Lowell's industry caused a decline. Factory buildings were abandoned or underutilized.

In the early 1970s, however, the city began to realize that perhaps its most important asset was its past: the derelict mill buildings, machinery, and canal systems that, to many, were just eyesores. Through a Model Cities program several local groups showed an interest in preserving this asset. They developed the idea of making Lowell into an Urban National Cultural Park and a State Heritage Park. This was the first time that an urban-park concept had ever been proposed. A group of interested city residents and outside consultants set out to formulate more specific plans. The concept was explored further by private groups aided by grants from the National Endowment for the Arts and other sources.

The following revitalization objectives were established:

- The use of the city as a learning laboratory utilizing the existing buildings, manufacturing machinery, and engineering artifacts to illustrate industrial history.

- The improvement of the environment by rehabilitating existing buildings and support facilities to reinforce this unique historical theme.

- An increased respect for the cultural heritage of Lowell's people to reinforce pride in the diverse nationalities and backgrounds of former mill workers.

- The preservation and enhancement of these historic resources as a strategy for economic revitalization to encourage tourism and associated industries.[1]

Local, state, and federal governments are contributing to this project. The city adopted the cultural-park theme as the centerpiece of its planning efforts. By 1977, Lowell had already invested more than $1.6 million in downtown street improvements to reinforce the area's nineteenth-century flavor. Building owners in the central business district can use the free design service provided by the city's Division of Planning and Development if they wish to restore or renovate their facades. The canal system and surrounding area, as well as the central business district, have been designated local historic districts.

On the state level, $9.1 million has been committed to the development of the Lowell State Heritage Park aimed at preserving and developing the recreational potential of Lowell's canal system and riverbanks. Another $10 million is currently being used for improvements in the city, including landscaping and pedestrian amenities adjacent to the canals and in the historic districts.

Federal support has come through grants from the National Park Service for renovations of historic buildings and in-depth studies. Both local historic districts are listed in the National Register of Historic Places. According to a recent report, "over $26 million in local, state and federal monies is already expended or committed in projects either integral or supportive of the Cultural Park."[2] The same report proposes a future federal commitment of $40 million in capital improvements for building restoration and exhibits, and a yearly operating budget of over $1 million to establish and administer the Lowell National Cultural Park.

George L. Duncan, Executive Vice President of the First Bank and Trust Company in nearby Chelmsford, Massachusetts, and a resident of Lowell, recognized a problem early in the planning for Lowell's urban revitalization: local financial institutions were reluctant to lend money for major restorations, renovations, and even for new construction in the central busi-

ness district; and potential borrowers were also hesitant to seek loans to renovate their businesses in an area of depreciating real estate values and poor retail trade.

Duncan had observed the successful economic results of Boston's and nearby Newburyport's restoration and preservation efforts, and believed in the concept of the Lowell Cultural Park. In 1975, he set out to establish the Lowell Development and Financial Corporation (LDFC) to provide building owners and tenants with low-interest loans to renovate and restore their properties in accordance with the concept. LDFC's purpose was to provide attractive and consistent design in the downtown area, and at the same time, to improve business, raise property values, encourage investment, and build community pride.

Execution The Lowell Development and Financial Corporation, chartered in December, 1975, by the Massachusetts legislature, has been set up under guidelines established by the U.S. Small Business Administration (SBA) for the creation of state and local development corporations. A local development corporation, defined in Section 502 of the Small Business Investment Act of 1958, may be established under applicable state corporation law "to improve the local economy by encouraging community effort to assist small businesses, and to provide the necessary financing."[3] Often, a local banker will help to form a local development company to bring together resources of business, industry, local, state, and the federal government to jointly develop the economic potential of the community. Local residents or business people must own and control the corporation, which may be either profit or nonprofit, but must have at least 25 stockholders.

In its first effort, LDFC has sold more than $350,000 in $50 non-dividend shares to ten local banks in the Lowell area; its ultimate goal is $2 million. This money is being loaned to small businesses in the central business district for facade and interior renovations. Renovation work must be consistent with design guidelines established in accordance with the State Heritage

Park and the proposed Urban National Cultural Park. A nineteenth-century theme is recommended and, as noted, the city's Division of Planning and Development provides a free design service to ensure consistency.

The LDFC charges 4 percent to 5.5 percent interest on these loans to cover losses on defaulting loans and to allow the corporation to break even. The funds are available under three programs:

	Building Owners Facade & Interior Renovation Program	*Building Owners Facade Program*	*Tenant/Lessee Facade Program*
Maximum Amount of Loan	$33,000 or 30 percent of entire facade and interior improvements, whichever is greater	$12,000 or 75 percent of facade improvements, whichever is greater	$12,000 or 75 percent of facade improvements, whichever is greater
Rate of Interest	4 percent	4 percent	5½ percent
Maximum Terms	25 years or same length of first mortgage, whichever is greater	10 years or same length of first mortgage, whichever is greater	10 years or the remaining term of the lease, whichever is greater
Other Source of Funding	For all of the above programs up to a maximum of $4,000, there is funding for 25 percent of the costs of approved facade improvements available from the Division of Planning and Development for those buildings in the historic district. This is an outright grant which does not have to be repaid.		
Bank Financing Available if Needed	First mortgage	First mortgage or improvement loan	Leasehold improvement loan

By mid-1977, the LDFC program was operational. To date, four projects have been completed including a delicatessen, a beauty salon, a taxicab company, and a jewelry store. Six other projects are scheduled for completion by the end of 1977.

The A&L Taxi Company is an interesting example. Lucian Petren, the owner, rented space on Bridge Street, and for more than ten years, watched the abandoned building across the street deteriorate and blight the neighborhood. When the property came up for sale for the tax title, he bought it and began renovating it using materials to which he had been accustomed, like plastic coverings and neon signs. He was approached by the LDFC and told that he could get a $30,000 loan at 4 percent interest if he followed the city's design guidelines. In addition, he would be able to receive an outright grant of $4,000 for facade improvements. Since the 4 percent rate was considerably lower than the 9 percent he was getting from the banks, he signed up. Petren removed the plastic and signs that he had erected and re-renovated using brick and black and gold trim signs. The recent project is not meant to be a pure restoration, but it complements the existing architecture. In addition to his taxi operation, Petren leases space to other businesses and plans to build a new building on adjacent property, also in keeping with the nineteenth-century theme. According to Petren, "I had the opportunity to move out, but I believe the town is going to pick up. People have to work hand-in-hand to do it."[4]

Since the LDFC is structured as an SBA-recognized development corporation, it is also eligible to obtain SBA loans and loan guarantees which can total up to $500,000 per project. Once the initial $350,000 has been committed, the LDFC intends to broaden the scope of its activities to include even high-risk development—possible under a variety of SBA programs—bringing together banks and borrowers to achieve the preservation goals established for the downtown redevelopment.

The Petren building after renovation. (Lowell Division of Planning and Development)

Costs LDFC's overhead is minimal; administrative services are donated by its members. Figures for these costs were not available.

Problems The problems to date have been administrative and logistic. In the beginning, it was difficult to get the ten banks, the local business community, and the political structure to agree on a theme and direction. It has also taken time to encourage local participants to contribute by buying shares. In addition, processing applications, a service which is currently donated, places some administrative burden on corporation officers. Nevertheless, according to George Duncan, "The entire operation is functioning smoothly and the results are much better than we originally anticipated."[5]

Benefits This type of business involvement forms an interested coalition, spreads the risk, and increases the impact of preservation activities. It also elicits local, state, and federal funds through matching grants and loans, which increase the program's scope and effectiveness. "For every dollar invested by the LDFC," says Duncan, "three additional dollars are invested in the downtown from other sources. This kind of leverage can be a key factor in improving the economic and visual vitality of the downtown."[6]

The Company The following financial institutions have purchased shares in the LDFC:

B. F. Butler Co-operative
10 Hurd Street
Lowell, Massachusetts 01852

Lowell Institution for Savings
18 Shattuck Street
Lowell, Massachusetts 01852

Middlesex Bank
174 Central Street
Lowell, Massachusetts 01852

Lowell Bank and Trust Company
489 Merrimack Street
Lowell, Massachusetts 01852

Union National Bank
61 Merrimack Street
Lowell, Massachusetts 01852

The Lowell Five-Cent Savings Bank
34 John Street, PO Box 440
Lowell, Massachusetts 01852

First Bank and Trust Company
44 Central Square
Chelmsford, Massachusetts 01824

First Federal Savings & Loan
15 Hurd Street
Lowell, Massachusetts 01852

Lowell Co-operative Bank
18 Hurd Street
Lowell, Massachusetts 01852

Central Savings Bank
50 Central Street
Lowell, Massachusetts 01852

For further information contact:
George L. Duncan
President
Lowell Development and
   Financial Corporation
722 East Merrimack Street
Lowell, Massachusetts 01852

Footnotes

1. *Report of the Lowell Historic Canal District Commission to the Ninety-Fifth Congress of the United States of America,* January 3, 1977, p. 20.
2. *Ibid.,* p. 23.
3. U.S. Small Business Administration, *Urban Neighborhood Revitalization,* (Washington, D.C.: U.S. Small Business Administration, n.d.), p. 4.
4. INFORM interview with Lucian Petren, Owner, A&L Taxi Company, June, 1977.
5. INFORM interview with George L. Duncan, President, Lowell Development and Financial Corporation, June, 1977.
6. *Ibid.*

Textron, Inc.

Summary Textron, a diversified manufacturing company, is the largest equity participant in one major renovation project and the developer of another in downtown Providence, Rhode Island, its home city. By mid-1977, Textron and three other local businesses had purchased the defunct Biltmore Hotel, and had begun renovations to transform it into a first-class 360-room facility. The city had also named Textron to renovate and develop the Providence Union Station complex, and negotiations were underway to obtain clear title to the land and buildings. The Union Station project will require ten years to complete. Over $60 million in public and private funds will be invested in the planned revitalization of seventy-acres of Providence's downtown area. Textron's projects will require over $46 million. Although the company's return on investment in these two reuse projects will probably be less than in its regular business ventures, the effort is expected to bring new vitality to the downtown area, thereby attracting further new investment.

Plot plan for Kennedy Plaza area in downtown Providence showing location of Biltmore Hotel and Union Station. (William McKenzie Woodward)

The Biltmore Hotel on Kennedy Plaza in downtown Providence. (Warren Jagger)

Background Providence (population 170,000) is Rhode Island's capital and business and financial center, as well as its largest city. Nearly 82 percent of the state's 923,000 residents live in its metropolitan area. A nineteenth-century textile and manufacturing center, Providence declined with its industries after World War II, and began to lose population to the suburbs. During the 1950s, Interstate 95 bisected the city, destroying nearly forty acres of mid-nineteenth-century neighborhoods. Urban renewal and Model Cities programs have also wiped out important commercial and mill buildings in and around the city. Since there has been relatively little new high-rise construction in the last ten years, most of the important nineteenth-century central business district still exists, but suffers from neglect.

Large-scale work to revitalize the Providence business district did not begin until the early 1970s. In 1973, Professor Gerald Howes and his transportation-planning students at the Rhode Island School of Design completed a study titled *Interface: Providence,* which assessed the city's accessibility and vitality, as well as the impact of the automobile on it. The following year, the Providence Citizens Lobby, which grew out of a series of forums prompted by the study, was formed to promote a revitalization program for downtown. At about the same time, newly-elected Mayor Vincent Cianci, Jr. filled the post of City Planner, which had been vacant for twelve years.

In 1975, the Providence business community formed its own group to assist in the revitalization effort. Led by Mr. G. William Miller, Chairman of

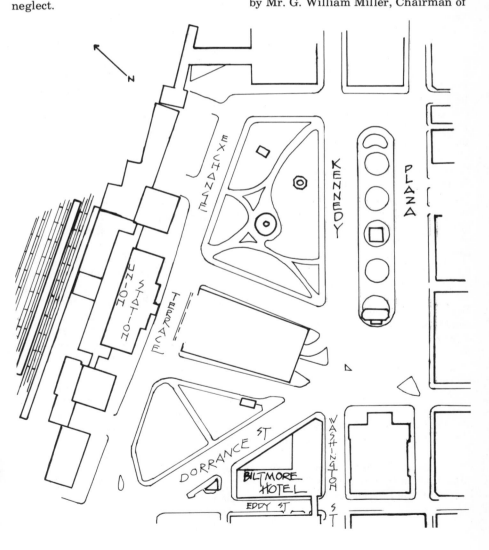

Textron, eight prominent firms—four local businesses and four banks—formed the 21st Providence Group.

During this same period, the Chamber of Commerce formed the Providence Foundation, a nonprofit corporation funded by thirty business, religious, philanthropic, and educational organizations to encourage citizens, businesses, and government officials to work together to attract new downtown investment. Through the Providence Foundation, the city's business community has helped develop the necessary planning and marketing feasibility studies to determine the course of future redevelopment. The Foundation's first project was a City Options Program, funded in conjunction with a grant from the National Endowment for the Arts and the City of Providence, which identified possibilities for future downtown development, and selected individual target areas. The Foundation is working closely with business and local and state government leaders to implement projects identified in the City Options Program. In 1975, the Foundation helped to fund a feasibility study for the adaptive reuse of the Providence Union Station, an underutilized four-building complex, as a transportation, office, and retail/entertainment center. Once the study was complete, the Foundation obtained federal Economic Development Administration grants to start the renovation work. Other projects include feasibility studies on renovating the Arcade, a nineteenth-century shopping mall, and the conversion of the Ocean State Theater, a recently refurbished rococo movie theater, into a performing-arts center. The Foundation is also attempting to persuade the state to locate a $24 million court complex in Providence's central business district.

Redevelopment will begin in the Kennedy Plaza/Burnside Park area, a major downtown open space near City Hall. The City Hall's exterior has already been cleaned, and renovation of the interior is underway. Textron, in cooperation with several other local firms, has agreed to help renovate two structures on this plaza: the Biltmore Hotel and the Providence Union Station.

Execution *The Biltmore Hotel.* The Biltmore Hotel was completed in 1922 at a cost of $7 million. It was partially financed by $2.5 million in preferred stock sold to local businesses by the Providence Chamber of Commerce. The hotel, designed by the New York architectural firm of Warren and Wetmore—architects for New York's Grand Central Station—employed highly advanced design techniques. The completely fireproof, nineteen-story structure with 500 guest rooms was Providence's second skyscraper. The Biltmore's simple, almost "modern" exterior contrasted sharply with its classically inspired interior public spaces. The ceiling of the main two-story lobby is covered with elaborate geometric coffering richly detailed with classical motifs. Public function rooms and a grand ballroom on the top two floors possess similar elaborate decorative detail. Throughout it history, the Biltmore has been the gathering place for Rhode Island's social, business, and government leaders. However, in the late 1960s, the hotel fell on hard times, and it finally closed in January, 1975.

Recognizing the destructive effect of a highly visible empty building and the need for a first-class hotel downtown, members of the 21st Providence Group formed a limited partnership to restore the Biltmore to active use. It purchased the hotel building in September, 1976. The general partners, Textron, the Outlet Company, a local retail store, the *Providence Journal*, a local newspaper, and the Business Development Company of Rhode Island, a nonprofit business development firm which loans money to local businesses, all developed subsidiaries to participate in the project. This consortium retained Hotels of Distinction, Inc., a hotel-management company which currently operates the Copley Plaza in Boston, to supervise the renovation and manage the hotel. The Boston architectural firm of Shepley, Bulfinch, Richardson and Abbot, and Providence architects Sturgis, Daughn and Salisbury, and Morris Nathanson Design have been retained for the project.

After examining several reuse options for the building, the new owners decided to restore the Biltmore as a first-class hotel catering to business travelers and corporate meetings. The public rooms will be elegant, the guest rooms, spacious. Relatively few exterior changes are planned, with the possible exception of a new glass elevator on the outside which will serve the public function rooms on the lower floors and the restaurant and the ballroom on the upper two stories. Interior renovation work will respect the character of existing detail. One major change will be the removal of the marble staircase in the main lobby to create a three-story entrance lobby with a registration desk on the ground level. Many of the original 500 rooms will be enlarged, reducing the total to 360. The smallest rooms will contain 225 square feet; the largest, 550 square feet. Most of the existing tubs and tile work will be saved, but other plumbing and lighting fixtures will be replaced. All new room furniture, carpeting, and draperies will be installed. On the top floor, several windows will be enlarged to provide restaurant patrons with a panoramic view of the State House and the Union Station.

Since the new owners acquired the property, work has moved forward on an exacting schedule:

September to October, 1976—Financial feasibility studies were completed for a variety of potential uses, and the hotel option chosen as the most attractive.

November, 1976, to April, 1977—Architectural drawings and specifications were prepared.

May, 1977—Demolition and renovation work began.

June, 1978—Grand opening scheduled, 56 years after the original opening party.

Providence Union Station. Completed in 1898 by the New York, New Haven & Hartford Railroad, the Union Station is built on a low man-made hill. The platforms are reached from the main terminal through underground passageways. The complex originally consisted of five buildings, laid out symmetrically, with the main passenger terminal in the center connected by colonnades to flanking buildings. A fire in 1941 destroyed the easternmost building. The station, built of yellow mottled brick with red sandstone trim, was designed to harmonize with the Renaissance-inspired architecture of the City Hall and the State Capitol. The original plans called for a boulevard running under the complex, connecting it with the State Capitol and the City Hall. This boulevard was never executed. The space between the rear of the station and the foot of the capitol terrace, planned as a park, is now used as a parking lot. In addition, compounding the design problems, the

Aerial view of Union Station prior to renovation in 1977. Elevated parking deck is in the foreground with railroad tracks behind. (Dennis P. Albert)

Artist's rendering of the Union Station complex after renovation with elevated parking deck removed.

city had built an elevated parking deck in front of the main terminal obscuring the view of the building from Kennedy Plaza, the prime open space in the area.

As train travel diminished during the 1950s, the station suffered from neglect and lack of maintenance. Many described it as a "Chinese Wall" cutting through the city center. However, recent efforts to improve service in the Northeast Rail Corridor have increased use of the terminal facilities. Under the Amtrak Improvement Act, federal funds are now available to renovate stations as transportation centers. In early 1977, the Federal Railway Administration allocated $13.2 million to repair the central terminal building, improve vehicular access to the complex, and add nearly 1,200 new parking spaces (480 in a new parking garage) around the station. Of the total new investment in the station, $6.4 million will be used to upgrade the central terminal. Improvements planned for the building include: installation of new mechanical systems; replacement of the porte cochere (an iron and glass structure extending from the main terminal's entrance over the adjacent driveway), removed in 1954; and addition of new escalators and direct access passageways to rail platforms. The city will also remove the elevated parking deck in front of the main terminal.

The city named Textron as the commercial developer for the Union Station in February, 1977. Redeveloping the complex and the 55-acre surrounding area is expected to take ten years. The renovation and adaptive reuse of the station itself is the keystone of the project. Textron is obligated to go forward with the station-complex renovation if a series of conditions are met, including improvement of the Kennedy Plaza area by the city.

Major elements in the company's redevelopment plan include the following:

1. Within the next three years, subject to a number of conditions, Textron will renovate the four-building, 120,000-square-foot Union Station complex located on 4.3 acres. Amtrak will be the major tenant in the center building, with the remaining space rented for government offices, retail shops, and a restaurant.

2. Textron will explore the feasibility of constructing a 400,000-square-foot high-rise office building on land adjacent to the station complex. The company would use about 100,000 square feet for its headquarters, doubling its present space. The remaining space would be leased to other tenants. Completion of the office tower would follow the station-complex renovation by several years.

3. If the station complex renovation and the office tower are successful, Textron will explore the feasibility of building a 200,000-square-foot retail center in the vicinity.

4. Textron will undertake long-range planning for use of the remaining land between the State House grounds and the Union Station. This land, currently used as parking lots, could be developed for park, recreational, commercial, and residential purposes, including luxury condominiums.

As of mid-1977, attempts were being made to resolve the intricate ownership problems so that the city could gain unchallenged title to the railroad property and sell it to Textron. Textron is interviewing architects to plan the station renovation. If the title problems can be cleared, financing arranged, and the necessary leases signed, construction work could begin during winter, 1978.

Costs *The Biltmore Hotel.* Textron and its partners purchased the hotel for $925,000 in September, 1976, and plan to invest another $10.5 million in the renovation. This represents a new investment of $31,740 per room, approximately half the expenditure required to build a new hotel of similar size, though not of similar quality. It would be impossible to duplicate the quality in some of the public function rooms at almost any price today. If the hotel maintains a 65 percent occupancy level at a $34 average room rate, it will break even. While the venture is not expected to show a tremendous return, Textron and its other partners do not expect the hotel to show continuing losses.

The Rhode Island Historical Commission has nominated the Biltmore Hotel to the National Register of Historic Places. If the nomination is accepted, and the renovation plans are approved by the National Park Service, the building will be eligible for accelerated depreciation benefits under the Tax Reform Act of 1976. The current equity investment in the hotel is $1.75 million, of which Textron has supplied $1 million. The partners hope to raise a total equity of $2.5 million and obtain a first mortgage from a consortium of five local banks for $6.5 million. These banks have agreed to provide the construction funds for the renovation and to grant a 25-year mortgage at less than conventional rates when the work is complete. The remaining $2.5 million will come from the U.S. Economic Development Administration which will provide a 25-year second mortgage at 7⅞ percent interest.

Providence Union Station. Textron estimated that a $35.5 million investment will be required to complete the first three phases of the station project, including:

1. $7.5 million for the renovation of the four-building station complex. Since Textron expects to purchase the buildings from the city for a nominal price, nearly all the funds will be used for improving the facility. Textron expects to invest $1 million to $2 million, with the remaining funds coming from government grants or loans and conventional financing from local banks. As in the Biltmore renovation, other local businesses may join Textron as equity participants.

2. $20 million for a new high-rise office tower. This figure represents a cost of approximately $50 per square foot for the new construction.

3. $8 million for a 200,000-square-foot retail complex.

Problems Both the Biltmore Hotel and the Union Station are high-risk development projects which require a developer with substantial financial strength and staying power. In both projects, there is great uncertainty about the required total renovation cost and whether the necessary market exists for the hotel, restaurants, shops, and office space. Although the hotel has already been granted preferred tax status for ten years, both projects must receive long-term property-tax concessions. Similar ventures in other cities have been successful, but there is no guarantee that they will work in Providence.

In the Union Station project, Textron and the city are having difficulties obtaining clear title to the property. The company has invested substantial legal and administrative personnel time in ownership negotiations. If a clear title for the station complex cannot be achieved, the project may be killed and Textron will lose its investment. Textron also still has to negotiate a satisfactory arrangement with Amtrak for use of the main building and be satisfied that the remaining 55 acres can be developed in a satisfactory and harmonious manner.

Benefits The long-term benefits of these projects to both the City of Providence and Textron are not entirely related to each project's "bottom line." According to John B. Henderson, Textron's Senior Vice President—Policy Planning, who is guiding the company's involvement in the Biltmore and the Union Station, the completion of the two renovations should serve as a catalyst to attract further new investment into the downtown from both the public and private sectors. Textron would like to build a major high-rise building to house its corporate headquarters and believes that when revitalized, the Union Station area would be an extremely attractive site. If the number of people using the downtown can be increased markedly, then the dependent retail, cultural, and entertainment sectors can grow as well. By making the downtown a better working environment, the company is in a better position to retain and attract top-quality employees.[1]

A major advantage of the renovation over new construction is the reduced time and money required to complete it. If completed on schedule, the Biltmore will be operating only nineteen months after purchase: less than half the time (and cost) required to build a new hotel.

The Company Founded in 1923 in Providence as the Franklin Rayon Company, Textron today is a highly diversified multi-national corporation with 181 plants and 64,000 employees (3,200 in Rhode Island). In 1976, sales reached $2.6 billion up from 1975's figure of $2.45 billion. Net income over the same period rose from $95.9 million to $121 million. Textron's products include helicopters, zippers, snowmobiles, greeting cards, and metal machinery, as well as fire and casualty insurance.

For further information contact:
John Henderson
Senior Vice President
Textron, Inc.
40 Westminster Street
Providence, Rhode Island 02903

Ron Marsella
Executive Director
Providence Foundation
10 Dorrance Street
Providence, Rhode Island 02903

Footnotes

1. "Project Seen Benefiting Both Textron and City," *Providence Evening Bulletin,* 10 February 1977.

Summary Trend Publications, the largest publisher of business periodicals in the South, is developing a former cigar factory in Ybor City, the Latin section of Tampa, Florida, into a multi-use commercial center, named Ybor Square. Trend purchased the 90,000-square-foot complex of three buildings in 1972. Since that time, it has created modern offices for itself on the top floor of one building; an arcade of specialty shops and a restaurant on the ground floor of the same building; and a Nostalgia Market, where vendors sell antiques and collectibles from small open cubicles, in another former factory building. The development is attracting both local shoppers and tourists to an area rich in Hispanic ethnic history. The retail shops opened in late 1974, and by 1978, the complex is expected to be operating in the black.

Background V. M. Ybor, a cigar manufacturer, originally moved his factory from Cuba to Key West. In 1885, he founded Ybor City after purchasing forty acres outside Tampa. There, he built another cigar factory and later invested $500,000 to create a model city for his workers. In the 1890s, Cubans, fleeing the harsh treatment of the Spanish, flocked to Ybor City, and it became a center for cigar making. Cuban patriot Jose Marti spoke on the steps of the Ybor Cigar Factory in 1893 to rally American support for Cuba's fight against Spain. In 1898, Teddy Roosevelt and his Rough Riders stopped in Ybor City on their way to Cuba. Once larger than downtown Tampa, Ybor City is now part of that city.

In recent years, the urban-renewal bulldozer has destroyed much of the early factory-worker housing in Ybor City. In its place now stand the functional buildings of the Hillsborough Community College. However, most of the historic commercial structures in the area have been saved, although some show signs of severe neglect.

The three buildings of the original Ybor Cigar Factory, once the largest cigar factory in the world, are located between 8th and 9th Avenues and 13th and 14th Streets near the Community College. These Victorian brick and timber commercial structures contain 90,000 square feet of space on one-and-a-half acres of land. They adjoin each other in a U-shape configuration around a Spanish-style central courtyard. Interior beams are heart pine, as are the wide floor boards. The latter are commonly four inches thick. The complex is listed in the National Register of Historic Places and is a Florida Monument.

The original Factory Building, erected in 1886, is three stories tall, with the exception of a one-story north wing. Tobacco was graded on the first floor, and the fine Havana types were stored in the basement humidor along with the finished cigars. On the two upper floors, more than 500 workers hand rolled cigars while a reader, known as "El Lector," entertained, educated, and propagandized from his elevated box. Each worker paid a quarter per week for the reader's services. Arriving tobacco ships were sighted from the cupola on the top of the Factory. Adjacent to the Factory, a three-story Stemmery Building, where the tobacco-leaf stems were removed, was added in 1902. At the same time, a warehouse was constructed across the courtyard from the Factory. This one-story structure with 24-foot ceilings was served by a small-gauge railroad which delivered tobacco from the harbor. A garden patio connects the Stemmery and the Factory.

In 1955, the American Tobacco Company sold the buildings—acquired in an earlier transaction—to the Havatampa Corporation, which continued to make cigars there until the mid-1960s. The buildings became obsolete with the introduction of modern mechanized cigar-production techniques, and they were sold to Trend Publications in December, 1972.

Execution By 1972, Trend Publications had outgrown its Tampa offices, and was looking for a site for expansion. Behind the peeling paint of the severely neglected old buildings, Trend President Harris H. Mullen envisioned a unique corporate home, a combination office, retail, and entertainment complex that would house artists, writers, antique dealers, galleries, and boutiques, attracting both local residents and tourists. The integrity of the historic buildings was to be maintained, while the interiors were updated with modern facilities. Trend established a real estate division to develop the complex.

Relying on his own intuition, not feasibility studies, Mullen's first project was to create new offices for Trend Publications. Architects Friedman and McKenna of Tampa were retained to develop drawings for the conversion. However, as the planning process stretched into the second year, Mullen recognized that if the total project were to be successful, he must demonstrate that there was a market for his idea. In summer, 1974, the first floor of the Factory Building was cleaned out, and 28 individual wire cubicles were built, each containing 200 square feet of storage space. The cubicles were rented on a monthly basis to individual collectors, antique dealers, and artisans. Every Saturday and Sunday since October, 1974, these vendors have sold their wares in the courtyard and from the cubicles. This Nostalgia Market has become a major event in Ybor City, attracting several thousand spectators and collectors. All the cubicles are rented, and there is a waiting list for space. Each dealer pays $62.50 per month.

By July, 1975, Trend's new offices on the third floor of the Stemmery Building were complete, and the company had moved in. A new glass-enclosed elevator was built on the exterior of the wing between the Factory Building and the Stemmery. The interior brick in the wing was cleaned, and a new three-story staircase was installed, providing a modern entrance way to the firm's offices. To create Trend's 12,000 square feet of contemporary office space, interior designers Dean-Redman of Tampa exposed and sandblasted interior brick and timber, and sanded and refinished the pine floors. The building materials provide the major elements of interest in the offices. Modern furnishings and paintings decorate the major rooms, which are defined by partial walls and flow easily into each other. There are several meeting rooms, individual offices for executives, and plenty of light and open space for editors and layout artists.

By October, 1975, the interior brick and timber on the first floor of the Stemmery Building had also been cleaned, and a mini-shopping mall had been created there. This was accomplished by placing a series of ten-foot partitions between the supporting posts. The fourteen specialty shops in the Stemmery Arcade offer a variety of merchandise, including candles, antiques, candy, jewelry, stamps, children's toys and clothes, plants, Cuban coffee and sandwiches, and, of course, hand-rolled cigars. Each shop contains approximately 380 square feet of space. By mid-1977, all the shops were occupied, although only about half were original tenants. Arcade tenants pay about $9 per square foot per year for shop space, plus a percentage of gross sales over a specified minimum. Gross sales for the Stemmery Arcade shops average approximately $20,000 per year, and some of the more successful enterprises are expected to pay percentage rentals in 1978. Utilities and services are prorated for tenants.

The Stemmery Arcade also contains the Rough Riders Restaurant, a bar and grill, run by a local entrepreneur, which serves delicatessen fare. The restaurant has steadily built its clientele, and now attracts 250 for lunch daily. By fall, 1977, renovation work on the second floor of the Stemmery will be complete, and the Rough Riders will expand into 4,000 additional square feet. Also on the second floor, a large open display space is planned, where dealers and individuals can sell antiques.

The central courtyard was landscaped to create an entrance way for the complex and in 1976, vintage Ybor City streetlights were installed. Throughout the year, arts and crafts festivals, antique shows, and photography exhibits are held in the courtyard. Local performing groups entertain the shoppers in the outdoor theater each weekend.

Aerial view of Ybor Square complex.

Arts and crafts show in Ybor Square courtyard with Factory Building in the background.

Future development of Ybor Square will continue in stages as market demand permits. With renovation work in the Stemmery complete, Mullen plans to upgrade the cubicles on the first floor of the Factory to more sophisticated shops similar to those in the Stemmery Arcade, and perhaps build additional cubicles on the second and third floors. The garden patio between the Factory and the Stemmery will be landscaped. Development plans for the warehouse are still uncertain. At one point, Mullen considered building a 256-seat theater in it, and creating additional floors for apartments. Townhouses on the second and third floors of the Factory have also been contemplated. The theater idea has been abandoned, but Mullen would still like to build some residential units in the project, if it can be done profitably.

In 1976, Trend's total income from the Ybor Square rentals was approximately $80,000.

Costs Trend would not disclose the amount of its investment in Ybor Square. The company paid cash for the land and the three buildings in 1972, acquiring them for substantially less than the $250,000 asking price.[1] Renovation work in the Stemmery cost approximately $20 per square foot. Construction costs were financed by a local bank at a floating rate 3 percent over prime. The construction loan was recently refinanced with an $800,000 long-term mortgage.

Trend spends approximately $20,000 per year promoting the complex, including $10,000 for media advertising. While the project income has yet to cover the yearly expenses, Mullen expects Ybor Square to be operating in the black by 1978.

Problems Although Ybor Square has been developed nearly as originally planned, the timetable for completion has been lengthened from two or three years to six or eight. Trend began construction work on the project in early 1974, just as the country entered its most severe recession since the 1930s. During the same period, the company was starting its new magazine, *The South*, and its own financial resources were strained. Money was very tight, and the construction loan, floating at 3 percent above prime, reached 15 percent at one point.

Another problem has been attracting a clientele to Ybor Square. The complex is small compared to the regional shopping centers, and inconveniently located. In addition, local prejudices about inner-city neighborhoods have had to be overcome. There were also problems during the initial phase of the Stemmery Arcade, since many merchants were first-time shop owners. Half the original tenants are no longer there, and a series of new ones had to be found.

Benefits Although Ybor Square has been slow to pay its own way, during the first five years the depreciation deductions and losses did provide some tax savings for the company. Mullen projects profitable long-term development. Recent appraisals indicate that the market value of the property is appreciating faster than operational losses.

For Harris Mullen, the chief benefit of Ybor Square has been the satisfaction of seeing his vision become reality. At the same time, Trend employees have gained a very special working environment. For Ybor City, the development has brought new visitors, new revenues, and new life to an area that had been deteriorating for several decades.

Florida Governor Reubin Askew recognized Trend's development at Ybor Square and its many cultural programs by naming it the 1976 recipient of the Annual Governor's Award in the Arts.

The Company Trend Publications is the South's largest publisher of business periodicals, textbooks, books, and pamphlets about the region. Its two major publications are *Florida Trend*, a monthly magazine with a circulation of 30,000 featuring articles on Florida business and finance; and *The South*, a monthly magazine with a circulation of 50,000 featuring articles of general interest about the South.

Harris Mullen is the publisher and major stockholder of Trend, which he founded in Tampa in 1957. The company employs 28 people and maintains headquarters at Ybor Square, as well as branch sales offices in Atlanta and Fort Lauderdale. All stock is privately held, and financial information is not available.

For further information contact:
Harris Mullen
Publisher
Trend Publications
P.O. Box 2350
Tampa, Florida 33601

Footnotes

1. Robert Fraser, "Monumental Faith," *St. Petersburg Times*, 10 December 1972, p. 5-H.

Once viewed as a genteel pursuit for aristocratic matrons, preservation today has meaning for everyone from inner-city residents to jazz buffs. Residents of Boston, New York, Richmond, San Francisco, and cities and towns across the country are discovering that they too have roots. Today, there are over 6,000 local historical societies in the United States.

Yet, business support for preservation, in such forms as outright donations of money, goods, or services has always been limited and indeed, by some measures, may even be decreasing. A 1976 survey by the Business Committee for the Arts, a nonprofit organization interested in stimulating corporate giving, found that business contributions to the arts increased overall from $144 million to $221 million between 1973 and 1976, and the number of times "historical and cultural restorations" were cited as recipients by participating companies increased from 10 percent in 1973 to 32 percent in 1976. Nevertheless, the amount of each charitable dollar contributed to preservation actually declined from 5 cents to 3 cents over the same period,[1] representing a decline from $7.2 million in 1973 to $6.63 million in 1976.

INFORM's study indicates that business would have much to gain by reversing this apparent trend. For the twenty companies profiled, the donation of money, property, materials, and publicity to preservation causes has always produced a return: either literally, in tax write-offs of business expenses or charitable tax deductions; or figuratively, in enhancing the company's image.

The firms profiled here represent a cross section of American business. They include large and small companies from the steel, tobacco, oil, and printing industries, as well as consumer-oriented businesses and public utilities.

These firms have donated funds to support a wide variety of projects: an archeological dig in Virginia, a photographic survey of U.S. county courthouses, an architectural analysis of important buildings in Mississippi, and the restorations of a grist mill in New Jersey, an opera house in Wilmington, Delaware, and a Moravian village in North Carolina. The companies have contributed property, including historic houses in Louisiana and Virginia, an 1883 office building in Troy, New York, and surplus gas stations in various cities and towns. They have given publicity support in several forms, ranging from Flanigan's underwriting of short films on historic local structures to Pinaire's production of four-color posters on preservation themes.

INFORM found that the motives behind contributions to preservation projects were frequently quite complex. In thirteen cases, location was a determining factor. R. J. Reynolds Industries' long association with Winston-Salem, for example, helped prompt its donations to Old Salem, Inc., a nonprofit group dedicated to the preservation of that city's Moravian heritage.

Nine of the companies studied reported that they were motivated by a sense of social responsibility, either on a local or national scale.* This "enlightened self-interest" encouraged Atlantic Richfield's gift of abandoned gas stations to community groups, providing the groups with

*Although not directly related to INFORM's study, a survey of 309 corporate chairmen and presidents conducted by The Conference Board of New York found self-interest (defined as public service necessary for the long-range survival of the corporation as an institution) was the second leading motive for corporate public-service activity.[2]

General Preservation Support

meeting places and relieving the company of abandoned properties which earned no income.

In six cases, INFORM found executive interest in preservation to have played a major role in the company's decision to contribute. Reynolds Metals, for example, preserved several stone canal locks in Richmond partly because a company Vice President saw the benefits of a revitalized river front to both the company and the city, and persuaded management to save them.

Among the companies studied, the indirect public-relations and economic benefits gained by contributing to preservation were found to have varied. Seventeen of the twenty businesses received significant favorable publicity of one sort or another. Flanigan's, to give one example, was cited by the City of Rochester, the State of New York, and the Business Committee for the Arts for its work on behalf of preservation in upstate New York. This furniture company sponsored films, distributed reprints of articles on preservation, helped develop articles on the same subject, and sponsored an essay contest on area landmarks. Bird & Son has been cited in the *Congressional Record* as well as by national columnists Bob Considine and Don Oakley for its national matching-grants awards to preservation groups.

Most companies studied by INFORM were reluctant to reveal tax benefits gained from contributions to preservation. However, Union Camp did disclose that it took a $26,000 tax deduction from its gift of the Tower Hill Plantation and ten surrounding acres to the National Trust for Historic Preservation. It had acquired the Plantation and surrounding woodlands in 1960 as part of a routine expansion of its holdings. The company instituted a program of donations of ecologically or historically important lands in 1975.

Sometimes, companies deducted the cost of their donations as part of their operating expenses, as Pinaire Lithographing did in the design and production of its two preservation posters.

In general, the contribution process has gone smoothly, with few problems encountered by the companies involved in preservation support. While those problems that arose were usually peculiar to the individual case, one which was common to several projects turned out to be administration. Two companies established their own support mechanisms without realizing that administering a nationally oriented program can be a full-time job. Bird & Son, a building-materials manufacturer, discovered this to be true in distributing a series of grants to preservation groups across the country.

All the contributions described here were handled by the companies themselves. However, some companies have established foundations to administer donations. This mechanism is especially appropriate for businesses whose earnings fluctuate dramatically, since it insures funding continuity even in bad financial years.

As of mid-1977, there were about 1,500 company-sponsored foundations in the United States. Although the Tax Reform Act of 1969 imposed a 4 percent levy on recipients of foundation grants and required more detailed financial disclosure from foundations, the number of foundations has not noticeably decreased.

The most important piece of federal legislation affecting business support of preservation is the Federal Revenue Act of 1935. Under this law, a corporation may donate up to 5 percent of its pre-tax income to charitable causes and deduct contributions as an expense for income-tax purposes. (An amendment to the Act later extended the same benefit to banks.) Companies may also deduct business expenses—including charitable contributions of facilities, employee time, products, services, and advertising—from taxable income. Nevertheless, the Commission on Private Philanthropy, a privately sponsored group consisting of representatives from business, community groups, and government, issued a report in 1975 which found that the average corporate charitable contribution has been about 1 percent of pre-tax net income in recent years. The Commission, chaired by John H. Filer, Chairman of Aetna Life & Casualty, reported that half of the annual $1 billion contribution by business to philanthropic causes is generated by the 1,000 largest corporations. It estimated that perhaps another $1 billion is given in other ways, such as donations of in-kind services, use of facilities, investments in urban revitalization, and support of job-training programs for the underprivileged or handicapped. The Commission's primary recommendation was that "corporations set as a minimum goal, to be reached no later than 1980, the giving to charitable purposes of 2% of pre-tax income."[3] Not everyone, of course, favors what amounts to public subsidy of corporate and private giving via tax benefits. However, the Commission, which generally favored this approach, recommended a "disappearing floor" for tax deductions only when donations amount to 1 percent or 2 percent of pre-tax income; a 10 percent tax credit if donations exceed an established level; and a 2 percent "philanthropy needs" tax which corporations or the federal government could distribute to charitable causes. Others feel that a social audit of business expenditures should be instituted. They prefer a fixed-percentage tax of corporate income for charitable causes.

The Business Committee for the Arts (BCA), founded in 1967 and backed by corporations, is also trying to stimulate company giving. It counsels both cultural institutions and businesses about effective programs, and presents annual awards in cooperation with *Forbes* magazine (they were formerly given in conjunction with *Esquire*) to businesses for contributions to the nation's cultural life. Of the companies profiled in this book Exxon, Reynolds Metals, Atlantic Richfield, Eastman Kodak, Flanigan's, and Seagram's have received such awards.

Business support of preservation has a significance beyond its direct and indirect benefits to company and community. It also helps shape broader public attitudes. As James Biddle, President of the National Trust, pointed out in *Preservation News*:

Actively promoting historic preservation or merely suggesting that old buildings are culturally significant, has a lasting effect on American attitudes. Just as "new, modern and improved" were key adjectives in advertising copy in the 1950's and 60's, so "enduring, antique, old-fashioned" and even "renewed" are the top sellers of the mid-1970's.[4]

Footnotes

1. Business Committee for the Arts, *Business Support for the Arts—1976* (New York: Business Committee for the Arts, 1976).
2. James F. Harris and Anne Klepper, *Corporate Philanthropic Public Service Activities, 1976* (New York: The Conference Board, 1976), p. 17.
3. Commission on Private Philanthropy and Public Needs, *Giving in America—Toward a Stronger Voluntary Sector* (Washington, D.C.: Library of Congress, 1975).
4. *Preservation News,* November, 1976, p. 5.

Anheuser-Busch, Inc.

Summary   In 1972, Busch Properties, Inc., a wholly owned subsidiary of Anheuser-Busch, Inc., contributed more than $150,000 to support archeological surveys conducted at Kingsmill on the James, a new residential community near Williamsburg, Virginia. This money, given directly to the Virginia Historic Landmarks Commission, supports efforts to identify and document early settlement on the property as far back as prehistoric times. Busch Properties is developing the 2,900-acre site under a master plan that will accommodate up to 5,000 homes and still leave more than 40 percent of the land as greenbelts and open spaces. The results of the survey have caused the developer to revise many of the original plans to avoid encroaching on newly uncovered historic sites. These changes have cost additional time and money, but have helped provide a good public image and a unique marketing approach for the new community.

Background   In the late 1960s, Anheuser-Busch wanted a new location in the mid-Atlantic region of the United States for its diverse operations including a brewery. The company was invited to the Williamsburg area by the leadership of the Colonial Williamsburg Foundation, which is responsible for the direction, administration, and support of Colonial Williamsburg. Anheuser-Busch was interested in the area because of its proximity to the major metropolitan markets of Richmond, Norfolk, Newport News, and Hampton, Virginia, as well as Washington, D.C., and because of its rail, truck, and ship-transport accessibility. Anheuser-Busch acquired approximately 3,600 acres of land—most of it from Colonial Williamsburg—for the site of its ninth brewery, for Busch Gardens, a family entertainment attraction featuring exhibits, rides, and wildlife, for the Kingsmill on the James residential development, and for a Busch corporate-center complex.

When Colonial Williamsburg sold the property to Busch, it stipulated in the purchase agreement that a review committee, consisting of Foundation and community representatives, was to be established to ensure that Kingsmill would be developed in harmony with the present character of Colonial Williamsburg and its environs. With the help of well-respected planners such as Carl Feiss, Grady Clay, and Conrad Wirth, tight environmental and aesthetic controls regulating land use and building design were developed and implemented. Kingsmill was not to compete with Colonial Williamsburg, but was to preserve the historic character of the land. By controlling and overseeing the development of the Kingsmill property adjacent to its new brewery, Anheuser-Busch could ensure maintenance of the high quality, character, value, and use of its immediate neighborhood. The company hired the well-known planning and landscape-design firm, Sasaki, Daw-

The remains of the eighteenth-century Kingsmill Plantation.

son, and Demay, which in conjunction with local planners and community representatives, developed a master plan for the site. Ecologically sensitive areas were identified, and major construction, with the exception of unobtrusive pedestrian and bicycle trails, was prohibited.

It was widely known that the remains of historic sites existed on the property. However, these sites, except for the extant outbuildings of the Kingsmill Plantation, were not considered in the original master plan. Their archeological value was overlooked until a major discovery was made. Early in 1972, Dr. William H. Kelso, an archeologist with the Virginia Historic Landmarks Commission (VHLC), discovered an old well eroding away from the steep banks of the James River on the Busch property. He obtained a $10,000 grant from Anheuser-Busch to excavate and survey the well. Wells are excellent archeological resources, since they contain a preserved time line of layers of sediment and discarded objects that clearly illustrate the history of settlement. The artifacts found in this well, dating back to the early 1700s, prompted Busch Properties to offer $150,000 to the VHLC to survey other parts of the Kingsmill property. Kelso and a team of assistants have been working on the project ever since, and the company has continued its support beyond the original grant.

Execution   Since 1972, more than 34 sites have been surveyed at Kingsmill by the VHLC. Under the direction of Dr. Kelso, teams of students from the Department of Archeology at William and Mary, as well as from other colleges and universities, together with several state archeologists, have traced the historic settlement of the Kingsmill property back to the early seventeenth century, just after Jamestown was colonized in 1607. In addition, the Department of Anthropology at William and Mary, supported by grants from Busch Properties, has surveyed fourteen prehistoric sites, some dating from as far back as 3000 B.C. Oysters, abundant in the James River, attracted early Indian settlement. Shell middens, or waste pits, indicated the presence of campsites. Artifacts, such as stone tools and projectile points, were also found, as were the outlines of one-room oval dwellings.

Major historic sites that have been excavated include:

- Littletown, the early-seventeenth-century plantation of Colonel Thomas Pettus. Pettus was a prominent landowner and public official. The site includes the remains of the mansion house, several outbuildings, and a well. Among the artifacts recovered from this site are a bottle seal bearing the initials of Pettus, a copper tobacco-can lid, and a Spanish silver coin.

- The Bray Plantation, the eighteenth-century residence of James Bray II, a burgess and justice of the peace from James City County. The remains of the mansion house together with five other buildings and a well were found. Artifacts from this site include a number of family wine-bottle seals; a pewter spoon bearing the name of David Menetrie, a Williamsburg brick mason; a sheet-brass lion's paw; and a sealed bottle more than 200 years old and still half-filled with milk.

- The Kingsmill Plantation, an eighteenth-century structure, and one of the grandest in the colonial Tidewater region. This was the most elaborate site surveyed and included the foundation of the mansion house flanked by two extant outbuildings. The site also yielded the remains of an earlier seventeeth-century building which contained one of the most valuable Kingsmill artifacts: a seventeenth-century pipe bowl bearing a carving of a small ship. The remains of a nineteenth-century dwelling were also found. This site yielded high-quality ceramics and cutlery.

The artifacts found at these and other sites have been publicly exhibited in the nearby Anheuser-Busch Hospitality Center. Several excavation sites have been preserved as parks within the development area, but are only open to residents of Kingsmill and guests.

While William Kelso first recognized the hidden value of the land and the means of preserving it, a number of other people contributed greatly to the effort's success. Among them were Walter E. Diggs, Jr., then President of Busch Properties, who recognized both the responsibilities and benefits of such a project, and Junius R. Fishburne, Jr., then Executive Director of the VHLC. The VHLC has encouraged corporate participation in several important preservation projects in the Commonwealth of Virginia (see Reynolds Metals, Ethyl, and Union Camp).

Costs
Direct

- $10,000 for the excavation and documentation of the Harrop Well "kick off" project urged by Dr. William Kelso.

- $150,000 for the initial contract with the Virginia Historic Landmarks Commission to conduct the archeological survey.

- $10,000 for archeological surveys of the prehistory of Kingsmill conducted by the College of William and Mary.

Indirect
Figures for the cost of the time and effort spent revising original plans for the development, and the donation of personnel and equipment to help with survey excavations were unavailable.

Problems   The most difficult problems for Anheuser-Busch were the costs caused by delays and plan revisions necessitated by the discovery of significant archeological sites. These meant that the designs for road and building-site placements had to be redrawn.

Benefits Anheuser-Busch and Busch Properties have received extensive favorable publicity for their archeological efforts at Kingsmill. Although Busch bought the property primarily because of its location and the resulting "spin off" benefits of being situated in a major historic tourist area, the archeological project was an additional bonus, creating community goodwill and attracting people to the site. Several of the Kingsmill homesites were sold as a direct result of articles written about the archeological activities. Kingsmill is no longer just a development in a unique environment. It incorporates a rich legacy of art and artifact that no competitive new residential community can offer. Materials and information found in the surveys are incorporated in advertising and promotional campaigns. (The Kings-

mill logo was developed from a seal found on an early-eighteenth-century wine bottle found in one of the excavations.) The local economy has been bolstered by the additional business and employment generated by the new brewery and Busch Gardens. Anheuser-Busch also pays approximately 25 percent of the county's taxes. In a report to the community in February, 1976, Anheuser-Busch noted that its combined Williamsburg operations had a direct impact on the local economy of just under $80 million in 1975. The approach of the Kingsmill development has stimulated other improvements such as cleanup of the James River in the area. Flood, erosion, and pollution control are also receiving more attention from local and state agencies.

Moreover, in documenting and pre-

Brass harness ornament was unearthed at an area called the Littletown Quarter. Several outbuildings at the site were associated with the Bray Plantation. The winged lion was the Bray family crest. The artifact is 5⅝ inches high.

Map of Kingsmill on the James with major archeological sites.

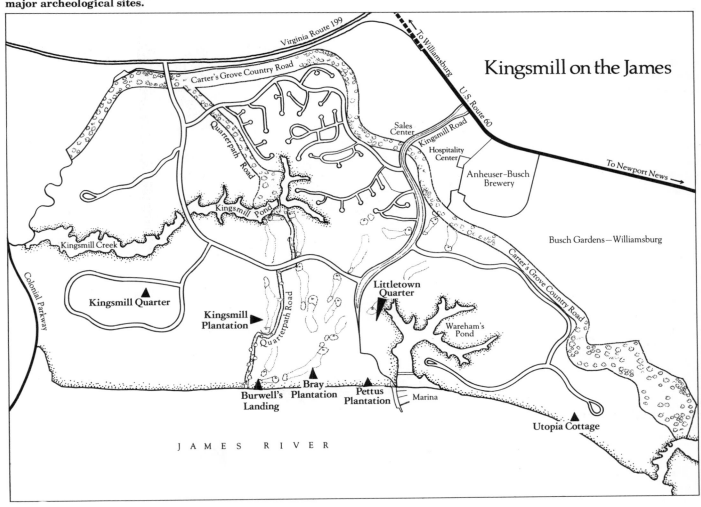

serving a part of U.S. history, the project has proved valuable to the Commonwealth of Virginia and to all those interested in a greater understanding of the country's past. The Commonwealth's educational institutions have used the excavations as a training ground for archeological scholars and as a source of data on Virginia's early rural history. In a report on his findings at Kingsmill, Theodore R. Reinhart of William and Mary's Department of Anthropology praised corporate support for this project:

The concern for the preservation of the historic and prehistoric resources and data of the Kingsmill property demonstrated by Anheuser-Busch, Inc., and Busch Properties, Inc., serves as an outstanding example for all developers and business organizations at a time when American archeology faces an acute "crisis" of its own.[1]

The Company Busch Properties was established in 1970 as a land-development subsidiary of Anheuser-Busch. In addition to the Kingsmill residential community, Busch Properties is developing 155 acres of land in Columbus, Ohio, as a business center for office, warehouse, and light industrial use. This project, known as Busch Corporate Center-Columbus, will provide new facilities for more than 57 companies and institutions. A second Busch corporate-center development is now underway at Williamsburg adjacent to Kingsmill on the James.

Anheuser-Busch began its brewery operations in St. Louis in 1852, when Adolphus Busch joined in partnership with his father-in-law, Eberhard Anheuser. Today, it is the world's largest brewer, with ten breweries throughout the country and an annual production capacity of more than 42 million barrels of beer. The company also produces industrial products such as baker's yeast, and owns and operates two Busch Gardens. Anheuser-Busch ranked 127th in the 1976 list of *Fortune* 500 companies. The company's net sales were $1.6 billion in 1976 and $1.4 billion in 1975. Net income came to $84.7 million in 1975 and $55.4 million in 1976.

Other Preservation Activities. Anheuser-Busch has also preserved its original brewery facilities in St. Louis which date from the founding of the company in 1852; this complex includes three historic landmark buildings listed in the National Register of Historic Places: Stables (1885), the Brew House (1891-1892), and the adapted Executive Office, formerly the Lyon Elementary School (1868). The company has also supported preservation through donations of money and property. In Clinton, Missouri, for example, an old Anheuser-Busch beer depot was turned over to the local historical society for use as its headquarters.

For further information contact:
Richard G. Knight
General Manager
Busch Properties, Inc.
100 Kingsmill Road
Williamsburg, Virginia 23185
Dr. William H. Kelso
Virginia Historic Landmarks
  Commission
221 Governor Street
Richmond, Virginia 23219

Footnotes

1. Theodore R. Reinhart, "The Prehistory of Kingsmill," (unpublished report, College of William and Mary, Department of Anthropology, October, 1974).

This 1860s schoolhouse, shown here in earlier years, is now the Main Office Building for Anheuser-Busch in St. Louis. (Boehl & Koenig)

Atlantic Richfield Company

Summary In 1973, Atlantic Richfield, one of the largest integrated U.S. oil companies, developed a Service Station Conversion Program to dispose of surplus gas stations, and help improve the environment. Under this Program, the company funds the recycling of the gas stations and donates them to communities. Plans call for five conversions in 1977. To date, Atlantic Richfield has spent approximately $250,000 on the Program.

Background In recent years, because of changing traffic patterns and relocation of the population, Atlantic Richfield realized that many of its gas stations were not profitable and closed them. These abandoned gas stations became graffiti-covered eyesores, strewn with garbage. To alleviate the problem, Atlantic Richfield decided to explore ways of utilizing these properties. Some of the stations had been put up for sale, but their deteriorated condition made them undesirable.

Execution In 1973, the company proposed a plan to convert its abandoned gas stations to community use. Atlantic Richfield first ascertains from local government officials which community groups or organizations might be interested in the property, then confers with them to determine what plans they envision. Upon approval, the company offers its advice and spends from $5,000 to $10,000 on the conversion. Refurbishing, which the company oversees, takes from two to six months, depending on the size of the project and the weather. The property is then usually donated to the community.

From 1973 through 1976, the project resulted in twelve conversions; five more are projected for 1977. A few examples illustrate the Program:

- In North Plains, Oregon, a remodeled gas station is now the Senior Citizens Community Center. Behind the Center, members cultivate a vegetable garden.

- In Long Beach, California, a former service station has been converted into a mini-auto clinic. Under the auspices of the Inner City Ministries (ICM), unemployed adults and high school students are taught automobile mechanics. ICM is responsible for maintenance and leases the old gas station from Atlantic Richfield for $1 a year. ICM trainees have made further improvements in the building, which is also used for concerts and other civic functions.

In most cases, Atlantic Richfield has found local government authorities or community groups receptive to its Program. Only one municipality has refused the offer, because the station in question was located in a proposed redevelopment area.

Costs Through 1976, Atlantic Richfield had spent about $250,000 on the Service Station Conversion Program. Since each gas station conversion is handled differently and involves several departments, a company official said that it was too complicated to provide a breakdown of financial figures.

Typical surplus gas stations: #1) Before. #2) After.

Problems The pilot project indicated that most community groups prefer to tear down the station and build a mini-park, garden, or new building. However, as new-construction costs continue to soar, more gas stations may be adaptively reused.

Benefits Atlantic Richfield is improving the quality of the areas where it has undertaken gas station conversions by providing a useful structure in place of an abandoned eyesore. The company is able to dispose of its surplus gas stations, and receives tax benefits for its contributions. The Program also helps create community goodwill.

The Company In 1976, Atlantic Richfield, a major integrated oil company, saw revenues increase 16 percent from $7.3 billion to $8.5 billion, and net income rise 28 percent from $450.4 million to $575.2 million. The company's sales break down as follows: domestic petroleum 87 percent, foreign petroleum 4 percent, and chemicals 9 percent. In January, 1977, the company acquired the Anaconda Company, a copper and aluminum producer.

Other Preservation Activities. In 1974, the company donated its former headquarters in Philadelphia to the Philadelphia College of Art. This contribution of a 21-story landmark building resulted in a $7 million tax deduction.

The Atlantic Richfield Foundation has also contributed to the following preservation efforts:

1. Donation of $15,000 in 1975 to the Grays Ferry Community Council in Philadelphia toward the adaptive reuse of a vintage church as a community center.

2. Donation of $5,000 in 1974 and 1975 to the Trinity Square Repertory Company in Providence, Rhode Island for conversion of an old movie theater into a playhouse.

3. Donation of $25,000 in 1977 toward a survey of noteworthy Victorian structures in Cape May, New Jersey, a turn-of-the-century seaside resort. Measured drawings were prepared, and photographs were taken during the summer of 1977 by a local group. The study will be published and will include a section on how to restore Victorian structures. Matching funds for the study were provided by the National Endowment for the Arts.

For further information contact:
Gene Owings
Senior Representative
Special Projects Development
Atlantic Richfield Company
515 South Flower Street
Los Angeles, California 90051

Bird & Son, Inc.

Summary   In 1975, Bird & Son, Inc., one of the nation's largest producers of building materials, awarded $100,000 in preservation matching grants. Projects involving historic homes and houses of worship received about 40 percent of the funds, but almost all types of structures and landscapes were represented, including a six-story wooden elephant constructed in 1881. The company received nationwide publicity as a result of its Historic Grant Program, and in 1975, became the first member of the National Trust's Corporate Associates Program. In 1976, Bird & Son followed up its Program with a donation of $125,000 to the National Trust for Historic Preservation for production of a film on preservation. In 1977, in cooperation with the National Trust, it contributed $140,000 in support of a program to revitalize U.S. "Main Streets."

Background   Bird & Son was founded in 1795. Its long association with American institutions is both a source of pride and publicity for the firm. Thus, when Bird's President Ralph E. Heim directed that the firm develop a public-service program for the nation's Bicentennial, some kind of preservation effort seemed appropriate.

According to Program Administrator D. Stuart Laughlin, Bird wanted to "give something back to the country in which we grew."[1] In addition, the company wanted a program which would provide maximum public exposure. Bird sought the assistance of the Society for the Preservation of New England Antiquities (SPNEA), the National Trust for Historic Preservation, and the Boston-based public-relations firm of Newsome & Co., Inc.

Once the decision to support preservation had been made, Bird first had to determine whether to turn the program over to some outside concern, or to keep the entire operation in-house. Donating money to an outside group, such as the National Trust, has the advantage of avoiding the bureaucratic complications usually attendant with program administration. On the other hand, a large contribution to an outside organization has the drawback of being a one-shot affair; the publicity it generates comes at a high price and can be short-lived. An in-house project, for the same price, might produce both more sustained coverage and a closer association of the company with the service.

Bird opted for the in-house alternative, but still had to determine the program which would best suit its objectives. For a large building materials manufacturer, the first alternative was obvious: to donate its own products to preservation projects. However, it rejected this alternative, because, as Laughlin explains, "We thought that giving away our own roofing and other products would appear too crass and commercial. We wanted to get away from that kind of thing."[2] Consequently, the company shifted its emphasis from product give-aways to simple cash grants. It then had to face the problem of how best to award the money.

Execution   An early suggestion was that Bird donate $1,000 to the most attractive historic house in each state; this proposal opened the door to myriad problems. Long consultation with SPNEA and the National Trust finally produced a plan which also won the approval of Newsome & Co., the public-relations firm. Under this proposal, Bird would award $100,000 to preservation projects on a regional basis. Panels of experts would judge the projects and select the winners. All funds would be available only as matching grants.

Bird officials claimed three major objectives for their program. First, and most obvious, their goal was to make money available for restoring and preserving America's historic landmarks. Second, they hoped to stimulate a "greater general awareness of the nation's historic sites, as well as of the financial needs of organizations attempting to preserve those sites."[3] Finally, they wanted to "develop a model

Lucy, a six-story "white elephant" located in Margate, New Jersey.

program in the field of historic preservation on which future efforts by corporate sponsors could be based."[4]

Actual planning for the Program began in June, 1974. At this time, Bird distributed a broadside to over 5,000 organizations throughout the country stating that matching funds up to $5,000 ($100,000 was allocated for the entire Program) would be provided for "any project designed to visibly improve the exterior of historic properties . . . to make them more accessible, understandable, or environmentally compatible to the public they serve."[5] The company established the following guidelines for eligibility:

1. Any nonprofit incorporated group in America can apply for up to $5,000, providing they can present matching capabilities.
2. The chosen site must be registered, or under consideration for registration, by the National Register of Historic Places.
3. There should be public access to the property.
4. The proposal should refer to an exterior-improvement project that had not yet been started (as of December, 1974), but could logically be completed by January, 1976.
5. Only one proposal per organization would be accepted.

After nearly five months of deliberation, Bird & Son's Historic Grant Program was announced on November 21, 1974, at separate press conferences in New York and Boston.

To begin an application, Bird required a letter of intent describing the project and plans for obtaining matching funds. If review of this preliminary material was favorable, then the submitting group would receive an official application. The firm set a March 31, 1975, deadline for receipt of completed applications.

In order to ensure success, Bird instructed Newsome & Co. to publicize the nature and progress of the Program. Meanwhile, with the aid of the National Trust, regional judgings were organized. Six panels of three persons each would participate in the initial screening according to geographic region. The company sought highly qualified people from many fields, including history, preservation, architecture,

conservation, education, and business, to serve as judges. The judges would recommend projects on the basis of overall merit, which Bird defined as "community interest and support of the project [a prime reason for the matching funds stipulation], a realistic assessment of costs, and a responsible plan of execution."[6] These recommendations were, in turn, passed to a national screening board for final review. Members of this group included historian Alistair Cooke, James Biddle, President of the National Trust, and William Murtagh, Keeper of the National Register of Historic Places. Regional panelists met during late April and early May, 1975, in Boston, Philadelphia, Charleston, Chicago, New Orleans, and Portland, Oregon.

Response to the Program was overwhelming: Program staffers acknowledged over 4,000 inquiries; 811 formal applications, requesting more than $3.2 million in grants were received from all 50 states and the District of Columbia. To lessen the difficulty of selecting winners, Bird officials, in consultation with preservation authorities, sent letters to all groups that had received preliminary approval, asking if they would accept partial grants so that other projects could be recognized. They agreed, and final awards were announced at a press conference on June 3, 1975, in the courtyard of Washington's historic Decatur House, headquarters of the National Trust. Bird & Son subsequently presented checks to 115 organizations.

The following examples illustrate the variety of projects that received grants: $600 went to the Brush Creek Bicentennial Commission to refurbish a unique Octagonal Schoolhouse in Sinking Springs, Ohio, dating from 1831; $500 was given to the Save Lucy Committee, Inc., to help preserve Lucy, a six-story wood and tin elephant, constructed in 1881, in Margate, New Jersey; $500 went to the Cullman City Commission to maintain the Clarkson Covered Bridge in Clarkson, Alabama; and $1,500 was donated to Historic Hannibal, Inc., to restore Main Street in Hannibal, Missouri, Mark Twain's boyhood home and the setting for several of his novels.

Costs

- $100,000 for individual matching grants distributed among 115 projects.
- $50,000 (approximately) for company administration of the Historic Grant Program.

Problems The Program's most serious drawbacks for Bird & Son were logistical. No one knew exactly what kind of reaction the Program would elicit. Certainly few anticipated the enormous number of inquiries and applications that were forthcoming. The project was "frightfully time-consuming,"[7] says Laughlin. While much of the difficulty certainly stemmed from the fact that methodology was being tested for the first time and modified as circumstances required, Laughlin believes that the administration of such a comprehensive nationwide program is inherently costly. "I had intended to spend only part-time on the project," he says, "but as the months wore on I found myself devoting almost all my energies to it."[8] When company executives evaluated the Program to determine a future course of action, it was felt that the grants could continue only if Bird employed a full-time administrator. "And at that time, we weren't prepared to do that,"[9] notes Laughlin.

According to Laughlin, "The main concern with the project was that it was too little in a well where there is no bottom. We wanted to do something to create a greater awareness of the need for preservation."[10] Bird has had only limited success in developing a model program of corporate donation to preservation. As Laughlin explains, "Every company wants to be original. This was our program, and we took credit for it. Companies are usually hesitant about following someone else's lead."[11]

Benefits From a preservationist's point of view, the Program represented a major step forward in corporate involvement. Stan Smith of the SPNEA, who worked closely with Bird & Son in the Program's development, reports that the company was highly responsive to suggestions and criticisms. The grants themselves, although too small in most cases to cover the total costs of restoration projects, nevertheless did serve as catalysts and incentives for further work within the communities receiving them.

From Bird & Son's perspective, the major benefit of the Program was clearly the favorable exposure it produced. Among the accolades received were a personal letter from Vice President Nelson Rockefeller praising Bird's commitment, a certificate of official recognition from the American Revolution Bicentennial Administration, and a special citation read into the *Con-*

gressional Record by Congressman John Moakley:

I think in a time of spiraling inflation and high unemployment that Congress would not look very happily on any kind of restoration project, and I think a private sector has to involve itself. . . . I just hope this action of theirs [Bird's] is contagious and that other corporations take a note out of their book.[12]
—*John Joseph Moakley*
U.S. Congressman
9th District, Massachusetts

In addition, the Program received massive coverage by both print and electronic media in all fifty states: from syndicated articles by Bob Considine and Don Oakley to numerous television appearances by Heim, nationally syndicated wire stories, countless local articles, and feature pieces in a number of specialty publications.

The Company Bird & Son, Inc., is one of the nation's leading building-materials manufacturers. Established in 1795, the company had sales in 1976 of $236 million, a 23 percent increase over 1975's sales of $191 million. Over the same period net income declined from $18.1 million to $16 million. Its three main divisions employ over 3,600 people in thirty plants and offices located in fourteen states.

Other Preservation Activities. In June, 1975, Bird became the first Corporate Associate of the National Trust for Historic Preservation. The Corporate Associates Program seeks corporate support for preservation through a minimum $1,000 annual contribution to the National Trust. In addition to this donation, Bird also sent all companies on the *Fortune* 500 list a pamphlet describing Bird's historic grant program and a letter from Heim asking for a donation to the National Trust.

The Octagonal Schoolhouse in Sinking Springs, Ohio.

Over 100 companies have since become Corporate Associates.

In 1976, the company sponsored—at a cost of $125,000—a film on historic preservation, entitled *A Place in Time*. The film, made by John Karol of Apertura, Inc., will be nationally distributed through the National Trust.

In 1977, Bird contributed $140,000 to the National Trust's Main Street Project, a three-year program designed to encourage small municipalities to revitalize their central business districts. This project focuses on three model demonstration communities selected from among 69 in a ten-state competition. Professional consultants will prepare master plans utilizing historic-preservation techniques. A handbook, film, and workshops will be developed.

SPNEA's Stan Smith believes that Bird could also make a lasting contribution to preservation in another way:

Bird & Son is one of America's leading building materials manufacturers, and nothing is more crucial to preservation work than the proper materials. If you've ever looked around, you know that the materials available today are simply ill-suited to the task. I have already consulted with Bird & Son on some product development ideas of designing high quality materials for use in preservation projects. I believe that there is a real market for such products. The tremendous response to the grants program proved that.[13]

Officials at the company are considering his suggestion.

For further information contact:
D. Stuart Laughlin, Jr.
Administrator, Historic Grant
    Program
Bird & Son, Inc.
Washington Street
East Walpole, Massachusetts 02032

Footnotes

1. INFORM interview with D. Stuart Laughlin, Administrator, Historic Grant Program, Bird & Son, Inc., April, 1976.
2. *Ibid.*
3. Bird & Son, Inc., "The Bird & Son Historic Grant Program, Information Sheet," (mimeographed, Bird & Son, Inc., n.d.), p. 1.
4. *Ibid.*
5. *Ibid.*
6. *Ibid.*
7. INFORM interview with D. Stuart Laughlin, Administrator, Historic Grant Program, Bird & Son, Inc., April, 1976.
8. *Ibid.*
9. *Ibid.*
10. INFORM interview with D. Stuart Laughlin, Administrator, Historic Grant Program, Bird & Son, Inc., May, 1977.
11. INFORM interview with D. Stuart Laughlin, Administrator, Historic Grant Program, Bird & Son, Inc., April, 1976.
12. John Joseph Moakley, *Congressional Record*, (Washington, D.C.: U.S. Government Printing Office, July 15, 1975), E3811.
13. INFORM interview with Stan Smith, official, Society for the Preservation of New England Antiquities, April, 1977.

CertainTeed Corporation

Summary In fall, 1973, CertainTeed Corporation, a manufacturer of building materials located in Valley Forge, Pennsylvania, developed its Building Restoration Program, which donates roofing products to historic buildings around the country. Since the Program was implemented in spring, 1974, CertainTeed has given its materials to over 23 projects, and plans to continue the contributions. The Program has been an excellent source of public-relations material for the company.

Background CertainTeed began its Building Restoration Program as a public-relations activity and to help preserve historic structures which reflect the social, political, and/or economic development of the United States. The Program was designed to help projects that needed the materials, but lacked the funds to pay for them.

Execution Each year, in response to articles and editorials in local newspapers, historical-society publications, and magazines such as *House Beautiful* and *House and Garden*, CertainTeed is contacted by up to 500 historical societies wishing to submit projects for consideration in the Program. These applications receive a color pamphlet outlining the Program and submission procedures, as well as before-and-after photographs of buildings already reroofed with CertainTeed's help. Review sessions are held every four months to choose additional sites.

The 1860s Honolulu House in Marshall, Michigan, reroofed with shingles donated by CertainTeed.

Each building, which must be owned by a nonprofit organization, is evaluated for its historic and/or architectural attributes as they reflect the growth of the United States. Geographic location is considered to assure equitable regional distribution. The building's condition and the financial stability of the operating organization are also factors in the review of applications. The selection of new sites is administered by CertainTeed's public-relations firm, Lewis and Gilman, Inc., of Philadelphia. The entire procedure from application to donation can take up to eighteen months.

Upon approval and establishment of a re-roofing date, CertainTeed donates its asphalt roofing shingles. Contributions range from 12 to 110 squares (one square equals a hundred square feet). The recipient selects the kind of shingle, usually CertainTeed's best product, which looks like a wooden shake and does not distort the historic integrity of the structure. Fiberglass-base shingles, which carry the highest fire rating available, are also occasionally selected.

Although CertainTeed only donates and does not install the materials, it will make available technical experts if guidance is needed. On request, it will also suggest local roofing contractors from whom bids can be solicited. Operating organizations may either pick up the shingles from their local outlet on a credit billing system, or from a CertainTeed dealer, if one is nearby.

Many organizations have used the value of the roofing to obtain matching grants from local, state, or federal sources.

To date, 23 sites have been selected to receive materials. Those which have already been re-roofed include: Thomas Edison's birthplace (1841) in Milan, Ohio; Poe Cottage (1812), Bronx, New York; Fort Mifflin, a British fort built in 1772 in Philadelphia; and Honolulu House (1860) in Marshall, Michigan, the only example of Hawaiian architecture extant on the mainland. Many of the sites are in the National Register of Historic Places.

Costs Information on the cost of the program and possible tax benefits gained by the donation of the materials was not available.

Benefits The gifts create goodwill between the historical societies and the company. In addition, CertainTeed has received extensive local and national exposure through radio broadcasts and magazine and newspaper articles. The historic structures also provide a showcase for its products.

The Company CertainTeed is a leading manufacturer of building products, including fiberglass insulation, polyvinyl-chloride and asbestos-cement pipe, asphalt roofing, and other items used in construction and underground utilities systems. CertainTeed had 1976 sales of $665 million, representing a 20 percent increase over 1975 sales of $553 million. Net income rose 88 percent over the same period, from $19.5 million to $36.6 million.

Other Preservation Activities. CertainTeed is currently sponsoring an exhibit demonstrating changes in housing technology at the National Museum of History and Technology of the Smithsonian Institution in Washington, D.C. The exhibit includes reconstructions of a "balloon frame" house developed during the mid-nineteenth century, and Hart House, a seventeenth-century home.

For further information contact:
Tom Newton
Director of Community Relations
CertainTeed Corporation
Shelter Materials Group
P.O. Box 860
Valley Forge, Pennsylvania 19482
Walter Rowen
Account Executive
Public Relations Division
Lewis and Gilman, Inc.
1700 Market Street
Philadelphia, Pennsylvania 19103

Ethyl Corporation

Summary In 1973, the Ethyl Corporation, a chemicals manufacturer, undertook the restoration of an 1861 foundry building in Richmond, Virginia. The building had been part of the Tredegar Iron Works, which was called the "Arsenal of the South" during the Civil War. Although Ethyl has not yet completed the restoration, and at present, has no specific plans for the structure, the project has already brought the company national and local recognition.

The Tredegar restoration and Reynolds' Kanawha Canal restoration, a few hundred yards downriver (see Reynolds Metals), mark the initial attempts to improve Richmond's James River waterfront.

Background Chartered in 1837 and located on the James River in Richmond, Virginia, the Tredegar Iron Works received its first U.S. government contract for artillery shells in 1839. By 1848, Joseph Reid Anderson, a West Point graduate, had purchased a controlling interest in the company. Under Anderson, Tredegar started producing iron rails and locomotives for the growing railroads. At the outset of the Civil War, the plant returned to munitions production, this time for the Confederacy. Tredegar provided 1,100 cannons and millions of projectiles, and may have built the first iron submarine. The company also supplied the iron plating used to clad the Merrimac-Virginia, the famous ship that fought the North's Monitor in the first battle of iron warships off Hampton Roads, Virginia.

After the Civil War, Tredegar returned to peacetime production, including spikes, angle bars, railroad-car wheels, practice shot for the Union, industrial castings, and horseshoes. However, munitions were still manufactured in wartime, from the Spanish American War to the Korean War.

By the early 1950s, the Tredegar buildings were beginning to show signs of age and deterioration. Steel had replaced iron, and a large part of Tredegar's market disappeared. The plant remained in operation until 1957, although a fire destroyed two of its large machine shops in 1952. After the sale of the historic property to the Albermarle Paper Manufacturing Company (which later became the Ethyl Corporation), Tredegar's owners, descendants of Joseph Reid Anderson, moved operations to Chesterfield County, Virginia. The old Iron Works buildings were abandoned, and, according to the National Register:

Vacant and fire ridden, the several structures that housed the mills and foundries in various stages of ruin, and a majority of the large rooms stand open or partially open to the sky.[1]

The old Foundry which Ethyl hoped to restore was in a badly deteriorated condition. After the collapse of one of its trusses, its slate roof had been removed to prevent the great weight from causing the building's walls to crumble.

The 1861 Tredegar Foundry Building in the process of restoration. (Al Cothran Studio)

A recent photo of the partially restored building. (Al Cothran Studio)

Execution The impetus for Ethyl's restoration of the 1861 Foundry was provided by Hurricane Agnes in 1972. After the flood caused by the hurricane, a city inspector called the company's attention to the advanced state of decay of the Tredegar buildings. Ethyl decided it was time to take a stand, and commissioned Property Manager Roy E. Johnson to study the Foundry's history and condition. After consultation with the Virginia Historic Landmarks Commission, the company decided:

Several of the buildings were, in addition to being in execrable condition, of uninteresting early 20th century construction. Other older ones had been so battered by hard use and the elements that they were beyond saving. But the jewel of the complex, a vast foundry building erected in 1861 was definitely restorable as well as another antebellum structure used for pattern storage. The decision was to save the latter two, and raze the rest though leaving buttresses and arches of exceptional interest.[2]

The building under restoration is the principal building, or Foundry. The 61-foot by 125-foot red-brick structure was built in 1861 to help Tredegar meet its tremendous wartime work load. Although the building had a strictly functional use, it includes decorative brick corbeling, fancy gable ends, and iron detailing.

Ethyl hoped the Tredegar restoration would turn the area into one of Virginia's most desirable pieces of real estate:

This restoration project will enhance both the appearance and the historic value of the area, as well as add a new dimension to the cultural value of downtown Richmond.[3]

The restoration of the Foundry included major brick-masonry work. The 21-inch-thick walls were stabilized, and in some cases, completely rebuilt. Ethyl has also constructed a replica of the original chimney stack which ventilated the large air furnaces used to melt iron for casting. The original chimney was dismantled earlier in this century. The roof too had to be fully reconstructed, since the original had been removed to prevent the walls from

crumbling. The trusses supporting the roof were duplicated using castings from the originals. Taylor and Parrish were the restoration contractors; Garrett Brothers did the brick-masonry restoration and reconstruction; and Carneal and Johnston were the architects. All firms are from Richmond. The project was designed to take approximately one year, but has taken much longer because the initial plans did not include restoration of chimney and air furnaces. To date, the project remains unfinished.

Costs The company did not release any figures for the cost of restoring the Tredegar Iron Works' main building.

Problems Because the original trusses did not comply with the Richmond Building Codes, the Building Department initially rejected the company's plans to duplicate them. Ethyl and its consultants reminded the Department that the trusses had supported the roof until deterioration necessitated their removal. A grandfather clause in the Building Codes, establishing historic precedence, permitted their restoration.

Benefits Ethyl as yet has not made specific plans for the restored building, so company rewards for the effort are conjectural. However, a valuable piece of architecture has been saved, pleasing preservationists. Junius R. Fishburne, Executive Director of the Virginia Historic Landmarks Commission, praised the project:

I think Ethyl Corporation should be commended for what it's doing. Not many companies are willing to do this type of thing. The easiest and cheapest thing would be to just bulldoze it.[4]

In addition, in August, 1976, the American Society for Metals selected the Tredegar Iron Works as one of its National Historic Landmarks. The National Register of Historic Places accepted the Ethyl Corporation's nomination of the Tredegar Iron Works in 1973. James Wamsley, writing in *Commonwealth*, described the site:

In ruins . . . the old Tredegar represents not only a 19th century industrial complex, but also a contemporary expression of the picturesque spirit which thrived on romantic ruins. The walls which once supported the broad roof spans are now free standing arcades and their Romanesque manner conjures up the images of a far earlier age. The old Tredegar works have a tremendous potential as a part of Richmond's redeveloped riverfront.[5]

The Company In 1962, the Albermarle Paper Manufacturing Company of Virginia, a paper and chemical producer, purchased Ethyl Corporation, a manufacturer of gasoline additives. Albermarle changed its name to Ethyl Corporation and now produces chemicals, plastic, aluminum products, and energy-related products. Ethyl sold its paper interests in April, 1976. Sales for 1975 were $930 million and increased 19 percent in 1976, to $1.11 billion. Net income for 1975 was $61 million, and was up 13 percent in 1976 to $69 million.

For further information contact:
Charles H. Zeanah
Director—Corporate Public Relations
Ethyl Corporation
330 South Fourth Street
Richmond, Virginia 23219

Footnotes

1. James W. Moody, Jr., "National Register of Historic Places, Inventory, Nomination Form," 10-300, (Washington, D.C.: Department of the Interior, National Park Service, December 18, 1970), p. 5.
2. James S. Wamsley, "Tredegar: Where Pioneer Industrialists Worked Iron, Restoring Begins," *Commonwealth*, May, 1973, p. 45.
3. *Ibid.*, p. 42
4. Laurence Hilliard, "Walls of 'The Works' Haven't Changed Much," *Richmond Times-Dispatch*, 1 April 1973, p. 6.
5. Wamsley, *op. cit.*, pp. 45-46.

Exxon Corporation

Summary Exxon, the world's largest oil company, has contributed to preservation efforts throughout the United States. Its activities have ranged from financing Historic American Buildings Survey (HABS) teams and publishing the results of their studies in Texas and California, to contributing money and expertise to help maintain an old General Store in North Carolina. In addition, Exxon has donated funds to: recycle New York's 1890 Federal Archives Building; maintain the recycled quarters of Boston's Institute of Contemporary Art; and create a park in New York's South Street Seaport. These contributions have helped improve company-community relations, and have strengthened awareness of the vital link between community and corporate prosperity.

Background Exxon is particularly interested in activities which are related to its products—notably, those concerned with energy conservation and the environment—but has supported projects related to education and broad social concerns as well.

Exxon prepares an annual budget for charitable contributions based on advice from all departments and field locations. Whenever possible, contributions are identifiable items in the budget, but budget additions are periodically approved for specific projects proposed to the company. Most projects are either national in scope or are in areas where Exxon has significant operations or concentrations of employees. National projects are usually brought to the attention of the Public Affairs Department in Houston or New York City, while local or regional projects are evaluated by local Exxon officials. Projects near Exxon facilities or involving Exxon employees receive preference.

In most instances, a community advocate for a proposed project has sought out a local or district Exxon official or public-relations representative. For example, in the Benicia case (see below), a member of the local historical society proposed to Exxon's oil-refinery manager that the company fund a study by the Historic American Buildings Survey. Since the required amount of funding was beyond the district office's budget, the manager submitted a proposal to the Public Affairs Department in Houston, which granted the funds.

Several examples of Exxon projects are described below.

Reprint of a 1910 post card of Benicia, California's Main Street. Most of these structures are still standing. (Stumm Photo)

Execution

Funding of the Historic American Buildings Survey Texas Catalogue. Since 1933, the Historic American Buildings Survey (HABS), part of the National Park Service, has been documenting the nation's historic structures through measured drawings, photographs, and research reports. Teams of architects, historians, and draftsmen have studied and documented vintage buildings in diverse locations, and published the results of their findings. To date, about 12,000 structures have been recorded.

In 1974, Exxon donated $8,000 to the State of Texas to finance publication of a Texas survey of over 200 buildings. The resulting catalogue includes drawings, photographs, and text describing the architecture and historical importance of each structure. Selected buildings were photographed inside and out. The most significant entries in the catalogue are illustrated with measured drawings. The catalogue sells for $5, and is available from the Trinity University Press in San Antonio. Exxon is also funding a similar study of historic structures in Arkansas.

Funding a HABS Survey, Benicia, California. In summer, 1976, the significant structures in Benicia, a historic California city, were studied and recorded by a HABS team under a $12,000 grant from Exxon and matching federal funds. Since Benicia is the site of an Exxon oil refinery, the company also volunteered its facilities for the HABS team's headquarters.

In 1847, Benicia was planned as "the Queen City of San Francisco Bay." In the 1850s, it became the site of the first U.S. Arsenal on the West Coast and grew substantially. Originally encompassing 252 acres, the Arsenal covered 2,700 acres by the time it closed in 1962. Many nineteenth-century structures remain there, complemented by Benicia's Victorian houses and commercial buildings.

When the Arsenal closed, the citizens of Benicia organized and raised the funds to convert the site into an industrial park. Today, it includes about 100 factories and distributors.

The HABS team surveyed the town's historically and/or architecturally significant buildings. Following the recommendations of the Benicia Historical Society, several vintage structures were selected for detailed measured drawings and analysis:

1. *The Camel Barns.* These warehouses of native sandstone date from the mid-nineteenth century, and once housed camels imported from the Mediterranean and the Far East in the early 1860s for the U.S. Army's Camel Corps. The animals were used briefly in the arid Southwest but their stubbornness made them unsuitable for service. Some of them were brought to Benicia for auction and berthed in these two barns, which also have the distinction of possessing one of the first elevators designed by Elisha Graves Otis.

2. *The Powder Magazine.* Built of local sandstone, with four-foot-thick walls, the structure dates from 1857, and considering its function, has an interior which is particularly rich in detail. The building has a vaulted ceiling supported by Grecian pillars.

3. *The Clock Tower.* Originally constructed as an arsenal in 1859, this building was California's first federal bastion. It was gutted by fire in 1912, and only two of the three floors and the tower, with its huge Seth Thomas clock, remain.

4. *St. Paul's Episcopal Church.* The Church was built in 1860 of California redwood and has been extensively remodeled through the years.

5. *Benicia State Capitol.* This impressive brick building with Doric columns was originally built in 1853 as the City Hall, and once housed the California legislature before it moved to Sacramento.

In addition to these extensively researched buildings, twenty others were studied and photographed. The HABS team also helped property owners by providing information about the finer details of their structures, such as the origin of the brass and building materials. Plans called for the publication of the Benicia survey in summer, 1977.

Donation to Help Save a General Store in North Carolina. In Valle Crucis, North Carolina, a town of about 25 people, a general store that had been the center of Appalachian life since 1883 was in danger of closing. In its heyday, the Mast Store "sold everything from cradles to caskets,"[1] and was particularly famous for its cured hams. A rambling 8,700-square-foot structure, with chestnut walls and clapboards, the site was considered important enough to be nominated for inclusion in the National Register of Historic Places in 1973.

In 1970, because of the owner's age and because profits were sagging, the Mast Store was sold to two absentee owners, who hired inexperienced managers to run it. Conditions worsened, and finally, in 1975, the decision was made to close the old store.

In an effort to prevent the closing, local residents formed the Friends of the Mast Store. They brought the problem to the attention of one of Exxon's sales representatives, when he called at the Exxon station next to the store. He, in turn, approached the company's Public Relations Manager for the Southeast Region. These two Exxon employees suggested establishing a foundation to raise funds to preserve the historic Mast Store.

The Appalachian Association for the Preservation of Important Places was launched with a $3,000 grant from Exxon. Others have contributed as well. The Appalachian Association is helping the present owner to make the Mast Store profitable and to make improvements in the century-old structure. The Association's Board, consisting of the owner and three other members, must approve any improvements or new undertakings. To date, indoor plumbing has been installed, additional heating units have been added to assist the coal potbellied stove; and the walls and ceiling have been insulated to save energy. One of the previous owners, an experienced businessman, has moved to Valle Crucis and taken over as President of the Mast Store.

Today, the Mast Store is flourishing. The seven-foot cast-iron potbellied stove is the center for the display of groceries, household items, medicines, and clothes. On weekends, country music is played outside. The emphasis remains on serving local customers, but the new Manager/President has

SOUTH ELEVATION

NORTH ELEVATION

FEET 1/4" = 1'-0"

METERS 1:48

MATERIALS:
FOUNDATION: BRICK
WALLS: BRICK AND WOOD SIDING
ROOF: ASPHALT SHINGLES
FASCIA: WOOD

Line drawings from the Benicia Historic American Buildings Survey: (above) the 1870s Carr House, and (below) the interior vaulting of the 1855 Arsenal. (Historic American Buildings Survey)

ISOMETRIC VIEW OF INTERIOR VAULTING

FEET 1/4" = 1'-0"

METERS 1:48

ambitious plans to promote the store by opening a restaurant, a delicatessen, and a crafts center.

Contribution to the New York Landmarks Conservancy. In 1977, Exxon gave $30,000 to the New York Landmarks Conservancy, a nonprofit organization, to study and promote the adaptive reuse of the 1890s Federal Archives Building in Greenwich Village. The building was designed by Willoughby J. Edbrooke, supervising architect of the U.S. Treasury and architect of the Old Federal Post Office in Washington, D.C. The Federal Archives Building is a one-block-square, brick building designed in the Richardsonian-Romanesque style. Its arcaded base is its most distinctive feature. Future plans for the building include a mixture of revenue-producing and community uses, such as housing and a retail arcade. Currently, a number of designs have been submitted and are being considered.

Bicentennial Gift to Boston, Massachusetts, for the Institute of Contemporary Art. In July, 1975, Exxon donated $25,000 for maintenance of the Institute's headquarters in a recycled Romanesque Revival police station built in 1886. The project's architect, Graham Gund of Cambridge, gutted the old interior and designed a modern decor. The vintage police station now boasts a five-story center staircase and interiors displaying outside exhibits as well as the Institute's artwork.

Support of the South Street Seaport Museum Park. Exxon donated $200,000 to build a park at the entrance to the South Street Seaport Museum. Located on a thirty-acre site, this museum depicts the history of the nineteenth-century Port of New York. The completed mini-park was dedicated in April, 1977. Its focal point is a 1913 lighthouse.

Costs Exxon, the largest corporation in the United States, donates more money to charitable causes than any other American corporation. In 1976, the company's contributions totaled $22 million, an increase of 20 percent over 1975.[2] However, this is less than 1 percent of Exxon's pre-tax income. Individual projects are itemized in the "Execution" section. Exxon did not break down its contributions to preservation.

Benefits Exxon, through its support of these various preservation-related projects, believes it is helping to improve employee and community relations, while at the same time, contributing to a greater public awareness of the American heritage.

In a recent company publication, Exxon comments on its charitable contributions:

At Exxon, we feel that it is in the best interest of business to continue to meet public expectations in these areas and to show through its actions that we believe the prosperity of any business is clearly related to the vitality of the community in which it functions.[3]

The Company Exxon, the world's largest oil company, had gross sales of $51.6 billion in 1976 and a net income of $2.6 billion, representing an 8 percent increase in sales and a 5.5 percent increase in earnings over 1975. Its sales breakdown is as follows: 44.1 percent petroleum and natural gas operations in the U.S.; 36 percent foreign exploration and production; 7.9 percent foreign refining and marketing; 8.2 percent chemicals; and 3.8 percent miscellaneous, including nuclear, coal, minerals, and land development.

For further information contact:
Contributions and Program
  Development
Public Affairs Department
Exxon Company, USA
P.O. Box 2180
Houston, Texas 77001

Public Affairs Department
Exxon Corporation
1251 Avenue of the Americas
New York, New York 10020

Footnotes

1. Downs Matthews, "Saving Mast Store," *Exxon USA,* Fourth Quarter, 1975, p. 9.
2. Written communication from Robert E. Kingsley, Senior Advisor, Communications and Cultural Programs, Exxon Corporation, to INFORM, August 12, 1977.
3. Exxon Corporation, "Introduction," *The Other Dimensions of Business: A Report on Exxon's Participation in Areas of Public Interest,* (New York: Exxon Corporation, 1977), p. 1.

Flanigan's

Summary Flanigan's, a furniture retailer in upstate New York, has supported the preservation movement in a variety of ways, ranging from financing the preparation and distribution of films and articles on preservation, to helping establish a local business committee which supports the arts. The company's efforts on behalf of preservation, which since 1974 have entailed a total expenditure of $12,000, have been due essentially to the interest and involvement of its President, Alan Cameros.

Background The association of furniture with the preservation of historic homes and other landmarks is, of course, a natural one. In addition, Alan Cameros has long been a supporter of preservation causes.

Execution Flanigan's has given its support to five particular projects since 1974. They are:

TV—Mini-Documentaries. It sponsored a series of five-minute shorts about the history and preservation needs of some of Rochester's landmarks. These were aired at various times between 1974 and early 1976 on a local public broadcasting station. In addition, the company donated a total of $2,000 to the six

landmarks featured in the television series. The landmarks featured were: the Stone Tolan House, the Erie Canal aqueduct over the Genesee River, St. Luke's Church, the Frank Lloyd Wright House, and Rochester's Federal Building.

American Lifestyle Films. These three-minute films, narrated by E.G. Marshall, depict the lives and homes of famous people, such as Thomas Jefferson and Monticello, Brigham Young and the Beehive House, Will Rogers and his ranch, and Andrew Jackson and the Hermitage. Originally financed and produced by Bassett Furniture Industries, the films provide a

A winning entry in Flanigan's Landmark Essay Contest.

1st

Our Neighborhood Cemetery

This cemetery is really old. I visited the cemetery last week. I saw a grave of a baby boy who lived only one day, on a plaque. The plaque was old. This cemetery started before 1821. I saw a plaque that fell down but I could read it. The plaque said death 1821 but I do not know when he was born. Soldiers who died in the Civil War are

buried there. On Memorial Day some one puts flags on their graves. It is called the Brighton Cemetery, and it is near East Ave and Winton Road South. The cemetery is very big and I like to walk there.

Kenny Lukacher
Third Grade
Hillel School
age 8
442-1442

brief view of practical preservation efforts. Flanigan's obtained two sets of the ten-part series and has made them available without cost to local schools and organizations. It is also sponsoring the series on commercial television. Distribution began in 1974 and is an ongoing project.

Article Distribution. In 1976, Flanigan's distributed free 6,000 copies of "A Preservationist's Guide," a featured article in *House and Garden*'s "Guide to American Tradition, 1976," a special Bicentennial issue. Written by Billie Harrington, Director of the Landmark Society of Western New York, the article provides information about the Society's projects in a nine-county area around Rochester, as well as about its basic preservation policies and methods of implementation.

Flanigan's has received a number of additional requests for this reprint, which is also being distributed by the National Trust for Historic Preservation and the Preservation League of New York State. The Business Committee for the Arts is using it to assist in soliciting funds for preservation activities.

The Landmark Essay Contest. In 1974, Flanigan's sponsored and organized an essay contest. Promotional ads in local newspapers were headlined: "Rochester has its famous landmarks, too. Why not enter Flanigan's Landmark Contest and tell us about your favorite Rochester area landmark." Contestants were asked to write 100 to 300 words on their candidate. Nine prizes of Flanigan's gift certificates amounting to $1,000 were awarded winners in three categories: grades 3 to 6; grades 7 to 12; and over 18 years of age. Winners and runners-up were guests on local radio and television shows.

Preservation issue of Scene. In 1974, a local monthly emphasizing the arts devoted an entire issue to historic preservation in the area. Underwritten, and largely written by Flanigan's staff, the issue included an introduction by Cameros on the goals of preservation, as well as articles on the adaptive reuse of commercial buildings and stately residences, area landmarks, the relationship of vintage and modern buildings, and an examination of architectural details of area commercial buildings.

In addition to company contributions to the Landmark Society, Flanigan's President Alan Cameros has personally been involved in preservation activities. He is currently on the Society's Board of Directors, and has encouraged Flanigan's employees to volunteer their time and solicit funds for the Society from the local business community.

As a result of his contributions to preservation, Cameros was also invited to join the Business Committee for the Arts, a national organization of business leaders that encourages business and industry to assume a greater share of responsibility for the support, growth, and vitality of the arts. Based on his experience with the national organization, Cameros founded a local prototype in August, 1976. This new organization currently consists of a participating membership of twenty-one local businesses. Cameros served as its first president.

Costs Flanigan's doesn't itemize the cost of its preservation projects. The company stated that each of its six projects cost about $2,000, totaling $12,000 to date. Funds are allocated on an *ad hoc* rather than annual basis.

Benefits Because of its numerous preservation projects, Flanigan's has received awards from both the City of Rochester and the State of New York. A company spokesman said that it was not possible to ascertain any direct effect of these projects on furniture sales. Nonetheless, many customers have remarked favorably on the company's involvement with preservation causes.

Although Flanigan's would not divulge how the costs of its preservation projects were treated for tax purposes, it is likely that such items were written off against advertising expenses or deducted for charitable contributions.

Alan Cameros expressed his philosophy of corporate responsibility:

We feel the responsibility of business goes beyond "making the sale"—a long range view must be taken to preserve the heritage and character of our community itself. Only if Rochester and the surrounding area have the fiscal ability to maintain and care for their resources will the community in its entirety prosper.[1]

The Company Flanigan's dates back to 1925, when William Flanigan started a moving and storage company that later expanded into retail furniture. Bought by Edward Cameros—father of the current President—in 1940, Flanigan's grew under its new management, and currently has four locations: three in the Rochester area and one in Buffalo. Today, Flanigan's is western New York's largest furniture retailer. The privately held company had recent sales amounting to about $9 million.

For further information contact:
Alan L. Cameros
President and Chief Executive Officer
Flanigan's
845 Maple Street
Rochester, New York 14611

Footnotes

1. Alan Cameros, "Preserving the Past: The Past is Alive and Well and Living Just off East Avenue," *Scene*, November, 1974, p. 1.

Hercules Incorporated

Summary In 1974, Hercules, a major chemical producer headquartered in Wilmington, Delaware, since 1912, pledged $50,000 toward the restoration of the city's century-old Grand Opera House. The Hercules gift was the first corporate contribution to this restoration, and spearheaded other contributions by the business community. The $5 million effort, completed in 1976, returned the Grand to its original use, and has served as a catalyst for further revitalization of downtown Wilmington.

Background The Masonic Lodges of Delaware laid the cornerstone for the Grand Opera House in 1869. Construction was financed by a $100,000 public subscription, and completed in 1871 under architect Thomas Dixon of Baltimore.

The Grand is one of the finest extant examples of French Second Empire architecture. The brick structure, measuring 211 feet long, by 92 feet wide, by 78 feet high, has a richly decorated cast-iron facade and a mansard slate roof topped by three cupolas. The design of the building both inside and out, incorporates the symbolism of the Masonic Order, based on the numbers three, five, and seven:

The facade was divided in 5 basic sections. The center section became number 3 when the sections were counted from left of center. . . . On the storefront level, each store comprised 3 sections. . . . On the second and third floors, each of the 5 sections included 3 arches and 3 keystones.[1]

Among the noteworthy features in the interior were the drop curtain painted with a romantic Italian scene, which was designed by Russell Smith, an eminent nineteenth-century theatrical designer, and the frescoed ceiling depicting the muses. At the time of its completion, the Grand Opera House boasted the second largest stage in the nation, and its acoustics were considered exceptional.

Through the years, the Grand gained a national reputation as a showcase for such performers as Little Nell, Edwin Booth, Ethel Barrymore, and George M. Cohan. President Ulysses S. Grant attended a "Fair" there in February, 1873. It was also the setting for diverse forms of entertainment, including symphonies, operettas, readings, minstrels, balls, and variety shows.

In 1897, an Edison Vidascope was installed. The Warner Brothers movie chain became manager of the Grand in 1930. Through the years the fabric of the once elegant theater grew shabby. A fire in 1934 destroyed the roof and the three cupolas. To meet fire regulations, in 1943, a false ceiling had to be added beneath the frescoed ceiling. Faced with dwindling receipts, the Grand closed in June, 1967, with the film, *The Game Is Over.*

Drawing of the Grand Opera House in the 1870s.

Execution Local groups attempted to keep the Grand open as a theater. But, gradually, the idea evolved to restore the once elegant building as a performing-arts center. Support was obtained from twelve area organizations representing the symphony, opera, and drama, and from volunteer groups. In 1971, a successful Centennial Gala Evening, marking the landmark's 100th year, brought together interested groups who established volunteer committees, cleaned up the debris, researched the history of the Grand, sponsored entertainment, and publicized the restoration efforts.

Three studies of the Grand were undertaken:

1. To investigate thoroughly the structural integrity of the building and propose new construction enabling the theater and office areas to meet 20th Century safety codes and artistic requirements.

2. To research all facets of the original house to permit authentic restoration of the theater as an historical landmark.

3. To determine the economic feasibility of embarking on a multi-million

dollar restoration project that would lead to a self-supporting center for the performing arts in an area that had not previously benefited from such a facility.

These aims required five years of planning. While the feasibility studies were being completed and the required financing obtained, live performances again began taking place on the stage of the Grand. National, state, and local groups and celebrities filled the hall with the sounds of jazz, symphonies, operas, and modern music. Ballet companies performed, and film classics were screened.

The studies and the eventual restoration cost $5 million. A sixty-member Board of Directors was responsible for raising this money. One of its members was a Hercules officer, and through his efforts the company agreed to pledge $50,000 toward the restoration endeavor. This represented the first major corporate contribution and encouraged gifts from other corporations. Besides corporate community support, funding for the restoration was also provided by individuals, the Greater Wilmington Development Council, the Delaware State Arts Council, the Masonic Hall Company,

the state, county, and city, and the National Endowment for the Arts.

The restoration of the Grand was carried out in two phases. In mid-1974, the exterior was restored as a visual symbol for the project, while the theater remained open. When removing the false storefronts, some of the original cast-iron facade was exposed. In several areas, the cast iron was missing, but it was duplicated and replaced. The mansard roof was re-slated, and the three cupolas and the grillwork were replaced. The rest of the building was cleaned and painted its original white. Most of the exterior restoration was completed by the end of 1974.

On May 1, 1975, the theater was closed so that interior renovation—scheduled for completion within a year—could begin. During this time, 26 different trades worked on the Grand. Plans called for blending the old with the new. The original seating plan, with a capacity of 1,144, was retained, but backstage facilities utilized the most modern theater technology. In addition, a computerized lighting system was installed; one of the first in the country. Right on schedule, the renewed Grand Opera House was rededicated on May 1, 1976.

Missing sections of the Grand's original cast-iron facade were recast and replaced.

Reconstruction of the Grand's interior.

Costs Hercules' pledge of $50,000 was made in 1974, payable in three annual installments in 1975, 1976, and 1977. In addition, the company donated more than $4,000 to the Grand Opera House for the feasibility study's operating budget.

Benefits Hercules was able to take tax deductions for its charitable contributions and its pledge of support, as indicated above, prompted other corporations to donate funds to the Grand. Besides serving as a cultural center for the greater Wilmington area, the restoration and revival of the Grand Opera House has spearheaded other revitalization projects in the inner city, notably a new downtown shopping mall on Market Street, the street on which the Grand is located. In addition, a new federal, state, and city office complex has been built; and a community college which opened downtown in 1974, is rapidly expanding.

The Company Hercules produces a broad range of specialty chemicals. In 1976, the company had sales of $1.6 billion representing a 13 percent increase over the 1975 figure of $1.4 billion. Net income jumped from $32.5 million to $106.8 million. The company's sales break down as follows: specialty chemicals, 45 percent; agricultural and industrial chemicals, 29 percent; plastic materials, 21 percent; and aerospace and defense products, 5 percent. Foreign markets account for about 40 percent of sales.

For further information contact:
John M. Martin
Chairman
Hercules, Inc.
910 Market Street
Wilmington, Delaware 19899

Lawrence J. Wilker
Executive Director
The Grand Opera House
818 Market Street Mall
Wilmington, Delaware 19801

Footnotes

1. Toni Young, *The Grand Experience* (Watkins Glen, New York: The American Life Foundation for the Grand Opera House, Inc., 1976), p. 39.

A copy of the original ceiling fresco reinstalled.

The restored Grand Opera House.

Summary In August, 1976, Liggett Group, a major tobacco and consumer-products company headquartered in Durham, North Carolina, donated 71 acres of the 3,400-acre Stagville Plantation, including its house and out-buildings, to the state. This site is listed in the National Register of Historic Places. Now, with partial funding by Liggett, it has become the home of the first state-owned preservation center in the country.

Background The Stagville complex consists of the Bennehan House dating from 1787, four antebellum slave houses, an eighteenth-century barn, and a cottage dating from about 1776. One of the oldest homes in Durham County, the Bennehan House was built by Richard Bennehan who first bought property in the area in 1766. Bennehan was a prosperous plantation owner and merchant, an early trustee of the University of North Carolina, and a commissioner responsible for planning the capital city of Raleigh. His descendants were also successful and civic-minded. By 1890, their land holdings were among the largest in the South.

Liggett Group purchased the Stagville holding in 1954 because of its rich tobacco land, and installed a caretaker on the site. The Historic Preservation Society of Durham, established in 1972, wanted to preserve and utilize the historic property for community use. To accomplish this, the staff of the North Carolina Division of Archives and History conceived the idea of establishing an educational research facility there: the Stagville Center for Preservation Technology.

Execution The Preservation Society and the Division of Archives and History approached Liggett Group and asked for the donation of the property. Liggett consented, and its donation in August, 1976, was the largest gift of its kind ever received by the state.

The North Carolina Division of Archives and History will administer

The Stagville Plantation House. (Stagville Preservation Center)

the Stagville facility. Dr. Larry Tise of the Division describes the Center's purpose:

We hope that the Stagville Center for Preservation Technology will help more people understand and get involved in the practical side of historic preservation. This will not be a place where people just learn from books. The historic property itself will serve as a study laboratory for people—not just professionals, but other interested citizens—to learn by working with artifacts, 18th and 19th century buildings, and real problems in preservation. Professionals will come to the center to exchange opinions and ideas and to study new preservation techniques.[1]

John B. Flowers III, Executive Director of the Stagville Center, has established a curriculum, and classes began in spring, 1977. At present, there are four staff members, but Flowers hopes to add more. Experts in preservation technology will be brought in from all over the country to teach the nuts and bolts of conservation practices. The Center will offer short courses, those leading to a certificate, and in time, a degree offered in conjunction with neighboring universities. The first courses offered in spring, 1977, under the City of Durham's Continuing Education Program were "A Survey of North Carolina Architecture from 1700 to 1939" and "A History of Stagville." North Carolina State University will offer course credit for an archeological survey to be undertaken on the property in summer, 1977. A ten-day preservation seminar is being arranged for the fall.

Flowers is also overseeing the physical development of the Center. The Bennehan House is now restored, and efforts are underway to obtain contributions of period pieces to furnish the rooms now used for meetings and classes. A Board of Directors has been established, consisting of state officials, community leaders, and members of the business coummunity, including the President of Liggett Group.

Costs Information on the initial purchase price paid for Stagville by Liggett Group is not available.

Benefits The gift of Stagville will provide Liggett with a tax deduction of about $250,000. Further tax benefits will derive from the company's additional contributions to help finance the Center for several years (amount undisclosed).

The donation of 71 acres of the Stagville Plantation is furthering better community relations by returning a bit of history to the public domain.

The Company Liggett was initially a tobacco company but started diversifying in 1964 through acquisitions and internal growth. It now markets a wide range of consumer products. Revenues break down as follows: tobacco products, 43.8 percent; spirits and wines, 19.7 percent; pet foods, 25.3 percent; and other products, 11.2 percent. For the year ending December, 1976, this international company had gross sales of $851.9 million and a net income of $36.2 million. This compares with 1975 figures of $813 million and $36.2 million respectively.

Other Preservation Activities. Liggett Group also contributed land to the state of North Carolina for a tobacco museum in Durham which opened in spring, 1977.

For further information contact:
Robert H. Fasick
Vice President and Assistant to the
   President
Liggett Group Inc.
4100 Roxboro Road
Durham, North Carolina 27702
John B. Flowers III, Executive Director
Stagville Preservation Center
Box 15628
North Durham Station
Durham, NC 27704

Footnotes

1. Liggett Group Inc., "Liggett Group Donates Historic Site to North Carolina," *News Release,* August 5, 1976, p. 2.

Summary In 1974, this Mississippi public utility funded the research and publication of two books on the archeological and architectural heritage of Claiborne County. Mississippi Power & Light undertook this project in conjunction with the preparation of a federally mandated Environmental Impact State for a nuclear plant it wished to build. Five buildings in the County have been added to the National Register of Historic Places as a result of the architectural survey, now in its second printing. The nuclear plant is scheduled for completion in 1977.

Two structures included in the Architectural Survey of Claiborne County: a house in Port Gibson (c. 1885) and the Windsor Ruins (c. 1860). (Mississippi Department of Archives and History)

Background In January, 1972, Mississippi Power & Light announced its intention to build a nuclear generating plant in Claiborne County, Mississippi. The Federal Power Commission required an Environmental Impact Statement evaluating the effects of the plant on the local ecology before construction could begin.

In addition, the Mississippi Department of Archives and History recommended that the power company survey the archeological remains and historic buildings not only of the area immediately surrounding the plant site, but of the entire County. Mississippi Power & Light agreed to fund the research and the eventual publication of two books.

Execution Mississippi Power & Light contracted with the Mississippi Department of Archives and History for two two-man teams to conduct the two studies. The research took about eight months. One book, *Architecture in Claiborne County, Mississippi: A Selective Guide,* was the result of the following process. In summer, 1972, the research team, an architectural historian and a historian, examined the records of the local historical society, the courthouse, local newspapers, and private sources to determine what sites in the County were important. These properties were visited and photographed. The resulting 110-page publication surveys the architectural history of Claiborne County; presents pictures of structures that have been demolished; and describes extant structures. This latter group includes:

churches; a synagogue; government, commercial, and educational buildings; plantation houses; vernacular dwellings; and ruins. The *Guide* contains black and white photographs depicting the exteriors, interiors, and architectural details of the historic buildings, and maps giving the exact locations of the entries. It also indicates whether sites are open to the public. The entries are rated in four categories: national significance, major significance, local significance, or valuable parts of the local scene. The criteria for each category is spelled out:

Those with national significance are either important works by nationally famous architects, are included in The National Register of Historic Places *because of their architectural qualities, or are unique examples illustrating the architectural development of the United States. Buildings with major significance are either outstanding examples of the work of important architects or builders, unique or exceptionally fine examples of a particular style or period, or important examples of construction techniques. Those of local significance are important examples of the architectural styles which make the greatest contribution to the overall character of their surroundings, or buildings which best show local developments in style and change of taste. The buildings judged valuable as part of the local scene are not in themselves examples of distinguished architecture, but are, nonetheless, important elements in their environment because of style, material, scale, and increasing age.*[1]

The *Guide* discusses 119 important structures, including 3 of national significance, 29 of major significance, 55 of local significance, and 22 of value to the local scene.

Initially, 1,000 copies of the book were printed. They were distributed through the Mississippi Department of Archives and History for $3.50 a copy. Because of unexpected demand, there was a second printing of 1,000 copies in 1975. These books are being sold at $5.00 per copy. Proceeds go to the Department of Archives and History.

Costs   Mississippi Power & Light provided $25,000 for research and publication of the *Guide,* which was published by the Mississippi Department of Archives and History.

Benefits   The architectural survey has increased awareness of the diversity of Mississippi's architectural heritage. Because of the interest generated by the *Guide,* five properties have been placed in the National Register of Historic Places. The survey has saved the Mississippi Department of Archives and History considerable time and expense. Robert Bailey, a Department official, said the survey would have taken much more time to complete if it had to await financing by the state. The state also benefits from the proceeds of the sale of the book, which help finance the Department's other publications. The company's involvement in historic preservation has encouraged many employees to take an active role in restoring houses in Claiborne County. In addition, Mississippi Power & Light has gained public-relations benefits by undertaking the two surveys. Articles about the projects have appeared in the *Jackson Daily News,* the *Jackson Clarion Ledger,* and the *Port Gibson Reveille.*

The Company   Mississippi Power & Light, a subsidiary of Middle South Utilities, a large public-utility holding company, provides electric service to the western half of Mississippi. Revenues for 1976 amounted to $308.8 million, a 28 percent increase over 1975's figure of $240.1 million. Net income for the same period increased 25 percent, from $20.8 million to $25.7 million. Revenues break down as follows: commercial and industrial, 38 percent; residential, 31 percent; and other, primarily sales to other utilities, 30 percent.

Other Preservation Activities. Mississippi Power & Light also funded an archeological survey of Claiborne County. From June to July, 1972, two archeologists examined the 2,200-acre tract where the proposed nuclear plant would be built. One significant mound site was discovered, and its excavation, later in 1972, was funded by the company. Pieces of ceramic and prehistoric tools were among the artifacts unearthed. From August through October, 1972, the same team carried out a surface analysis of archeological sites in other parts of Claiborne County. They identified 86 sites dating from 7000 B.C. to 1000 A.D. In 1973, the findings were published as the *Archaeological Survey of Claiborne County, Mississippi,* which sold for 50 cents. There was an initial printing of 1,000 copies. A second printing costing about $2,000 was financed by the Mississippi Historical Society and the Mississippi Department of Archives and History. Proceeds of all sales go to these organizations.

For further information contact:
Alex McKeigney
Vice President for Information
 Services
Mississippi Power & Light Co.
Box 1640
Jackson, Mississippi 39205

Gregory B. Free
Restoration/Preservation Specialist
State of Mississippi
Department of Archives and History
P.O. Box 571
Jackson, Mississippi 39205

Footnotes

1. Ed Polk Douglas, *Architecture in Claiborne County, Mississippi: A Selective Guide,* (Jackson: Mississippi Department of Archives and History, 1974), p. 4.

Nabisco, Inc.

Summary In 1976, Nabisco, the country's largest specialty baker, donated $75,000 to Waterloo Village, New Jersey's only remaining "colonial village." The funds were earmarked for restoration of a 1760s Grist Mill. The company researched and provided colonial recipes that are cooked in the Dutch oven in the recently restored Mill, and donated the Nabisco memorabilia on display there. Nabisco employees are charged a reduced admission fee at Waterloo Village, with the company making up the difference.

Background Located in western New Jersey, Waterloo Village was settled as a farming community by the English about 1740. In 1763, when an iron forge was constructed, Waterloo began to prosper. During the Revolutionary War, the iron produced there was used for gun barrels for the colonial troops. Although the iron forge subsequently stopped production for lack of wood, the town again prospered with the construction of the Morris Canal in 1824. Waterloo, one of the main depots along the Canal, flourished until the rise of the railroad after the Civil War.

The railroad brought the town's growth to an abrupt halt. Waterloo became nearly a ghost town. Then in the late 1960s, Percival Leach and Louis Gualandi gradually bought up most of the existing historic buildings. They recreated the early American village and the nineteenth-century transportation center on the Morris Canal by restoring and furnishing numerous historic structures, including: the Canal House (c. 1760), the Wellington House (c. 1859), and the Old Stage Coach Inn (c. 1740 with an addition c. 1830). Waterloo Village, open to the public, also provides ex-

hibits and demonstrations of early American crafts and trades. The Waterloo Foundation for the Arts, a nonprofit organization partially subsidized by the State of New Jersey, administers the Village. It relies primarily on admission fees to cover its operating costs. Leach and Gualandi have proceeded with restoration of the Village's historic buildings as time and money have permitted.

The Grist Mill was an integral part of the original Village. During the heyday of the Morris Canal, its flour was shipped throughout New Jersey. At the time of restoration, the sturdy stone structure still possessed the grinding stones needed to process the flour, but at some point, the waterwheel had disappeared.

The Grist Mill at Waterloo Village.

Execution In fall, 1975, Nabisco moved its executive offices from New York City and set up a new world headquarters in East Hanover, New Jersey. At the time the company was searching for a suitable method of observing the nation's Bicentennial. Although numerous projects and events were suggested, Nabisco sought a project which would have lasting value and which, preferably, would be related to the State of New Jersey. Early in 1975, the producers of a Nabisco sales-promotion film shot several scenes on location at Waterloo Village, acquainting company executives with the work of restoration underway there. The Grist Mill seemed an appropriate Bicentennial gift. Nabisco contributed $75,000 for materials, and Leach and Gualandi obtained another $75,000 for labor under the federal government's Comprehensive Employment and Training Act (CETA).

Research for the restoration was not difficult since the mill was still standing. Rotting beams and other structural remains provided evidence of the building's original appearance. The recollections and expertise of an elderly local resident, whose father had operated the Grist Mill, were also helpful. Charles Howell, one of the world's experts on grist mills, and a professional miller, supervised the entire restoration.

After a feasibility study, restoration began with replacement of the eighteenth-century supporting beams, the underprop for the heavy grinding machinery. New beams were cut down and sized from nearby oak trees. The new props measure from 9 feet to 27 feet in length and the heaviest ones weigh over 1,000 pounds. The millstones were treated and returned to working order; a new wooden waterwheel, 10 feet in diameter and 6 feet thick, was constructed. With the waterwheel generating power, and the supporting machinery sound, the Grist Mill was once again operational.

A Dutch oven, used for baking goods in colonial times, was installed to complete the milling operation, and Nabisco researched and prepared colonial recipes. Tourists at Waterloo Village can now view the entire baking process from whole grain to baked goods.

The second floor of the restored Grist Mill contains an exhibit of early farm implements and Nabisco memorabilia, such as paintings done for advertisements and packaging used through Nabisco's history.

Costs Nabisco spent $75,000 for the restoration of the eighteenth-century Grist Mill, and CETA funds provided another $75,000. Costs of the time spent researching colonial recipes, and the value of the donation of the company's advertising art and memorabilia were not available.

Benefits Another attraction has been added to historic Waterloo Village while Nabisco has obtained public-relations benefits. A flier distributed at the Grist Mill and a plaque on the building credit the Company for its contribution. The exhibit of Nabisco memorabilia is another advertising vehicle, and company Christmas cards have featured a painting of the Grist Mill. The reduced admission plan has encouraged Nabisco employees to visit Waterloo Village, bringing additional revenue to the site. The company did not disclose information on any tax benefits gained from its $75,000 gift or its other contributions.

The Company Nabisco had sales of over $2 billion and a net income of $77 million in 1976, an increase over 1975's $1.97 billion in sales and $59 million in net income. Its products include cookies and crackers, pharmaceuticals, toys and games, pet foods, and confectionaries.

For further information, contact:
Glenn Craig
Director of Public Relations
Nabisco, Inc.
River Road and Forest Avenue
East Hanover, New Jersey 07936

Percival H.E. Leach &
  Louis Gualandi
The Historic Village of Waterloo
Stanhope, New Jersey 07874

Niagara Mohawk Power Corporation

Summary Niagara Mohawk, the largest public utility in upstate New York, has headquarters in an Art Deco building dating from 1932. Proud of this landmark, the company provides guided tours of it and a descriptive pamphlet. In spring, 1976, Niagara Mohawk assisted the Everson Museum in Syracuse in mounting a major Art Deco exhibition, including photographs and measured drawings of its headquarters. The company has also built an architecturally compatible addition to its building.

Background The modern architectural style called Art Deco had its roots in the *Exposition des Arts Decoratifs et Industriels* held in Paris in 1925. Utilizing modern technology and materials, Art Deco buildings are sleek, streamlined, and incorporate geometric designs. The style also employs many of the period's innovations in lighting techniques, such as reflective lighting, cove lighting, and spotlighting.

In the 1920s, at the suggestion of the Buffalo architectural firm of Bley and Lyman, Niagara Hudson, a predecessor of the present company, built several of its new smaller offices in the then popular Art Deco style.

The structures reflected the company's growth, and served as showcases for many new lighting systems. Niagara Mohawk's headquarters is an imposing building with a facade of black glass and stainless steel. Completed in 1932, it became a central New York attraction. The building resembles a ziggurat, the Assyrian or Babylonian temple-tower, rising from a large base in multiple steps to a central tower. It measures 208 feet by 88 feet at ground level, and extends 114 feet to the tower. Flanked by three steps, the tower is 28 feet high and 20 feet wide; it is graced with a helmeted, winged figure called the Spirit of Light. The statue, made of stainless steel, is believed to be one of the first instances of this metal's use for outdoor sculpture.

Lighting, used to emphasize building structure and detail, was a significant part of the overall design. Helium tubes supplemented incandescent lamps in illuminating the building's exterior. Hidden floodlights highlight the Spirit of Light at night, and when fully lit, the building itself can be seen for miles. In the tower, there are 16,000 pounds of heat-resistant glass with thousands of watts of floodlights. Since World War II, however, reasons of economy and energy conservation have prevented the use of much of the original lighting.

The interior of the building is particularly rich in Art Deco ornamentation. There are four fused-glass murals in the lobby depicting Gas, Illumination, Generation, and Transmission, thereby visually explaining the company's operations. A photograph by Margaret Bourke-White, the famous photographer, depicting the Schoellkopf Station in Niagara Falls was used as the model for the Generation panel. The stainless steel elevator doors are etched with applied geometric designs characteristic of Art Deco. To fully appreciate the building one must walk through the interior and observe the way the lighting changes the visual impression of the decorative ornamentation.

Execution Through the years, the Niagara Mohawk building has been nicknamed Early Jukebox, Steel Wedding Cake, and Aztec Temple. In recent years, however, Art Deco has become recognized as an important architectural style, and the company, in response to the many requests received from architectural and art students to view its building, began conducting tours and distributing a descriptive brochure, *Niagara Mohawk's Art Deco Building.*

In spring, 1976, Niagara Mohawk assisted the Everson Museum of Syracuse in preparing a major exhibit on Art Deco, in which the company's building served as a central example. Niagara Mohawk's employees helped mount the show, and the company provided numerous photographs, a photo essay in mural scale, and measured drawings of its building. In conjunction with the exhibit, Niagara Mohawk arranged special tours of the landmark building.

Niagara Mohawk's Art Deco headquarters in Syracuse.

Costs The utility did not provide cost figures for its work on the Everson Art Deco exhibit, the descriptive brochure, or the guided tours of the building.

Benefits Maintenance of this vintage building and the educational program on its history and merits help create a good public image for Niagara Mohawk. The building has been written about in many publications. Ada Louise Huxtable, the *New York Times* architectural historian, discussed the building in an April, 1974, article on Art Deco architecture. In addition, Niagara Mohawk's headquarters received a citation from the Landmark Preservation Board of the City of Syracuse.

The Company Niagara Mohawk is the major public utility serving upstate New York. Revenues for 1976 amounted to $1.1 billion, reflecting an 11 percent improvement over 1975 revenues of $972 million. However, net income declined from 1975's record results of $114.8 million to $108.4 million. Approximately 82 percent of the company's revenues are derived from the sale of electricity, and the remaining 18 percent from gas. Electric sales break down as follows: residential, 31 percent; commercial, 32 percent; and industrial, 24 percent.

Other Preservation Activities/ Western Division Headquarters in Vintage 1913 Building. The Buffalo headquarters of the company's Western Division are also located in a landmark building with terra cotta decorative details. Completed in 1913, the thirteen-story tower was modeled after the Tower of Light, the central attraction of the Pan-American Exposition held in Buffalo in 1901. The Tower of Light, a Classical Revival structure, elaborately illuminated and decorated, was crowned by the Goddess of Light

statue. Buffalo General Electric Company, one of the present corporation's predecessors, used the Exposition building as a prototype for its headquarters. The extant structure, with a three-tiered tower of classical details, resembles a wedding cake. It is still economical to operate, and is a downtown Buffalo landmark.

Niagara Mohawk News. Niagara Mohawk publishes this magazine eight times a year for its employees. Besides containing articles on the public-utility industry and on company operations and employees, it has included features on upstate history and on historic structures. The *News,* which has a circulation of 17,000, has been published continuously since 1930 (except during the Depression years of 1932 to 1938).

For further information contact:
Jack L. Mowers
Supervisor
Photography
Niagara Mohawk Power Corporation
300 Erie Boulevard West
Syracuse, New York 13202

A view of elevator doors with Art Deco motifs.

A glass mural from a picture by Margaret Bourke White.

Summary Between 1975 and 1976, this offset printer, in Louisville, Kentucky, produced two posters promoting preservation causes and explaining aspects of the printing process. The posters, which cost $4,000 to produce, have received national acclaim, and demonstrate how a business enterprise can promote preservation as well as its product. Because of the success of these posters, the company is currently designing a series of Ethnic Heritage posters to commemorate Louisville's 200th anniversary.

Background In 1975, Pinaire asked its designers to create a poster as a handout for a business exposition in Louisville. The poster was to be visually arresting and reflect the quality of the company's work.

Execution Pinaire's designers, Julius Friedman and Nathan Felde, produced a two-sided color poster. One side depicted four interior details of a vintage house: two stained-glass windows, a Classical Revival newel post and staircase, and some rich Victorian paneling. The poster was headlined "When we build let us think that we build forever." The other side of the poster showed the top of the newel post in several amplified pictures. Its purpose was to explain the technical aspects of pictorial reproduction utilizing dots in various sizes, colors, and positions. The poster was distributed at no cost and was well received.

Because of the first poster's popularity, Pinaire decided to produce a second for the Bicentennial observance. The same designers focused on two important issues of the times: urban problems and historic preservation. One side of the poster, headed "Fight Urban Decay," is illustrated by a fresh tube of toothpaste marked "Preservation" flanked by a glass of water and a toothbrush. The other side is entitled "Preserve for the Future" and stresses the importance of printing in preserving the past and promoting progress in the future. The picture depicts a mason jar containing a Georgian Revival house, an apple, an apple slice, and a knife.

The poster was also used as an ad in a Bicentennial publication on preservation in Louisville prepared by the local Chamber of Commerce. This publication was sold at the National Trust for Historic Preservation's bookstore in Washington, D.C. The Trust received many inquiries about the ad and its availability in poster form. In response to these inquiries, the Trust obtained the Bicentennial poster from Pinaire at a discount, and sold it as two separate $4 posters. Mention of the poster in the Trust's monthly publication, *Preservation News,* resulted in additional sales.

Costs The cost of each poster was about $2,000.

Benefits By allowing printing of these posters and permitting the National Trust to sell them, Pinaire has gained national exposure for preservation, its product, and itself. The company has also been able to deduct the cost of the posters from its advertising expenses. The success of Pinaire's effort has led the company to plan another poster project—this time a series commemorating the 200th anniversary of Louisville.

The Company Pinaire has been in existence for about thirty years. Its offset-printing plant produces quality reproductions of collector prints, advertising brochures, annual reports, and books. Since Pinaire is privately held, financial figures are not available.

For further information contact:
Jack Ernwine
Sales Representative
Pinaire Lithographing Corporation
175 West Jefferson St.
P.O. Box 1060
Louisville, Kentucky 40201

A Pinaire preservation poster.

Summary In October, 1974, Republic Steel Corporation donated the Burden Iron Company Office Building, built in 1882, and two acres of land in Troy, New York, to the Hudson-Mohawk Industrial Gateway, a nonprofit educational organization founded in 1972 to study and help preserve local industrial buildings and sites, as well as nineteenth-century industries. The Gateway commissioned an architectural firm to study the structure in 1975, and is currently renovating it as its headquarters. Republic has received tax write-offs and favorable publicity by donating a "white elephant" building to an interested group which recognizes the value of preserving and recycling historic industrial structures.

Background In the early part of the nineteenth century, the area north of Albany at the confluence of the Hudson and Mohawk Rivers, expanded rapidly as an industrial and transportation center. Abundant waterpower, excellent shipping, and later, railroad facilities brought many iron and metal works, textile mills, and manufacturers of scientific surveying instruments to the area.

Henry Burden, a Scottish immigrant and well-known inventor, took over the Troy Iron and Nail Factory in 1848. Powered by Burden's timely inventions, which included the first machine capable of mass producing horseshoes, a unique railroad spike and production process, and the first American improvement in the process of manufacturing wrought iron, the company rapidly expanded. It was the sole supplier of horseshoes to the Union forces during the Civil War. In 1864, the Troy Iron and Nail Factory became Henry Burden and Sons. When Burden died in 1871, the company was employing about 2,000 people, and was one of the largest employers in New York State.

In 1881, the company, now the Burden Iron Company, began building a new headquarters building. New York City architect Robert H. Robertson, who had designed Burden's country house in the then popular Queen Anne style, was commissioned to design the headquarters adjacent to the lower works and the railroad.

This building, eventually donated to the Hudson-Mohawk Industrial Gateway, was designed in a combination Queen Anne/Richardsonian Romanesque style. It measures 86 feet long and 68 feet wide, and is of brick construction, with pressed-brick decorative elements. The gable over the entrance has a pressed-brick arch with a hand-carved stone floral garland beneath it; above the garland, the company name appeared in gilded letters. Two flanking brownstone panels with floral motifs stand over the doorway. The building is crowned by a galvanized iron cupola and four molded, corbelled chimneys. Its original roof was tile. The interior was lavishly paneled with cherry wood, including walls, floors, and ceilings. Most of the labor was provided by employees of the iron works.

The office building's interior prior to renovation. (Hudson-Mohawk Industrial Gateway)

The Burden Iron Company continued to flourish until the deaths of Henry's sons just before World War I. About this time, steel was replacing iron. Since the Burden Company did not produce steel, it gradually declined, until it was liquidated in 1940.

Republic Steel bought the lower works in 1940 and operated a steel blast furnace there until 1972, when it closed and demolished the plant because of declining markets, soaring costs, and antipollution requirements. Between 1940 and 1972, the office building was used as a storage facility and was stripped of most of its cherry wood paneling. After the plant closed, the abandoned office building soon began to decay. Today, the only other buildings remaining are parts of a horseshoe warehouse and factory, and the steel frame of a rolling shed.

Hudson-Mohawk Industrial Gateway. The Hudson-Mohawk Industrial Gateway is a nonprofit educational organization founded in 1972 to study the industrial development of America during the nineteenth century, and to preserve nineteenth-century industries and buildings along the Hudson and Mohawk Rivers. Gateway tries to encourage the continued operation of these industries, preserve their buildings and sites through adaptive reuse, and attract tourists to them. It also counsels companies on the rehabilitation or recycling of buildings.

In 1975, Gateway staff advised the W. & L. E. Gurley Company, manufacturers of scientific and surveying instruments, on the rehabilitation of the company's original 1862 buildings in Troy. In the same year, it provided technical assistance on masonry problems encountered in converting the Cohoes Harmony Mills, a textile mill complex dating from the 1830s to the 1860s, into space usable by smaller manufacturers.

The organization, financed by donations, state grants, memberships, and receipts from tours it conducts, has five employees and a current budget of $60,000. The Gateway also publishes a quarterly newsletter for its 550 members. In 1976, about 1,800 people participated in the Gateway's tours, which are conducted from May through November.

The Burden Iron Company Office Building. (John Peckham)

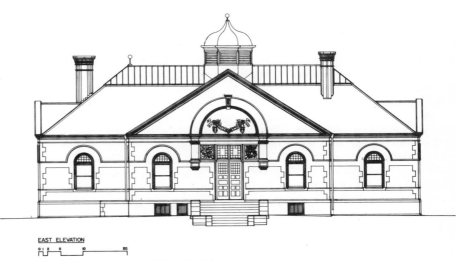

EAST ELEVATION

The Burden Iron Company Office Building. East elevation. (Hudson-Mohawk Industrial Gateway)

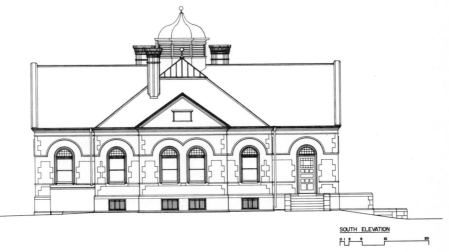

SOUTH ELEVATION

The Burden Iron Company Office Building. South elevation. (Hudson-Mohawk Industrial Gateway)

Execution In 1973, the Hudson-Mohawk Industrial Gateway received funds from the National Endowment for the Arts to survey important industrial buildings and sites in the Troy area. The Burden Iron Company Office Building, listed in the National Register of Historic Places in 1972, was among the buildings it surveyed. Gateway realized that the abandoned Burden building, although in need of renovation, would be ideal for its headquarters. The group prepared a feasibility study on the adaptive reuse of the building, and in spring, 1974, asked Republic Steel officials if they would contribute the unused structure. Republic Steel's legal department studied the possibility of donation, and in October of that year, the company gave the building, as well as two acres of land, to Gateway. Republic's real estate department drew up the deed describing property lines and Gateway's rights of access.

In July, 1975, Gateway commissioned the architectural firm Mendel, Mesick, Cohen to prepare a report on the history of the Burden Iron Company, the construction of the office building in 1881 and 1882, the present condition of the building, the measures needed to arrest its decay, and appropriate techniques for adaptive reuse as Gateway's headquarters. One immediate recommendation by the architects was that the asphalt roof, which had replaced the original red tile one, be repaired or replaced. The roof was leaking and causing water damage to the fabric of the building. Ultimately, many changes had to be made. The mortar in some sections of the brickwork, and some of the brick, had to be replaced, as did the old wiring, heating, and plumbing systems. The skylight had to be sealed, and to arrest vandalism and increase security, the doors and windows had to be made secure. The architects' report suggested, as a further security measure, installing an apartment for a full-time resident. Repair and construction—the first phase of the recycling project—began in December, 1976, and was completed in June, 1977.

The second phase will be remodeling the Burden Office Building as headquarters for Gateway. If sufficient funds can be raised, work will begin in late 1977 and be completed by 1979. To date, Gateway has raised $160,000: a $110,000 Historic Preservation Grant from the National Park Service and $50,000 from the City of Troy's Community Development budget.

Although only a few remnants of the cherry wainscoting remain, structurally, the interior is in relatively good shape. The renovated interior will include offices for the staff, a library, an exhibition and reception area, an auditorium, and meeting rooms; and even the paneling may be reproduced. The renovated Burden Office Building will house lectures, social gatherings, and exhibitions, and will serve as the orientation center for numerous tours run by Gateway.

Costs The architects' report, plan, and specifications cost $3,500. Republic would not divulge the value of the building and surrounding property.

Benefits The adaptive reuse of the historic Burden Iron Company Office Building will functionally and symbolically serve the objectives of the Hudson-Mohawk Industrial Gateway. The renovated building will serve as a visual symbol demonstrating that "the fullest future of the area rests in large measure on the successful restructuring of these historic industrial resources in the revitalized fabric of the urban environment."[1] Based on Gateway findings, several other industrial structures have been recycled by businesses.

The residents of Troy will benefit from the increased interest and tourism the complex will create, as well as from the recycling of an abandoned building. In addition, the building's use as an education and exhibition center will enhance the quality of the nearby residential neighborhood.

Republic Steel took a tax deduction for the donation, based on an independent appraisal. The company considers this confidential information and would not reveal the amount.

The company's donation of the Burden Iron Company Office Building to Gateway has been featured in several publications, including the *Troy Times Record,* the *Albany Times-Union,* the *Albany Knickerbocker News,* and *Fortune* magazine.

The Company Republic Steel Corporation, the fourth largest steel company in the U.S., is involved in all aspects of the manufacture of steel. It provides raw materials and a variety of finished products to a broad range of national and international markets. The company's sales break down as follows: autos, 25 percent; distributors, 15 percent; machinery and equipment, 15 percent; construction and contractors' products, 8 percent; forging, 11 percent; and oil and gas, 7 percent. In 1976, Republic had net sales of $2.5 billion and a net income of $65.9 million; comparable 1975 figures were $2.3 billion and $72.2 million.

Other Preservation Activities. On July 2, 1974, the company donated 36 acres of land, including a lake, near the old Burden Iron Company Office Building, to the City of Troy for use as a park. It also gave a 65-ton Whitcomb diesel locomotive, an 87-ton diesel rail crane, and an old-style ladle car, all dating from the 1920s, to the Mohawk & Hudson Chapter of the National Railway Historical Society. The ladle car is presently on loan to Gateway.

For further information contact:
A. F. Connors
Director of Public Relations
Republic Steel Corporation
P.O. Box 6778
Cleveland, Ohio 44101

Tony Opalka
Historical Researcher
Hudson-Mohawk Industrial Gateway
5 First Street
Troy, New York 12180

Footnotes

1. Letter from Tony Opalka, Historical Researcher, Hudson-Mohawk Industrial Gateway, to INFORM, May 12, 1977, p. 1.

R. J. Reynolds Industries, Inc.

Summary Since 1950, R. J. Reynolds Industries has made several grants for the renovation and preservation of Old Salem, a historic Moravian town which is now part of Winston-Salem, Reynolds' home city. A $452,800 grant made in 1976 is financing the reconstruction of the Single Brothers Workshop. The company is helping to preserve some of Old Salem's heritage, and in so doing, has received a good deal of favorable publicity.

Background In the mid-eighteenth century, the Moravians, a German-speaking group of Protestants, immigrated to Pennsylvania. Part of this group eventually settled in Salem, North Carolina, in 1766. The town prospered as a religious community until the mid-1800s, when there was a relaxation of the religious laws excluding non-Moravians.

By the 1940s, many of the buildings of the eighteenth-century town of Salem had either been demolished, modernized and used for commercial purposes, or left to decay. In 1947, a local grocer announced plans to construct a large supermarket in the heart of the historic area. Fearing the total destruction of the last remaining Moravian buildings, local citizens formed a nonprofit organization dedicated to the restoration and preservation of the Moravian town.

Since its inception in 1950, Old Salem, Inc., has restored or reconstructed seven Moravian buildings as exhibit areas: Single Brothers House (1769), Miksch Tobacco Shop (1771), Salem Tavern and Barn (1784), Boys' School (1794), Market Fire House (1803), John Vogler House (1819), and the Winkler Bakery (1800). These buildings are furnished with period pieces and are open to the public. Old Salem, Inc., administers the Winkler Bakery, Salem Tavern, and an old country store, all of which sell German-style food and goods.

Old Salem, Inc., is a multi-faceted organization whose main goal is education. Its tours and lectures, given by hostesses dressed in period costumes, cover all aspects of Moravian life. It also sponsors crafts demonstrations, concerts, archeological digs, and student summer programs, and publishes many descriptive pamphlets and brochures.

Old Salem is a residential community, as well as a historic attraction. Many of its 96 renovated properties are now either owner-occupied or rented to tenants by Old Salem, Inc. The Village is a registered National Landmark.

Execution Executives of R. J. Reynolds have served on Old Salem, Inc.'s Board of Trustees and Executive Committee since the restoration effort began more than 25 years ago. During the 1960s, the company made several grants totaling $414,000 to Old Salem's capital fund program for general restoration and operations. It also donated a substantial sum toward the restoration of the Miksch Tobacco Shop in 1957. Several members of the Reynolds family have personally made large contributions to the project.

Early in 1975, archeological research conducted by the Department of Restoration of Old Salem uncovered the original foundation, bake oven, and surviving building materials from the Single Brothers Workshop. The Workshop was built by the Moravian Single Brethren in 1771. The original building stood behind the Single Brothers House, and measured 71 feet by 31 feet. The one-and-a-half-story log structure rested on a stone foundation. The roof was covered with wooden shakes and boasted three molded-brick chimneys. The center section of the building was of half timber construction with brick infill, and contained a bake oven. In 1771, the Workshop housed a baker, a joiner, a weaver, a blacksmith, and a tailor. In the next century, it became a toy shop and general store. By 1921, the building had fallen into ruin, and the last remains of the wooden structure were demolished to make way for an apartment house. By the 1970s, this too had been abandoned.

In October, 1975, the Campaign Organization of Old Salem approached R. J. Reynolds Industries' Contribution Committee for a grant to remove the remains of the apartment house and reconstruct the Workshop. The proposed grant was submitted to the company's Board of Directors, who voted to approve $452,800 for the reconstruction, beginning with $55,000 to remove the remains of the apartment house still standing on the site.

Old Salem's Department of Restoration researched the project and is supervising the reconstruction. Original eighteenth-century architectural plans and drawings, written in German, were translated and studied to ensure an authentic reproduction of the building.

In the past two years, the site has been cleared, and the stone foundation of the original building has been repaired and reinforced. Oak logs needed for construction were, as of mid-1977, in the process of being secured and trimmed. Once completed, the Workshop, under the direction of the Old Salem Department of Education and Interpretation, will house a Learning Center with an eighteenth-century kitchen and dining room, a Moravian classroom, and a "best room" which will be furnished with period or reproduction pieces. In these areas, visitors will be able to learn about and gain first-hand experience in crafts such as soap making, spinning, and weaving.

Costs R. J. Reynolds Industries has contributed $452,800 for the Single Brothers Workshop reconstruction. Of this amount, $55,000 was donated for site preparation and demolition; $7,800 was set aside for archeological excavation; $315,000 to be contributed in two annual installments will be used for the actual reconstruction; and $75,000 has been reserved for furnishings and educational materials.

Problems Old Salem has found the preparation of the oak logs to be used in the reconstruction both costly and time-consuming, since it is done by hand.

Benefits Completion of this long-desired reconstruction will be an important visual addition to Old Salem Village. The project will also serve as an educational exhibit on the unique heritage of Winston-Salem, Reynolds' home city. Old Salem's efforts have had the positive effect of attracting many people to live and work in the area, providing an increased tax base, and boosting the town's economy. R. J. Reynolds has gained much publicity from the grant. Old Salem is frequently mentioned in the local and national media. It has been featured in articles in such magazines as *Reader's Digest* and *Seventeen*, in local newspapers and in papers as far away as Phoenix, Miami, Atlanta, Wilmington, and Cleveland as well. In 1974, Old Salem received an award from the North Carolina Literary and Historical Society for its significant contribution to the preservation of North Carolina history.

The Company R. J. Reynolds Industries, Inc., is a diversified international corporation and the largest tobacco manufacturer in the United States. Its 1976 sales were $5.75 billion, compared with $4.8 billion in 1975. Its 1975 earnings were $338 million. Its products include tobacco, petroleum, package foods, and aluminum products.

For further information contact:
Mark Gutsche
Assistant Public Relations
   Representative
R. J. Reynolds Industries, Inc.
Winston-Salem, North Carolina 27102

Frances Griffin
Director of Information
Old Salem, Inc.
Drawer F, Salem Station
Winston-Salem, North Carolina 27108

Miksch Tobacco Shop, Old Salem. (Old Salem, Inc.)

Reynolds Metals Company

Summary The Reynolds Metals Company, a leading producer of aluminum, has preserved a stretch of the historic James River and Kanawha Canal in downtown Richmond, Virginia, acquired in the purchase of additional facilities. This first canal system built in North America represented a major link between the Atlantic Coast and middle America. The preservation site includes two of the five stone locks that made up the Tidewater Connection linking the Canal and the tidewaters of the James River, and is considered an early American engineering landmark. In all, more than three-and-a-half acres along the James River have been incorporated in Reynolds' restoration and beautification project, which includes signs describing the Canal's history and picnic facilities open to the public.

Background The history of American interest in navigating the James goes back to the first permanent English settlers who landed at Jamestown in 1607. After only ten days on this continent, and many long months in ocean voyage, they had progressed 125 miles westward up the James until they reached the impassable seven miles of falls at what is today the City of Richmond.

Richmond grew as the commercial hub of the area, because it was the link to the River and transportation to the coast. Waterpower from the River and the Canal supplied many mills which later produced a large portion of the country's flour. Until the middle of the nineteenth century, however, most of the products of these mills could not be shipped to the West without a great deal of trouble and expense.

The James River and Kanawha

Canal were part of the Great Central American Waterway conceived by George Washington as early as the 1740s. Then a surveyor, Washington proposed a connection between the James River and the Ohio and Mississippi Rivers to the west. In 1785, the Virginia Assembly created the James River Company charged with clearing and improving the River, and named Washington its first president, although he served only in an honorary capacity. Initially, two short canals were built, one around the falls at Westham, west of Richmond, and the other from the River into the city itself. At the eastern terminus of the latter canal, in the heart of Richmond, a Great Basin was completed in 1800 to permit boat turning. In 1810, construction on a connection—consisting of thirteen wooden locks—between this basin and the tidewaters of the James was initiated. Later, in the 1840s, these wooden locks were replaced with five granite locks of such exact specifications that they can truly be considered great engineering artifacts. By the 1850s, the complete canal system was open to navigation, from the harbors of the Atlantic Coast to the town of Buchanan, Virginia, some 197 miles away. There, a short overland connection to the Great Kanawha River led to the Ohio and then the Mississippi. The

Each of the five locks of the Tidewater Connection had a lift of 13 feet 8 inches, for a total lift of 68 feet 4 inches from 13th Street to 9th Street.

A schematic of the Tidewater Connection and the Great Basin of the James and Kanawha Canal.

The remains of the James River and Kanawha Canal Company's works cover over 480 miles from Richmond, Virginia to the Ohio River.

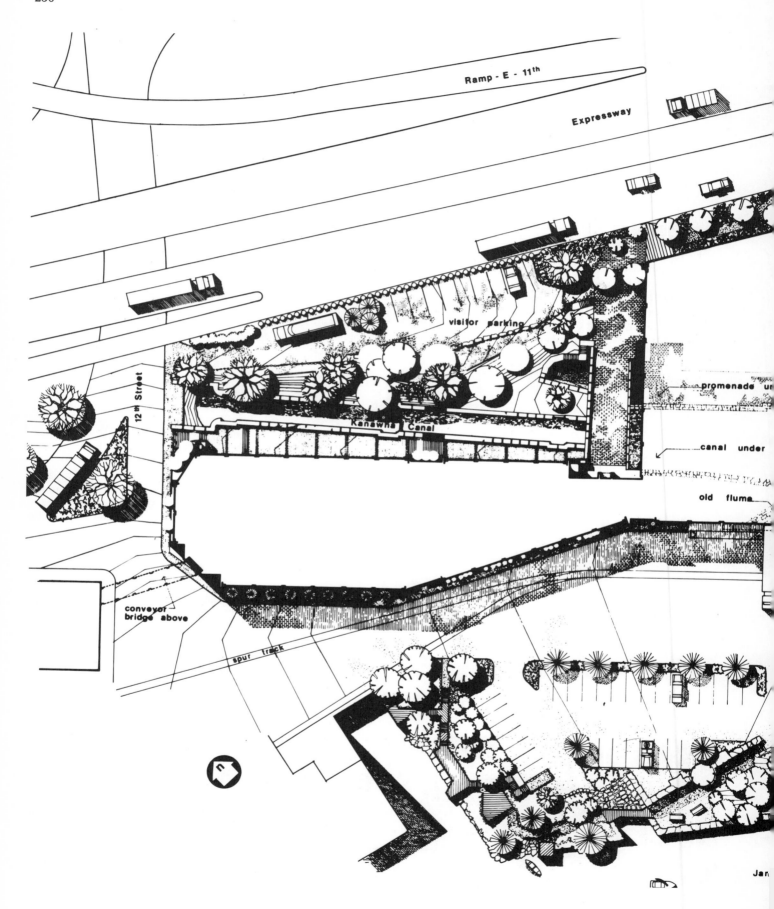

Ramp - E - 11th

Expressway

12th Street

visitor parking

Kanawha Canal

promenade u

canal under

old flume

conveyor
bridge above

spur track

Jan

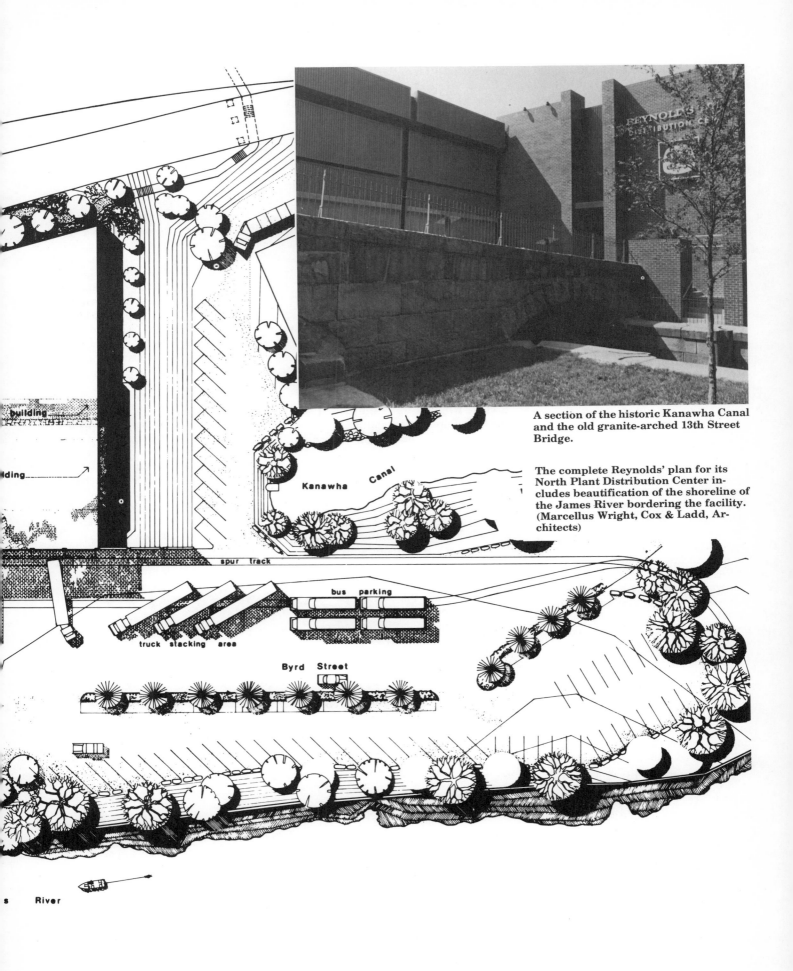

building

ding

Kanawha Canal

A section of the historic Kanawha Canal and the old granite-arched 13th Street Bridge.

The complete Reynolds' plan for its North Plant Distribution Center includes beautification of the shoreline of the James River bordering the facility. (Marcellus Wright, Cox & Ladd, Architects)

spur track

bus parking

truck stacking area

Byrd Street

s River

Canal's heyday lasted from the 1850s to the 1860s, when it was severely damaged by Union forces during the Civil War. Competition from newly developed railroads prevented its revival following the War, and it was sold to the Richmond and Allegheny Railway Company in 1880.

In the wake of "progress and development," much of the Canal had been filled in or left to collect trash. Local historians recognized this, and through their efforts, the Canal was included in the National Register of Historic Places in 1970. The Nomination Form for the James River and Kanawha Historic District—from the Great Ship Lock to Bosher's Dam— stated:

The range of local interest in the canal is illustrated, on the one hand, by the plans of Reynolds Metals Company to incorporate the two lower locks of the Tidewater Connection into their new plant, and on the other hand, with the threatened demolition of the upper three locks of the Connection by the Richmond Metropolitan Authority's expressway.*[1]

Reynolds purchased an old factory complex along the James River in the 1940s, and adapted it for use by their Packaging Division. In the late 1960s, needing more warehouse space, the company acquired additional property in Richmond. This included two of the Tidewater Connection's granite locks, just east of Reynolds' present facility. At that time, the locks and other original stonework were not an obvious concern, since a building previously constructed on the site covered over much of them. Fortunately, however, the building's architect had anticipated eventual interest in the Canal, and had constructed his building without disturbing the artifacts below. When Reynolds razed this building, it found the preserved stonework, and decided to design the new distribution facility to incorporate it. The 1860s granite-arched 13th Street Bridge was also incorporated in the design, and the new warehouse took its shape from these historic artifacts.

* It has since been reported that the Richmond Metropolitan Authority had numbered, disassembled, and removed the stone locks for reassembly and display at a later date.

Execution From the beginning, Paul Murphy, Vice President and General Manager of the Packaging Division, was convinced that preserving the Canal would be an asset to the company and the city. He persuaded the company to hire the architectural firm of Marcellus Wright, Cox, Cilimberg & Ladd to design the warehouse building. Reynolds' own staff did the working drawings and site supervision. The granite works were reassembled where necessary, and Mr. Steven Slaughter, a 74-year-old stonemason who had worked on restorations at Williamsburg, was brought in to assist with the work. The Virginia Historic Landmarks Commission lent technical assistance, and advised the company on historical accuracy.

At about the same time, the 100-year-old wooden 9th Street Bridge was being demolished to make way for a new bridge. Reynolds bought the old bridge's wrought-iron railings to use in the Canal project. In addition to the restoration, the company opened the entire project to the public and installed signs describing the Canal's history, as well as restroom facilities and a picnic area. A film on the Canal is also planned. Phase I of the project was completed in 1973, and work continues on further improvements, including restoration of the wooden locks.

Costs Because the costs of restoring the Canal and locks were incorporated in the total cost of building the new warehouse facility, Reynolds is not able to provide an exact figure for the project's cost.

Problems The only special problems resulting from Reynolds' plans for restoring the Canal were technical difficulties in actually executing the project. Some of the original granite walls had caved in and had to be reassembled.

Benefits The benefits to the city and the public are clear. The company has received considerable favorable publicity, and the tourist site enables it to reap additional public-relations benefits. Reynolds, in cooperation with the Metropolitan Richmond Chamber of Commerce, has instituted a "Lunch at the Locks" program, serving lunch to tourist groups. Preservation activities by Reynolds and other companies along the James have encouraged the city to plan major improvements in the riverfront area to make it more accessible to the public. Several new buildings, including the Federal Reserve Bank of Richmond and the First & Merchants National Bank, have recently been constructed there. The Ethyl Corporation, just upriver from Reynolds, is also restoring a historic property, the Tredegar Iron Foundry, which made Civil War armaments.

The Company Reynolds Metals is the country's second largest producer of primary aluminum and the world's largest producer of aluminum packaging materials. In 1976, it had net sales of over $2 billion and total assets of more than $2.3 billion. More than 325 people work at Reynolds' North Plant facility in Richmond, and approximately fifteen new jobs were added by the company's decision to build the new Distribution Center.

For further information contact:
A. R. D. Perrins
Director, Creative Services
Reynolds Aluminum Packaging
  Division
Reynolds Metals Company
Richmond, Virginia 23261

Footnotes

1. Tucker H. Hill and William Trout, "National Register of Historic Places, Inventory, Nomination Form," 10-300, (Washington, D.C.: U.S. Department of the Interior, National Park Service, June 23, 1971), p. 7.

Walkway open to the public between the Distribution Center and the Canal.

Summary Safeway, the largest supermarket chain in the nation, made a rather unique contribution to preservation: during the month of September, 1976, it placed a message about the National Trust for Historic Preservation on its milk cartons. About 900,000 of these cartons were distributed in northern California and Nevada. The Washington, D.C.-based National Trust believes this campaign increased awareness of and interest in the organization.

Background In July, 1975, the National Trust's San Francisco office staff indicated to Safeway that the organization was in need of more exposure on the West Coast. Safeway, which for many years had placed messages on milk cartons for public-service and environmental organizations, such as CARE, the Red Cross, and Johnny Horizon, suggested that the recently opened National Trust Regional Office might want to take advantage of the same service.

Execution The National Trust provided the copy for the message, and Safeway's ad agency did the layout.

Costs Each impression for the message cost about ½ cent, and there were three impressions per carton, making Safeway's donation (not including the costs of layout by the company's ad agency) approximately $13,500.

Benefits The advertisement brought the National Trust many inquiries about membership, although the exact number of new members the organization gained through this exposure is not known: Safeway has received many favorable comments from preservationists.

The Company Founded in 1915, Safeway became a corporation in 1926. Originally a Western supermarket chain, it has expanded to 29 states and now has outlets in England, Canada, West Germany, and Australia. Stores number about 2,440. Sales reached $970 million in 1975, and topped $1 billion in 1976. In the same period, net income declined from $148 million in 1975 to $105 million in 1976.

For further information contact:
Felicia Del Campo
Manager, Public Relations
Safeway Stores, Incorporated
4th & Jackson Streets
Oakland, California 94660

The National Trust for Historic
  Preservation
740-748 Jackson Place, N.W.
Washington, D.C. 20006

National Trust for Historic Preservation advertisement on Safeway milk carton.

Joseph E. Seagram & Sons, Inc.

Summary

To celebrate the United States Bicentennial, Joseph E. Seagram & Sons has originated a project documenting the County Courthouse across the country from the inception of the county system to the present. In the development of the country, the Courthouse is undoubtedly the single most important building type.

Specially commissioned photographs by fine photographers will form the core of the archive. Work selected from the body of material and essays on the social and political role of the county seat and the architecture of the courthouse will be assembled in the form of a book and a national exhibition.[1]

The above is an excerpt from a questionnaire and letter sent in February, 1975, to county clerks, state bar associations, historical societies, and any other source that was thought to be interested. Seagram's allocated $250,000 for this study and will finance publication of the book.

Joseph E. Seagram & Sons, Inc., is the largest subsidiary of The Seagram Company, Ltd., the largest producer and distributor of distilled spirits and wines in the world.

Background At a meeting of Seagram's executives in 1974, Ms. Phyllis Lambert, an architect and the sister of Mr. Edgar Bronfman, the company's Chairman and Chief Executive Officer, was given the job of choosing an appropriate way for the company to mark the Bicentennial.

Ms. Lambert decided that the Bicentennial project should take the form of a survey of a particular type of building in some way symbolic of the growth and development of the country. The choice was the county courthouse, and the means of preservation, photography. Ms. Lambert enlisted the help of Mr. Richard Pare, who teaches photography in Chicago, to prepare a feasibility study and report to Edgar Bronfman.

Execution Mr. Pare devoted two months to drawing up a proposal. The courthouses of Indiana were the pilot project. After receiving the approval of the Board, Mr. Pare relocated to New York to coordinate and plan the project.

In February, 1975, 5,000 letters and questionnaires were sent to county clerks, state bar associations, historical societies, and state organizations, requesting photographs or postcards and information from an architectural, historic, and social viewpoint on the presently used courthouse, and any predecessors, if such structures were still standing.

Seagram's commissioned 24 photographers to photograph over 1,000 courthouses, roughly one-third the number of existing courthouses in the 48 contiguous states. This group of photographers worked systematically all over the country in an attempt to survey the architecture and the present status of the buildings. Shooting began in spring, 1975, reached a peak of activity that summer, and concluded in January, 1977.

Seagram's located and recorded many remarkable buildings. One—in King William County, Virginia—was the oldest courthouse still in use today, dating from about 1725. Built in Flemish bond brickwork, it is surrounded by a boundary wall.

Also documented was the oldest frame courthouse, which dates from 1749, and is located in Plymouth, Massachusetts. Besides its occasional use as a courthouse, this building now functions as a museum known as the Old Towne House.

Some courthouses were photographed as they were being demolished. Others have fallen victim to the bulldozer since being photographed.

Because the courthouse is often a focal point of the community, it was viewed as more than simply a structure, and was photographed both in detail and in the context of the surrounding area. Extant courthouses that are no longer serving their original function were also included. Over 8,000 pictures of interiors and exteriors, as well as photographs of other pertinent architectural details, have been taken. Not every county or state will be included in the book, though all of the 48 contiguous states are represented in the archive.

A book, drawing on the archive, was scheduled for publication in 1978. It will be primarily pictorial, utilizing about 300 photographs. Three essays will accompany the pictures: the first, by Henry-Russell Hitchcock and William Seale, on the architecture; the second, by Paul Reardon, Associate Justice (Ret.), Supreme Judicial Court of Massachusetts, on the history of the county system; and the third, by Calvin Trillin of the *New Yorker,* on the genre and folklore of the courthouse and county offices.

Richard Pare has negotiated a contract for the publication of the book, which will retail for about $35. Seagram's will pay for the cost of production, and will share the royalties generated by the sale.

Several exhibitions have taken place, including a major exhibition of 86 prints in St. Louis in March, 1976. A touring exhibit is being planned in collaboration with the American Federation of the Arts and the National Trust for Historic Preservation. Changing exhibits drawn from the archive may be seen in the reception area of Seagram's national headquarters in New York City. Also in New York, 64 photographs in an exhibit called "Courthouse" were on view at the Museum of Modern Art from April to July, 1977.

256

Costs The Board of Seagram's committed $250,000 for the study; this sum financed the photography and paid all expenses, including travel, photographic materials, and salaries. The company will also finance the book of 300 of the best photographs, paying the editor's salary, the essayists' fees, and the bill for archival materials purchased to accommodate the photographs and information gathered. Indirect expenditures include use of an office at Seagram's headquarters in New York, salary for a secretary, mailings, and administrative services.

Benefits Seagram's undertook this project as its contribution to the Bicentennial in the hope that the photographic documentation of courthouses throughout the United States would encourage more research in similar areas by other groups.

The Company For the fiscal year ending July, 1976, Joseph E. Seagram & Sons had sales of $1.7·billion and a net income of $32.2 million, compared to sales of $1.6 billion and a net income of $29.1 million for the previous year. Seagram's sales account for 20 percent of the distilled-spirits market in the United States. The company also is involved in oil and gas exploration and production through its subsidiary, Texas Pacific Oil Company, Inc.

Other Preservation Activities. The company's headquarters are presently the subject of a preservation effort. In October, 1976, Seagram's applied to New York City for landmark status for its headquarters building on Park Avenue. This bronze-and-glass tower was designed by the well-known architects Mies Van Der Rohe and Philip Johnson, and was completed in 1958. Reputed to be among the finest metal curtain-wall buildings, the Seagrams Tower has served as the prototype for similar structures all over the world.

Seagram's application for official landmark status is the subject of lively discussion among preservationists, since the present New York Landmarks Preservation Law stipulates that a structure must be at least thirty years old before it can be considered. Seagram's decision to seek landmark

status is also interesting because owners of buildings usually fight landmark designation. Seagram's request is currently under review.

Phyllis Bronfman Lambert, the originator of the courthouse project, has recently purchased and successfully renovated the vintage Biltmore Hotel in Los Angeles, California.

For further information contact:
Richard Pare
General Editor
Phyllis Lambert
Director
Caroline Sederbaum
Assistant to the Editor
United States Bicentennial Project
Joseph E. Seagram & Sons, Inc.
375 Park Avenue
New York, New York 10022

Footnotes

1. Letter from Richard Pare, General Editor, United States Bicentennial Project, Joseph E. Seagram & Sons, Inc., to county officials, state Bar Associations, historical societies, and other interested parties, February, 1975.

Courthouse (c. 1877) in Lake City, Colorado. (William Clift)

A view of Pittsburgh's Allegheny Courthouse (c. 1880), designed by Henry Hobson Richardson. (Richard Pare)

Summary

In 1972, Standard Oil Company (Indiana) donated the historic Destrehan Plantation House, and four acres of the surrounding land, valued at $160,000, to the River Road Historical Society of Destrehan, Louisiana. The company also contributed an initial $12,000 toward renovating the eighteenth-century mansion. The gift has enabled the Historical Society to begin the work of preserving the house. Partly due to the success of this project, the Society is administering another newly restored plantation.

Background

The Destrehan Plantation House was built in 1787 for a French sugar and indigo planter named Robert Antoine Robin De Logny. De Logny hired a free mulatto named Charles Pacquet to construct the house according to his specifications. It was completed by slave labor in 1790.

The house contains two stories: the top floor, reachable by two mahogany staircases, contains the main living area, including the dining room and bedrooms; the service areas, added later, are on the lower floor. In 1812, two two-story additions were made on either side of the main house.

The galleries were supported by masonry Tuscan columns, and the roof over them by painted wooden columns. At the time of the house's construction, there were no levees for the Mississippi River, and flooding was a regular occurrence. As a result, the house originally had no lower floor, but was supported by masonry columns. In 1840, when the levee system for the River was completed up to Baton Rouge, the lower floor was enclosed for use as a service area. During the Greek Revival period—about 1840—both sets of columns were replaced by massive Doric columns.

The house has been a local landmark since it was built. In 1973, it was included in the National Register of Historic Places. The nomination form explained a bit of the Destrehan Plantation's uniqueness:

The house is one of the oldest in Louisiana and one of the best documented structures of the colonial period. It represents three major phases of construction and illustrates the changes in architectural style in Louisiana from the original eighteenth century colonial structure to the post colonial addition of the detached wings, to the ante-bellum Greek Revival alterations in the colonnade and interior details.[1]

Upon his death in 1792, Robert De Logny willed the plantation to his daughter, Marie.

Later, Marie married Jean Noel Destrehan. Jean Noel constructed the two additions to either side of the house to accommodate Marie's and his fourteen children, and he officially gave his name to the plantation. It was after Jean Noel died in 1823 that Stephen Henderson purchased the property for $187,294. Pierre Adolph Rost, the adopted son of Stephen Henderson, resided in the plantation house until 1914.

During Rost's occupancy, rumors sprang up around Destrehan that the house grounds were haunted by the long-deceased pirate, Jean Lafitte, who had been a frequent visitor to Destrehan in Henderson's time. This rumor gave rise to the belief that Lafitte may have buried a part of his booty somewhere in the plantation house or grounds.

In 1914, the Mexican Petroleum Company bought the house and grounds for $40,000, and built a refinery on the property. The company subsequently sold the house, refinery, and grounds to the Pan Am Southern Corporation, a predecessor of Standard Oil. Standard Oil furnished the house and maintained it during its 44-year occupancy. Before World War I, the house served as a club for employees who resided on the plantation grounds. Later, it served as the offices of the refinery accounting department. In 1958, Standard Oil closed down its refinery operations in Louisiana and the building was vacated.

During the fourteen years it remained vacant, the plantation house was totally stripped of valuables, both inside and out, by vandals. They believed the story of hidden treasure, but found none. Instead, they took everything removable: shutters, mantelpieces, doors, windows, cisterns, woodwork, pipes, and whatever furnishings remained.

Some local residents, fearing the entire mansion would be destroyed through neglect, formed the River Road Historical Society in 1972. Their aim was to preserve and restore what was left of the old plantation house.

Execution

In 1971, Standard Oil had the house and grounds appraised; the house was appraised at $74,000, and the land at $86,000, for a total of $160,000. The next year, at the insistence of the Historical Society, Standard Oil donated to it the mansion and four acres of the surrounding land. However, the newly formed Historical Society was having difficulty in raising the money to begin the restoration. Standard Oil donated $12,000 for a new roof and structural reinforcement, badly needed to halt further interior and exterior deterioration until more money could be raised. In May, 1973, Standard Oil discovered the original plantation bell, mentioned in a 1792 inventory, and mounted it near its original position.

In November, 1972, the River Road Historical Society held its first annual Fall Festival on the plantation grounds in order to help raise $500,000, the estimated cost of complete restoration. The *Torch,* a magazine published by Standard Oil, described a later Fall Festival:

More than 20,000 people attended the event, which was based on the Bicentennial theme. Local artisans made, displayed and sold their works, which were produced in the same manner as they were in the days when the house was being built. Louisiana foods including piquante, jambalaya, gumbo, and "dirty" rice were served by the potful.[2]

By the time of the third annual fair, which brought in $38,000, the first phase of the restoration project was completed. The Society had succeeded in raising $104,000, which was spent in clearing the land around the mansion, restoring the wooden columns, and reinforcing the structure.

Since then, the River Road Historical Society has raised an additional $50,000 toward its goal. The money has been used to paint most of the exterior, and to replace every window and door, as well as the stolen hardware and shutters. In addition, the parlor and dining rooms will be refurbished and repainted, and the floors will be refinished. To date, only one interior room has been completely restored. This room, which was the wine cellar, serves as an antique shop to raise funds for the Society.

The River Road Historical Society has received contributions from other major corporations such as Dupont and Shell Oil. It has also succeeded in placing Destrehan in the National Register of Historic Places, making the project eligible for matching funds at both the state and federal levels. Through the Society's efforts, the mansion is now open to the public, and an estimated 2,000 people visit it each month.

Costs Aside from providing a figure of $12,000, which represented its donation for early restoration work, Standard Oil gave no other financial details on its involvement in the Destrehan project.

Problems The major difficulty in the restoration was replacing all the portable valuables stolen by vandals during the house's fourteen-year vacancy. According to Ann Little, Destrehan's current Administrator, "What nature couldn't do in two centuries, man has done in fourteen years."[3]

Benefits Standard Oil's image has been enhanced by the public-relations material the donation has generated; the Destrehan restoration has been prominently featured in the local media. Information on tax benefits the company gained by donating the property is not available.

The River Road Historical Society was at last able to begin the restoration it had long hoped for. As a result of its success with Destrehan, the Society has recently become administrator of the newly restored San Francisco Plantation in Garyville, Louisiana.

The Company Standard Oil is the leading petroleum-products company in the Midwest, and distributes to all other states under the AMOCO name. The company also markets natural gas, and agricultural and chemical products. In 1976, Standard Oil's revenues were $11.5 billion, an increase of 16 percent over 1975 revenues of $10 billion. Net income, over the same period, rose 11 percent from $787 million to $893 million. Of the company's earnings, 78 percent came from U.S. petroleum and natural gas; 9.2 percent from Canada; and 12.5 percent from overseas.

For further information contact:
S. L. Paffenrath
Staff Writer, Communications Division
Public and Government Affairs
  Department

Standard Oil Company (Indiana)
200 East Randolph Drive
P.O. Box 5910-A
Chicago, Illinois 60680
A. Rush Little
Administrator
Destrehan Plantation House
P.O. Box 5
Destrehan, Louisiana 70047

Footnotes

1. Samuel Wilson, Jr., "National Register of Historic Places, Inventory, Nomination Form," 10-300, (Washington, D.C.: U.S. Department of the Interior, National Park Service, July 14, 1972), p. 4.
2. Rod Taylor, "Destrehan Rides Again," *Amoco Torch*, January/February 1976, p. 23.
3. INFORM interview with Ann R. Little, Administrator, Destrehan Plantation, March, 1977.

The Destrehan Plantation House. (River Road Historical Society)

Union Camp Corporation

Summary In March, 1976, this leading wood-products producer donated the historic Tower Hill Plantation in Virginia with ten acres of land to the National Trust for Historic Preservation. The donation of this property, dating from 1775, was significant for two reasons: it was the first corporate gift of a historic house and property to the National Trust, and it was the first such gift by Union Camp, which had previously given away vast tracts of historically and ecologically important woodlands.

Tower Hill, appraised at $55,000, was donated to the National Trust for use in its asset real property program. The property will be sold subject to protective covenants that will prohibit subdivision of the land and alterations to the house without the Trust's consent.

Background The Tower Hill property marks the second donation made by Union Camp under its Land Legacy Program set up in November, 1975. Two years before, Union Camp had made its largest single land donation ever. It had given its entire holdings in the Great Dismal Swamp of Virginia, involving almost 50,000 acres valued at $12.6 million. This swampland, rich in ecological and historic resources, is now part of the National Wildlife Refuge System of the U.S. Department of the Interior. The contribution was officially completed in January, 1975, and Union Camp received in return a federal tax reduction of approximately $6 million over three years.

The Land Legacy Program was established as an expression of the company's ongoing interest in making donations of land and resources. Alexander Calder, Jr., Chairman of the Board of Union Camp, stated the corporation's preservation philosophy:

There are many companies such as Union Camp whose business activities involve the ownership of large landholdings. In our case, as a forest products firm, trees are our major natural resource. . . . Thanks to the nation's tax laws, which . . . entitle companies to the normal deductions for charitable contributions, investor-owned corporations are able to . . . participate with conservation agencies to assure the safekeeping of these lands [of unique ecological and historical significance] for future generations.[1]

The Land Legacy Program's role was to administer company donations. Under it, several of Union Camp's grants have been made through The Nature Conservancy, a nonprofit agency that accepts and makes donations of land and acquires land for government and other conservation bodies. The other four gifts, in addition to the Tower Hill property, made under the Land Legacy Program have included:

Turtle Island, South Carolina (1975)—Located at the mouth of the Savannah River, this 1,700-acre island is the southernmost barrier island in South Carolina. It was given to the South Carolina Wildlife and Marine Resources Department in December, 1975, and is maintained as a wildlife area. Donation of Turtle Island and the Great Dismal Swamp represent a contribution valued at $13 million. This was the first contribution under Union Camp's Land Legacy Program.

Chowan Swamp, North Carolina (1976)—This 3,800-acre tract will eventually become an environmental-studies center for educational and public use under the auspices of the State of North Carolina. The donation was made in April, 1976.

Hall's Knoll, Georgia (1976)— Located about thirty miles from Savannah in Midway, this site was the home of Dr. Lyman Hall, a signer of the Declaration of Independence and the first Governor of Georgia after the Revolutionary War. In July, 1976, the Land Legacy Program donated 88 acres to the Liberty County Historical Society which plans to establish a wildlife sanctuary. In time, trails and markers will indicate the numerous species of plants and trees indigenous to the area. Since Lyman Hall's house was burnt by the British during the Revolutionary War in 1782, the Society will undertake an archaeological dig to determine its exact location.

Crescent Lake, Florida (1976)—In November, 1976, the company contributed 2,850 acres to the Florida Department of Natural Resources Endangered Lands Program. The Department will maintain the land as a wildlife preserve. Appraised at $955,000, this ecologically valuable land abounds in wildlife, including bald eagles.

Execution The second donation under the Land Legacy Program was Tower Hill. In 1968, Union Camp bought the plantation tract and woodlands to which the Blow family had retained title for nearly 200 years. The one-and-a-half-story frame house on a raised brick foundation had originally been built in 1775 as the plantation manager's residence. With its exposed end chimneys, laid in Flemish bond brickwork, Tower Hill House is an excellent example of Virginia architecture of that period. It is a relatively small house with five dormers that have unusual jerkin head roofs.

The four-room house, with two rooms on each floor, was remodeled in the twentieth century. However, its interior still boasts a central staircase with a molded handrail, turned balusters, and square newel posts, and the dining room retains its original chair rail molding. After the larger plantation house burned, this smaller house served as the owner's residence. In recent years, the company rented it to local organizations.

The Tower Hill tract has historic significance; the property was once owned by the Harrison family, which gave the United States two Presidents, Henry Harrison, the 9th President, and Benjamin Harrison, his grandson, the 23rd President.

Union Camp continually analyzes its properties for historic and ecological significance. When the company realized the importance of Tower Hill, it approached the National Trust which gladly accepted the gift. The house is presently on the real estate market.

Benefits When the property is sold, the National Trust will be able to use the funds received for further preservation activities, while the restrictive covenants assure that the historic house's architectural integrity will be protected.

Union Camp earned from this donation a $26,500 reduction in its federal income taxes, in addition to public-relations benefits.

The Company Union Camp Corporation, a major natural-resources company, owns about 1.7 million acres of woodlands in Alabama, Florida, Georgia, South Carolina, North Carolina, and Virginia. The company's product lines consist of paper, packaging, building materials, and specialty chemicals. In 1976, for the first time, Union Camp's sales totaled more than $1 billion, representing a 20 percent increase over 1975 sales of $835.9 million. Its net income showed a 34 percent improvement, from $88.7 million to $118.6 million.

Other Preservation Activities. In early 1977, Union Camp offered to pay half the cost of membership in The Nature Conservancy for any of its employees who wished to join.

In line with the company practice of researching its vast holdings for ecological and historic significance, Union Camp recently co-sponsored an archaeological dig that took place on a fifteen-acre site belonging to one of its mills in Michigan. The site was the scene of a battle between British soldiers and Indians and American troops in January, 1813. The dig was conducted in cooperation with the local historical society and resulted in unearthing such items as lead rifle balls and arrowheads.

The company is currently analyzing its holdings in the South to ascertain if any important Civil War events took place on them.

For further information contact:
John G. Gregory
Director of Resource Development
Union Camp Corporation
1600 Valley Road
Wayne, New Jersey 07470

J. E. Moody
Vice President, Real Estate and
 Legal Services
National Trust for Historic
 Preservation
740-748 Jackson Place, N.W.
Washington, DC 20006

Footnotes

1. Union Camp Corporation, "Union Camp Corporation Donates Plantation Homesite of Patriot Lyman Hall, Declaration of Independence Signer [Who] Was Governor of Georgia," *News Release*, July 1, 1976, p. 2.

The Tower Hill Plantation House.

APPENDIX

INFORM identified many more business-supported preservation projects across the United States than are profiled in the body of this book. For those on which some information was available, a short description of the project is included below. The organization of this section mirrors that of the full case studies. It is divided into three sections: recycled buildings, community revitalization, and general preservation support. Where possible, contacts are provided for readers wishing to obtain further information.

Recycled Buildings

Project: Restoration of the Lockerly Plantation House (c. 1839) as a guest complex

Company: American Industrial Clay Company
433 North Broad Street
Elizabeth, New Jersey
07207

In 1963, the American Industrial Clay Company purchased Lockerly Hall, located in Baldwin County, Georgia. The company completely restored the lavish antebellum plantation house for use as a guest house for visiting technicians, scientists, and manufacturers interested in kaolin. Kaolin is a kind of white clay used in the production of ceramics, paper, and textiles. It is mined by the company nearby.

The house, built in 1839 by Daniel Tucker, a local judge, remained a residence until the 1963 sale. The company restored the building, and the late Edward Grossman, company President, placed his private collection of Southern antiques on display there.

Project: Reuse of a Victorian mansion (c. 1886) as corporate offices

Company: Atlantic Coast Life Insurance Company
149 Wentworth Street
Charleston, South Carolina
92401

Contact: Robert Scarborough
Secretary-Treasurer

In 1940, the Atlantic Coast Life Insurance Company purchased the 13,883-square-foot Rogers Mansion located on the edge of Charleston's historic urban core. This ornate four-story Victorian house was originally built for a wealthy merchant by architect Daniel C. Waynes at a cost of approximately $200,000.

Atlantic Coast Life renovated the structure and adjacent stables for $225,000, or $16 per square foot. According to the company, operating costs on the building are high due to high ceilings and maintenance, but the only way "to preserve Charleston is to save the old buildings and keep them on the tax rolls."

Project: Reuse of a vintage residence as corporate offices

Company: Atlantic Mutual Life Insurance
17 West Mcdonough Street
Savannah, Georgia 31401

Contact: Ann Connor
Secretary

In 1954, Frederick Wessells, Jr., President of Atlantic Mutual Life Insurance and several other companies, purchased the Moses Eastman Mansion in Savannah, Georgia, to house the offices of his many businesses. This project was the first adaptive reuse of a vintage residence for office space in Savannah.

The three-story brick and stucco structure, built in 1843 by Eastman, a wealthy merchant, includes a porch with a two-story rounded colonnade. In 1893, a fourth story was added, and the raised basement was converted to use as the first floor. The Mansion remained a residence until 1939 when it became a millinery shop. In 1946, it returned to residential use.

Atlantic Mutual Life discovered that the Mansion required little renovation. All systems were in working order. A vault was added to the raised basement, several walls were removed from the upstairs bedrooms, and the interior was painted. Several outbuildings, including an old garage and outhouse, were demolished to provide parking spaces. The office furnishings are contemporary, although the original lighting fixtures and crystal chandeliers remain. An intricate iron fence, featuring the faces of famous men, surrounds the house.

Today, the first floor houses the Southern Bank and its vaults. The second floor has been kept exactly as it was when Wessells first purchased the house. The library and drawing room remain as period rooms. The third and fourth floors serve as the offices of Wessells' other companies.

Project: Use of a museum building (c. 1861) as a retail clothing store

Company: Bonwit Teller
234 Berkeley Street
Boston, Massachusetts
02116

In 1947, the New England Mutual Life Insurance Company purchased the New England Museum of Natural History building and site which were adjacent to its company offices in Boston's Back Bay. The Museum was moving to new quarters, and was vacating its 1861 classical landmark building. New England Mutual Life contemplated demolition and new commercial construction, but Walter Hoving, then President and owner of Bonwit Teller, a retail clothing chain, agreed to lease the old museum and convert it into a specialty store. Bonwit Teller has been located in the building ever since. High real estate taxes—at an assessed value much greater than the market value of the property—have caused the company some concern, but it is pleased with the prime location and image of the historic structure.

Project: Reuse of an old bookstore as newspaper office

Company: The Boston Globe
Old Corner Bookstore
50 Bromfield Street
Boston, Massachusetts
02108

The Old Corner Bookstore, a brick structure built about 1718 at the corner of School and Washington Streets in the heart of Boston, was originally a private home. It was later adapted as a bookstore by Ticknor and Fields, publishers of Longfellow, Stowe, Emerson, Holmes, Thoreau, Whittier, and many others. In the twentieth century, the bookstore declined. The building was last used as a pizza parlor before its existence was threatened by the urban-renewal bulldozer. In the mid-1960s, Historic Boston, Inc., an *ad hoc* group of concerned citizens, was formed to purchase and restore the building. The group was supported in its efforts by a contribution of more than $100,000 from the *Boston Globe*, the city's major newspaper. The *Globe* also signed a long-term lease for use of the building as the company's in-town office, insuring the project's financial success.

Project: Continued use of a historic hotel

Company: Braniff International Hotels, Inc.
P.O. Box 35001
Dallas, Texas 75235

In October, 1974, Braniff International Hotels, Inc., a subsidiary of Braniff Airways, purchased the Driskill Hotel in Austin, Texas. The 1886 structure long served the city as a center of social and political life. In 1964, President Johnson watched the televised results of his election there, and the hotel served as the White House Press Center whenever the President was at his nearby ranch. In 1966, the building was designated an official state historic site and a Texas Historical Medallion was awarded; however, by 1969, it was closed for financial reasons. A group of local preservationists fought to save the old hotel. After two years, they raised enough money to purchase and renovate the building, through the sale of $500,000 in stock in the Driskill Hotel Corporation. The hotel was reopened in 1973. Braniff purchased the building from the Driskill Hotel Corporation in 1974 and committed at least $350,000 to restore and remodel the lobbies and general ballroom space.

Project: Reuse of three factory buildings for office space

Company: Burroughs Corporation
Burroughs Place
Detroit, Michigan 48232

Contact: Robert Farkas
Manager, Press Relations

The Burroughs Corporation's world headquarters in Detroit consists of three renovated factory buildings. Between 1967 and 1972, the buildings were stripped down to their steel-reinforced concrete frames, and unified by enclosure in concrete, glass, and aluminum walls. The new five-story complex contains more than 600,000 square feet of floor space. The reuse scheme was executed by the architectural firm of Smith and Gardner of Detroit.

Project: Reuse of the Hale Houston House as corporate offices

Company: R.W. Byram Company
706 Guadalupe Street
Austin, Texas 78701

Contact: Chuck Christensen
President

In 1969, R.W. Byram Company, which publishes oil- and gas-industry trade publications, purchased the Hale Houston House at 706 Guadalupe Street in Austin, Texas. The house is on the Bremond block (see Appendix: Texas Classroom Teachers Association), a street which contains six of the city's oldest homes, all listed in the National Register of Historic Places.

The Hale Houston House was built in 1850 by John Bremond, a wealthy merchant. The original section of the house is a one-story Greek Revival structure which includes a central hall, five bay windows, and a gallery with Doric columns. The ceilings are ten feet high, and the interior boasts fine wainscoting. In 1873, Bremond's son, Eugene, added the second story, consisting of three bedrooms and a screened porch. The house today has five fireplaces and one-and-a-half-inch-thick oak flooring.

Byram adapted the building for its offices and constructed a two-story, 2,400-square-foot addition to house its printing offices.

Project: Renovation of the Joseph Foster House as a branch bank

Company: Cape Ann Bank and Trust Company
154 Main Street
Gloucester, Massachusetts 01930

Contact: William F. Bonney
President

In 1972, the Cape Ann Bank and Trust Company purchased the Joseph Foster House in Gloucester, Massachusetts, as a facility for its expanding trust department. The house, built in 1760 by Colonel Joseph Foster had been continuously occupied most recently by a confectionery and a dental office. It had been divided into four apartment units prior to the bank's purchase. The bank's original renovation plan was expanded at the urging of then bank President Kendall to include an accurate restoration of the house. The interior was returned to its original proportions. The original chimney and main entrance sites were found and suitably reproduced. Much of the original wooden paneling was salvaged and reused. The interior doors are all replicas of a door found in the house and believed to be an original. The new interior blends eighteenth-century atmosphere and modern banking conveniences. According to the bank, the restored building is a highly satisfactory facility, as well as a source of community pride and good public relations.

Project: Reuse of pre-earthquake San Francisco office building

Company: The Chartered Bank of London
California Branch
465 California Street
San Francisco, California 94104

In 1976, this British bank, like many American banks in Europe, established operations in a renovated historic building. The bank spent more than $250,000 to restore and adapt the 1905 Merchants Exchange Building in San Francisco. The Exchange, designed by Willis Polk and Julia Morgan, long a San Francisco landmark, is one of the few buildings to survive the earthquake of 1906.

Project: Renovation of 1902 bank building and construction of a compatible contemporary addition

Company: Citizens Savings and Loan Association
700 Market Street
San Francisco, California 94102

Contact: Casey MacKenzie
Community Relations Manager

In 1964, the Citizens Savings and Loan Association completed renovation and new-construction work on its building near the intersection of Market, Kearny, and Geary Streets in San Francisco. The original 1902 structure, built in the French Renaissance style, was one of the few buildings to survive the 1906 earthquake and fire. The original twelve floors were completely refurbished and extended to connect with a new service-tower corner designed to complement the style of the older building. Clark and Beuttler, with associates Charles W. Moore and Alan E. Morgan, were the architects. The cost of the alterations and addition was $2.25 million, or approximately $24 per square foot.

Project: Conversion of a church into a temple of finance

Company: Consolidated American Life Insurance Company
National Headquarters
308 North West Jackson Street
Jackson, Mississippi 39205

Contact: George W. Pickett
President

The First Baptist Church, built in 1843, was one of the few buildings not burned by the Union Army as it pushed through Jackson, Mississippi, during the Civil War. In the early 1900s, the building was converted into a dormitory and classroom facility. Later, it became an apartment house, a church again, and finally, in 1959, the home office of the American Liberty Life Insurance Company (now merged with Consolidated American).

The temple-like structure is today one of only four publicly used buildings still remaining from Jackson's pioneer days.

Project: Renovation of Federal Reserve branch for office use

Company: Crispin Company
22 World Trade Center
Houston, Texas 77001

In 1973, the Crispin Company, an international trading company specializing in steel products, moved its headquarters into an old branch of the Federal Reserve Bank of Dallas. The 1922 structure, located in Houston's central business district, is limestone-faced with terra cotta detail. Architect for the renovation Howard Barnstone highlighted the building's grand main-floor area by using glass walls for office partitions and marble designed to blend with the original decor. The former vault has now become a conference room.

Project: Conversion of industrial buildings to offices

Company: Fibreboard Corporation
55 Francisco Street
San Francisco, California 94133

Contact: Ron Kaufman
The Kaufman Companies
55 Francisco Street
San Francisco, California 94133

In 1970, the Montgomery/North Block was an abandoned and unattractive group of industrial buildings located in the North Waterfront area of San Francisco. Although it was separated from the established downtown by several blocks, developer Ron Kaufman felt that the buildings and the area had recycling potential. Kaufman convinced the Fibreboard Corporation of this potential, and the company agreed to take a fifty-year lease on 100,000 square feet in one of the buildings for use as its world headquarters. The cost for the space was about 30 percent to 40 percent less than the cost of similar space in a new building. Other major businesses, including the Western Contract Furnishers and the Victoria Station restaurant chain, have also leased space in the complex.

Project: Relocation and reuse of two houses as bank branches

Company: Franklin Savings Association
P.O. Box 1723
Austin, Texas 78767

Contact: Charles Betts
President

In 1974, in Austin, Texas, the Franklin Savings Association bought a historic house threatened with demolition, moved it to a new location, restored the exteriors, and adapted the interiors for use as a branch bank. The project cost $150,000 (including banking equipment). In 1976, the Association followed a similar process with another historic home. This relocation and renovation cost $345,000. The bank's efforts have resulted in extensive publicity and savings deposits above expectations.

Project: Modernization of Goodyear's vintage corporate headquarters

Company: Goodyear Tire and Rubber Company
1144 East Market Street
Akron, Ohio 44305

Contact: Howard P. Tolley
Manager, Community Relations

In 1970, Goodyear Tire and Rubber began a multi-million-dollar renovation of its approximately sixty-year-old corporate headquarters, located in a commercial district of Akron, Ohio. The facade of the seven-story building was covered with bronze-tone aluminum, and rows of tinted-glass windows were installed. A new factory gate house and main entrance were also built. Interior additions included construction of a terraced lobby and a seventh-floor cafeteria. A system of moving rubber ramps, instead of conventional elevators, takes employees between floors. Several factory buildings were renovated as well. They were retrofitted with the same bronze-tone aluminum as was used on the corporate headquarters to create a unified look.

The project was completed in 1973. Goodyear estimates that the cost of these renovations was approximately one-half what it would have been for similar new construction.

Project: Reuse of historic inn as a bank branch

Company: Home Federal Savings and Loan Association
419 Main Street
Worcester, Massachusetts
01608

Contact: Charles M. Zettuck
Senior Vice President

In 1974, the Home Federal Savings and Loan Association relocated and restored historic Stearn's Inn in Worcester, Massachusetts, as a branch bank. The two-story frame inn, which originally served as a stagecoach stop on the Boston to New York run, was believed to have been built in 1812. However, during its relocation, architectural evidence suggested the possibility of its dating from about 1750. The taproom of the inn has been set aside for banking operations, but all the other rooms (except the kitchen, which houses the bank's safe-deposit vault) have been restored as accurately as possible, and are open to public tours. A porch, added after 1750, was removed, and the building's exterior was painted ivory white. The original window frames were restored, and the few panes of glass surviving since 1750 were preserved. New paneling in the banking section matches existing paneling in the rest of the rooms, and wallpaper and carpets were chosen in keeping with the period.

Project: Adaptive reuse of a Victorian mansion as corporate offices

Company: Indianapolis Life Insurance Company
North Meridian and 30th Streets
Indianapolis, Indiana
46208

In 1923, Edward B. Raub, founder of Indianapolis Life, purchased the Fairbanks Mansion to house the offices of his new business. The 26-room, Renaissance Revival Mansion, built in 1913 by Charles Warren Fairbanks, a former U.S. Vice President, is constructed of Indiana limestone on a brick and steel foundation. Indianapolis Life's adaptation of the building left the first-floor library intact. The company's offices on the second floor still feature the original decorations, fireplaces, and mirrors. Air conditioning and central heating were installed in the mid-1950s.

Project: Reuse of a nineteenth-century mansion as magazine offices

Company: Industry Media, Inc.
311 Steele Street
Denver, Colorado 80206

Contact: Charles W. Cleworth
President

Industry Media, Inc., publishers of *Plastic Machinery and Equipment Magazine,* is headquartered in a late-nineteenth-century house in Denver. Charles W. Cleworth, President and Publisher, wanted his company to have its own building. He purchased the house and land for $36,000. Renovation of the 2,900-square-foot building (not including a carriage house used for storage), cost $57,000. Calculated with the purchase price, this made a $32-per-square-foot cost for the overall space.

Project: Renovation of the Grove Park Inn

Company: Jack Tar Hotels, Inc.
403 South Akard Street
Box 5235
Dallas, Texas 75202

The Grove Park Inn, completed in July, 1913, was built in Asheville, North Carolina, for E.W. Grove, owner of the pharmaceutical firm manufacturing Bromo-Quinine. Grove wanted the structure built from the stone of nearby Sunset Mountain, and finally entrusted the work to his son-in-law, Fred L. Seely, a former newspaperman. Seely designed and constructed the five-sectioned, terraced structure using lichen- and moss-covered boulders, just as they were taken from the mountain. After almost a year of labor by local artisans and Italian stonemasons, the hotel boasted a great hall, 120 feet long and 80 feet wide, 400 rugs made at Aubusson, France, 700 pieces of furniture, and over 600 solid-copper lighting fixtures. William Jennings Bryan spoke at its opening. Other distinguished visitors included the Franklin Delano Roosevelt family, Henry Ford, John D. Rockefeller, and Woodrow Wilson. During World War II, the State Department used it as an internment center for Axis diplomats, The Philippine government-in-exile was also located in one of the cottages on the sixty-acre tract.

Jack Tar Hotels, Inc., bought the Grove Park Inn on September 28, 1955 and made considerable effort to restore the resort to its original state. The finest of the original furnishings were renewed and retained, and additions were made to facilitate its use as a resort and convention center.

Project: Reuse of a Victorian mansion as insurance offices

Company: Kling Brothers Insurance Company
43 W. King Street
York, Pennsylvania 17401

In 1954, Ralph and Earl Kling purchased a neglected sixteen-room Victorian mansion in York, Pennsylvania. The house, built in 1870, features a circular cherry staircase and wooden mantels. The Klings renovated it as an office for their insurance business, and mounted their large Currier & Ives print collection on the walls. Originally, the prints, which the brothers bought from local farmers, were intended only as period decorations for the mansion. However, by 1963, word of the collection had spread. Tour guides of the Pennsylvania Dutch area began to mention it as one of York's attractions. The collection, now open to the public, attracts as many as 200 visitors a day.

Project: Adaptive reuse of a century-old hardware store as newspaper offices

Company: Logan Leader/News Democrat
120 Public Square
Russellville, Kentucky 42276

Contact: Robert Stuart
Publisher

In 1973, the *Logan Leader/News Democrat* purchased a hardware store built in 1876 by the Ryan family, the most affluent family in Russellville, Kentucky. The two-story brick structure housed the Ryan's food and hardware business until sometime after the turn of the century. At that time, it became a tractor dealership. The *Logan Leader* purchased the building for $70,000. The renovations, which cost $90,000, included sandblasting the exterior, the creation of a staircase, and the construction of partitions. The latter were made from the original oak flooring removed from one of the rooms. All new electrical, gas, and water systems were installed, and the floors were refinished.

Street-floor plan Logan Leader Building.

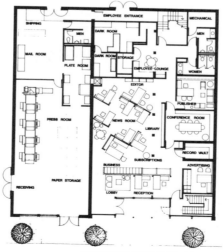

FIRST / STREET FLOOR PLAN

Second-floor plan.

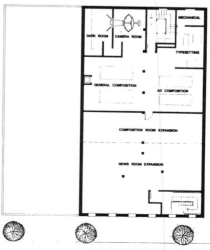

SECOND FLOOR PLAN

Project: Renovation of the Samoa cookhouse and the preservation of a historic lumber town

Company: Louisiana Pacific Company
Samoa Division
Samoa, California 95564

Contact: Lois Lee Bishop
Public Relations Manager

In 1973, Louisiana Pacific Company became the owner of the Hammond mill complex located in Samoa, California, one of the few remaining company towns in the U.S. Samoa has been a lumber town since 1892, when the first mill, built by John Vance, was put into operation. By 1912, the complex was sold to A.B. Hammond, and was known by the Hammond name until its purchase in 1956 by the Georgia Pacific Company. Later, Louisiana Pacific became independent of Georgia Pacific.

Samoa is a 600-acre complex containing 105 homes dating from 1900. It was isolated until several years ago when a new road opened it to tourist trade. Today, the town and its logging museum, a recent addition, are popular attractions, and the renovated eighty-year-old cookhouse has become a popular eating spot.

Project: Continued use of a vintage winery

Company: Paul Masson Vineyards
Brown Vintners
505 Beach Street
San Francisco, California
94133

Contact: Lois A. Leal
Assistant Publicity Manager

At the turn of the century, Paul Masson, son-in-law of the winery's founder, planted a vineyard in the Santa Cruz Mountains near San Jose, California, and built a fortress-like stone winery in the hills. After the earthquake of 1906 left San Jose's St. Patrick's Church in ruins, Masson purchased a twelfth-century Romanesque arch, which was shipped from Spain for use in the church, and included it as part of the winery's facade. The winery was damaged by fire in 1941, but was restored to its original design. The Paul Masson Winery is registered by the State of California as a Historic Landmark.

Project: Renovation of the Willard Carpenter Mansion as Medco's corporate offices

Company: Medco Corporation
405 Carpenter Street
Evansville, Indiana 47703

Contact: Glenn Medcalf
Director of Communications

In 1974, the Medco Corporation, which operates 25 nursing homes, purchased and began renovation of the Willard Carpenter Mansion in Evansville, Indiana, as its corporate headquarters. Carpenter, who made his fortune in merchandising and real estate, built the Mansion in 1848. Subsequently, his home was a stop on the Underground Railway for blacks fleeing the South.

The Mansion is built in the Greek Revival style, the only building of this style extant in Evansville. The two-story structure is made of brick, covered with stucco scored to imitate dressed stone. The original tin cover on the pitched roof was later replaced by asphalt shingles. The main entrance is located behind a small porch, supported by pairs of pillars and pilasters.

In the Medco renovation, the building's exterior was patched and repainted, and as much of the interior as possible was restored. However, the interior design was altered to accommodate functional office requirements. The lower two floors house the executive offices, accounting department, computer room, and meeting rooms.

Project: Conversion of the Brewmaster's House, Zang Brewery, to offices

Company: Mood Music Systems, Inc.
2345 7th Street
Denver, Colorado 80211

Contact: Keene Z. Smith
President

In January, 1972, Keene Z. Smith, President of Mood Music Systems, distributors of jukeboxes and other music systems, purchased the Zang Brewery's Brewmaster's House in Denver. The two-story brick house, built in 1855, is one of the few remaining structures of the old brewery. Mood Music Systems restored the house to its original appearance, installing only modern plumbing and wiring, and a fire escape. The company moved to the ground floor of the building in April, 1973. It leases the upper floor as offices for architects and engineers. Space in the Brewmaster's House rents for $6.50 to $7.50 per square foot, comparable to downtown rentals. According to the company, the carefully restored environment has improved employee morale and seems to have boosted productivity.

The renovated Willard Carpenter Mansion, now Medco's corporate offices.

Project: Reuse of farm buildings as commercial and office space

Company: Nashua Federal Savings and Loan Association
157 Main Street
Nashua, New Hampshire 03060

Contact: Charles F. Rutter
President

In 1976, the Nashua Federal Savings and Loan Association, with the help of Royal/Longstreet, a development firm specializing in bank buildings, restored and adapted as offices a farmhouse and barn dating from the 1730s. The bank's branch office is located in the reconstructed barn, which includes a silo. The office space in the restored farmhouse is leased to other tenants. The project required a $500,000 investment. The branch has attracted more than $2 million in deposits, exceeding the $1 million to $1.5 million originally projected.

Project: Conversion of a railroad station to a newspaper office

Company: The Naugatuck Daily News Corporation
195 Water Street
Naugatuck, Connecticut 06770

Contact: Frederick Hennick
Publisher

In 1964, Rudolph and Frederick Hennick of the *Naugatuck Daily News* purchased the Borough of Naugatuck's vintage railroad station for use as their paper's offices. The 1910 red-brick building cost $1 million; an additional $2 million was spent on improvements. Renovations were carried out by W. J. Megin and Company of Naugatuck, and took one-and-a-half years to complete. Except for replacing the original badly decayed Spanish-tile roof, all efforts were made to preserve the building's original form, while accommodating the facilities of a modern newspaper.

Project: Reuse of an 1813 bank

Company: North Carolina National Bank
Box 120
Charlotte, North Carolina 28201

In 1968, the North Carolina National Bank relocated and readapted as a branch bank a building constructed in 1813 to house the State Bank of North Carolina. The State Bank opened in 1814, with William Polk its first President occupying the structure both as an office and residence. In 1873, the bank sold the building to Christ Church. The structure served as a rectory, and more recently, as a Sunday school. In 1968, the North Carolina National Bank purchased the building and hired Arthur McKimmon II of McKimmon & Rogers, a Raleigh architectural firm, to research and plan for the restoration. The actual restoration was done by Williams Realty, also of Raleigh. The building was moved about 100 feet, and its interior was stripped of all plaster and woodwork. All windows and doors were replaced, and the wood molding, cornices, and wainscoting were reproduced and replaced where necessary. Flooring from demolished historic houses was installed, and the original entrance was restored. The bank provides full banking services, and has added a drive-in window.

Project: Continued use of the Oneida Mansion House

Company: Oneida, Ltd., Silversmiths
Oneida, New York 13421

Contact: Elaine McCoy
Assistant Manager, Public Relations

The Oneida Community Mansion House was built in 1861 by John Humphrey Noyes and his followers. Noyes, a religious leader who taught a perfectionist ideal, founded the Oneida Community in 1848. The 400 Community members lived as one family in their House, the center of all phases of life and work. To support themselves, the members manufactured and sold such useful items as canned goods, traps, bags, and silverware. Although the Community prospered, it abandoned its religious and social goals in 1880, forming a joint stock company to carry on business operations.

Today, the 475-room Mansion serves as an apartment complex and guest house. It also hosts local gatherings.

The three-story brick structure boasts three-arched windows, both gabled and flat roof sections, a balustraded deck, and four-story projecting towers. Built in High Victorian and Second Empire styles, the Mansion has been preserved almost as it was during the days of the Oneida Community (there are several period rooms), with only the addition of a library in an old school room. It is listed in the National Register of Historic Places.

Today, Oneida, Ltd. (formerly the Oneida Community, Ltd.), is the world's largest producer of stainless-steel flatware and a leading producer of silver and silver plate.

Project: Construction of a compatible modern building for switching equipment

Company: Pacific Northwest Bell Telephone
421 S.W. Oak Street
Portland, Oregon 97204

Contact: D. L. Gunderson
Vice President—Oregon

In 1973, Pacific Northwest Bell installed modern electronic switching equipment in a new brick building located in the historic mining town of Jacksonville, Oregon. The building is constructed of structurally reinforced concrete and concrete block veneered with brick. The street facade's arcade is modeled after the design of the nearby Table Rock Saloon, and includes space for a display of early telephone equipment. The building's size, color, and brickwork conform to those of the surrounding structures, and its exterior lighting consists of recreations of the town's original gas streetlights. Professor D. Marion Ross, Architectural Historian of the University of Oregon, was retained as consultant on the project.

Pacific Northwest Bell's switching installation in Jacksonville, Oregon.

The Oneida Community Mansion House.

Project: Renovation of the "oldest food store" in America

Company: Piggly Wiggly
101 Broad Street
Charleston, South Carolina
29401

Contact: F. Marion Brabham

In 1969, Piggly Wiggly, a supermarket chain, purchased a vintage food store on Broad Street in Charleston. The store had been in continuous operation since it was chartered as a grocery in 1847.

Charleston's beautification program establishes strict standards for any new construction or renovation in its historic district. These include the maintenance of a harmonious color scheme, the elimination of inappropriate signs, and the installation of gas streetlights. The renovated structure has nineteenth-century-style windowpanes, and features a turn-of-the-century-style snack shop, a tobacco shop, a bakery, a gourmet food shop, and a wine cellar.

The renovation won awards from the Charleston Chamber of Commerce and the Charleston Historical Preservation Society in 1970.

Project: Continued use of an 1881 flour mill

Company: The Pillsbury Company
1162 Pillsbury Building
608 Second Avenue South
Minneapolis, Minnesota
55402

Contact: Robert G. Walker
Assistant Vice President

For the past five years, the Pillsbury Company, a large producer of baking goods, has allocated $50,000 annually for the renovation and upkeep of its A Mill. Completed in 1881, the mill was once the largest and most advanced flour mill in the world. It was originally one of five mills owned by the Pillsbury-Washburn Company. The stone and concrete structure has been in continuous use since 1881, and over the years Pillsbury has maintained the exterior facade. The portion of Minneapolis where the mill is located is being gradually converted into a waterfront "old town." Preservation of the A Mill has been an important contribution to the restoration of this historic area.

Project: Continued use of the oldest hardware store in Maryland

Company: Quynn's Hardware Store
10 and 12 East Patrick
Street
Frederick, Maryland 21701

Contact: Katherine C. Anders
Co-owner

Quynn's Hardware Store has been in continuous operation on the same corner of Patrick Street since 1796, when Frederick, Maryland, was a stop on the Cumberland Trail going west from Washington to the Cumberland Gap. Quynn's sold westbound pioneers flour, sugar loaves, guns, tobacco, and countless other items. It was only in the late 1800s that the store began to specialize in hardware.

Descendants of Allan Quynn, the original proprietor, retained ownership of the store until 1977, when Dr. William G. Quynn sold the property to Mr. William H. B. Anders, Jr. Mr. Anders has maintained the Quynn name and tradition. The store is located in a small two-story structure laid in Flemish bond brickwork. Its facade has hardly changed over the years, except for the replacement of the original frame windows with plate glass, and the addition of an occasional coat of paint. The store has five rooms on the ground floor. Several rooms in the basement and on the upper floor are used for storage.

Project: Reuse of vintage railroad stations as restaurants

Company: The Santa Fe Railroad
80 East Jackson Boulevard
Chicago, Illinois 60604

Contact: Bill Burke
Vice President, Public
Relations

In 1972, the Santa Fe Land Improvement Corporation, a subsidiary of the Santa Fe Railroad, leased a two-story vintage railroad station in National City, California. The building was converted into a restaurant called The Depot. The restaurant includes a main dining room on the first floor, two smaller dining rooms, a wine cellar, and a freight room. The latter boasts a bar made of railroad ties. The restaurant, which can accommodate 147 people, is entered through an authentic railroad club car.

The Depot Steak, another restaurant, was opened in a vintage train station in Berkeley, California. The depot's ticket windows now serve as a salad bar, and the interior is lit with railroad chandeliers. The restaurant seats 110 customers in the main area, and 35 at the bar.

Project: Reuse of 109-year-old house as corporate offices

Company: Schlegel Corporation
1555 Jefferson Road
Rochester, New York
14623

Contact: Richard Turner
Chairman and President

In 1974, Schlegel, a leading producer of perimeter and area sealing systems for the construction and automotive industries, was looking for additional office space and for a new location for its corporate headquarters. The Rochester, New York, company began to explore the feasibility of constructing a new headquarters facility, while at the same time investigating the option of relocating in existing buildings. In summer, 1976, Richard Turner, Schlegel's Chairman, learned of the availability of the 109-year-old Hiram Sibley House. It contained the 15,000 square feet needed for the corporate headquarters. Schlegel took an option on the building and commissioned a feasibility study comparing the conversion of the historic house with new construction. By the early fall, the company's Board of Directors had approved the renovation, and work is now in progress. Although it was not a factor in Schlegel's decision, the rehabilitation may qualify for accelerated depreciation under the new federal tax law, making the cost for the renovation lower than originally anticipated.

Project: Restoration of part of the William Aiken House

Company: Southern Railway System
920 15th Street, N.W.
Washington, D.C. 20013

Contact: William F. Geeslin
Assistant Vice President
Public Relations and
Advertising

In 1973, the Southern Railway System restored part of the second floor of the William Aiken House in Charleston, South Carolina. The part of the floor which was not restored had been utilized as a display area for the National Railway Historical Society.

William Aiken, the first President of the South Carolina Canal and Railroad Company, built the three-story brick and white stucco house between 1807 and 1811. He added an East Wing in 1831. In 1863, his son sold the house to Aiken's company, which used the building as its offices. At the turn of the century, Southern Railway acquired the company, and the house became its Charleston offices. The building still serves that function today. In 1977, the company donated space in the house to the National Trust to serve as the Trust's Southern Field Office. The building was designated a National Landmark by the U.S. Department of Interior in 1964.

The second floor renovation took three years and cost approximately $50,000. A drawing room, the main stairway, and another room across from the drawing room were restored to their original appearance, and now serve as offices. The ballroom is now a meeting room. Simons, Lapham, Mitchell and Small were the architects who advised the local contractors on the project.

Restored ceiling and light fixture in the downstairs hallway at Aiken House. (Savannah Chamber of Commerce)

Project: Adaptive reuse of a vintage railroad station

Company: Southern Railway System and the Savannah Chamber of Commerce
Southern Railway System
P.O. Box 2202
227 West Broad Street
Savannah, Georgia 31402

Contact: Savannah Chamber of Commerce
P.O. Box 530
301 West Broad Street
Savannah, Georgia 31401

The Central of Georgia Railroad, a subsidiary of the Southern Railway System, had no further need for its 1860s brick station in Savannah and donated it to the city. In 1973, the Savannah Chamber of Commerce raised $200,000 from local businesses to renovate the building as a visitors center. (Visitors spend more than $500 million annually in Savannah.) The actual renovation cost $300,000, and to make up the difference, the Chamber of Commerce is paying $25,000 annually to the city. Architects Gunn and Meyerhoff designed the adaptation and renovation. The center, which opened in 1975, now includes a theater, an exhibit area, offices, a lounge, and rest-room facilities. Tourist parking is also available. Southern Railway maintains a small railroad museum complete with a restored locomotive in a former station shed.

Project: Restoration of the Stewart Building, erected in 1884

Company: Stewart Title Insurance Company
P.O. Box 1540
Galveston, Texas 77553

The Stewart Building, built by the Stewart Title Insurance Company in 1884 as its corporate headquarters, is a four-story red-brick structure designed in the Neo-Renaissance style. It is located in the Strand National Historic Landmark District of Galveston, a ten-square-block area that was the financial center of Texas during the nineteenth century.

In summer, 1976, Stewart Title, aided by a $20,000 matching grant from the Texas Historical Commission, began restoring the exterior of the building, including the reproduction of a cornice which was destroyed by a hurricane in 1900.

The first two floors of the building serve as company offices. Plans call for adapting the remaining two floors as apartments.

Project: Continued use of Syracuse Savings' landmark headquarters

Company: Syracuse Savings Bank
1 Clinton Square
Syracuse, New York 13203

Contact: Frederick Schwartz
Vice President, Marketing

The headquarters of the Syracuse Savings Bank is located in an 1876 banking hall designed by Joseph Tyman Silsbee and built by master builder John Moore at a cost of $281,000. The six-story building, once the tallest in Syracuse, is constructed of buff- and red-colored sandstone. It was modeled after the Palace of the Doges in Venice, and is a combination of Venetian and Gothic architecture. The building has pointed arches and Gothic moldings. Its interior carvings were executed by Italian stonecutters. The structure's 170-foot tower also boasted the first public elevator in Syracuse.

The building has been renovated several times. Part of the second floor has been removed to increase the height of the ceiling in the first-floor lobby to forty feet. In 1975, the bank began installing air conditioning and a new heating system. To date, it has spent $1.5 million on the renovations, which are still in progress.

Project: Renovation of the Arizona Biltmore Hotel

Company: Talley Industries, Inc.
3500 N. Greenfield Rd.
Mesa, Arizona 85203

In June, 1973, Talley Industries purchased the Arizona Biltmore Hotel in Phoenix. The building, designed by Frank Lloyd Wright, was constructed in 1927. Talley immediately closed the hotel and began installing a sprinkler system in accordance with Phoenix fire codes. However, before the installation was completed, a fire broke out, destroying the roof and damaging some of the hotel furnishings. Talley hired Taliesin Associated Architects of the Frank Lloyd Wright Foundation to design and supervise the reconstruction of the damaged floors as well as the refurnishing and decoration of the main building. The work was carried out under the direction of Mrs. Franz G. Talley, wife of Talley's owner.

The hotel was built of precast concrete blocks, the first time this material was used in the construction of a large public building. It featured a roof made of Arizona copper, and boasted the largest gold-leaf ceiling in the world, located in the main lobby and adjacent areas. Some of the gold leaf had to be replaced due to fire damage. Other renovations involved creating a cocktail lounge and bar in an area previously known as the Sun Room. Talley is also considering erecting a free-standing addition that will contain eighty rooms and a convention meeting room.

Project: Conversion of a nineteenth-century mansion to office space

Company: Terracor Company
529 East South Temple
Salt Lake City, Utah 84103

Contact: Dan Cunningham
Director of Public Relations

In 1969, Terracor, a development company, converted and restored the historic nineteenth-century Brown Mansion in Salt Lake City for use as its headquarters. A University of Utah class, under Owen Olpin, Professor of Law, and lawyer E. Scott Savage, conducted an economic feasibility study. The study revealed that, given current zoning requirements, renovating the existing building would bring greater benefits than new construction on the same site. The existing building contains 25,600 square feet, and the zoning code would have permitted only a 23,973-square-foot new building.

Project: Adaptive reuse of three Victorian mansions as the Association's offices

Company: Texas Classroom Teachers Association
700 Guadalupe Street
Austin, Texas 78701

Contact: C. E. Saunders
Executive Director

In 1958, the Texas Classroom Teachers Association purchased four vintage Victorian buildings originally owned by a wealthy merchant family in Austin. The buildings, which the Association is presently using as its offices, include: the John Bremond Home (c. 1888), the Pierre Bremond Home (c. 1890), the Walter Bremond Home (c. 1886), and a carriage house of the same period. Apart from minor repairs, refurnishing, and the replacement of some of the original fixtures, little alteration of the three homes was made by the Association. However, the carriage house was completely renovated as a residence for the Association's President.

The Bremond buildings had been used by community organizations prior to their purchase, and the John Bremond Home remains a meeting place for the YMCA, the Texas Medical Association, and the Elks Club.

Project: Continued use of 1924 bank building

Company: Union Commerce Bank
917 Euclid Avenue
Cleveland, Ohio 44115

The bank's 1924 building in downtown Cleveland, Ohio, contains one of the world's largest banking halls. Designed by Chicago architects Graham, Anderson, Probst, and White, the hall is sixty feet high and contains 27,000 square feet. In 1974, the bank, encouraged by architect Peter van Dijk, decided to restore rather than remodel the grand hall as part of business's overall commitment to the redevelopment of downtown Cleveland.

Project: Continued use of nineteenth-century railroad depot

Company: Union Pacific Railroad Company
1416 Dodge Street
Omaha, Nebraska 68102

Contact: Barry B. Combs
Director of Public Relations

In 1966, the Union Pacific Railroad Company undertook exterior restoration of the Union Pacific Depot, the oldest Union Pacific property in Cheyenne, Wyoming. Built in 1886 at a cost of $100,000, the Richardsonian Romanesque building was designed by architects Van Brunt and Howe of Kansas City, Missouri. It is constructed of red and grey sandstone blocks of random size, laid on a wood and iron frame. The interior of the building is finished with native red oak and yellow pine. In 1890, a tower clock was added, and in 1922, a one-and-a-half-story restaurant was attached to the Depot's eastern end. Today, the latter addition, known as Hicks Hall, serves as office and meeting space. In 1929, the wooden supports of the building were replaced with steel, and the half story over the east extension was remodeled as a functional third floor. New train sheds were added to the south end in 1937 as part of Union Pacific's $375,000 improvement of the Depot and surrounding yards. A park originally located directly to the north was replaced by a Greyhound Bus Terminal in 1940. The original slate roof was replaced in 1952 with asbestos. In the 1966 restoration, the entire exterior was sandblasted, cleaned, and restored. In 1976, Union Pacific funded the complete remodeling of the second and third floors of the building. The Depot at Cheyenne was nominated for inclusion in the National Register of Historic Places in 1972.

The Union Pacific Depot at Cheyenne, Wyoming.

Project: Reuse of a textile mill for production and company offices

Company: Ursula of Switzerland
31 Mohawk Avenue
Waterford, New York
12188

Contact: Hudson-Mohawk Industrial
Gateway
5 First Street
Troy, New York 12180

In 1972, Ursula and Richard Garrow of Ursula of Switzerland, a women's-apparel manufacturer, purchased the Laughlin textile mill, built in 1894. The five-story red-brick structure located in Waterford, New York, includes corbeled brick cornices and a brick tower which houses a water tank.

Thus far, the Garrows have renovated three of the mill's five floors to serve as their manufacturing plant and offices. Windows were replaced, and the roof was repaired, along with other minor refitting. Old textile machinery was removed; the wooden floors were sanded and oiled; and the mechanical systems were improved.

Offices were created and partitions erected to form a design studio, cutting area, sewing and finishing workshop and storage space for finished garments.

Eighty employees currently use the three floors of the mill.

Project: Restoration and conversion of an old hotel into a modern bank

Company: Van Horn State Bank
P.O. Box 728
Van Horn, Texas 79855

Contact: J. E. Billingsley
President

In the mid-1970s, the Van Horn State Bank purchased the rundown El Capitan Hotel in Van Horn, Texas. The bank renovated and restored the building, which now houses the bank, an office of the Border Patrol, a florist, and a jewelry store.

The El Capitan Hotel was opened in 1930 as part of a chain extending from El Paso to San Antonio. In 1963, the building was sold to a developer who planned to convert it into an apartment complex. The developer later abandoned both the idea and the hotel. Vandals tore up the property, removing windows, doors, and plumbing. The Van Horn State Bank purchased the building for $30,000.

The renovation of the two-story concrete and brick structure cost the bank $250,000. It involved 16,000 of the hotel's original 30,000 square feet, and included a total revamping of the wiring and heating systems. The former lobby serves as the bank's service area; an old coffee shop is now the bank's note department; and the basement has been converted into offices for the Border Patrol. The original walk-in cooler now serves as a jail. The two wings of the building house the Wallis Jewelry Store and Stephen's Flower Shop.

Community Revitalization

Project: Community revitalization in Camden

Company: Campbell Soup Company
Campbell Place
Camden, New Jersey
08101

Contact: Gabe Danch
Director, Community Relations

Campbell Soup, the food-products company, is helping revitalize its hometown of Camden, New Jersey. In 1967, the company spearheaded the formation of the Camden Home Improvement Program (CHIP), a non-profit organization backed by local business. The CHIP bought, renovated, and sold about 550 turn-of-the-century row houses, before it was terminated in 1975 due to the cessation of federal financing for prospective low-income buyers.

At present, Campbell Soup is subsidizing the State Street Housing Corporation, an organization similar to the CHIP, which is purchasing and remodeling about 300 deteriorating houses. The State Street Housing Corporation also arranges mortgages for home buyers with eight Camden banks. Campbell Soup has committed $70,000 to the mortgage pool.

To further commercial redevelopment, the company helped form the Camden Community Loan Plan, which provides financial assistance to minority businesses in conjunction with the federal Small Business Administration. Campbell Soup's staff also counsels these new businesses about management and finance.

Project: Founding of the Community Preservation Corporation

Company: 34 Major Banks
Community Preservation Corporation
641 Lexington Avenue
New York, New York
10022

In 1974, 34 major commercial and savings banks with headquarters in New York City founded the Community Preservation Corporation (CPC). This organization, a nonprofit housing finance corporation, was established to provide a mechanism through which banking and other financial interests could join the government in an effort to preserve New York City's housing stock. Initially concentrating on Crown Heights in Brooklyn and Washington Heights in Manhattan, the CPC began financing the rehabilitation and preservation of one- to four-family homes through short-term and permanent mortgage loans. It also offers first and second mortgages at up to 90 percent of value for periods of up to thirty years. Mortgages are either conventional or insured by the Federal Housing Administration, the New York City Rehabilitation Mortgage Insurance Corporation, or the Veterans Administration.

The 34 members of the CPC have contributed: $400,000 capital to cover operating costs; an $8 million revolving fund for short-term construction financing; and $32 million in permanent financing through the purchase of the CPC's collateral trust notes. The CPC has two offices located in Crown Heights and Washington Heights. Each is staffed with a full-time mortgage officer.

Project: Donation of $3.8 million to the City of Akron for neighborhood revitalization programs

Company: B.F. Goodrich Company
500 South Main Street
Akron, Ohio 44318

Contact: Timothy W. Early
Community Planning Administrator

In 1964, B.F. Goodrich gave Akron, its home since 1870, $300,000 to finance a feasibility study on the revitalization of the city's downtown industrial district, which was beginning to deteriorate. To help implement the study's recommendations, the company donated an additional $3.5 million in June, 1965, to the Opportunity Park Project. This revitalization project called for the creation of a new residential district to include garden, townhouse, and high-rise apartments, new factories, shops, two large parking decks, new churches, a new school, an elevated highway (Akron's first), and an industrial park.

B.F. Goodrich is also spending several million dollars to modernize its headquarters, and is planning to purchase several parcels of land in Akron as part of the revitalization effort.

Project: Residential and commercial
redevelopment in
Minneapolis

Company: Honeywell Corporation
Honeywell Plaza
Minneapolis, Minnesota
55408

In the early 1970s, Honeywell began a
housing-renovation program in the
neighborhood around its plant and
corporate offices in Minneapolis. The
company purchased, renovated, and
sold houses in the area to low-income
families, with prospective buyers receiving support and assistance from the
Model Cities and other federal programs. Honeywell wanted to break
even, but actually lost from $2,500 to
$5,000 on each project. Since 1971, the
company has completed more than
fifteen houses, concentrating on the
area's worst buildings to stimulate
other owners to improve their properties. In 1957, Honeywell converted a
former thermostat factory into its corporate headquarters and remained in
the city instead of following many
other Minneapolis corporations to the
suburbs.

Project: Renovation of Newburyport's
downtown

Company: Institution for Savings
93 State Street
Newburyport, Massachu-
setts 01950

Contact: John Pramberg
President

In addition to maintaining its offices in
an elegant Victorian building constructed for the bank in the 1870s, the
Institution for Savings has been a
preservation leader in the historic seaport town of Newburyport, Massachusetts. Utilizing a recent state law called
the "leeway bill," allowing banks to
invest a portion of their earnings in
any projects they wish, the bank has
purchased, renovated, and rented several old buildings in the downtown
historical area. Its latest project, the
adaptive reuse of the Knight Grain
Building, an urban redevelopment
property in the waterfront area, was
completed in 1976.

Project: Commercial renovation in
an Iowa town

Company: Pella Rolscreen Company
102 Main Street
Pella, Iowa 50219

Contact: H. S. Kuper
Vice President

Pella, Iowa, a small town settled by
pioneers of Dutch descent in 1847, is
the home of the Pella Rolscreen Company, a producer of windows and doors.
The company has contributed funds for
a "Dutch Fronts" project, which provides $500 grants to individual store
owners to remodel their storefronts
according to an approved design. This
helps to preserve the original Dutch
character of the town and its architecture, and to improve the physical
condition of the main commercial
center. Pella Rolscreen provides design
and planning services through Des
Moines architect William Wagner and
interest-free loans of up to $5,000 to
store owners who wish to do more
complete remodeling.

The company also provides about
one-third of the financial support for
the local historical society, and has
purchased and restored the town railroad station.

Project: Renovation of the Hotel
Florence and other buildings
in the Pullman Historic
District

Company: Pullman Incorporated
200 South Michigan
Avenue
Chicago, Illinois 60604

Contact: Barbara Lahnum
Assistant Secretary—
Contributions and Stock
Plans

In 1963, Pullman, Inc., donated $1,000
to the Historic Pullman Foundation to
help renovate the Historic Pullman
Center, a former Masonic Lodge. In
1975, the company donated $25,000 to
the Foundation for the renovation of
the nearby Hotel Florence dating from
1881. Both buildings are located in a
part of Chicago called the Pullman
District.

The Pullman District was originally
a separate company town built in 1880
by George M. Pullman, owner of the
Pullman Palace Car Company, a
railway-car manufacturer. In the
1890s, an economic crisis depressed
business, and Pullman lowered his
wages without lowering his rents. This
led to the Pullman strike in 1894 and
the court-ordered assimilation of the
District into the City of Chicago.

The Historic Pullman Foundation
was founded in 1973 as a nonprofit
organization dedicated to the preservation of the Pullman District's buildings. The area itself has been recognized as a Historic District by the
city (1972), state (1969), and federal
(1970) governments. The Foundation
has succeeded in renovating three
buildings to date: the old Masonic
Lodge, the Market Hall, and the Hotel
Florence.

The Hotel Florence was named after
George Pullman's favorite daughter.
He himself maintained a private suite
in the building. The Queen Anne-style
hotel, designed by architect Solon Be-
man, has 49 guest rooms and a large
dining area with a capacity of 100. It
has been back in operation as a hotel
since July, 1975, and the Pullman
Suite has been restored.

Project: Revitalization of Trustees' Garden section of Savannah

Company: Savannah Gas Company
114 Barnard Street
Savannah, Georgia 31401

In 1945, Hansell Hillyer purchased the Savannah Gas Company and, with it, ten acres of some of the worst slums in Savannah. The site, known as Trustees' Garden, was planned by James Oglethorpe, Georgia's founder, and the Trustees of the Colony of Georgia in 1733. It was the first experimental garden in the country. Over the years, Trustees' Garden became a residential community. In 1945 Hillyer was about to tear down the area's deteriorated houses, when his wife convinced him to let her try to restore them. Mrs. Hillyer, with support from the company, soon turned Trustees' Garden into one of the most sought-after residential sections of the city. In 1953, when the use of natural gas eliminated the need for the gas-manufacturing plant on the site, Mrs. Hillyer and the company converted the plant buildings into modern apartments.

Project: Contribution to the Stevens Neighborhood Housing Improvement Program

Company: Seattle Trust and Savings
804 Second Avenue
Seattle, Washington 98104

Contact: Rick Hooper
Stevens Neighborhood Housing Improvement Program
522 19th Avenue E.
Seattle, Washington 98112

The Stevens District Neighborhood Housing Corporation, sponsor of the Stevens District Housing Improvement Program, was established in 1976 to encourage the residents of Seattle's Stevens District to bring their single-family frame homes up to present building-code standards over a five-year period. In December, 1976, Seattle's City Council allocated $100,000 to the Program in Community Development Block Grand funds. The city will also subsidize low-interest loans at 4 percent to 7 percent for those residents in a "high risk" loan category.

As of 1977, Seattle Trust and Savings is paying the salary of the Program's Director, providing office space, and financing publicity. The bank also provides the services of an administrative secretary and loan officers, and technical assistance when needed. The Stevens Neighborhood Housing Improvement Program will process Seattle Trust loans, and both the Program and the bank will process subsidized loans from the city's Rehabilitation Program. In addition, Seattle Trust has initiated an Energy Conservation Loan Program offering home-improvement loans at 8¾ percent interest (compared to a 9½ percent conventional rate) to all homeowners in the Seattle area who are willing to include energy-related improvements in their remodeling.

Project: Neighborhood revitalization in several Vermont towns

Company: Vermont National Bank
100 Main Street
Brattleboro, Vermont
05301

Contact: Jean A. Hubner
Marketing Officer

The Vermont National Bank has been involved in several preservation efforts, including support for town-scape improvement in Bellows Falls, Bennington, and Springfield. In Springfield, the company renovated a vacant A&P store in a blighted area, converting it into a branch bank and a shopping mall. The bank uses about one-third of the building and rents the rest. The branch opened in 1977. The entire project was coordinated with Downtown Springfield Beautification's plans for a landscaped pedestrian mall area.

Project: Distribution of Iowa Landmark Calendars

Company: American Federal Savings and Loan
Sixth and Grand Avenues
Des Moines, Iowa 50308

In 1960, American Federal Savings and Loan Association, the largest savings and loan in Iowa, began distributing Landmark Calendars to its patrons. The Calendars contain thirteen (the number may vary) illustrations of Iowa's historic buildings drawn by Des Moines architect William J. Wagner. Sites depicted have included: the Drake University Administration Building, the Langworthy Home, the Frank Lloyd Wright Hotel, the Des Moines Old Federal Building, the Manning Mansion, and the Keokuk Post Office and Federal Court Building.

The Landmark Calendars have been popular with bank patrons: the bank finds it often cannot print enough to meet demand.

Project: Distribution of a guidebook to the "Governor's Mansion"

Company: Banker's Trust Savings and Loan of Mississippi
P.O. Box 918
Jackson, Mississippi 39205

In 1976, Banker's Trust of Mississippi helped fund and distribute *An Historical Guide to the Governor's Mansion.* The Greek Revival structure, a Jackson landmark, was completed in 1841 at a cost of $50,000. The first residents were Governor Tilghman Tucker and his family, who took possession in 1842, and the Mansion was continuously occupied until 1971, when it was declared unsafe. At that time, the State of Mississippi appropriated $1.5 million to restore the building. Architects Charles E. Peterson and Edward Vasson Jones restored both the interior and exterior, and added a modern townhouse. Work was completed in 1975.

The guide book, distributed by Banker's Trust Savings and Loan, included color photographs of the Mansion's interior and exterior and short biographies of its inhabitants. Funds received from the sale of the $3 book (over and above production costs) are donated to the Executive Mansion Commission. The Mansion is also open to the public. As of March, 1977, Banker's Trust is no longer distributing the *Guide,* since it has filed a bankruptcy claim, and has been in receivership since spring, 1976.

Project: Restoration of the Pemberton House

Company: The Coca-Cola Company Incorporated
P.O. Drawer 1734
Atlanta, Georgia 30301

Contact: Beverly Lee Taylor
Historic Columbus Foundation
P.O. Box 5312
Columbus, Georgia 31906

In 1969, the Coca-Cola Company, the largest manufacturer of soft-drink products in the United States, underwrote the Historic Columbus Foundation's restoration of the Pemberton House in Columbus, Georgia. Dr. John Styth Pemberton, inventor of the formula for Coca-Cola, lived in the house from 1855 to 1860, and is believed to have developed the formula there. The Foundation restored the building to its original 1850s form: later additions were removed; the gingerbread facade was taken down, and the home was furnished with mid-Victorian antiques and replicas. The backyard kitchen, removed from the house to prevent fires, was restored as an 1850s apothecary shop. Both buildings are administered by the Historic Columbus Foundation and function as a museum open to the public.

Project: Restoration of the Marland Mansion, a private home in Oklahoma

Company: Continental Oil Company (Conoco)
1000 South Pine Street
Ponca City, Oklahoma
74601

The Marland Mansion was built between 1926 and 1928 by E. W. Marland, a wealthy oil magnate and President of Marland Oil, now part of Conoco. The 55-room stone structure was modeled after the Renaissance Davanzatti Palace in Florence, Italy, and built at a cost of $2.5 million. The Mansion has terrazzo floors, wrought-iron doors, fancy ironwork railings, richly carved wooden paneling, and ornate mosaic ceilings. John Duncan Forsyth, a prominent architect, designed the building, and hired a team of architects to execute the detail work. Over 100 craftsmen were brought in to work on the construction. At its completion, the Mansion was reported to be the largest home in Oklahoma and the largest air-conditioned home west of the Mississippi.

Marland and his family lived in the Mansion until 1941, when he sold it to a Catholic religious order for $66,000. Several religious groups owned the property subsequently. In 1975, the home was purchased by Ponca City, with Conoco donating half the purchase price to the city. The House was vacant at the time of purchase, but has since been refurnished with period furniture, some of which originally belonged to the estate. Opened to the public in April, 1976, the Mansion, now houses seminars and meetings, and on April 23, 1977, hosted the Lieutenant Governor's Ball of Oklahoma. The city plans to turn one of the buildings on the estate's grounds into a petroleum museum.

Project: Awards program for renovations

Company: Esco Corporation
2141 N.W. 25th Avenue
Portland, Oregon 97210

Contact: Nello J. Vanelli
Director of Public Affairs

Since 1969, the Esco Corporation, a steel foundry, has given four awards each year to businesses in and around Portland, Oregon, which "remodel their buildings to enhance the beauty of the area." These plaques and certificates are given to both the owners of the buildings and the architect(s) responsible for the design.

Project: Donation of an eighteenth-century house and funds to the Preservation Society of Charleston

Company: First Federal Savings & Loan Association of Charleston, South Carolina
34 Broad Street
Charleston, South Carolina 29402

Contact: Howard F. Burkey
President

The First Federal Savings & Loan Association of Charleston donated the Frederick Wolfe House and an adjacent lot to the Preservation Society of Charleston in spring, 1973. The donation was made with the understanding that the house, which stood in the First Federal parking lot, would be moved to the adjacent lot (First Federal donated the $6,400 necessary for the move), and there be renovated as a residence by the Society. The 1796 house, typical of Charleston architecture, is a two-and-a-half-story, wood-frame structure with a two-story piazza containing Doric columns. There are three dormer windows on its pitched roof.

The renovation cost $49,800, and was carried out by the H.A. DeCosta Company under the Preservation Society's supervision. It included the installation of new mechanical systems, wiring, and roofing. Renovation also required metal work, masonry, plumbing, carpentry, weather stripping, painting, and the removal of enclosed portions of the piazza.

Project: Restoration of an 1890s statue and fountain

Company: The First National Bank and Trust Company
Third and High Streets
Hamilton, Ohio 45012

Contact: Richard Shutte
Vice President, Marketing

In 1975, the First National Bank and Trust Company of Hamilton, Ohio, agreed to finance the complete restoration of a statue and drinking fountain which had been out of use since 1928. The statue of Herbe, the Greek nymph of streams and brooks, was installed in front of the First National Bank Building in 1890. The fountain had pumped water into street-side bowls, a large one for horses, a smaller one for dogs, cats, and other animals, and had provided a continuous stream for people. The statue itself was conceived by Bartel Thorvaldsen, whose original is located in Copenhagen, Denmark. Hamilton had recently developed a central water supply, and the statue symbolized this achievement.

The fountain was utilized for 38 years, until the bank began construction of its new central office building. The statue was removed from the front of the bank, and for a time, was used by a former Hamilton police sergeant as a garden ornament. It began to rust, and eventually both arms broke off. Then, in 1975, the statue was rediscovered by the First National Bank and the Hamilton Foundry. The bank paid Theodore Gantz, a sculptor from Cincinnati, to supervise the restoration and recreate the missing pieces. The Hamilton Foundry agreed to cast and replace what was needed. The restoration returned the statue to its original appearance, but water is only piped to the human drinking fountain.

Project: Relocation and renovation of the century-old Bashford House

Company: Food Maker Industries, Inc.
9330 Balboa Avenue
San Diego, California
92123

Contact: Ken Kimsey
Director
Prescott Historical Society
415 W. Gurley Street
Prescott, Arizona 86301

In 1973, Food Maker Industries, owners of the Jack-In-the-Box fast-food chain, purchased the land on which the 100-year-old Bashford House, one of the oldest buildings in Prescott, Arizona, was located. At this time, the Prescott Historical Society, a state museum, and the Sharlot Hall Historical Society, a sister organization, began a fund raising drive to finance moving the house to the museum grounds where renovation as a community meeting house would begin. After three months, $25,000 was collected, including $1,000 donated by Food Maker. The house is now located on the museum grounds and serves as a combination art gallery and community meeting house.

Project: Creation of the Genesee Country Museum

Company: The Genesee Brewing Co.
P.O. Box 762
Rochester, New York 14603

Contact: Mark Holdren
Public Relations Manager

In 1967, the Genesee Brewing Company, led by John D. Wehle, its Board Chairman, and several of his associates, founded the Genesee Country Museum. The Museum is a nonprofit educational organization established to develop the early American Genesee Country Village. It seeks to identify historically significant farm and village structures, and relocate them on the 55-acre Village site in Mumford, New York. The Village's cost, calculated at $3 million over a ten-year development period, was financed almost entirely by charitable contributions from Genesee Brewing, and from the Louis A. Wehle Foundation. The Genesee Brewing Co. is also providing engineering and restoration assistance.

Over thirty early street plans of upstate New York towns were studied by the Museum's staff to ensure an accurate reproduction. Development plans called for a village of forty buildings. To date, over thirty buildings have been moved to the site, including a ten-room inn, a Greek Revival mansion, several office buildings, a farm, a blacksmith shop, a printer's shop, and a store, as well as other shops and residences, all dating from 1799 to 1859. There are also crafts demonstrations. Once moved to the Village, each building is completely restored and furnished.

Genesee Village opened in 1976, and attracted 64,000 tourists in its first five months. The Village has been featured in many newspaper articles and on several TV news shows. In 1977, John L. Wehle received the Rochester Chamber of Commerce's Business in the Arts Civic Award.

Project: Contribution of $1,000 to the Utah Heritage Foundation

Company: Kearn's Tribune Publishing Company
143 South Main Street
Salt Lake City, Utah 84111

Contact: Stephanie Churchill
Director
Utah Heritage Foundation
355 Quince Street
Salt Lake City, Utah 84103

In 1977, Kearn's Tribune Publishing Company contributed $1,000 to the Utah Heritage Foundation. The Foundation, a nonprofit organization, was established in 1966 to identify and preserve Utah's historic buildings. It buys historic homes, and resells them on the condition that they be restored. The Foundation will also move a house threatened with demolition. Its headquarters are located in Salt Lake City in the renovated Thomas Quayle home, a one-story frame structure built in 1884.

Project: Donation of $50,000 to the Community Triangle Project

Company: Mississippi Chemical
P.O. Box 388
Yazoo City, Mississippi
39194

Contact: Jo G. Pritchard
Library Chairman
Ricks Memorial Library
Yazoo City, Mississippi
39194

In 1974, Mississippi Chemical contributed $50,000 in the form of a matching grant toward the Main Street School/Ricks Memorial Library Community Triangle Project. The other $50,000 was to be donated by local merchants and residents. Mississippi Chemical's President, Tom C. Parry, is helping to spearhead the fund-raising drive. The Community Triangle Project, requiring $600,000 over a three-year period, is attempting to renovate and reuse the 1904 neoclassical Main Street School as a community center and expand the 1900 Beaux Arts-style Ricks Memorial Library. The latter is listed in the National Register of Historic Places. Plans also call for the creation of a landscaped triangle joining the two buildings. The Project is slated for completion late in 1977.

Project: Donation of a nineteenth-century magneto switchboard and building to the Virginia City Historic District Commission

Company: Nevada Bell Telephone
645 E. Plumb Lane
P.O. Box 1911
Reno, Nevada 89502

Contact: James Riley
Public Relations

On June 14, 1975, the manually operated 1882 magneto phone system in Virginia City, Nevada, was replaced with a modern, totally automated switching system, providing dial service. That same year, Nevada Bell donated the original magneto switchboard, building, and land to the Virginia City Historic District Commission. The old telephone building is now open to the public. Nevada Bell's new system is located in a new two-story frame switching station built to blend in with the 1860s Gothic buildings in Virginia City, a gold and silver boom town which is today a popular tourist attraction

Project: Commercials featuring the painting of "Great American Homes"

Company: Sears & Roebuck Company
Sears Tower
Chicago, Illinois 60684

Contact: Glenn Spaerl
Manager, Marketing
Public Relations
Home Improvement
Group

In 1971, Sears began its "Great American Homes Program" to promote its best interior and exterior latex house paint. Under the Program, Sears paints landmark buildings, such as the homes of famous Americans. The projects are filmed for use in Sears commercials.

Most structures are owned by non-profit organizations, are open to the public, and are listed in the National Register of Historic Places. Those chosen so far have included the homes of John Quincy Adams, Mark Twain, Casey Jones, and Betsy Ross.

The buildings are painted their original colors or as close to them as possible. In addition, Sears does any necessary exterior carpentry work. The company receives approximately three applications per week from organizations wishing to have their homes considered. The Program is now in its sixth year.

Project: Donation of the Melrose and Southdown Plantation buildings to historical societies

Company: Valhi, Inc.
1010 Common Street
New Orleans, Louisiana
70112

Contact: The Association of Natchitoches Women for the Preservation of Historic Natchitoches
P.O. Box 2564
Natchitoches, Louisiana
71457

The Terrebonne Historical and Cultural Society
P.O. Box 2095
Houma, Louisiana 70361

In 1971, the Southdown Land Company (now Valhi, Inc.) donated the Melrose Plantation in Louisiana and several acres of land to the Association of Natchitoches Women for the Preservation of Historic Natchitoches. The company had purchased the Plantation and its pecan orchards for $2.2 million the previous year. The donation was made after Southdown had auctioned off the Plantation's furnishings.

The complex, originally called the Yucca Plantation, includes the Yucca House, the African House, the Ghana House, and a barn. It was built in 1776 by a former black slave, who later became a slave owner, Marie Therese Coin Coin Metoyer. The wooden plantation buildings with steep thatched roofs are the only African-style buildings extant from this period. In 1833, Marie's grandson, Louis, constructed the "Big House," now known as the Melrose Plantation House. The House is built in Louisiana French colonial style, with Greek Revival details.

In 1973, the Southdown Land Company donated the Southdown Plantation House to the Terrebonne Historical Society of Houma, Louisiana. The House was built by W.J. Minor, founder of the Southdown Sugar Company, in 1848. The Plantation includes: the main house, constructed mostly of brick, with two rounded Gothic turrets; a two-story structure connected to the main building by several walkways, which is thought to have been part of the slave quarters built in 1848; a stable complex; and a carriage house.

Both the Melrose and Southdown Plantations are listed in the National Register of Historic Places.

Methodology

This book is designed to be a tool for both businesses interested in building reuse and neighborhood preservation, and preservation and community groups interested in soliciting business support for these causes. Through a series of 71 case studies, the achievements of business in preservation are defined and illustrated. An appendix listing of 71 more projects substantiates the scope of the effort. The examples selected were chosen for their variety, scale, and geographic location, as well as for the degree of company cooperation.

The methodology used to identify business participation in preservation involved travel, periodical review, and follow-up interviews. In spring, 1975, the authors made several trips to Washington, D.C., to confer with federal officials, including officers of the U.S. Department of Housing and Urban Development and the Environmental Protection Agency. In addition, the authors met with members of the staff of the National Trust for Historic Preservation. These visits were made in an effort to identify important issues in the area of business contributions to preservation. An advisory board for the project was established to review concepts and offer direction.

In summer 1975, the study authors visited thirty states and talked personally with State Historic Preservation Officers (SHPOs), their staffs, and local preservation and business leaders. (Each state has a Preservation Officer appointed by the Governor to oversee preservation matters.) More than 100 examples of business involvement in preservation were identified from this effort.

In fall, 1975, letters and questionnaires were sent to all the SHPOs not personally contacted that summer, and to State Preservation Coordinators of the American Institute of Architects (AIA). (Two AIA-designated architects coordinate the organization's preservation activities in each state.) The questionnaires generated about fifty additional examples. That same fall, the National Trust for Historic Preservation distributed flyers at its annual conference in Boston. Several people wrote in response to the flyers.

In August, 1976, letters were sent to *Fortune* magazine's list of the 500 largest U.S. industrial corporations. Approximately 5 percent of the companies responded to the mailing, producing several interesting projects. Additional companies carrying out preservation projects were identified via a variety of sources, including periodicals, books, and word of mouth.

In January, 1977, INFORM sent a questionnaire to the over 200 companies identified over the previous year and a half as having preservation projects. Approximately 20 percent replied. In all, 71 projects were selected for profiling. Follow-up phone calls to these companies continued throughout spring and summer, 1977.

Other useful sources of information on the projects in this study were: newspapers, including *Preservation News,* the newspaper of the National Trust, the *New York Times,* the *Wall Street Journal*, and local papers; and periodicals, like *Fortune, Business Week,* and *Architectural Record.*

Many publications helped provide an overview of the situation. Several were particularly important in surveying relevant legislation. They include: the National Trust for Historic Preservation's *A Guide to Federal Programs for Historic Preservation,* published in 1974, and supplemented in 1976, and *A Guide to State Programs,* published in 1972, and revised in 1976; the U.S. Department of Housing and Urban Development's *Neighborhood Preservation;* the National Endowment for the Arts' *Neighborhood Conservation*; and the National Center for Urban Ethnic Affairs' *Neighborhood Reinvestment.* Much information about business involvement in preservation support comes from publications of the Business Committee for the Arts, including its 1976 survey, *Business Support for the Arts,* and Gideon Chagy's *The New Patrons of the Arts.* The Filer Commission's Report, *Giving in America,* and the Conference Board's *Annual Survey of Corporate Contributions* were also helpful in their analyses of business contributions to preservation. Frederick L. Rath, Jr., and Merrilyn Rogers O'Connell have produced a useful preservation bibliography entitled *Historic Preservation: A Bibliography on Historical Organization Practices.* Ronald Lee Fleming and Vision,

Inc., of Cambridge, Massachusetts, will soon publish a survey of corporate design in historic areas.

The case-study format was finalized, and most drafting of profiles was completed in winter and spring, 1977. In April, 1977, the project's advisory board reviewed the format and offered suggestions on the shape of the cases and the project. In the months that followed, first drafts were sent for verification of factual material to companies profiled, and often to local preservation groups for review and comment. Changes were incorporated when appropriate.

Chapter introductions were written in summer, 1977, incorporating findings from the case studies, as well as materials from outside sources. Sections on legislation affecting community-revitalization and recycling programs were reviewed by experts in the field.

The information presented in each case study was supplied by the companies involved, their architects or contractors, community groups, or nonprofit organizations. It is the result of friendly questions, and depends for its accuracy on these groups' cooperation.

Glossary

AIA the American Institute of Architects, a national professional organization of architects.

AID American Interior Designers, a national professional organization of interior designers, now part of the American Society of Interior Designers, (ASID).

Art Deco a decorative style stimulated by the Paris Exposition Internationale des Arts Decoratifs et Industrieles Modernes of 1925. Widely used in American architecture and decorative arts of the 1930s, Art Deco was a glorification of technology. It placed emphasis on gleaming steel and sharp angular or zigzag surface forms.

Art Nouveau a decorative style of architecture and applied art developed in France and Belgium at the end of the nineteenth century. Essentially an aesthetic movement, it featured organic, dynamic forms and the luxuriant use of curving designs and whiplash lines.

balloon frame a wood frame in which the vertical members run continuously from the lowest horizontal member to the lower edge of a sloping roof.

balustrade a handrail supported by miniature columns, or other forms, called balusters. In the Georgian and Federal periods, balustrades were often placed on the edge of roofs of houses.

Beaux Arts historic and eclectic design on a monumental scale, featuring elaborate exterior decoration. It originated at the Ecole des Beaux Arts in Paris in the nineteenth century.

bracket an overhanging member projecting from a wall or other body to support a weight acting outside the wall. Brackets also often serve a purely decorative purpose.

cantilever a structural beam which projects horizontally out beyond its supporting member.

Chicago skyscraper style a tall multi-story commercial-building style that flourished particularly in Chicago at the end of the nineteenth century. It was based on the development of steel structural framing in the 1880s.

Classic Revival an architectural movement based on the use of pure Roman and Greek forms. It was popular in England and the United States during the nineteenth century.

Colonial a broad term covering a variety of architectural styles developed during the American Colonial period. Based on English, French, Dutch, and German styles of the seventeenth and eighteenth centuries, Colonial was essentially a transfer of these designs to the New World. Its features vary by region, but can include brickwork, steeply pitched roofs, and half-timbering.

column a supporting pillar, basic to much of classical architecture. A column consists of three parts: a base, a shaft, and a capital.

Doric column the oldest and sturdiest type of column, the Doric is distinguished by a thick shaft with a flat capital.

Ionic column distinguished by its scroll-shaped capital.

Corinthian column characterized by a slender shaft and a capital of carved leaves.

Tuscan column a Roman simplification of the Greek Doric column, usually featuring smooth shafts.

Community Development Block Grant the funds granted to communities for their use and disbursement under Title I of the Housing and Community Development Act of 1974, which replaced many different federal renewal programs. These funds are allocated in a lump sum rather than for individual projects, and allow local governments greater autonomy.

console a decorative projection from a wall designed for support.

corbel a supporting projection for a floor or overhanging member. If the corbel is one of a series, each is stepped progressively further forward from the wall.

cornice a molded, projecting, horizontal member which crowns a structure.

cottage style an eclectic architectural style of small, simple, typically rural residences, usually one or one-and-a-half stories, prominent in the nineteenth century.

cove lighting a method of lighting in which a light source is concealed by a horizontal recess or cornice below it and directs light up at a reflecting ceiling.

cupola a small domed turret, usually centered on the ridge of a roof.

curtain wall a wall supporting only itself. The weight of the roof or floor above is supported by the framework of the building.

dry grit a method of cleaning the exterior of a building by forced air through a directing nozzle using some form of grit (e.g., sand, silica, copper slag). Although this type of cleaning has been used on many of the buildings discussed in this book, it is not recommended for exterior cleaning as it can destroy the building surface, encouraging deterioration.

FAIA Fellow of the American Institute of Architects.

Federal an architectural style in vogue in the United States after the Revolutionary War until about 1830. The English architect Robert Adams was the primary influence on the Federal style, which was characterized by the use of classical forms and details such as columns and pilasters.

flashing sheet copper or another substance used to make an intersection between units weathertight.

Flemish bond a pattern of brickwork in which headers (bricks laid so that the end appears on the wall face) and stretchers (laid so that the side appears) are laid alternately in each row.

frieze the decorated band along the upper part of a wall immediately beneath the cornice.

gallery an intermediate floor projecting out into an enclosed space from one of the enclosing walls.

gazebo a small, fanciful, garden summerhouse.

Georgian an architectural style of eighteenth century England. Georgian emphasized the use of classical symmetry and form. Pilasters, balustrades, and brick were common. It was popular in America from 1720 to 1790.

gingerbread style refers to the elaborate woodwork of Victorian-style houses.

Gothic European medieval architecture of the late twelfth to sixteenth centuries characterized by the use of the pointed arch and ribbed vaults.

Gothic Revival a style which resulted from a conscious attempt to revive medieval forms. It was popular in the United States and Europe from 1820 to 1870, and was distinguished by pointed-arch windows with tracery.

Greek the architecture of ancient Greece, characterized by the use of the column and the lintel as supporting elements, marble as a building material, and symmetrical forms.

Greek Revival a style stimulated by the Greek fight for independence, Greek Revival was marked by a use of Greek and Roman forms. It was popular in England and the United States in the first half of the nineteenth century.

HABS Historic American Buildings Survey, established by the federal government in 1933 to record and document important buildings and sites.

HAER Historic American Engineering Record, founded in 1969 to record and document important industrial and engineering sites and structures.

heart pine mature pine from approximately the center of the tree.

HUD the United States Department of Housing and Urban Development.

jerkin head roof a roof in which the end of the top of the roof is cut short, and a secondary slope is formed.

joist one of a series of parallel horizontal timber beams upon which floor boards or ceiling supports are fastened.

lintel a horizontal piece of stone, timber, or masonry spanning an opening.

mansard roof a roof which slopes on all sides, with the lower slope generally steeper than the upper one. A feature French in origin.

measured drawings drawings to scale of a given structure.

mortise a cut-out hollow in one member, often a timber, meant to receive and hold another corresponding part, or tenon.

National Register of Historic Places the federal inventory of historic buildings, sites, and districts of national, state, or local importance. It is administered by the National Park Service. Nomination must first be approved by the appropriate state historic-preservation officers.

National Trust for Historic Preservation the national organization which furthers preservation activities in the United States. Chartered by Congress in 1949, it is a nonprofit organization backed by federal and private funding.

neoclassical a style which dominated Europe and America in the late eighteenth and early nineteenth centuries. It was characterized by the monumentality of its buildings, and the sparing application of detail and strict symmetry.

Neo-Renaissance a style which came about in the mid-nineteenth century as a reaction to the Gothic Revival. Neo-Renaissance is characterized by a division of the building facade into a base, middle, and top, and the use of carved stone and sculpture.

newel post the posts at the bottom and top of a staircase.

NHS Neighborhood Housing Services, a nonprofit partnership of local residents, government, and financial institutions whose purpose is revitalizing neighborhoods through financial counseling, loan programs, and education.

nogging the filling-in of brick between closely spaced vertical members of a frame wall or partition.

outbuilding a small separate building whose function depends on a main structure.

pediment a surface used ornamentally over doors or windows, usually triangular but sometimes curved.

piazza an open public space surrounded by buildings.

pilaster a shallow column usually projecting from but engaged to a wall.

pressed brick smooth-faced brick molded by mechanical pressure.

Queen Anne an eclectic style of domestic architecture popular in England and America in the nineteenth century. The term is a misnomer since the style is a mixture of Gothic and Renaissance characteristics.

redlining refusal by a financial institution to make loans in a given area regardless of the qualifications of the potential borrower.

Regency a type of architecture popular in England during the regency and reign of George IV. It was a colorful neoclassical style which often combined Oriental motifs with stucco and balconied terraces.

Richardsonian Romanesque a style named after its foremost practitioner, American architect Henry Hobson Richardson (1838 to 1886). Richardson integrated Romanesque elements, such as large rounded arches, into strong solid buildings symbolic of the burgeoning growth of American capitalism. He also emphasized asymmetrical design and rusticated masonry walls.

riser the vertical piece between the horizontal treads of a staircase.

rococo a mid-eighteenth-century style, French in origin, rococo emphasized profuse curved decoration expressed in light colors and fanciful forms.

Romanesque a term generally used to cover European architecture during the time between the Roman and the Gothic styles. Based on Roman forms, rounded arches and semicircular vaulting were typical.

Second Empire a French architectural style, popular in the 1860s and 1870s, which employed neoclassical motifs and mansard roofs primarily on public buildings. It was named after the French Second Empire of Napoleon III (1852 to 1870).

shake a type of hand-split shingle.

shingle-style a style of American architecture, popular in the late nineteenth century, whose foremost proponent was the firm of McKim, Mead and White. The style emphasized the use of shingles on roof and walls, and large open interior spaces.

spandrel a panel covering of an exterior wall in a skeleton frame building between structural supports and window openings.

terra cotta cast and fired clay used for wall facings and architectural ornamentation. It was popular in the United States in the early twentieth century.

terrazzo floors floors consisting of marble chips cast in cement and then ground and polished.

travertine a cream-colored limestone used as a building material.

truss the triangular frame structure used to support a roof or floor.

turnbuckle a device with screw threads at both ends, or a screw thread at one end and a swivel at the other, that is turned to bring ends closer together. It is usually used to tighten rods.

vernacular folk buildings or decorations characteristic of an area.

Victorian a broad term referring to eclectic and revival buildings and decorative arts during the reign of Queen Victoria (1840 to 1901). The main characteristics include low-pitched, bracketed roofs, asymmetrical design, towers, and sometimes round-arched windows.

wainscoting a wood, stone, or masonry overlay of a wall surface, usually less than half the height of the wall.

About the Authors

Raynor M. Warner is an architectural designer with Cambridge Seven Associates, architects in Cambridge, Massachusetts. He holds a Master's Degree in Architecture from the Harvard Graduate School of Design and a Master's Degree in Historic Preservation from Columbia University School of Architecture. He has designed and developed several renovation projects in Boston and served as a consultant to the National Trust for Historic Preservation. Mr. Warner has written and spoken extensively on preservation subjects and is currently a director of Preservation Action. A graduate of the Citadel, he was formerly an account executive with two New York advertising agencies, Young & Rubicam and D'arcy McManus.

Sibyl McCormac Groff is the author of *New Jersey's Historic Houses—A Guide to Homes Open to the Public*. A member of the National Trust for Historic Preservation and the Victorian Society of America, she has lectured extensively on preservation. Ms. Groff is also a member of the board of the Jacob Riis Settlement House in New York City. She is a graduate of the Emma Willard School and Wells College and has studied in the Columbia University School of Architecture's Historic Preservation Program. She was formerly a stockbroker and securities analyst in New York and London.

Ranne P. Warner is currently developing a U.S. real estate investment program for Commercial Union Properties, the real estate subsidiary of the London-based Commercial Union Assurance Company. She received a Master of Business Administration with Distinction from Harvard University Graduate School of Business. Ms. Warner has lectured and written extensively on preservation, corporate involvement in social issues, and U.S. real estate. A director of Preservation Action, she has been a consultant to the National Trust for Historic Preservation and developed several renovation projects in Boston. Ms. Warner has been a Research Associate at the Harvard Business School and an account executive at two New York advertising agencies, Benton and Bowles and Marsteller, and at Burson-Marsteller, a public relations firm. She is a graduate of the University of Missouri School of Journalism.

INFORM Publications

Studies

Energy Futures: Industry and the New Technologies
(Ballinger Publishing Co., 660 pages, $22.50)
A survey of corporate research and development of 17 new energy sources and technologies, including solar, wind, geothermal, trash-to-energy, coal gasification, and nuclear systems. Environmental impact is evaluated, federal programs assessed, and corporate investment analyzed for each technology. Over 200 major R&D projects of 142 firms are individually profiled, including technical achievements, and obstacles to commercialization.

Promised Lands
Volume 1: Subdivisions in Deserts and Mountains (560 pages, $20)
Volume 2: Subdivisions in Florida's Wetlands (540 pages, $20)
Volume 3: Subdivisions and the Law (535 pages, $20)
An analysis of the environmental and consumer impact of the land sales and subdivision industry. The study examines practices at nineteen large-scale "new communities" located in the states of Arizona, California, Colorado, Florida and New Mexico. Laws in these states and on the federal level are analyzed for how effectively they regulate abuses, such as consumer fraud and degradation of water resources. Guidelines for upgrading subdivider's practices are proposed.

Business and Preservation: A Survey of Business Conservation of Buildings and Neighborhoods (300 pages, hardcover, $22, paperback, $14)
An illustrated survey of 71 projects undertaken by American business to restore and preserve buildings and neighborhoods. Projects analyzed include adaptive reuse and rehabilitation of historical buildings for new purposes, neighborhood conservation efforts, and general preservation support.

Handbooks and Summaries

A Clear View: Guide to Industrial Pollution Control
(235 pages, hardcover $12.50, paperback $4)
A citizen's handbook on assessing factory air and water pollution problems and bringing about improvement.

What You Should Know Before Buying A Lot: Consumer Guide to Subdivisions (50 pages, $1.75)
Questions to ask and facts to consider before making a downpayment on a lot in a "planned new community."

Planner's Guide to Subdivisions
(50 pages, $6)
A guidebook for county planners, planning professionals, and concerned citizens on how to evaluate the environmental impact of a new large-scale subdivision. A series of environmental standards are described, with precedents from localities across the country for using each.

Business and Preservation, Summary Report

(30 pages, $6)
Highlights from the study.

Energy Futures Abstract
(20 pages, $6)
Major findings of the study described above.

Promised Lands 1 & 2, Summary Report
(30 pages, $6)
Major findings on impact of nineteen subdivisions in five states.

Promised Lands 3, Summary Report
(30 pages, $6)
Major findings on effectiveness of government regulation of subdivisions.

To obtain any of these publications, or information on a subscription to all INFORM publications including its newsletter, contact INFORM, 25 Broad St., New York, N.Y. 10004, 212/425-3550.

SUBSCRIPTION RATES: Corporations, institutions (two copies of each study, summaries, newsletter), $500; Government (one copy of each study, summaries, newsletter), $125; University and community libraries (one copy of each study, summary), $60; Individuals, non-profit groups (summaries, newsletter), $25. Donations are tax-deductible.

Index